Sabbats

An Essential Guide to Yule, Imbolc, Ostara, Beltane, Midsummer, Lammas, Mabon, and Samhain

Your Free Gift
(only available for a limited time)

Thanks for getting this book! If you want to learn more about various spirituality topics, then join Mari Silva's community and get a free guided meditation MP3 for awakening your third eye. This guided meditation mp3 is designed to open and strengthen ones third eye so you can experience a higher state of consciousness. Simply visit the link below the image to get started.

https://spiritualityspot.com/meditation

Table of Contents

Part1: Yule

The Ultimate Guide to the Winter Solstice and How It's Celebrated in Wicca, Druidry, Christianity, and Paganism

Introduction

Despite occurring in the middle of winter, when days get as cold and dark as they come, pagans have learned to honor Yule early on. Pagans knew that after the longest night of the year, the darkness finally reached its pinnacle, only to be defeated by light soon after. The winter solstice, as this night is known in the pagan communities, marks the rebirth of the Sun. Just as the earth seems to succumb to darkness, it comes back out again, and by spring, it slowly becomes more vibrant than ever. The knowledge that this is what comes after this night brought so much joy into people's lives that they knew that this date in the pagan calendar needed to be marked by a special celebration.

The pagan tradition of celebrating Yule has since spread widely and been adopted by many cultures, both pagan and non-pagan. Nowadays, Yule is once again becoming one of the most celebrated holidays, for it promises us the return of light, both in the sky and in our hearts. Because our lives are so stressful these days, it is easy to succumb to darkness, especially during the winter when the weather seems just as gloomy and cold as we feel on the inside. By celebrating Yule in a pagan way, you can learn that this darkness is necessary to make you stronger, just as it is crucial for nature to rest before awakening again to provide us with sustenance in the coming year.

This book outlines several things you can incorporate to clear away the cobwebs and celebrate this new beginning. Your mood will improve as soon as you start thinking about what to prepare to welcome the light back into your life. Whether you are a solitary practitioner or prefer group practice, there is a special pagan way for you to celebrate Yule and express yourself. There is a broad range of activities to choose from, and you can take as many days as you need or have available to prepare for this holiday. On the night of the Winter solstice, it is entirely up to you whether you do a quick cleansing and prayer ritual or follow the traditional 12-day Yuletide calendar with Yule-related activities for each day.

To celebrate this magical holiday, pagans across the globe gather in large communities to celebrate by sharing their bounty with others. And even if you do not have a pagan community nearby, you can still involve those around by giving. You can share the handmade crafts you create or donate food to those in need as you would share your bounty after a successful harvest. This way, you'll share the light with many people who might not be aware of its approach.

As with all pagan practices, whatever your choices for celebrating Yule, they must resonate with your spiritual needs. Let the spirit of Yule awaken your soul by following the winter solstice celebration tips from this book. If you are just starting your pagan spiritual journey, honoring Yule is the best way to start your spiritual development. After all, nothing makes your soul grow stronger than hope for a new, better life.

Chapter 1: From Yule to Christmas

The Yule festival is a popular celebration that dates back centuries. Although its origins are somewhat murky, the Yule festival likely has pagan roots. Today, the Yule festival is celebrated by Christians and non-Christians alike. It is a time to come together, celebrate life, and enjoy the company of loved ones. So, what is the Yule festival? And where did it come from? Read on to learn more about the history and origins of this festive occasion.

What Is the Yule Festival?

Yule is a winter festival falling on the winter solstice originally celebrated by the Germanic people. This festival is feasting and merrymaking during the darkest, coldest time of the year. It marks the end of a long, bleak winter and the rise of spring. People would decorate their homes with greenery, such as holly and ivy, light logs, and feast on special holiday foods. The festival typically lasts for 12 days, beginning on December 21st, the day of the winter solstice, and ending on January 1st, known as the yuletide. Winter solstice has been a very important day in Germanic and Norse pagan tradition and other pagan cultures worldwide.

Why Is the Winter Solstice Significant to Pagans and the Yule Festival?

The winter solstice is the shortest day and longest night of the year and marks the official start of winter. At this time of year, the sun is at its lowest point in the sky and turning back towards the earth, giving the appearance of a wheel turning. This is how Yule derives its meaning of "wheel" in old English. For many pagan cultures, this day is interpreted as the sun's death and rebirth. It signifies the sun's return after months of darkness and cold weather and is a welcome sign that spring will eventually arrive.

For pagans, this is a time to celebrate the natural world and the cycle of. Pagans believe that the earth is alive and that everything has a spirit, including animals, plants, rocks, and land. Winter Solstice is a time to honor these spirits and to give thanks for the gifts and blessings they have given us. It is a time of hope, rebirth, and renewal. It is also a time to celebrate the goddess of fertility, who brings new life to the earth after a long winter period.

Etymology

The word "Yule" is derived from the Old Norse jól, one of the title names of the Norse god Odin. It is also sourced from an old English term, géohol, which referred to a hunting season following the harvest. "Geol" was later replaced by the Old Norse word "jól," with the same meaning. "Jól" eventually became the modern English word "Yule." The word "Yule" is also used in many other languages, including Swedish, Danish, Norwegian, Icelandic, and German. In addition to referring to the holiday season, the word "Yule" describes Christmas trees and decorations. It is even used in some Pagan and Wiccan traditions. The festival is said to have originated in ancient Scandinavia and Germania and is often related to Norse mythology.

Similar Festivals to Yule

Different cultures have different names for the winter solstice festival. Although many practices were situated in different geographical locations, their celebration was very similar.

Ra God Ritual

Winter solstice in ancient Egypt was celebrated as the homecoming of Ra, the sun god, to thank him for keeping the land and crops warm. The ancient Egyptians celebrated the winter solstice in several ways. People would offer prayers and sacrifices to Ra during the festival, and boats decorated with sun symbols and olive leaves were sailed down the Nile.

Saturnalia

The Saturnalia festival was a Roman holiday every December 17th - 23rd to honor the god Saturn. It was a time when people could let loose and have fun. The festival was very similar to the Yule festival celebrated by the Germanic people. Both festivals lasted for several days and involved feasting, decorating their homes with greenery and lights, and exchanging gifts. However, Saturnalia was also a time when social norms were turned upside down. Slaves and masters would switch roles, and people dressed up in costumes. The Saturnalia was an opportunity for people to celebrate life and enjoy themselves before the cold winter months set in. It was similar to

Yule and Christmas celebrations.

Inti Raymi

Every December, people around the world celebrate the winter solstice. In the Northern Hemisphere, this marks the shortest day of the year and the beginning of winter. The Southern Hemisphere marks the longest day of the year and the start of summer. The Inca people of Peru also celebrated the winter solstice. They called it Inti Raymi, which means "Festival of the Sun." Inti Raymi was a time to thank the sun god, Inti, for his life-giving warmth and light. The festival was held in June, the onset of winter in the Southern Hemisphere. Like many other winter solstice celebrations, Inti Raymi included feasting and dancing. But it also included some unique Inca traditions, like processions through the streets and sacrifices to gods and goddess statues. Despite being separated by hundreds of years and miles, Inti Raymi and the modern-day festival of Yule have many similarities. Both celebrate the winter solstice with feasts and entertainment and involve special displays or decorations that honor their respective sun gods.

Similarities between Yule and Christmas

Yule festival was Christianized and transformed into Christmas.
https://pixabay.com/images/id-791110/

The Yule festival was a Pagan celebration later Christianized and transformed into Christmas. Around the 4th century, Roman Emperor Constantine declared Christianity the empire's official religion. This profoundly impacted how Christmas was celebrated, as many Pagans were converted to Christianity. Christmas was an attempt by the emperor to persuade Pagans to convert to Christianity by insinuating the birth of Jesus into the Yule celebrations. In the 9th century, King Hakon of Norway introduced Christianity to Scandinavia. He banned Pagan celebrations by forcing them to abandon the Yule festival in favor of Christmas but allowed them to follow some of the regional Yule customs like drinking ale. These two events helped to shape Christmas into the holiday we know today. While the original Pagan origins of the holiday have been largely forgotten, they still influence many ways we celebrate Christmas today. Here are some similarities between Yule and Christmas customs.

1. **Timing:** Both holidays are celebrated around the winter solstice. Yule is celebrated for 12 days from the winter solstice, which falls on December 21st in the Northern Hemisphere. In comparison, Christmas is celebrated on December 25th.

2. **Decorating with Greenery:** One of the most popular decorations for Yule and Christmas is evergreen branches and wreaths. No tree would survive except the evergreen trees in Scandinavia due to harsh winters. So, Viking natives used to decorate and carve evergreen trees to resurrect the spirits of other trees because evergreens symbolize life and growth, which is especially important during the dark winter months. Post Christianization of Yule, the tradition of decorating an evergreen tree is still evident when celebrating Christmas.

3. **Santa Claus:** During the Yule celebration, children in Germanic regions filled their boots with straw and placed them outside their house to be filled with gifts by the Norse god Odin. Legends say that a bearded Odin would ride on his eight-legged horse Sleipnir and deliver gifts to good children. After the Christian takeover, the title and character changed to Santa Claus.

4. **Gift-Giving:** The practice of giving gifts has been enjoyed by people for centuries, and it continues to be one of the most popular aspects of Christmas and Yule. For many, giving a gift is a way to express love and gratitude and is often seen as a gesture of goodwill. Gift-giving is so important to Christmas and Yule that it has become one of the defining features of these holidays.

5. **Feasting:** Of course, no holiday is complete without a feast. Whether you enjoy a traditional Christmas dinner or a more festive Yule feast, spending time with family and friends around good food is always a cherished tradition.

6. **Spending Time Together:** Lastly, the most important similarity between Yule and Christmas is that they are both holidays about spending time with those you love.

Key Difference between Yule and Christmas

Christmas and Yule customs vary greatly from culture to culture. In some cultures, Christmas is a time of joy and celebration, and Yule is a time of reflection and contemplation. However, some key differences between the two customs should be noted.

- Christmas is a Christian holiday that celebrates the birth of Jesus Christ, while Yule is a pagan festival that honors Norse gods like Odin, Thor, and Freya.

- Christmas is celebrated on December 25th, and Yule is typically celebrated for 12 days between December 21st or the day of the winter solstice and January 1st.

- Christmas means Christ's mass, or "feast of rejoicing. " The term mass is derived from the Latin word "massus," which means "to make or generate." Yule or Jul has multiple meanings. In old English, it is sometimes referred to as Odin or the wheel reference to sun movement.

- Yule customs mention the burning of logs during celebrations, whereas Christians light candles during the birth of Christ celebration. Yule festival typically involves activities like burning large Yule logs, decorating evergreen trees, sacrificing animals, and drinking ale. Christmas focuses on decorating personal evergreen trees at home, exchanging gifts, feasting, and attending religious services.

Yule Then

The ancient Yule traditions of Germanic and Scandinavian people were some of the most fascinating and unique in history. These cultures have long since disappeared, but their customs and beliefs surrounding the winter solstice are still remembered and studied today.

They celebrated Yule, a 12-day festival that coincided with the Winter Solstice, with many traditions that may seem strange and familiar to us today. One of the most well-known Yule traditions is burning a large log in the hearth. It brings light and life into the home during the dark winter months. The logs were to burn for the whole 12 days guiding light until the complete resurrection of the sun. Other common decorations included evergreen wreaths, mistletoe, and branches, symbols of fertility and rebirth.

However, the most important part of the Yule season was the feast when families would get together and feast on roasted meats, fresh bread, and sweet desserts. They also drank plenty of ale, mead, and cider to stay warm and ward off evil spirits. After the feast, it was customary to spend time singing songs and telling stories around the fire.

In some cultures, animal sacrifices were also part of the Yule celebrations. These could be anything from burning cows and pigs in giant bonfires to leaving food for wild animals.

One of the most popular traditions during Yule was the exchange of gifts. This was a way to show love and appreciation for friends and family. It was also seen to bring good luck in the coming year.

Yule Now

Modern pagans celebrate Yule with many activities, ancient and modern. Many of these activities focus on the winter solstice. Modern pagans also celebrate this day as the sun's rebirth, decorating homes and workplaces with evergreen trees and wreaths, lighting candles, feasting, and giving gifts to loved ones.

Modern pagans also participate in more specific activities related to their beliefs, such as performing rituals or meditating. Whatever activities are chosen, they typically aim to bring about a sense of warmth, happiness, and hope during the dark winter months. While there are many similarities between ancient and modern pagans celebrating Yule, there are also some differences. One of the most notable is that ancient pagans would have celebrated for a full month. In contrast, modern pagans typically celebrate for a shorter period, probably because people now have busy lives and do not have the time to commit to a month-long celebration. Another difference is that ancient pagans often used log bonfires as part of their celebrations. Modern pagans are more likely to use candles and electric lights and make log cakes to signify the importance of log burning rather than burning them.

Wiccan and Druid Perspective of Yule

As it marks the point at which the sun returns after the longest night of the year, Wiccans believed that the winter solstice is a time of great importance. For many Wiccans and Druids, Yule is a time to celebrate the light and life that will soon return to the world. Wicca is a sect of neopaganism. Its festivals include the Moon's cycles, known as Esbats and generally linked with the female deity of the triple goddess, and the sun's cycles, known as Sabbats, associated with the male deity of the Horned God. They share a common belief with druids regarding the Oak King and the Holly King.

Wiccans and Druids believe in the Celtic legend of the battle between the Oak King and the Holly King. According to the legend, the Oak King represents the light and warmth of summer, while the Holly King represents the darkness and cold of winter. Every year, they battle for supremacy. The Oak King eventually triumphs and brings summer back to the world. However, the Holly King is reborn at Yule and takes over again. This cycle of light and dark, life and death, is a metaphor for the cycle of the seasons.

As winter always gives way to spring, so will darkness eventually give way to light. For druids, Yule is a time to celebrate this eternal cycle and give thanks for the light that always returns.

Important Yuletide Symbols

- ## The Yule Log

Since ancient times, the Yule log has been a symbol of light and protection. In Scandinavia, the Yule log was traditionally used to ward off evil spirits and keep homes safe during the long, dark winter. The log was often decorated with images of animals or plants and was believed to offer protection from harm. The Yule log is still used to symbolize light and protection during winter. Many people burn a Yule log in their fireplace on Christmas Eve, and some even decorate it with images of Santa Claus or other holiday characters. Whether you burn a Yule log in your home or simply use it as a decoration, this age-old symbol will surely bring a touch of light and protection to your winter celebrations.

- ## The Yule Goat

In Scandinavia, the Yule goat symbolizes Thor, and it was traditionally sacrificed before Yule. The Yule goat was associated with fertility and renewal and was thought to bring good luck. The Yule goat was originally a straw goat used as a decoration during the winter solstice celebrations. Over time, the Yule goat became associated with Santa Claus and a popular Christmas decoration in many parts of the world as a symbol of magic and light. The Yule goat is often depicted as a white goat with antlers, which represents the spirit of the winter season. It is also associated with trickery and mischief; if you are not careful, the Yule goat will play tricks on you.

- ## The Yule Mistletoe

Mistletoe has been used as a holiday decoration for centuries. The Druids believed that mistletoe possessed magical powers and used it in their ceremonies. The mistletoe's white berries were thought to represent the Oak King, while the green leaves represented the Mother Goddess. The mistletoe was also seen as a symbol of fertility and often used in love spells. In addition, mistletoe was popular among Nordic pagans to protect them from evil spirits and was often used to broker peace deals. Today, mistletoe is still a popular holiday decoration. While its magical properties are debatable, its symbolic meaning remains clear; mistletoe is a sign of goodwill and peace.

- ## The Yule Wassail

During the Yule season, ancient Germanic and Nordic people would brew a special drink called wassail. This drink was thought to bless the earth and drive away evil spirits. The word wassail comes from an Old English meaning "to be of good health." People would wander through their crops, pouring wine on the ground and yelling to scare away evil spirits. Wassail was also drunk as a toast to good health and prosperity. It is recognized as a symbol of warmth and well-being by the pagans.

- **The Yule Boar**

The Yule boar is a tradition dating back to Pagan times. Freyr is the goddess of the harvest and rides a boar with golden bristles. During Yule, Pagans sacrificed wild boars, hoping the goddess would bless them with children, love, and a bountiful harvest. Current people use ham instead of sacrificing boar. The Yule boar symbolizes fertility, prosperity, and good fortune. It is also a reminder that we are connected to nature and the cycle of life.

- **The Yule Candle**

The Yule candle symbolizes light and life and has a long history dating back to ancient times. The Yule torch was used to light the Yule log and provided light for the banquet. As people started observing rituals inside their houses, the torch was replaced with a candle. The Yule candles became a sign of protection against evil spirits and were thought to fill the home with comforting light. In ancient Scandinavia, the Yule candle was burned, and the leftover wax was placed on the plow blades in hopes of a fruitful crop in the New Year. Today, the Yule candle is still a symbol of light and life, an important part of many holiday celebrations.

- **The Yule Ivy**

Ivy is a sign of rebirth since it thrives after the host plant dies; it represents eternity because it does not turn brown in the winter. Man was represented by the ivy, while the holly represented women. Pagans used ivy to make wreaths for Yule, as wreaths ornamented with both ivy and holly were thought to represent life. Ivy was also associated with marriage and was frequently worn as a crown during the Yule festival. Ivy is still used for decorating homes during the holidays and is also popular for wreaths and centerpieces for Yule and Christmas. Take a moment to appreciate the history and symbolism of ivy the next time you see it.

- **The Yule Ginger Bread**

Gingerbread is a holiday tradition dating back centuries to pagan celebrations. The word "gingerbread" comes from the Old English root "gingifer," meaning "preserved ginger." Ginger, a popular spice in ancient Europe, was used for its flavor and medicinal properties. Gingerbread was originally made using only ginger and honey, but other spices like cinnamon and nutmeg were added to the recipe over time. These spices were considered warming and healthful, making gingerbread the perfect winter treat.

- **Yule Symbol of Holly Tree**

The holly tree is a popular Yule symbol for a good reason. The evergreen plant is associated with new life and growth, making it a natural choice to represent the season of renewal. Holly also has a long history as a decoration, dating back to Germanic pagans to ancient Roman times. In many cultures, the plant is seen as a sign of good luck and is often used to ward off evil spirits. After Christianization, the sharp leaves of the holly tree represent the thorns of Christ's crown, making it a popular symbol of Christmas. Whether you view it as a representation of new beginnings or as a sign of good fortune, there is no doubt that the holly tree is an important part of the Yule season.

While both holidays have their roots in ancient pagan celebrations, they have evolved into very different festivals over the years. Christmas has become a time of joy and celebration, while Yule has retained its more reflective and contemplative nature. Whether you celebrate one or both of these holidays, enjoy the season.

Chapter 2: Yule Lore and Deities

As with most lore traditions observed worldwide, the festival of Yule is rooted in ancient beliefs, stories, deities, and historical figures whose relevance has survived the test of time for centuries. Many of these vestiges from old pagan, Germanic and Scandinavian cultures laid the basis for what billions of people now cheerfully celebrate as Christmas, which explains the continued interest in various legends around the solstices and paganism, Wicca, and Norse mythology. Learning about these founding myths and their associated deities and symbolisms will pave the way for a better understanding of Yuletide in its ensemble of rites and practices.

This dedicated chapter explores the most defining stories of Yule lore. We will begin with the one surrounding the birth of the Sun by Sunna, the eternal goddess of the Sun, and mention its parallelism to the birth of Jesus Christ in modern Christianity. Next, we will tell the riveting story of the battle between the Oak King (bearer of light and ruler of summer) and the Holly King (commander of the darkness and winter). Then, our discussion will touch on the folkloric theme of the Wild Hunt and its significance in the context of the winter solstice. To finish, we will delve further into how various deities spanning different traditions find their place in the origins of the Yuletide, including Odin, Saturn, and Krampus.

The Birth of the Sun

The duality between light and darkness is a fundamental pattern in ancient lore. Specifically, the transition from one to the other is often the underlying motive for popular religious celebration. In the context of the winter solstice, as observed in the pre-Christian era, the passage from darkness to light is precisely what the festival of Yule is about. It is a period of seasonal change and renewal, honoring the welcoming of the sun and the lengthening of days until summer, which in the Northern hemisphere signifies warmth, bountiful harvests, hope, comfort, and good health for all ancient folks and their families. This duality notably explains why so many groups throughout history, from the Egyptians to the Celts, held the sun in such high esteem and even worshipped it.

The birth of the sun is a defining aspect of Yule as it has been celebrated for millennia. At its core lies ancient Celtic pagan beliefs, the rebirth story of the Sun god, an allegory of the sun who would bring enlightenment to the world after months of darkness and hardship. Every year on the winter solstice, the goddess of the Sun would re-emerge from the Underworld and birth a son who was to become the new Sun god or king. The Sun god matured and continued to grow throughout the new winter and spring, with the sun rising north again, symbolizing the rich fertility he brought along with him. At the peak of the growing season, when flowers bloom and crops ripen for harvest, the strong and handsome son would become his divine mother's lover. They committed to one another romantically and would later mate. From that point on, the Sun god grew old and frail as crops were exploited for sustenance until he eventually died, and the sun returned to favor the south. On the next winter solstice, Sunna would give birth to their son, who replaced his father-brother and became the new Sun god. And on and on it goes. According to the ancient Celts' beliefs, this perpetual cycle of birth and death defines the annual rebirth of the sun, which still influences several traditions centuries later.

While Christianity appeared much later, we can draw certain parallels between the sun's perpetual rebirth story and the birth of the Messiah. The most obvious resemblance is that both events occur around roughly the same winter solstice period when days are the shortest and daylight is scarce. This possibly indicates a time of much-needed renewal and reinvigoration for believers in terms of symbolism. Whereas Jesus Christ was born of immaculate birth by the Virgin Mary, the Sun god was essentially the product of incest, a widespread and accepted practice across pantheons at the time. Despite this great difference in conception, both birth stories have a supernatural dimension as a pillar of these respective faiths.

In addition, the Messiah's documented portrayals as Savior and Light of the World (according to the New Testament) further reinforce the symbolic ties between the arrival of Christ and the birth of the Sun-god in ancient lore. It shows that, despite evolving traditions and syncretism, the sun as a celestial representation of renewal on Earth has been an integral part of both religious belief systems and folklore throughout the ages. Similar accounts can be observed with the Persian savior god Mithra and Hercules, the legendary Greek hero. His twelve back-breaking labors symbolized the sun's movement throughout the year across the zodiac.

The Two Kings

From a mythological viewpoint, the story of the Two Kings yet again illustrates the fierce, eternal battle between darkness and light, the underlying purpose of Yule. At that time, kings were the ultimate commanders of authority in the mortal realm, which explains why they were often featured in ancient legends. In Druidic mythology specifically, the light and darkness duality opposed the periods of the waxing year (from summer to winter) and the waning year (from winter to summer), over which ruled two king brothers, eternal sons of the Goddess. Their bi-annual confrontation is a common re-enactment theme in pagan festivals and rituals until today. It tells a story of life cycles, growth, death, and renewal, all rhythmic by the sun's mighty and life-altering revolutions.

The Oak King, who rules during the waxing year, assumes the leadership at the onset of the winter solstice. He is a representation of new light and life. A youthful symbol of health, vigor, development, and innovation, he fights and defeats his adversary by cutting off his head during an annual battle held on Yule. His victory marks the start of winter and the lengthening of days, bringing warmth and fertility until it peaks in mid-summer. In contrast, the Holly King is the embodiment of darkness and death. His reign is considered a time for learning, reflecting, contemplation, and deliberation. His rule lasts throughout the waning year, starting at Litha, the summer solstice when daylight becomes scarcer and uncertainty ensues due to widespread famines. At another yearly battle, he conquers the Oak King and rules for six months until the following Yule. The cycle then repeats. (Other accounts claim that the brothers simply "surrender" their life and compete for the favors of the Sun goddess mother, and, ultimately, they are the same.) Therefore, Yule allows us to learn the lessons of our experiences, lighting candles and bonfires to start anew while celebrating with a festive and generous feast lasting for 12 or 13 days.

Another lesser-known yet well-documented variation of this story is found in another Northern European mythology. The brothers' rivalry gave way to a ritual animal hunt this time. According to Irish lore, the little King of the waning year assumes the shape of a wren (a small yet clever bird). As the prey, he hides in an ivy bush (or Holly bush) to escape his predators. Soon enough, the King of the waxing year, personified as a hope-inspiring robin redbreast, finds him and kills him, ushering in the new bountiful winter season. Every six months, the hunt occurs until one kills the other, perpetuating the light-darkness cycle ad vitam æternam ('til Kingdom come).

The Wild Hunt

The legend of the Wild Hunt is one of the most common themes in European folklore. While it goes by many names and is most popularly cited in old Germanic (Wilde Jagd, Wütende Heer) and Norse cultures (Oskoreia, Odensjakt), the story quickly spread to the rest of the continent, from Spain all the way to Eastern parts of Europe. We even find various accounts as far as Quebec. The Wild Hunt is generally regarded as an announcer of catastrophe and is believed to precede dramatic events like wars, famines, and plagues – and is an omen of chaos and death. Although this is not the only interpretation, it blurs the line between the living and the dead.

Picture yourself lost in a forest on a cold, stormy night in the middle of winter. You gaze up to the dark sky and witness a morbid, spine-chilling sight. Riding above you is a horde of spectral hunters and their ferocious hounds, birds, Valkyries, elves, fairies, and other supernatural creatures, led by a ghostly mythological figure. The sound of the wind howling is deafening. Anyone unfortunate enough to cross their path or who dares to address them is destined for doom or worse. Sometimes, they will abduct you, transport you far away, and drop you somewhere unfamiliar, conscious, or otherwise. They will sometimes decide to enlist you in their ranks and take you to the Underworld, where great perils await. The sinister procession can also wreak havoc in towns and homes, stealing food and beer and terrorizing local folks. According to common themes, these night-roaming spirits were dead souls doomed to wander as a way to purge themselves from their mortal sins and wrongdoings.

Now, who can the leader of this fearful crew be? If one is to believe popular folktales, the Wild Hunt is led by various mythical characters, kings, historical figures, and heroes. In German folklore, the procession is commanded by the god Wotan and his werewolves. Instead of attacking innocent bystanders, they would loot villages and spread chaos. Further north in Scandinavia, the hunt was known as the Asgard ride and was led by Odin (Oðinn). Although rarely seen, its passage was recognized by the barking of his vicious dogs. One story has it that Odin roamed the night skies in an oxen-pulled carriage and that one must throw themselves to the ground to avoid being snatched or hurt. In early medieval England, the Wild Hunt was portrayed as a demonic party but later romanticized and said to be led by fairies. Its leaders notably included King Arthur, King Herla, Herne the Hunter, Nuada, and Wild Edric. In Wales, legend has it that Gwyn ap Nudd, ruler of the Underworld, was in charge of the nocturnal procession. Last but not least, in Irish mythology, the Fairy Cavalcade, as it is locally known, was commanded by well-known mythological heroes.

However, originally the myth featured a god and goddess leading a visit hunt to nearby lands during the holy holiday. They brought blessings and also accepted offerings from the local people. It is said that the two sky-riding deities could be heard despite the howling wind, but for some reason, they later became known as an ill-intended pack of ghouls. This initial version of the legend allows us to tie the significance of the Wild Hunt to the winter solstice, which, as we know, promises the return of light against darkness. The procession is seen as an allegory for the wild forces of nature that bring the year's cleansing tide, clearing away all that is undesirable and making way for new life. For this reason, the Wild Hunt neatly falls under the winter solstice's hallmark as a time for renewal, transformation, and change. It teaches us to let go of everything holding us back to start afresh, thrive in the coming season, and continue repeating this cycle.

Yule Deities

Yuletide certainly would not exist without the divine intervention of various deities. This final section covers some of the most relevant gods and goddesses across European traditions, from Old Norse culture to Wicca. We will investigate their symbolic influence and how they are related to Yule through their respective mythologies. Their portraits should provide plenty of insights into the fascinating folktales of this centuries-old festival and help draw interesting parallels with modern-day Christmas.

Odin

Also known as Jólfaðr ("Yule Father") and Jólnir ("Master of Yule") in Old Norse, Odin is the god of the dead, war, creativity, and wisdom. He is prevalent in Anglo-Saxon and Norse mythologies, bearing numerous names and taking various forms depending on local tales. As one of the most celebrated deities of the Yuletide, he is thought to be the precursor of modern-day Santa Claus. In stark contrast to the latter, Odin is commonly depicted as a thin, old, white-bearded traveler donning a cloak with a broad hat or hood over his head. His face is covered in mysteries, and he doesn't look too approachable. As mentioned in the legend of the Wild Hunt, Odin roamed the windy night sky of the Nine Worlds in search of knowledge and wisdom. Alongside him were packs of gods, beasts, and other spirits and creatures facing ice giants and heroically combated dark forces. He was notably known for flying an eight-legged horse named Sleipnir. The deity punished those who provoked his wrath and showered those he favored with gifts and good fortune. In opposition to many Christian portrayals, Norse folks knew Odin to be a generous and benevolent god who would grant humanity valuable presents during winter. Given these associations, Odin plays a defining role in Yule's beliefs.

Saturn

Saturn was the god of agriculture.
https://pixabay.com/images/id-2326787/

While the sixth planet of the solar system may immediately come to mind, Saturn was initially a deity in the Roman pantheon. He was the god of agriculture, celebrated on the occasion of a mid-December pagan festival known as Saturnalia. This was perhaps the most popular holiday of the Roman calendar, deeply rooted in the legends of the winter solstice. As with other defining deities, the god Saturn is honored with feasting, drinking, gift exchanging, and a spirit of collective joy to celebrate fruitful harvests. During this week-long feast, roles were exchanged, and slaves temporarily became masters. The symbol behind it was certainly to humble the powerful and empower the powerless. So, again, the theme of changing seasons and welcoming in a new light after the perils of darkness appear.

Cailleach Bheur/Beare

In ancient Scottish and Irish lore, this goddess is most commonly known as Beira. She also goes by the title Queen of Winter. The reign of this female deity begins in the late fall, when sunlight is scarcest and the earth infertile, and ends shortly before the summer solstice. She is often depicted as an old one-eyed woman who brings storms and havoc. Her appearance during Yuletide explains her association with the festival and winter solstice. She would purge the world of all frailty and defects to allow it to start fresh in the coming season.

Frau Holle

According to Scandinavian myths and legends, Frau Holle is the goddess who symbolizes the Yule season, the evergreen plants, nighttime, and snowfall. She is also commonly associated with rebirth and fertility. Frau Holle is often portrayed riding across the dark sky, driving her wagon, and accompanied by various creatures. If the similarities between her and Odin are not strikingly clear yet, she is also known to visit houses to distribute divine blessings to those she favors.

Thor

In today's popular culture, the name Thor generally invokes images of superheroes and titan-slaying warriors. Originally, Thor was a god in Scandinavian and Icelandic mythology. Many folktales depict him as a benevolent and protective god with a fun-loving and jolly nature. His connection with Yule is mainly owed to his precious goats, who carry the elves as they go from home to home, bestowing gifts to villagers. A parallel can be drawn between modern-day representations of the reindeer and Thor's goats, which, in Yule celebration, are decorative straw animals.

The Horned God

According to modern Wicca, Yule is celebrated yearly at the winter solstice to honor the rebirth of the Horned god, an allegory for the newborn solstice sun. As the god of hunting, his connection to the myth of the Wild Hunt leaves no doubt about his ties to Yule. The Horned god is also typically associated with wilderness, sexuality, and life cycle. He is often depicted with a beast's head wearing horns or antlers, further reinforcing the association with winter and its dangers.

Krampus

Lastly and similarly, the figure of Krampus, who does not technically fall under the deity category, is one all children dreaded around that time of year. Originating in Alpine folklore, Krampus is a hairy, beast-like horned figure who appears during the Christmas season to scare little ones who have misbehaved and punish them with birch rods. He sometimes accompanies Saint Nicholas, a European folklore personage and patron saint of children, in early December on what is known as Krampusnacht (Krampus Night) in Germanic lore. We find several variations of this bestial figure in regions of Germany and Austria.

Ultimately, the stories and folktales surrounding Yule lore are plentiful. They encompass many traditions and customs from all corners of Europe and beyond. Cultures worldwide continue to observe this time of year by honoring unique deities and engaging in a multitude of rituals. As we have seen in this chapter, the Yule festival honors the return of the sun and the lengthening of days of the winter solstice, symbolizing rebirth and renewal. It is a time of celebration and hospitality where communities of worshippers get together to feast, drink, and make offerings or sacrifices to their favored deities.

As illustrated in these founding stories, mythological gods and goddesses play a central role in the legends of Yuletide. Whether they bring light or sow chaos, give gifts, or inflict punishment, their symbolism is a great part of what Yule represents until today. Now, while keeping track of them all is certainly no easy task, as you go about your research, you'll start to see patterns and parallels emerge between different traditions. With Yule lore covered, the next chapter will introduce you to traditional Yule crafts and decorations, so you can celebrate Yuletide and honor the gods as it was meant to be.

Chapter 3: Yule Crafts and Decorations

Yule traditional crafts and customs are common among different cultures due to their widespread recognition during Christmas. The Yule tree is used for decorations and other activities like hanging the wreath to celebrate this special time. In this chapter, we explain the measures you can take to celebrate the Yule tradition in a pagan way and explore the pagan spiritual symbolism of the Yule Tree and Yule wreath. We will also draw parallels with Christianity's symbolism of these particular customs.

Furthermore, we explain how you can create various pagan ornaments to add to the tree. We also provide step-by-step instructions on creating and decorating Yule wreaths and how to hang them. Finally, we focus on plants and trees that produce green materials often used for pagan decorations.

The Yule Tree

The Yule tree, also known as the Christmas tree, is usually decorated to mark a special occasion in many cultures. This tree is an evergreen conifer species like fir, pine, juniper, cedar, or spruce. The tradition of using this tree for celebrations has roots in ancient civilizations in Europe, the Middle East, and Asia. The modern custom was popularized in the 19th century. The Yule tree is often decorated with bright colors and lights symbolizing religious events, spirits of the deceased, and stellar objects.

In the US and other countries, lighting the Christmas tree is an annual event used to celebrate the Christmas holidays. The tree is decorated with lights of different colors, and its lighting marks the beginning of the festive season.

The Yule tree is also viewed as a crucial symbol in pagan tradition. Among the early pagans, it represented the World Tree or Tree of Life. During the ancient periods, people used to decorate the tree with the gifts they expected to receive from the gods. It was usually decorated with natural ornaments like berries, pinecones, different fruits, and other symbols sacred to the goddesses and gods. Berries and popcorn were hung around the trees so birds could feed.

Pagan Spiritual Symbolism of the Yule Tree and the Yule Wreath

Yule has its origins in European traditions, especially in pre-Christian Germanic. When the nights became longer and the days grew colder, the ancient people gathered around fires and lit candles to lure the sun back. They would also take out their food to enjoy the festivities, often accompanied by dance and song, and people also took pride in decorating their homes. These Yule traditions are similar to the present Christmas celebrations. The following are common Yule traditions designed to accompany end-of-year celebrations.

The Yule Log

Build a Yule Altar

The Yule altar is an important component of the winter solstice, and its purpose is to honor the sun's return. A candle is crucial on the altar since it symbolizes the sun. The altar should also have winter symbols like cedar, evergreen boughs, wreaths, and pinecones. Use sweet grass or sage to cleanse the altar.

Wreaths

In ancient times, wreaths were traditional items that symbolized the wheel or the completion of a cycle. Evergreens were used to make wreaths and decorated with berries and cones. They were hung in different places around the home as decoration. Wreaths were also presented as gifts to symbolize friendship, goodwill, and joy.

Bells

Bells were rung in the morning during the Winter Solstice to eliminate demons that could have surfaced during the dark periods of the year. They also herald the brighter and warmer days brought by the solstice.

Caroling

Caroling was another common Yule tradition observed by young children via song to honor the Winter Solstice. The children would move around the village singing, and the villagers would give them sweets and other tokens of appreciation. The small gifts symbolized the food provided by Mother Goddess.

Evergreens for Yule

Evergreens were used as symbols of renewal, life, and rebirth. These were believed to possess power over death since they were always evergreen, and the color never faded. They were used to stop death and destruction and defeat winter demons. Evergreen plants also encouraged the return of the sun. Various nature symbols are used for Yule, including Oak, Holly, Ivy, Mistletoe, Bayberry, Laurel, Frankincense, Blessed Thistle, Sage, Pine, and Yellow Cedar.

Other Yule Symbols

Different foods are used for Yule, including fruits, cake, gingerbread, spiced cider, nuts, berries, turkey, pork dishes, ginger tea, eggnog, and wassail. The common colors of Yule are red, green, white, gold and silver. White symbolizes purity, while green stands for the waxing Oak King, and silver represents the moon. Gold symbolizes the sun and warmth.

Similarities with Christianity's Symbolism of These Customs

Christianity copied many aspects from the Pagan winter festivals, like the 12 days of Christmas. Pagan festivals usually last 12 days, and Yule strongly connects with December 21st. Yule has a strong cultural history, and it is celebrated together with the modern-day Wicca. Yule still refers to Christmas in Nordic regions, and the holiday is believed to be Nordic or Germanic in origin. It was celebrated for several centuries before the creation of Christmas by Christians in the 11th century AD. Christmas is meant to celebrate the birth of Christ, while Yule was used to honor the land spirits, ancestors, and gods. People would ask for protection from the spiritual world during the colder months. Yule was also used to celebrate the past year and new beginnings.

Christians adopted several traditions from the pagan people they conquered when they spread their religion to entice more people to join Christianity. They also decided to celebrate the birth of Christ during the same period of the year as Yule. During its early days, Christians did not want the Christmas holiday associated with Yule or practice or pagan traditions since they were associated with dark forces. The Christians imposed their religion to gain dominance over other cultures. The idea behind pagan Christmas is noble since it is meant to celebrate the new light, hope, and good fortunes brought by the year. Many people in Nordic countries are reclaiming their old pagan and Yule traditions after realizing that they are not demonic or evil. While an effort was made to demonize the pagan belief system, Yule and Christmas shared several things in common.

As a result of the shared history of Yule and Christmas, several pagan traditions have been adopted in the modern celebrations of Christmas. Yule traditions mainly included feasts and setting better intentions to serve the gods in the coming New Year. However, these have been transformed into Christmas celebrations and New Year's Resolutions. Christmas tree, caroling, and offering gifts are some practices with pagan origins.

Pagan traditions and Christmas share many things, like decorating the Christmas tree around December 21st. Yule trees were collected and decorated with candles and other ornaments to symbolize the sun, stars, and the moon and were also used as remembrances for the departed. The candles were mainly used to celebrate the sun's return and light. Candles are still used in celebrating Christmas occasions.

In short, Christmas is for Christianity, while Yule is celebrating the Wheel of the Year. However, several religions have adopted pagan rituals, which is why Christians settled on December 25th to celebrate the birth of Jesus Christ. Hence, the occasion coincides with pagan festivals that honor the pagan gods.

How to Create Pagan Ornaments

Various pagan ornaments can be added to a Yule tree for the Winter Solstice holiday. The following are a few ornaments that you can hang on your Yule tree.

Magical Ornaments

You can create different things using salt dough, like Sabbat ornaments. You need to use a cookie cutter to make these magical items and attach them to your tree. Cinnamon spell ornaments are ideal for your magical holiday project. Cinnamon smells and tastes good and has been used for various purposes. For example, the Romans burned it during funeral ceremonies since it was believed that the smell it produced was sacred and pleased the gods.

When you design an ornament, write a symbol of your intent on it using a toothpick. Also, consider natural items from nature as your decor. Simple things like feathers, seeds, and acorns are easy to use, and you can make many interesting things from them. Chenille stems can be used to create pipe cleaner ornaments, which are easy to use. For each pentacle, you need three chenille stems that are easy to bend. So, once you teach your children, they can handle the task. Plastic or glass, fillable ornaments can also be used to create spells that you can hang on your Yule tree.

Pentagram Stars

Pentagram symbols have spiritual meanings, and you can add them to your Yule tree. Use paper to fold stars, wood, or yarn. These symbols represent the moon, light, and sun and are great options you can add to your tree. You can also use orb decor and faux candles since they represent solar energy.

Herbal Sachets

Herbal sachets include using scrap fabric, giving your home an amazing aroma. These are simple pouches or bags made of cloth stuffed with various aromatic blends of flowers, herbs, and other pleasant-smelling goodies. Choose sacred plants commonly associated with the Yule tree, like holly, mistletoe, or evergreen, to create your herbal sachets.

Solar Symbols

The winter solstice marks the sun's return, so you can use different solar symbols to decorate your holiday tree. It is also a wonderful way to spend quality time with your kids making these decorations. Use construction paper and paper plates to make simple symbols, or purchase wooden discs from your local craft shop and paint them bright orange or yellow. Another way to create these symbols is using modeling clay or salt dough.

Witch Balls

These beautiful balls are specifically meant to protect your home and its inhabitants from harm. You'll get protection and good luck when you make a witch ball every year. Although you can hang a witch ball anywhere, a Yule tree is an appropriate place. Some people use clear bulbs that provide a luminescent shine and fill them with herbs and flowers. You can also add anything meaningful like a rune or personal note.

Fertility Symbols

Although Neopaganism rarely associated Yule with fertility, the early pre-Christian societies linked fertility with the winter solstice. They would perform fertility rites underneath the mistletoe, and the concept of wassailing also originated from pre-Christian European activities. You can hang different items like cups, antlers, and eggs to pay tribute to fertility deities. However, these are not usually honored until Beltane.

God's Eyes

God's eyes are versatile crafts and one of the easiest to make since you can use any color. For your Yule crafts, create them in green, red, white, or gold. Cinnamon sticks are great for these crafts since they provide the season's scent. Natural items are also perfect for decorating your tree. You can collect feathers, twigs, acorns, berries, bark, and pinecones to hang on your tree. These are believed to be natural gifts and provide luck and a protection shield from harm.

Make an Evergreen Yule Wreath

Wreaths provide ornamental decorations associated with Christmas and are commonly made from twigs, evergreen leaves, or flowers organized in a ring.

Building a wreath using winter evergreens like juniper, fir, cedar, and pine is a great way of honoring the season. Evergreens were associated with prosperity and protection in ancient pagan cultures, making them popular options for celebrating the end of the year.

Over the years, countless wreaths have been created and hung over mantels and used to adorn doors and walls. These wreaths are made from various materials, including natural greens, pinecones, straw, coffee filters, fresh cranberries, and Christmas ornaments. Although wreaths are commonly associated with Christmas, they make great decorations all year round. A door with a pinecone wreath looks inviting and warm, while cranberry wreaths in winter provide a colorful contrast to the bare trees and white skies.

Satin rosebuds consisting of ribbon-wrapped wreaths add fine details to springtime events. In summer, seashells in different sizes and shapes can be collected and used to decorate various places around your home. The options to fabricate new wreaths are endless.

How to Make an Herb Wreath

Herb wreath.
https://www.pexels.com/photo/wreath-of-grass-on-lilac-background-7195270/

If you want to make a wreath from reeds, gather them together, check if the size is appropriate and use them to form the base. Keep a container with different wreath-making materials so that you can experiment with various tools. If using greenery, use floral wire of different gauges as well as tape in different colors, floral pins, twine, craft glue, and pins to form the wreath. Use pruning shears to shape your greenery, and cut your wire and shape it using wire snips. You'll also need nose pliers to reach tight crevices.

Bend your twigs or reeds and create some flexibility using the chosen wire. Tie the materials together and secure them using wire. Bring the two ends together and use more wire to secure them to each other. Make sure you loop the end of the wire around the wreath many times and tighten the twist. When the wreath's shape is formed, you can add different materials to decorate it. There is no strict formula for making a wreath, so create anything that suits your needs.

Hanging a Wreath

You can display your wreath on the entrance door for everyone to see. Make sure that you avoid creating unsightly holes on your walls or woodwork surfaces. Use a sturdy ribbon or mono-filament to suspend the wreath on your door. Using ribbon provides a bold and bright display. Hang the wreath at the desired height. A fishing line is also ideal for a seamless and no-show appearance when you hang your wreath. Hanging hardware, including screw eyes, D rings, picture hooks, and nails, can also be used for your project.

Magnetic and command hooks are ideal for hanging your wreath in your preferred location. An adjustable wreath hanger can also hang the wreath on your door. If you want to hang a heavy wreath with a ribbon, first attach the mono-filament capable of supporting the weight, then put a ribbon on top to decorate it. Hanging a wreath is not a special deal since you can apply any formula you deem necessary.

Other Important Yule Symbols

Besides wreaths, consider other essential Yule symbols like the Yule goat, commonly used as a Christmas symbol and tradition in Scandinavian and Northern European regions. As discussed in chapter one, it originated from Germanic pagan, and modern Yule goats are representations created using a straw. The celebration of the Yule goat is connected with the Norse god Thor who rode in a chariot drawn by two goats, Tanngnjostr and Tanngrisnir, to the sky. The last sheaf grains in a harvest were also bundled and credited with magical properties and saved for Yule celebrations, where the Yule goat also featured prominently.

The Yule goat is also connected to other traditions, like the sheaf of corn. It is viewed as an invisible spirit in Sweden, and it would appear before Christmas to ensure the Yule preparations were carried out correctly. Any straw or hewn wood object could be considered the Yule goat. In Scandinavian communities, a popular Christmas prank was to take a Yule goat and place it in someone's house without being noticed, and the pranked family would also use the same method to get rid of it.

The purpose of the Yule goat has changed throughout history. In the Scandinavian custom, like the English tradition of wassailing, which was held during Christmas or Epiphany, the young men would dress in costumes and walk around performing pranks, plays, and singing songs. This tradition was common in the 17th century and continues in certain areas. The characters often included a Yule goat which was scary and sometimes demanded gifts.

The Yule goat is known as the best Christmas ornament in Nordic countries. The modern version of the Yule goat is a decorative figure made of straw and is tied with red ribbons. This goat is often found on or under the Christmas tree. In towns and cities, the larger version of the Yule goat ornament is erected strategically. This practice started in the 1960s and continues to be observed in different places.

Yule Feasts

Yule feasts are significant symbols since they are meant to celebrate the Wheel of the Year. It is the ideal time for people in different places to invite family and friends to a table with favorite holiday dishes in honor of pagan traditions. The dishes mainly consist of seasonal foods preserved in earlier months or those harvested in winter despite the frost.

Different foods are associated with Yule. For instance, the fiery spices, including cloves, ginger, cinnamon, and turmeric, symbolize the heat from the reappearing sun. Additionally, root vegetables like carrots, beets, potatoes, parsnips, and turnips are included in the feasts since they can withstand the frost. Root vegetables can still be harvested under biting conditions. Preserved and dried fruits are also incorporated into various Yule dishes. Winter squashes are essential components of the Yule table. They can be harvested in autumn and are usually kept throughout winter.

Most Yule festivities are accompanied by alcohol. Fermented beverages are often brewed in warmer months and aged to maturity in preparation for the feasts. Beer, wine, and mead are the common alcoholic beverages used to warm the Solstice feasts. Wassailing is another tradition celebrated to bless the fruit trees that brew alcohol.

In this chapter, we have covered a variety of Yule crafts and decorations that can be used for Christmas and winter solstice celebrations. The next chapter focuses on the trees and plants that produce green materials used for pagan decorations. It also highlights the significance of Yule-colored candles in the homes of different pagans, not only Wiccans.

Chapter 4: Sacred Trees and Plants

Countless species of flora have been held sacred by countless groups of humankind throughout the ages. Flora is the name of a Roman deity, goddess of spring, and all flowering plants that bear fruits and vegetation. Trees were often worshipped in ancient cultures. At other times, they depicted existing gods, goddesses, deities, and sacred things. They were mediums between the worshipper and the worshipped that dwells in them. They represented values, traits, natural phenomena, and metaphysical concepts. Trees were metaphysical at times. Similarly, plants and flowers have had many meanings, and their different qualities gave rise to various symbolisms.

The very essence of trees and plants, the cycle of their existence, their beginnings and ends, were contemplated by humankind, prompting similar meanings and symbols shared across many cultures. Their growth and regenerating leaves saw birth, life, rebirth, and immortality. Death, decay, and mortality were seen in their conclusion.

These very symbols are at the heart of the Yule celebrations. Yule is analogous to rebirth, transformation, renewal, and new beginnings. In many ancient cultures, Yule celebrates the sun's rebirth, marking the return of light and the approaching spring. It seems only fitting that trees and plants would be recurrent symbols associated with Yule and Yuletide celebrations.

Evergreens

Yule Trees

The cyclical nature of plants and trees is never-ending. The forces of nature giving rise to one another invoke continual life and immortality, perhaps the most important theme in the winter solstice. What is better to depict this eternal life than the very trees that never lose their leaves or their green color?

The original use of evergreen trees around the winter solstice period can be traced back to many ancient cultures across Europe and all over the world. In ancient Rome, temples were decorated with evergreen trees, symbolizing immortality, and the continuation of life, in honor of Saturn, the Roman god of time, wealth, and agriculture. Homes were also decorated with evergreen boughs and branches. They surrounded their homes with lamps to keep away the evil spirits of darkness. A common Christmas tradition, exchanging gifts also took place in the ceremonies. These rituals became known as Saturnalia, the most popular and remarkable festivity in the Roman Empire. Some of its traditions served as precursors to subsequent rituals and ceremonies in Europe.

Evergreens were very powerful symbols of renewal, rebirth, and immortality for Celtic Druids and Old Norse people. The first accounts of entire trees being cut down and brought home are contested, but traces figure in many Celtic and Norse traditions. They were adorned with coins, nuts, and fruits to bring luck, fortune, and fertility in the next spring.

Evergreen trees were worshipped in Norse mythology. Nordic people saw in them the depiction of the sun god Balder, son of Odin and Frigg. They decorated their trees with food and small carved figures and runes. The evergreens, widely abundant in the Nordic forests, also gave them the promise of a new life and the coming of a fruitful spring. Forests, especially those full of evergreen trees, were considered sacred places in most Northern Germanic and Celtic cultures. Before Yuletide celebrations, groups of people went to the forests, searching for the best trees they could find for the Yule log.

Trees, boughs, branches, plants, and branches of evergreens held a significant place in ancient mythologies and gave birth to traditions that still hold true to this day. Some theories also suggested that the Norse's mythical "Tree of Life," Yggdrasil, is a precursor of the Yule tree tradition.

To understand why evergreens were so cherished and held in very high esteem in Nordic and Celtic cultures, we should remember that winters of the Northern hemisphere are usually extremely dark and cold. The only glimmer of hope for many people had been those evergreen trees standing tall and green in the middle of the dead, decaying forests.

Light over Darkness

The powerful symbolism of the evergreen trees and plants is one of the defining aspects of the Yule and Yuletide celebrations. The celebrated sun's rebirth signals the return of light and brighter days leading to spring. Evergreens, symbols of rebirth and renewal, are a reminder that life will go on, days will be gradually longer, and spring will eventually take over the darkness of winter, just like the year before and the year before.

During the winter solstice's dark days, the sun's gradual return is celebrated, and hope for a fertile spring is restored. While tales around specific evergreen trees vary across cultures, these same key symbolisms overlap between many cultures and make up the essence of Yuletide.

Yule Logs

As mentioned in chapter one, burning the Yule log is a popular tradition worldwide that goes back thousands of years. This ritual also has its roots in ancient European cultures, namely Celtic, Norse, and Germanic. At winter's peak, the darkest day of the year, they would set fire to the log to cast out the dark and evil spirits. By doing this, they sought to bring luck, fortune, protection, and fertility for the coming spring. The trees from which the logs are cut down were carefully selected. They wanted the logs to remain on fire for the whole midwinter period, twelve days. In many local Northern traditions, it was mostly considered a bad omen and a sign of tragedy and sadness to come if the log ceased to burn before the end of midwinter. Others believed that failing to light a log from the first attempt would also bring bad luck. Yule logs were actually entire trees, cut down, brought into families' fireplaces, and, in some Nordic traditions, burned for twelve days. Since evergreen is an extensive family of trees and plants, various evergreen woods were used during the winter solstice to light bonfires. They all held various symbols depending on the traditions and cultures. However, they mostly shared the concepts of protection against evil and darkness.

- Oak

Oak tree.
https://pixabay.com/images/id-2018822/

These long-living trees are symbols of endurance, strength, and wisdom. Many myths and lore are associated with the Oak tree.

- **Holly**

In addition to protection, holly logs are linked with visions and revelations. Along with Oak trees, holly is highly sacred in many European traditions and the source of some of the most famous pagan tales.

- **Birch**

Birch trees are a powerful symbol of rebirth and regeneration. In the dense Northern woods of Europe, birch is among the first to recover from the various disasters that can affect forests. It can also grow in very harsh conditions. So, the birch tree signals new beginnings and a promise of life after death.

- **Yew**

Once worshipped in Germanic traditions, yew symbolizes aging, death, and resurrection, regarded as the Tree of Rebirth by ancient Northern Germanic cultures.

- **Ash (Evergreen)**

These fast-growing, mystical, and sacred trees symbolize everything from life and rebirth to strength, growth, health, and healing. They are closely associated with many gods and deities and portrayed in some of the most remarkable myths and allegories, particularly Yggdrasil or the allegorical Tree of Life.

- **Conifer Trees: Pine, Fir, Cedar, Spruce**

These pleasant-smelling trees, longtime providers of warmth, shelter, and refreshing energy, are admired for their restorative abilities. Besides protection, they are symbols of healing, cleansing, joy, and hope, among other things.

Mistletoe and Holly

The two iconic evergreen shrubs are the root of many popular traditions, as well as ancient myths and lore. Their significance to Yule traditions is huge, as they profoundly connect to the winter solstice's most central concepts.

Mistletoe

Mistletoe has held many symbolisms throughout ancient times. Due to its leaves remaining green all year, even though its host is dead or leafless, it symbolizes life and immortality, much like evergreens. In addition, its unique reproductive system and ability to bear colorful fruits, even in winter, made it a symbol of fertility.

The most cherished mistletoe in some Northern European cultures, notably Celtic, was the one found on Oak, the widely-worshipped tree at the time. In that event, it is seen as the soul of the Sacred Oak. A whole Celtic ritual revolved around this specific sight. On the sixth day of midwinter, they would gather, led by a high priest, and harvest the mistletoe with a golden sickle. Mistletoe fruits, though poisonous, were believed to bring health and luck and were picked using large pieces of cloth lest they touch the ground and bring bad luck. Mistletoe was also brought indoors on the winter solstice to protect and chase away evil spirits.

The mistletoe was the central element of two very popular traditions and myths.

Kissing under the Mistletoe

Although later adopted by Christianity, this famous romantic tradition is believed to be of Scandinavian origin. It simply says that a couple who meet under a mistletoe must kiss, and they are then bonded by eternal love. It also traces back to ancient Rome, precisely during Saturnalia. War enemies were gathered under the mistletoe to reconcile, although not to kiss, under the mistletoe. The origins of this tradition are unclear, but it is aligned with the mistletoe's ancient symbolism of love and fertility. Mistletoe's love symbolism can also be related to Frigg and Baldur's captivating motherly love tale.

Sacred Plant of Frigg

One of the earliest accounts of mistletoe's love symbolism is the classic Old Norse tale of Frigg, the goddess of love, and her son Balder, god of the summer sun. Frigg wanted to protect her son at all costs for fear of the total annihilation of all life on Earth. Other versions of the tale suggest that Balder had many nightmares foretelling his demise. Either way, Frigg took an oath with every element of nature so that her son would never be harmed. However, she overlooked mistletoe when making her pact. Loki, the god of evil, took advantage and eventually ensured Balder was killed by an arrow made from mistletoe. Frigg's mourning tears became the mistletoe's berries. In the end, strangely enough, they came to symbolize love and rebirth. The connection to the mistletoe's kiss is observed in other versions of the story. One is that Frigg revived Balder. She declared that all those who pass under the mistletoe deserve protection, love, and a kiss.

Holly

The sparkling green holly leaves and the glaring red berries make up the holly tree that enchanted many ancient cultures throughout history. Holly's significance in the winter solstice's celebration of the sun's return already places it among the holiest and most cherished plants in pagan mythology. The Holly King and the Oak King's eternal battle speaks for that. Much like mistletoe, the sacred holly was revered for its evergreen qualities. Holly is often used for Christmas decoration, adopted from earlier traditions, and made to represent Christ's thorns, Crimson berries illustrating his blood, and the holly tree representing eternal life. However, Holly's spiritual symbolism dates back to various earlier mythologies. It was considered a sacred tree, a symbol of rebirth and protection from evil and darkness. Its thick and convoluted branches were believed to block the evil forces from passing through. Early Europeans commonly used holly branches as winter solstice decoration for protection. For some, holly was so sacred they had to make an offering to be able to cut down branches.

Holly and Oak were seen in many pagan traditions as the Earth's sole rulers, putting one another down with every coming season. Holly was regarded by Celtics as the most sacred tree, after Oak. However, it found its way to most European mythologies at the time as a prominent symbol for Yule and winter solstice celebrations.

Ivy

Along with mistletoe and holly, Northern Europeans highly regarded ivy, especially among the Druids. Ivy was the center of a couple of mythological tales. It mostly symbolized strength, determination, and protection from evil, due to its thick, complex branches and ability to grow in relatively harsh conditions. Its evergreen characteristic also makes it a symbol of eternal life. Ivy branches were used as decoration in many ancient feasts, including Yule, often formed into wreaths and garlands by Celtics. As an evergreen climbing plant able to cling even to dead trees, ivy was also viewed as the eternal soul of the dead and deceased. They represented rebirth, resurrection, and immortality because they could grow back after being cut down.

Ivy was a recurrent symbol in many other ancient cultures, namely Greek and Roman. The Greek god of wine and pleasure, Dionysus, was portrayed as covered in ivy. His Roman counterpart, Bacchus, the god of wine, also wore ivy crowns to protect himself against intoxication, becoming a symbol of protection.

Ivy and Holly

Ivy became primarily associated with holly in Christian traditions; the combination of the two was popularized by the famous Christmas carol "The Holly and the Ivy." However, this association had its origins in pagan mythology. Celtics viewed holly as a male plant and ivy as a female plant, often bringing them together. Young Celtic women used to carry ivy branches to bring fertility and luck during Yuletide. Coupled with holly, the two represented faithfulness and fidelity.

Birch

Birch has been a venerable evergreen since time immemorial. It has been shared across many cultures, and many deities are closely associated with it. The Old Norse Freya and Thor, the old Irish Brigid, the white goddess, and the Roman Venus are closely connected to the tree. It stands to reason. Birch is the miraculous evergreen that can survive the harshest conditions. It is the first to regrow and stand tall after the most destructive catastrophes. It signals new beginnings and gives new hope that all is not lost and life carries on. Birch was also cherished for its medicinal properties.

Birch was among the first trees to be used as Yule logs for the winter solstice by many North European cultures. It was also thought to cast away evil and darkness and help people be brave and courageous. It was admired for its elegant, feminine presence. It was particularly connected to motherhood, portrayed as tender and graceful.

Yew

The enduring yew trees were sacred throughout most of the Celtic Druid history. Their fascinating capacity to regenerate, creating new trunks when their branches touch the ground, makes them a powerful symbol of rebirth and resurrection. Due to their highly toxic alkaloids, yews also symbolized death in Celtic mythology. This continued with the Christians, who sometimes buried yew sprouts with their deceased. Yews were also among the most recurrent trees in churchyards.

In ancient Greek mythology, the goddess and Titaness Hecate, and the crone of the triple goddess, are depicted in yew. Together, they guard the worlds of death and the afterlife, influencing many later portrayals of yew.

In many ancient traditions, yew was believed to be a connection between the world of the living and the world of the dead. During midwinter, yew was a symbol of protection against the otherworldly forces of darkness. It was quite common for Yule logs from yew to be brought home and burned during the winter solstice. That signaled the death of the year. Sometimes, they were saved and used for protection against thunderstorms.

Oak

Oak was by far one of the most universally sacred trees in ancient times. Oak was possibly the longest-lived European tree at the time, and many cultures cherished it. There were many accounts that the great Tree of Life, Yggdrasil, was an oak tree standing at the center of the cosmos.

Oak trees symbolize strength, resistance, luck, and protection across many cultures. In some cultures, they were depictions of gods and goddesses. Oak trees symbolized the Greek god Zeus, the Roman god Jupiter, the Celtic god Dagda, and the Germanic god Thor. Oak trees are associated with protection from thunder mainly because these gods were, too. We have already mentioned how mistletoes are most cherished when they grow on oaks, especially those hit by thunders. Druids viewed those mistletoes as a divine gift from the gods. They harvested them and offered them as a blessing.

Among Druids, oaks were very sacred and often worshipped. Oak groves and forests were holy places frequented by Druids in search of knowledge and wisdom. Druids are sometimes suggested to be "disciples" of trees, going to oak forests and listening to the wind rustling oak trees to acquire revelations. They also gathered there to discuss important societal matters and solve issues.

During the winter solstice, oak trees held a steady presence throughout many Northern cultures. Particularly in Celtic culture, branches of oak trees were used as decoration. Even bigger, entire trunks were cut to make the Yule log. It would eventually burn through the 12 midwinter days. For druids, the sun stood still during that entire period. Burning the Yule log was necessary to push away the darkness and the evil spirits – and oak was the most preferred tree for the Yule log. The other significant connection between oaks and Yule celebrations is the Oak King's never-ending battle with the Holly King.

Yuletide celebrations are, in their very essence, a celebration of nature. They are anticipation of a fertile spring to wash away the cold, dark winter. Amid all the darkness and long nights, evergreens are the only glimmer of light left in all those leafless, dead forests. It explains how they are at the heart of Yule's symbolism. As a result, most rituals revolved around them, and most cultures cherished them, worshipped them, and linked them to deities. The spiritual value of trees and plants is truly universal. Different mythologies are packed with themes of nature and eternal life. Yule is but another reminder that life will go on, and hope will emerge even in times of decay.

Chapter 5: Setting up Your Yule Altar

The ending of a year has its importance in almost every religion. It symbolizes the time passed and the time still to come. Religions around the world have their own set of traditions and rituals according to their beliefs. These rituals are old but are still practiced and performed. As time has progressed, they have taken the shape of a tradition or culture, culminating in a diversity of celebrations or rituals occurring around the globe every year. People celebrate the end of the year, keeping their religion, culture, and traditions in mind. As the calendar year comes to an end, it is pretty special.

What Is Yule, and When Is It Celebrated?

Pagans uniquely celebrate the end of the year and the winter solstice. This celebration is called Yule. However, due to the different hemisphere seasons, the Yule celebration for pagans varies depending on where they live. People living in the northern hemisphere celebrate it on December 21st. But these celebrations occur in June if you live below the equator in the southern hemisphere. The winter solstice is considered the longest night of the entire year. During this time, at night or following the sun's rise, pagans light a log or make an altar, which must be lit for a full 12 days.

This celebration welcomes the New Year by symbolizing the sun's return. Although all pagans don't have altars, having one is always a good idea. Individuals can have varying beliefs; some consider an altar a strong aspect of their belief system. The Yule altar is a crucial part of the winter solstice celebration. The primary purpose of this altar is to honor the returning of the sun, so for this purpose, an altar always has a candle symbolizing the sun's return. As it symbolically represents the sun, the candle's color needs to be golden or yellow. Candles of other colors can be used, but a yellow flame is much more preferred.

Benefits of an Altar

An altar allows you certain experiences in life that you can not have otherwise. Religious people often wish for a connection with the divine, which does not matter how you view the divine or your religion. An altar allows you a direct connection with the divine regardless of how you view divinity. Life is complex at the best of times, and looking at life from different angles and perspectives is immensely important. An altar helps to view life from several perspectives. You can think of any situation you are in from multiple angles, giving a better understanding of the world. One of the biggest advantages of having an altar is that it allows you to fight off negativity.

Even if you do not have a deep connection with your religion or any religion, you'll feel a spiritual connection and fill that void in your heart with the help of an altar. Making an altar can be incredibly relaxing, and you have a sacred place in your house for praying and meditation. It has innumerable benefits. If you like crafting, placing your crafting objects on your altar is incredibly rewarding. However, one of the biggest benefits of an altar is that it creates a positive energy flow throughout your home. Moreover, if you are a parent, building an altar is the perfect way to help your children understand the concept of divinity. They can actively participate, which will help you introduce spirituality to your children.

How to Make an Altar

The best part about an altar is that it can be as creative as you want. They are your expression, so make an altar however you want. It can be crowded with various elements and objects or as simple as you wish. It all depends on what you want the altar to be. You should make one that helps you create a better connection with whatever you want to embody in life. An altar usually depends on intentions. You must think deeply about why you are making the altar and your intention. Once you set your intentions, you'll get an answer, and you can use that to create positivity in your life.

If you like to write, the easiest way to make an altar would be to write down your intentions on a piece of paper. Once you have written them, you will know what you wish to accomplish or call into your life. It could be the energy you wish to embody or even call for support from your ancestors. When you know your intentions, collect items that give you the same vibe similar to what you wrote down.

Once that happens, you can collect various objects to be placed on your altar. These could be objects that match your intentions and give you a feeling or a vibe that matches what you have written down. Imagine that you wish for support from your ancestors. You need to collect items that make you feel connected to them.

Here is a list of items that you can place on your altar.

1. Photos of ancestors
2. Crystals

Crystal assortment.
https://www.pexels.com/photo/close-up-photo-of-assorted-crystals-4040644/

3. Candles
4. Flowers
5. Statues
6. A journal
7. Incense
8. Cards
9. Pictures that remind you of your ancestors
10. Books

You can place anything that gives you a feeling of connection with your ancestors.

How to Set Up a Yule Altar Properly

Deciding where to set up your altar can be an overwhelming process. Usually, the altar needs to be where you feel the most spiritual, inside the home. Moreover, you need to set up an altar where you are quiet and not disturbed by anyone. It is all about where you place your altar. Ensure that you place your altar where you feel active, energetic, present, happy, and spiritually connected. Therefore, you can set it up on a table or a corner in your home where you feel the most at peace.

If you are considering setting up an altar for Yule, you'll need to understand how best to decorate it and what to use. You will need the right place to set the altar up properly and enough space so the objects are not congested. The altar can be placed inside your home or in the open air in your garden. If you do not wish to place the altar at your home, you can find a small place not far from your home with a shelter and where it is safe to be alone. However, keep in mind that the altar's placement has significance. Make sure the altar and its objects are safe and protected and that it is at a location where you can observe or check up on it from time to time. Most people prefer to keep it inside their home or garden. The whole structure and features of the altar need to symbolize the sun's return or the winter season. Here is how you can decorate your Yule altar.

Set a Cauldron

Setting a cauldron is crucial for a Yule altar. If you can not find a cauldron, use a bowl or any other vessel and place it at the center of your Yule altar. The placement of the cauldron is important because it symbolizes a goddess' womb. Place a pillar candle inside the vessel. The candle's color can be of your desire, but it is best to use a color like gold or yellow that symbolizes the sun. The candle symbolizes the sun's rebirth coming out of the cauldron. If you desire to make your candle more special and attractive, you can paint or draw solar symbols on it. Use cinnamon oil and rub it all over the candle. When you have everything ready on your altar, leave it until the Yule ritual begins or the eye of the winter solstice.

Colors of Winter

Since Yule falls in winter, the colors of winter are used. So, cold colors are better suited to decorate your altar. These colors include blue, silver, and white. You should also find a way to include other colors like red, white, and green as they also belong to the winter season. Add dark green to the mix is also recommended because evergreen boughs are a great feature for a Yule altar. The colors you add to your Yule altar all symbolize something particular. In modern pagan concepts, the color red is associated with passion. However, it is not the case with everybody. Some people consider red to be a color of prosperity. If you look at it from the Chakra perspective, red is associated with the root chakra, and the location is at the base of your spine. This is a healing chakra, and many experts believe that this chakra helps us connect to the Earth and gives us energy.

As mentioned above, every color needs to symbolize something. If you have chosen the color white on your altar, consider using it for purification rituals. If you are using white, consider hanging white snowflakes and stars. White symbolizes keeping the environment spiritually clean. As the winter solstice is all about the sun's return, it is a good idea to hang a few gold suns around your home. They can be hung to pay tribute. Moreover, we know that the association of the sun or light is usually with gold or yellow color. Therefore, using yellow or gold candles is necessary for some individuals.

Symbols of Winter

As the winter solstice's longest night celebrates the sun's return, adding solar symbols to your altar is a great option. You can use anything bright and shiny to represent the sun. Mostly, people use gold discs and yellow candles to symbolize the sun. Some people also opt for a large pillar candle and then add solar symbols. That could also be a great idea if you're space-conscious and wish to confine the altar to a small place rather than adding solar features all around your home.

Evergreen boughs are also an amazing addition to your Yule altar and also symbolize the winter solstice. You can add items like reindeer or even a small statue of Santa Claus. Moreover, adding pinecones and a Yule log is also an excellent choice. Another great idea is to use sacred plants associated with the winter solstice, and the evergreen family has many plants you could use. Here is a list of the plants:

1. Pines
2. Juniper
3. Cedar
4. Fir

These plants are associated with safety, security, and prosperity. Moreover, these plants also symbolize renewal and the continuation of life as we know it. Hanging these plants around your house will ensure the safety and prosperity of your family and those who live in it.

Other Signs of Winter

You can use innumerable things and objects to symbolize the winter for your Yule altar. The only thing that can restrict you is the space for your altar. You can add a bowl of dry fruit and nuts like walnuts and pecans. If you wish to use fruit, place oranges and apples on your altar. Since the winter solstice is about rebirth, if your intent is about fertility, then add something associated with fertility and abundance, such as mistletoe. The addition of bells can be both promising and profound. Even though bells and candies are traditionally used for Christmas, they are also associated with winter, so they can also be used for a Yule altar. Adding bells is great because, in ancient pagan times, bells were used to scare or drive away evil spirits. However, on Yule, you can use them to symbolize the coming of prosperity and peace to your home. Many people worldwide also use sun wheels to depict how the sun has begun its journey back to Earth.

Symbols of Nature

If you are making an altar, you can not skip Mother Nature. You'll need to put specific symbols or objects depicting nature's rebirth during the Yule celebration. Forest animals are one of the best symbols of nature, so use them to represent nature's rebirth. The best one to use is a Stag because it symbolizes the Wiccan god. You can also use other symbols like snowbirds and squirrels. Keep in mind that the altar needs to be meaningful to you. Any addition you make symbolizing the season, sun, or rebirth can be used as long as it has meaning to you.

Decoration of the Altar

The altar's decoration must be aligned with the festival or celebration. Once the altar is ready and you wish to decorate it according to the festivities of Yule, you need to keep several things in mind. The festival deals with reflection, rest, and the returning of the sun, which is symbolized by light, meaning that the sun has a major role and deserves the most time and decorations to its name. However, it does not mean that you can put up any object resembling or symbolizing the sun. You need objects that have a connection with you. Below is a list of colors mainly used for a Yule altar.

1. Gold or yellow for the sun
2. Silver for the moon
3. Red for blood, symbolizing life
4. Green of rebirth or nature or coming back of the crops
5. White for peace, tranquility, and new beginnings

After the colors, you'll need a set of objects to honor all the elements. Here is a list of all the elements you may need for this purpose.

1. A chalice or kettle used to hold water.
2. Evergreens or stone for the earth
3. A sword and incense for the atmosphere, environment, or air.
4. A staff or candles to symbolize the sun

You can also use a variety of herbs or oils for this purpose. Cedar has healing properties, which are usually associated with healing and protection. Moreover, cedar can also be used for cleansing. Pines can be used for longevity or immortality. This tree has a unique purpose. Even though humans are not immortal, this tree symbolizes having the courage to handle all the setbacks in life. It symbolizes the inner strength and positivity needed to overcome life's difficulties. Cinnamon is associated with the sun so that it can be used as an element of fire. Cinnamon can be highly beneficial because it makes you feel cozy and warm where your altar is placed.

Placement of the Altar

The placement of the altar holds immense importance. As it symbolizes the sun's return and the Yule festival is celebrated in winter, you need to place the altar facing north because the north is aligned with the winter season. You can drape your altar with a cloth or scarf. However, ensure that the cloth you use is of the seasonal color, red, green, or gold.

The Finishing Touches

If incense is unavailable, you can find different ways to honor the various elements. One idea is to use pine and cedar sticks and place them on your altar. If you can not find anything yellow or golden color, you can always use oranges to symbolize the sun. Moreover, decorate the altar according to your intent by keeping objects of value to you and having a deep connection. They could be anything, as long as they symbolize something regarding the Yule festivities, and you feel a connection with them. If you are a staunch believer of any deity, you can even add offerings required by that deity.

How to Take Care of Your Altar

You must understand that an altar is not a dead piece of wood or simply made up of "some objects". It is alive with energy because an altar comprises the same elements that make up our bodies. If not taken care of, the altar can die over time. The flowers get burnt, and the offerings dry up and evaporate. The altar's candle and incense will burn out, and all that remains are the ashes. Therefore, it is imperative to take care of your altar.

You need to regularly dust your altar and clean it of ashes to keep your altar alive and well. If you see some plants or flowers drying up or dying, replace them with new and fresh ones. The water placed inside the chalice or bowl can dry up or get polluted, so add fresh and clean water. You can even change the photos you have put on your altar. These can be changed with changing seasons so that you can follow Mother Nature.

If you use the same altar for a long time, you might need to replace almost everything. The Yule log can dry up, and sometimes even termites will attack or infest it. So, it is best to add new objects to your altar to keep it updated and new.

A Yule altar can be used for various purposes. Once you have properly set up a Yule altar, you can use it for many rituals and spells. Adore your altar, and it will give you a sense of pride and accomplishment. It should be in a place where you feel fulfilled and spiritually active. When you have constructed your altar, you can move on to experiencing new things with it, like magic spells and rituals. It can be a new way for you to view the world positively. It is not only relaxing and peaceful, but you can also experience the world in an entirely new and exciting way. Practicing magic spells and numerous other rituals using your altar will be an amazing way to keep yourself connected with the spiritual world.

Chapter 6: Recipes for a Yule Feast

Our pagan ancestors combined the symbolism of foods harvested during winter and the celebration of a new year by designing the Yule feast menu. Ancient gatherers created pastries shaped like the sun to pay homage to Lugh, the Celtic sun god, and hunted wild boar to offer tribute to Freyr, the Norse god.

The Yule holiday season is the perfect time to fill your stomach with dishes that ignite the body and complete the soul. The winter solstice holiday offers rich, comforting, and calorific (calories do not count during the holidays) foods to the table.

We celebrate this season with hearty recipes from specific seasonal ingredients you will not find during any other celebration. Festive roasts and meat-stuffed pies, delicious soups prepared with care, scintillating salads that pop with flavor, mouth-watering sweets, crumbling cookies the whole family can share, and drinks for the adults.

The bulk of these festive foods is made with seasonal ingredients like foods sourced from the earth like potatoes and carrots or ground spices such as ginger, cinnamon, nutmeg, vegetables, and fruits, like oranges, pears, and citrus fruits.

It is the time of year when traditions are honored, celebrations made, and respect paid through the foods we eat. Join in on the solstice tradition and create a scrumptious Yule-themed feast.

Yule Centerpiece Main Course

Yule dinner traditions dating back hundreds of years revolved around hunting, roasting, and feasting on boar. Our ancestors would spear and roast the whole pig on an open fire as a sacrificial display of honor to the gods.

Our cooking methods are a little more refined these days, but we can still enjoy a traditional Yule feast with roasted or baked ham. How you prepare your meat is up to you. Either cook it in the oven or barbecue it in the garden.

Ginger Glazed Ham

Cooking Time: 4.30 hours

Preparation Time: 15 minutes

Serves: 8

Difficulty: Easy

Ingredients:

- 1 joint of mildly cured ham
- 1 quart of ginger ale
- 4-1/4 oz of ginger preserve
- 3 tablespoons of mustard
- 4-1/4 oz of brown sugar (soft)
- 1 tablespoon of cloves (ground)

Method:

1. Place the ham in a large pan and pour over the ginger ale. Bring the pan to boil and slightly lower the heat to a swimmer for around 5 hours. Just before the 5 hours, preheat the oven to 230C.

2. While waiting for the oven to heat, prepare the glaze. Put the ginger preserve in a bowl and stir together with your chosen mustard. Add the brown sugar to the mustard and add the ground cloves.

3. Take the cooked ham from the pan and place it on a tray lined with foil. Cut away the skin leaving a thin layer of fat. Spread the glaze on the ham and cook in the oven for 30 minutes. Serve when hot for a hearty meal or cold in a sandwich.

There are plenty of Yule-themed recipes for ham. Try adding any of these other glazes for a scrumptious meat centerpiece.

Flavor with ginger glaze, maple glaze, Dijon maple, cider glaze, orange or apple glaze, brown sugar, honey glaze, raisin sauce, or pineapple rights for an added Yule spirit.

New England Lamb Bake

Cooking Time: 3 hours

Preparation Time: 30 minutes

Serves: 8

Difficulty: Easy

Ingredients:

- 1 tablespoon of canola oil
- 2 pounds of lamb, sliced into 1-inch cubes
- 1 sliced onion
- 2 sliced carrots
- 3 cups of chicken broth
- 2 tablespoons of fresh parsley
- 2 leeks (white portion), sliced in 1.5 inches
- ¼ cup of flour
- ¼ quarter teaspoon of thyme
- ¼ teaspoon of pepper
- ½ teaspoon of salt
- 3 tablespoons of butter, melted and divided
- 3 potatoes, peeled and sliced

Method:

1. Preheat your oven to 230C. Place lamb and onion in a large cooking pot and cook the meat, stirring continually until browned. Add flour and stir until blended with the meat. Pour in the chicken broth and bring to a simmer until thick. Stir in leeks, carrots, and rosemary, 1 tbsp of parsley, thyme, salt, and pepper.

2. Grease a large baking dish and add the lamb. Place the sliced potato on top and cover with 2 tbsp of melted butter. Cook in the oven for 1 hour, remove to add the remaining butter over the potatoes. Place back in the oven, and bake for around 1 hour, until golden. Leave to sit, then sprinkle the remaining parsley.

Winter Solstice Casserole (Vegetarian Option)

Cooking Time: 1 hour

Preparation Time: 10 minutes

Serves: 4

Difficulty: Easy

Ingredients:

- 6 sausage/vegetarian substitute
- 3 hash brown potatoes
- 7 eggs
- A handful of mushrooms
- 1 onion, diced
- 1 green onion diced
- 1 tomato, diced
- A handful of your preferred cheese
- Sage and rosemary
- 2 tablespoons of butter

Method:

1. Preheat your oven to 230C. Set a frying pan at medium heat and melt the butter.
2. Sauté the onion and mushrooms
3. Stir in the potatoes and cook until brown
4. Pre-grease a large casserole dish, and spread the mixture evenly along with the dish
5. Grab a bowl and mix the sausage, eggs, cheese, and preferred seasoning. Pour over the potatoes
6. Place the dish in the oven for around 40 minutes. After 10 minutes, remove the dish and sprinkle cheese to cover the mixture
7. Garnish with sliced tomatoes and green onions.

Celebrate Yule with these hearty centerpieces that keep you in a festive mood all day long.

Winter Solstice Soups

Try a soup packed with traditional ingredients if you prefer something lighter or a cozy afternoon tea. Continue the Yule theme of paying respect to pagan gods by preparing and eating food generated through the soil.

Slow-Cooked Winter Soup (Vegetarian)

Cooking Time: 5-1/2 hours

Preparation Time: 15 minutes

Serves: 5

Difficulty: Easy

Ingredients:

- 1 cup of split red lentils
- 1 diced onion
- Bay leaves
- A handful of your preferred cheese
- 4 diced celery stalks
- 2 ½ tablespoons of extra virgin olive oil
- 4 diced carrots
- 3 zucchinis chopped into chunks
- Fresh thyme
- 3 zucchinis chopped into chunks
- 240 ml of chopped tomatoes
- 4 potatoes chopped into cubes
- 6 cups of chicken or vegetable broth/stock
- 3 cups of sliced cabbage

Method:

1. Add the following ingredients to the slow cooker: chicken/veg stock, olive oil, tomatoes, onion, thyme, celery, bay leaves, carrot, cheese, zucchini, potatoes, red lentils, and season to taste.
2. Cook on low heat for 10 hours or high heat for 5-1/2 hours.
3. 1 hour before cooking time ends, add and stir in the cabbage

Garnish with a sprinkle of cheese, parsley, and a drizzle of olive oil

Solstice Seafood Stew

Cooking Time: 2 hours

Preparation Time: 30 minutes

Serves: 6

Difficulty: Medium

Ingredients:

- ½ pound of cleaned squid, slice the tentacles in half and slice the bodies into rings
- 1 pound of sliced white fish like cod, hake, bass, or halibut
- 1 pound of shrimp
- 1 pound of clams
- 1 pound of mussels
- 2 cups of vegetable or seafood broth/stock
- Add red-pepper flakes for preferred taste
- 4 cloves of garlic
- 1 cup of fennel
- Dried oregano
- 1 cup of chopped onion
- ½ cup of celery
- 2 tablespoons of extra-virgin olive oil
- 1 tablespoon of tomato paste
- 1 baguette
- 1 tablespoon of tomato paste
- Canned tomatoes
- Clam juice
- Parsley
- Unsalted butter to taste
- 1 cup of white wine
- Bay leaves
- 1 tablespoon of lemon zest

Method:

1. Heat a large pot over medium heat, add olive oil, chopped celery, onion, and fennel, then add salt and pepper to taste. Mince some

garlic and add this with the pepper flakes. Stir the mixture for around 8-10 minutes.

2. Simmer the mixture and add the squid. Cook for around 20-30 minutes and stir occasionally. Add the oregano and tomato paste and stir for 1 minute.

3. Raise the heat a little, add the wine and cook until half of the liquid is reduced. Add stock, tomatoes with juice, clam juice, and bay leaves. Bring to the boil, reduce heat, cover, and cook for another 30 minutes. Season to taste.

4. Take a bowl and add the butter, lemon zest, and 1 tbsp of parsley. Cut the baguette in half, toast both sides, and spread the flavored butter on each side with the remaining garlic.

5. Add the clams to the pot, cook for 5 minutes, and stir in the mussels and shrimp. Place the fish on top of the cooked stew and cook for 5 minutes. Serve and season to taste

Yule Salads

Nutritious salads are the ultimate winter comfort food. Dense with roasted vegetables and citrus fruits, making the festivities magical.

Roasted Winter Salad Bowl

Cooking Time: 40 minutes

Preparation Time: 20 minutes

Serves: 5

Difficulty: Medium

Ingredients: (Salad)

- 9 oz. of quinoa

- 14 green beans, sliced

- 2 oz. of green onions

- 1.75 oz. of toasted seeds (your preference)

- 4 garlic cloves

- ½ avocado

- ½ tablespoon of extra-virgin olive oil

- 3 potatoes, chopped into chunks

- 1.75 oz. of kale

Ingredients: For the dressing

- ¼ cup of extra-virgin olive oil
- ¾ oz. of maple syrup
- ¼ cup of red wine vinegar
- ½ oz. of mustard

Method:

1. Preheat the oven to 200C and place green beans, garlic cloves, and chopped potatoes in a large roasting tin. Season with olive oil and salad and pepper to taste. Place in the oven and roast for 20 minutes.

2. Remove the tin from the oven and give the vegetables a flip, then roast in the oven for a further 15-25 minutes until nicely browned.

3. Boil the quinoa for around 15 minutes until fluffy.

4. Mix the ingredients for the dressing in a bowl.

5. Remove the roasting tin from the oven, separate the garlic cloves and mix them into the dressing.

6. Take a large mixing bowl, add the beans, potatoes, quinoa, green onions, and kale, then coat the vegetables with the dressing. Season to taste.

Beverages

Our ancestors did it right. What better way to recover and quench their thirst after a winter solstice hunt with large bowls of mead and punch?

These days many more are options available to us, but we still pay homage by re-creating pagan beverage traditions during the festivities.

Wassail

Wassail is translated from Old Norse as "be fortunate" or "be in good health." This Yule drink is filled with festive spices and fruits, with endless possibilities. Add or remove spices, flavors, and liquid to suit your holiday needs. You can make it with or without alcohol.

Ingredients:

- Apple cider
- Orange juice
- Lemon juice
- Granulated sugar
- Allspice berries
- Cinnamon stick

- Fresh ginger- peeled
- Cloves or 1 tablespoon of ground cloves
- Water

Method:

1. Take a large saucepan or stock pan and place over medium heat. Add water and sugar to taste. Boil for around 10 minutes.

2. Remove the mixture from the heat. Drop in a cinnamon stick with the ginger, cloves, and allspice berries.

3. Then stir in the apple cider, lemon, and orange juice and place over low heat to warm. Your house will smell amazingly festive after this. Thank us later.

   The Yule festivities will not be complete without delicious desserts. Why not stick to a time-honored tradition and go with a classic?

Yule Log

The Yule log was born from the origins of Norway. Pagan rituals called for a family tradition in honor of the winter solstice. They would search the woods for the healthiest-looking Oak tree and burn it on the fire at home to celebrate life and deference to the gods. The ashes would be scattered around the family home as protection against spirits.

Cooking Time: 15 minutes

Preparation Time: 20

Serves: 6

Difficulty: Easy

Ingredients: For the sponge

- 3 eggs
- 1 teaspoon of baking powder
- 3 oz. grams of plain flour
- 3 oz. grams of caster sugar
- 2 ½ tablespoons of cocoa powder

Ingredients: For the icing and filling

- 1-1/4 cup of cream
- 2 0z. of butter
- 1 ½ tablespoon of golden syrup
- 5 oz. of chocolate

Ingredients: For the mushrooms

- Piping bag (Buy or make your own)
- Cocoa powder
- 3 tablespoons of sugar
- 2 eggs
- 2 oz. grams of melted chocolate
- A dash of tartar

Method:

1. Heat the oven to 230C. Line a large baking tray with a non-stick baking sheet and whisk the caster sugar and eggs together in a mixing bowl

2. Mix the baking powder, flour, and cocoa powder, and fold in the mixed eggs. Then pour the mixture into the baking tray. Bake for 15 minutes

3. Place a layer of non-stick baking sheet on a flat surface and tip the baking tray onto the sheet. Roll the cake up from one edge to the other. The paper should remain

4. Melt and mix the chocolate and butter for the icing and pour in the syrup and 6 tablespoons of cream. Mix until smooth.

5. Unfold the cake, spread the remaining cream on top of it, then roll it back up again.

6. Take a spatula and spread the icing over the entire cake. Use a fork to add a tree bark effect. Dust some powdered sugar to give the log that wintery feel.

Method: For mushrooms

1. Preheat the oven to 230C and mix the tartar and egg white into a large mixing bowl.

2. While whisking the eggs, sprinkle in the sugar. Mix until stiff peaks are formed.

3. Transfer the mixture into the piping bag and pipe into stems onto a baking tray to resemble mushroom stems and small dome shapes for the mushroom caps

4. Cook the "mushrooms" for around 3 hours

5. Remove the tray from the oven and wait for the "mushrooms" to cool. Dip the caps into the melted chocolate and attach the stems. Decorate your log with the "mushrooms" however you want and dust with powdered sugar

Decorate your masterpiece with red ribbons or green holly for a deep midwinter feel and candles to honor the deities.

How to Imbue Your Food with Yule Magic

The winter solstice celebration is a tradition dating back hundreds of years. It is a time to exchange and share recipes, eat delicious foods, and pay homage to our pagan ancestors. There are many ways to recreate the traditional pagan methods of belief and respect during Yule.

It is a time for hibernation and regeneration. Until the daylight returns and the heat from the sun thaws the frozen soil, light your candles and fires to symbolize the internal flame of life within the home. The pagans of ancient days used fire and light during solstice to ward off evil spirits and resurrect a source of light through the darkness of winter.

While you decide on what recipes will suit your Yule celebration, consider caroling as a way to involve yourself further in the culture of your ancestors.

To prepare for the winter Wassail recipe ingredients, pagans would gather together to sing and play instruments around the apple, orange, and lemon trees to generate healthy and plentiful yields. To prepare for your Yule feast, find an orchid or meadow and spread your Wassail upon the greenery to imbue nature with sacred and magical attributes in preparation for next year.

Decorate your house or table with sun images to bring luck and banish evil. The gold, oranges, and yellows symbolize the successful conquering of the darkness as winter unfolded.

Do not ignore any plants you may have lying around. Instead, make a garland or a wreath to symbolize eternal life, and scatter some thistle, ivy, sage, or holly on your dinner table. For pagans, evergreen brought hope that not everything perished during the winter. The plants that survived winter brought to light and life into the homes that used them.

Kiss under the mistletoe? This tradition comes from the pagan symbol of love, peace, and fertility. Mistletoe was mixed with the sacrificial blood of an ox or boar and used as medicine and fertility treatment. Providing life and hope during the cold winters was an important factor for survival. Hang up some mistletoe to pay homage to the past traditions and imbue your feast with magic, love, and light.

Take the New Year's resolution and turn it into something more than an end-of-the-year tradition. Do it the pagan way and make a new year's resolution by paying respect to the meat on which you are about to feast. Lay your hands in the meat before carving it and commit to the next year.

The Yule recipes mentioned are only a few ways to bring pagan tradition into your home this winter. There are many different foods to add to your festivities. Remember, pagans hunted and feasted on wild animals, and while we are not recommending hunting, obtaining the exact sacrificial meat will imbue your feast with tradition.

Festive meats like venison, goose, and ham were sacrificed, roasted, served, and feasted on as a way to absorb gold wisdom and power. So, do not forget to pay respect to this method while you are enjoying the solstice.

Bring fresh and preserved fruit to the table to symbolize the foraging aspect of ancient pagan tradition. Giving them as gifts will hark back to the community aspect of surviving winter together.

Planting your own vegetables in preparation for winter is a great option. If you can forage for your own food, you are one step closer to your pagan ancestors and the rituals on which they placed so much importance.

Root vegetables like sweet potatoes, carrots, beets, potatoes, parsnips, and turnips could survive the harsh winter, providing an extreme source of sustenance for ancient pagans. The meals from these ingredients symbolized hope and health during the winter. When most things perished, these foods created and sustained life.

If you want to experience Yule as the ancient pagans did, preparing your Yule feast for the winter solstice should involve as many of the above traditions as possible. There will always be more things you can do to pay homage to Yule. Finding the right menu could be as simple as a modern-day feast coupled with the promise of the future with a traditional new year's resolution or a glass of Wassail at the end of a long day peeling potatoes.

Chapter 7: Yule Activities and Customs

You are walking through the mall and suddenly catch a glimpse of large logs and evergreen trees. You turn around and see a huge display of Yule decorations. You can not help but smile as you think about the upcoming holiday season. You start to plan the various activities you'll be doing to celebrate. You'll probably spend time decorating your home, baking holiday cookies, and wrapping presents. You might also attend a holiday party or two or even go caroling. Of course, you will also want to take some time to relax and enjoy the company of your family and friends. But, no matter how you choose to spend your holidays, one thing is certain, they will be merry and bright. Here are some of the most important activities to do with your family when celebrating the Yule festival. But first, it is also important to understand the essential value of the Yule festival.

Yule: a Festival of Giving Back

Many people think of Yule as a pagan version of Christmas, but it is so much more. While Christmas is a time of giving and donating to those in need, Yule gives back to nature, animals, and the poor and needy. It is a time to celebrate the cycle of life and remember that we are all connected. We are all part of the same web of life. When we give back to nature, we are really giving back to ourselves. When we give to the poor and needy, we are helping to create a more balanced and just world.

Decorate a Yule Tree

For many people, decorating an evergreen tree is essential for celebrating the Yule holiday. Decorating evergreen trees was a key part of pagan celebrations of the winter solstice. For pagans, evergreen trees symbolized new life and hope for the future. They were often decorated with items representing fertility, like berries and flowers. In some cases, pagans hung small pieces of food on the tree to offer thanks to the gods for a bountiful harvest.

When celebrating Yule with your family, there is something special about decorating the tree for the holidays. It is a chance to spend time with family, bond over shared traditions, and get creative. If you are thinking of decking your halls this year, why not start with a Yule tree? Here is a step-by-step guide to help you get started:

- First, gather your materials. You'll need a tree (real or artificial), lights, garland, and ornaments. Make cardboard cutouts of different foods or find plastic models in a store. Find lights that resemble glowing candles, berries, and flowers. Once you have everything you need, it is time to get started.

- Start by stringing the lights around the tree. Wrapping them around the trunk and branches in a spiral pattern always looks nice. Make sure that the lights look like upside-down candles because ancient pagans decorated the Yule tree outdoors and garnished them with hanging candles to symbolize the sun, stars, and the moon. Once the lights are in place, it is time to add the garland. Drape it around the tree in loops, starting at the top and working your way down. If you use ornament hooks, now is the time to add them to the branches.

- Next, it is time to hang the ornaments. Start with the larger ornaments and work your way down to the smaller ones. The ornaments can range from plastic fruit models to small flowers.

And, Voilà!! You have your Yule evergreen tree ready.

Make a Yule Greeting Card

The holiday season is a special time of year when family and friends come together to celebrate. One way to show your loved ones how much you care is by sending them a Yule greeting card. These cards can be homemade or purchased, but they should always be personal and thoughtful. For children, making their own Yule greeting cards is a great way to get them involved in the holiday spirit.

To make a Yule greeting card, first, gather your materials. You'll need some cardstock, scissors, glue, and any other embellishments you want to use (markers, glitter, etc.). If you are ambitious, you can make your own paper.

Next, it is time to start crafting. Let your children loose with the scissors and let them cut out whatever shapes they want. Once they have got a nice pile of cutouts, help them glue the cutouts onto the cardstock to create their masterpiece. If you are using other embellishments, now is the time to add them. They can decorate the cards with drawings or paintings and write beautiful messages inside. Not only will this create cherished memories for years to come, but it will also spread the holiday cheer. So, consider making and sending Yule greeting cards as a fun and meaningful way to celebrate the season.

Light a Yule Log

Lighting a Yule log is the most important part of a Yule festival.
Joe Malzone, CC BY-SA 4.0 <https://creativecommons.org/licenses/by-sa/4.0>, via Wikimedia Commons: https://commons.wikimedia.org/wiki/File:The_Yule_Log.jpg

The Yule log is an important part of the Yule festival, and lighting it in your home is a great way to enjoy the holiday with your family. The Yule log is the most important part of a Yule festival as it signifies the sun's power and would be lit for the full 12 days of Yuletide. Nowadays, it is very hard to practice burning Yule logs outdoors, mainly by lighting logs in the fireplace. Lighting the Yule log also brings good luck for the coming year. If you are looking for a way to add some extra magic to your Yule festival celebrations, decorate your Yule log with cinnamon stick, holly, and mistletoe. It is a fun way to enjoy the holiday with your family and friends and bring good luck for the coming year.

Are you looking for other fun and creative ways to celebrate the holiday season with your kids? Why not make your own Yule log right at home? You'll need three pieces of wood (same length but different diameters), bundling wire (wires are more secure, but you can also use a ribbon), craft straw, pine needles, leaves, and berries (alternative). Bundle the smaller diameter logs together with the wire or ribbon. Next, take the larger diameter log and place it perpendicular to the bundled logs. Finally, decorate your Yule log with straw, pine needles, leaves, and berries. This activity is a great way to teach your kids about the importance of nature during the holiday season. Not to mention, it is a whole lot of fun.

Engage in Yule Entertainment

The Yule festival is a great time to celebrate with family and friends and celebrate. One of the best ways to celebrate time to get together with family and friends is by engaging in Yule entertainment activities. Yule-themed movies are an excellent way to get into the festive spirit and teach kids about Yule customs and traditions. Reading books on Yule is another great way for kids to learn about this special time of year. Quizzes, puzzles, and games are also a great way to entertain kids and help them learn about Yule customs and traditions. Engaging in these activities is quality family time; your kids will enjoy the Yule season while learning something new.

Create an Evergreen Wreath

Did you know that decorating your home with evergreen wreaths is very important while observing the Yule festival? It might seem like a simple decoration, but it has great significance. The materials used to make the wreath, yew, holly, pine, mistletoe, and ivy, represent different things. For example, yew represents everlasting life, protection, and prosperity. Holly and ivy ward off negative energy, pine has healing magic, and mistletoe brings fertility and abundance. By hanging an evergreen wreath in your home, you invite all of these positive things into your life.

But why stop at a wreath? Dream big and make a solstice bush. This is a large evergreen bush decorated with all sorts of festive items. It is believed that your wish will come true if you make a wish while standing under the solstice bush. So, to bring some extra magic into your life this holiday season, decorate with evergreen wreaths and bushes.

Go on a Solstice Nature Hike

The winter solstice is the shortest day of the year, and for pagans, it marks the beginning of a new cycle. Celebrating the solstice with a family hike is a healthy way to connect with nature and feel the power of the season. Being out in the natural world, surrounded by greenery, helps you feel more connected to the earth and understand the true meaning of the Yule festival. Sitting in nature, feeling the sun on your face, and being one with the elements can be a very grounding experience. It will help you appreciate the changing seasons and connect with Yule's pagan roots. Taking your family on a winter solstice hike is an important ritual where you understand and appreciate this special season's true meaning.

If you want a realistic experience of the ancient Yule festivals, what better way to celebrate than spending a night outdoors beneath the stars? A nature hike is a perfect activity for getting everyone in the family involved. When night falls, build a bonfire and enjoy a feast, drinking ale or wine, listening to old legend Yule stories about Norse gods and their importance to the Yule festival. An evening under the stars is a perfect way to connect with your pagan roots and nature like ancient pagans did and learn more about the tradition. Plus, it is a unique experience your whole family will enjoy.

Give Back to Nature

The Yule season is a time for celebrations, and many people enjoy decorating their homes and yards with lights and greenery. However, it is also important to remember the true meaning of the holiday by giving back to nature. One way to give back is to scatter seeds for birds and other animals or plant new trees. You can also feed animals in your area or simply spend time enjoying the wildlife around you. By taking these simple steps, you can help preserve the ancient pagan traditions of Yule and show your appreciation for nature. In addition, these activities are a great way to teach your family about the importance of giving back to the natural world. So, this holiday season, take some time to thank nature by giving back in your unique way.

Exchange Gifts Inspired by Nature

The Yule festival is a time to celebrate the natural world and show appreciation for all it does for us. One way to celebrate is by exchanging nature-based gifts with our loved ones. Traditional items like evergreen wreaths and holly branches are significant symbols of the season and remind us of the importance of maintaining a connection to nature. Furthermore, giving gifts from the earth shows our gratitude for all it provides. Exchanging gifts can be a powerful act of intention that helps incline people more towards nature. So, this Yule, take a moment to connect with the natural world and express your thanks to it. It will be sure to bring some extra cheer to your holiday season. A few gifting ideas are:

1. Herbal Incense

Incense has been used for centuries in religious ceremonies and to create a pleasant-smelling environment. It is made from various natural materials, including fragrant flowers, plants, and herbs. Incense made from these materials is a great Yule festival gift.

One of the oldest known ceremonies is using herbal smoke to offer prayers to the gods. Make a variety of smells and mixtures, bottle or bag them, and gift them to friends in a colorful basket with an incense burner. Your friends will appreciate the thoughtfulness of the gift and enjoy using the incense in their homes.

2. Scented Candles

Anyone who has ever stepped into an Herbal Candle store knows the overwhelming power of fragrance. Whether you prefer the smell of fresh-cut roses, jasmine, or lavender, there is a scent for everyone. What better way to spread holiday cheer than with a scented candle? Herbal scented candles are the perfect Yule gift for anyone on your list. They add a pleasant smell to any room, but they can also illuminate your festive night. By dispersing the aroma of herbs, flowers, and other plants, you create the perfect atmosphere for your Yule celebration. So, look no further than an herbal scented candle for a unique and thoughtful gift.

3. Crystals

Natural crystals make a great Yule and Wiccan gift because of their magical properties. Crystals help relieve many problems, making them an ideal present for loved ones. For example, crystals help heal physical and emotional pain, promote relaxation, and protect against negative energy. They also cleanse and purify space, boost creative energy, and promote prosperity. Since they are so versatile and have so many different uses, natural crystals make a wonderful gift for almost anyone of all ages and cultures on your list.

4. Essential Oils

Herbal essential oils and magical oils make great gifts for any occasion, but they are especially well-suited for Yule and Wiccan celebrations. The healing properties of these oils are beneficial for the mind and body. Aromatherapy is popular for providing stress relief, improving mental clarity, and boosting energy levels. Since these oils are derived from natural plant sources, they are in harmony with nature, making them ideal for spell work and other rituals. Moreover, these oils' pleasant smells help create a festive and uplifting atmosphere.

Wassailing

Wassailing is an important custom and ritual performed while celebrating the Yule festival. The word "wassail" comes from the Old Norse "ves heill," meaning "be of good health." Wassailing is a practice that involves going from door to door, singing carols, and offering a toast to neighbors to spread good cheer and bring blessings for the coming year. The wassail cup was traditionally made of earthenware or pewter and filled with cider, ale, or wine, sometimes with spices or fruit added for flavor. The wassail bowl would be passed around, and each person would take a sip before moving on to the next house. Wassailing was a way to promote community and fellowship during the cold, dark winter months. It was also believed that the noise of the carolers would scare away evil spirits. Today, many people still enjoy wassailing as part of their Yule celebrations. It is a wonderful way to come together with friends and family and create lasting memories.

Perform a Wishing and Gratitude Ritual

A great way to get into the holiday spirit is by lighting candles and setting intentions for the year. Creating a cozy and festive atmosphere also helps you focus on your goals and visualize them coming to pass. Light a candle and speak your resolutions. Then, meditate with the candle and let it burn down as you visualize your ambitions becoming true. If you prefer, write down your resolutions beforehand so you can refer to them during your visualization. This Yule activity will surely motivate you for the year ahead.

Another way to make the season even more special is to take some time to reflect on all that you are grateful for. Lighting candles and writing down your gratitude is excellent for showing appreciation for the blessings in your life. You can also thank the nature spirits, gods, and your ancestors for their guidance and support. Expressing your thanks will bring you joy and attract even more abundance into your life. So, to make your Yule celebration even more meaningful, add some gratitude into the mix.

Singing Pagan Carols

There is something special about singing pagan carols during the Yule festival. Maybe it is because you can really let loose and be yourself without worrying about what others think. Or maybe it is because pagan carols are just so darn catchy. Whatever the reason, singing pagan carols is one of the most entertaining aspects of the Yule festival. There are plenty of great pagan carols to choose from, including "The Holly and the Ivy," "Deck the Halls," "Santa Claus is Pagan too," and "We Three Kings." So, whether you merely want to let off some steam or enjoy good old-fashioned holiday cheer, grab your friends and start belting out pagan carols. You are sure to have a blast.

The Holly and the Ivy

Many people are surprised to learn that the popular carol "The Holly and the Ivy" has pagan origins. The holly, with its evergreen leaves and red berries, symbolizes winter fertility, while the ivy, with its green leaves and white flowers, represents eternal life. Together, these plants represent the ever-renewing cycle of nature. The carol likely dates back to the medieval period when Europe was still largely pagan. Over time, it became increasingly popular in Wiccan Yule celebrations, likely due to its cheerful tune and optimistic message. Today, "The Holly and the Ivy" remains one of the most-played pagan carols during the holiday season.

We Three Witches

We Three Witches is a popular pagan carol many have enjoyed for centuries. The song tells the story of three witches who meet on Halloween night to perform their dark magic. While the lyrics may be lighthearted, the message behind the song is quite serious. The three witches represent the elements of earth, wind, and fire, and their meeting on the Yule night symbolizes the coming together of these forces to create a powerful spell. The song also pays tribute to the pagan holiday of Samhain, which was traditionally a time for honoring the dead and celebrating the changing of the seasons. Today, We Three Witches is still a popular choice for Wiccan parties and celebrations, and its popularity shows no signs of waning.

Santa Claus is Pagan too.

Santa Claus is a popular figure in Christian culture, and his image is often used to sell everything from toys to Christmas trees. However, some people view Santa Claus as a symbol of paganism, and the carol "Santa Claus Is Pagan Too" reflects this perspective. The lyrics of the carol state that Santa Claus is a pagan god who has been "whitewashed" by Christian churches. Furthermore, the carol suggests that Christmas is a pagan holiday that has been Christianized, reflecting the belief that Christianity has co-opted pagan traditions. Whether you view Santa Claus as a jolly old man or a symbol of paganism, there is no denying that he is an integral part of Yule culture.

These activities and customs are used during Yule festival celebrations to create a fun and festive atmosphere. Taking some time to slow down and enjoy the company of those you love creates lasting memories cherished long after the Yule season ends. Whatever your plans are for celebrating Yule, incorporate some of these time-honored traditions.

Chapter 8: Yule Rituals and Ceremonies

The Yule season is a time of great importance in many cultures worldwide. For many, it is a time to celebrate the winter solstice and the Sun's return. It is also a time to reflect on the past year and set intentions for the coming year. Many different Yule rituals and ceremonies have been practiced for centuries. These time-honored rituals, from decorating the Yule tree to singing carols around the fireplace, create a sense of unity and belonging. Each of these rituals has its meaning and purpose, but all are essential to celebrating this special time of year. But what is it about these activities that makes them so special? Let us find out.

Yule Log Ritual

The Yule log was a crucial part of winter solstice celebrations in many cultures. The holiday commemorated the return of the Sun and the lengthening of days. The Yule log symbolized the Sun's power, and its warmth was believed to ward off evil spirits. The Yule log represented the Sun, and people were hoping to encourage the Sun to keep shining by burning it.

Ancient pagans kept the log burning for twelve days, and a little ale, mead, oil, or salt was sprinkled onto it daily. On the last day, the head of the family would carry the log into the house and put it in the hearth. The next year, a piece of the old log would be used to light the new one. The ashes and remains of the Yule log were thought to have magical properties. They were scattered around the house and farm to protect against evil spirits. Today, the Yule log is often used as a decoration, but some people still carry on the old traditions. Whether you use it to ward off evil spirits or enjoy its warmth, the Yule log is a significant part of winter solstice celebrations.

Modern Yule celebrations differ a little from the ancient pagan rituals. Many places do not allow burning logs outdoors, so families resort to burning the log and conducting their rituals indoors in their fireplaces. Due to different wood types having varied magical and spiritual characteristics, logs from various trees are burned to achieve a range of results. A family aiming for a prosperous year might burn a pine log, while a couple seeking fertility might burn a birch log in their hearth. The great Oak indicates strength and knowledge, while the aspen is the wood for spiritual enlightenment. Many families combine various wood logs and bind them with ribbon to create a huge ritual log encompassing all their benefits.

All family members are asked to gather around the Yule log or fireplace when performing the Yule log ritual. The family's patriarch lights the log. The adults in the house begin their prayers when the log catches fire, saying:

"The Wheel has turned once more, and

the earth has gone to sleep.

The leaves are gone, and the crops have returned to the ground.

On this darkest of nights, we celebrate the light."

"Tomorrow, the Sun will return, its journey continuing as it always does.

Welcome back, warmth.

Welcome back, light.

Welcome back, life."

After this ceremony by the adults, all family members circumnavigate the burning log several times. Once they are settled back in their original position, children pray to the burning Yule log by saying:

"Shadows go away, darkness is no more,

as the light of the Sun comes back to us.

Warm the earth.

Warm the ground.

Warm the sky.

Warm our hearts.

Welcome back, Sun."

Once the prayer was completed, everyone in the family would come near the altar and express gratitude to every member. For example, to their mothers for providing food and taking care of them throughout the year or their kids for being a constant inspiration. When the ritual was finally done, it was mandatory to sit around the fire, sing songs, and tell stories about pagan legends and Norse gods. Some families keep their logs burning for 12 days in their fireplace to depict the ancient way of this practice. The ashes from the burnt log must be saved in a jar or sprinkled around their house and workspace. The ashes bring more luck for the coming year and ward off evil spirits.

Consider practicing the Yule log ritual with your family to add more meaning to your holiday season. It is a great way to show your gratitude and create lasting memories.

The Yule Ritual of Returning Sun

The Yule ritual is an ancient tradition that celebrates the return of the Sun. Originally practiced by the Druids, the Yule ritual has been adapted by many cultures over the centuries. The days during Yule are short, the climate is cold, and post-holiday blues set in. So, it is no wonder many cultures have winter festivals centered on light. After all, what could be more cheering than bringing light back into your home and life? Celebrated by Pagans and Christians alike, this holiday commemorates the winter solstice when the Sun reaches its lowest point in the sky. As a festival of light, Yule festivities often involve many candles, bright colors, solar symbols, or even a bonfire. Whether you are lighting a candle to chase away the darkness or gathering around a bonfire to watch the sunrise, the Yule ritual of returning the Sun is a great way to celebrate the end of the year's longest night. The Yule ritual reminds us that the Sun will always return, even in the darkest times. It is a time to come together and celebrate new beginnings.

Celebrate the return of the Sun by making various winter delicacies like cornbread, cranberry dressing, plum pudding, game stew, etc. Before the ritual, have the entire family dine together. When you have finished feasting, clean the area, and cover your table or altar with candles. Ensure to place the sun candle in the middle. A sun candle is merely a candle assigned in ritual to represent the Sun. It might be gold or golden in color and can even be engraved with sun sigils.

Turn off the lights and gather everyone around the altar. Facing the candles, pray:

"The wheel of the year has turned once more, and the nights have grown longer and colder.

Tonight, the darkness begins to retreat, and light begins its return once again.

As the wheel continues to spin, the Sun returns to us once more."

As you ignite the sun candle, say:

"Even in the darkest hours, even in the longest nights, the spark of life lingered on.

Laying dormant, waiting, ready to return when the time was right.

The darkness will leave us now, as the Sun begins its journey home."

Light the other candles, starting with the candles closest to the sun candle, and work your way outward. Say as you light each one:

"As the wheel turns, light returns.

The light of the Sun has returned to us, bringing life and warmth with it.

The shadows will vanish, and life will continue.

We are blessed by the light of the Sun."

When you have finished the ritual, reflect on all the good things that transpired this year. Consider your expectations and perceptions about the future and how the rising Sun will help you achieve everything you wish. After meditating, sit back and enjoy some eggnog and cookies while basking in the illuminating candlelight.

The Yule Goddess Ritual

The Yule goddess is a key figure in many pagan winter solstice celebrations. Also known as the Mother goddess of the Great Mother, she is seen as a symbol of hope and renewal. In many traditions, her role is to give birth to the new sun god at the winter solstice, marking the return of longer days and warmer weather. The Yule goddess is also associated with other aspects of nature, like plants and animals. Her symbols include holly and ivy in some traditions, representing fertility and rebirth. Rituals involving the Yule goddess often involve singing, dancing, and feasting. These activities help bring about a sense of community and belonging and provide a chance to connect with the natural world. The Yule goddess is a powerful reminder of the cycle of life and death and the importance of respecting and honoring nature.

How to Perform Ritual Solitarily

Solitarily performing a Yule goddess ritual is a great way to connect with the divine during the holiday season. Find a quiet space where you will not be disturbed. Next, light some candles and incense to create a peaceful atmosphere. Make sure to have candles in colors depicting nature like green, red, and yellow. Use incense sticks of cinnamon, myrrh, and frankincense for a feeling of nature. Then, sit or stand before your altar and take deep breaths to center yourself. Once you feel calm and focused, begin your invocation by calling upon the goddess of your choice. If you do not have a specific deity in mind, simply invoke the energy of the Yule season and whisper to the goddess:

"It is the season of the winter goddess.

Tonight, I celebrate the festival of the winter solstice, the rebirth of the Sun, and the return of light to the earth.

As the Wheel of the Year turns once more, I honor the eternal cycle of birth, life, death, and rebirth."

"Today, I honor the goddess of the forest, the Mother of nature, who rules the season.

I give my thanks to the beautiful goddess, whose blessings bring new life to the earth.

This gift I offer you tonight, sending my prayers to you upon the air."

Rituals for Groups

The Yule Lady is the reborn goddess; her tales of childhood represent the long dark winter nights. The Yule Lord is the Holly King, who rules over the light for half of the year. To perform the Yule goddess ritual, you'll need a small group of people, preferably four. You'll also need a decorated tree, some evergreen boughs, holly berries, candles, and a cauldron. Take a few moments to appreciate the tree's natural beauty before decorating it with the evergreen boughs and holly berries, and remember the goddess.

To begin, each person must take a moment to reflect on the story of the Crone and the Maiden. A person will each take the role of high priestess, Crone, and Maiden. Once the roles are assigned, it is time to light the candles and incense sticks. As you light each candle, say aloud:

"It is the season of the Crone,

the time of the winter goddess.

Tonight, we celebrate the festival of the winter solstice,

the rebirth of the Sun, and the return of light to the earth.

My season has ended, yet the season of the Maiden begins.

Thank you for the wisdom of your years and for seeing the season through to its end."

"You have stepped aside from that the new season may begin, and for this, we give you honor. We make these offerings tonight to show our love to you, O goddess. Please accept our gifts and know that we are entering this new season with joy in our hearts."

Once the prayers are over, sit closer to the evergreen tree or go out in nature. End the Yule ritual by feasting and drinking ale in honor of the goddess.

Yule Cleansing Ritual

Winter solstice, or Yule, is a time to celebrate the Sun's return and the natural world's rebirth. It is also a time for cleansing and purification, on a personal level and in our homes. One way to cleanse your home for Yule is to perform a ritual cleansing. It can be done on the night of the solstice or in the days leading up to it. To cleanse your home, you'll need a bucket of water, a handful of salt, a sprig of evergreen pine needles, sage, sweetgrass, mistletoe, and patience.

Start by casting a circle around your home, using salt water to create an invisible barrier that will protect your space during the ritual. Once the circle is cast, light some candles and incense, and say a prayer or invocation asking for guidance from the spirits of nature. Then, beginning at the front door, sprinkle saltwater as you walk through your home, banishing negative energy from each room. When that is done, combine a sprig of evergreen, sage, pine needles, and mistletoe and tie them with a ribbon. Use these plants to cleanse your house and smudge them in every corner. This is an ancient tradition to remove the evil and negative energies present in the house. You can do the same therapy on yourself and visualize all negativity being drawn out of your home and yourself and dissipating into nothingness. Finally, open all doors and windows to let in fresh cold air and bring in the positive energy. Some people, while cleaning, sing:

"Yule is here, and I smudge this place,

Fresh and clean, in time and space.

Sage and sweetgrass, burning free,

as the Sun returns, so it shall be."

After you've finished smudging, take a moment to appreciate the pleasant energy from having a clean physical place.

Yule Ritual of Blessing Your Tree

According to pagan beliefs, evergreen trees symbolize new life and rebirth. In the depths of winter, when the world is cold and dark, evergreens remind us that spring will come again. For this reason, evergreen trees have long been associated with the winter solstice celebrations. In many cultures, people would bless an evergreen tree as part of their solstice rituals, asking for its protection and fertility in the coming year. Today, people still bless evergreen trees as part of their Yuletide celebrations. They reaffirm their faith in the cycle of life and death and their hope for a prosperous new year.

When choosing the perfect evergreen tree, you must keep a few things in mind. First, consider the size of your home and choose a tree that will fit comfortably inside. Next, consider the type of tree that you want. If you want a traditional evergreen, opt for a fir or spruce. For something a little different, consider a pine or cedar. Once you've decided, it is time to head out to the tree farm.

When you get to the farm, take time walking around and examining each tree. Pay attention to the overall shape and size of the tree and ensure there are no bare spots. When you've found the perfect tree, cut it down, and bring it home. While cutting the tree, whisper:

"O evergreen, mighty tree, you who are full of life.

I am about to make the cut and ask your permission.

We will take you into our home and honor you,

adorning you with light in this season of the Sun.

We ask you, o evergreen, to bless our home with your energy."

Before decorating, you must bless the tree. Light candles and incense sticks when you bring the tree home. Create a casting circle around the tree. As you start your prayer, sprinkle saltwater on the evergreen tree and say:

"By the powers of earth, I bless this tree,

that it shall remain sacred, a symbol of life,

stable and strong in our home throughout the Yule season.

By the powers of the air, I bless this tree,

as the cool winter winds blow away the baggage of the old year,

and we welcome the brightness of the new into our hearts and home.

By the powers of fire, I bless this tree,

as the days have gotten shorter, and the nights grew dark,

yet the warmth of the Sun is returning, bringing with it life.

By the powers of water, I bless this tree,

a gift I give, that it may stay bright and green for us a bit longer

so that we can enjoy the harmony and peace of Yule."

Now it is time to decorate, and this is where your family can bring out their creative juices. String up some lights, hang homemade ornaments and berries. Do not forget about the garland and tinsel. These final touches will really make your tree shine.

Yule Blessing Ritual for Donation

Yule is a traditional winter festival celebrated for centuries. The Yule blessing is part of the Yule tradition, a ritual where people offer donations to those in need. The Yule blessing dates back to ancient times when the winter solstice was when the veil between the worlds was thin, and spirits could cross over into our world. The Yule blessing was a way to provide protection and goodwill to vulnerable people. Today, the Yule blessing is still practiced by many to give back to those in need. It reminds us that, even in the darkest times, we can all help make the world a little brighter.

You may be wondering how the Yule blessing ritual for donations is conducted. All the donations are combined in a casting circle. This circle is marked with four direction points representing fire, earth, water, and air. From these points, each circle member prays and blesses the donations. To conduct this ritual, you'll need candles and a symbolic representation of each four points. For instance, a vessel with stones, salt, and sand represents earth; a ritual bowl with burning camphor or a log represents fire; an incense stick represents air; a vessel like a chalice or a cauldron filled with water or wine represents water.

Once you have placed materials at each point, start accumulating all the donations inside the middle of the circle. Place four people with candles on the four points and pray.

The member on the earth symbol lights the candle and revolves around the circle, saying:

"May the power of earth bless the donation.

Earth is the home, the land, and the foundation of community.

Nurturing and firm, solid, stable, and full of endurance and strength,

This is the base upon which we build our community.

With these powers of earth, we bless this donation."

Once the member representing earth finishes his prayers and returns to his position, the member with fire lights his candle and revolves in the same way, praying:

"May the powers of fire bless this donation.

Fire is the heat, the fertility of action, the bringing of change,

Strong will and energy, the power to get things done,

Fire is the passion that drives our community.

With these powers of fire, we bless this donation."

Prayer of the Air Ritual

"May the powers of air bless this donation.

Air is the soul, the breath of life in a community.

Wisdom and intuition, the knowledge we share freely,

Air carries away troubles from our community.

With these powers of the air, we bless this donation."

Prayer for Water Ritual

"May the powers of water bless this donation.

Cleansing and purifying, washing away ill will,

Carrying away with it need, want, and strife.

Water is what helps to keep our community whole,

With these powers of water, we bless this donation."

After the blessings have been given, the donations are given to those in need or for funding charitable organizations. Either way, the goal of the Yule blessing is to bring happiness and joy to others during this holiday season.

Following the Yule rituals mentioned, you can celebrate the Yule festival precisely as ancient pagans did. It is a great way to connect with your heritage. Decorating your home and preparing festive meals and rituals increases your sense of well-being and create lasting memories with loved ones. So, why not give some of these ancient Yule rituals a try? You could find they bring a little extra warmth and happiness to your holiday season.

Chapter 9: Yule Spells and Blessings

Love, peace, wealth, and knowledge. Reasons for casting a spell are not few. The proper spell attracts what you need the most or repels anything you loath.

Blessings also have magical outcomes. However, they are not as powerful as a spell. In short, a blessing is merely a form of acknowledging a higher power source. They are prayers and serve as an alternative to saying "Thank you." It is a way to express your gratitude and commitment to life in the universe.

The right blessings and spells at the right moment can grant wonderful results. Since Yule is such an important celebration is undeniably categorized under this "right" moment.

This festivity includes its own sets of prayers and charms. Adding them to the overall celebration is not "just another" decoration. They are as important as any ritual and deserve attention, respect, and a touch of seriousness.

Consider this idea of seriousness not as a rigid, boring task. On the contrary, it is a beautiful and even fun activity to connect deeper with the universe's energy. However, rules need to be followed precisely for maximum efficiency.

The first rule: The use of spells on other people without their consent is not allowed. The witchcraft and pagan community discourage this act completely. Bear in mind that a spell is a powerful tool. Therefore, the spellcaster runs the risk of failing and achieving results that were not expected. Luckily, this is a worst-case scenario and most likely not to happen. One way or another, interfering in someone else's life, desires, thoughts, and habits is a wrong deed. Always ask the other person before casting a spell on them, even if you have the best intentions. Once they give their consent, you are free to do as you please.

The second rule: Take a session of meditation. Starting with a moment of mindfulness is a key aspect. After all, the benefits of meditation and breathing exercises are many, embracing long and short terms equally.

Nonetheless, the reason for a meditation session is simpler. The goal is to clear the mind of any distractions. Consider how relevant thoughts and ideas are for these activities. Troubled thoughts lead to troubling outcomes. So, a clean, undisturbed mind must be the aim when working with magic. When the head is free from ordinary, regular thoughts, our being is well-prepared for proper focus. We are relaxed, ready to control, and clearly convey sharper ideas in our minds. Therefore, meditation is recommended before any ritual or spell.

Although the goal is to merge with nature, using technology for guidance is allowed. For example, background music is a good tool that complements meditation wonderfully. Headphones also help. As long as it does not distract you, you can give anything a try.

The time recommended for the meditation is a minimum of 10 minutes. Whether you want to extend the time or not is up to you. The idea is not the quantity but the quality of the meditation.

The instruction for the meditation is as follows.

Either sit or lay down comfortably on a couch, a blanket on the floor, the floor itself, or any natural surface like sand or grass. If you feel relaxed, then you are on the correct path.

Once you have found your ideal position, close your eyes. Take deep breaths in and out through the nose. Lead the air to the lungs, feeling the purity of the element within your body, gently let it out. Repeat the process at your own pace; there is no need to hurry. Feel your hands, feet, and chest. Notice how much you relax the more you keep doing it. Each breath leads you closer to total relaxation.

In your mind, visualize a winter biosphere. Describe it. What does it look like? Are there plants and animals keeping you company? Is it snowy? Are you in a forest or a plain desert? Is there a gentle breeze touching your skin? Are the sun rays looming through the trees? Are there sun rays fully embracing you? Can you hear anything memorable? Ask yourself these questions and answer them in your mind with visual images. There are no wrong answers. Each individual has a version of their own; just make sure that it is a wintery day.

Think about the winter solstice and how it's the shortest day of the year. Reflect upon the last half of the year. Think about your achievements. Your favorite moments. Which moment are you the proudest of? Then, focus on the six months ahead. What are your goals? What do you want to accomplish? What do you want to experience? What do you want to create or manifest? How would you like to feel? Visualize them. Remember, there are no wrong answers.

Lastly, come back to the present. Keep breathing in through the nose, then gently exhale. Move your toes and fingers. Move your arms and feet. Feel them. Once you are done, open your eyes. Slowly, stand up and be grateful for the experience. You can say this prayer to count your blessings:

"I am grateful for that which I have

I am not sorrowful for anything I do not

I have more than others, and I have less than some,

but regardless, I am blessed

with what is mine."

If you happen to have a pagan prayer bead or any similar object, it would be great to use it for the prayers. More specifically, count each blessing with the beads. Take a moment to remember everything you are grateful for or anything you thought about in the previous meditation. Enumerate them as a list. Once again, there are no wrong answers. You could be grateful for your food, your roof, a new friend or lover, a job opportunity, a happy memory, a book you have read, or meditation. The ultimate goal is to fill you with positivism.

Now you are ready to continue with any of these spells.

Yule Jar Spell

The Yule Jar is an easy and relatively quick spell that can be done anytime. It is created to manifest love, charm, good luck, success, and prosperity. You'll need a sealable jar. It doesn't need to be too big. The smaller, the better. If you are unsure whether the jar is correct or not, check the ingredients below. You will realize which size suits you best.

The elements to be placed in the jar are as follows:

First is chamomile, great for attracting luck. Then, cloves, which also manifest luck and financial prosperity. Add ginger for self-assurance and sensuality and nutmeg for love and passion. Cinnamon also attracts passion, so add a whole stick to the jar. Notice that you must add and not replace these elements.

Also, find either orange zest or some orange oil, which guarantees health, and rosemary for clarity.

Lastly, cardamom pods and four or five sage leaves.

However, there are three more items needed for a successful spell:

- **Coins:** Eight, to be more precise. These represent the wheel of the year. They can be any coin, not necessarily high-value coins.

- **A Crystal:** No specific crystal. It has to be one of your preferences. It works better if the crystal's energy is correlated with your desires (rose quartz for self-love, citrine for wealth, etc.).

- **A Color Ribbon:** This will be tied to the jar at the end of the process. Use the ribbon you like the most.

When you have the items, head to your altar and light some candles. Call for your god or goddess. If you are unsure whom to call, you can call the universe or the energy of the elements instead.

Place each natural element in the jar. Do it as you like, but I encourage you to do it as gently as possible. Treat it as a piece of art. Imagine you are painting or building a sculpture. Approach it as a recipe, too. Why not? The intention is to create a relaxing, therapeutic-like atmosphere. Attention to detail leads to concentration, which ultimately helps a stronger manifestation. While putting the elements inside the jar, reflect upon your wishes.

This next step is not mandatory but is strongly encouraged for better results. Grab a piece of paper with your manifestation written on it. A phrase, a list, you choose. Just make sure to put it in the center of the jar when you finish.

Now, scatter the coins inside the jar. The crystal should also be placed in the jar but on top of the elements. As soon as you finish, say this prayer:

"I call upon the deities I follow to give me luck and blessing while the warmth returns.

Let there be love and plentifulness here and on every land.

Earth, I give you this offering as thanks for a prosperous and happy year and a new turning of the wheel."

It's worth mentioning that "Earth" can be replaced with the name of the goddess or god of your preference.

Close the jar and tie it with the color ribbon. Place your hand on top and apply your energy to it. Finally, mention these words:

"Binding these herbs and hopes for the future,

let there be luck in all to come.

Blessed be."

The spell is cast, and the jar can be placed on your altar or a shelf. Once your desires have been manifested, empty the contents of the jar into a natural environment. However, keep the crystal and the coins, so the soil is not polluted.

Sweeping Spell

Yuletide season commemorates the victory of good against evil. It is a moment to cleanse negative energies from the last year and open the door to the brand new, positive year.

You open the door for energy to enter with this spell.

It is believed that both front and back doors must be opened on the very first day of the year. It is an invitation for darkness to leave your house (or cleansing negativity) and simultaneously give a warm welcome to light and prosperity.

In other words, the back door is the exit to evil, and the front door is the entrance to happiness.

This spell requires only two elements, a lighter and a scented candle (replace with an incense stick if you prefer).

Head to the back door and open it. Open any windows, too.

If you happen to have two or more floors, go to the top of your house (the attic is a good place to start). The idea is to go from top to bottom. From there, head to any room and turn the scented candle on. In each room, walk anti-clockwise, leaning the candle on the walls, valuable objects, pictures, and the corners repeating this mantra:

"The old year fades away now, please, clear out the negative energy today."

Repeat the process in every room. Go down one floor and start again until you finish the entire house. The last room you must visit is the one with the back door open. At the door, say goodbye to the old, the negative, and the sorrows.

Exclaim, *"So mote it be!"* Then close the door and windows.

You are halfway through. The next thing is opening the front door. Similarly, you must pass the lighted candle on every object and corner throughout the house again. However, this time walks clockwise.

Say out loud, *"New start, new year. Bring me peace, prosperity, and happiness."*

When you have visited each room, go upstairs and repeat the process. You decide when you have gone through the entire house, place the candle anywhere, leave it on, or put it off. Head to the front door one last time, and say, *"Prosperity is welcomed in this home. Let them be."* Then close the front door.

It is worth pointing out the importance of the clockwise and anti-clockwise walk. The anti-clockwise serves as a negativity remover. It is a way of "going back" through the previous year, departing evil and darkness. On the contrary, strolling clockwise has the opposite effect. It brings prosperity and good luck. It manifests what is to come in the near future. So, this is a very important step, do not forget.

Magical Festive Fragrance

Infusing your house with a sweet scent is already enough to bring happiness. Who doesn't like the smell of an aromatic home?

A regular scent works marvelously, but why not make two friends with one gift?

Try a magical scent. It will provide protection and prosperity accompanied by a delicious smell.

All you need is a saucepan filled with water. Add one or more of these elements:

- **Cinnamon Sticks:** Two or more for passion, success, and prosperity.
- **Cloves:** Between eight and twelve for increased wealth.
- **Ginger:** You can add a couple of slices for confidence and prosperity.
- **Orange:** It can be sliced or use a few peels, although I recommend using a whole orange for health and positivity.

Choose the ingredients according to what you wish to attract. Pour the ingredients into the pan and heat it at a low temperature. Then, stir clockwise (preferably with a wooden spoon) while repeating these words, *"These ingredients filled with magic power, success, luck, and prosperity will shower."* When the pleasing scent starts to fill the house, turn off the heat and leave it standing for a while. A wise idea would be to share the liquid in your garden when you are finished. Plants will be thankful for it, and you'll be giving back to nature what she gave to you.

Spell for Love and Prosperity in the Following Decade

This spell requires a candle, a lighter, and, if possible, glitter and cinnamon oil. The colors of the candle and the glitter could be green, red, white, or golden.

Call upon your goddess or god. Ask for the universe to share its eternal energy with you. Say prayers and blessings, the ones you resonate with the most. Thank the universe for this moment. Subsequently, rub the candle with the color glitter and cinnamon oil. If you prefer, carve a legend in the candle's body related to your deepest wishes. Do it before anointing the candle; otherwise, it will not be easy with the glitter and oil. When you finish, light the candle, and say this prayer out loud:

"While I'm sitting in reflection upon the longest winter night,

I welcome with this candle the return of warm light.

Towards the New Year, rebirthed and renewed.

Love, prosperity, and luck,

will guide me through."

Let the candle burn the rest of the day and night. If possible, light other candles you have at home. If there is a candle in almost every room, better yet!

The Magical Snow

Snow is a source of fun and playing. Create snowmen and snowwomen, throw snowballs to your friends, and lay down and make snow angels. The possibilities are endless.

However, we forget that snow is also a source of magic. Although, it is not much of a surprise, considering that snow is formed from one of the main elements. The properties are there, waiting to be used.

The snow magic interferes with those habits we want to get rid of. It is a way of "freezing" patterns that drag us down to focus solely on what's good for us. The best part of this spell is its straightforwardness. All you need is a pencil or pen, a piece of paper, and a snowy day.

Write down the habit you want to take out of your life on the paper. Use a color pen if you wish, especially if the meaning of that color is related to the new habit you want to forge. Once written, go outside and say the bad habit out loud. Say how you will no longer be chained to it. Then, gently bury the paper in the snow, and leave it there.

Eventually, the snow melts, carrying with her your bad habit. The water washes the habit away, and a new year of possibilities awaits ahead.

A common occurrence is to wander in our heads, not being sure where to start. Should I start with the strongest spell? Should I stick to more than one? Should I force myself to do one despite not having all the elements? I will answer all with just three words, *"Take it easy."* Rushing only disturbs the mind and distracts you from the true outcome. Crafting a spell is a serious deed, but no one claims that it should not be fun or relaxing. When in doubt, start with the one you consider the simplest, or ask a friend or family member to provide help. If you fail, you can always give it a second chance.

Moreover, we wish you a happy Yule, a happy year, and happy life. Good luck, and may the universe work in your favor.

Chapter 10: Your 12 Days of Yuletide Calendar

Our beloved green Earth gives us millions of reasons to celebrate nothing and everything. Celebrations remind us that no matter how much we struggle, how difficult and dark our days can be, or how life seems unfair at times, we can always pause for a second and admire the things that surround us. We can always reflect on ourselves, our lives, family and friends, and the universe. We can hope for better days to come and set out on a path to change our lives and search for meanings in our existence. Celebrations bring us together with our loved ones and incite us to rejoice and share happiness with the world. When celebrations become traditions and rituals, joy is no more shared among us than it is passed to future generations, inherited from ancestors.

This is the very spirit of Yule, the ageless festivity observed by many cultures for thousands of years. It is the celebration of the returning light, the sun's rebirth. It is a reminder of the never-ending cycle of life and the continuity of existence, light after darkness, death after life, and life after death. It is also a remembrance of immortality and all things eternal. Gods and goddesses or the regenerating nature excellently embodied in the unchanging evergreen trees, a powerful and defining symbol of Yule.

Yule is truly universal and timeless. This chapter will suggest how you can celebrate the twelve days of the winter solstice to help you delight in an astounding observation of Yule. We will be bringing up the tales and myths behind each day.

Preparations

Clean/Cleanse Your Place

Clearing your living space and cleaning everything is a great way to start the New Year. It is symbolic of washing away the past, banishing negative energy, or scaring away the evil spirits if you are not particularly friends with them. If you want to do it in style, use a besom, the classic witch's broom. Do not worry if you are not a witch; the besom is for everyone.

Set Up an Altar

Besides reveling in a gorgeous sight, building an altar is a celebration of the sun's rebirth. Set it up by the fireplace if you have one. Otherwise, place it in a central place, like a wall.

Burn a Log

(But only if you can pull it off!) We have discussed how evergreens are powerful symbols of life, rebirth, and immortality. Use an oak log or evergreen.

Decorate

What would be better than having a bunch of boughs, branches, and flowers, taken from sacred plants and trees to decorate your altar? Additionally, you can make a nice wreath, also from evergreen. Use pine, cedar, or other conifer trees for a pleasant smell. There are plenty of cool ideas to decorate the house or the altar further, so be creative. Carved runes, little statues, coins, and fruits are a few examples.

First Day | Mother's Night

The first Yuletide night could pretty much be a festival on its own. This night was dedicated to the All-Mother, Frigg, goddess of love, birth, motherhood, marriage, family, and many others in most Germanic traditions. All ancestral mothers, mothers of clans, and other female deities and spirits, also called Disir, are honored in this celebration.

Baldur's Rebirth

Mother's night occurs on the evening before the solstice, December 21st. It is the darkest day of the year. According to Norse mythology, this was the night when the mother goddess Frigg gave birth to the sun god, Baldur. Baldur's rebirth is celebrated as it slowly brings the light as the days become gradually longer. This is reminiscent of other Celtic traditions where the sun's return, represented by the Holly King, was celebrated.

The Battle of the Two Kings

Many Celtic and Wiccan cultures celebrated the first night of winter solstice because it marked the sun's rebirth. The Holly King, or Sun King, defeats the Oak King, or Dark Lord, thus bringing the light again. This renewal of the year was a promise for the coming of spring.

First Night Rituals

• Honor the Mothers

Since this is Mother's Night, regardless of your beliefs, it is a perfect opportunity to honor mothers, ancestral and alive. Frames of your mother and grandmothers are obviously the best fit. If you prefer, add a picture or statuette of the mother goddess Frigg.

• Light Candles around the Altar

This is the time to light one or many candles by the altar. The candles are an excellent way to welcome the sun and the return of light. Lighting a big candle to represent the sun is a good choice. Alternatively, light as many candles as you want to represent the light. Ensure that you have a special, bigger candle representing your sun. How about including a symbol of the sun because, well, it is fitting.

• Burn the Yule Log

Arguably the most iconic Yule ritual, the first night is where the Yule log is set to burn. We suggest that you use candles to light it. If you are with family or friends, each can hold a candle, or everyone holds the same candle. Bringing everyone together for this ritual is highly encouraged.

• Recite Prayers

Depending on your beliefs, you may recite prayers in honor of mothers. For instance, Pagan prayers to Frigg and the Disir are very fitting. After all, it is her day.

• Perform Rituals to Welcome Back the Sun

Before, during, or after lighting the candles, look up nice rituals to celebrate the sun's return. There are many traditional prayers you can check out.

• Make an Offering

Pick your offering. It could be anything, like an animal, roses, petals, etc. Recite rituals as you make your offering. Dedicate it to Frigg or mothers in general. Consider making a little speech in appreciation if your mother or grandmothers are around.

• Have a Feast

The first day of Yule is a day for feasting and rejoicing. Dedicate this feast in honor of the All-Mother and ancestral mothers. The feast can be anything but consider offering food to the deities. Place a plate of food close to the altar. The feast usually comes after all the rituals have taken place.

- **Exchange Presents**

Now is the best time to open gifts. Thoughtful gifts to show how much your close ones mean to you would further brighten the mood, making the first night of Yule a real joy for you and everyone.

Second Day | Night of the Wild Hunt

The second night of Yule is mostly about protection and courage. Many Norse traditions say it is best not to go out alone, lest your soul be taken by the All-father Odin and his dead company. It is also a night where you face your fears and set out to overcome them in the next year. This night was associated with one of the Nine Noble Virtues in some cultures, truth.

The Wild Hunt

According to many Germanic traditions, it is very unfortunate to be found by the Wild Hunt riders during the second night of Yule. A host of the dead riding on horseback, led by the All-father Odin, and accompanied by howling dogs, take the souls of the unwanted spirits, the fallen, and the lonely wanderers on their path. They swept the land with strong storms and wind sounds and were furious. They sometimes invaded villages, broke into houses, stole food, *and sometimes children*! People have stayed indoors during this night and tried not to annoy Odin and the dead. They left sacrifices by the door and offered something for the Wild Hunt riders to feed on, so they would leave their own.

Second Day Rituals

- **Make an Offering**

Make the Wild Hunt's journey easier by offering a drink to Odin and his riders outside your front door. You don't want to take any chances.

- **Ask Odin for Protection**

Say prayers or perform rituals to ask Odin for protection during these dark times. Odin and the dead are said to bring fertility as they pass. If it is an issue for you, why not try anyway?

- **Make a Feast**

You can dedicate this feast to Odin.

- **Build a Wooden Sleipnir**

Odin's eight-legged horse is a classic creature. Why not craft one yourself and put it near the altar?

- **Watch a Horror Movie**

The Wild Hunt is out there, and it is scary. You should be fine as long you are not seen by the raging host of Odin. You can enhance the spooky atmosphere by watching a Yule horror movie. Movies like Krampus and the

Hogfather come to mind.

- **Share Spooky Stories**

Gather your close ones and read horror tales. Given the right setting, reading stories from Creepypasta works like a charm.

- **Face Your Fears**

We have told you how the twelve days of Yule are days of self-reflection. So, get into the next year with a clear mind, having contemplated and overcome your fears. Fear hinders our spirits and ambitions, so it is best we do without it.

Third-Day | High Feast of Yule

The third day of Yule is sacred to Thor and Frey.

Thor and the Yule Goat

The closest connection of Thor to Yule is the tale of his feast with the human children Thjalfi and Röskva. Loki accompanied Thor on a visit to Jotünheim on a chariot pulled by his two loyal goats, Tanngrisnir and Tanngnjóstr. He met Thjalfi and Röskva's family, who welcomed them to dinner. In return for their hospitality, Thor treated them to a great feast, feeding them his special goats, only to resurrect them the next day. He asked the family to take good care of the goat's hides and bones. However, Thjalfi was careless and split a leg bone in two. The goats were resurrected, and Thjalfi was crippled. Thor was furious and made a deal with the family to take Thjalfi and his sister Röskva to work for him.

Third-Day Rituals

- **Make an Offering**

Thor's Yule Goat is symbolic of his power and ability to protect humans. Instead of showing the family his wrath, he devised a way to spare them. Offer a drink and some food to Thor in return for his protection.

- **Make a Special Feast**

While you do not have to make a great feast for each of the twelve nights, the third day's feast may well be your best, as a testament to your hospitality.

- **Invite People Over**

Despite the eventual inconvenience, the god of war and fertility appreciated the family's hospitality. He blessed them with his protection in return. This night is as good a time as any to invite people over or unexpected welcome visitors and treat them to a nice meal.

Fourth Day | Feast of Ægir, Njörd, and Freya

This day is sacred to the Vanir god and goddess Njörd, Freya, and the jötunn Ægir. The Vanir gods are associated with nature and fertility, making this another great day to celebrate the gifts of nature. Ægir is the god of oceans and brewing, the former being another essential element of nature. Njörd is also the god of the sea. Ægir was very close to the gods and goddesses and often brewed special drinks to welcome them.

The Aesir/Vanir Hostage Exchange

Following the war between the Aesir and Vanir deities, Njörd, the father of the deities, set out on a journey to Asgard with Frey and Freya to exchange hostages with the Aesir. He built a great home called Noatun on the shore, having quietened the storms and tempests stirred by Ægir. He cast his protection over all the fishermen and spent much time there watching the ocean, which he loved.

Fourth Day Rituals

- **Honor the Vanir Deities**

In honor of the Aesir gods, offer something to them. You can also carve runes of Njörd and Freya.

- **Brew Something**

As Ægir did, why not brew something? Beers are very fitting, although you can brew juice if you prefer. Offer something to the Vanir gods and have a nice drink with your partner, friends, or family. Do not forget to make a toast.

- **Go to the Ocean**

Another perfect idea to celebrate the feast of Ægir, Njörd, and Freya, is to spend time at the sea or the ocean. A lake could also work if you are far from the sea. Oceans and seas are very soothing, so having a feast is bound to wash away intensity and stress.

Fifth Day | Feast of Community

This day is sacred to the community. It is a great time for people to be brought together to help each other out and make lives a little easier.

Fifth Day Rituals

- **Help People Out**

If you are outdoors and you see someone gardening, why not lend them a hand? If you see an old man or lady on their way home with some groceries, why not carry the bags for them? You get the idea. It is a great time to help people in your community.

- **Collaborate with People**

Whether you want to have today's feast in your home or are invited somewhere else, make sure everyone chips in with a little something and helps each other in any way. Cook together, prepare the little ceremony together and have fun.

- **Give to the Poor**

Before your evening gathering, consider going out with a group of people to give the poor and needy food and clothes. If possible, sheltering the homeless for a night would also be a virtuous thing to do.

Sixth Day | The Feast of Eir

The sixth day of Yule honors Eir, possibly the goddess of healing. It is the perfect time to wish health and well-being to your loved ones for the coming year.

The Beloved Healer

It is contested whether Eir is a goddess or a Valkyrie. She was the handmaiden of Freya and Odin, and gods and goddesses revered her. She was thought to have powers over life and death and was called on to heal the sick and injured deities. In Norse mythology, those who healed the sick were mostly women. It makes sense since Eir shared her healing knowledge and expertise with many women.

Sixth Day Rituals

- **Tend to the Sick**

As a token of appreciation to Eir's healing powers, take care of sick family members, make them happy every way you can and visit hospitalized relatives.

- **Stay Healthy**

No matter your diet, be extra healthy this day. There is no reason to make a heavy feast. Fasting is also a great way to cleanse your body from toxins, but if you are eating, prepare light and healthy food and eat in moderation. A vegetable soup and herbal tea can work wonders.

- **Do Exercises**

You can do a million good physical activities individually or in groups on this day. Walking or running a few miles, working out, practicing sports, or doing yoga are great ways to stay healthy.

- **Ask for Blessings**

Pray to the deities for blessings and speedy recovery for the ill.

Seventh Day | Feast of Thor

Not unlike the third, the seventh Yule night is sacred to Thor. We have seen the symbolism in Thor's Yule Goat. This day is another opportunity to be hospitable and generous.

Seventh Day Rituals

- ### Pay Tribute to Thor and Frey

Consider carving the runes Þ or Þᛰᚱ to honor Thor. A model of Thor's hammer or a little statue of Thor wielding his hammer is a very cool decoration idea for this night. A great place to put them is by the burning log or the lighted candles.

- ### Have a Feast

It does not have to be as big as your third day's feast. Have a nice evening meal with whoever is with you or invite people over if you can. You can also make an offering.

- ### Ask for Protection

On this night, you can ask Thor to cast his protection over your home and family.

- ### Watch a Cool Thor Movie

This night is very fitting for a nice movie around Norse mythology, particularly Thor. "Thor: Ragnarok" is a captivating and visually stunning movie.

Eighth Day | Feast of Skadi and Ullr

This night is also a contemplation of winter and darkness. The sun's return is celebrated during the winter solstice, but that does not take away the importance of winter. The light can only exist as long as there is darkness. Skadi and Ullr are winter gods and are honored during this night.

Skadi's Revenge and Unhappy Marriage

Skadi is all about winter, cold, ice, snow, etc. Previously a giant, she was portrayed as a beautiful goddess walking with a gorgeous wolf through ice and snow, wearing her iconic snowshoes, and marked by a desire to revenge her father slain by the gods in an unsuccessful theft attempt. Seeking justice for her father, the gods were patient with her and offered her amends. Odin turned her father's eyes (Thjazi's) into two stars. The gods accepted her impossible challenge to make her laugh and asked her to marry a god of her choice based on the sight of her feet alone.

Loki eventually made Skadi laugh by tying his testicles to a goat using a rope before wrestling him and falling off. Skadi wanted to pick the beloved

Baldur for her husband and picked the most pleasant feet before her. Sadly, Njörd's feet were pretty nice, and she married him.

After a glorious wedding, Skadi wanted to live in the extremely cold high mountaintops, and Njördr wanted to live in his beautiful coastal home, leading to an unhappy marriage.

Eighth Day Rituals

- **Go Hunting**

Humans have spent most of their existence hunter-gathering instead of settling in houses, villages, and towns. Unless you do not eat meat: Make sure it's hunting season, prep your gear and equipment, and make sure that you have the required documents.

- **Make an Offering**

Honor the gods of the hunt, Skadi, and Ullr, by offering food in the middle of nature or hunting grounds. Do not worry; it will not go to waste. At least an animal or two would be quite happy.

- **Decorate**

If you have arrows, bows, spears, or hunting guns, this day is perfect for using them as decoration.

Ninth Day | Feast of Odin

The ninth day is sacred to Odin, the central god of Norse mythology. Odin has it all. He is the god of war, death, wisdom, poetry, runes, magic, etc. This day is a great opportunity to learn new things and gain knowledge. Odin sought knowledge in the most spectacular ways.

Odin's Sacrifice

Odin went to great lengths in search of wisdom and knowledge. He arrived at Mimir's well, the Well of Urd, the well out of which the great Yggdrasil tree grows and is associated with knowledge and wisdom. Mimir's wisdom was unparalleled; he knew it all. Odin asked Mimir for a drink from the well. The latter refused unless Odin offered his eye in return. Odin cut his eye and finally had a drink.

Odin's Other Sacrifice

Odin sacrificed too much for wisdom. He had already lost an eye, but that did not stop him from wanting more knowledge. His second big sacrifice was none other than himself. The runes originated in the Well of Urd and were only revealed to those worthy of such wisdom. Odin hung himself using a Yggdrasil branch, pierced his chest with a spear, and fell into the well's water. He stayed there for many days until he finally perceived the runes.

Ninth Day Rituals

- **Represent the Yggdasil and Odin's Eye**

A drawing, painting, or model of the Yggdrasil would be a great decoration. If it is a model, consider representing the Well of Urd. You can figure it out. A statue or picture of Odin and a representation of his eye would be great, too.

- **Learn**

Every day is a great day to learn new things. Particularly, on this day, a good symbol of Odin's eternal quest for wisdom.

- **Read the Hávamál**

The Hávamál is a great resource for many Norse myths and tales. It is a collection of Old Norse poems, one of which tells the story of Odin's sacrifice.

- **Make Runes**

It is a perfect day to carve runes and use them to decorate your surroundings. It will give a rather mystical atmosphere.

Tenth Day | Feast of Sunna

In Yule, we celebrate the sun's return, and the tenth day is a reminder. The goddess of the sun, appropriately named Sunna, is honored on this day. This night is also sacred to the ancestors. It is a great time to celebrate the eventual coming of spring and contemplate our origins, paying tribute to our ancestors.

Sunna's Life

Daughter to Mundilfari and sister of Mani, Sunna was named after our shining star. Deities did not like this and sent her from Earth to the Sun. She eternally rode a chariot pulled by two horses and brought day and night as she went. She had a shield named Svalinn to keep the sun from burning everything under the sun. A wolf, Sköll, kept chasing her, and an eclipse was formed when it got really close to her. Eventually, she will be caught and devoured at Ragnarok. However, she will have given birth to a daughter by then, taking her place when the new world is created.

Tenth Day Rituals

- **Make a Sun-themed Evening**

Nothing will beat symbols, drawings, or crafts of the sun to decorate your altar on this day. Portrayals of Sunna are also a good idea.

- **Remember the Ancestors**

Make a toast and raise glasses to ancestors. It is a good way of remembering how we came into existence.

Eleventh Day | Feast of the Valkyries

This night is sacred to the Valkyries and all the goddesses.

Choosers of the Slain

Valkyries, or "choosers of the slain," are Odin's female warriors who rode horses, wolves, or boars, going from one battlefield to another, deciding the fate of fallen warriors. They would take the dead to Freya and Odin to choose who was worthy of Valhalla. Freya was always the first to choose and would take half of the dead to her realm. The Valkyries chose the other half on behalf of Odin. Valkyries will fight beside Odin and come to Ragnarök.

Eleventh Day Rituals

- **Portray Valkyries**

Valkyries are such iconic creatures, and there are many of them. Having each one portrayed is the perfect way to decorate your altar.

Twelfth Day | Oath Night

This marks the end of the winter solstice and the beginning of the New Year. The journey has been enthralling; by this time, you will have celebrated new beginnings in the best possible way. This day is sacred to every god and goddess, notably the Æsir & Dísir. It is an end to what we hope was a wonderful year and a start to bright future days. It marks an end to a series of amazing feasts and festivities, but with a final celebration that ought to be worth remembering.

Twelfth Day Rituals

- **Take an Oath**

The New Year is a new beginning. Welcome it by making a promise that you'll definitely fulfill. Set your mind to achieve the things you want and spare no effort to get there. If you, like our ancestors, believe oaths are divine promises that must not be broken, refrain from taking oaths that you are not sure you can fulfill.

- **Have One Final Feast**

Yule traditionally ends with a boar feast, but you can do it with something else. Make sure you gather as many people as you want for this final gathering until the next celebration.

- **Praise the Things You Hold Sacred**

Offerings, prayers, and toasts to all gods, goddesses, and sacred beings are a great way to end the festivities packed with tributes and remembrances.

- **Take Out the Fire**

Now you can let the sun do the rest of the work. If you burned a big log, hopefully for twelve days straight, consider saving some of it for next winter. Do the same with the candles you lit each day.

With the year gone, another chapter begins, full of promises and possibilities. We shared some insights into what was behind our beloved Yule celebrations. Bear in mind that there are always a million ways to celebrate anything. In particular, Yule's observations are very personal. We perceive these celebrations differently, and we have shared a few ideas and insights into the mythology that underlies Yule celebrations. Do not forget to get creative with your own ideas. Make this year's Yule an experience worth remembering. May the light be with you wherever you go.

Conclusion

The winter solstice is one of the most celebrated traditions across the world. Also known as Yule, it is honored in many different ways and across diverse religions and spiritual practices, such as Paganism, Druidry, Wicca, and even Christianity. The latter adopted Yule customs, slowly incorporating them into Christmas celebrations. While this adaptation brought in some different traditions, the essential purpose of the holiday remains the same. It gives people the opportunity to gather and spend time with their nearest and dearest, as well as their community, as it was done in ancient times.

However, as you have learned from this book, for pagans, the winter solstice means much more than family feasts and decorations. The holiday marks nature's descent into darkness, only to emerge again after this day. According to pagan lore, the night of the winter solstice is the time when the Goddess gives birth to the Sun, an event remarkably similar to the Christian arrival of the Messiah. This night also marks the moment when the Oak King (the pagan representation of summer and light) defeats the Holly King (the ruler of darkness and winter), allowing nature to be reborn again.

If you want to celebrate Yule, begin by making your own unique decorations. This will help you get into the true pagan spirit of the holiday and express your beliefs and creativity. Whether you choose to make adornments for a Yule tree, assemble a Yule wreath, or display Yule symbols in any other way, is entirely up to you. Using the sacred plants and trees in your decorations can also bring you closer to nature's spirit.

Another thing you can do is to set up an altar dedicated to this holiday. Even if you do not actively practice the magic as a pagan, you can still take advantage of this sacred space when commemorating holidays like Yule. Active practitioners will be happy to know that casting spells and performing small rituals at their altar will make the magic even more potent. Spiritual cleansing practices and ceremonies for welcoming the Sun are particularly effective at this time of the year. Performing them increases your natural abilities and intensifies your spiritual development.

Most of the rituals can be performed by both solitary practitioners and groups. One of the most well-known is the Yule log ceremony, which you can do with your family and friends, or, if you prefer, in the sanctity of your own company. You can use the spells and charms we introduced to you or create your own to customize your rituals. Preparing a delicious Yule feast, as well as crafting decorations, brings family and friends together. Add in some traditional activities with a modern twist, like giving gifts or making donations to people in need, and you can involve your entire community in the preparations. You can add this and all the other activities listed in this book to your Yuletide calendar, which is essentially a schedule for what to do for the 12 nights before the winter solstice. Remember, behind each day is ancient lore representing a milestone in a pagan's spiritual development, so be sure to include activities that symbolize your view of the holiday.

Part 2: Imbolc

The Ultimate Guide to Brigid, and Candlemas and How It's Celebrated in Christianity, Wicca, Druidry, and Celtic paganism

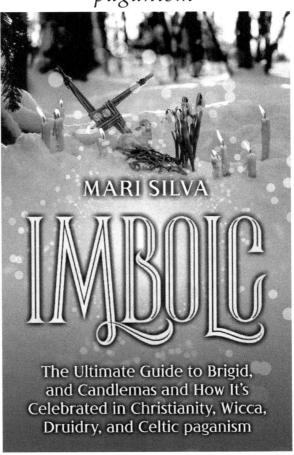

Introduction

The desire to celebrate Imbolc is one of the purest. It's not ego-based or rooted in a desire to become more interesting or attract more attention when speaking to people. It's rooted in a genuine connection to nature, Brigid, or both. It's also an act that is rooted in love. Without this level of authenticity, all we get is another empty tradition void of meaning.

When reading about Imbolc (or other pagan festivals, concepts, deities, and other studies like astrology and numerology), we often notice hints toward subjective misinformation, either intentional or not.

For one, it's really hard to find credible sources, and, in almost all cases, it takes a seasoned practitioner to provide guidance and source references. Otherwise, it's a process of trial and error. Especially when it comes to spirituality, this can be exhausting if not dangerous.

It's also hard to pinpoint one's intention from their writing. Some authors don't care about those who read their books and blogs. They may omit or cherry-pick information to appeal to the readers. They may also be using paganism to glorify themselves, which is one of the factors behind misinformation.

On the other side of the coin, there are many old-school authors able to provide a treasure trove of information. However, they tend to miss the mark when explaining rituals and spells because of the inaccessible ingredients many of them use.

Then, there are the authors who speak about spirituality from their perspectives, which, of course, is appreciated. Nevertheless, it can alienate many who don't view things in the same light or who don't connect to the same deities, herbs, plants, and rituals as they do, which creates the false belief that the spiritual journey is a straight line with strict practices. It divides the pagans who practice "right" and those who practice "wrong."

These issues are exactly what we do our best to avoid in this book. Rather than get caught up with what's on the surface of Imbolc practices, we delve deep into what this early spring festival is about. After fleshing it out, we take each aspect of the festival, from its associated herbs to the crafts and spells. That way, we give each part of Imbolc the attention it deserves.

More importantly, because we understand how complex spirituality is, we made sure we have provided enough alternatives so everyone can find something with which they connect. What one person may feel called to do may not be how others feel, and this is the approach we will be taking throughout this book.

Before we start, you're invited to keep your mind and heart open to what your instincts and your guides communicate to you throughout the book. Remember that the universe communicates with us in the most subtle things and the most mundane ways.

Now, without further ado, let's start down the path to explore this beautiful festival and everything it stands for.

Chapter 1: Introduction to Imbolc

Imbolc celebration.

Imbolc is a significant pagan festival heavily rooted in ancient Celtic culture. While nowadays, it's more commonly known as St. Brigid's Day and is also celebrated as a Christian holiday. The origins of this holiday go back to pre-Christian Ireland, Scotland, and the Isle of Man.

The pagan Wheel of the Year consists of eight seasonal festivals. Four of these festivals occur on the two solstices and the two equinoxes. These four events mark the beginnings of the four seasons based on the position of the Earth from the sun:

- Yule is celebrated with the winter solstice on 21st December.

- Ostara is celebrated with the spring equinox on 20th March.

- Litha is celebrated with the summer solstice on 21st June.

- Mabon is celebrated with the autumn equinox on 22nd September.

Meanwhile, the other four festivals are called cross-quarter days and occur between the four main festivals or sabbats. These are:

- Imbolc - celebrated on 1st February between Yule and Ostara.

- Beltane - celebrated on 1st May between Ostara and Litha.

- Lughnasadh - celebrated on 1st August between Litha and Mabon.

- Samhain - celebrated on 31st October and 1st November between Mabon and Yule.

Because it's celebrated on the 1st of February, between the winter solstice and the spring equinox, Imbolc represents the "coming" of spring. It's the time of the year during the tail end of winter when people start to notice signs of the coming of spring.

Of course, after a cold and hard winter where the nights reached their darkest, the days their shortest, and life was made dim by the cold, the signs of spring are more than worthy of celebration. It was especially so in the distant past when people depended directly on the seasons to plant or hunt, and this festival was held in very high regard.

Imbolc's Cultural Significance

The culture that ruled pre-Christian Ireland, Scotland, and the Isle of Man was mainly farming-oriented. The lands had plenty of greenery and fertile soil, so farming was the easiest way to sustain life and make money. Of course, certain birds, animals, and cattle came with farming.

In winter, the world naturally grows cold. This means that, for any warm-blooded creature to survive, their bodies need to exert extra effort to maintain their blood temperature at a reasonable level. The stronger winter gets, the harder it is for animals to maintain their temperature.

All warm-blooded creatures try to find ways to cope with this great inconvenience. Some animals migrate to a warm place because life becomes too unsuitable for them. Others hibernate to avoid dealing with the temperature difference, and others decrease their activity levels to conserve their resources.

The same goes for plants. The plants' enzymes don't function well in cold temperatures. And, because a decrease in temperature means slower movements on an atomic level, roots don't absorb nutrient particles as efficiently. So, instead of wasting their energy making new leaves, plants shut down photosynthesis and dedicate all their resources to survival.

As you see, in winter, the world becomes an inhospitable place for the warm-blooded. It's a time to survive rather than thrive. Nevertheless, this difficult time and the collective human despair and frustration that come with it usually end with the promise of spring. This is where Imbolc draws its cultural significance.

On Imbolc, the whole community would celebrate that the time to survive was coming to an end. They no longer needed to store or conserve food, and they didn't have to worry for their lives. Plants start growing their leaves around that time, so it's a sign that Mother Earth's womb is ready to receive and produce seeds.

In addition to that, animals are nearing their last months of hibernation. And some animals even give birth around or shortly after this time because it is when a newborn can tolerate the weather.

With all of that being said, it's obvious why everyone used to come together to celebrate this particular day. It's also obvious why festivals had very significant roles back then. They often coincided with agricultural events that affected the region as a whole. So, regardless of one's religion or beliefs, they all had the same core reason to celebrate.

Imbolc's Historical Significance

If you take a look at Celtic sagas and mythologies, you'll be able to see the influence of the rural culture. Among the most glorified creatures in Irish mythology were two in particular; Glas Gaibhnenn, a cow that produced near-infinite amounts of milk, and Manannan mac Lir's immortal swine, which always came alive the next morning after it had been killed.

Both reflected the wishes of kings and commoners alike and reflected how deeply people valued these specific animals; the well-fed swine and the cow that produces plenty of milk. Because the grass grows faster in spring, cows produce the most milk in spring (milking season), and pigs gain the most weight. Because Imbolc was associated with fertility, growth, and regeneration, it gained a lot of historical significance.

The legendary Hill of Tara, where the stone of destiny, Lia Fáil, stands, was and is a sacred historical location according to Irish tradition. In close proximity to it lies a burial mound called the "Mound of Hostages."

The entrance to the Mound of Hostages is positioned so that it would be in alignment with the sun on two occasions; Imbolc and Samhain. At the start of the two festivals, the sunlight makes its way through the entrance and to an engraved stone at the back of the chamber and then lights it up for about a week.

Imbolc's Spiritual Significance

Culture and history aside, Imbolc has a strong spiritual significance for all pagans. One of the pillars of paganism is one's connectedness to nature and the earth, which is one of several reasons the eight festivals on the Wheel of the Year were created. They were ways for the first worshippers to tune into the Earth's cycle around the sun and its effects on all life forms and forces.

Another reason was that Imbolc was a spiritual event worthy of celebration. As the Earth orbits the sun, the land reaches a point farthest from the planet's main source of energy and life. On a physical level, this natural phenomenon creates the winter season.

This phenomenon stands for darkness and death on a mental and spiritual level. This is not necessarily an evil type of darkness and death but the natural end of a cycle and the natural opposition to light and life. It's a time to rest and work on shedding harmful behaviors and thoughts.

It can also be a time of deep depression and frustration as we lose touch with our light source. On a biological and chemical level, this can cause vitamin D deficiency and trigger seasonal affective disorder where the individual experiences depression-like symptoms.

This disconnection from the fire element can trigger a decline in one's energy and passion on a spiritual level. It can manifest in a loss of joy and passion, a lack of ambitions and motivation, and a decline in libido (sex drive).

All in all, it doesn't sound like a great time. Granted, it can be beneficial for some people as it can push repressed emotions and trauma to the surface so they can be released. However, that doesn't mean that winter is only a tough and joyless time.

This is why, as it nears its end, we celebrate Imbolc. After such an intense season where people have gone through the process of shedding beliefs, processing trauma, and grieving losses and absences, it's only fair to celebrate that we have made it through. Not just that, but it also makes sense to celebrate the coming season, the return of the light, and the rekindling of the fire within us. This is also why Imbolc is considered one of the four fire festivals.

Celebrating Imbolc marks this wonderful beginning of a new cycle. It allows us to reflect on the past and set intentions and hopes for the future. It also allows us to cleanse ourselves and our surroundings and let go of everything we wish to leave behind. That way, we can wholly embrace the new cycle in a much better way.

Not just that, but celebrating such a day allows individuals to deepen their connection to the cycle that influences us and rules the elements around and within us. This brings a deeper sense of spiritual alignment and allows people to make the most out of each phase and its influences.

One can start planting seeds for new thoughts and behaviors on this day. It's also when they can start acting on their New Year's resolutions or planning for them. We all make the mistake of holding ourselves to our resolutions while forgetting that winter is not the time to grow anything.

Each year, the fact that we get to celebrate Imbolc presents us with the promise that there will come a time when we feel energized and motivated to act. It's a comforting message, especially for those who can't stay still or don't feel comfortable losing their motivation. It's a message from nature that says, "There is a time for everything. Don't worry. It wasn't yet your time to move forward, but it will soon be."

For Wiccans, Imbolc holds an almost identical, albeit slightly different, significance. In addition to everything mentioned above, Imbolc represents the transformation or the role shift that the Goddess goes through.

The Goddess is a Wiccan triple deity who takes on three forms; the Maiden, the Mother, and the Crone. Each represents certain aspects of female energy and expresses the divine feminine.

The Crone is the form that the Goddess takes during wintertime. It's her elder aspect that brings forth wisdom and represents death. At the same time, it represents rebirth and transformation as the Crone is reborn into the Maiden at the start of spring.

Imbolc is also considered a celebration of this transformation. It takes time to reflect on the wisdom attained during the past year. And, just like the Crone gracefully embraces her rebirth as the Maiden, Imbolc presents an opportunity to become humble and open oneself up to the new cycle.

The Festival's Etymology

Imbolc is a variation of the Old Irish words "*i mbolg*," which, when translated, means "in the womb."

Now, the name is part-metaphorical and part-literal.

As we've mentioned, Imbolc marks the start of spring. It marks a time when life and warmth are just returning to the Earth. The living conditions are just starting to become suitable enough for animals and birds to give birth to their babies. We should also mention that people take this time to prepare for sowing their seeds. This is the literal part as, during this time, seeds are planted in the womb of the Earth. Animals, too, start to reach the peak of their development inside their mothers' wombs before coming out into the world during springtime.

As for the symbolic part, what's signified by the womb is the beginning of life. In the winter season, trees stop growing leaves, animals hibernate, many crops go out of season, and people refrain from making much effort to preserve their energy. The pace of life significantly slows down. Imbolc marks the time when the wheels of life start to move again, when the Earth as a whole begins to, once again, wake up and rejuvenate itself.

This is what Imbolc celebrated and still celebrates. Although, between back then and nowadays, there are a few differences in how people approach the festival.

Imbolc in the Past

One fundamental difference that separates how people used to celebrate Imbolc in the past from how they do now is in their connectedness to nature.

In the past, we were almost at one with nature. There was nothing separating people from their surroundings. People lived on the land and from the animals they had. There weren't as many divisions or layers between them and nature as there are now with corporations, mass production, etc.

People were also at the mercy of the elements. The sun was their main source of light. Meanwhile, nowadays, we might turn on the lights when it gets too cloudy outside. And, if you get cold in your insulated house or apartment, imagine how cold it was inside a clay/wooden house and under a straw ceiling.

This is why, back then, more and more people celebrated the festival. Not only did it impact pagans on a spiritual level, but it impacted everyone on all levels. They rejoiced that soon there was going to be plenty of food, that the nights were only going to get warmer until Samhain, and that the light would get brighter.

As a result of the festival's national presence, it was customary for people to gather around huge bonfires, feast, and dance. It was a way of further summoning the light and awakening the dormant fire element. At the same time, it celebrated the end of winter.

Among the other traditions observed by the public was the preparation of the land so that, come springtime, it would be ready for planting. Around this time, it was also common to see people doing their share of spring cleaning around their houses to prepare for the new year.

People would also visit holy wells, pray for fertility, health, and blessings for the new year and leave offerings for the gods. Water from these wells was considered holy and taken home as a source of blessings for the house and whoever drank it.

Last but not least, people also used to pour milk and porridge into the rivers and seas or the ground as an offering to the gods and goddesses of nature and fertility.

Imbolc Is the Present

Nowadays, what's common isn't a connection to nature but a disconnection. So, for one person to have this connection, they must have worked to nurture and maintain it. Imbolc has lost its popularity the more advanced our way of life has become.

It's reached the point where the only people who celebrate Imbolc are pagans and Wiccans. Of course, there are Christians who celebrate St. Brigid's day, but while it takes place on Imbolc, it's not entirely the same.

From a purely pagan lens, the traditions associated with Imbolc have undergone a great shift from the physical to the mental and spiritual. Instead of preparing the land, people take this time to cleanse their bodies, houses, minds, and spirits. Instead of planting seeds, people take the time to meditate on or journal about the ideas, projects, beliefs, thoughts, etc., that they'd like to plant within themselves.

Some people take the time to plan for their New Year's resolutions, and others even skip New Year's and make their resolutions on Imbolc.

Nevertheless, the core concepts remain unchanged even with the differences, and it shows primarily in the symbols. People drink and eat milk and baked goods on Imbolc to celebrate the milking season. They light bonfires and candles to invoke the fire element within themselves and celebrate the sun's return.

People also prepare food to special recipes for an Imbolc feast and come together to recite poems and prayers. On the one hand, it's a celebration of the coming of light and spring. On the other hand, it's a tradition that allows people to reflect on the past and let go of any baggage that may hold them back.

Last but not least, Imbolc is one of the ways for modern pagans to nurture their connection with Mother Nature and attune themselves to its cycle.

Imbolc and Current Associations

The Imbolc Festival has many associations, whether with symbols, colors, herbs, deities, tools, crystals, or animals. Throughout this book, we will discuss them in detail, but giving you a roadmap, here are the most prominent things linked to Imbolc.

Symbols

- Brigid's Cross
- Brigid Doll

- Milk
- Baked goods
- Snowdrop flowers
- Fire
- Candles

Colors

- Red
- Orange
- White
- Green

Deities

- Brigid
- The Wiccan Goddess

Herbs and Plants

- Bay Leaves
- Heather
- Rosemary
- Angelica
- Basil

Tools

- Hearths
- Bonfires
- Altars
- Special offerings

Crystals/Stones

- Amethyst
- Sunstone
- Peridot

Animals

- Cows
- Sheep

Having named these items, you need to remember that everything is highly subjective, especially when it comes to spirituality. You may feel drawn to certain items not mentioned within this book, and that's okay. In fact, you should welcome that.

Many of us prefer to use herbs other than rosemary for their cleansing effects. Meanwhile, some people can just be drawn to particular stones and crystals as they embark on a new cycle. This freedom, openness, and harmony are all about the spiritual experience.

More importantly, it's an incredibly personal and diverse experience. Rules or pre-appointed symbols cannot control our souls and how we relate to the spiritual. So, keep your mind and heart open to how you feel as you read on. Do what feels right to you, and remember that nothing is set in stone.

Chapter 2: Brigid, Goddess, and Saint

Earlier in the previous chapter, we mentioned that Imbolc is also called St. Brigid's Day. Then we said that they were not entirely the same. Now is the time to expand on both statements.

Imbolc is the time and festival in which pagans also celebrate the Irish goddess Brigid. Not only is she seen as a goddess of fire and a herald of spring, but she's also a triple goddess with a maiden aspect that shines at the beginning of the yearly cycle.

When Christianity came to Ireland and the surrounding countries, the missionaries declared Brigid a saint. It was an attempt to gain the favor of the local population while making their transition to Christianity easier and smoother by including a familiar face.

It is, however, important to say that some scholars genuinely believe that St. Brigid bore no relationship to the goddess. Instead, they think she was an abbess (Mother Superior) who was granted sainthood after managing to found a convent of nuns in Kildare.

As a pagan celebrating Imbolc, whether you're focused on the nature-related, spiritual, or divine aspects of the day, the foundation of your rituals and traditions will be somewhat the same. That's why interchangeability is acceptable here.

However, as a Christian celebrating St. Brigid's Day, your rituals' intentions and foundation will differ, even if your traditions share similarities with pagan ones. This is why we maintain that Imbolc and St. Brigid's Day are not entirely the same.

In Imbolc, Brigid is a central figure to the pagans who choose to worship and revere gods. Not all pagans worship the gods. Some are simply animists who believe that all things have spirits and an influence on humans. As we said before, there is no gate-keeping when it comes to spirituality. It's all about what we feel drawn toward.

For those who feel drawn toward Brigid on this day, it's because of the goddess's captivating identity.

Brigid

In Irish mythology, Brigid was the daughter of the Dagda (the father god of all Irish deities) and The Morrigan (the triple goddess of war). In addition to her unique identity, many of her qualities were shaped by her parents, their abilities, and their characteristics.

Brigid is known first and foremost as a goddess of poetry and wisdom. Being also a goddess of healing and the daughter of an all-father, she is an advocate for peace. In her stories, she married Bres simply to keep the peace between the gods and a race of giants.

However, as much as she's willing to do for peace, she can prove to be a fearsome warrior if need be. After all, she was the daughter of the Morrigan. Brigid also draws her protective instincts from her mother, which fuels her reputation as the guardian and protector of women in combination with her feminine side.

Brigid plays a central role for more than one reason when it comes to Imbolc. First of all, she is a fire goddess and brings warmth after the cold months of winter. Secondly, she's associated with fertility in women and crops. People even used to invoke her name when they needed their cows to produce milk. Thirdly, wherever she travels, she travels with Glas Gaibhnenn, the sacred cow that produces infinite amounts of milk.

Spring is a celebration of fertility. Animals give birth and produce milk. Famines end as seeds turn to plants, and plants grow lush leaves full of life. Poems are sung in celebration, as warmth and new birth return to the Earth. And so, Imbolc is the day to invoke Brigid, the one goddess associated with all it is that makes up spring.

Nevertheless, this is not all there is to Brigid. This triple goddess is a complex entity with multiple aspects and associations. Understanding her relationship with Imbolc and how to honor her during this time is crucial to understanding who she is. More importantly, don't forget to reflect on what you learn, so you can understand who she is to you.

The Triple Goddess

The most important part of Brigid's identity is her three-fold form. Each of her aspects presents a different side of her. And each trinity represents a different part of Brigid's identity.

First off, Brigid's not only a goddess of poetry but also a goddess of healing and a goddess of smithing. She floats between these three forms, exalting one at a time but housing all of them at all times.

Second, Brigid is often illustrated as holding fire in her hand. It's an expression of her being a fire goddess and a bringer of light. In alignment with her three-fold form, she represents the three fires:

- The fire of the hearth represents fertility, a warm and blessed home, and healing.

- The fire of the forge stands for crafting and smithing.

- The fire of inspiration represents her wisdom and identity as a poet and an inspiration for wise men and poets.

This is why the physical representation of Brigid's complex character is fire. It's also why people often burn fires for Brigid to invoke her spirit and her blessings.

In the past, a burning hearth was at the center of every house, spreading warmth to the people who lived in the house. The people who put time and effort into tending the fire were a manifestation of that love. And travelers who, from afar, saw a hearth fire burning inside a house were filled with a sense of hope and relief. They also knew that whoever was inside would offer them food and a place to stay. This was healing after a long journey, just as warmth is healing after a long winter.

Once again, Brigid's warmth, love, healing, hope, and relief are all associated with what Imbolc gives us, from the promise of light to the bounties that come with the season.

The Goddess of Poetry

Brigid, the goddess of poetry and inspiration, offers us herself as a muse during Imbolc. Inspiration is the seed of poetry, but one has to start with a blank page to create. Similarly, to think clearly and prepare for new experiences, you need to let go of old influences, outdated perceptions, and other forms of baggage; only then can you truly get the most out of it.

After a long winter filled with demotivation, a lack of inspiration, and sluggish energy, the coming of the sun and Brigid's fire of inspiration give us a much-needed push into the opening world of a new season. Spring is the perfect time to connect with Brigid, ask for her blessings, and receive her energy. It's the best time to give birth to new ideas because this is when the mind is as fertile as the Earth.

So, don't hesitate to start creating, planning, or taking action. Your decisions will see fruition as Brigid's fire of inspiration glows brighter, chasing away winter.

The Goddess of Healing

Fire represents purification and healing. It's a symbol of the sun and the coming of spring. Brigid is the goddess to which you can connect when you want to heal after grieving during winter. She's also there to help you purify, cleanse, and ready yourself for the new year cycle.

Because of her ability to heal illnesses and cleanse, Brigid is also associated with the element of water. Whether you take water from her wells or charge a coin with your intentions and throw it inside as an offering, you'll receive her blessings and healing.

The Goddess of Smithing

Brigid's third aspect and form are her as a goddess of smithing and the forge's fire. She's an inspiration, a muse, and a source of strength to creatives and crafters.

One of Brigid's first inventions was the whistle. It was a magical whistle designed to be used at night. It made a noise so loud that it drew people towards the whistleblower. It was her contribution to protecting women from assault.

Her energy and influence emanate through fire, and it's common to feel more driven and inspired as spring draws near. What's more, you won't meet as much resistance by starting your projects or working with the goddess during this time. In fact, you won't feel like you're working against the grain at all. Your ideas will flow, and crafting will be a joy, not a burden.

The Maiden

The goddess Brigid is known for her love, compassion, and generosity. In the past, pagans believed that life followed her everywhere she went - that flowers sprung under her feet and trees bore fruit at her touch. She is a fearless young goddess who brings life and healing everywhere she goes. With unquenchable fire as her element, no wonder Brigid was immediately associated with spring and birth.

One aspect of Brigid was her identity as a maiden. Using the Wiccan perspective as an example, let's say that Imbolc and spring are the beginning of life. They resemble a youthful maiden.

Summer resembles the maternal aspect of the divine feminine, the matron or the mother. After all, it is the lushest time of the year when there's plenty of everything, from crops, fruits, and flowers to animals.

Meanwhile, winter resembles the crone or the hag – the wise old lady who has lived a lifetime and is dying. She grieves her own death and sheds her current identity to prepare for rebirth with the coming of spring.

Cailleach is the ancient crone associated with and accredited with creating winter and landscapes in ancient Gaelic myths.

Cailleach was a giantess with a staff that froze the ground it touched and formed mountains when she accidentally dropped some rocks from her basket. She was the one who collected the clouds and covered the Earth with snow.

Cailleach ruled the winter months while Brigid ruled the summer months. At the end of winter, the crone turned herself into a stone pillar and made way for Brigid and the new life that came with her.

While the winter months bring to us destruction, the promise of Brigid's return brings a sense of warmth and hope. Around Imbolc, we start seeing signs of Brigid's return: blooming flowers (especially snowdrops), warmer nights, longer days, singing birds, and bumblebees.

Brigid's return also reminds us that death, depression, and loss don't last forever. New life always grows back.

Imbolc is also a great time for women and men to connect with the divine feminine through Brigid the maiden. It's a time to connect with her love, compassion, and powerful life force. Of course, one can also turn to the goddess for their mother and crone needs. However, during this time, Brigid's maiden aspect is at its peak.

The Saint and the Sacred Flame

A girl was born to a Druid father and a Christian mother one day. Her name was Brigid, and, like her father, she was dedicated to the worship of the Irish gods. However, she dedicated her life to honoring her namesake, Brigid, at a young age.

On the hill in Kildare, it was said that she gathered a group of nineteen priestesses, and, together, they kept a hearth fire burning to honor the goddess. Brigid then created this sisterhood which tended the goddess's fire, keeping it lit until the sixteenth century.

This fire was known as the sacred flame. It stayed alight, invoking Brigid's presence and spreading her blessings all over Earth as long as it remained.

When St. Patrick came into Ireland and proceeded to spread Christianity throughout the land, Brigid's mother invited him to talk to Brigid. Eventually, he convinced her to become Christian, and she dedicated her life to Christianity.

She started a convent in Kildare, where she used to tend the fire and, even there, she still kept the fire burning. As time passed, the Catholic Church's hold grew strong enough for the pope to order a full transition from paganism to Christianity.

The sacred flame was extinguished when pagan temples and artifacts were shut down and destroyed. Then, it was re-lit in 1993 in the market square in Kildare by the Brigidine Sisters. Brigid's fire is still tended until now in a place of worship called Solas Bhirde, Kildare, Ireland.

This is the story of Brigid and the sacred flame, which became a form of veneration and worship practiced by all of the goddess's followers. However, there are several theories about who Brigid, the human, was.

Because Brigid, the goddess, could shapeshift and assume different forms, it's believed that she was St. Brigid, except that, back then, she transformed herself into a little girl who grew up to be a saint. It was all because her people needed her to appear in this form at the time, like when she assumed the form of Maman Brigitte for her people who moved to Haiti and the Caribbean Islands to fit with their needs.

Had she retained the identity of Brigid, the goddess, her people would not have been able to practice her worship or feel her influence. It was illegal to practice any form of pagan worship or celebrate any pagan festivals. However, once Brigid had taken a saint form, she became accessible to her people again.

Not only that, but she became accessible to everyone who believed in St. Brigid, Christians and pagans alike. It's only fitting to reiterate what we said at the beginning of the chapter: Brigid is a complex goddess.

The last theory developed by scholars was about Christianity merging the Irish goddess and everything that represented her with Christian imagery. It was a common method used by the Catholic Church throughout Europe and Scandinavia.

Maman Brigitte

Another facet of Brigid's identity is the death loa, Maman Brigitte.

Maman Brigitte is a spirit in Haitian Vodou religion. When the New World was created, many Irish, English, and Scottish people - women in particular - entered into indentured servitude contracts.

This type of slavery was based on the barter system. The wealthy offered to pay the travel costs for the poor who wanted to migrate to the New World. Those people would work as enslaved people for the rich for a specified time.

As the Celtic peoples migrated to the Caribbean Islands and Haiti, they brought with them their traditions. Because most were women, they brought Brigid Dolls as a protection charm with them. After all, Brigid is the protector of women.

This was how Brigid, the Irish goddess, adopted a new aspect, Maman Brigitte, the death loa.

In Haitian Vodou, a loa is a spirit. Maman Brigitte is the Haitian death spirit primarily associated with guardianship and cemeteries. Back then, she was believed to live in the trees within graveyards, and she was invoked for multiple reasons.

Similar to Brigid, Maman Brigitte was a protector and a deliverer of punishment when the need arose. She was invoked when a woman needed to get justice but was unable to because the law didn't favor her. When it came to punishment, Maman Brigitte was a spirit to be feared. Given that historical time period, she was an ancient symbol of female empowerment.

She was also called upon by families who wanted her to protect their kin fighting wars abroad. She was also invoked whenever someone needed healing. Because Maman Brigitte was a great healer, she was the spirit people depended upon when they were desperate. They knew that she would step in and either heal the sick or relieve them by making their death a painless one.

Maman Brigitte is heavily associated with the fire element like her Irish counterpart. People worship and honor her using blue and purple candles, as these are her colors. And, according to tradition, she appreciates offerings of extremely hot peppers, especially when steeped in a glass or container of rum.

During the time of Imbolc, if you feel drawn to work with Maman Brigitte, you'll get the best results if the intent of your magic is oriented towards:

- **Love**

Whether it is romantic love, passion, connection, or communication, Maman Brigitte's energy and influence can be strong in these matters specifically, as this is her time of blooming.

- **Authority**

Maman Brigitte is a dominant figure and one of authority. She commands death and bestows punishment as she sees fit. She can help when it comes to matters of authority, power, control, and developing self-confidence.

- **Fire**

Any magical workings related to fire will be exalted during the time of Imbolc. Some people choose to practice divination with fire, while others practice fire scrying. Both are very good methods to connect with Maman Brigitte's influence.

- **Healing**

There is none other than Maman Brigitte to resort to when it comes to health, protection, and fertility. She is the protector of women, the commander of death, and a master healer.

Can you see the similarities between Brigid and Maman Brigitte? It is believed that Brigid saw that, at the time, her people needed her protection and guidance as they were enslaved in foreign lands. However, they needed it in a particular form, so she took on the form of Maman Brigitte.

On Imbolc, we celebrate Brigid with all her aspects, facets, and forms - her entire complex identity. Because she is a fire goddess associated with light, life, and healing, we focus on her during the coming of spring. We honor her, express our gratitude, and allow her exalted influence to impact our lives where we most need it.

Chapter 3: Candlemas and Imbolc

Candlemas is a Christian festival also celebrated on the 2nd of February. It's known as the feast of the presentation of Jesus Christ. It's also known as the feast of the purification of the Blessed Virgin Mary. Meanwhile, in French, it's referred to as Chandeleur, which comes from the word *"chandelle,"* meaning candle. Also, it's alternatively known as *la fête de la lumière"* or the festival of lights.

As you can see from some of these names, this festival is also associated with light, purification, new beginnings, and the element of fire which, in a way, makes it almost the same as Imbolc or St. Brigid's day. However, the jury is still out on whether they are the same holiday.

There are various opinions about the matter. Some people believe that Candlemas and Imbolc are different names for the same holiday. Others believe that they're different holidays. Meanwhile, some people argue that it's a Catholic adaptation of a pagan holiday.

Who is right? There's no telling. And not only that, but it's also not important. At the end of the day, what makes a festival are the intentions of the ones celebrating. However, what is important is understanding where the various opinions come from.

This chapter will discuss the differences between Candlemas and Imbolc and the complete Christian origins and traditions of Candlemas. So, if you feel you want to form an opinion on the matter or feel you're a little bit curious, this chapter will answer all your questions. It may even add a little bit of depth to how you celebrate Imbolc and inspire you to adopt a specific tradition.

Candlemas for Christians

Before we delve into the debate of whether or not Candlemass is Imbolc, we need to understand everything about Candlemas, its meaning, and its significance in Christianity.

Understanding the significance of Candlemas is no simple matter because many names know it, and each name highlights a different aspect of the celebration.

The Feast of the Presentation of Jesus Christ

You should remember this event from Jesus Christ's childhood if you're familiar with the Bible.

Forty days after Jesus was born, he was taken by Mary and Joseph to a temple in Jerusalem.

According to the Laws of Moses, if the firstborn child was a male, he should be presented and dedicated to God and give a sacrifice. The sacrifice consisted of a pair of doves or pigeons.

The origins of the law go back to when Moses was leading the Israelites out of Egypt. Exodus 13:2 says, "*Consecrate to me every firstborn male. The first offspring of every womb among the Israelites belongs to me, whether human or animal.*"

And this is what Mary and Joseph did. They took their firstborn to the temple to dedicate him and his life to God's service. More than that, however, Jesus was the son of God, and he came to Earth to save his people. So, his coming to the temple was not just a passive action following an ancient tradition.

Jesus's birth represented the arrival of the Savior on Earth. His coming to the temple was a confirmation of the fact that things were about to change. It was the first step that set many events in motion. In a way, the child had connected with his life path and was set on it.

So, one significant aspect of Candlemas is the celebration of the beginning of a life in the service of God. This aspect, however, is four-fold. It was a celebration of the start of Jesus's journey to serve God, which ended with him dying on the cross to save mankind. Two, it's a day for Christians to remember to dedicate their lives and focus on God rather than the material world. Three, it's an opportunity to act on this remembrance and either start the journey or get back on track.

Four, the church is often regarded as a mother in the eyes of its people, given its role in nurturing, guiding, and providing safety. Ephesians 5:25, "*Husbands, love your wives, as Christ loved the church and gave himself up for her,*" is only one verse where the church is personified as a wife and a mother.

Just like Mary, the mother, came to the temple to present her child, so did the church during this time. A church regards that day as one to call upon its people and present them to their service to God.

The Feast of the Purification of the Blessed Virgin Mary

Another Law of Moses that the Israelites observed is mentioned in Leviticus 12:2, "A *woman who becomes pregnant and gives birth to a son will be ceremonially unclean for seven days...*"

After seven days of giving birth to a male, the woman was to soak in water to purify herself. Then, she was to wait for 33 days. She couldn't worship, touch anything sacred, or visit a temple in those days. This period was called a "purification period," it doubled if the child was a girl (14 days before soaking in water and a 66-day purification period afterward).

When this purification period was over, the woman had to take a year-old lamb and a pigeon or a dove to a priest so he could sacrifice them on her behalf. The lamb was to be given as a burnt offering, a general sacrifice, and a sign of her devotion to god. The pigeon was to be given as a sin offering.

Jewish and Christian teachings refer to birth as a process where a mother creates life while staring death in the face. She endures a great deal of pain and suffering, which, on many occasions, ends with joy and relief. However, there is still the possibility of other outcomes.

According to Christian and Jewish beliefs, when individuals have made close contact with death, they need to go through a purification process. The ritual, which includes cleansing, a waiting period, and a sacrifice, is intended to purify the mother and connect her to life and God.

When Mary and Joseph took Jesus to the temple, it was 40 days after his birth which meant it was after Mary's purification period was over. At the time, she also had to offer her sacrifices to God to undo her separation from the living world.

This is why the feast is taken as a time to celebrate the Virgin Mary and her purification. Not only that, but it also is considered by the church a time for purification. Before giving one's life to God, a person needs to be pure from sin. They need to recover from the separation that being away from God causes and connect to him. The church considers this an opportunity to encourage its people to purify themselves.

The Festival of Light

John 8:12 goes, *"Jesus spoke to them, saying, 'I am the world's light.'"*. You can already see where the symbolism originates. Now, let's consider what candles represented in ancient times.

We've already discussed how the sun was the main source of light, only replaced by hearth fires or candles. In the wintertime, when nights were long, the fire was what people depended on to see and to work.

Candles gave people hope. Sometimes they helped guide travelers and gatekeepers and provided a sense of safety in the darkest of times.

Because Candlemas is a celebration of the day Jesus was presented to God in the temple, it also became a day when people celebrated the arrival of the light of the world - the son of God. He would then guide people to salvation and go on to die for their sins.

Candlemas Dates

Traditionally, Candlemas is celebrated on the 2nd of February, just like Imbolc. This day is also the 40th day of Christmas (Jesus's birth on December 25th), aligning with the Christian post-birth purification tradition. This is only the official festival, however.

Different churches tend to have different dates during which they celebrate the specific episode of the presentation of Jesus and not Candlemas as a whole. However, in the 5th century, the Roman Catholic Church was the first organized church to celebrate the episode during Candlemas on the 2nd of February.

Traditions

How Christians celebrate Candlemas can vary from one country to another and even from person to another. Like countries and churches, individuals create or add their own twists on traditions depending on the festival's meaning. This section, however, refers to the most common traditions observed by the Christian public.

Church

Most people go to church on this day to get into the spirit of Candlemas and connect with the meaning and intention behind it. The churches are often decorated with a near-infinite number of candles to celebrate the day.

Many people go to ask for purification or to dedicate themselves to God. Like it's common to consider New Year's Day as a day for new beginnings, many Christians take Candlemas as their day of new beginnings.

Candles

Another reason people go to churches is to either get candles that have already been blessed or get their candles blessed.

They then take their blessed candles home and light them throughout the year whenever they need divine help, hope, or guidance.

Traditionally, families also have feasts where they light candles to celebrate the arrival of Jesus at the temple.

Pancakes

While pancakes/crepes are mainly common in France and Belgium, they were a tradition adopted during the reign of the Roman Empire. At the time, Pope Gelasius I used to go down to the streets and pass galettes (savory crepe-like pastry) to the travelers who came to celebrate Candlemas in Rome, even though, at the time, it was not yet an official festival.

These galettes soon became a symbol of the festival. They were round and golden, representing the sun - the universe's main light source. Then, over the years, galettes were exchanged for the more famous crepes and became the traditional meal to have on the day of Candlemas.

Festivals and Processions

- ## Peru

The Virgin Mary has a lot of significance to many nations in South America. She first became known to them when the Spanish came to conquer Latin America. Gradually, the natives were converted to Christianity. That was when they were introduced to the maternal side of the Virgin Mary. To them, she was a protector of the oppressed, a source of strength for women, and a source of healing. This is why more than one country/city has adopted the Virgin Mary as a patron saint.

In Puno, Peru, the Virgin Mary is known as the Virgen de la Candelaria, which translates to the Virgin of Candles. While the main day of celebrating her is February 2nd, the Festival of Virgen de la Candelaria lasts for two whole weeks, from January 24th to February 13th.

It's one of Latin America's three largest festivals, next to Carnaval in Rio de Janeiro and El Día de Los Muertos (The Day of the Dead), a continent-wide festival.

- ## Puerto Rico

In Puerto Rico, the Virgin Mary is known as Nuestra Señora de Candelaria, which translates to Our Lady of the Light.

On Candlemas, the whole country celebrates her and the theme of light that is attached to the festival. A statue of the Virgin Mary is carried or driven through city streets all day. Then, the procession ends with the Holy Communion in a church.

Afterward, there are feasts, fireworks, dancing, and singing. People also light bonfires and candles to celebrate the Lady of the Light.

- Luxembourg

Just like Jesus, the child is the center of the story of his presentation at the temple. The children in Luxembourg are the main stars of Candlemas. They light candles and lanterns and walk down the streets in a tradition that resembles iconic parts of both Christmas and Halloween. They stop at each door to chant traditional songs, and, in return, they are given candy.

Candlemas and Imbolc

Having understood the three things that Candlemas stands for and its significance for Christians, we can now explore its relationship with Imbolc.

First of all, it's important to pinpoint the beginnings of the two festivals since it'll help you when considering one festival's potential influence on the other.

Pope Sergius I declared Candlemas an official festival in the 7th century. Nevertheless, historical evidence clearly shows that it had been celebrated for at least two centuries before that. Pope Gelasius I assumed the papacy in the year 492 A.D, and in his years, there was already a Candlemas procession.

Perhaps it was not official yet, but many have already celebrated the festival. And it was in those years that a Candlemas tradition of eating crepes developed.

Meanwhile, there isn't a specific date when Imbolc became a festival. Because the majority of literature on paganism and Irish mythology was either burnt, destroyed, or hidden during the Christianization of Ireland and England, resources are limited on the matter.

However, St. Brigid was born in the 5th century, and her name was based on Brigid, the Celtic goddess. This means that Brigid must have been known well before the 5th century, and if Brigid was known before that time, it must have been the same way with Imbolc.

So, the first piece of information is that Imbolc came before Candlemas in the 5th century, while Candlemas could have started before that. Now, this sort of vagueness can be frustrating, but there is one fact that could shed light on why the timings are close to each other.

Rome and Ireland were not Christian countries but pagan ones in the ancient past. They had temples, druids, altars, sacrificial grounds, and everything they needed to worship the gods. This went on up until the 4th century.

In 313 A.D., Emperor Constantine granted freedom from persecution to Christians. It started making its way to the top, and ten years later, it became the Roman Empire's official religion. When the tables turned, the Catholic Church and the Christian public started persecuting and forcefully converting unwilling pagans.

Pope Gregory I was one of the popes who led a diligent campaign dedicated to converting England and the rest of Europe. At first, he sent messengers, but they took too much time, so he ordered that the process be made faster through threats, violence, and the destruction of temples.

Then, one day in 597 A.D., he wrote a letter to the third Archbishop of Canterbury, Abbot Mellitus, telling him to stop the violence. "*Tell Augustine that he should by no means destroy the temples of the gods but rather the idols within those temples. Let him... place altars and relics of the saints in them.*"

He then says, "*[S]ince it has been their custom to slaughter oxen in sacrifice... Let them, therefore... on the feast of the martyrs whose relics are preserved in them, build themselves huts around their one-time temples and celebrate the occasion with religious feasting. They will sacrifice and eat the animals not anymore as an offering to the devil, but for the glory of God to whom, as the giver of all things, they will give thanks for having been satiated.*"

This speaks to a specific conversion technique employed by the church, which was to take something familiar to pagans and replace it with a Christian alternative. If this were done back then during the Christianization of Anglo-Saxon England and in Ireland starting from the 5th century, it could have taken place in post-313 A.D. Rome.

After all, it would explain the similar themes of purification, new beginnings, and the coming of the light. If the question were so easily solvable, it wouldn't have been a matter of debate for this long a time.

It's been long-debated because while the Christianization theory does explain certain similar themes, it indirectly nods to the very real possibility of Candlemas' independent existence.

After all, if Imbolc had truly been replaced, there must have been something to replace it. Perhaps the Christianization could have shaped some of Candlemas's traditions as the church hoped to create a more familiar environment for pagans. However, it's nearly impossible to say that Imbolc and Candlemas are different names for the same holiday or even different holidays until new data comes to light.

Candlemas, at its heart, is rooted in the Bible and the story of Jesus's presentation and Mary's purification. It's been a long-celebrated tradition since the Israelites were still making their way out of Egypt.

On the other hand, Imbolc is a celebration of the coming of spring, the end of winter, and the fertility and bounties associated with this time of year. Not just that, but it's also a celebration of the coming of Brigid with the summer months. It's also a long-celebrated pagan tradition with roots that go back to the time of myths which could go as far back as 4000 years B.C., if not further.

Either way, as we've said before, how you observe Imbolc or Candlemas is solely up to you. So, whatever your opinion of the two festivals is, the most important part of it is what it means to you. If you lose this personal and spiritual connection to the festival, it won't matter which belief or opinion you subscribe to.

Chapter 4: Flowers, Herbs, and Trees

Since Imbolc is the festival of the beginning of spring, many plants, herbs, flowers, and trees are associated with it. This chapter will go over all the plants associated with the festival and the goddess Brigid.

Some of these plants are known for being among the earliest signs of spring, and others are closely related to Brigid and Maman Brigitte. Meanwhile, others have an impact on one's energy and space, which can prove beneficial for pagans, witches, herbalists, and anyone else who celebrates the spiritual aspect of Imbolc.

As you read this chapter, you may be tempted to burn some herbs or work with some of these flowers. Of course, you should do what you feel called to do, but since we can't tell when this may be, here are the guidelines for working with any plant or herb:

- Always ground yourself before doing any spellwork. Because spells work on psychic, psychological, and physical levels, they need you to be in a focused frame of mind. In other words, you need to be centered and grounded, so you won't experience a sudden drop in your energy, physical pain, fatigue, or any other symptoms. This can be through meditation or any other technique - it's completely up to you. We will also expand on this in the spells and rituals section of the book.

- If you're going to use your herbs in a bath, you'll want to make sure they are clean before you allow them to contact your body.

- Always research the plant you are about to consume, apply it to your skin, or work with since some may be toxic or come with precautions.

- Make sure you are not allergic to the herbs and flowers you'll be using, especially their oils. The best thing to do is keep track of any symptoms, and with oils, you'll want to conduct a small test - which you'll find at the end of the chapter - before you use it.

With this being said, get ready to strengthen your connection with Imbolc as we explore its various plants, their symbolism, and how they're used to celebrate and honor the season and its goddess.

Flowers and Plants

Snowdrops

Snowdrops.
https://pixabay.com/images/id-1166564/

Snowdrops are one of the most famous plants associated with Imbolc. Think of it as the equivalent of Christmas and mistletoe.

The whole plant is small with a white flower. Out of the earth, the stem emerges, surrounded by two green leaves. Then, there's a white, drooping bell-shaped flower at the end of the stem.

It's the first flower to bloom at the end of winter, so it's so significant. Spotting snowdrops is one of the earliest signs that spring is on its way. It's a symbol of hope and a reminder that even the coldest and darkest days will end and give way to brighter and better ones. Last but not least, it's considered a sign of Brigid's return.

Coltsfoot

Coltsfoot.
https://pixabay.com/images/id-1274956/

Coltsfoot is another flower commonly associated with Imbolc and Brigid. Like snowdrops, they too bloom in the early spring. Their flowers are a stunning yellow, similar to dandelions in shape.

Coltsfoot is associated with Brigid, and its corresponding planet is Venus which, like Brigid, also has a heavy association with the divine feminine. This is why Coltsfoot, too, is known for its use in spells related to love, healing, and wealth. It's a great flower to burn during divination, as well.

Overall, if you want to work with Coltsfoot, Imbolc is the time since it's during their season and the season of their goddess.

Be careful when working with Coltsfoot because it contains a group of alkaloids (to defend itself against predators) that have been shown to cause liver damage. You can only become affected if you consume the flower.

Blackberry

Blackberries are very closely associated with Brigid for more than one reason. They are Brigid's sacred fruit, and because they fall under the planetary influence of Venus, blackberries represent everything that has to do with the divine feminine.

Just like Brigid and Venus are associated with healing, love, and prosperity, so are blackberries. Primarily, however, during Imbolc, blackberries are used for their healing and rejuvenating properties. Whether they are put in baked goods, eaten by themselves, or used in spells, blackberries can be quite potent when used at this time.

Chamomile

Chamomile is a popular and effective ingredient used in many spells and rituals. It's associated with the element of water - one of Brigid's elements - and is known for its ability to purify and protect. Not just that, but it's also associated with many sun gods.

With the coming of spring, it's important to purify one's space and energy as one embraces the arrival of the sun and the Earth's revival. Purification can put you in the right headspace to accept what the spring has for you. It can also bring you a sense of peace and balance due to its properties relating to the water element.

The best part is that Chamomile is a very versatile flower. It can be brewed into a tea, put in a bath, burnt, steeped in water, sprayed for protection against spirits, candle magic, etc.

Tansy

Tansy.
https://www.pexels.com/photo/a-close-up-shot-of-tansy-flowers-6891103/

The word Tansy is derived from the Greek word *athanatos* which means immortality. It's all because the flower does not die easily and can survive various temperatures. They die late in the winter, letting their seeds fall into the ground, only to be born again.

They are a symbol of rebirth and the fact that death only makes way for a new birth. This makes it a true parallel of the cycle of life and the season change from winter to spring. In addition to its connection with Imbolc, the flower can be associated with Brigid, who is known to represent rebirth and renewal.

Tansies are mainly used in longevity spells. Tansy flowers and oil are sometimes used to honor the bodies of the deceased. Last but not least, they are added to dairy-based baked goods to celebrate Imbolc.

What's crucial for you is that eating Tansies can harm you. They are toxic in large amounts, and as little as ten drops of the oil can cause death. So, make sure you abide exactly by the recipe.

Lavender

Lavender is a calming herb with cleansing, healing, and calming properties, especially when combined with other herbs. It's the perfect herb if you are determined to get in the right frame of mind for Imbolc.

You can burn it, brew a tea out of it, or use it in baths to take away the negative energy from yourself or your space and calm yourself down. It is a great way to ground yourself and practice self-care on this day, especially if you've had a tough winter. And, if you feel called to work with Brigid, you can always prepare a cup of lavender tea for yourself and another for the goddess.

If you consume too much lavender, you may have to deal with a few minor side effects such as constipation, diarrhea, and headaches.

Daffodils

Daffodils bloom late in the winter or very early in the spring, making them one of the most closely-related flowers to Imbolc. Their bright white and yellow colors are also a strong reminder of the coming of light.

Looking at, growing, and meditating on daffodils can help you connect with the bright spirit of Imbolc. It will help you get in tune with nature and its patterns. Not just that, but they're also one of the perfect plants to add to your altar if you want to channel that essence of Imbolc.

Celandine

Celandine, specifically Greater Celandine, is a little bright yellow flower associated with the sun and the element of fire. Needless to say, it's also closely tied to Imbolc and Brigid.

The name is derived from the Greek khelidōn, which translates to the bird species, the swallow. In Ireland, the swallows arrive in the spring (April). Celandines get their name because they start to bloom a little while before the swallows migrate back to Ireland.

The flower is known for its protective properties, especially in legal matters. Nevertheless, it's also known for its powerful toxins if consumed raw - even in moderate amounts. When using it, herbalists make sure to calculate an exact dosage, so if you use it, make sure you always get the dosage right or follow the exact recipe.

Iris

Irises are beautiful flowers known for their large petals, delicate but showy. They are the birth flowers of those born in February, which makes them one of the main symbols of Imbolc.

The meaning of the Greek word iris is rainbow. This speaks to the symbols attached to the flower, like hope and the coming of spring. Not just that, but Iris was also the name of one Greek messenger of the gods. She was the link between the physical and spiritual worlds.

That is why it was common to find purple irises planted over graves, especially those of women. It was an offering for the goddess to help the dead navigate their new environment. The same flowers were also taken to symbolize Maman Brigitte and her identity as a death spirit.

While Irises can smell heavenly, they can also be toxic because they contain the compound iridin, which can cause nausea, diarrhea, pain, and vomiting when ingested. Some Irises can irritate your skin when their leaves or roots are touched.

Violets

Like purple irises, violets are also considered one of Maman Brigitte's favorite offerings. They are also known as February's birth flowers, especially because they bloom during the late winter and early spring. They are a reminder that Imbolc is the time to bloom or start blooming.

As for their uses and associated meanings, the flower's beauty makes it a perfect ingredient for love and fortune spells. Meanwhile, the flowers can be great protectors as their beauty overwhelms and scares away malicious spirits.

Last but not least, there are many ways to consume violets. They can be eaten alone, sautéed, or steamed. They can be put into soups, herbal teas, and baked goods. You can even glaze them with sugar and eat them candied.

Herbs

Bay Leaves

One little-known fact about the silvery leaves of the fascinating bay leaf is that you can use it for cleansing just as you would use sage and palo santo. This makes them a perfect way to welcome Imbolc.

As powerful and potent as they are, they are also gentle leaves that can be written on and burnt to release or manifest. Primarily they are associated with growth, cleansing, and healing.

They can be used with salt to cleanse a house or in a bath to cleanse one's energy. They can also be used to attract abundance, wealth, and good fortune.

Heather

Heather is known as a plant that stands for growth. It's ruled by Venus and the element of water, which is why it reflects certain aspects of Brigid, mainly rebirth, new beginnings, beauty, and peace.

It's a powerful herb to be used when preparing for Imbolc, especially because this is the time to begin anew and start planning ahead. Heather also attracts positive energy and can provide protection.

Finally, it's one of the best ways to bless a new couple, a new relationship, or a new endeavor.

Rosemary

Rosemary is a very powerful herb, one of the most powerful, in fact. Its association with Imbolc comes from its cleansing and protective properties. Given that Imbolc is the time to shed whatever is old and harmful to make way for the new, it's a perfect time to use Rosemary.

You can burn it alone or in a bundle to cleanse your space and magical belongings (wands, tools, etc.). Rosemary oil is great for cleansing objects, as well. As for the raw herb, you hang it somewhere for protection or use it to make decorative wreaths that you can charge with intention.

Angelica

Angelica
https://www.pexels.com/photo/delicate-angelica-archangelica-with-small-leaflets-5349219/

The Angelica flower's Latin name is Angelica Archangelica. It's a flower deeply associated with angels and archangels. Needless to say, anything like that would be a great source of protection in preparation for any endeavors you want to attempt during the spring.

While the leaves can break spells and hexes and be put in protection bags with other herbs to keep you safe, the roots and stem are also quite magical. Tea can be made from the roots. You can also put them in your shoes to make sure you attract the people and energy for which you're looking. Lastly, the stems can easily be turned into a flute.

Basil

Basil is a beautiful herb that packs quite a punch behind it. It's used for protection. Some people argue it can draw out scorpion venom. Meanwhile, others associate it with evil, so they believe you must curse the ground it grows in for the plant to grow properly.

To protect yourself, you can put basil in your house. You can also keep a leaf or two in a prosperity bag to attract wealth. The sweet and enchanting smell of basil is also why it's a great choice for love spells.

Vanilla

Vanilla is a plant deeply connected to Venus and elemental water. It has a sweet, calming, and pacifying effect that provides a sort of healing warmth. This makes vanilla incense a great choice to have around during Imbolc. After all, it's when internal warmth is just as needed as external warmth.

If you work with spells or feel drawn to them, you'll get the best results from vanilla when you use it for fortune, love (even self-love), sex/desire-related rituals, and spells.

Ginger

Have you ever eaten ginger and felt a burn? Just like you feel this physical burn, you should also feel a metaphysical burn as ginger helps ignite one's internal fire. Given that the element of fire rule it, this makes the use of ginger very fitting during Imbolc.

Ginger's fiery nature makes it very effective in achieving spiritual and mental clarity by purifying and healing. If you're in a relationship or are looking for one (or even a fling), putting ginger in a spell bag for attraction will heat things between you and your crush or your significant other(s).

Thyme

Thyme is one plant that has been widely known and used by various cultures throughout the ages, from ancient Egyptians to the Greeks. It's been used in embalming bodies, purifying, cleansing spaces, and even incense.

If you're planning on doing some self-healing during winter's last days, thyme is an herb you'll want by your side. When you're about to take on new tasks and need prosperity and good fortune, thyme is the way to go, too. Also, it's one of the best herbs to use if you want to clear out negative emotional energy, perhaps after a fight, a rant, or after releasing pent-up emotions.

Trees

Oak

Ages ago, the oak was a sacred tree to druids. They provided a sense of security and protection. Because they often lived for centuries and had a maximum lifespan of 500 years, they were also a symbol of wisdom and strength, not to mention that people depended on their wood in nearly every aspect to survive, from houses to weapons.

Because the oak is masculine and feminine, it is a great tree to work with if you are trying to connect to either of your aspects. More importantly, it's a great tree to have at your altar or to have your altar made of, especially if you want the aid of what the oak represents as you approach the spring.

Rowan

Rowan is a sacred Celtic tree deeply associated with the tree of life, and it's a symbol of protection and wisdom. In the Celtic tree calendar, it's the one associated with February. People used to plant a rowan in front of their house to protect them in the past. Others used a simple sprig.

The rowan tree is also associated with the maiden aspect of the triple Goddess, which corresponds to Brigid. So, whether you want to celebrate Imbolc, honor Brigid, or appreciate the delicate solemn nature and powerful influence of rowan trees, make sure to set aside time to work with tree sprigs or even plant new seeds.

Willow

The willow is closely associated with the divine feminine and the sun, among other planets. It is associated with sensitivity, intuition, emotions, and introspection. At the same time, it is associated with the maiden aspect of the triple goddess.

It's a beautiful reminder that even though winter is hard, it is not a time to escape but be taken advantage of. The tree also presents an invitation for you to work with it and reflect upon your previous winter so you can learn your lessons before beginning the summer seasons. The willow also invites you to connect your divine femininity with the coming of spring.

Resins

Myrrh

Myrrh is a gum-resin extracted from a type of tree called Commiphora myrrha. It's one of the staples for rituals, spells, and veneration of gods and goddesses. Some people link it to the element of fire, but its healing properties make it more of a water-type.

The resin is used in protection and banishing spells which are two things many of us need, as they cut ties with what doesn't serve them, be it toxic relationships, a malicious spirit or person, or something else. In ancient Egypt, the resin was also used when asking Isis for help or working with her.

Having read this list of plants, their connection to Imbolc and Brigid, and how they can serve you during this time, there is one thing you should keep in mind. The list, truly, is endless. These are the most popular plants, and the ones we feel help us celebrate and connect to the spirit of Imbolc.

Your practices, beliefs, and what you feel drawn to on your spiritual journey should guide you when selecting or experimenting with herbs and flowers. This chapter was only a roadmap and a list of suggestions. All the decisions are completely up to you.

Oil Allergy Test

Before experimenting with the plants and their oils, it's important to conduct this simple allergy test to avoid any mishaps or grave consequences.

1. Dilute the oil by adding a few drops of essential oil to twice the amount of water.

2. Wash your arm with unscented soap for sensitive skin.

3. Add a few drops of the diluted mixture to a small area of your skin.

4. Place a bandage over that area to prevent the oil from getting washed away. Keep it on for a day. If you notice any symptoms, like itchiness, redness, etc., then take off the bandage, rinse the area immediately, and stay away from that oil. You can also place a few drops on a band-aid and apply that for a quicker alternative to the bandage test.

5. If your skin doesn't react in 24 hours, you're free to enjoy all that your oil of choice offers.

Chapter 5: Crafts and Decorations

Decorations are not put up just so your house can look better. It does feel that way sometimes, but it really isn't. It's the equivalent of dressing up for a special occasion. You know that you're about to go out to celebrate something, you feel happy, and you're in a good mood. Perhaps you want to take some pictures to remember the event, too. So, to express all of this, you dress nicely.

Making crafts and decorations for Imbolc is a form of self-expression. When you're celebrating a season or a milestone in the year cycle that is/has become so important to you, it's natural to want this happiness and excitement to reflect on your space. After all, our space reflects who we are and what we value.

More importantly, it's a way of connecting to Imbolc on a very deep level. When you're making crafts, you're not just making objects. You're making things similar to those made by ancient pagans hundreds of years ago. These things bear deep meaning and beautiful emotional and spiritual significance – and they are/have been used in rituals that not only honor Imbolc but the goddess Brigid.

Making crafts and decorations can be really fun, especially if you have kids. Fun is important on Imbolc. Perhaps some of us can get carried away with the mental and spiritual side of Imbolc, and others can feel like they are being called to do something else. Of course, we all celebrate in different ways, but don't forget that we are celebrating the coming of spring at the end of the day.

While it is easy to lose oneself in the serious aspects, remember that fun is an intrinsic part of Imbolc. It's a festival that should be joyously celebrated. So, take the time to reflect on your winter, plan for your spring, and purify your space, but also allow yourself to have fun and get excited about spring and the coming of Brigid. Then, allow this excitement to show in the form of decorations.

This chapter is all about creating crafts and decorations from scratch. We will talk about the most popular decorations of the occasion, their connection to Imbolc, and what exactly is done with these objects.

St. Brigid's Cross

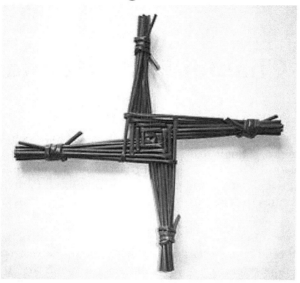

Saint Brigid's Cross.

Culnacreann, CC BY 3.0 <https://creativecommons.org/licenses/by/3.0>, via Wikimedia Commons: https://commons.wikimedia.org/wiki/File:Saint_Brigid%27s_cross.jpg

St. Brigid's cross, also known as the Celtic sun wheel, is one of the most famous Imbolc decorations. Not only that, but it is a form of adoration and a way to honor Brigid. After all, this cross is her symbol, and it represents the sun, of which Brigid is a goddess.

The symbol may look like a cross, but it is a set of spokes that connect at the center. These spokes reference the sun wheel, the solar disc, or the wheel of fire which all connect to Brigid.

Before Imbolc, these crosses are made to honor Brigid and her return. After the winter months, the goddess brings the sun with her to spread warmth on the earth. So, in celebration of this act, we make these crosses to remind ourselves of the goddess's blessings and celebrate the spring's return.

The cross can also be your way of asking for the goddess's protection and blessings on your home and loved ones. It's up to you, your relationship with Brigid, and the intentions you set.

Materials

- 17 12-inch reeds, pipe cleaners, straw, or rushes. You can use one of these materials for the cross. It's completely up to you to choose, although we recommend a natural material rather than an artificial one.

  The number of reeds you use will determine the size of your cross, so it's also completely customizable. If there is a number that represents something to you or that you particularly connect to, it's a great idea to use it.

- Four pieces of string - these will only be used to tie the arms of the cross at the end, so you can substitute the pieces of string with more reeds or rushes if you know how to tie them.

Spiritual Preparation

- The St. Brigid's cross ritual started on the 1st of February at midnight in the distant past. When the reeds were gathered, the people would welcome Brigid as they brought the reeds into the house. Of course, now we understand that the gods and goddesses care about what's in our hearts more than what we do. So, if you'd like to, you can welcome Brigid in your own way as you bring the reeds into the house (during your preferred time of the day).

- After you've gathered your materials, cleanse them in warm water (if you can) and clean your space. If you are a Wiccan, feel free to cast a circle to outline your sacred space - or not if you feel like you don't need one.

- Take a little bit of time to ground yourself, then gradually shift your focus to Brigid. Because this cross is an act of love for the goddess, you'll want to put intention into your creation. So, before you start, take a few minutes to set your intentions and focus on your relationship with Brigid.

Instructions

1. Take one reed and hold it horizontally with your thumb and index finger. This will be the main reed - the spine - and we will place all the rest around it. One of your hands will be used to keep the reeds tight around the center.

2. Take another reed with your other hand, fold it in half over the main reed to create the letter "T," and keep it tightly in place with your thumb and index finger. The fold should be facing you, and the separate ends should be facing the ground.

3. Make a 90-degree turn (anti-clockwise) so that the main reed is vertical and the second reed is pointing to your right.

4. Grab another reed and fold it over the second reed. It should be parallel to the main reed, and the loose ends should be pointing downwards.

5. Make another 90-degree turn and fold another reed over the main reed in the same way as before. Make sure it's tight around the center.

6. Then, make a 90-degree turn to complete the circle and fold another reed over the last one you placed.

7. Repeat this process until you get the size you want or until you're down to your last reed - you'll need one reed to secure the rest of the reeds in place before you tie them.

8. Once you've done this with your reeds, don't let go. Make sure to keep them held tight; otherwise, they will go all over the place.

9. With the last reed, the process will go a bit differently. Instead of folding the reed in half, wrapping it around the cross's arm, and keeping the ends loose, trap the ends inside the folded reed. The last reed should make a 90-degree angle with the folded reed it's trapped in.

10. Make sure all the reeds are tight around the center, then bundle together the ends that make up each arm of the cross.

11. Tie each arm with a piece of string or with a long reed.

Uses

Brigid's cross doesn't only have to be used during Imbolc. There are many uses for this beautiful symbol. In addition to its being a celebration of Brigid and a source of protection and blessings, you can place it on your altar or in a space to keep Brigid's presence near you. You can also burn it as an offering to the goddess.

After Imbolc

Because St. Brigid's cross is a sacred symbol and one that may absorb negative or malicious energy to protect you, you must dispose of it correctly. At the end of the year (next Imbolc), or if you're permanently leaving your space, you must burn the cross and bury its ashes in the earth as an offering.

Don't forget to express your gratitude to the cross and Brigid.

The Brigid Doll

The Brigid doll is a symbol of Brigid, the maiden. Imbolc is also a celebration of Brigid's rebirth and the transformation from crone to the maiden, so this doll represents this new beginning.

It's a way to invite the maiden's fertility, abundance, potential, life force, confidence, and curiosity into your house. Not just that, but it's also a way of observing and celebrating these qualities in the goddess herself.

In the early days, the Brigid doll was made using woven wheat or oats to celebrate the earth's fertility. Although, these materials may be hard to find now. If you can find them, by all means, go ahead and get some. However, if you can't, there are other options, like straw and corn husks.

Materials

- Corn husks or Straw - a few hours before you start, put your straw in warm water and let it soak to make it bendable.

- Yarn

- Cotton balls (only for corn husk dolls)

Spiritual Preparation

- Take some time to relax your thoughts, become calm, and set your intentions for making the doll. Since it is a celebration of Brigid's maiden aspect, that's what we recommend you focus or meditate on before starting. However, what you focus on is still your decision, so trust in yourself.

Instructions
Corn Husk Dolls

1. To make the head, you'll need to take a husk, fold it in half, and put in a few cotton balls, ideally two. It depends on how big you want the head to be.

2. After putting the balls in, lift the husk around them, and apply a little pressure right above to trap the cotton balls and twist the husk. Then, take a piece of yarn and tie a tight knot to create the head. Make sure you leave a length of husk from the front and back to make the torso.

3. Take two husks, fold them in half - or as much as you need - and tie a knot half a centimeter (less than half an inch) away from each end. The husks should form the arms, and the small, spread-out parts should form the hands.

4. Tuck the arm/hand husks into the torso husk, twist to trap the arms and tie a knot to form the waist.

5. To form the skirt, put two slightly overlapping husks on a dry surface, place your doll on them, and place another two husks on top (also slightly overlapping. Make sure you align the tops of the husks with the doll's waist.)

6. Press the tops of the husks together around the waist and tie a tight knot to connect the skirt to the waist.

7. Gently pull the doll's skirt down from its face and arrange it how you'd like it to look. You can also take a pair of scissors to the skirt and even it out, or even give it a distinctive design.

Straw Dolls

8. Take many straws (10 -15) and tie them together about half an inch from the end. This will make up the head's length, width, and size, so you can customize the number of straws and where you place your knot from the straws' end. We recommend you try it out first as it helps you to understand how it works.

9. One by one, bend the straws upwards at the knot, folding each straw into itself.

10. Flip the straws upside down and tie another knot around the bundle that forms at the top. You've just created the head and the body.

11. Take half the number of straws you used for the head and tie a knot down their middle to create the arms.

12. Part the body straws evenly and place the arm straws in-between. Make sure you hide the middle knot with the straws that make up the body.

13. Slide the arm straws to the height you'd like. Ideally, you want it to be close to the head knot to stabilize the arms. After you're satisfied, tie a knot under the arms to keep them in place.

14. Tie two knots, one on each arm just a little ways from the end, to create the hands. If you don't like the length of the arms, tie the knots wherever you'd like on the arm, then cut the extra straw with a pair of scissors. Make sure you leave a small bit of straw to create a noticeable hand.

15. To create the bottom half, spread out the leftover length of body straws, then trim the excess to create a proportionate bottom. For a better-looking doll, make sure your knots are very tight.

16. An optional step is to color your doll or decorate it with herbs.

After Imbolc

Like with St. Brigid's cross, if you ever want to or need to dispose of your Brigid doll, burn it in a fire and present its ashes to the ground.

Brigid's Bed

If you're planning to make a Brigid doll, then there's nothing better than Brigid's bed to go with it.

On Imbolc, Brigid comes to visit her people and bestow upon them her blessings. Just as a Brigid doll is a symbol of the goddess, the bed is a welcoming gesture, and it's something that Brigid truly appreciates.

Brigid's bed is a miniature resting place for the Brigid doll. Once you make the bed, place the doll in it and either place it by the fire - if you have one- or in your kitchen next to the cooker/oven.

Materials

- Wicker basket
- A receiving blanket, a small bed sheet, or any type of soft cloth
- A small blanket

Spiritual Preparation

- If you're planning to go through this much effort to receive Brigid into your home, she must be one of two things; a beloved old friend or a new friend you're looking forward to meeting. Keep your mind on how Brigid would react upon seeing the bed you're making for her. This will help you keep your intentions focused on this act of love.

Instructions

1. Line your wicker basket with a receiving blanket or any other type of soft, delicate material to serve as a bedsheet.

2. If you have a miniature pillow, put it in there. If you don't, you can make one by sewing together two pieces of cloth around some cotton or any soft and fluffy material.

3. Fold a small blanket and keep it at one end of the wicker basket for Imbolc night.

Uses

If you want to invite Brigid into your home as you're having Imbolc dinner, place your doll in the bed with the blanket over her and a candle, or a few, next to her - make sure you observe fire safety precautions.

Some people prefer to make a ritual out of it and put the Brigid doll in the bed as they sleep at night.

Regardless of what you choose to do, Brigid will see your intentions and efforts, and she will bless you and your household.

Ice Candles

Ice candle

Wannikw7, CC BY-SA 4.0 <https://creativecommons.org/licenses/by-sa/4.0>, via Wikimedia Commons: https://commons.wikimedia.org/wiki/File:Ice_candle_festival.jpg

Ice candles are a fascinating creation. More than that, they are a perfect symbol of what happens on Imbolc. The sun starts approaching, gradually melting winter's ice, and banishing its cold.

Materials

- A double boiler or a pot and a steel bowl - you can substitute the bowl for a pan, but it wouldn't be as ideal.

- Paraffin wax or chunks of used candles

- A large, empty milk carton

- Wick

- Mold sealer

- Small chunks of ice

- Colored dye (optional)

Ratios: The ratio in this recipe is equal parts ice and wax. The amounts depend on the size of your container. For example, if you'll be using a quarter of a 32-ounce milk carton, then you'll need four ounces of each.

Spiritual Preparation

- If you'd like to set any intentions while making your candle, you can either do that before you make the candle or when it's done.

Both are good options, but they are different. We recommend you channel your energy and intentions or ask a deity to bless your candle before you make it. This makes the experience rather personal and uniquely intimate.

Instructions

1. To make the candle mold, cut the top off the milk carton leaving only the size of your desired candle.

2. Make a very small hole with a pin or a needle at the bottom of the carton. Make sure it's right in the center.

3. Slip the wick into the hole and gently drag it out from the other side until there's an extra inch of wick extending from the top of the carton.

4. Coil what's left of the wick at the bottom of the carton, press it against the carton and cover it with a mold sealer to make sure the wax and ice don't leak out.

5. Turn the carton so that it's sitting on its bottom. Place a pencil or a chopstick across its edges, then coil and tie the extra wick around this pencil while ensuring it's taut. This is important since it'll guarantee a straight wick.

6. After that, it's time to prepare the candle. Cut your paraffin wax or old candle wax into small blocks using a knife, a hammer, a chisel, or a screwdriver.

7. Fill up about a quarter of a pot and place the metal bowl or smaller pot/pan inside it. You don't want the water to touch the surface of the second pot. As you heat the water to a boil, the steam will heat the pot and melt the wax.

8. Pour the wax chunks into the double boiler, then when the wax melts, that's when you can add the dye to color your candle. If you use old candles, you'll already have an interesting mix of colors.

9. When the wax is ready, take your ice out of the freezer and arrange it inside the carton. Make sure it's snug around the wick, and make sure that the wick is centered. Then, pour in the wax. Ideally, you'll want to place a large container lined with aluminum foil under the carton to control the damage in case of any leaks or accidents.

10. Ice candles usually take about an hour and a half or two to cool down completely. Leave yours to cool before you peel off the carton. And make sure you peel the carton over a sink to avoid spilling any remaining water.

11. Completely trim the bottom wick.

12. Trim the top wick to a quarter of an inch.

13. Leave the candle to dry completely before using it, and then place it in a shallow bowl or another container to catch the molten wax and enjoy!

Uses

- The beauty of an ice candle is that it can represent more than one thing. It can represent the coming of spring. It can represent Brigid's return. It can even represent you or your life. Perhaps this winter has been a hard one, or perhaps you suffer from a seasonal affective disorder that drains you. The candle can symbolize your fire that will soon burn bright.

- You can also use the candle on your altar or when you're meditating.

- The candle could be a perfect accompaniment to the Brigid doll and Brigid's bed as it can represent the goddess's dual elements: fire and water.

Chapter 6: Setting Up an Imbolc Altar

Imbolc ritual altar.

As important as they are, altars are not for all pagans or practitioners. How we interact with the gods and nature depends on how we prefer to interact. Many of us consider altars a safe and sacred space where they worship, pray, and more. Meanwhile, other theist pagans simply don't feel the same way. Some don't worship deities (non-theistic pagans), so they don't have a pressing need for an altar. Last but not least, some pagans tend to steer clear because altars can be triggering for them.

This is all to say that the importance of an altar is not an objective one but a very subjective one. If you're new to paganism, you deserve to form your opinion on altars. You'll want to read through this chapter as we will discuss altars in general before delving into Imbolc altars.

On the other hand, if you have already figured out your stance concerning altars, this chapter will serve you greatly, or it will just be an interesting read and nothing more.

In this chapter, we will discuss how to keep an Imbolc altar or decorate your existing altar for Imbolc and everything that has to do with altars.

Altars

An altar is a sacred space for you to worship in any way you please. In our modern world, they are not just for pagans and Wiccans but also used by organized religions. However, this doesn't mean that they belong to one and not the other. The concept of an altar is a neutral one that you can give whatever meaning you like.

Imagine a "secret spot" where you usually go to meet a friend or to be alone and think for a little while. This spot is comfortable and has a few of the things that you like around it. And, when you go there, you experience a feeling of calm almost instantly, or you can't help but remember your companion who often goes there with you. An altar is exactly like that.

It's a place for you to nourish your spirit and tend to your spiritual needs. It's also a place for you to worship your deities of choice, connect with them, and ask for help. More importantly, it's a physical manifestation of your deities' spiritual presence, which can put a smile on your face whenever you look at it, better yet, help you when times get tough.

When it comes to witches and Wiccans, altars serve another purpose besides the rest. They are a sacred and safe space charged with energy and intentions where the person can perform spells and practice their craft.

What the Altar Should Look Like

There isn't really one standard altar set-up even though, in the past, there was a traditional approach to Wiccan altars.

The more humanity has grown in understanding, the more we've come to grips with the fact that the look of one's altar should depend on what one wants to do with it.

If you want to worship deities, it makes sense to include some of their symbols, perhaps a picture, a symbol of their element, plant, and anything else you may want.

If your ancestors are the ones you'd like to ask for guidance, then you may want to place some of the objects that deeply connect you to your family upon your altar.

If you intend to connect with the universe and its energy, you'll want to have a few natural items - crystals, seashells, feathers, herbs, flowers, etc.

If you'd like to keep your altar a workspace so you can practice witchcraft, it makes more sense to go easy on the symbols and keep more of your frequently used ingredients and tools, like candles, Tarot cards, mortar, and pestle, etc. On your altar.

If you'd like to celebrate a particular occasion or an event, like Imbolc, you can create a new set-up (or exchange your existing one) that resembles how you feel about the event.

So, as you see, an altar's look is not fixed. It can change to suit your purposes and intentions, what you're currently drawn to, or what you need.

As for how cluttered/fancy your altar should be, we'll tell you the same thing we said since the beginning of the chapter. It's up to you and the resources at your disposal. At the end of the day, what an altar looks like is nothing compared to what it means and the power it holds.

Keeping Your Altar

Your altar reflects your spiritual side, and this is why we keep recommending that you follow your instinct. Whatever you are drawn to will shape your altar, and as you grow and build a connection to your special space, it will change to reflect this growth and connection.

Here is an outline and a loose guide to help you create your own altar, as we've done before. We'll leave the customization to you.

The Purpose of Your Altar

The purpose of an altar will determine how you proceed with the next steps, which include finding a location, building, decorating, cleaning, and so on.

We've already tackled the various purposes of an altar, from worship to witchcraft, but finding your own purpose can be a bit challenging.

Some of you may have that purpose clear in your head. Others may feel strongly drawn to building an altar, and that's it. Now, there are two approaches to finding the purpose of your altar. One is to narrow down your choices, and the other is to embrace the infinite possibilities.

To narrow down your choices:

Consider how you feel when you get the urge, though, or call to make one.

Do you feel a sense of excitement or safety? If so, what makes you feel that way? Some people feel excitement at the thought of getting to explore their relationship with certain deities. Others feel like they yearn for the safety and warmth of a space they can dedicate to their complex range of spiritual needs.

In addition to exploring your feelings, it's always helpful to explore your imagination. What do you see yourself doing at the altar? Are you meditating? Burning incense? Talking to some spirit or deity? Grounding yourself? Asking for help? Perhaps you imagine doing all of these or none of them.

To embrace the unknown:

The purpose of your altar could be to explore your spiritual aspects. Some people like to know what they're going to do on a trip. Others like traveling without an itinerary because it leaves room for them to do what they truly feel like doing.

Because your altar is yours and only yours, it can be that safe place that allows you to explore what feels right for you. Embracing the possibilities means creating this blank canvas, paying attention to the colors you're attracted to, and listening to what your soul, heart, mind, and body feel like painting.

If this seems a little vague now, don't worry. You'll understand more with each paragraph.

The Location of Your Altar

An altar is sacred, and so are the items on it. So, the ground rules are:

- Don't put it somewhere where it's easy to bump into it.
- Don't put it somewhere where it may be desecrated.

Now, these may be rules, but they are also things that simply make sense.

You wouldn't put a new crystal vase in your cat's favorite place to bask in the sun. It would get knocked down in less than a day.

If you get a new chair knowing that your dog often has "accidents" because he doesn't believe in peeing outside, wouldn't you take the necessary extra precautions?

That said, let's talk about where you should put your altar.

Location is about safety. In each of our homes, there is always that place we're attracted to the most. It's a place we feel comfortable. It's also a place where we can sit all day, especially with a nice drink or something after a hard day. This is the type of place you want for your altar.

This place could be somewhere in your bedroom, your living room, by a window, in the attic, or in your favorite corner/nook. In the far distant past, people used to keep their altars in the kitchen. Even now, kitchen altars have their own unique signature that differentiates them from other altars.

Because the kitchen resembles the heart of the house - it's where food is cooked and where the fire is constantly burning - it was always considered a great place to set up an altar. Nowadays, a kitchen is not just that, but it's also where we get to touch, smell, listen to, taste, and feel nature's many elements.

A kitchen altar can serve as a reminder that there is worship even in life's most routine and mundane aspects. It can bless and protect your kitchen and the meals you prepare. Moreover, it can help you further connect with nature, its magic, and the magic of combining different ingredients and creating a whole new thing. Finally, it's a great way to celebrate Imbolc for many reasons that we will delve into later in the chapter.

Unfortunately, some of us don't have the luxury of publicly practicing our beliefs, so your favorite spot in your bedroom will do just fine. You can even use a small or foldable surface as an altar, and that way, you can store it and take it out whenever you want to.

The Building Process

An altar consists of two main things, a surface and sacred items. Some people choose to put a tablecloth over their altar's surface for decoration, to protect the surface, or because the color or design of the cloth means something to them. However, it's not at all necessary. In fact, it can be a nuisance if you'll constantly need to clean it from melted wax.

Another group also considers an offering plate as essential, and it is, but only for them since offerings are a big part of their worship.

So, the rule of thumb when it comes to your altar is that if you don't want it, then you don't have to have it.

Now, without further ado, let's explore the two main components of an altar.

- ### The Surface

This could be a surface you have in the house, like a counter, a coffee table, the top of a microwave, a shelf, or even a lazy Susan. It could also be a make-shift surface, like a wooden box, a cardboard box, a crate, a shoebox, etc. As long as it will be able to carry your items, it'll be perfect.

This is where your items will go, and if you are using the altar for practical purposes, it'll be where you work. That means that based on the purpose of your altar - or what you think it is - you'll have to decide how much space you need. This may sound like a crucial point, but it isn't. The worst-case scenario is that your altar will be a bit cramped, and that's okay, as long as you're comfortable with it.

- **The Sacred Items**

Now that you've got yourself a surface, all you need are a few sacred items, and you'll be good to go.

This is the most fun part about creating an altar for many because imagination is your limit. As long as you feel connected to the items you put on it, you're doing it right. So, what sort of items are we talking about here?

People who design their altars to reflect their love for nature and the universe like to include one item to represent each of the four elements:

- **Earth**: A stone or a crystal
- **Fire:** Candle
- **Water:** Shells, sea glass, sand dollars, sea/ocean water (or any kind of water)
- **Air:** Feathers, bird-shaped pins/statues/trinkets, incense

Nature-oriented pagans also like to include plants like sunflowers, lavender, roses, violets, etc. A plant is also a great choice if you plan to work with a deity who a particular plant symbolizes. You can place a dried leaf, a small branch, or a twig onto your altar.

Speaking of deities, pagans who work with and/or connect to specific gods decorate their altars with pictures or statues of the gods or of animals that represent them. For example, if they worship Odin or the Morrigan, they'll put a crow to symbolize them.

They may also add plants or symbols associated with the gods onto their altar. For instance, if they worship Brigid, they'll put Brigid's cross or a piece of oak.

Some people choose to put one or two items from their childhood. Perhaps, a special item connects them to an ancestor or one they always saw magic in. It could also be an item that provided them with a sense of safety when they were children.

Then some often use their altar to speak to their ancestors and ask for help and guidance. These people add pictures of their deceased loved ones and perhaps some items which belonged to them.

The list of items you have to choose from is endless, which can put a little pressure on you. Remember that it's okay to expand your altar, have more than one, or even replace one item with another. And as for the placement, it's completely up to you.

Remember, what you choose to put on your altar shouldn't have to abide by others' standards, and it shouldn't have to be "cool," "eclectic," or "eccentric." All it needs to be is something that you feel will be appropriate. More importantly, remember that your altar's magic and power come from within you and not from the objects.

The Cleansing Process

Cleansing is an important part of keeping an altar. Just like anything else, the items on the altar can absorb negative energy, especially if you put them there with that intention. At some point in time, the environment around your altar will become saturated with this negative energy.

There are many reasons to cleanse your altar:

- When you feel that the energy has become too negative.
- The first time you make an altar.
- When you bring a new item or use a new surface.
- When you change the purpose of an altar, like when you're celebrating Imbolc.

There are also many ways to cleanse your altar. The two most popular ways are:

- You can burn sage or myrrh and let the smoke absorb the energy. Make sure that you leave a window open so the smoke will have a chance to leave the house.
- You can spray seawater or holy water (water and salt that has been blessed in the way you feel is right for you) or water left under a full moon for a night.

Imbolc Altars

Imbolc altars are not much different from normal altars. The only difference is the sacred items you put on it, which are purely determined by your relationship with Imbolc. With Imbolc altars, you'll find that you can be more detailed with what you put on them since celebrating Imbolc is a very specific purpose.

When decorating your altar for Imbolc, apply everything you've learned so far in this chapter to choose a location, a surface, and your sacred items.

Altar Preparation

If you already have an altar, you don't have to make a new one. You can cleanse it, remove the items that don't fit with your way of celebration, adding those ways that do.

On the other hand, if you don't have an altar, you can have the Imbolc altar as your first or set up a kitchen altar if you'd like to. Don't forget to choose a place that reminds you of life, rebirth, the coming of spring, or

Brigid. You don't have to change your altar's location, but it may add a different flavor.

As for kitchen altars, all you need is a lazy Susan or a tray as a surface and your choice of sacred items. Because the kitchen is Brigid's domain - it's the heart of the house and where the fire is - it's a perfect place to set up an altar for her. And, because Imbolc is when plants and animals come to life, you can include nature-related sacred items to celebrate spring and the fruitfulness that comes with it. It'll serve as a beautiful reminder of how connected to nature you are - what you're cooking came from the earth, which is made fertile by the sun's return, which is what you're celebrating.

Imbolc-Related Sacred Items

There are two main types of objects you can add to your Imbolc altar. Depending on your beliefs and what you feel comfortable with, you can choose these items.

Brigid-Related Items

These are the items that symbolize Brigid or that are associated with her.

- Brigid's cross
- Bull statue, picture, etc.
- A piece of oak bark
- A statue, a painting, or a drawing of Brigid.
- A crescent (The first phase of a new moon, which represents the maiden aspect of Brigid.)
- Candles, especially red, white, and green
- Red or orange crystals/stones, like amethyst, sunstone, and peridot
- Snowdrops
- An offering plate

Nature-Related Items

Imbolc, after all, is a celebration of the return of spring which makes it a celebration of nature.

- Plants, like daffodils, snowdrops, Irises, and rowan trees.
- Animal statues, specifically cows and sheep.
- Candles
- Incense
- Crystals/stones
- Tarot cards (It could be a way to set intentions for the spring.)
- Runes

- A miniature bonfire

After Imbolc

After Imbolc, all you have to do is figure out what you want to keep and what you want to throw away. Whatever you'd like to keep, cleanse it, and keep it in a safe and clean place. Then, cleanse your altar like you'd cleanse a new altar and put your day-to-day items.

Now, disposal of offerings, sacred items, and altars is one issue that plagues almost everyone who keeps an altar. Setting up an altar for a one-day occasion seems like a whole impossible ordeal. Because everyone deserves to celebrate Imbolc without worrying about the day after, here is your comprehensive disposal guide.

Organic or Degradable Objects

When it comes to anything degradable, it's okay to burn the object and bury it in the ground. Before that, however, make sure that it won't harm the earth, soil, or plants. Suppose it will; maybe *compost it* instead of burning it.

Inorganic or Non-Degradable Objects

When it comes to anything that won't decompose on its own or that will pollute the atmosphere if burnt or buried, it's best to cleanse the item however you see fit and then find a different way to dispose of it.

You can give it away or swap it with someone if it's a statue. If it's a used candle, you can melt it with a little extra wax (or more used candles) to make new candles. If it's a recyclable object, recycle it. Always remember to cleanse your items before you dispose of them, though. You don't want to pass on anything unwanted to anyone unaware.

Offerings

Different traditions have different tips on how to dispose of an offering. First of all, there is no specific waiting period that you must leave an offering for so that the gods can eat it. For the gods, it's all about the intentions and the essence.

Second, there are many ways to dispose of an offering. As long as yours is respectful and environment-friendly, you can do what you want:

- You can eat the offering.

- You can burn it and then present it to the ground.

- You can throw your offering into a body of water.

- You can feed it to an animal.

- You can compost it.

Chapter 7: Recipes for an Imbolc Feast

One of the beautiful things about Imbolc is that it's one of the very food-orientated Sabbats. Since spring is the time when most foods grow, animals reproduce, and milk production flows, Imbolc has long been associated with the coming of not just the season but with everything it has to offer.

This abundance of food-inspired ancient pagans to create recipes based on what was most popular with the coming of spring to celebrate the land. Nowadays, we still celebrate this tradition, even though the recipes may have changed a little - or a lot.

Imbolc Recipes vs. Regular Recipes

What separates a regular recipe from an Imbolc recipe are the ingredients used and the blessings and intentions added. Neither cuisine nor cooking method nor dietary restrictions can make your meal less "Imbolc."

The coming of spring celebrates an increase in milk production, which means that an Imbolc recipe should include milk and/or other dairy products. It also celebrates the time chickens start laying eggs, which makes eggs a part of the celebration. Third, it's a celebration of the Earth becoming fertile again, which opens the door to oats, potatoes, wheat, vegetables, and the flowers and herbs we mentioned earlier in the book.

As you read through the recipes, you'll notice that there are some ingredients more common than others. It's also why the cooking style isn't the be-all and end-all - and the ingredients, too, if we're being honest. Granted, the ingredients have some significance, especially for people who love tradition, but it's a celebration of nature at heart. As long as nature is involved, you're on the right track.

As for the cuisine, our recipes are mainly Celtic because Imbolc was primarily celebrated among Celtic cultures. However, keep in mind that paganism did not represent and is not strictly tied to Celtic cultures. Imbolc is a celebration of nature, making it a festival for all peoples and cultures. This means there's always room for you to celebrate with the cuisine you like most.

Things might have been different if you were honoring Brigid or preparing an offering for her on this day, though. In this case, it makes more sense to prepare Irish or Celtic recipes since Brigid is an Irish goddess. Even then, an offering is more about what the food holds and represents rather than the food itself, so many would argue that it still won't matter what cuisine you cook.

Well, what if you can't cook at all? Well, that's no problem. This chapter has a selection of easy recipes that are guaranteed to become firm favorites for you and the people you celebrate with.

Side Dishes

Rosemary Potato Rolls

This vegetarian recipe is a great Imbolc dish if you're a fan of herbs and if you want a little extra cleansing and protection. To get ready for the spring, rosemary can help you start fresh. As for the potatoes, they're a classic Imbolc food, just like the butter and milk in the recipe, which are also a celebration of Brigid.

Ingredients

Yield: 14 rolls

- 3 oz. (approx. 90 ml) or ⅓ cup and ½ tbsp. butter
- ¼ cup sugar
- ½ tsp salt
- ½ cup milk
- An egg
- ½ cup mashed potatoes
- 2 & ½ cups all-purpose flour
- 1 tbsp. finely chopped rosemary

For the yeast mixture:

- 1 & ⅛ tsp or 4 grams of yeast
- ¼ cup warm water

Preparations

- Boil and mash the potatoes.
- Beat the egg.

Instructions

1. Heat your milk until it starts to bubble, then set it aside.

2. While the milk heats, add the yeast to the warm water and stir carefully to ensure the yeast is properly distributed in the water. You should see foam in the cup within five minutes. If you don't see foam, try with a new pack of yeast.

3. Mix the sugar, salt, and butter in a mixing bowl, then add the milk when the mixture gets too lumpy.

4. Gradually pour half a cup of flour into the mixture as you stir.

5. Add the egg into the mixing bowl along with the yeast mixture.

6. Mix in the potatoes and the rosemary.

7. The dough should be in a more liquid form than a solid one, so stir until it's completely smooth before adding what's left of the flour, then keep mixing.

8. Sprinkle a little flour, just enough to cover your work surface, before transferring the dough from the bowl. You want to prevent the dough from sticking, but you don't want to use too much flour that dries it out.

9. Knead the dough until there are no more lumps. As you knead, pay attention to your dough. If it's too sticky, add more flour. If it keeps crumbling, use a teaspoon to add more milk.

10. Use oil or butter to lightly coat the inside of a bowl, then put the dough into it, cover it with a cloth, and leave it for 45 minutes to rise in your oven or microwave - or any warm place.

11. After the dough has risen, lightly coat a cupcake or muffin tin with oil, then pinch off medium-sized chunks from the dough, ball them up, and place two to four balls in each slot.

12. Cover the tin (or tins) with clean cloths and leave it in a warm place to rise again for about 30 more minutes.

13. At the 20-minute mark, preheat your oven to 375 F or 190C.

14. Bake the rolls for 15 minutes or until you can insert a toothpick in the middle of a roll, and it comes out clean.

Possible Variations

- The best thing about herbs is that you can put them in anything. Because this is a sort of sweet bread, you can add lavender, vanilla, or violets.

- For more savory bread, you can decrease the sugar (to taste) and add a sprinkle of pepper, then add your choice of herbs. Thyme, basil, and bay leaves are great additions.

- If you don't have the time to make mashed potatoes, you can use instant mashed potatoes instead.

Savory Dishes

Colcannon

Colcannon is a traditional Irish salad-like dish made of potatoes and kale or cabbage. It's an Imbolc dish that showcases potatoes and celebrates spring's effect on the soil.

Ingredients

Yields: 5 servings

Because this dish doesn't depend on the ratios of its ingredients, you can get as creative as you want with the amounts.

- 2 russet potatoes
- Half a bunch of kale
- 3 spring onions
- Ice
- Salt
- Pepper
- 1/2 cup or 4 oz. unsalted butter

Preparations

- Peel and quarter the potatoes.
- Chop your onions - you can add texture to your dish by varying your chopping styles.

Instructions

1. Bring a pot of water to a boil, then let it simmer.
2. Add a dash of salt, put in the potatoes, and let them cook until they are soft in the middle. A knife should be able to slip easily through the potato.
3. While the potatoes cook, bring another pot of water to a boil, then throw in your kale. Let it flash-cook for a minute, then take it out and put it in a bowl of ice-cold water.
4. When the kale's temperature goes down, leave it to drain.

5. In a blender, throw in 2 chopped spring onions (⅔ of the entire amount) and add the kale. If you want texture, pulse for a few seconds until everything is roughly mixed. If you want a smooth kale-onion mix, work the blender for a little more, or use a food processor.

6. Go back to the potatoes. Drain them, but keep them in the pot if they're done.

7. Add butter to the potatoes and mash with a masher, a spatula, or even using the bottom of a mug.

8. Add the kale and onion mixture to the potatoes and any other spices you might want.

9. Season with salt and pepper, and enjoy.

Possible Variations

- This recipe is great because it leaves so much room for creativity. You can add your own herbs, vegetables, and even spices. If there's something you feel like you need to try, go ahead and chuck it in there. We recommend you try basil, rosemary, and thyme.

- Cheese is a great addition to this recipe, whether it's added when you're mashing the potatoes or as a topping. Ideally, go with a salty cheese to balance out the butter.

- You can add a little protein to your dish by frying bacon or cooking minced meat or chicken. Simply toss it in when you have mixed all the ingredients.

Cheese Pasta

This is a simple dish that most of us can cook in our sleep. It also happens to be a modern Imbolc dish. The ancient Irish didn't necessarily depend on mac and cheese in their daily lives, but cheese on its own was almost a necessity. Even better, cheese, among other dairy products, is an Imbolc food. And what's pasta made of? Wheat that comes from our fertile earth.

Ingredients

Yields: 7/8 servings

- A 1 lb. (500g) bag of pasta (any shape)
- 4 cups (1 quart) of cream
- 8 ounces or ½ a pound (250g) of goat cheese
- 2 tbsp rosemary
- 1 clove garlic

- Salt
- Pepper

Preparations

- Crush and peel the garlic
- Chop the rosemary
- Chop the goat cheese into cubes.

Instructions

1. Bring a pot of water to a boil, add 1 tablespoon of salt (or 1 and a ½), then throw in the pasta. Let it cook until it's al dente - until it's mostly soft but still has that bite to it. Then, drain the pasta.

2. Over medium-low heat, pour the cream into a large saucepan, then add your rosemary and the clove. You can also add any other spices.

3. Let the cream simmer by keeping the heat medium-low until you notice little bubbles on the surface. You don't want a full-blown boil because then the cream may curdle.

4. When the cream thickens, add the goat cheese cubes, and stir.

5. Gradually, the goat cheese will start to melt, and you'll have your sauce.

6. Salt and pepper to taste, then add your sauce to the pasta in the pot or vice versa. Then, mix well and enjoy.

Possible Variations

- This recipe is a vegetarian one, but you can add cooked chicken to the sauce before combining it with the pasta.

- Once again, you can add as many herbs as you want depending on what you like or the benefits you need.

Desserts

Lemon Almond Cake

This recipe is butter-free which is great since most Imbolc foods tend to rely heavily on dairy. However, that's not the best thing about it. The light-yellow color of this cake is a beautiful reminder of the sun. Not just that, but the almond flour also serves as a nice nod to Imbolc since almond trees start blooming during this time. As for the lemons, they provide a beautiful, refreshing flavor that, unlike other desserts, won't make you want to keel over and slip into a food coma.

Ingredients

Yields: 7/8 Servings

- 1 1/2 cup (144g) finely ground blanched (without almond peels) almond flour
- 1 tsp baking powder
- 1/2 cup (100g) white sugar
- 4 large eggs separated into whites and yolks (see how below)
- Zest from two medium or large lemons
- 1/4 tsp ground cardamom
- 1 tsp white vinegar
- A pinch of salt
- Powdered sugar

Preparations

- Over a small bowl, crack an egg, but hold it vertically as you separate the shell to keep the yolk from falling. Then, gently pour the yolk into the empty half of the shell. Repeat a few times until all the egg white is in the bowl. Transport the yolk into a separate bowl and repeat with the other three eggs.
- Preheat the oven to 350 F or 170 C and grease a pan of your choice, preferably an 8-inch mold, with oil or butter.

Instructions

1. Put your yellow ingredients - the yolk and the lemon zest - into a bowl and a quarter cup of sugar. Whisk or mix until smooth.

2. Then, it's time to mix your dry ingredients. In a separate bowl, add the flour, cardamom, baking powder, and any other dry ingredients you'd like to add - vanilla powder, instant coffee, etc.

3. Add your dry ingredients to the egg yolk mixture and whisk until they're one thick, uniform mixture. It should look a little crumbly, like wet sand.

4. You can use a manual whisk for this step, but it would be much easier to use an electric one. Start beating the egg whites slowly at first, then work up to a faster speed. Once you see bubbles, add a pinch of salt and vinegar to help your egg whites turn quickly into a fluffy cloud-like mixture. Add the sugar. Once the mixture turns into this cloud-like texture, add the rest of the sugar and mix. Only stop when the mixture is strong enough to form peaks when you lift up the whisk.

5. Gradually add the meringue (egg white mixture) dollop by dollop into the cake mixture. Fold every dollop of meringue added to the mixture until there's nothing left. Don't whisk because you don't want the fluffy meringue deflating.

6. Pour/scoop your batter into the mold, level it, and bake for 30 minutes - or until you can stick a toothpick through the center and it comes out clean.

7. Let the cake cool before you slice it.

8. Top with powdered sugar, lemon curd, or lemon whipped cream.

Possible Variations

- You can turn this recipe into a cupcake recipe by baking at 400 F or 200 C for less time.

- Lavender can be a great addition to this recipe, especially if you'd like to offer a slice for Brigid.

How to Imbue Your Food with Magic

There are two good ways to give your food an extra magical kick.

Focusing Intentions

We always hear about food being made with love, but no one ever takes it seriously. It's just something we say. What if it isn't just that? What if there's a little more meaning to the phrase? Because there is.

Love is a force. It's a vibration. It's transferable. You can send it to other people, and, in the same way, you can also send it to objects.

The simplest way to imbue food with happiness, gratitude, warmth, love, etc., is by focusing on your intentions and channeling your energy into the food.

You simply need to ground yourself (through meditation, breathing exercises, or any of your preferred methods), then channel your energy into your ingredients before you start working.

When you're working, try to stay connected with this energy. The easiest way to do that is through music. You can play love songs, happy songs that make you feel safe and calm, etc.

After you're done, do the same with the end product as you did with the individual ingredients- you don't have to touch it; hovering your hands above it is enough.

Sigils

Sigils are a simple and effective way to imbue food with magic, and they cover a much wider range of attributes than transferable intentions because they can embody magical intentions. You can have sigils for protection, prosperity, growth, peace, happiness, etc.

You need to draw your sigil of choice on your food with a toothpick.

There are two ways to go about sigils. You can use pre-existing sigils and runes based on your own beliefs, or you can make your own sigils, and here's how:

First, you've got to ground yourself. Take a few moments to find your center and calm yourself.

Then, when you're ready, start shifting your focus toward your intention. What effect would you want your food to have on those who eat it? What do you want to give them? When you find the right words, say them out loud.

The key here is to say them as facts. In other words, speak from a place of trust in the power of your sigil. For example, "This cake brings abundance to those who eat it,' instead of "I hope this cake brings them abundance."

If the words feel right, grab a pen and a paper, and write them down. You can write a full sentence as in the past example or just the magical intention, abundance.

Ultimately, sigils are symbols. So, you need to create a symbol from the letters of the sentence or the keyword. You can use all or only a few. It doesn't matter as long as it feels right to you. Remember that this part is purely creative, so there is no right or wrong.

Once you've created your sigil, it's time to conduct an activation ritual.

Go to your altar. If you don't have an altar, just create a safe spiritual atmosphere somewhere in your house - you can light up a candle and burn some herbs or sage.

Sit in front of your sigil and speak your full intention out loud, just like you did before. Repeat your intention a few times - if there's a number that bears significance to you, have it be your number of repetitions. By doing this, you are affirming the sigil's purpose.

Once you've finished, fold the four corners of the paper inwards and seal the paper with wax - preferably sealing wax, but regular wax works as well. This part is parallel to the symbolic sealing of the sigil's meaning.

After this step, place the folded paper on your altar.

Your sigil is now ready to be used, so feel free to draw it on your food, skin, air, or wherever you want.

Chapter 8: Imbolc Family and Group Activities

A huge part of Imbolc is the community with which you celebrate. Now, this doesn't mean that those who prefer to celebrate alone or have no choice in the matter should miss out on the essence of the festival.

Celebrating alone is different from celebrating with a family or a group. Alone, you can introspect and delve as deep as you want into your thoughts and emotions. You can also worship in a way you feel comfortable. You get a fully customizable experience and, if you choose to, a rather deep one. You also get to cook your own foods and spend one-on-one time with nature and your deities.

On the other hand, with a group or a family, you get to share the experience with other people who have a similar special relationship with nature. As one, you get to be together, celebrating the coming of spring and/or Brigid.

Perhaps you won't have as deep an experience, but you'll have a broad one. You'll get to listen and witness how other people celebrate Imbolc, and if you have children, then you'll get to see them spiritually growing. Overall, you'll feel an overwhelming warmth and a sense of togetherness.

We recommend that, for Imbolc, you separate your day into two parts; one for celebrating alone and one for celebrating with your community. And, because we've spoken about solitary festivities significantly more than group ones, we will flip the scales in this chapter.

Throughout this chapter, you'll get to read about many group activities, not just for adults but for children too. You can feel free to do them as they are, add your twist, or use them as a building block to build your own unique traditions.

Spring Cleaning

Spring cleaning is a very popular tradition in many parts of the world, especially in the U.S. Without knowing its origins, you may have thought that the event is a tad too random. After all, why spring? What happens during that time that makes it customary to do some deep cleaning?

Well, each culture has its own reasons. For pagans, however, we choose to clean on Imbolc because it's our new beginning. Like death gives way to life, winter gives way to spring, and we consider that return of light our new beginning.

As the light returns, as life starts to bloom once more, and as we come to life after a season of low activity and demotivation, we start cleaning our houses and cleansing our bodies. It's a way of saying, out with the old and in with the new.

Spring cleaning for Imbolc can be fun, especially if you have kids. You can try so many ideas that won't make it feel anything like a chore.

Make a Playlist

Whether you want to make an Imbolc playlist or a spring-cleaning playlist, all you need to do is add a bunch of songs on the days leading up to Imbolc and crank up the volume on the day.

You can even use Spotify to create a collaborative playlist, share the link and have every member of your family/group contribute with their own picks. Your playlist will have something for everyone, from "Here Comes the Sun" by The Beatles to "Irreplaceable" by Beyoncé.

Raise the Stakes

The best defense is a good offense. You've got to raise the stakes if you want to take spring cleaning for Imbolc to a whole new level. We suggest you make a game plan, assign each person a role, a room, or a domain, and then pick out rewards for the best performance.

You could add points for creativity, points for taking no prisoners - as opposed to hoarding, and points for thoroughness. The criteria are up to you but don't forget to make the reward worth it.

If you enjoy it, this could become an annual family tradition - your own version of the Olympics.

Clean with Purpose

There's a difference between cleaning as a reaction to a dirty house and cleaning with a set purpose. Of course, when Imbolc cleaning, the purpose is to declutter your space and let go of what you don't use anymore. It's also to make space for what is yet to come to you that year.

Taking a little time to connect with that purpose can do you wonders. You can have your family or group sit in a circle and then go around saying what you want to get from this year's spring cleaning.

Lighting a Fire

We've already spoken about the significance of fire during Imbolc, so we'll talk about how you can light one safely and what to do in a gathering around the fire.

Campfire

If you have a wood burner or a fireplace, chances are you already know how to use it. In this case, you don't have to light a campfire. However, if you do have access to the open space and would like to be with nature on this day, then a campfire is exactly what you want.

You'll Need:

- A level piece of dirt-covered ground
- Rocks
- Tinder - small twigs and dried leaves
- Kindling - slightly larger twigs and thin branches
- Firewood
- A matchbox or a lighter
- Water

Find a dry, dirt/sand-covered ground or a flat rock. If you can't find an area like this, you can clear out a patch of grass - although we don't recommend that for obvious reasons. The point is that you can't light a fire on a flammable object, so you need dirt or rocks.

Then, place medium or large rocks in a circle to create your fire ring and gather some tinder in the middle.

Over the tinder, place two pieces of kindling in a crisscross shape. You can also place eight pieces of kindling, two to each side, in the shape of a square.

Light up your tinder and tend to the fire, adding more tinder until it's big enough to burn the kindling. Blow on the base of the fire to make it burn stronger.

When the fire is strong enough, add in your firewood.

Last, and most importantly, don't leave your fire unattended. Always keep it under control, and keep some water - or a small fire extinguisher - next to you at all times.

Fire-Oriented Activities

- **Fire Manifestation**

This is a simple ritual you can have with your group where you write your goals and wishes on bay leaves, then throw them into the fire.

You can either go round the circle, share your wishes out loud, or keep them to yourself and connect to the energy and focus that come with group settings.

- **A Reflective Sit-Down**

Fire is a great element to meditate on and to be used for divination. It can help you get into a trance state, and it can help start conversations among people. This makes it the perfect time to reflect on your past year, share your thoughts and anxieties about the future, and share what you love about Imbolc. There are also dozens of Imbolc prompts online that can help start a dialogue between you and your family or community.

Organizing a Feast

Who doesn't like food, especially when it's with the people you love and celebrating a festival that you love? Also, food is also a way to bond with other people. You can exchange recipes, learn techniques, and eat food inspired by different cultures and imaginations.

Now, you can prepare all the food and take care of everything feast-related, but that can be a little too much effort. Instead, you can prepare a menu with your family and have everyone come up with a dish or a course and prepare it. Especially if you have kids, this can be a great idea. Don't leave your younger kids alone in the kitchen, though. You can also have a dish party where every group member gets to bring in a dish.

Imbolc Cooking Challenge

You already know a few ingredients that we consider Imbolc essentials. Instead of having an ordinary dish party, you can turn the heat up. You have two options to do that - both are great fun.

With each option, you'll need a few pieces of paper (as many as the participants) and a pen. For the first challenge, you're going to write the name of an Imbolc-related herb or flower on each piece of paper. Carefully fold the pieces of paper enough so that no one can see what's written inside. Then, mix up the papers and let each person draw a piece of paper.

People will have to prepare their dishes while ensuring that they include that one ingredient on their piece of paper.

The second challenge goes the same exact way except that, instead of an herb, you'll put a list of ingredients on each paper, and these must all be included in the dish.

Group Divination Ritual

Divination is also a great group activity to practice with your people. Not to mention, Brigid is a goddess associated with divination, especially fire divination. Plus, rather than practice it alone, your people will help you get in the zone. You can all help each other focus while, at the same time, doing this act of love for each other. Overall, it will help you get closer and get in tune with each other's life journeys.

Fire Scrying

A bonfire is perfect if you want to go into a trance-like state. So, if you'd like to, you can practice fire scrying, but only if that's a form of divination you're comfortable with practicing. An advantage of fire divination is that you can light a fire and plan your entire evening around it.

Tarot Cards & Runes

There are also Tarot cards and runes, both of which can engage the whole group and help strengthen the bonds between its members. This sense of community is very important, especially in a world where practicing paganism can get a little lonely.

Stream of Consciousness Writing

Another method that can work for people who don't practice divination or scrying is a stream of consciousness writing. It's where you take a piece of paper and start writing out your thoughts. They don't have to make sense. They only have to be your authentic thoughts.

It's a psychological technique that's supposed to help you be mindful of the thoughts going on in your head and your senses. Nevertheless, it can also help you get through to your deepest thoughts, inner child, and higher self.

At the end of the day, it's not about the technique itself; it's about the quietness and the active awareness that the exercise provides. It creates an environment of openness that will allow you to listen to or access the area you want to access inside you.

Bardic Circle

A bardic circle is essentially an artists' get-together. In the past, bardic circles were where bards used to sit together in a circle, often around a fire, and live performances and recite poems. It was a celebration of the imagination, creativity, and the arts. It was also a celebration of Brigid, the muse of all poets and the goddess of inspiration, wisdom, and poetry.

In your own bardic circle, you can have it as a purely artistic gathering, or you can also include Brigid. Remember that you don't have to honor Brigid if she's not a goddess you work with or if you don't feel comfortable.

If your people are already in touch with their artistic side, you can have them each bring one of their works (or create a new one) to show the group and speak about it for a bit. You can also ask your group to bring their instruments and tools for impromptu performances.

Last, you can propose a particular theme or a natural element to make your bardic circle more interesting. A common element will bring out each person's genius and unique perspective. As people start seeing how they look at the same thing, they'll begin appreciating their creative side even more.

On the other hand, if your people aren't really in touch with their bardic side, you can pass out papers and pens - you can also use your phones - then give out a prompt.

This prompt could be a complete sentence, like "And as life coursed through nature and plants rose from the ground, one didn't." It could also be an incomplete sentence, "Mother Nature caressed her cheek and smiled, then said..." There are also dozens of online poem/story prompts.

Inspired by these prompts, your people should start writing their short stories or poems. Give them a good five minutes, then ask everyone to stop. Afterward, let them read out their creations. You don't have to worry about things like grammar and structure. This is only a creative writing exercise that's supposed to engage one's imagination and help people connect over their stories.

Before you start a bardic circle, you must create a safe space for your people to share their art. It may help if you agree on a few ground rules before you begin or if you go around stating intentions before you begin. Remember that you can't expect someone to share openly if they don't feel safe enough to do so.

Planting Seeds

What's more festive than planting new seeds? When celebrating this joyful coming of spring and the signs of new growth in nature, it's only fitting to grow your own trees or plants.

The best part is that you don't need any special tools or requirements. You can plant trees in your community garden, in the forest, in the backyard, or in your coven's garden if you have one.

If you have kids, or if your kids are new to Imbolc, this activity will be more than perfect because it will help them tune in to nature and its cycles. It will also help them understand what Imbolc is about.

There are many seeds to choose from, so we'll classify them into fast-growing and slow-growing - all of which can be planted on Imbolc.

Fast-Growing Seeds

- Spinach (winter varieties)
- Lettuce
- Sunflowers
- Basil
- Cilantro

Slow-Growing Seeds

- Cactus
- Coneflowers
- Sage

If there's a plant you feel particularly attracted to, don't hesitate to research it and see if you can plant it in February. By all means, don't feel limited to this list.

After deciding on a seed to plant, you can practice adding intentions to the seed. And, as your plant grows, don't forget to talk to it and give it love, whether through touch or kind words. According to a study done by Deepika Choube and Shubham Sharma, positive and negative words directly impact a plant's growth.

Candle-Making

For starters, candle making is a fun activity that will help you get rid of your used candles and get you a cool new one.

Candle making is also a great activity that resembles rebirth. Over the year, you use up your candles until they're no more. Then, during Imbolc, you experience your own return of the light as you turn your spent candles into one whole candle.

Now, what makes group candle-making great in particular is the end product.

If you melt your own candles, you'll probably have an idea of what colors you'll end up with. However, when you melt candles with a group, there's no limit to the colors involved. There's also no way to predict the end result.

Imagine if five people put all their year's used candles into the mix. That's at least five colors, assuming they're not avid white candle fans.

As for the process, it's almost identical to making ice candles. The only difference is that you skip out on the ice here.

Ask your friends to cut their wax into small chunks and bring it with them.

Then, you can either have people choose their colors and melt the wax accordingly or just pour everything into the double boiler and mix well.

You can add colored dye if you want to introduce a whole new color. You can draw a sigil to imbue the candle with magic. Or, you can add fragrance oil to make the extra candle special.

You can also use mason jars or reuse old jars as containers for your candles. You have to clean the jar and let it dry while you make the wax. Then, attach the wick to the bottom of the jar by dipping it in hot wax and quickly pinning it to the bottom of the jar. The wick should hold steady as long as you don't pull on it aggressively.

Keep your wick straight using the pencil method as you pour the wax into the containers and leave them to dry.

Meanwhile, you can sit with your friends and eat, talk, or do any of the activities we mentioned above. For example, you can even make a classy event out of the whole evening, candles, and lavender wine. And, at the end of the day, everyone gets to go home with a new treat for their altar or house.

Chapter 9: Spells, Rituals, and Baths

In some of the past chapters, we've discussed how to celebrate Imbolc on a physical level. We've talked about the most popular Imbolc foods and the crafts and decorations. Even when we spoke about altars, we didn't delve deep enough into the spiritual side of Imbolc festivities. In this chapter, however, we will go as deep as we can into the spells, rituals, and spiritual baths that can be done during Imbolc.

Now, Imbolc is one of the best times to cast your spells and practice divination, especially if you channel the element of fire into your practices. Brigid's association with healing and magic, combined with her powerful return during Imbolc, can give your spells a special kick.

Main Themes

At Imbolc, we try to focus on spells and rituals that have to do with the main themes of this event. The whole of nature - and the universal energy - goes through the cycle that comes with the seasons. This is why certain spells will naturally be more effective than others if their purpose and intention happen to be in sync with the natural cycle.

Throughout the book, we've discussed Imbolc's main themes:

- Rebirth
- The coming of light
- New growth
- The end of winter/darkness
- Abundance
- Fertility

- The return of fire

These are the themes we'll draw inspiration from in this chapter, and they're also the themes that you can build your spells on.

Keep in mind that each theme bears influence on so many of life's aspects that there's a near-infinite number of magical intentions you can extract:

- New opportunities
- Banishment
- Attraction
- Release
- Cleansing
- Healing
- Rejuvenation
- Motivation
- Fertility
- Fortune
- Abundance
- Focus
- Motivation

These are only a few, and we'll try to provide you with spells and rituals for as many intentions as we can. For the rest, we'll provide you with an all-purpose spell that you can customize depending on what you need.

Spells

All-Purpose Candle Spell

This spell is a great choice if you're still a beginner or if you have too specific an intention that you'd like to realize. Given the use of candles, it's a very fitting choice for Imbolc, especially if you like or are interested in working with Brigid. Fair warning - the spell can be a little time-consuming.

Ingredients

- A taper candle - can either be a plain white candle or a colored one. If you associate a certain color with a particular intention or a question, you can use that. If you don't want to, that's fine. It's completely up to you.
- Pen or a small blade
- A match or a lighter

- The moon (optional)

Instructions

1. Start at nighttime. Prepare your ingredients, cleanse your space, and set the mood, so to speak.

2. Ground yourself. This spell takes a lot of focus and concentration, and it requires you to be mindful of your intentions. It always helps to be calm when doing this sort of spell.

3. Figure out your intention and make it known. You can do this by speaking it out loud and repeating it a few times. Then, hold your candle in your hands and channel this intention into the candle.

4. Take your pen or small blade and write/engrave the thing you wish to attract or banish on the candle. For attraction purposes, to attract wisdom, for example, write the name of the thing from top to bottom. To banish something, like pain or jealousy, write the name from the bottom up.

5. Place the candle in front of you and light it. As it burns, focus on your intention, and envision it coming true. Try to remain focused for as long as you can.

6. When you feel like you've spent enough time or when you start losing your focus beyond return, blow out the candle.

7. Give gratitude to the candle and the universe and any deities you've asked for help (if any), then burn what's left of the candle and throw it away. If you've used soy wax, coconut wax, or beeswax, you can bury the candle in the ground. Paraffin wax, on the other hand, can be harmful to the soil.

Additional Information

- If you feel a special connection with the moon and would like to include it in your spell, time your spell with the phases of the moon. A new moon will help you attract what you want. A waning moon will help you get rid of what you don't want.

Abundance Spell

This spell is a beautiful source of abundance, especially if you need something quickly. It works great for job/career opportunities and decisions that are out of your control. Keep in mind that this is a candle spell, so make sure you're safe.

Ingredients

- Enough gold candles to form a circle (about eight)

- A picture where you're smiling

- A medium-sized mirror

- Lighter or matches

Instructions

1. As with all candle magic spells, start yours at night too. Choose a place where you can prop up your mirror later while doing the spell, then cleanse that space.

2. Sit by yourself, find your center, and connect with your intention.

3. Arrange your candles in a circle and make sure they're stable enough so that they don't fall.

4. Place a smiling picture of yourself in the circle's center.

5. Start lighting up the candles slowly. Light one at a time in a clockwise direction and speak from your heart. You can chant a verse you've composed about the return of the light and the igniting of your own fire. It can rhyme, but it doesn't have to. You can also say what you specifically want. It doesn't matter what you say as much as your intentions.

6. Repeat your words or channel intentions while lighting each candle.

7. Stabilize the mirror against a wall or a surface to see the whole circle. Then, ask for twice the fortune or twice the abundance.

8. Sit with the candles for as long as you can maintain your focus. Then give gratitude and, ideally, let the candles burn out. Blow them out if you're not comfortable leaving the candles overnight or until they burn out.

9. When the candles are out, clean your mirror while chanting everything you chanted the night before. Then, pick out a place where the sun enters your house and prop the mirror so that it can reflect the morning light.

10. Every time you pass the mirror, stop and look into it and say, "I will thrive with the abundance I am given," or anything with the same meaning.

Rituals

Starting a ritual
https://unsplash.com/photos/x5hyhMBjR3M

When it comes to rituals, the guidelines are much looser than spells since they're all about you and your psychology, spirituality, and psychospiritual. Meanwhile, spells involve working with energies, deities, and different types of magic.

As you read through these rituals, feel free to customize them.

Fertility Ritual - Brigid's Cross, Doll, and Bed

The Brigid doll represents the goddess, and it carries her blessings, most of all, fertility. The bed is a gesture and a symbol of welcoming the goddess, and therefore her blessings, into your house. As for the cross, it's a celebration of Brigid's power, and it serves as an offering for Brigid and a request for her protection.

Combined together, these three objects can be of great power, whether you decide to put them on your altar, near your fireplace, or in the kitchen.

All you have to do is:

- Put your intentions into making the three objects, and don't hesitate to ask Brigid out loud what you want while doing so.

- On the eve of Imbolc, before you go to bed, put the doll in her bed and ask Brigid one more time to bless you or your household with her fertility.

- As an offering, you can leave a cup of milk for the goddess.

- You can also leave the cross as an offering or hang it somewhere in your house to receive Brigid's protection. Of course, you can also make two crosses and do both.

Thought Seeds Ritual

Imbolc is a great time to start harnessing your drive, planning your way and acting on your thoughts, turning them into habits. This ritual embodies the spirit of Imbolc and the new growth it brings into people's lives. It should be mentioned that this ritual includes keeping a plant alive. If you can't do that, it's recommended that you stick to our modified version.

Growing new seeds is a real-life parallel of how our thoughts can turn to helpful habits that finally bloom/bear fruit. In this ritual, you'll charge a few seeds with intentions, and, as a result, their growth will reflect on your life.

Requirements

- Your choice of seeds
- Empty plant pots
- Soil mix (suitable for your seeds)
- Pen
- Bay leaves

Instructions

1. Write what you'd like to grow within yourself on the bay leaves - one thing for each leaf. Keep your intentions focused as you write, and make sure to keep your language growth-oriented and not oriented towards dispelling.

2. Fill less than half of each pot with soil, then focus your intentions on more time and give the bay leaves your gratitude as you place one in each pot.

3. Fill up the rest of the pot and plant your seed.

4. Water the seed, tend to it, and care for it. As you do and as you care for yourself too, you'll start seeing the plants growing with your intentions and feeding your drive more and more.

Modified Version

The modified version of this ritual focuses on the psychological aspects of the ritual instead of anything else. So, here, you'll simply plant the seeds without including the bay leaves.

What makes this a ritual is that it will mark the starting point of your journey. As you plant the seed, picture the thought seeds you planted in your own head, whether by working on yourself, healing, or practicing a new skill - it could be something personal, relational, or professional.

Tending to the plant will remind you to tend to yourself as the days go by. More importantly, noting the small signs of growth in your plant will help you notice the signs of growth within yourself. And, on the next Imbolc, the fully grown plant will help you reflect on where you were and where you are now.

Overall, the ritual will keep you mindful of your journey and your growth so that:

1. You wouldn't neglect yourself.

2. You wouldn't make the mistake of undervaluing your work and the effort you've dedicated to your journey.

Divination

Divination is the practice of seeking knowledge. It could be about the future or the present and about a major life decision or a feeling you've struggled with. You could even practice divination for someone, although it's important to get their full consent.

So, with divination, the possibilities are endless. What you need to remember is to be as specific as you can. When you ask someone for help, you would tell them what you want help with and how they can help, right? With divination, it's the same thing. You can't ask a deity or the universe for specific answers if you're not giving them a specific problem.

Specificity aside, how you practice divination is completely up to you. There are many ways and methods, so it's all about what makes you feel comfortable.

Tarot

Tarot cards are a great way to practice divination. They're fun, easy to use, and the medium allows for answers that don't require much interpretation.

You'll Need:

- Tarot deck
- Your cleansing method of choice

Instructions

1. Cleanse your deck and your space before you do your reading.
2. Ground yourself and find your center.
3. Hold the cards between your hands, channel your energy into them, and ask the cards your question.
4. Shuffle your cards until you feel satisfied.
5. Fan out the cards and choose the one you feel drawn to.
6. Pull out the card without flipping it over or turning it around and place it face down on the surface in front of you.
7. Flip your card right or left side up to reveal it.
8. Note the card's position (inverted or upright), read up on its meaning, and reflect on the answer you received.

Additional Information

- There are various types of spreads, from the three cards representing your past, present, and future to the 10-card Celtic cross, which delves deeper into questions.

Fire Scrying

Scrying is the act of looking deep into an object or a space to attain a trance-like state and connect with the answers or visions you're looking for. Fire is a great way to do that, especially on Imbolc, because it's when the element's influence is strong.

You'll Need:

- A candle or a fire

Instructions

1. Prepare a clear and safe area for yourself and ensure it's free of distractions. Cleanse your space, turn off your phone, and take care

of any responsibilities that may break your focus.

2. Ground yourself through breathing exercises, meditation, yoga, or your method of preference.

3. When you feel ready, light your fire, and sit in front of it.

4. Take deep, slow breaths as you gaze into the fire. Don't put pressure on yourself to do it the right way. You'll know it's right when it is, and it will come to you naturally. Until then, simply look at the fire. Rest your eyes where it feels right, and see how the fire tongues dance and flicker. Note its colors and how it moves with the air around it. Listen out for the sound of the burning flames.

5. As you relax and grow more comfortable starting into the fire, you'll feel more and more ready to initiate this step. Connect with the energy of the fire and draw it towards you.

6. Keep your eyes, ears, and mind open to any visions, sounds, or thoughts you experience. Don't get distracted and start chasing ideas and thoughts. Remain present and mindful. Even if you decide to explore a thought that comes to you, do so by choice and because it feels right and not because you can't help it.

7. You should spend as much or as little time as you want in front of the fire. Stay in tune with your body and mind, and they will tell you when it's time to end the session. You'll either feel satisfied or a tad uncomfortable and distracted.

8. Toward the end of the session, look away from the fire and take a few moments to calm down and, once more, ground yourself. Show gratitude to your fire and the energies, spirits, or deities you've asked for help. Then, put out the fire/candle.

Additional Information

- Scrying can be done using any shiny object. You can use a water surface, a crystal ball, crystals with reflective surfaces, and the list goes on.

- If you're planning on scrying more than once, start keeping track of the messages that come to you. After each session, jot down your notes in a notebook. With time, you may start seeing certain repetitions and patterns.

A Brigid-Aided Divination

If you are interested in working with Brigid, this next divination ritual relies heavily on the help of the goddess.

You'll Need:

- An altar for Brigid
- A red candle
- Candle/Match

Instructions

1. Set up an altar for the goddess. You can use your Brigid doll, bed, and cross, among other items.

2. Ground yourself and find your center before speaking to Brigid.

3. Light the candle, greet Brigid and invoke her presence. You don't need any special words. Your sincerity is enough.

4. Stay mindful of your internal environment as you note how the goddess responds to you.

5. As you start noticing Brigid's presence around you, thank her for responding to you. Then, ask her your question. Be as specific as you want and give her as many details about what you need help with as you need to. If you have an idea of the solution, share that with her.

6. After you've finished talking to the goddess, thank her and then, when it feels right, blow out the candle.

7. Pay attention to your feelings and surroundings in the following days. Remember that the goddess won't turn the sky red and split the earth in half to send you a message. She will subtly communicate with you. It could be a sighting of an animal, a plant, or an angel number. It could also be through a feeling or an experience. Remember to keep your mind and heart open and trust that your answer will come.

Baths

Just as Imbolc is a time to cleanse your space and your mind, it's also a time to cleanse and tend to your spirit and energy. Spiritual baths can help you relax on a spiritual level. They can also help cleanse you of negative energy and rejuvenate your energy reserves.

Now, all baths are done in the same way. The effects, however, vary depending on the herbs and ingredients used. So, to start, we'll discuss the method first.

General Instructions

1. It doesn't make sense to cleanse your spirit and energy in a dirty tub or a cluttered bathroom. So, prepare by cleaning your bathtub and organizing the space around it.

2. Figure out what you want from your bath - healing, energy, cleansing, etc. This will help you set the scene for your bath. Let your intuition guide you throughout this preparation process.

3. If you'd like to do something specific while bathing, figure it out to prepare for it, whether by buying a bathtub tray or clearing out a spot for it.

Some people are more vision-oriented. They like to have things like candles and flower petals all around them.

Others are more smell-oriented, so they burn essential oils or incense.

And others are sound-oriented, so they like to have their phone, tablet, or laptop nearby to pick up their music.

There's no rule on engaging all your senses either. It's all up to you and what relaxes you most.

1. Prepare your environment, then turn on the hot water and let it fill the tub. Add your salts and, in a cheesecloth, put your herbs of choice, tie the cloth, and let it steep. You can also add your herbs directly into the water, but the cloth saves you the effort of collecting the leaves afterward.

2. Once the water has cooled down to your preferred temperature, it's time for you to soak.

Healing Bath Recipe

- Two generous handfuls of Epsom salt or pink Himalayan salt (cleansing)
- Lavender (calming)
- Chamomile (healing)
- Orange blossoms (relaxing)
- Rosemary (cleansing)
- Rose petals (relaxing)

Rejuvenating Bath Recipe

- Eucalyptus (refreshing)
- Mint (energizing)
- Jasmine (mood-boosting)
- Meadowsweet (mood-boosting)
- Dandelions (refreshing)

Chapter 10: Poems, Prayers, and Blessings

While Imbolc is for everyone, it has a special value for writers and poets. Not only is it the beginning of the spring - arguably the most beautiful season, but it is also tied to Brigid, a poet's goddess and muse.

Since Brigid is the goddess of poetry and wisdom, writing is a wonderful way of celebrating Imbolc and honoring the goddess.

Throughout the years, there have been poems written about Imbolc and Brigid. Not just that, but prayers and blessings too.

This chapter is all about poems, prayers, and blessings. It's dedicated to those who would like to recite a few verses in Brigid's honor and those interested in composing their own poems.

Poems

These next few poems are from a collection published by Jill Hammer in the Journal of Feminist Studies in Religion.

Imbolc

'Imbolc' gets off to a rather tragic start as the author doesn't shy away from describing the sense of despair, weakness, and hopelessness that she experiences during winter. It's a very relatable piece for those who experience hormone imbalances or Seasonal Affective Disorder during winter.

"Easier

if once having given birth

the new fawn straggled off to Eden

so much harder

to carry her with

her stick legs
over snowfields
if there were a brook
a fig left lying in the snow
a trickle of sap from a tree
to make the journey easier
o lady of the well of life
pity one who bears herself
through cold winter
Show yourself
though you dwell beneath frozen water
tap the ice until it breaks."

In this poem, the author calls upon Brigid to break the veil of winter and show herself. The poem starts with the author describing herself as a fawn and comparing her state during winter to that of a newborn deer. She starts pleading for Brigid to aid her by shattering the winter.

The author likens herself to a newborn fawn in the first and second stanzas. She also likens her emotional state in winter to the fawn's near-impossible journey from the land of the ice and snow to an Eden-like place. She wishes that spring would come soon, but like the fawn that journeys on weak legs, she too must travel across the metaphorical snowfields.

In the third stanza, she wishes for the slightest signs of spring and life to hold her over until she crosses the fields. She hopes to see a brook, a fig, or the faintest trickle of sap.

In the fourth and fifth stanzas, she outright calls for Brigid, the lady of the well of life. She asks the goddess to take pity on her as she tries to survive the bleakness of winter. She pleads for strength at first, but then she invokes the goddess's presence and asks her to break winter's hold.

The Feast of Brigid

This is a much brighter poem than the one before. It's a celebration of the coming of spring and of the role that Brigid plays in it.

"The red-haired girl draws milk
in a pail from the earth.
The earth is a spotted cow
with teats that are geysers
and anthills and rotten logs.
The red-haired girl
strokes and strokes

the dark soil.

When the milk rises in spurts

she catches its arc of white froth

to give out to visitors.

At the gate of the farm

the world holds out its hand,

while in a field rimed with frost

the first snowdrop toddles from the ground."

In this poem, the author celebrates spring and Imbolc with a set of beautiful imagery that likens the earth to a cow and Brigid to the red-headed girl that provokes the cow to release milk - a symbol for spring.

The poem opens with a red-haired girl milking the earth into a bucket. The red-haired girl here could easily be a symbol for Brigid herself. Overall, the image introduced in the stanza is unusual, but it's attention-grabbing, thought-provoking, and allows the author to elaborate in the next stanza.

In the second and third stanzas, the author elaborates on the first stanza by explaining that the world is a spotted cow and that the earth's features are its teats. Meanwhile, the red-headed girl continues to stroke the soil - just like Brigid brings the spring to its people.

In the fourth and fifth stanzas, milk erupts from the earth, and the girl catches it in her bucket. She then gives it to the people of the world who have gathered around the farm where the girl is.

The poem ends with a description of a snowdrop growing in a snow-covered field just as milk erupted from the earth. This part further confirms the theory that Brigid is the red-haired girl.

Prayers and Blessings

As a rule of thumb, the best prayers are the ones said and spoken from the heart. Of course, Brigid loves a good verse, but not at the cost of your authenticity. Ultimately, a verse is only a pretty vessel for what's truly important, which is the essence.

You can memorize and repeat prayers and blessings and still mean them with all your heart. This is why we will include and discuss a few of those. However, as you recite them, don't forget to do so with intention.

A Prayer of Thanks

"We welcome the season of Brigid

She who protects our hearth and home.

We honor and thank her

for keeping us warm as we eat this meal.

Exalted One, bless us and this food,

and protect us in your name."

This is a simple prayer that you can recite alone or with your family members. You can also recite bits and pieces of it as you go about your day or as you notice the subtle signs of spring.

A Prayer for the Coming of Light

"Blessed Brigid, shine your light

Bring us warmth from your fire,

And healing from your holy well."

This, too, is a simple prayer that you can say to invoke Brigid's presence and her strength. It can come in handy during tough times when the winter seems endless. It also doubles as a nice prayer of gratitude and a celebration of Brigid's strength when uttered during Imbolc and in spring.

How to Write Your Own Poem

Writing your own poem is a unique and wonderful way to express your feelings about Imbolc and Brigid. Poems can also be quite a special offering for the goddess.

Now, most people believe that it's hard to write poetry. The truth is, it's simple once you forget about all the pressures, rules, and judgments that come with doing any creative work.

So, take a moment to connect with yourself and think about an aspect of Imbolc that you feel drawn to – or the one that you love the most. Once you have that, you can flesh it out by exploring it even further. Perhaps, think about your favorite scenes in nature, your favorite aspects of Brigid, and why you like these things. What do they mean to you?

As you're exploring the premise of your Imbolc poem, try to incorporate all of your senses. Jill Hammer prodded her readers' imagination by invoking an image in' The Feast of Brigid. This made her poem much more vivid and interesting because it engaged our sense of sight. You can also focus on the smells, sounds, and even textures that you note during this time to draw a whole portrait.

When you've finished brainstorming, sit down, and let your feelings and intuition guide you. You can write a line a day or a poem a day, as long as you feel what you're writing and are not tapping a keyboard or scribbling on a paper.

Although, if you haven't written before, you might need to write a lot without "feeling" until you get the hang of writing. Once you're comfortable enough with the imagery and the phrasing, you'll be relaxed enough to let your feelings guide your writing.

That's all there is to it. And remember to write from the heart and try not to judge your writing. This is a form of expression. It's an act of love, and it can only thrive in a safe environment.

Conclusion

For pages and pages, we have explored all the aspects of Imbolc, from its earliest origins to its connection with Brigid. We have also included poems and prayers that can be recited to celebrate the event. And while there are no more words to say, the truth is, this book hasn't come to an end yet. In fact, it never will.

This book is about the physical, psychological, and spiritual aspects of Imbolc and Brigid, and these are not limited topics. They're ever-growing and ever-evolving.

With every person who reads this book, every scholar and researcher who explores the Celtic culture, traditions, and history, and every individual who celebrates Imbolc and Brigid, our collective knowledge of Imbolc grows.

Whether it is through new archeological evidence found, new spiritual experiences, spells, rituals, or even dishes, every person adds pages upon pages to this book. So, while this is a conclusion, think of it as a conclusion to only the part written by us.

Every pagan who celebrates Imbolc is writing down parts right now. It's time for you to start writing your part, too. So, take the information from this book, but don't stop there. Delve deeper within yourself, reflect on what you've read, and ask questions. Direct your hunger and curiosity toward exploring what Imbolc means to you and what it could mean to you.

Before you know it, you'll be creating your own rituals and spells. You'll start having your own traditions and dishes. You'll be able to start a conversation with, "I don't know about you, but Imbolc for me is about..."

And, for some of you, maybe it will come to you as a slow realization that Imbolc is not your festival. That's perfectly fine, too. What you celebrate doesn't define you as a human or as a pagan. Perhaps you feel more connected to a different festival. Perhaps you feel connected to none of them.

At the end of the day, all festivals are human-made. We give them meaning. So, now, it's up to you to find out what Imbolc means to you. Have a beautiful journey, and blessed be.

Part 3: Ostara

The Ultimate Guide to Spring Equinox and How It's Celebrated in Wicca, Druidry, and Paganism

Introduction

The art and practice of Wicca have become more widespread in the past few years, and many people are learning about its singular holidays and traditions. Given the chaos of the new decade and the level of uncertainty the new century has thrown us into, it is not at all surprising that Wicca would make a comeback of sorts. It's difficult to find another belief system that can compete as a way to connect with nature, feel the seasons, celebrate change with less anxiety, be calmer and at peace.

The Ostara is one of the most important Wiccan holidays, celebrated to commemorate the beginning of the spring equinox. It is a hopeful holiday that encourages people to mark nature's capacity for rebirth and renewal and the cyclical nature of life.

Unlike other guides to the Spring Equinox available on the market, this book does not take the study for granted, nor does it offer gimmicky, trendy introductions to Wicca. In your hands is a tome that is easy to comprehend and intended to make the study of this important season readily available to everyone. This is an ancient holiday celebrated for centuries by Druids, Wiccans, and pagans. While it is crucial to take this important tradition seriously and place it in its proper context, this does not preclude beginners or newbies to the religion from discovering this joyous holiday. After all, the Ostara or Spring Equinox is part of a long string of celebrations meant to honor the cyclical nature of human life. In effect, it is one of the eight sabbats on the Wiccan Wheel of the Year, and the idea of fertility and rebirth is taken further to honor the God and Goddess' creation of the Child of Promise.

This guide will help introduce you to all the wonderful elements that make this holiday unique. Actually, there are quite a few elements that have been passed down through history from the celebrations of the Equinox, unbeknownst to us. Just as mistletoe and other traditions remind us strictly of the Yuletide, the Ostara comes with many beautiful holiday symbols. Hot cross buns are more than the source of a nursery rhyme; they are shaped in a way that honors the Norse symbol for the wheel of life.

Likewise, many of the animals that we associate with spring originate from pagan era celebrations of Ostara. The bunny rabbit may be our most beloved symbol of Easter, and chocolate companies have made bank on its image for centuries. Still, history tells us that this symbol has been around since time immemorial. The celebration also wouldn't be complete without violets, daffodils, and all the delicate, colorful flowers that the spring months can offer. Therefore, celebrating Ostara acknowledges the change in weather and an important element of human history that sometimes falls by the wayside. Luckily, this book is dedicated to illustrating the key concepts of Ostara and reviving it for a new generation in the most accessible way possible.

Chapter 1: Introduction to Ostara

When the light that is reignited at Yule, a festival observed by the Germanic peoples and linked to Odin, the Wild Hunt, and the pagan Anglo-Saxon Mōdraniht, balances and then overtakes the darkness, this signifies the time of the year that we know as Ostara. Many witches and pagans worldwide celebrate the eight renowned festivals represented in the Wheel of the Year.

Ostara celebrates the coming of spring and the Spring Equinox. At that time of the year, the sun moves across the line marking the equator. During that day, the day and night are balanced. They both last for equal hours of the day. In the Southern Hemisphere, the Spring Equinox usually falls on the 23rd of September. However, Ostara typically falls on the 21st of March, which is relevant to the Northern Hemisphere's Spring Equinox.

Spring comes to life when Saint Bridgit's day, marked as Imbolc on the Wheel of the Year, arrives. Non-surprisingly, the symbols that we associate with Easter and springtime, such as rabbits and eggs, are also significant characteristics of Ostara. Ostara, or Eostre, probably sounds a lot like Easter to you. Well, it does, and there's a very good reason for it. It seems that Easter started out as Ostara. The church Council of Nicea dictated that

Easter would take place on the Sunday right after the first full moon that follows the Spring Equinox, in 325 B.C.E.

As we just mentioned, Eostre, the Celtic goddess of dawn, along with spring fertility, is celebrated through Ostara. The goddess' name happens to be very similar to the word "Easter." It also means "East," which is the direction of the sunrise. This is why this time of the year, along with its Celtic celebration, is ideal for goal-setting and action.

It must be noted that the popular celebration of Ostara has gone through various changes throughout history. Similarly, it had different meanings and symbols tied to it over the years. In fact, modern-day traditions suggest that the holiday celebrates the day that Pan, the Horned God, is reborn, and therefore gets to meet his consort, the goddess.

Another reason why Easter is thought to be derived from Ostara is that merriment and feasting are significant aspects of the celebration. This festival is also when people tend to conduct ritual cleaning, which helps them get rid of old, unhelpful patterns and make space for renewal.

The origins of Ostara date back to Celtic and Germanic peoples. The festival hails from stories that they used to share about the goddess. The spring equinox, also known as the vernal equinox, wasn't only celebrated by the Celts and Germanic peoples or even entire Northern Europe. In fact, the spring equinox is a significant occurrence in many countries and cultures worldwide, including India, Nepal, Portugal, China, Kurdistan, Uzbekistan, Egypt, Persia, Rome, Turkey, and Afghanistan.

The Ancient Romans celebrated the Hilaria, which were religious festivals that honored Cybele, the mother of the Gods. The followers of this goddess believed that she had a consort who was born through a miraculous virgin birth. The consort was named Attis, and he was resurrected every year following his death during the spring equinox of the Julian Calendar.

A pyramid called El Castillo, located in the Mexican Mayan city Chichen Itza symbolizes the alternation of day and night. This pyramid was dedicated to the Indigenous Mayan serpent deity Kukulkan. Each fall and spring equinox, the sun shines on the northern staircase of the 79-foot-tall pyramid and creates an illusion of a serpent slowly creeping on it during the late afternoon. The snake continues to go down the pyramid until it meets with a huge sculpture of a serpent's head, located at the base of El Catillo. For ten centuries, the indigenous Mayans of Central America have celebrated their own spring equinox festival.

To this day, many Persians celebrate the equinox as the new year or Nowruz. The Achaemenians, a Persian dynasty of kings, celebrated the vernal equinox with the No Ruz festival. No Rus translates into "new day," a celebration of renewal and hope, a common theme revolving around spring. Persians also celebrate the spring equinox with another festival right before Nu Ruz. This celebration, namely Chahar-Shanbeh Suri, involves purifying homes and leaping over fires. It's incredible how these countries may have so little in common yet hold relatively similar beliefs about a specific period of the year. This just shows how incredible the coming of spring is.

In this chapter, we will explore the history and cultural origin of Ostara. You'll also find all about the connection between Ostara and the Druid's Alban Eilir. This chapter explains how Ostara is considered one of the eight sabbats on the Wiccan Wheel of the Year. Finally, you'll come across the key features of this holiday.

History and Cultural Origin

Have you ever thought about holidays and a Holiday? Well, it's safe to say that approximately each March 21st is a Holiday- a commonly recognized celebrated day. As you know by now, it marks the birth of spring and the end of winter. Not only is it the vernal equinox, but it is also Ostara. The vernal equinox and Ostara fall on March 21st this year.

Ostara, a pagan holiday, celebrates the day that serves as a global symbol of awakening, rebirth, and new life. Since the daytime and the nighttime are an equal length on the spring equinox, it is also considered a midpoint between the two extremities: light and dark.

The forthcoming spring celebration is a very popular practice among many ancient and modern customs across various nations and customs. Seemingly, Wicca has appropriated many of these beliefs and their symbols for Ostara. Like its counterparts, Ostara is associated with renewal, fertility, and rebirth. The time of the year signifies the start of a new agricultural cycle when farmers would plant their seeds.

Numerous symbols of Ostara are deeply rooted in other traditions. For example, the use of rabbits and hares, which we will delve deeply into throughout the following chapters, are examples of these emblems. The March hare was perceived as a symbol of fertility and spring in medieval Europe. This is because rabbits are a nocturnal species for most of the year. However, they come out in March, as it is their mating season, which is why they can be seen at any time of the day. Furthermore, female rabbits and hares can become pregnant with their second litter while still pregnant with the first. This should explain why they're perceived as a very significant symbol of fertility.

To celebrate the coming of spring, modern-day Wiccans and pagans typically go outdoors to meditate. They may also conduct a simple ritual that honors the occurrence. Others may plant seeds or include seasonal candy, like chocolate rabbits and peeps, as part of their familial celebration. This always helps get the kids in the spirit of the Holiday.

Common Misconceptions of Ostara

Ostara is probably the most misunderstood Neo-Pagan Wheel of the year holiday (more on that later). Many Pagans may not be aware that the popular concepts behind the symbolism and history of Ostara are based on speculations that lacked sufficient evidence that arose during the nineteenth century. Either way, one must keep in mind that it shouldn't matter if a specific spiritual practice is not based on solid evidence, as it doesn't strip it away of its spiritual significance. However, understanding the history of the Holiday can help clarify common misconceptions about the celebration.

The history we know of the Ostara today is rather gnarly. The roots of the Holiday can be traced back to the olden Proto-Indo-European days. But before we explore the origins of Ostara, it only makes sense that we touch upon the popularly held beliefs about this celebration. The most pervasive is that the goddess Eostre, which the holiday was named after, may have been an adaptation of Astarte or Ishtar. Astarte was the West Semitic goddess, particularly the ancient Middle East great goddess, and the deity of important Mediterranean seaports like Sidon, Tyre, and Elat. She was also thought to be the queen of heaven, which is why the Canaanites used to burn her offerings and "pour liberations" (Jeremiah 44). Ishtar is Astarte's Akkadian counterpart.

There are many stories regarding the association between modern-day Easter celebrations and Ostara. One of them suggests that the Easter bunny and eggs are adaptations of the Pagan symbols that represent fertility and are linked to the goddess Eostre and Ostara, which we will explain in greater detail later. It is believed that these symbols go all the way back to Ishtar.

Others claim that the Easter bunny comes from an Eastern mythology hare. In accordance with this conception, modern-day Ostara celebrations choose to honor the Eostre and the coming of spring. They celebrate the fertility that appears in the vast lands of Earth, hence usually commandeering the egg and bunny symbols of today's western Easter Holidays.

The issue with either interpretation is that they're not historically based or evident. So, what do we really know about traditional Ostara and Spring Equinox celebrations, and where do our beliefs come from?

The Origins of the Holiday

Unsurprisingly, the Spring Equinox is significant among many ancient Eastern and Indo-European cultures and religions. The Babylonians, Persians, Romans, and others based their calendars on the spring Equinox being the start of the year. On March 1st of every year, an order of ancient Rome priests dedicated to Mars and known as the Salii held public festivals.

A spring festival known as Akitu was also prevalent during that time in Babylonia. Akitu surrounded the imprisonment and escapade of Marduk, a god, and his marriage to Ishtar the Earth Goddess. When he arrived at "Bet Akitu," Marduk started to celebrate with both world gods, the upper and the nether. He decorated a huge table with their statues during the event. He then returned to the city at night to celebrate his marriage to Ishtar. This was considered where both earth and heaven and the gods unite. The purpose behind the marriage was to bring this union to life by occupying the throne before everyone. They even recited poems on occasion. Their love was believed to create life during springtime.

Common Practices and Beliefs

Ostara is very closely linked to the Easter Christian Holiday. In fact, Easter is considered a variation of the equinox Holiday. Ostara and Easter, its posterity, get their names from Oestre or Eastre, the Teutonic goddess of Spring and the dawn.

Unlike Christmas, Thanksgiving, Halloween, St. Patrick's Day, and other common holidays, Ostara doesn't fall on a fixed day of the year. Depending on when the first full moon appears, Ostara generally falls between March 19th and 22nd of each year.

Ironically, most of the imagery and symbols that most Christians link to Easter actually originate from the ancient fundamental concepts, like life and rebirth, of Ostara. For instance, candy, bunnies, Easter baskets, eggs, and even new clothes are traditions that have been long devised with the Pagan holiday. It may also come across as a surprise to learn that painting and dyeing Easter eggs even dates back to ancient Egypt, where eggs were painted and eaten to celebrate the festival of Isis, the mother goddess. People used to gift each other painted eggs on the spring equinox.

Not many people know that the egg, which is among the most popular symbols of spring and Easter, is originally a very powerful symbol of life. An article in the Massachusetts Daily Collegian explains that according to Pagan legends, there is an incredibly horrible history behind the traditional symbol of Easter.

In old Europe, people commonly decorated eggs and offered them as gifts, as they believed that they would bring prosperity, abundance, and blessings around during the coming year. However, as Christianity spread and the "old religion" practices were abandoned, people began to hide the eggs and have children find them. Hence, the egg hunt game each Easter. This made all the children in the village look around everyone's gardens, fences, and other hidden spots at the same time. It was believed that people who sought out the heretics and heathens used to threaten children or bribe them with coins so that the person with the uncovered egg on their property gets accused of practicing the old religions. However, it's important to note that this is just a common piece of Pagan lore, and there is no documentation of this ever happening.

Traditionally, Ostara feasts include variations of ham and other meats. This goes back to the ancient celebrations of the holiday. People didn't slaughter animals during the winter back then, so they had to eat them sparingly. They also had to use a lot of salt to cure their meat. They did, however, welcome the spring season with fresh meat and an abundance of green options like nettles, asparagus, and dandelion greens. People ate them with zeal because they were easily accessible in the spring. Even in modern times, many Pagans prefer to eat sparingly at certain times of the year. However, they do it out of choice and not because it's a necessity. They eat a clean diet and avoid eating food containing manufactured chemicals and other toxins to maintain their health and purify their bodies.

Giving candy is a widespread tradition in the spring holiday, making the celebration popular with kids of all ages. The difference between Ostara and Easter is that many Pagans don't support the idea of rabbits dropping baskets full of candy for kids to enjoy. Instead, a fairy legend is widely exchanged. Parents tell their kids that it's only right to leave offerings to the spirits during the holidays to remain in their favor. So it happens that sweets are traditional gifts on Ostara. It was believed that if the fairies were not offered gifts, mischief would befall them.

Ostara and the Druid's Alban Eilir

If you think about the most prominent events that ancient peoples and cultures celebrated, you'll find that agricultural holidays are among the most significant. In modern times, the Druid tradition opts to create a Wheel of the Year that rebuilds a set of holidays more in tune with the changing seasons and terrestrial practices. This is why most druids celebrate the "Wheel of the Year," a group of eight holidays that happen every seven weeks. These holidays include the equinoxes and the solstices. According to the Druid Revival tradition, each has a unique name. The wheel also accounts for four fire festivals, which serve as the midpoint between equinox and solstice and vice versa.

If you wish, you can look up a chart of the druidic holidays or wheel of the year to get a clearer picture. The wheel of the year progresses from Alban Arthan (roughly December 21st), the Winter Solstice, and the time when darkness looms, to Imbolc. From there, it goes to Alban Eiler (the spring equinox), Beltane, and finally, Alban Hefin, which is the Summer Solstice (roughly June 21st), and when the light shines the brightest. Alban Arthan and Alban Hefin lie right across from each other on the wheel. Lughnasadh follows right after, then comes Alban Elfed (the fall equinox), then Samhuinn, and back to Alban Arthan. Alban Eiler and Alban Elfed serve as the two midpoints, providing balance during the year, making the light and dark equal. The other six holidays that we had just mentioned sit within either the dark or light halves of the year. Compost, growth, rebirth, and harvest are among the most recurrent themes and symbols throughout the Druid wheel of the year. Wiccan traditions have a similar wheel, which we will be covering in this chapter, in which Ostara takes the place of Alban Eilir.

As the celebrations of the wheel of the year begin, most druids start to feel a heightened sense of proximity to nature, as well as a deep appreciation toward the changing seasons. The existence of the Wheel of the Year, whether Druid or Wiccan, provides us with a sense of balance. It is a great way to keep track of the alternating seasons and the passage of time. This is one way we can pay closer attention to what we can learn from each season.

The Druid Wheel of the Year is typically celebrated in different ways, either physically and terrestrial or through more mystical and spiritual activities.

Like Ostara celebrations, Druids celebrate Alban Eilir through food, gatherings, and grove rituals. They may also start planting seeds, helping other people out, participating in environmental cleanups, engaging in wildcrafting, writing, music, or painting, conducting a personal ritual, meditating, or reflecting.

Alban Eiler can be translated into "Light of the Earth." Like Ostara and Easter, this holiday is celebrated during the spring equinox. It is one of two "balance" celebrations. At this time of the year, Druids pay extra attention to the significance of planning, creating projects, coming up with new ideas, growing, planting, and nurturing. They view it as their shot to bring balance into their lives and realize the significance of harmonizing their activities in the larger landscape. They aim to remind themselves that they aren't walking the path of life on their own.

Ostara and the Wiccan Wheel of the Year

The wheel of the Year represents the eight Sabbats of the Wicca and Neo-Paganism movement. The Sabbats are holidays celebrated by pagans and witches worldwide through various practices. The sabbats are considered the eight pillars of the circle of life. In that case, that circle is an unending cyclical pattern of nature. This is exactly what the placement of the Sabbats on the wheel of the year symbolizes. Even though scientific breakthroughs have established that time is linear, we still can't help but recognize the cyclical essence of life.

You can think of the Wheel of the Year as a form of a calendar split into eight sections instead of 12 months. The Sabbats divide the year into eight equal sections, signifying the beginning of each season, and, as you already know, their midpoints. There are two categories of sabbats. The first one is the sun or lesser Sabbats, including Yule, Ostara, Litha, and Mabon. These, as we mentioned, are known as solstices and equinoxes, and they mark the starting of each season. In other words, the four solar or lesser festivals are the Winter Solstice, Spring Equinox, Summer Solstice, Fall Equinox. Other categories include the earth festivals, the moon, or Greater Sabbats. These are Imbolc, Beltane, Lammas, and Samhain. These signify the midpoints of every season. Unlike the first category, which includes Ostara, the moon Sabbats always fall on a certain day. You may have noticed that some terms are common or similar to the Druid Wheel of the Year.

As opposed to the modern-day Wiccan traditions and beliefs, there is no solid proof of an existing ancient Wheel of the Year, at least in its current form. However, it is safe to say that the Celts still celebrated the festivals marked on the wheel thousands of years ago. They were just as significant then as they are today, even if they were known by different terms.

The Wiccan Wheel of the Year goes as follows:

31st October - Samhain

20th - 25th December - Yule

1st - 2nd February - Imbolc

20th - 23rd March - Ostara

30th April - 1st May - Beltane

20th - 22nd June - Litha

1st August - Lughnasadh

20th - 23rd September - Mabon

The eight festivals or Sabbats were made to focus on everything that is continuously being obtained and then lost during the cyclical turns and alternatives of the years. In the ancient Egyptian civilizations, along with many others, the Celts thought that ingratitude was some type of "gateway sin." They believed that being ungrateful could lead to the darkness of resentment, pride, and even self-pity. However, these eight Sabbats force us to take a moment to observe and reflect on everything surrounding us. It allows us to express gratitude for all we have been given during the year. It also allows us to process what we have lost and make peace with it. It is the only way to find and maintain balance in ourselves and the world around us.

Key Features of the Holiday

By this point, you are undoubtedly well-versed in the holiday's symbols. Bunnies, fertility, and eggs are the symbols that come to mind when the word "Ostara" is mentioned. Besides the fact that we've been talking about these symbols for the majority of the chapter, we still have Easter and the continuity of this holiday to thank for Ostara becoming one of the most popular pagan holidays. Nonetheless, we are positive that you'll encounter some symbols that you probably had no idea about.

The Hare

The hare is among the most significant features of Ostara, and it is all for a good reason! The next chapter will teach you more about the connection between the hare and Eostre, the goddess. As we mentioned earlier, hares are also known for being a symbol of fertility, considering the number of offspring they typically have. Hares are also often associated with the moon.

Eggs

Eggs are symbolically representative of "birth," which makes sense, considering that many creatures lay eggs instead of giving birth. Eggs are also associated with the sun, abundance, and fertility. They are usually incorporated into rituals to help lift curses and make wishes in funerary rites and kitchen witchery.

Hot Cross Buns

While hot cross buns are a popular Easter symbol, they are also a part of the Wiccan tradition, as they have relevant significance to witches and pagans. They are also typically representative of the four elements of earth, water, air, and fire. Some believe they represent the major phases of the moon (dark moon, waxing moon, full moon, and waning moon) as well as the wheel of the year's four fire festivals (Imbolc, Beltane, Lammas, and Samhain).

Serpents and Dragons

The snakes come out of their winter hibernation during the time of Ostara. They roam around in the daylight, shed their skin, and lay their eggs. There are numerous reasons why serpents are easily linked to Ostara. The shedding is representative of birth and renewal. These creatures are also incorporated into several creation myths. Dragons are also symbols of Ostara, as they're associated with the worship of the sun and renewal.

Spring Flowers

Spring flowers make the ideal choice for altar decorations regarding Ostara celebrations. Many pagans also like to use them as offerings to their deities. Daffodils, celandine, catkins, crocuses, violets, primroses, and hyacinths make great spring flower choices. These flowers bloom during springtime and represent life, as they come around after long, harsh winters. Hyacinths make the most popular symbols of Ostara.

In the ancient Celtic culture and other various cultures, time was thought to be exclusively cyclical. It was apparent that the seasons alternated, and even people died. Yet, nothing was permanently lost because things came back around in one way or another, keeping the natural cycle alive. Springtime has also been one of the most celebrated seasons around the world, as it is associated with fertility and the agricultural season.

Chapter 2: Eostre and the Hare

Celebrations of the Ostara are intertwined with stories of Eostre and the Hare. This isn't merely a game of phonetics - all the words sound slightly similar, and that is because they share the same roots in Anglo-Saxon pagan traditions. To fully appreciate the magic of the Spring Equinox and why it has become such an important tradition for many Wiccan practitioners, it is important to delve deeper into its history and learn more about the goddess Eostre, from whom many of these beliefs have evolved.

More than Just a Name

According to German lore, Eostre is the Germanic goddess of the dawn, and she is shown in various writings and images as celebrating the Spring Equinox. In fact, according to the old Germanic calendar, the month most similar to what we now know as April was previously referred to as "Ōstarmānod," which roughly means "Easter-month." If you take a moment to re-read these words and say them aloud, you can clearly tell that they are related. Easter essentially predated the dawn of Christianity as a holiday and was initially named the Spring Equinox celebration.

To take it a step further and allow for the connecting of the dots, so to speak, we should devote a bit more time to Eostre and the iconography most associated with this goddess. In terms of symbols, she is commonly associated with the egg and the rabbit. According to legend, the goddess Eostre found an injured bird in the dead of winter, so she transformed the bird into a hare to save its life. However, there was one quirk: even though it was no longer a bird, the hare could still lay eggs and continue the feature of abundance and joy that serve to be markers of the spring season.

We will delve deeper into this fantastic story later in the chapter, but suffice it to say, many of the words or traditions common to the English language and Judeo-Christian in a broader sense have their roots in this pagan history. The connections are preserved in the linguistic asides and symbols humanity has maintained and cherished over the centuries. Further proof that celebrations of the Ostara bring us even closer to our shared history than previously thought.

The Goddess

Historians have recorded Eostre's unique story for centuries, and of course, there have been a few vagaries in between. Unlike other gods and goddesses we may be familiar with, an image of her visage was not used as often in Renaissance paintings or sculptures as, say, Medusa or Hercules. The few clear visual representations of Eostre herself - rather than the symbols she is often associated with - indicate a goddess with a benevolent face, flowers in her hair, and dressed completely in white. She stands in clear contrast to the wintry and dark image usually floating behind her. As a goddess meant to be an antidote to the cold and dark, she has often been represented as exactly that: generous, calm, and bright.

Eostre is a goddess often associated with fertility, spring, flowers, and all the elements that come to flourish in the wake of a barren winter. As previously stated, her name is used interchangeably with "Eastre," which has become known as Easter - without alluding to the goddess herself, of course - and "Ostara." Then, in the 1400s, under the reign of Charlemagne, Germans referred to her as "Ostaramonath." To avoid confusion when it comes to celebrating Ostara, the goddess will be referred to as *Eostre* in this chapter and throughout the book - though it does help to highlight the extent to which these traditions are so deeply intertwined.

For centuries, historians have argued about the origins of belief in Eostre. While there is a clear connection between her and Anglo-Saxon religions and myths, her name is rarely mentioned in popular literature. Again, the matter is complicated by the lack of a specific trace for Eostre in terms of her revival in paintings, sculptures, or works of art. In fact, her name appears in written records for the first time in the late 1200s, in a document written by St. Bede, an English Benedictine monk who lived at the monasteries of St. Peter and St. Paul in the Kingdom of Northumbria of Angles. Beyond that, her presence has primarily been felt through the linguistic vagaries people have held onto over time, as well as the numerous traditions associated with the pagan holiday that inevitably became part of Judeo-Christian folklore years down the line.

Unlike other gods and goddesses, the extent to which Eostre was worshiped in the same way as a deity is a bit uncertain. St. Bede, in his journals, had reported that pagan Anglo-Saxons in medieval Northumbria had held festivals in her honor during the month of April. However, beyond this formative text, we don't know much else about here and the extent to which the pagans honored Eostre. In any case, whether or not she was a singularly worshiped deity, by the 19th century, Eostre had become a huge part of German culture, appearing in much of its folklore and popular art.

Festivals for Eostre

Going by the texts that have survived, written by historical figures such as St. Bede, we have at least some glimpse into how the pagans honored Eostre. Unsurprisingly, festivals held in her honor are remarkably familiar to us now. Eggs would be brought and decorated, painted with bright colors and intricate drawings. There would be egg hunts and plenty of cooking because communal feasts were an important part of the holiday. Wearing flowers in your hair and creating floral wreaths for homes to inaugurate the beginning of the festival were de rigueur for all pagans who worshiped her.

Typically, bonfires would be lit in the evening before the major celebration would begin the next day. The following morning, water would be drawn from wells or the nearest water source, followed by a prayer to the goddess. According to literary sources, women - or young maidens specifically - were encouraged to wear all white to honor the spirit of the celebration. Much like it is now, Spring was regarded as a blank slate back then, a time for renewal and rebirth. Therefore, white and soft pastel colors have become synonymous with the season and Ostara in general. They indicate the rock, mountains, lush harvests, and the wealth of natural resources representing the ancient goddess. In turn, these are the colors we now most associate with Easter, acting as further proof that these things do not happen in a vacuum and that most current traditions have their roots in our shared history.

Besides the collective celebrations, pagans would create an altar in their homes and give thanks to the goddess of Eostre according to their own rituals. Smudge sticks were often used, just as they are today, and the prayers vary according to the personal preferences of the practitioners, but the baseline of giving thanks remains.

The Spring Equinox celebration includes a basic acknowledgment of the changes that occur over time. The ceremonies attribute these changes to the higher powers that manifest themselves in the form of the Gods and Goddesses. During this important time, the Gods and Goddesses of the Spring Equinox are sometimes referred to as The Green Man and Mother Earth. Yes, another way to refer to the Goddess Eostre has traditionally been Mother Earth. According to recorded history, the Green Man is typically said to be born of Mother Earth in the depths of winter, and he is then thought to live the rest of the year till the next equinox.

During the festivities, a woman and a man may be chosen to play the roles of Spring God and Goddess, play-acting courtship scenes and symbolically planting seeds. Then there are egg races, egg hunts, egg painting, and, of course, plenty of egg-based dishes to round out the holiday's unique festivities.

Story of the Hare

The story of the hare and how it has colored our perceptions of Eostre and Easter is rather interesting. While it is not exactly an ancient holiday, it is not a contemporary one either. Many people have erroneously perceived that the Easter bunny - or hare - is a product of the greeting card companies, like Valentine's Day. On the other hand, some believe the story of the hare and spring is as old as time, and it is one of our most ancient myths. The truth is somewhere in between. One thing is certain: the Easter bunny was never meant to be a rabbit; it was always a hare. It is uncertain why and how the hare transformed into a rabbit, even though the only conceivable difference is that the former are much larger animals, with long legs and ears commonly associated with popular depictions of the Easter bunny.

The essence of the origin of this story is that the goddess Eostre transformed a bird into a hare, who then responded by laying many eggs of beautiful, bright colors for her at her spring festival. While some writers claim that this story is incredibly old, others claim it was created as early as the 1980s. This decade arguably saw the nexus of the hyper-commercialization of the Easter holiday and the renaissance of the Wiccan religion.

Earlier in this chapter, the delineation was made between Ostara, the Ostre, and the Eostre - all words related to a similar concept. Many historians took St. Bede's word for it, believing the story of Eostre, an Anglo-Saxon goddess whose history is rarely, if ever, documented in pagan sources but rather appears in his own work documenting early Christianity. According to St. Bede and folklorist Jacob Grimm, who later expanded on the famed theologian's work, Eostre is a more localized version of a famous Germanic goddess named Ostara. St. Bede and later Grimm wrote extensively about Ostara - or Eostre - and how she was worshiped. Some historians have also pointed out that Eostre could simply have meant "east." However, this does not necessarily solve the mystery of the hare and the ways all Anglo-Saxon words share the same phonetic and linguistic roots.

According to stories written by later folklorists and archivists who have been trying to uncover the history of Easter, the exact story of how Eostre transformed a bird into a hare may be a bit convoluted, and there are different variations on the same theme. In all cases, a simple child's tale may hold the answer. This version will be summarized here:

Every Spring, the goddess Eostre would hold a massive celebration celebrating the end of the winter darkness. Animals and children the world over would gather to pay their respects to her and bring small gifts to express their appreciation for the change in seasons. One year, the hare wanted to bring Eostre a gift a day before the celebration was held, but it realized it had nothing to give her. It had been an especially difficult winter, and the hare hadn't been able to harvest much of anything and had barely enough to eat. While rummaging through the forest for some food, the hare found an egg in the grass, which tempted the hare considerably as they battled severe hunger pains. Instead of eating it, the hare decided that the egg would make a wonderful gift for Eostre since it symbolizes birth and the Spring season. So, the hare decorated the egg and prepared the present for the goddess. Eostre was so impressed with this beautiful object, with the selflessness of the act, that she decided from here on out that the hare would be responsible for delivering intricately decorated eggs to the world's children every spring till the end of time.

Does this sound familiar? Well, it should, since this version of the tale bears some resemblance to the more Christianized versions told later on. There is another way in which the story of the hare has been told and ties more specifically to the pagan spirit of things, as it were. Here is that version of the story:

The goddess Eostre celebrates the Spring Equinox every year by holding a massive festival in a lush, green meadow. One year, Eostre was late, and thus the spring season itself was delayed. This occurred because Eostre found a dying bird in the snow, which cleaved her heart in two. To help heal the bird, she brought it back to life as a white hare and named it Lepus. Eostre gave it the power to lay eggs for one day every year to pay tribute to the hare's original form as a bird. From then on, every year, the hare was allowed to give away its eggs to those attending the Ostara festival.

This version is far closer to what Wiccans these days celebrate when it comes to the Ostara. It is clear to see the ways Easter has evolved from this tale, and it's also clear to see how dear the hare is to the whole celebration of the spring. Eostre did not only bring a dying animal back to life, but she also transformed it. This story of shapeshifting reveals not only one but two magical acts of renewal key to our understanding of the entire season. Dying plants or roots in the ground are transformed into trees, flowers, fruits, vegetables, and so on. The connection is clear both emotionally and conceptually.

As such, it may be interesting to consider why the hare? Any other animal may have been chosen for this story if we are to take things strictly on a narrative basis. In reality, hares have always shown up as popular motifs in folklore, and they have been named time and again as familiars for witches, most probably because of their unique speed, which makes them difficult to catch. Some witches, such as the 17th-century Scottish witch Isobel Gowdie, have been documented as saying that they transform into hares when they need to escape.

Interestingly, in many other traditions, the hare is considered a moon creature, so its conflation with spring in Anglo-Saxon myth is rather intriguing. For example, the ancient Egyptians felt that the hare could easily switch genders during the moon cycle, making the animal a particularly androgynous figure. Likewise, in China, the popular adage of "the man in the moon" is replaced by "the hare in the moon" since the hare is seen to be a moon goddess's messenger. It is also tasked with guarding all wild animals, and it works to grind up the elixir of eternal life with a mortar and pestle. In fact, they are also tied to fertility in Chinese folklore since it is said that the hare can become pregnant by crossing the water in the moonlight or touching the rays emanating from a full moon. While it is surprising that the hare in Anglo-Saxon tradition is tied to the spring, the animal has always represented fertility and metamorphosis of some kind in the grand scheme of things.

Fact or Fiction?

There is little debate regarding the fact that pagans, druids, and Wiccans have always celebrated the Spring Equinox in one form or the other. The real debate is the extent to which the Goddess Eostre in all her manifestations - Ostara, Eastre, and so on - and the hare are real. Truthfully, Gods and Goddesses have historically served as conduits by which certain characteristics or difficult to pinpoint changes are made manifest in an easy-to-identify form. Therefore, the figure of Eostre may have been a way of communicating the significance of the spring season rather than an actual Goddess worshiped by the early pagans. Other folklorists and historians have pointed out that St. Bede may have simply misrepresented the festivities he witnessed centuries ago and misheard the word for "East" as "Eostre," but it is difficult to say.

Of course, this also means that the story of the hare is also quite debatable. While it is a beautiful story, regardless of the different versions out there, it may also be a convenient vehicle for expressing the uniquely transformative nature of Spring after a long, cold, and dark winter. Nevertheless, in history, the hare appears as an important animal for early pagans worldwide, and witches have historically looked to them as carriers of a powerful aura, one that allows them to take on altering guises in the face of fear or hardship.

What has never been debated is the fact that celebrations of the Spring Equinox are a constant in Anglo-Saxon tradition and world cultures more generally. While modern-day Wiccans are encouraged to pay homage to Eostre and tell the tale of the hare, it is only one part of an ancient celebration that has been taking place for centuries. The fact that some of these stories and traditions became a part of Christianity and the celebration of Easter is no accident: the Ostre has been an important part of our shared humanity for a long time, and the traditions, like other holidays celebrated by pagans, are difficult to shed because they are infused with so much meaning.

Chapter 3: Making Eggs Magical

Transitioning from the previous chapter, where you have learned about the association of the goddess Eostre with Ostara and the hare, this chapter will discuss how eggs are related to this topic. Eggs have been present as a symbol of Ostara in many Wicca and Pagan traditions, albeit the origin of symbolism goes far beyond the existence of these belief systems. The use of eggs in healing, protection, and spring celebrations has been present since the rise of Ancient Eastern cultures. An egg can be used for these purposes, raw and cooked. The shells can be made into powder - or in case of symbolizing the spring equinox - painted and decorated with different motives.

The Magical Eggs of Ostara

In many cultures, the egg symbolizes life, and some link it to the origin of the entire universe. In ancient times, members of clans exchanged eggs in the spring, which was thought to bring a plentiful harvest come autumn. In some cultures, eggs were given to be consumed in Eostre's honor, while in others, they were displayed in a sacred place of a home. Not only that, but eggs are considered to have magical powers, which are amplified at the beginning of spring when nature is reborn, and life begins anew. Eggs are thought to bring fruitful lands and chase away the dark part of the year. For this reason, they have been used in various forms to protect their owners or provide them with what they need in life. For example, in some Celtic and Pagan cultures, a red egg is given to newlyweds, enhancing their fertility.

But how exactly are eggs tied to Ostara? The answer to this question is twofold. For one, being the vessel for a new life makes eggs one of Eostre's most helpful tools for maintaining the fraternity of nature. According to the legends, Eostre's sacred hare has given her eggs as a gift. The hare presented the eggs in a nest he found them in, but he enchanted them with vivid colors instead of the usual brown or white ones.

The other explanation for the egg symbolism in Ostara is much more mundane and is related to the hare. Hares are creatures living in the wild, and before giving birth, they form nests to protect their young from the elements and predators. When the young grow up, they abandon the nests, and they are often reoccupied by plovers who use them to lay their eggs. When people found bird eggs in hare nests, the connection was attributed to magic.

The Use of Eggs in Magical Spells and Rituals

Eggs have been used by witches who wished to gain protection or heighten their powers for centuries. It is believed that eggshells can help rituals and spells come to fruition - especially during sabbats. Other creatures, including malicious spirits, can also use the magic of eggshells. To prevent these creatures from putting eggshells to use, a witch should either destroy their eggshells or protect them. The most common way to do this is by grinding the broken and dried eggshells down in a mortar. The resulting powder can then be used in protection, rituals including dressing candles for candle magick, casting circles, drawing sigils, carrying around spell bags, and much more. Throwing broken eggshells on the roof or placing them around the four corners of the house are also great ways a witch can protect their home from harmful spells.

Being a symbol of Ostara, painted eggs can be used in magical acts designed to appease deities and spirits. After the eggs are decorated, they are left either by the foot of trees or hung as ornaments on trees and other indoor plants. This ensures the home is protected, and its inhabitants will receive an abundant supply of everything they need. Another traditional way to use eggshells is making them into candles before Ostara. Burning eggshell candles during this sabbat results in similar magical benefits as decorating the eggs.

Dyeing Your Eggs with Natural Colors

In many cultures, decorating Eostre's eggs is one of the most common ways of celebrating Ostara. Feel free to try it out if you also want to pay homage to this sabbat by making your own colored eggs. However, for the magic of the eggs to become as powerful as it can be, it's recommended to use only natural color sources. Fortunately, there are plenty of magical herbs and plants that can be used for these purposes - and many of them can already be found in households. The items you don't keep in your home can be found in local health food stores or supermarkets. This way, the only thing you'll have to focus on is choosing which type of dyed eggs you want to make and letting your creative juices flow. There are two main types of dyed eggs: full and blown out.

Creating Normal Dyed Eggs

Originally, dyed eggs were left out in the open air to dry out naturally. Therefore, raw eggs were used for this process. If you live in a large home with a large garden or field attached to it, this may still be a viable option for you. However, if your only option is to place the eggs inside your home, you must cook them before decorating them. While some recipes require placing the eggs in boiling water to apply the dye, the eggs may not cook through during this process, so you may want to pre-cook them a little bit. Here is a step-by-step instruction on how to color whole eggs:

1. **Prepare Your Dye:** Take the plant material you are using for the different colors and place them in individual pots. Make sure you use plenty of them for each color. Pour water over them, add a tablespoon of vinegar, then bring to a boil. Let it boil for at least 20-30 minutes before placing the eggs inside. Check the intensity of the color before doing so.

2. **Prepare the Design:** While the dye is being made, you may prepare a design for your eggs. Pour vinegar onto a cotton swab, then rub

the eggs with it to remove any grease that will prevent the dye or the stencil from sticking to the surface of the shell. If you are using them, you may create stencils from herbs such as rose petals, cilantro, or rosemary. Press the herbs on the eggs and pull a piece of pantyhose over them to keep the stencil in place. If you are using onion peels and cabbage leaves, you won't need to use a stencil as these will leave your eggs colored in different shades, which can be decorative on their own.

3. **Dye the Eggs:** There are two main ways to go about dyeing your eggs. The first is to take raw eggs and boil them in the dyed water. Slowly place the eggs (with or without a stencil) into the boiling dye, lower the heat and let them cook for 10-12 minutes. After that, turn off the heat and check the intensity of the colors. If the eggshells haven't reached the desired shade, leave them in the dye until they do. The second option is to place already hard-boiled eggs into a cooled dye and let them soak. This allows more control over the intensity of colors and ensures you don't end up with half raw eggs.

4. **Finishing Touches:** When you are satisfied with the color of the eggs, you can remove them from the container with the dye. Tap them dry with a paper towel, then let them air dry for a couple of minutes. Once they are dry, you can remove the stencil (if you used one) with a pantyhose and enjoy your colored eggs.

Making Blown Out Eggs

After dyeing raw eggs and letting them dry naturally, the next best thing is coloring hollowed-out eggs. Once their inside is removed, the eggshell dries much quicker. What's even more important is that you can literally leave these lying around in your home all year round if you feel like it. They can make for beautiful ornaments or decor items, and you can even give them away as presents to your friends and family around Ostara.

Blown-out eggs can be dyed in several ways. You can color them the same way you did the whole eggs - by boiling or soaking them in dye. However, hollow eggshells float, so you may experience problems keeping them immersed. One of the solutions to this problem is to simply color the eggs before blowing them out. Another option would be to place a strainer or small bowl over the eggs to prevent them from coming up to the surface. You can also get creative and hand dye the eggs instead of dipping them.

Whichever method you choose to dye the hollow eggs, blowing them out may take some practice to learn. Here is how to do it:

1. **Gather the Supplies:** You'll need a syringe or an infant medicine dropper, both of which are available at a pharmacy. You'll also need a pin and a paper clip.

2. **Prepare the Eggs:** Whether you are saving the inside for cooking or throwing it away, you need to clean the egg's surface before making a hole in them. Before starting, the eggs should be kept at room temperature for a couple of hours. You may want to put them in warm water for 10 minutes just before beginning the process.

3. **Pierce a Hole:** Hold the egg in one hand, the pin in your other one, and using a winding motion, make a hole in one end of the egg. Twist the pin a couple of times as if you were trying to screw it, push it in, then repeat the process on the other end.

4. **Scramble the Inside:** Take the paperclip and unfold it to create a longer pin. Stick it inside the egg and move it in a circular motion to scramble up the yolk. This will make it easier to remove it easily later.

5. **Squeeze Out the Inside:** Take the syringe or the infant medicine dropper and place it over one of the holes you have created earlier. Hold the egg over a bowl with its uncovered hole facing down, and start squeezing the syringe. The inside of the egg should come out on the other hole. You need to put the paperclip back again and scramble the egg a little more if it doesn't. You can also shake the egg gently to break the resistant yolk.

6. **Rinse the Eggs:** Don't try to get every bit of the egg out by blowing in more air because this could make your egg explode. Instead, fill up the syringe with warm water and squeeze this inside the shell. Shake the egg to make sure everything is washed off and blow the water out. Repeat the process if you need to.

7. **Let the Shells Dry:** Once hollowed out, you need to let the eggs dry at room temperatures for a couple of hours. Place them in an egg holder to keep them safe. When the eggshells are dry, you can keep them at room temperatures until you are ready to decorate them.

If you are dyeing hollow eggshells by submerging them in water, they will be filled with dye on the inside as well. After taking them out from the water, let them cool to room temperature, then gently blow out the dye water. When the water is out, let them dry a little bit more before getting crafty and adding a few more decorations to them.

A List of Natural Colors

Colors can have a powerful effect on your magic. They can even determine the success of your spells and rituals. Each color has its own power and can be used for different purposes. As you would use a color of candle or crystal for a particular spell or ritual, you can use different colored eggs to manifest your intention. Here is the list of natural sources and their symbolism:

- **Black:** While the use of plain black eggs may symbolize dark magic, there is no reason why you should decorate them with golden or colorful symbols. When employed alongside colorful protection symbols, the color black can be an incredibly powerful tool to ward off negative energy and malicious spirits.

- **White:** White is the most powerful color to use in magic. It can substitute any other color and has cleansing properties. Since there is almost no way to color eggshells white with a natural color, you may want to get white eggs to begin with and treat them as a blank slate. You may draw on them with any other color as you do on the black ones.

- **Green:** It is the color associated with nature; therefore, it symbolizes everything earthly and natural. Placing green eggs at the altar or space you are using can ensure you have the best start possible if you are trying out a new magic act. It promises abundance in everything you need in life to become a better human being.

- **Blue:** The color blue can help you get into a relaxed state of mind, making your practices much more successful. Blue eggs can be used to achieve clarity, so your intention is always well defined when casting a spell or doing a ritual. They may offer you protection or symbolize other creatures that do.

- **Purple:** If your magic requires you to tap deeper into your intuition, but you feel unable to do so, the color purple can help you out. Often associated with royalty and higher power, purple can elevate your spells and rituals to a whole other level. There is no better way to show off your creativity than dyeing your eggs purple.

- **Pink:** Using pink color is also a great way to show love. However, because it's more gentle than red, it may just be the perfect color for self-care. It can be helpful if you feel the need to be kind and more understanding towards yourself so you can heal from any past trauma and your magic can flourish once again.

- **Red:** While nowadays, the color red seems to be associated with passion, it was originally the symbol of fertility. Not only that, but red is the color that everyone loves receiving in gifts. If you want to offer protection for someone, you can simply give them a red egg. You can also use the egg to cast a protection spell for a specific person.

- **Orange:** Like yellow, orange can also brighten up your day. Dye a couple of eggs orange, and you'll also get your creative juices flowing so you can come up with new spells and rituals and find solutions to all your problems. This raises your confidence, further enhancing your magical powers, and you'll never get stuck again.

- **Yellow:** The color yellow can do wonders on lifting your spirit when you are feeling down and unsure whether your spells will turn out as they should. Painting your eggs yellow ensures that you'll always have sunlight in your home. It's the next best thing after going out to soak in the natural sunlight.

Natural Dye Sources

Here is the list of natural dye sources, along with the type of plant matter that contains them:

Yellow: Straws, onion peel, saffron, and dandelion flowers.

Orange: Goldenrod and Crocus petals.

Red: Plums and red beets.

Green: Moss, spinach, grass, and buckthorn berry.

Blue: Huckleberry, sunflower seeds, and logwood.

Purple: Elderberry or blackberries.

Brown: Walnut husk, alder cones, and coffee.

Black: Alder bark and walnut shells.

Pink: Pokeberry.

As with extracting natural dye for any other purposes, you can use hot water and vinegar to facilitate the process of dyeing your eggs. You can even make a batch of dye ahead of time and freeze them. The frozen batches of color can always come in handy if you can't find all these plants around Ostara.

Decorating the Eggs

You may leave your eggs the color they come out after being dyed. Some dyes will color the eggshells according to their natural pattern (similar to tie-dye), which means you'll already have some additional decorations on your eggs. That said, if you want to add a few more elements to them, feel free to do so. If you wish to use the eggs in a magic ritual, drawing sigils or runes on them can enhance their powers. The simplest way to add additional details to colored eggs is to use a different color to draw the desired symbols to your eggs. You can take a specific egg painting tool or a small art brush to make the small strokes. If you are good at freehand painting, you can do this without much preparation. Otherwise, you may want to sketch out the pattern you want to use on paper, then slowly repeat this on the egg with a pencil. Once the outline is drawn, you can proceed with painting the symbol.

If you want to use them as ornaments, you can add string, ribbon, or twine to them. You simply need to thread these through the existing holes using a large needle or a paperclip. These can also help you enlarge the hole to get everything through safely. Once the string sticks out on both ends of the egg, tie off one end, and decorate the other one. You can either make a simple loop out of it or add a few beads to cover the top hole and knot. This way, you'll have a much nicer egg to display for Ostara. Solid-colored eggs look the best with beads or small crystals added to them. If you are using the eggs for a spell or ritual, you may also want to add a charm or the symbol of the spiritual guide you are trying to evoke.

Chapter 4: Ostara Crafts and Creations

Since the Spring Equinox signifies the end of the winter, its celebration is usually a joyous occasion. All that greenery that awakens when the spring comes also reinforces the upbeat vibe of this sabbat. However, as with most holidays and celebrations, preparing for it can become quite overwhelming and stressful. Not to mention that sometimes the awakening in nature is still not visible yet around Ostara - or perhaps we cannot enjoy it fully due to our busy schedules. One of the best ways to remedy this is to create handcrafted ornaments and items that will remind us of the true meaning of Ostara. Even witches who are aware of the importance of performing mindfulness exercises can use these to focus and enrich their magic during the sacred sabbat of Ostara. Renewal, rebirth, fertility, hope, and balance are some of the most meaningful things in life in general. This chapter contains a few creations you can make to celebrate Ostara and brighten up your days even after the sabbat has passed.

Ostara crafts use items that can remind the creator about sunshine, spring rain, flowers, animals, harvest, and all the other beautiful things they can look forward to during those long months until the winter arrives once again. According to Pagan and Wiccan originating from Europe, the jovial nature of this sabbat is due to the extremely harsh winters people had to endure on this continent. People considered themselves fortunate if they could make it through the cold months, and once they did, they were more than happy to celebrate it. They thought being able to experience the inherent beauty of the warmer months is a blessing not to be taken for granted. They often spent the winter preparing gifts for Ostara to celebrate it when spring arrived. Plus, making the fun crafts had given them something to do during winter, as they couldn't tend to the fields, garden, or hunt.

Ostara Crafts Are for Everyone

It's no secret that those who dabble in Wicca and Paganism consider Ostara one of the largest celebrations throughout the year. However, you don't have to share these or similar belief systems to celebrate this sabbat by decorating your home. In addition, most people decorate their altar or the place they consider the sanctuary of their home. But feel free to bring spring into every room of your house if you want. You can even share the joy with your family and friends by preparing handcrafted and dedicated gifts for them for Ostara.

While you are probably familiar with the tradition of decorating eggs and making hare nests with eggs during this time of the year, there is so much more to Ostara than this project. Some of the creations you'll see in the continuation of this chapter were traditionally created by witches, while others aren't even witchcraft-related. Even if you aren't inclined to deepen your spirituality, immersing yourself in crafts can help you reconnect with nature. After all, spirits aren't the only ones who can generate positive energy. You also have the power to do this - and this power comes from nature itself.

Choosing Crafts for Ostara

Ostara is generally regarded as a celebration of nature and the awakening of the outside world, but it is also a celebration of possibilities. Crafts can symbolize your ability to achieve anything you want; you just need to find the right project for you. The selection of images, symbols, and items with magical associations you can encounter is vast. For this reason, finding the right project for you may prove challenging - especially if this is your first time celebrating Ostara.

In nature, many of them are born or reborn in the spring, making them the perfect choice for Ostara projects. All you need to do is find the closest piece of nature, step into it and look carefully for any inspiration. Grass, flowers, the sun, and even fruits and veggies grown in early spring can be included in your craft projects. Or, you can also add products and symbolism, such as eggs or anything else related to farm animals, wildlife, or otherworldly creatures. These are all connected to Ostara - and so are seeds, potted plants, or gardening tools.

When it comes to flowers, the most natural choices for this occasion are lilies, tulips, daffodils, snowdrops, crocuses, vervain, lilacs, carnations, daisies, clovers, lotus flowers, and violets. Out of the herbs associated with Ostara, your choice may fall on mint, dill, thyme, tarragon, parsley, tansy, lemon balm, rosemary, or lavender. Craft projects made for these can be used for various purposes, from candle dressings to protection spells to cleaning rituals. Furthermore, incorporating elements of spring cleaning can enrich all of your projects and inspire you to take on the task of beautifying your home with a much more positive spirit.

The color you'll be using is a matter of personal choice. Some prefer to use more earthy colors and even colder ones to signify the change in the outer land space from wintery to sunny. Others use brighter flower colors to remind themselves of the joyful nature of this celebration - and that life is just as full of possibilities as the color palette flowers come in. If you keep the finished products at your altar, you can also design your crafts to complement the aesthetics of the space. All in all, when it comes to choosing the Ostara creations you can make, the sky's the limit.

Ostara Egg Tree

As you would have learned from the previous chapter, the egg and its symbolism are the grandest hallmarks of Ostara celebrations. You were also able to see that there are various ways to color and decorate eggs and how plain ones can be used in magical spells and rituals. One of the projects where you can use your freshly decorated eggs is the Ostara egg tree. It does not have to be an enormous tree, nor do the ornaments have to be perfect. It will be sitting indoors, and apart from reminding you of the changing seasons, it should also symbolize the benefits of a new beginning. As long as you are having fun when preparing it, it will already begin to fulfill its purpose. And if you want to keep it on your altar, you should definitely keep the proportions smaller.

The Material You'll Need:

- Spanish moss
- Lightweight branches
- A vase
- Florist foam
- Acrylic paint
- Spring decorations

Instructions:

1. Decorate the vase or the pot with a design that reminds you of spring, such as flowers, butterflies, or eggs. Feel free to freehand paint the design, or even use your fingers to do so. The latter can be a ton of fun for children or any group of creative friends.

2. Allow the paint to dry before filling the vessel with florist foam. You'll need to hold the pot firmly in one hand and press the foam down so it molds to do inner walls.

3. Press the branches into the foam one by one and arrange them in a way so they will look like a tree. Use as many branches as you need to achieve the perfect tree shape and size that fits your space.

4. Once you are satisfied with how your tree looks, you can cover the top of the foam with Spanish moss.

5. Start hanging the eggs and the other spring decorations on the branches. You can also add ribbons and the cookie-shaped salt dough to the tree.

6. When the tree is completely decorated, you can use it as a tabletop or keep it on your altar. Or keep it on the table and only place it on the altar when you are doing rituals or spells.

Always use branches that have already broken off and not the ones still attached to live trees. The goal is to celebrate life and nature, not to destroy it. The only exception to this rule is the branches you get from pruning the trees. This procedure allows new growths to become stronger, so not only will you not harm the tree, but you'll also help it thrive.

The Flower Crown

In medieval times, flower crowns were worn by maidens who celebrated their youth, fertility, and springtime. Creating flower crowns is another way to bring fun into the Ostara celebration. Wearing them can help you feel more connected to spring on a personal level. After all, what could bring you closer to nature than wearing it? In addition, self-adornment is a great way to express your beliefs. And there is no better way to display how you feel than rocking a luscious flower crown with confidence. This will also enhance your powers if you are doing witchcraft.

The Material You'll Need:

- Floral tape
- Wire cutters
- 3-5 stems of silk flowers
- A piece of wire
- Scissors
- Needle nose pliers
- A thin ribbon

Instructions:

1. Start by cutting off most of the plastic flower blossoms from their stems. Be careful not to squash the flowers and leave a tiny length of the stem behind.

2. Use the pliers to curl both ends of the wire towards themselves until they almost touch each other.

3. Place a silk flower at one end of the wire and start winding a floral tape around its leftover stem. After that, wind the tape around the wire as well, so you can secure the flower onto it.

4. Take the next flower and repeat the process from the previous step, then do the same with the remaining ones until you arrive at the middle of the wire.

5. Move to the other end of the wire and start attaching flowers there as well, working your way back to the middle.

6. Once your entire wire is filled with silk flowers, you can tie a ribbon through each end of the wire. This will help you fit the crown to your head better.

Feel free to substitute the silk flowers for real or dried ones to make the crown even more true to nature. If you are using a real one, you can dry these later and use them in your practice. You can do the same if you're using flowers that are already dry, or you can preserve the entire crown for next year's Ostara celebration.

Spring Snake Wreath

As Christianity spread throughout Ireland Under St. Patrick's influence, it slowly pushed Paganism out of the country and the rest of Europe - an event that Pagans began to refer to as the snakes being chased away. They began to wear and decorate their homes with snake symbols to protest this. Nowadays, this practice has been reduced to wearing a small serpent pin on St. Patrick's Day and during the entire Ostara season. Those who more liberally embrace Paganism decorate their front door with a Spring Snake Wreath.

The Material You'll Need:

- A hot glue gun
- Rubber snakes
- A wreath form
- Spring greenery, such as ivy
- Ribbon
- Florist wire

Instructions:

1. Start by winding the ivy around the loop of the wreath. Be careful not to use too much greenery so you can have enough room left for the snakes as well.

2. Next, start placing the snakes between the greenery. When you are satisfied with their arrangement, secure the snakes to the wreath with hot glue.

3. Once all your snakes are in place, you can add a few more items, such as ribbons. You can just loop them around or make them into a bow and secure them with the florist wire.

4. Lastly, add a loop of wire to the top of the wreath to hang it up when all the glue has solidified.

Depending on the size of the loop, you'll need anywhere from 6 to 12 rubber snakes. You want to have enough of them to fully represent the message the wreath is conveying, but not so much that you can't add ribbons and the other decorations you are using to spruce the ornament up. Another tip is to pipe the glue to the wreath and gently push the snakes into it. Doing it the other way around, you would risk touching the rubber with the metal tip of the hot glue gun, which would melt it.

Crystal Eggs

Crystals have a unique energy and have been used for healing and protection for centuries. Witches can use them to enrich their magic or simply help them manifest the intent in spells and rituals. Crystal eggs are a craft project that requires baking the gems into an egg-shaped dough. The eggs can be used during the traditional Ostara games, which involve children looking for eggs the adults have hidden around their homes. When the child finds an egg and cracks it open, they will find the hidden treasure, which they can keep as protection.

The Material You'll Need:

- ½ cup of salt
- 1 cup of all-purpose flour
- ¼ cup of clean sand
- ¾ cup of warm water
- 1 cup of used coffee grounds
- Gemstones or crystals
- Cooking spray
- Acrylic paints

Instructions:

1. Start by blending coffee grounds, salt, flour, and flour, then slowly add the water and mix until well combined. You should end up with a thick dough.

2. Spray the crystal with cooking spray to prevent the dough from sticking to it. Take a small scoop of dough into your hand and put the crystal into the center of it.

3. Shape the dough into an egg shape and place it on a baking tray lined with parchment paper.

4. Bake the eggs at 350 degrees for about 12-15 minutes. Let the eggs cool after taking them out of the oven.

Depending on the environment you let them sit in, your eggs may take 1-2 hours to cool as the clay-like dough tends to hold on to heat. Once they have cooled, they will be rock hard, and you can paint them or decorate them as you like. After the paint dries, you can either display the eggs on your altar or hide them for the children to find.

Seed Packet Greeting Cards

With the arrival of the spring, it comes planting season. Even if you only have room for a few pots around your kitchen, there is something magical about growing your own plants. Seeds represent the promise of a new life, and by gifting them to your friends and family, you can bestow this promise to them. Seed packet greeting cards are a wonderful way to surprise your loved ones around Ostara. In modern times sending personalized greeting cards has become a lost art, but people who will receive yours will more than appreciate the gesture. Not only will they appreciate receiving a handwritten note from you during a sabbat, but the attached seeds will surely tempt them to try out gardening if they haven't done it before.

The Material You'll Need:

- Envelopes
- Pre-cut blank greeting cards
- Seed packets
- Pens and markers
- A glue stick
- Other craft supplies

Instructions:

1. Write a list of people you want to send a greeting card to, and choose a packet of seeds for each card.

2. Attach the seed packet to the front of the card. Use only a small amount of glue, so it wouldn't get onto the seeds but make sure you secure the packet so it can be handled safely.

3. Take a pen or a marker and write an upbeat message on the inside of the card. Feel free to decorate around the text with glitter and other art supplies.

4. Once the glue you have used is dry, place the cards into an envelope marked with the name of the person you are sending it to.

While giving seed packets for Ostara can be a great time to connect with friends and family, you don't need an excuse to send them a card or two once in a while to show you are thinking of them. Plus, seeds can be planted all year long. Birthdays or other momentous occasions at any time of the year could also merit sending these cards.

Cascarones

The tradition of making Cascarones for Ostara hails from Mexico. These hollowed-out eggs filled with herbs, confetti, perfume, or other items are also used to celebrate other holidays. Cracking open a Cascarone egg above the head of a loved one is said to bring them many blessings, luck, love, and happiness in the coming year. Pagan witches use a Cascarone during their rituals and magic spells for similar purposes.

The Material You'll Need:

- Craft paint
- A dozen eggs
- Tape
- Paintbrushes
- Material for the filling
- A funnel

- Tissue paper
- A wooden spoon

Instructions:

1. Take a wooden spoon and crack one end of the egg slightly open. Be careful not to hit the egg with too much force so it would break open completely. If you are going to use the insides, make sure to wash the surface of the eggs before cracking them open.

2. Let the inside out, then rinse the inner walls of the egg with water. Do this by slowly adding soapy water from a cup and leaving the shells to soak for a couple of minutes.

3. Once the eggshells are clean, place them onto a tray and leave them to dry overnight.

4. Use paint to decorate the eggs with magical symbols, or however you like, then let everything dry again.

5. Place a small funnel at the shell's opening and add the filling to the egg. Once the eggs are full, stick a piece of tissue paper into the hole to prevent the inside from spilling out.

6. Use tape, paint, and craft decoration to cover the crack, and your Cascarone will be finished.

The most popular choice for filling used by witches is dried herbs. Due to their magical affinity, herbs have a strong association with spells and rituals - and can be a useful tool for enriching your witchcraft. By choosing the right herbs and plants for their filling, Cascarones can be turned into a magic spell or become part of any ritual. Some options include lily of the valley, lavender, marjoram, thyme, lilac, purple clover, rose hips, and sunflower seeds.

Chapter 5: Setting Up an Ostara Altar

One of the joys of Ostara is that it's a season when many people choose to create an altar for their practice. An Ostara altar can be as simple or elaborate as you want, with the only limitation being your budget and time.

What does one need for an Ostara altar? A lot of creativity and a little bit of knowledge. That's all the supplies needed to create a beautiful, spiritual, and sacred space for this spring holiday. To build your own Ostara altar, you should have items from nature such as fresh flowers or fragrant herbs, candles in appropriate colors (purple is typical), crystals corresponding to the sabbat energies (carnelian may be a good choice), eggs, seeds, and other objects representing qualities associated with Ostara.

The Significance of the Ostara Altar

An Ostara altar is a physical representation of the spiritual connection we make to the natural world. It can be used as a place to focus our prayers and intentions and connect with the divine. The items on your altar should be chosen specifically for this purpose and placed in such a way that they create an aesthetically pleasing display.

When setting up your altar, consider the following:

- What theme or feeling do you want to evoke with your altar?
- Which aspects of Ostara are most important to you?
- What objects or symbols represent these aspects?

Ostara Signifies Balance

Balance is an important theme during Ostara. It falls on the equinox when the day and the night are the same lengths.

This holiday represents the balance of night and day, winter and spring, darkness, and light, culminating in rebirth or resurrection. In nature, it means that before we can have new growth, there must be dormancy as well - this is represented by the time between Yule (Winter Solstice) and Ostara.

The equinox is a time of transition, and as such, your altar should reflect this. You may want to include both dark and light elements or images of the goddess in her various aspects. As the season progresses and we move closer to Beltane (May Day), your altar should become more celebratory with bright colors and symbols of new life.

An altar is a place where we can work on our personal balance by honoring all aspects of ourselves. We can include both light and dark symbols and items representing the feminine and masculine aspects within us. The most important thing is to be true to yourself and create an altar that feels authentic for you.

Ostara Is a Time of New Beginnings

For many, Ostara marks the beginning of the new year. It's a time when we can set our intentions and goals for the coming months and begin to put them into action. An altar is a great place to start, as it provides us with a space to focus on what we want to manifest in our lives.

The items on your altar can be used as visual reminders of your intentions, and you can write these down and place them near your altar for daily contemplation. As you work towards your goals, it's important to stay positive and focused, and the Ostara altar can help keep you on track.

Themes for an Ostara Altar

There are many possible themes for an Ostara altar. Some of the most common are:

- Fertility
- Growth
- New Beginnings

- Springtime
- Joy
- Rebirth

When choosing a theme, it's important to consider the qualities you want to invoke during this time of year. If you're looking for increased fertility in your life, then an altar with symbols of fertility on it is one way to help achieve that goal. It's also important to make sure the items you choose for your altar appeal aesthetically and spiritually.

Choosing Items for Your Altar

When selecting items for your altar, there are a few things to keep in mind:

- The colors of the candles, crystals, and other objects should correspond with the energies of Ostara.

- Choose objects that represent qualities or aspects of the holiday that are important to you.

- Make sure the altar is aesthetically pleasing to you.

- Consider the space you have available for your altar and choose accordingly.

If possible, try to gather items from nature to use on your altar. This can include things like fresh flowers, branches, or leaves. If you're not able to get outside, consider using items that represent nature, such as pictures or artwork.

The Ostara Altar: Practical Considerations

Depending on your space and budget, an altar can be as big or as small as you want it to be. If you're looking for a place of honor in the home to set up an elaborate display, then consider one of these options:

- Create a permanent altar in a place of honor like your living room. This allows you to build upon it each year and continuously create new memories for your family.

- If space is an issue, consider setting up an altar on the ground floor of your home where everyone can see it as they pass by. You might want to set aside one evening per week (or more) to spend time at the altar and focus on your Ostara rituals.

- If you're traveling or don't have a lot of space, consider creating a small, portable altar that can be easily packed up and transported with you. This could include a few simple items like a candle, some crystals, and an egg.

How to Use Your Ostara Altar

Once you've created your Ostara altar, it's time to start using it! Here are a few ideas:

- Place fresh flowers or herbs on the altar as an offering to the natural world.

- Light candles and incense to create a sacred space for meditation and prayer.

- Set out specific items and focus on them one at a time.

- Place an item you regularly use (like your athame) in the center of the altar as a way to connect with it every day.

- If there are children in your home, consider placing toys or games on the altar for them to play with when they visit. (Just make sure to clear the items off before using the altar for a more serious purpose).

- Place pictures of loved ones who have passed away on your altar. Make sure they're displayed in an area where everyone can see them. This is a wonderful way to honor their memory during Ostara and beyond. Many people also choose this time to release any grief or sadness they may be feeling.

- Draw a tarot card every day from the Ostara Tarot deck and use it as a focus for your altar rituals.

Creating an altar is a wonderful way to connect with the energies of Ostara and create a sacred space for yourself during this time of year. It can be as simple or as elaborate as you want it to be, and there are no rules that say you have to use it in a certain way. Have fun with it, and let your creativity flow!

Elements of the Ostara Altar

As you prepare for Ostara, think about the types of objects that are most important to your holiday rituals. These could include:

- Pictures and artwork representing fertility – This can be anything from images of goddesses like Ishtar or Freya to flowers in bloom (such as tulips). The idea is to choose symbols that appeal aesthetically to you and make you feel connected to the holiday.

- Candles in colors that correspond with Ostara, such as yellow, green, or pink

- Crystals representing new beginnings, growth, and fertility, such as amethyst, rose quartz, or peridot

- Items related to nature, such as branches, leaves, or flowers
- Herbs and spices to add a scent that connects you with the holiday, such as cinnamon sticks, pine needles, or mint leaves
- Fresh fruits like pomegranates (to celebrate Persephone), apples (for their symbolism throughout history), or oranges (symbolizing abundance) – you can also use chocolate eggs, a popular symbol of Ostara.
- Anything else that feels special to you and has a personal meaning related to the holiday.

Here are some more details on colors, gemstones, and flowers associated with Ostara.

Colors of Ostara

There are a few colors that are associated with Ostara, and you may want to consider using them in your altar decorations:

- **Green** is the color of new beginnings and growth. It represents the fertile earth that is coming back to life after winter.
- **Yellow** is the color of sunshine and happiness. It symbolizes the bright future that awaits us all.
- **Orange** is the color of warmth and vitality. It represents the fires of spring that bring new life to the world.
- **Pink** is the color of love and compassion. It reminds us of the importance of giving kindness to others during this time of year.
- **Purple** is the color of royalty and magick. It represents the power and mystery of Ostara.

Using these colors in your altar decorations can help to connect you more deeply with the energies of this season. Have fun experimenting with them!

Gemstones of Ostara

There are also a few gemstones associated with this holiday:

- **Amethyst** is the stone of spirituality and healing. It helps to promote calmness and clarity during times of stress. This can be especially helpful if you're going through any major life changes at this time, such as moving or having children! If your usual coping mechanisms aren't working, try bringing an amethyst with you to help restore your peace of mind.

- **Aquamarine** is the stone of courage and intuition. It can be used to increase feelings of empathy in difficult situations, which may come up during this time if there are children or family members who have a new baby (or babies).

- **Diamonds** are the stone of clarity and truth. You can wear a diamond or carry one in your pocket to help you see things clearly during this time, especially when making important decisions about your life path.

- **Emerald** is the stone of prosperity and growth. It helps us develop new ideas that we may not have had before.

- **Rose quartz** is the stone of love and nurturing. It can be used to promote feelings of compassion in others as well, which may come up during this holiday if you're dealing with young children or family members who have a new baby (or babies).

Birch Trees

Birch trees are often associated with Ostara because they represent new beginnings and growth. It also signifies love and fertility. If you have a birch tree nearby, consider using some of its branches in your altar decorations. You can also use dried leaves or flowers from other plants to create a similar effect. A birch besom (broom) can be used to spread the energies of Ostara around your home.

Lavender Flowers and Sprigs

Sprigs of lavender are often associated with this holiday, too. Like other flowers mentioned in this section, they're commonly used for their scent during rituals involving love and fertility (such as weddings). However, these flowers can also be used to promote relaxation and peace of mind. If you're feeling overwhelmed during this time, consider using a sprig of lavender on your altar or carrying it with you as a talisman.

What Cloth to Use for the Altar

If you have a white tablecloth, that would be perfect! If not, try using a piece of cotton fabric in any color. White or off-white colors are usually associated with Ostara, and they can help promote peace and clarity during this time.

White Candles for the Altar

Candle Magic is commonly associated with Ostara. You can use white candles to increase the energies of new beginnings and growth mentioned earlier in this post (for example, by increasing your confidence or self-esteem). If you have a specific goal for which you'd like more support during this time (such as getting pregnant), try placing a candle on top of a picture or drawing of that goal.

The Importance of the Rabbit in Ostara

The rabbit is a symbol of Ostara because it represents prosperity. In some cultures, it's also seen as a sign of fertility. If you feel drawn to this animal, you may want to consider including a statue or picture of a rabbit on your altar.

Eggs as Symbols of Ostara

Another common symbol associated with Ostara is the egg. This represents new beginnings, growth, and fertility. If you're trying to get pregnant, you may want to decorate your altar with eggs (or use them in candle magic) as a way of increasing those energies.

How Long Should You Keep the Altar?

There's no right or wrong answer to this question! Some people prefer to set up their altar and then take it down immediately after the holiday has passed. Others like to keep it up for a few weeks or even months as a reminder of the energies present during this time. Some others prefer to only use it during certain rituals and celebrations, such as Beltane (or May Day), which is often celebrated around this time in various cultures across the world. It all depends on what feels best for you.

If you are using perishable items on your altar (such as flowers or fruits), it's a good idea to take them down after a few days so that they don't go bad.

What Else Can Be Added to the Altar?

There are endless possibilities when it comes to adding items to your Ostara altar! You can use anything that feels special to you and represents the holiday's energies to you. Some other items that you may want to consider include:

- Stones such as amethyst, rose quartz, or moonstone
- A pentacle or other symbol of the five elements
- Herbs such as lavender, chamomile, or mint
- Feathers from a bird you like
- A handmade (or store-bought) wreath or crown made of flowers and/or plant materials
- Pictures, statues, or drawings that represent your goals for this time of year, such as getting pregnant; it can also be fun to include pictures of family members who have passed on!

It's important to note that you don't have to use all of these items if you don't want to. You can also add personal touches and symbols representing the energies, goals, or qualities you're looking for during this time of year! As mentioned earlier, the point is not really what's included on the altar as long as it feels right for you and helps manifest the qualities you want in your life.

If You're a Nature Lover...

There tend to be many opportunities for doing outdoor activities during this time of year, which can make it extra special for people who love nature and being outdoors! Try adding something related to nature (a plant or tree branch) to your altar if that sounds like you. You can also create a little vignette using items from nature, such as leaves and flowers that you've picked during walks outside.

Final Thoughts

What's included on your Ostara altar is up to you! The most important thing is that it helps you feel good and supports the manifestation of positive energies in your life. There is no right or wrong way to do things, so go with what feels best for you and enjoy the process!

Chapter 6: Magical Ostara Recipes

No celebration is complete without festive food. We can't celebrate a festival without serving some delicious mouth-watering dishes. Every celebration has certain dishes associated with it. For instance, can you imagine Thanksgiving without turkey? Is the 4th of July complete without apple pie? Certain foods make festivals, well, more festive. The Ostara festival is no different.

If this is your first time celebrating the Ostara festival, you probably want to serve some special dishes that will be perfect for this occasion. This chapter will bring you a few very delicious recipes that will make your guests rave about the food.

Many different ingredients go into making Ostara dishes. However, you'll find that some ingredients are used more than others, such as ham, eggs, mint, and spring produce. Eggs and Ostara share a connection because eggs have been considered a symbol of birth since ancient times. Christians were the first people to eat eggs during festivals like Easter, which they still do up to this day. They even make the eggs look more festive by dyeing and painting them. Therefore, to honor the spring festival, it makes sense to incorporate this symbol of rebirth and fertility in many recipes and eat it as a meal.

Ham is another ingredient that you'll find in many recipes. This is because our ancestors would use the preserved meat at the beginning of the spring. Another popular ingredient is mint, and it is incorporated in so many dishes because it symbolizes magic and wealth. Additionally, some people consider mint to have fertility energy, and its bright color makes it perfect for spring dishes. We will also use some seasonal fruits and vegetables in our recipes because they are abundant at this time of year. Chives are another popular ingredient because they have many benefits. They help lower your blood pressure and can be used as a remedy for ailments like lung congestion, cold, and the flu. Chives are also believed to be magical because they protect against diseases and evil spirits.

Recipes for Ostara Dishes

Deviled Eggs

Some people think that the word deviled is associated with or derived from the word "devil." However, there is no connection between the two words. The word deviled was first used in the 18th century to describe hot and spicy food.

We are starting with deviled eggs because they are incredibly easy to make.

Ingredients:

- 6 big eggs
- 2 to 3 tablespoons of mayonnaise (preferably full-fat mayonnaise)
- 1 or 1½ teaspoon of Dijon mustard (this is optional if you aren't a fan of mustard - either use less than what is in the recipe or not at all)
- 2 teaspoons of chives that are finely cut
- 1 teaspoon of apple cider vinegar
- Salt and fresh pepper
- Paprika

Instructions:

1. Boil the eggs until they are hardened. Since we are using large eggs, you'll need to boil them for about 15 minutes. However, if you want to use small eggs, then 9 minutes will be enough
2. Leave the eggs for a few minutes to cool down

3. Peel the eggs and split them in half

4. Remove the yolks from the eggs

5. Next, you'll need to mix the yolk with the rest of the ingredients - mayonnaise, vinegar, mustard, salt and pepper, and chives

6. If you are a fan of spicy food, you can add a small amount of tabasco to the mixture

7. Scoop the mixture and put it in the egg whites

8. If you want to add colors to your eggs, then you can sprinkle a small amount of paprika into your dish

That said, if you want the eggs to be pink, then boil them a day in advance and leave them overnight in beetroot juice.

Hot Cross Buns

Hot cross buns are a delicious pastry that people have enjoyed for years.

Ingredients:
Dough

- 3 cups of flour
- ¾ cup of sugar
- 1 cup of whole milk
- ¼ cup of melted butter or margarine
- ⅛ teaspoon of salt
- 1½ teaspoons of cinnamon
- ¼ teaspoon of allspice (this ingredient is optional)
- 1 cup of raisins (this ingredient is also optional)
- 1 cup of walnuts (also optional)

- 28 grams of dry yeast
- ¼ cup of hot water to dissolve the dry yeast
- 1 large egg, well-beaten

Frosting:

- 1 cup of orange juice
- 1 tablespoon of milk
- 2 cups of confectioner's sugar

Instructions:

1. Preheat the oven to 375 degrees
2. Combine all of the dough ingredients, except the hot water, egg, and yeast
3. Add the hot water to the yeast and let it dissolve
4. After the yeast dissolves, add the egg and the mixture
5. Mix them well altogether
6. After you finish mixing all of the dough's ingredients, cover it with a piece of cloth and leave it for an hour to rise in a warm place
7. Now that the dough is ready, shape them into round balls about 3 inches across
8. Place the balls about 3 inches apart on a lightly greased cookie sheet or a jelly roll pan
9. Now put the dough sheet in the oven
10. Wait for about 5 to 8 minutes
11. Open the oven and remove the buns
12. Using a knife, cut ¾ of an inch down into the dough and carve equilateral crosses on top
13. After you are done, put the buns back in the oven, and leave them to bake for about 15 to 20 minutes
14. When they turn to a brown-gold color, this means that they are done, and you can remove them from the oven
15. During the 20 minutes when the buns are in the oven, you can start making the frosting
16. Mix all of the frosting ingredients together and beat them until they are smooth and consistent
17. Add the frosting on top of the buns after removing them from the oven. It is important to drizzle the frosting when the buns are still hot

sprout Salad

Now it is time to take advantage of some of the spring's delicious and beautifully colored vegetables.

Ingredients:

- 2 chopped green onions
- 2 cups of baby spinach
- 1 cup of mung bean sprouts
- 1 cup of alfalfa sprouts
- ½ cup of craisins and dried cherries
- ½ cup of slivered almonds
- 2 teaspoons of honey
- 2 teaspoons of Dijon mustard
- 1 can of mandarin oranges (this ingredient is optional)
- ½ cup of mayonnaise
- A dash of lemon juice
- Fresh dill

Instructions:

1. Get a plate or a bowl
2. Place the baby spinach first so they will be at the bottom
3. Next, add the sprouts
4. Make sure that you spread the sprouts on the plate so they don't get clumped
5. Sprinkle the dill, almonds, craisins, green onions, and the mandarin oranges (if you aren't going to use them, then simply sprinkle the other ingredients and leave this one out)

6. Now prepare the dressing

7. Mix the honey, mustard, lemon juice, and mayonnaise well together

8. Drizzle the dressing over the salad

We know that some people don't enjoy the taste of mustard so much. In this case, you can add any dressing you want instead. Additionally, if you aren't a big fan of mayonnaise, you can use less of the amounts mentioned in the ingredients. If you are leading a healthy lifestyle and don't want to use mayonnaise, you can opt for white yogurt instead. This dressing can also be a very delicious dip for chicken fingers that your children will surely love.

Roasted Lamb

After winter is over and to welcome the warm spring, our ancestors would prefer to have lambs as the first spring meal, making this dish perfect for Ostara.

Ingredients:

- 1 cup of white cooking wine
- 1 teaspoon of rosemary, chopped
- 2 cloves of minced garlic
- 2 teaspoons of olive oil
- ½ cup of orange juice
- Pepper and sea salt
- Leg of lamb

Instructions:

1. First, you'll prepare the marinade
2. Mix all of the ingredients in a bowl except for the lamb

3. Using a whisk, blend them together
4. Put the mixture in a plastic bag
5. Put the leg of lamb with the mixture in the bag
6. Leave it overnight
7. Make sure that the lamb is at room temperature
8. Take it out of the bag and put it in a roasting pan
9. Pour the marinade juice as well
10. Put the roasting pan in the oven and let it bake at 450 degrees
11. Let the lamb roast for about an hour
12. After it is done, remove it from the oven and put it on a rack
13. Cover it with a foil and let it sit in the marinade juices for about 20 minutes
14. Now, it is ready to be served

You mustn't overcook your lamb. When you take it out of the oven, the middle should still be pink. Additionally, letting the lamb sit in its juice for 20 minutes is essential to prevent the meat from drying out.

Mint Chutney

At the beginning of this chapter, we have mentioned how important mint is and how it is used in various recipes. Using mint in this recipe makes this sauce a great addition to various spring and Ostara meals. It can go with many dishes, and it is perfect for the roasted leg lamb that we have just mentioned. It can also go with bread, vegetables, spicy food, pasta, and Mediterranean food, or you can simply eat it with a spoon because it is that delicious.

Ingredients:
- 1 small, chopped onion
- ½ cup of cilantro, fresh

- ½ cup of chopped red pepper
- ½ cup of parsley, fresh
- ½ cup of chopped green pepper
- 3 cups of mint leaves, fresh
- ¼ or ½ cup of olive oil
- ½ teaspoon of sea salt
- A dash of lemon juice
- Water

Instructions:

1. Blend all of the ingredients until they form a paste
2. Gradually add water to the mix in the blender to thin the paste out
3. Keep blending the paste and water together until it becomes smooth
4. You can either serve it right away or put it in the fridge to serve later

Ostara Peep Ambrosia

Ostara peep ambrosia is a dessert that is very easy to make. It is the perfect dish for the Ostara celebration.

Ingredients:

- 2 cans of pineapple tidbits
- 2 cups of shredded coconut flakes
- 2 cans of mandarin oranges
- 2 bananas, chopped
- 1 package of 12 marshmallow peeps
- 1 jar of maraschino cherries
- 1.75 grams of cottage cheese
- 1.5 grams of any dessert topping

Instructions:

1. Cut the peeps into small pieces
2. Squeeze the juice from the fruits mentioned in the ingredients
3. Combine and mix all of the ingredients together
4. Leave the mixture in the fridge for a few hours
5. Take it out of the fridge and serve it as a dessert

Lemon Bread

Ostara is during the time of year when the earth is just waking up excited to welcome the spring. It is the time of year when beautiful vegetables, fruits, and flowers start to bloom. It represents rebirth. The lemon bread is perfect for this theme as it reflects re-emergence.

Ingredients:

- 1 package of any lemon bread recipe (prepare the ingredients on the package)
- ½ cup of dried cranberries
- ½ cup of golden raisins
- 1 teaspoon of orange zest
- Vanilla ice cream
- A ring
- A shiny coin
- A crystal
- A piece of silver or gold jewelry

(These last four items will be added to the bread as a surprise gift)

Instructions:

1. Prepare the mixture of the bread as directed
2. After everything is mixed together, start adding the ingredients
3. Add the golden raisins
4. Add the orange zest
5. Add the dried cranberries
6. Fold in the crystal, coin, or ring, making sure to wash them first
7. Whatever items you choose, they must not melt in the oven
8. Bake the bread according to the directions on the packaging
9. Take it out of the oven
10. Leave it until it cools down
11. Add powdered sugar or any glaze that you prefer (this step is optional)
12. Add a scoop of vanilla ice cream on top of each piece
13. Slice the bread

Before serving the bread, you should let your guests know that you have hidden gifts inside so they don't choke on them. That said, if you are making this bread for small children, you should opt-out of putting any treasures or anything in the bread that they may choke on. This bread can work as an appetizer or snack.

Roast Potatoes with Rosemary

Ingredients:

- 700 grams of new potatoes
- 2 cloves of minced garlic
- 2 tablespoons of olive oil
- 1½ tablespoon of chopped rosemary, chopped
- ½ tablespoon of salt

Instructions:

1. Add water to the potatoes, make sure that the water covers all of them
2. Bring the potatoes to a simmer
3. Cook the potatoes for 5 minutes
4. Heat the potatoes until they feel dry on the outside
5. Add the rest of the ingredients - rosemary, olive oil, garlic, and salt
6. Put the potatoes in a pan in one layer
7. Put them in the oven
8. Bake them at 180 degrees
9. Leave them for about 15 to 20 minutes
10. When they look brown and crispy, it means that they are done

Lemon and Lavender Cake

This delicious cake is perfect for the Ostara festival and celebrating spring's arrival.

Instructions:

- 2 eggs
- 1½ cup of self-rising flour
- 1 teaspoon of lavender
- 1 lemon
- ½ teaspoon of vanilla extract
- ½ cup of butter
- ½ cup of sugar
- ⅛ teaspoon of salt
- ¼ cup of milk

Cake Liquor Ingredients:

- ⅞ cup of powdered sugar
- 1.5 lemons, juiced

Cake Glaze Ingredients:

- ½ cup of powdered sugar
- ½ lemon, juiced

Instructions:

1. Preheat the oven to 355 degrees
2. Get a 8 x 4 loaf pan
3. Butter the pan
4. Get a large bowl and add the half cup of sugar and the half cup of butter
5. Next, add the lemon zest and the 2 eggs
6. Then add the salt, vanilla extract, teaspoon of lavender, and the 1½ cups of flour
7. Mix all of them together
8. Add milk to the mixture
9. Stir until the mixture becomes thick
10. Put the mixture in the buttered pan
11. Bake it for about 45 minutes

12. Before the caking finish baking with about 10 minutes, start preparing the cake liquor
13. Add the 1.5 lemon juice and the ⅞ cup of powdered sugar in a small bowl
14. After the cake finished baking, poke a few holes on top of it, and pour the liquor on the cake while it is still hot
15. Let it cool in the pan
16. Now, prepare the glaze
17. Mix half of the lemon juice with the 1½ cup of powdered sugar in a small bowl
18. When the cake is cooled down, you can spread the glaze over it
19. Decorate it with one teaspoon of lavender

Lemon and Herb Cauliflower

The lemon and herb cauliflower can be a great side dish for the Ostara celebration.

Ingredients:
- 3 heads of cauliflower (try to opt for different colors)
- 1½ teaspoon of thyme, chopped
- 1 teaspoon of chopped basil
- 1 teaspoon of chopped parsley
- ⅓ cup of olive oil
- ½ teaspoon of black pepper
- ½ teaspoon of salt
- 2 lemons, juiced
- 1 lemon zest

Instructions:

1. You need to preheat the oven to 425 degrees
2. Wash the cauliflower, then trim it
3. Chop the florets into small pieces, make sure that the pieces are equal in size
4. Put the thyme parsley, basil, and olive oil in a large bowl
5. Put the cauliflower in the bowl
6. Mix together
7. The cauliflower florets must be all coated with the herbs and olive oil
8. Get a large, rimmed baking sheet
9. Line the sheet evenly with parchment paper
10. Sprinkle the pepper, salt, and lemon zest
11. Squeeze the lemon juice
12. Let it bake for about 40 to 50 minutes
13. When the cauliflowers are done, they will become brown
14. Take it out of the oven
15. Sprinkle it with the chopped parsley

You can use other herbs and spices if you want to experiment with something different.

Spinach and Feta Quiche

We have mentioned that eggs and spring vegetables are some of the main ingredients of many Ostara dishes. Therefore, combining them will make the perfect dish for the Ostara celebrations.

Ingredients:

Crust:

- 215 grams of all-purpose flours
- 3 tablespoons of cold water
- ¾ of kosher salt
- 170 grams of diced cold unsalted butter

Filling:

- 6 large eggs
- ¾ cup of soft cream cheese (make sure that it is room temperature)
- 283 grams of frozen chopped spinach, thawed
- ⅓ cup of each heavy cream and whole milk
- 100 grams of goat feta
- 1 teaspoon of kosher salt
- 1 cup of grated cheddar
- ½ teaspoon of ground black pepper
- 8 thinly sliced green onions
- ½ cup of grated Parmesan cheese
- Non-stick spray oil

Instructions:

Crust:

1. Blend the salt and flour in a food processor
2. Add butter
3. Add water while the machine is running
4. Stop once the dough is balled
5. Next, wrap the dough in plastic paper and put it in the freezer
6. Leave it for about 15 to 20 minutes
7. You want the dough to be firm, not hard
8. Get a 9x13 inch pan
9. Coat it lightly with oil
10. Add parchment paper at the bottom
11. Place the dough in the pan and press it in an even layer
12. Press the dough all around and let it extend a little over the edge of the pan

13. Now put the dough in the freezer again for about 20 minutes until it becomes solid

Filling:

1. Preheat the oven to 425 degrees
2. Get a large sheet of foil and coat it lightly with spray oil
3. Wait until the crust becomes solid
4. Then prick the crust using a fork and press the oiled side of the foil down against the dough
5. Fill the crust with rice, pie weights, or dried beans
6. Let it bake for about 20 minutes
7. Remove the weights and foil slowly and gently
8. Put it back in the oven and let it bake for 5 minutes or more
9. Now, prepare the filling using a whisk or an eclectic mixer
10. Beat the cream cheese until it becomes smooth
11. Slowly add the whole milk and heavy cream
12. Don't stop mixing
13. Whisk the eggs, two at a time
14. Squeeze the moisture out of the spinach
15. Break the feta and add it to the mixture
16. Stir in with the salt and pepper, cheddar, scallions, spinach, and parmesan
17. Don't turn off the oven after the crust finishes baking
18. Pour the filling on top of the crust
19. Bake the quiche for about 25 minutes until the crust becomes golden-brown and the filling is set
20. Leave it for about 10 minutes to cool down

Chickpea and Marjoram Frittata

Ingredients:

- 1 cup of cooked chickpeas
- 1 minced garlic clove
- 1 Spanish onion
- 4 eggs
- ½ cup of grated cheese
- ½ cup of milk

- Marjoram leaves
- Sea salt and black pepper

Instructions:

1. Slice the onion
2. Fry the sliced onions in butter or oil
3. Add the salt, pepper, and garlic
4. Now, remove it from the stove and thoroughly stir the herbs
5. Add the chickpeas
6. Keep stirring to combine the ingredients well
7. Pour the mixture into a pie dish
8. Now, add the grated cheese and the herbs
9. Beat the eggs
10. Stir in the milk
11. Then put them over the onions and chickpeas
12. Preheat the oven to 200 degrees
13. Put the mixture in the oven
14. Leave it to bake for about 20 minutes
15. When it is golden and firm, it means it is done

The great thing about making a frittata is that you can get creative with the ingredients and add whatever you want. For instance, if you are a vegetarian or a vegan, you can add rocket, corn kernel, or sweet potato. Meat lovers can also add salmon or ham. There are many spring vegetables to choose from, so play around and experiment with the ingredients you want.

Honey Fritter Cake

Ingredients:

- 2 eggs
- 2 teaspoons of cinnamon
- 2 tablespoons of honey (you can add more if you want to)
- 1 cup of milk
- 1 cup of self-rising flour

Instructions:

1. Using a fork, mix the milk, eggs, and honey together
2. Add the flour
3. Lightly mix the ingredients

4. Avoid over beating the ingredients, or they will become hard

5. Add the cinnamon (you can add other spices if you want)

6. Get a frying pan

7. Grease it lightly with butter or oil (preferable macadamia oil)

8. Heat the frying pan

9. Add spoonfuls of the mixture to the pan

10. Cook each side lightly

The right meal can make or break a festive celebration. If you are going to invite your friends and family to celebrate this magical Ostara with you, you need to choose dishes that reflect this beautiful occasion. Luckily, there are various fruits and vegetables waiting to be plucked and added to your ingredients at the beginning of spring. The recipes mentioned here will help you out when preparing meals for your first Ostara with your loved ones. Remember that you can always experiment with the ingredients. You are the chef here.

While preparing your meals, you should set intentions for the food you want to create. Setting intentions is a lot similar to praying but without formality. You choose the kind of experience you wish to have, which will help put you in the right direction. We cook almost every day, so it becomes more of a habit. We never really think beforehand about the kind of experience we want to have while cooking or our relationship with the food we are making.

Before you prepare your Ostara meal, get a pen and paper, and write down what you want to achieve from this meal: healing, nourishment, energy, or connecting with your family. Now take a look at what you wrote and choose the intention calling to you. For instance, if you hope that this meal will help you connect with your family, then set the intention "this meal will help me connect with my family" before preparing the meal. Setting an intention will help you choose the appropriate food and ingredients. It will also deepen your relationship with food because you'll see it as more than just a meal but as a method to help you achieve your goals.

Chapter 7: Magical Gardening

Ostara is a Wiccan holiday that marks the celebration of the return to life, renewal of the earth, and light. Being one of the eight Sabbats, Eostre represents spring and new beginnings. This time of the year marks the beginning of the farming cycle when farmers would begin to plant seeds. One way of celebrating Ostara or the renewal of the earth is to practice magical gardening.

The chapter discusses how you create garden charms to bless the soil in your garden, do seed blessings, and create magical fertilizers. It also highlights the instructions for creating the miniature greenhouse to grow Ostara herbs and other plants. The last section of the chapter provides a list of Ostara plants, herbs, and flowers. It also recommends magical ways to use each one.

Garden Charms

When preparing your magic garden, you should first consider blessing it with charms you'll bury in the soil. The following are some of the appropriate charms you can consider for your magic garden.

- Dried fruits preserved from the previous season
- Small pieces of apple to display the pentacle
- Solar symbols
- A Goddess figuring in wood, clay, or other organic materials
- Horns dedicated to the Horned God
- Whole eggs
- Yonic or phallic symbols
- Quartz crystals are associated with fertility and the energy of the Goddesses, such as Moss Agate, Rosophia, Gaia Stone, Citrine, Green Fluorite, Unakite, and others.

You must consecrate and bless your preferred items depending on your preferences. A quick way to bless a statue is to breathe life into it and make sure you do that with an intention. You can also perform a quick consecration with the charms, which you can bury at the corners of your garden. If you have a single charm, you can bury it at the center of your garden.

You must visualize the charms as providing the energy of fertility to the soil, promoting the growth of the plants, and delineating barriers that pests cannot cross. You can also consider other sympathetic and statuary charms like garden gnomes. This sympathetic magic is effective since it can attract nature spirits. You can also add a variety of garden decorations, including butterflies, bees, faeries, glass witch balls, wind chimes, and wreaths.

Old Magic

Other forms of old charm you can consider for your garden include broom leaping, dancing, or sex in groups or couples near the garden space. However, you should make your intention clear for embarking on these practices.

Deities

If you want to request blessings of deities in your garden, there are different options you can consider. Some of them include the following:

- Ceres
- Blodeuwedd
- Danu
- The Dagda
- Dionysus

- Demeter
- Freyr
- Kokopelli
- Isis
- Hermes (god of boundaries)
- Inari Okami
- Inanna/Ishtar
- Mars
- Kouzin Zaka
- Modron
- Meztli
- Osiris
- Pachamama
- Pomona
- Persephone
- Priapus
- Xochipilli
- Xochiquetzal

When you decide to use these deities in your garden, make sure you don't just randomly pick something. Before you choose any of these deities, it is better to do some research and learn something about their traditional offerings to help you make an informed decision. You should conduct background checks to see if there is anything that makes the deity odd. For example, the Mesoamerican deities used to be associated with human sacrifice, while Dionysus used to be known as driving people into cannibalism. Therefore, you must get an idea of what each deity represents before you get it.

Magical Fertilizer

Another vital component you should consider for your garden is magical fertilizer. There are different things you can sprinkle over your garden soil or mix with fertilizer or compost to promote growth in your garden. The following are some of the items you can consider.

- Broken eggshells, particularly Easter eggs
- Mead

- Consecrate wine
- Consecrated milk
- Handfasting or wedding cake
- Animal bones from meals (You can clean the bones first and draw magical symbols to bless them. You also need to enlist the influence of the animal spirits they belong to
- Consecrated food
- Yule tree remains
- Menstrual blood or semen (collect it using biodegradable material

You can also add some invocation as you prepare your magical fertilizer, like: "I call upon the earth's spirits."

Magical Gardening

When you have prepared all the fundamental tasks, the next step is to move to the fun part of magical gardening. This is a rewarding magical activity, but it involves some work, and plants do not grow randomly. You need to prepare the garden and the herbs you'll grow in your garden. You should consider various factors if you want to grow a successful magical garden.

Hardiness Zones

When you undertake a magical project, you should begin with non-magical things. In the case of preparing a garden, you should know the hardiness zone you are in. This includes the type of weather or climate in your area. You can use a map to gain insight into the zone where you belong. The climate in your area will determine the types of plants you can grow in your area. Other plants perform well in dry climates, while others prefer wet conditions. Therefore, choose herbs and flowers that suit the climatic conditions in your area.

Soil Type

There are different types of soils, and they are suitable for various plants. Common soil types include loam, dry soil, clay, hard, crossroads dirt, and others. You should have your soil tested first if you plan to start gardening inside or outside your yard. Your Home depot or garden supply store can test your soil to determine its pH to suit what you want to plant. Depending on the soil type, you may need to mix an additive, and you should also know how the soil traps moisture. For instance, sandy soil does not hold moisture longer, and clay soil requires plants with strong roots to break it.

Little Sunshine

All plants require a certain amount of sunshine every day to enhance growth. Other plants require full sun in different climates, while others can thrive in cool conditions. You should ascertain that the area where you plan to place your plants receives sufficient light. Note that the afternoon sun is more intense than morning sunlight. Make sure you choose the best location in your yard for your magical garden.

Determine the Purpose of Your Garden

You should determine the purpose of your garden like any other magical work. Define the reasons why you want to start a magical garden. Other people grow it to attract fairies, while others grow herbs to use in their workings. After you've determined your intention, you'll need to look for plants that fit your specific purpose. If you visit your local garden store, you'll find seed packs that match your specific theme.

Choose Your Seeds

When choosing your seeds, you need to remember if you'll keep them in a container or transplant them into your garden. You must do some research to determine the herbs that do well indoors or outdoors. If you buy heirloom seeds, you can regrow them the following year. GMO plants cannot produce seeds that you can use the following cropping season. If you want to create a green witch's paradise, you can consider strictly medicinal seeds. Apart from getting the desired seeds, you should also acquire pots to plant them, a pen and paper to write your intention, newspaper, or cardboard to lay on the floor if you want to grow your seeds inside.

Seeding for Success

When you acquire the preferred seeds, the next step is to plant them according to the instructions provided on the package. You should trust that your intention will succeed. If you want to plant outside, you need to create a small nursery for your seeds first. You must have a paper where you plot the growth stages of the plants until they mature. Have a map about how you'll plant the flowers or herbs and keep a timeline for transplanting them if you use an outside magic garden. There are different ideas you can consider when planning your magic garden.

You need to decorate your altar, home, or sacred space with the things that align with the Spring season. For instance, you can consider flowers like tulips, pussy willows, hyacinths, or anything from nature. Include colored eggs for fertility, citrine, and crystals such as rose quartz, green aventurine, aquamarine, and amethyst. If you want to use candles, green, pink, and yellow colors will be great.

Cleanse and Ground

When you prepare your nursery, you must cleanse and ground the space where you would like to plant the herbs or flowers. You can do this by smudging with incense or herbs or using your favorite essential oils such as rose, geranium, neroli, and lemon. Any material you use should pass through mist or smoke. Sit or stand, then start to create a connection with your breath. You should breathe slowly and consciously and make sure you feel your nervous system calming. Your body movement also needs to slow down when performing the cleansing and grounding ceremony.

You should meditate on your intention for your Spring magic garden, where you outline what you want to achieve. At this moment, you should feel your intention developing and growing inside your body. You should be ready to embody the creation you are making on this particular Equinox. You should ask for insight, clarity, and guidance. It is important to remain quiet so that answers can emerge from within. Write your intention down when you are clear about what you want to achieve.

Visualize

The next step is to hold your seeds and try to visualize your intention if it can come to fruition. You must not doubt your intention but feel the joy, excitement, peace, and pride. You should also feel the energy of wholeness, which you should use to feed the seeds, so they bear fruit. Remember to whisper your intention to the seeds as if you are sharing a secret.

Bless Your Soil

It is essential to bless the soil first, and you can achieve this by establishing communication with it. Dip your fingers into the earth and feel its liveness. This will transfer waves of gratitude and blessings into the soil where you'll plant your seeds. Blessing the soil also helps promote the fruition of your plants.

Plant Your Seeds

When you have blessed the soil, you can move on to plant your intention. Place the written intention at the bottom of the pot. Do the same if you use crystal and cover it with soil. Choose the day that corresponds with your intention before planting your seeds. You can cast your circle around your garden and call different elements of deities to help your garden thrive. You can also create a garden guardian, which you can place among the plants.

Another crucial thing you should know is that plants love music. Therefore, you can play your favorite music when growing the plants to raise power that will enhance growth. When planting seeds in the nursery, make sure to place them in a way that will allow them to sprout easily. You must push them to the depth in the soil as stated on the packet. While planting your seeds, you need to keep on stating your intention. Tell the seeds your intention to make them feel loved and appreciated. This also helps you transfer the energy you have requested into the seeds.

Once the seeds are planted, walk around the area, and introduce your guardian to the seeds and your intention. Your guardian in spiritual form should also tell you where you should plant the seedlings once they germinate. Keep on watering the seeds and sending gratitude and blessings to your seeds. Gently water the seeds to ensure you do not disturb them.

Transplant the Seeds

If you intend to grow your plants in an outdoor garden, you should transplant them when they are ready. When the enchanted seedlings are established and are free from the risk of weather elements such as frost, you can plant them in your garden. You can replant your written intention in the garden if you feel like doing so. Another important aspect to consider is having a diagram when planting the seedlings in the garden. Ensure they have enough space to grow and are not congested. As the plants grow, their foliage will also expand, and it can impact growth if there is no space.

Care and Trust

As indicated earlier, you need to choose the best site for the garden in your yard. The plants in the garden should get sufficient sunlight. You can also add crystals in the soil or around the pots to enhance the growth of your plants. You must check on the newly grown plants in your garden daily so they grow with your intentions and goals. Make sure your seedlings don't get excessive water since this can impact growth. You must water them as instructed by professionals.

Be Patient

We don't know how the plants will grow in most cases, but we are certain they will. At this stage, you don't need to focus on how the plants will grow but on the outcome. Nature does not hurry, but it will bear fruit in everything grown. You must have trust and patience. All you need to do is take time to nurture your growing plants and your intentions. Try to revisit your goals every day and send love to your planted seeds. Visualize your goal and send gratitude to the plants in the garden.

Like any other earth magic, plants in your magical garden take time to grow and bloom. You may also encounter setbacks that can impact your intentions. For instance, weather elements can impact your garden in different ways, but you need to find ways to address the challenges to salvage your plants. Insects can also attack your garden, so you need to take appropriate steps to control them. In some instances, you'll realize that other plants can thrive while others simply die no matter how you try to look after them well.

How to Create a Miniature Greenhouse to Plant Ostara Herbs and Plants

If you do not have appropriate outdoor space for your outside garden, you can create a miniature greenhouse. If it is too cold outside to plant seeds outside, you can get started indoors, where your seedlings can thrive. You must plan ahead of time to know what you want to plant. It is essential to give the plants a head start to sprout ahead of schedule. When the warmer weather finally arrives, you can transfer the plants to their intended space.

You can make a small indoor greenhouse, and you'll need the following items to make it.

- Disposable baking pan consisting of a plastic lid
- Seeds
- Potting soil
- Small peat pots

You should start by preparing your baking pan. These baking pans are available in grocery stores, and they come in black or foil. Foil pans can reflect light better than the black ones, so try to get these if possible. If you use a black pan, make sure you line it using an aluminum foil sheet. This sheet will help reflect light so that it does not affect the plants.

You also need to poke holes at the bottom of the pan for drainage. Make sure the holes are not too big so the pan can retain some water and moisture. And make sure the holes are not too small, as this can lead to excessive moisture, which can cause root rotting. You can start with a few holes and add more later, depending on the growth rate of the plants.

When you have prepared your peat pots, fill them with potting soil and line them to fit inside the baking pan. Place a seed in the soil inside each pot and cover it. When you place seeds in each pot, mix everything with water.

Place the lid on the baking pan and put it on a sunny window. When the interior of the baking pan warms up in the sun, condensation will develop on the lid. The heat trapped from the sun and condensation will aid the seeds sprouting inside the peat pots placed in the baking pan.

Do not remove the lid to allow the plants to grow. If you want to remove the lid to water the plants, make sure you do it over a short period. You can watch your seeds begin to sprout, and this can take a few days or weeks, depending on the type of plants inside. When you feel your seedlings are ready, you can transplant them into your garden. You only need to place the peat pot with the seedling into the soil. However, make sure to arrange your peat pots strategically so that the plants are not congested, which can stunt growth.

Magical Gardening Plants and their Purpose

There are different plants you can consider for your magic garden, and they can be used for various purposes. Other herbs and flowers thrive indoors. The following are some plants you can grow inside your home and their purpose.

- **Rosemary:** This plant offers cleansing and protective qualities, and you can use them for magical purposes. If you want to purify your home, burn the dried leaves, and the smoke can do wonders.

- **Basil:** This plant brings happiness, prosperity, and love. Having it in your home in different states can help you enjoy a happy life.

- **Oregano:** Another plant that promotes tranquility, joy, and health. You can use it in different forms to enjoy its immense benefits.

- **Thyme:** This is a herb that promotes self-confidence and courage. When you burn it, it wards off negativity, and it can also bring good fortune.

- **Mint:** It helps improve verbal communication and adds power to your prayer and words. When you take the herb orally, it can break negativity, misfortune, and bad luck. You can cook with these herbs, use them to make tea, or perform other forms of magic.

On the other hand, the common witchy herbs you can grow in the garden include the following:

- **Mugwort:** This is a wonderful plant that promotes lucid and psychic dreams. It is good to dry and smudge with.

- **Calendula:** It promotes love and joyful energy and is amazing for making salves.

- **Rue:** This garden plant consists of protective and cleansing qualities. If you are looking for protection against unforeseen elements, you can use this plant.

- **Lavender:** Promotes quality sleep, calms your nerves, and offers relaxation. The plant also produces a nice scent with healing and soothing properties to the mind.

- **Yarrow:** It is used for divination and to protect the auric field. If you want to know something about the future, you can use this plant. The herb gives you insight into different things you can encounter.

- **Garden Sage:** This plant is used for protection and wisdom. It can help you make meaningful decisions in your life. It is great for teas and culinary purposes in different dishes.

Magical gardening is one way of celebrating Ostara, and it symbolizes the renewal of the earth. You should consider different things like creating garden charms, blessing the soil in your garden, and creating magical fertilizer. However, gardening takes time, commitment, and work, just like loving someone. You may not always achieve your desired goals, but you need to keep trying. Instead, you should learn from your mistakes if you are concerned about achieving your goals. You should also consider several things when preparing your garden, as highlighted in this section. The next chapter focuses on prayers, invocations, and chants.

Chapter 8: Prayers, Invocations, and Chants

Besides the craft projects you can participate in while preparing for the arrival of spring, you can also get in the spirit of Ostara by reading and reciting some prayers, invocations, and chants. Preparing for such a momentous occasion can be stressful - and there is a lot to think of, especially if this is your first time celebrating Ostara. By reciting some Ostara-related chants, everything can become much brighter. You'll become full of energy to do everything you need to prepare for spring. And by singing some upbeat poems and chants while preparing Ostara dishes or decorations, your move will improve even more. The time will fly, and your tasks will be done before you even realize it.

If you have children, this is the easiest way to involve them in the process - and by doing so, you'll have even more fun. If you don't, you can still persuade fellow witches or friends and family to join you. For those welcoming the Spring Equinox as solitary practitioners, singing Ostara chants can be a great way to keep their minds filled with jovial thoughts during this period. These promote positivity and fertility in magic and professional life alike.

If you want to draw magic from the awakening nature or Eostre herself, you'll need to invoke them with chants and prayers. Since they require the focusing of your mind, chanting invocations and prayers for Ostara is the best way to get in tune with the true spirit of this sabbat. Prayers work best if recited in front of the altar or during meditation - when you are in a relaxed state of mind. They can help you form a deeper connection with nature and the spiritual world, particularly at this time of the year. By celebrating this season, you are bestowing a great honor to the greatest forces in the universe. In turn, they will allow you to synchronize your magic with Ostara's.

Preparing for Chanting Prayers, Invocations, and Chants

There isn't much preparation for chanting Ostara poems and songs, except learning the words and the meaning of each poem or song. After that, you'll be ready to break into your favorite Ostara song whenever the mood strikes you. Or you can organize a reading session with your fellow witches or social circle and read the poems aloud.

Now, with prayers, the situation is a little bit different. Prayers can invoke the most powerful magic on the exact day of the Spring Equinox. If you can, this is the best time to chant them. If you have decided to learn them just shortly before the arrival of this date - and you aren't able to recite the prayer just yet (or aren't confident enough to do so), you may do it after the spring has officially arrived. You are free to decide what feels right for you at a time, so you can determine when to start saying the prayer of your choice. Most prayers aren't for one-time use only, and you can repeat them as many times and whenever you feel like doing it. That being said, it's not advised to recite Ostara prayers with intent before the arrival of spring. No matter how you may be tempted by the warm weather and the bright sun, it's best to wait and only practice the prayer. If you are really inspired by seeing nature, come back to life, you may chant some invocations to natural spirits or Eostre. They won't mind being honored by you seeking them out and asking them to help you throughout the year that comes. Prayers, however, often have very different purposes. While they can also be used for asking for guidance, more often than not, they contain praises and words of gratitude. These have the purpose of further ensuring the help from the entity the prayer is directed to. This is another compelling reason for reciting them only when their magic is most powerful.

Stay still for a couple of more minutes after prayer, and reflect on how you feel. If you have used a smaller candle, you may let it burn out, and if you have used a larger one, save it for your next prayer. It's also a good idea to keep a symbol of the subject of your prayers nearby after your prayer. This will infuse it with your energy, making it more powerful for using them in spells.

Prayer for Ostara

On Ostara, the time of birth and rebirth,

Help me reconnect with what comes to life,

Help me receive the energizing magic of Nature and Earth,

So, when they come alive, I can do the same.

Help me recharge my magic,

Through the fertile energy that's taking over,

Until it becomes one with me,

And mine become one with it.

I am ready to accept a new path

So, bless me with a new life

And help me spread it around me.

Prayer for The Revival of Nature

Now that the deep sleep of winter is fading

And the hand of the frost losses

Nature may be revived once more.

May it come alive again,

And return to the fertile land.

Bringing spring on its way,

As it warms and the snow melts away.

The too soil warms and comes to life

Sprouting grass and flowers alike.

Let all life awaken and the earth reborn

So, spring can work its magic anew.

Ostara Garden Blessing

While the earth still looks dark and cold,

New life has already sprouted down below.

May our gardens be fertile and full come harvest,

May we have rain but be free of pests.
We welcome the nourishing Sun,
When our crops need energy, may it come,
May our soil be blessed now,
So, it becomes fruitful in autumn.
Let our garden thrive
Blessed be.

A Poem about Ostara

Ostara is the reflection of sunlight on the leaves,
It is in the music of the streams,
It is in the scent of blossoming flowers
It is in our dreams as they become reality.
Ostara can transform our sorrow into joy,
As it makes the darkness of the winter
into a warm spring day,
Everything bad fades away.
Ostara is what brings the change,
And grants new life a chance.
With all the new insects and birds chirping away,
Nature will never twice be the same,
They dance as plants and snakes follow,
And our life will never be shallow.
Praising the Goddess of Fertility
We hail to you, oh goddess of spring,
You who bring the warm winds,
Make flowers bloom and animals stir,
Help the soil awake so we can plant the seeds.
We praise you, oh goddess of fertility,
As we know that through the cycles of life,
You'll bring us a good harvest and bounty.
Only you can make us fertile in our work,
Through our hands and hearts.
We praise you for all your blessings,
And the hope you bring us,

We pray that you cover the land
So, this year can too come to a fruitful end.

Greeting Eostre

As we watch nature shed its winter cloak,
We welcome to the warmth that follows,
So, we greet you, Eostre, lady of Spring.
With our joyful hearts,
We dance at your arrival,
Goddess of the early sunrise.
We welcome the lively colors
And the blessing that follows
In abundance may we grow,
So, we can prosper now and tomorrow.
Grant us a mindful eye
So, we don't miss
The chance to thrive.
In you, we see the promise of a better tomorrow
Blessed be now and forever.

Prayer for Honoring the Goddesses of Spring

As the new life returns to the earth,
Everything is preparing to bloom,
And appear once more out of the nourishing soil.
So, we welcome you in,
Beautiful goddesses of spring,
Eostre, Flora, Cybele, and Persephone.
We see your magic in the trees,
You work in the soil that brings,
Flowers and grains,
And we know whom to be grateful to,
when it rains.

Goddess of Ostara Invocation

The Goddess of Ostara comes with the spring
Cloaked in the sunlight, she melts the snow,

Green leaves, flowers, and awakened animals,
She brings many gifts to the revived earth.
The Goddess of Ostara comes with the spring,
Fair Maiden, we seek to welcome you in.
We plant our seeds now, oh Goddess of spring,
And we will reap what we have sown in the autumn wind,
We ask you to guide us with your light touch,
As your kindness envelops us.
When she comes, she offers us the sacred egg,
Providing birth, fertility, and a circle that's complete,
The Goddess of Ostara comes with the spring,
Fair Maiden, we seek to welcome you in.

A Hopeful Chant for Ostara

Ostara, when springtime comes,
And when nature transforms,
Everything is new, and everything grows,
Everything will change, and we might cry,
But this day will be filled with hope no matter why.
A Chant for Celebrating Ostara
When the wheel of the year turns,
And the long daylight returns,
Here comes Ostara, the forebearer of spring.
As the Sun is regaining its strength,
The time with sowing will now be spent.
The goddess now bestows her blessings onto our lands,
She replenishes our sources,
So come winter, we have food again in our hands.

Creating Your Own Dedications to Ostara

Lastly, you should keep in mind that magic is highly personal. The power comes from within you, and it changes over time. If you are at the beginning of your magical journey, you may need to rely on existing prayers and chants for your spells and rituals. As you become wise in the ways of a witch and learn how to evoke more power, you'll be able to create your own magical aids. Ostara is one of the largest and most enchanting sabbats, which can also provide you with the most inspiration. Nothing can help you more in creating your own dedication to Ostara than observing as nature sheds its winter cloak and comes to life around you.

- **Decorating Your Altar:** You may add a potted plant to keep yourself close to nature at all times. Crystals, symbols, and candles that speak to you about nature are all helpful additions. Vivid spring colors usually help boost the vibe, but if you feel that you would rather use white, that's fine as well.

- **Learning the Symbols:** Ostara has more symbols than just the eggs and the rabbits it's known for. There are also seeds, snakes, wheat, and literally everything that comes from nature and may symbolize fertility. Learning them and using them in your practice is another great way to celebrate this sabbat.

- **Creating a Prayer:** Write your own prayer for Ostara and recite it every day in front of your altar. Light a candle while doing as the flames help carry the magic.

- **Getting Crafty:** There are plenty of craft projects you can do for Ostara, so you should have no trouble finding the ideal ones for you. Some are better suited for solitary witches, while others are great for families with children. Don't forget to add some of your creations to your altar.

- **Writing a Poem:** Even if you are welcoming spring on your own, this doesn't mean you can't get into the spirit of Ostara by coming up with a poem or chant of your own. And if you have children, they will love singing your Ostara songs while preparing for the sabbat.

- **Practicing Mindfulness:** While the spring is known for its abundance of activity, sometimes the only way to enjoy this is to slow down a bit by yourself. Find the closest piece of nature, stop for a couple of minutes, and do some mindfulness exercises while observing it.

- **Trying Out New Activities:** Seeking out an activity you always wanted to try will energize you, which will have a positive impact on your magic as well. Becoming committed to this activity during this time of the year ensures that you receive everything you need from Ostara.

Chapter 9: Spells and Rituals for Solitaries

Pagan traditions vary widely, and they focus strongly on rituals, spells, and magick to create change in individuals through physical actions and prayer. Practitioners may use multiple sources to follow a particular Pagan tradition. Other traditions include Wicca, a kind of religious witchcraft, Druidry, non-Wiccan religious witchcraft, and feminist Goddess worship. The rituals and spells mainly focus on observing natural cycles like seasonal changes, honoring a deity or deities, or celebrating passage rites such as birth, marriage, and death.

A participant is involved physically in the rituals that often include chanting, drumming, and dancing. While other rituals and spells are practiced in groups, solitary or individual practitioners can also do the same. This chapter discusses the spells and rituals for Solitaries in Ostara. It discusses different types of Wiccan and druid rituals and spells.

Solitary Practice

Although some Pagans practice in groups, many are solitaries implying they practice alone. Many pagans identify as solitary, and they only gather with small groups for special occasions. Most of them prefer to worship in private homes or outdoors. The solitary practitioners are known as Neo-pagans who follow diverse religions such as Wicca, traditional reconstructionism, and witchcraft. The following are some of the spells and rituals for solitaries.

Ostara Ritual

To perform this ritual, you need to use the season's symbols to decorate your altar. Spring represents fertility in the world, so you should decorate the altar with appropriate seasonal symbols. For instance, you can consider the colors you see in nature during this time, like plump tulips, daffodils, crocuses, and green shoots. You also need to include symbols of young animals like chicks, lambs, rabbits, and calves since they symbolize Ostara.

On top of decorating the altar, you can also perform the ritual outside early in the morning, where you can reconnect with the earth. You'll need a bowl of milk, three candles (one green, one yellow, and one purple), and a bowl of sugar or honey. The first thing is to focus on the air around where you should inhale deeply to smell if there is a change in the season. Since spring is a season of rebirth, the air will consist of a smell of fresh green grass, earthly and rainy aroma.

The next step is to light the green candle that symbolizes the blossoming earth and chant a few praising the coming of a new season. You need to light the yellow candle next, which represents the sun. As you light this candle, you must say a few words in appreciation of the warmth and light provided by the sun. The sun warms the land, promoting the growth of plants. Finally, you must light a purple candle representing the Divine force in our lives. This can be a god or goddess, and this candle stands for the things we cannot understand in our lives but are sacred. Focus on the Divine aspect of the candle as you chant something.

You should take a moment to meditate, focusing on the three flames before you and considering what they symbolize. You also need to determine how you fit between the three components: the sun, earth, and Divine symbolized by the three burning candles. Finally, mix the honey and milk, and pour the mixture around the altar as an offering to the earth. You may wish to say something as you present your offering. Stand for about one minute facing the altar once you make your offering and feel the sun on your face and the cool earth beneath your feet.

Grounding or Earth Meditation

Grounding meditation is one crucial and simple daily practice for many Pagans. It helps you connect with the energy of the earth and maintain emotional and physical balance. You must find a place to sit quietly – and make sure the sun is shining and nothing disturbs you from performing this meditation. Ensure that you locate an outdoor place where you can connect with everything that represents the earth. The practice of divination is another example of grounding meditation where you ask about the day ahead. Other Pagans use Tarot cards or runes while others consult astrology to gain access to sources of spiritual knowledge. Others can look for connections with the natural world through interactions with plants, animals, water, and wind to understand different patterns of the local environment.

Making an Eggshell Fertility Talisman

To make this talisman, you'll need:

- A needle and thread
- A small green circle cloth
- Eggshells
- A piece of paper with an image of your goal
- Some fertility herbs like carrot, bistort, nuts, wheat, rice, myrtle, barley, rye, acorns, pine cones, cedar, juniper, turnips, honeysuckle, and lemongrass

You can also include geodes or holey stones associated with fertility. Infuse all the ingredients with your desire for a baby. Place them in the green cloth and sew them. Holding the talisman between your belly and hands, begin to chant and ask your goddess for a baby. You should wear your talisman around your belly as much as you can. You can renew your intent by chanting appropriate words related to conceiving a baby.

Other Forms of Egg Magick

There are also other types of egg magick you can consider making positive changes in your life. For instance, you can sweep hard-boiled eggs from outside the house to the interior using a broom. This ritual is specifically meant to bring fertility and abundance. You can also use brown eggs to perform magick that will help in animal husbandry. The eggs will protect your livestock against diseases and provide healing power. Brown eggs also help ease the pets when giving birth. The other magic you can perform is to bury a rotten egg near a crossroad, which will cause abundance to shift from the enemy to you.

To ensure you have sufficient food in your home during winter, bury one egg at each corner of the cardinal point of your yard. This magick also helps keep your family safe by offering protection powers. Before you begin spring planting, make sure you bury some eggs in your garden. Decorated eggshells hanging from trees surrounding a particular place provide blessings of abundance.

Magick

Many Pagans exercise magick, which is different from the stage or other forms of fanciful magic in novels. In Paganism, magick is viewed as a spiritual practice that functions like prayer, and it comes with a more physical component. It aims to create change within an individual and in the world. When you practice magick, you should start by stating a clear intention and raising the required energy to support it.

You can achieve this through dancing and chanting, breath exercises, or concentration. The energy will be released into the world or an object that serves as the focus of the intention. The object can be a piece of jewelry, a candle, or any item on the altar. Pagans feel that magick should include a practical component to be successful. For instance, you need to complete an application for a successful job magick.

Candle Rituals

Pagans often perform a variety of rituals daily to strengthen their spirituality. Other rituals are simple since they only involve lighting a candle in the dark and meditating on the flame. You can give a cup of water to your ancestors and say a prayer. A verbal ritual or spoken intention is believed to be very powerful. It can bring change to the Pagan's life if properly said. You need to choose your words carefully if you want to achieve your life goals.

Personal Cleansing

The first thing you should do is to build an altar if you want to do personal cleansing. This is a sacred workplace, or a place of divinity used by Pagans to perform rituals in their homes. An altar can be in any convenient location inside your home or outside if your yard is big. Your altar should have ritual tools, natural objects, photographs of the dead, or other items of beauty and personal power. You can undertake a healing or personal cleansing at the altar, or you can present an offering of a deity. You can also make a herbal charm or meditate at your altar. Looking at the altar will remind you of your spiritual life.

Spiritual Cleansing

Spiritual cleansing is another spell you can perform to make your heart spiritually clean and healthy. It is essential to draw closer to God, who can do the spiritual cleansing since we cannot do it. Apart from asking God to cleanse your heart, you also need to cleanse your body from within. For instance, you can deep clean your mouth and remove negativity and pessimism. You should train your mouth not to say bad things. This also involves the decision to refrain from arguing or complaining.

Spiritual cleansing also involves the removal of dirty things from your mind. Garbage in your mind affects the way you think, so feed it with the word of God. When you renew your mind, you can enjoy inner peace, which will help you live happily. Make sure you clean all the hidden areas since concealed sin can destroy your peace or health. Another important step you can take to cleanse yourself is to release bitterness and unforgiveness.

If you keep bitterness, it will look like baggage you'll become too familiar with but not aware of how it might be hindering your life. Similarly, you should learn to get rid of anger, rage, slander, and brawling. Instead, learn to be compassionate and kind to other people. Open your life and allow the light of God to shine in your body. Other people are too serious about life, which can impact them in different ways. You must have some fun to relieve pressure.

A Cascarone Love Spell

Knocking someone on the head with a special egg called the cascarone is another way of blessing you. Cascarones consist of eggshells collected over several weeks before Easter and are hollowed out carefully. They are then filled with different substances and decorated. When the eggs are knocked on someone's head, the substances inside will shower blessings on the individual involved. The common items used as fillers include sage, lavender, flour or cornmeal, and perfumed herbs. While the idea is playful, this spell effectively makes magick and provides blessings to others.

To make cascarone eggs, you should empty them first, and you can do this by making small holes on both ends of the egg. Wash the shells with cold water and allow them to dry. Decorate the shells before you fill them. You can add herbs or confetti to fill the empty shells. Make sure you use a small kitchen funnel and be careful not to break the shell or make it full since it can cause discomfort when you know it on someone's head. When the eggs shells are full, seal them and store them in a cool and dry place while you wait for Ostara morning.

When you want to perform a cascarone love spell, follow the instructions highlighted above and fill the shells with magickal herbs such as yarrow, lavender, rose petals, apple blossom, willow, daisies, or rosemary. These herbs are commonly associated with attracting romantic love. As you create your cascarone, you need to visualize the contents as a love catalyst. This will make your desired lover notice you more than other people without impinging their desire to choose a preferred lover. You can shower the person you love with the cascarone on Ostara or break it in a flowing river while visualizing your intention being carried to your loved one's heart.

Use of Sacred Jewelry

Jewelry is another special tool you can use for your spells and rituals. The Wiccans usually wear jewelry consisting of pagan symbols like the pentacle, a five-pointed star. This pentacle is a symbol of life, and it reflects the union of different elements, including air, earth, fire, and water, with the spirit. However, the pentacle is often misrepresented and associated with evil in horror movies. Not all pagans use the pentacle.

Green Spells

Green spells are primarily concerned with healing and nurturing. They draw power from the earth and use flowers, herbs, and other plants as the source of spell ingredients. Nature also provides ritual content, and it is the most respected component by the witches. You can become a green witch if you have a gift of soothing and healing, are drawn to nature, and enjoy gardening as well as tending herbs and plants.

Solitary rituals and spells are mainly focused on celebrating the coming of the spring season, which symbolizes rebirth or new life. There are different types of spells you can perform alone, and you'll need certain elements to undertake them. However, your needs and aspirations will determine the rituals or spells you can perform. The next chapter focuses on spells and rituals for social pagans.

Chapter 10: Spells and Rituals for Social Pagans

There are different spells and rituals for social Pagans you can perform to celebrate Ostara, which marks the coming of springs and new life. The last chapter discussed the spells and rituals for solitaries, and this one discusses some complex spells and rituals since they will require a group to perform.

Ostara Rebirthing

This ritual involves rebirthing, and you can perform it as part of a group. Ostara is an excellent way to help you rededicate yourself to the gods celebrated in your tradition. There should be an Ostara altar and supplies such as a bowl of soil, a black sheet for each participant, incense, and a white candle to perform this rite. The High Priest or High Priestess (HP) is the only person who must be on the altar. Other members of the group should wait in another room until the HP calls them. If you are performing this rite outside, other participants should wait at a distance away from the altar. If you are called to cast the circle, you can do it as instructed.

The first person should wait outside the circle and be covered with a black sheet from head to toe to start the ritual. You can be nude under the sheet if the group permits. When the HP is ready, they will call the first person into the altar, create an opening in the circle as the participant enters, and close behind them. Still covered in the black sheet, the participant will kneel on the floor before the altar. The HP greets the member and says:

> *Today is the time of the Spring equinox.*
>
> *Ostara is a time of equal parts, light and dark.*
>
> *Spring has arrived, and it is a time of rebirth.*
>
> *The planting season will soon begin, and*
>
> *life will form once more within the earth.*

As the earth welcomes new life and new beginnings,

so can we be reborn in the light and love of the gods*.

Do you, (name), wish to experience the rebirth of spring and

step out of the darkness into the light?

The participant will then reply with an affirmative answer, and the HP collects salt from the altar and sprinkles it over the participant clad in a black sheet. The HP will say the following: "With the blessings of the earth, the life within the soil, you are reborn in the eyes of the gods." The HP will then take incense and pass it to the participant, chanting blessings of the air and asking knowledge and wisdom to be brought to the member.

The HP takes a burning candle and passes it to the participant, asking the burning fire of the spring sun to bring harmony and growth. They finally sprinkle water around the participant chanting something to the effect that water brings blessings and the darkness of winter be swept by the warm spring rains. The participant will slowly emerge from the black sheet when everything is done since this is a symbolic rebirth. When you move out of the black sheet, remember you are leaving behind your darkness and stepping into the light. You should take your time to reflect on the magic that will come with this ritual. The HP will welcome the participant, saying, "you have stepped into the bright area" and asking the gods to welcome you. There HP will repeat the ceremony on every member until they have been reborn. When everyone in the group has passed through the rebirthing process, they need to take time to meditate to get the balancing energy of Ostara. While meditating, you must think of the balance you wish to get in your life and consider how you'll work hard to find peace and harmony.

Stargazing

Stargazing is another rite performed by cosmic witches who largely focus on lunar energies to celebrate Ostara. This spell helps protect people against celestial events, and their practice is active even though they use star signs and birth charts. They use their knowledge to seek changes instead of just reciting what is in the public domain. If you are drawn to the skies, you can perform stargazing with other people.

Ostara Ritual for a Coven

A coven is a group of witches comprising practitioners who gather for rituals such as celebrating sabbats or Ostara. The number of people involved in these groups usually varies, although many believe 13 to be ideal. Their meeting place is called a covenstead. Any group consisting of less than three members is known as a "working couple" regardless of the gender of the people involved. When a coven becomes too big, it can be unmanageable, and it can be split. A High Priest and High Priestess jointly lead the covens, although some ceremonies are led by only one of them.

The practice of Wicca coven rituals is based on the notion of getting into contact with nature and worshiping a goddess or a god. The practice also involves using magic to celebrate the wheel of the year. This ritual involves the presentation of deities to the goddess. The Wiccans will use the ceremony to perform white magic that positively impacts life, not black magic.

Dance and Laugh Together

Ostara comes with a childlike kind of playfulness and fun. Dancing is not only exciting, but it helps magnetize blessings and gives you joy wherever you go. You must dance while barefoot and outdoors with others. Make sure you laugh at the wildness and silliness of the entire activity. You'll realize that dancing and laughing will fill you with the vibrant, buoyant, and springtime vibration that will energize you and make positive changes to your life. It is essential to ensure that you do this as a group to enjoy the benefits of this fun ritual to the fullest.

A Theatrical Ostara Ritual

The women's Ostara ritual aims to bring back spring and create a balance between life and death, day and night, and light and dark. The ritual involves different things, and it comes with a lot of activity in the center. Therefore, you should make sure you set your altar to the side so that it does not disturb the movement of people. The following are some of the activities you can expect before the ritual.

- **Dyeing Hard-Boiled Eggs** - Involves an egg hunt, which means there should be enough eggs for each member. Hide both plastic and real eggs before the ritual around the area where you'll conduct the rite.

- You may also need to prepare lyrics before the rite if you prefer using many songs and chants.

- If you want to play with puppets, make them in advance or assign the roles to participants if you want to have actors before the ritual.

- You can also make "spring fortunes" that are enough for each participant. You need to place these fortunes together with small chocolate eggs and candy-like jelly into plastic eggs.

When you have prepared the activities to perform before the ritual, you should also list the items you want people to bring to the ritual. The following are some of the required things for the ritual.

- Spring items like flowers, eggs, baby animal figures, budding twigs, and plants are required to decorate the altar.

- Musical instruments, particularly drums and rattles

- A walking stick, rain stick, or other items that can be used to wake the earth

- Dark cloak to cast off or festive clothes

The next thing is to create a sacred space where the ritual will be performed. Children and adults attend the ceremony, so it is important to create an efficient circle if many people attend the ritual. The space is purified by having two people walk the perimeter, wafting incense, sprinkling water and salt. The priestess can cast the circle with words, or a popular chant is used. When the ritual space is ready, the next step is to perform different rituals.

Awaken the Earth

The first ritual is to awaken the earth, and this can be done with little help. When the circle is cast, there may be a need to push it out to cover the entire area. The participants will walk around the yard to mark the beginning of the ritual. If some people show up with walking sticks, they can use them to tap the earth as they walk around. This is meant to wake up the earth. Everyone is encouraged to play their drum or shake the rattle. The participants will sing and chant, "And she will rise," as the awakening process continues. This song is fun but rousing, and it encourages mother earth to wake up. The participants will chant that "the earth is a woman is a woman, and she will wake up." The point of awakening the earth is to encourage spring energy to rise.

Awaken the Young Goddess and God

If there are kids around, they will become the center of attention in the process of awakening the young sun goddess and god after winter. If the young ones are timid to do this, a couple of adults can be requested to perform the task. The pair will lie in the center of the circle with a blanket or dark cloaks on them. The members will sing Whispers of Spring repeatedly to awaken the young god or goddess.

The couple in the center will finally spring up and cast their dark cloaks off. They will tell the participants that it is time to cast off the winter blanket, and everyone will throw away their winter coats in a typical fashion. Festive clothing is then revealed, accompanied by cheering and fun fare. This ritual is an excellent way to involve young children for them to understand its significance from a tender age. The rite does not require speaking but just acting to awaken the goddess. The song Whispers of Spring works perfectly well for this ritual, and it sounds magical when a group of people sings it in unison.

This is a nice way to involve some of the littlest kids, as it doesn't require speaking, just acting out the process of waking up. If you don't happen to have the (out of print) song, Whispers of Spring works just as well if you do it as spoken word. It sounds very magical when a whole group whispers it together in unison.

Conduct Some Spring Cleaning

Spring cleaning is one of the easiest rituals you can perform to celebrate Ostara. This simple ritual involves collective cleaning by people who don't honor the sabbats but clean their homes at the start of spring. Physical cleaning is a great way of removing stagnant energy from your home, impacting you to start afresh. When you clean your home, you are symbolically eliminating old things and paving the way for the new. This will give you a new lease on life, and the exercise brings joy and satisfaction.

Y0u can infuse your cleansing floor wash with pine needles and rosemary to purify the energy while removing dirt and debris from your floor. You can also sprinkle black salt to absorb negative energy before sweeping your home. When you finish cleaning the place, you can use sage to smoke cleanse all stagnant energy.

Take Nature Walk

Getting outdoors is the best thing you can do after a long cold spell. Since Ostara is more about the fertility of the earth, you must find an appropriate park where you can take some nature walks to observe new plant life and growth. Walking as a group, try to watch for animal activity, especially the rabbits and birds. The fun thing you can do with your kids is to walk around with them and let them show you signs of spring. You can also help them create a bird feeder to attract birds to your home. This exercise is good since it helps you celebrate spring as a group where you learn and share different things about new life.

Spring is the time of the year that symbolizes new life and rebirth. During this time, new life returns, and the theme of resurrection is dominant. Depending on your tradition, it can be observed that there are different spells and rituals for social pagans that are used to celebrate Ostara. The celebrations mark the arrival of spring and the fertility of the land, which characterizes agricultural changes.

Conclusion

Ostara is a magical time of light and balance in the universe. It is a pagan holiday that has morphed and transformed itself throughout the years, celebrated by Wiccans, but it also remains a touchstone of Druidry and paganism. Most people worldwide also celebrate this time of year, if only by another name to better suit newer theological or ideological frameworks. However, that has not robbed this time of the year of its joyfulness or color. In fact, it has only grown in popularity over time, and the renaissance or renewed interest in Wicca has only underscored this fact.

This book has provided an easy-to-follow guide for the various rituals and ceremonies attached to this wonderful holiday, and there are even more you can research and discover once you devote more time to your practice. Setting up an Ostara Altar is, of course, key, but there are other fun things you may consider exploring should you have the wherewithal. For example, there are wonderful nursery rhymes for kids to help them become more excited about the holiday. One called the "banishing ritual of the chocolate rabbit" is a funny rite for kids to practice. Still, it's one that the whole family can enjoy doing together if that's something you're interested in pursuing. Ostara magic is mostly wholesome and accessible for people of all ages, so you can get little pagans involved if that is a plan you're interested in exploring later on.

Part of the point of going through this guide is to underscore the historical significance of this holiday, render the complex rituals around it more accessible, and encourage serious study of other aspects of Wicca. One way to help you enrich your practice is to explore the folklore pertaining to the Ostara. Many tales regarding serpents, egg magic, spring flowers, and the bunny rabbit are worth your while. These stories divine the important symbolism contained within seemingly benign objects or beings - a daffodil, the March hare - and delve deeper into their history. If you thought the Ostara was simply the pagan prototype for Easter, then you are sorely mistaken. If you love celebrating St. Paddy's day, you might be surprised to learn about more connections between the Ostara and that holiday. The former doesn't have sole proprietary influence over the ever-elusive four-leaf clover. In fact, it is mentioned in some of the earliest known Ostara rituals.

So, now that you know everything you need to know about Ostara and how to honor this ancient tradition, you should feel empowered enough to do more historical research and readings. Also, no Ostara is complete without a true feast, so you might as well get the table ready and pay tribute to the coming of spring. Eggs, painted or not, are more than welcome, as is a fresh salad of spring greens and hot cross buns. Commercial treats aren't shunned either, so if you want to buy a bunch of colorful marshmallow Peeps, then go ahead! Just remember the origins of this unique celebration, and do your best to honor the arrival of spring.

Part 4: Beltane

The Ultimate Guide to May Eve and How It's Celebrated in Wicca, Druidry, and Paganism

Introduction

Paganism as a religion, and the various cultures that are part of this ideology, have a fascinating and intense history. For people new to religion, many aspects may no longer seem that important or valuable. However, only when you look into the history of these things do you realize what a monumental place they hold. *The festival of Beltane is one of those things that is quite underestimated.* It seems like a standard celebration with all the parties and festivities from afar, but, in reality, the roots are momentous.

While it is a celebration of spring, fertility, reproduction, and the sexual aspect of human existence, these concepts go even deeper. When we speak of things growing, developing, and eventually benefitting us, it is not only the material things we see in the physical world, like crops and children. Rather, this festival also encapsulates the idea of planting a seed of positivity, joy, happiness, and camaraderie within ourselves. It is about changing our perspective from simply consuming and benefitting from the things around us in life to becoming a source of positivity and good energy. It encourages people to create positive change and help people in need while also going the extra mile to do what we can in a personal capacity to make the world a better place.

This is also a festivity that celebrates the fact that we are all completely dependent on each other. In this world, existence itself is a chain of reactions, from the seeds that we plant and the fruit that we eat to the children that continue the human race – and including all the other resources that we consume in this process. Moreover, it is a time to realize that all living things go through these processes. We need to feel a sense of community to care for everything as a living thing and not just something we consume for personal gain.

In this book, we go through everything you need to know to understand what exactly Beltane is and how you can make this a powerful part of your life. We cover everything from the religious perspective of this festival to the various customs related to Beltane and how they have changed over time.

We look into various techniques on celebrating this fantastic time of the year with plenty of tips and techniques about how you can cook meals, decorate in theme, and celebrate.

If you live in a region where there aren't a lot of pagans to enjoy this time of the year with – or are new to the lifestyle and don't know what to do – you will find helpful advice in this book that is easy to implement. There are so many things you can make your own and put your family's unique spin on it. This will make the Beltane celebrations even more enjoyable.

This book helps you get started as a beginner with hands-on methods and easy-to-understand instructions. Get ready to relish in a holistic perspective of how different pagans celebrate the festival of Spring and how they prepare for the next part of the year.

Chapter 1: Introduction to Beltane

The Celtic calendar is marked by eight sabbats, four of which are of the utmost importance to those wishing to celebrate their Celtic roots and culture according to their pagan or neopagan beliefs. Being one of the greater sabbats and having a unique meaning behind it, Beltane is one of the most lavish Pagan holidays – and is celebrated accordingly by the modern Celtic Pagans and other Pagan cultures alike.

On the Witch's Wheel of the Year (equivalent to a calendar for those practicing Celtic Paganism), Beltane sits between Ostara, the sabbat signaling the beginning of the spring, and Midsummer, the celebration of the summer season. All three sabbats are associated with the celebration of life, and each has a unique significance in Pagan life. Rather than the awakening of nature or the ripening of its fruits, Beltane symbolizes the creation of new life.

Beltane is positioned opposite Samhain on the wheel and is the festival marking the very end of the harvest season. Albeit seemingly different, there are similarities between these sabbats. In the Northern Hemisphere, Beltane is also known as May Day – as it falls on May 1st, with the festivities often beginning on the last day of April. In the Southern Hemisphere, this sabbat is held on November 1st, with the gatherings starting on the last night of October. Apart from celebrating the turn of spring into summer, Beltane is associated with several other Pagan beliefs and their symbolism.

In this chapter, you will gain insight into the origins of Beltane and how it shaped the Celtic culture. In addition, you will be able to understand its symbolism and why this sabbat played a fundamental role in the life of the Celts for centuries. The knowledge you gain here is designed to serve you as a stepping stone for delving into the enchanting practices of Beltane you will encounter throughout the following chapters.

The Origins of Beltane

Ancient Celtic culture has lived on for centuries through traditions passed down to generations by word of mouth, but rarely in written form. Therefore, much of our knowledge about Celtic Pagan culture, including their sabbats, is known to us only from tales and myths, which may vary from one territory to another. This is the case with the celebration of Beltane, which, as Celtic mythology indicates, may come from various sources. However, most sources agree that Beltane is also a nature-based celebration, much like their other Pagan sabbats.

Some of these sources associate this holiday only with the celebration of nature, while others indicate a connection between Beltane and the Celtic sun deity Bel. In fact, the name Beltane has Celtic origins and can be translated as "the fires of Bel." Bel is also known as Belenus, one of the most powerful Celtic deities who is often associated with fertility. According to tradition, to honor Bel, the community extinguished all the fires, then relit with special fires for Beltane, marking the beginning of the festivities. Couples would jump across smaller fires together, hoping Bel would bless them with fertility. Feasts of nourishing spring foods were offered as people asked the deity for a small favor to make their lives more fruitful or productive in the coming months.

The fires of Beltane also honor the Sun as it is believed to support Bel's endeavors in providing plentiful harvest and the survival of the winter months. Not only does Bel need honoring, but the Sun also has to be flattered to join the side of humans. Otherwise, it may come out either too harsh during the summer or provide too little sunlight for the crops and animals to thrive on. As much as nature relies on water and nourishment, it wouldn't survive without the rays of the Sun.

Meals cooked over the Beltane fire are said to provide magical nourishment to sustain the body during hard work, battles, and everything it needs to endure in the coming year. Ashes obtained from the fire can be used in cleansing rituals and spread over animals, crops, and humans for protection. The Druids, the most educated class of Celts, were responsible for keeping their traditions alive. Beltane also honors their contribution by encouraging visitation to sites where the Druids held their rituals. To do this, one must follow the path of the Sun – by moving from East to West. This is another example of symbolism that emphasizes the role of the Sun in helping nature reach maximum fertility.

Beltane and Fertility

As the spring reaches its peak in April, nature prepares for the upcoming summer, and the land becomes the most fertile it will be throughout the entire year. The snow has melted, the showers become heavy, and longer hours of sunlight warms the land and produces greenery everywhere. Due to this, natural energies become the most active, and their power is the strongest. Beltane honors this life that bubbles with fertility so potently around this time of the year that, in most cases, results in the conception of a new life.

Due to their Celtic roots, the ancient Pagans have lived around the cyclical schedule, relying on weather conditions to survive. With the arrival of the harsh winter months, most work has ceased and is only to be resumed again when the abundance of fertile earth is presented in spring. To survive the winter, they had to harvest enough crops and hunt or cultivate enough animals during the summer to sustain them when they couldn't do this. And much of their ability to do this depended on whether nature was generous enough to provide their crops and animals the nourishment they needed. They have created Beltane, the celebration often associated with fertility and the possibility of a plentiful harvest throughout the year. However, to obtain this, nature has to be won over with fertility rituals, including bonfires, dancing, maypole setting, and much more. Beltane honors nature by donning its green cloak and asks for the unfurling buds and the newborn animals to be nurtured. This way, humans can build a suitable supply for the next winter season.

The time for sowing seeds and planting crops has come once again. The anticipation for the first flowers to appear in a few days brings to mind the symbolism of the cycle of life – from birth to death to rebirth. This concept of endlessly renewing fertility around Beltane is also often applied to pursuing other endeavors, whether it's work, conceiving a child, art, or even the practice of magic. The Celts believed that if something began on Beltane, it was bound to come to fruition. This point in the Wheel of the Year is considered the best time to conceive new ideas and reconsider old ones; after all, dreams can be manifested more easily while having fun at the same time.

According to yet another myth, the renewed fertility of nature represents the Spring god's devotion to Flora, the maiden goddess of Spring, and his transition from an initial admiration to a long-lasting commitment. The goddess reaching her fullness is said to start the events leading to most old and new Beltane traditions. As the god expresses his love for his goddess, their union is consummated in a Great Wedding, during which a child is conceived. The following year around Beltane, this child is destined to take over the place of his father, who dies during the winter, so he can sustain humans with nourishment. This symbolizes the cyclical nature of life, and the need for nature to die, in order for it to be reborn during the spring and summer. To honor the union of the god and the goddess, mortal weddings were banned at Beltane, but betrothals were acceptable, and couples often wandered off to create a magical child of their own. Rather than the reenactment of the Great Wedding, couples try to emulate the union representing passion, sensuality, and vitality. Symbols like the Green Man, the May Queen, and the Maypole were also created to celebrate this union and the resulting conception. Since its inception, the maypole has been regarded as an everlasting symbol of fertility, whereas the 6-8 ribbons attached to it are meant to represent life's spiraled nature.

Beltane and the Otherworld

Like Samhain, Beltane describes a certain and limited timeframe in which the veil between our world and the one beyond becomes diminished enough to permit communication between the living and the departed. Beltane is the ideal time to seek out spiritual guides and ask for their guidance and protection. This is particularly important because the kindred spirits of nature and the ancestors aren't the only creatures living in the Otherworld. There are plenty of malevolent or potentially dangerous entities that can also cross the thin veil between the worlds. They can ruin harvests, bring diseases to animals, and even attack people if one isn't careful enough. To avoid this, farm animals were driven through the smoke of the Beltane fire as protection from these creatures to remain healthy and fertile.

The Aos Sí

In the Celtic lore, The Aos Sí are depicted as fairy-like creatures with mostly neutral dispositions – with a few exceptions. One of these is the Ban Side (the woman of sìd), who, like Banshees, are the forebearers of death. If they appear in front of someone and begin to wail and shriek, the person has to take special precautions to avoid imminent death. The Sluagh Sídhe, or the fairy host, are other creatures with dark intentions. They are said to be airborne spirits representing the remnants of damned souls. To avenge their fate of never being able to move on to the afterlife, they lurk around for a chance to steal the souls of the innocent.

Beltane marks when grazing animals are moved to summer pastures, where they will interact with nature's spirits. Since not all spirits were good-natured, Celts asked benevolent fairies and spirits to protect them and their animals from the Ban Side. Leanan Sídhe, also known as the fairy lover, is often summoned during Beltane, along with the Cù Sìth, the fairy dog, and the Cat Sìth, the fairy cat. However, as even these Aos Sì can act maliciously, they must be appeased with offerings, including animal sacrifices, feasts, and other gifts. Baskets adorned with yellow flowers are said to appease Aos Sì, as is visiting holy wells. Wells are said to represent the closest way to reach the fairy mound, the home of Aos Sì. In Ireland, decorating these wells with ribbons, flowers, and shells is also associated with winning over the Aos Sì and the other spirits living in the Otherworld. Adornments were also placed around peoples' homes, inviting the spirits there and giving them small gifts as a sign of trust and good intention. This way, these creatures will grant the blessing of protection and answer prayers dedicated to them.

The Good Spirits

Fortunately, the malevolent spirits aren't the only creatures with which Pagans can interact. Many good spirits live in all the realms of nature, including this world. Some believe that the appearance of new flowers and animals around Beltane means that the good spirits and fairies are hard at work. Each new bud, seed, and birth is a testimony of their good deeds. Every small piece of nature can be seen as the magic of fairies making miraculous things happen.

There are countless rituals, customs, and games created by Pagan communities wishing to honor the spirit of nature and teach their importance to the next generations. After all, their positive energy is the force that makes it possible for us to sense the fertility of nature. They even allow us to engage in fertile endeavors by freeing our energy and becoming one with our spiritual selves. According to Celtic tales told to children, acorn caps represent discarded fairy hats, the flowers on the ground are left behind by their work. The moss on a riverbank or tree barks is the soft bedding where fairies sleep on their leaf pillows.

The Ancient lore warns against disturbing the work of the fae, and one should only approach them or their world with caution. Yet, the help of the fairies should be acknowledged as, without their help, nature wouldn't be able to don its luscious summer coat, nor would we have crops and new animals to sustain us. While fairies and good spirits don't usually tend to turn against humans, they will still appreciate the food and other gifts left out for them during Beltane.

Other Tales Associated with Beltane

According to some Wiccan traditions, Beltane is when the Queen of Winter and the May Queen enter into a battle to rule over nature. As spring turns into summer, the May Queen gets stronger and stronger, eventually establishing supremacy over the Queen of Winter. Each queen ruler is supported by their followers, who enter into a mock battle to gain victory for their own queen. Traditionally, the May Queen is captured by the followers of her enemy, and her own followers need to offer a ransom to get her back. The ransom is represented in symbolic offerings to nature and the May Queen herself and is said to help her gain the power she needs to win the battle.

Beltane festivities are also symbolizing the celebration of life in general. The Maypole, the May baskets, the flowers used for decorations, and self-adornment are all used to express gratitude for life. Pagans have long ago recognized that humans wouldn't be able to live happy and healthy lives without the fruits of nature. Representing these fruits of nature, gifting flowers, or using them as decorations and self-adornments can help restore the health of those recovering from an ailment and provide a long and well-balanced life for the young and elderly alike.

According to a somewhat different Celtic lore, the tale of the Spring goddess and the Spring god represents the oldest and the most hopeful love story on this planet. Rather than being united once and conceiving a child, the god and the goddess are separated every winter. When the late spring arrives, their glorious reunion is to be witnessed by the vivid colors unfolding around us and the bright sunlight empowering everything. Also, in this tale, the emphasis has been put on restoring the balance between the masculine and feminine energies. The cold winter represents the power of masculinity, while the vivid color in nature and human celebration act as its feminine counterpart. After their separation, the god and goddess come together to create a new life, and to bring balance to the existing one. Their reunion testifies to unbridled sensuality, yet it is said to inspire new ideas and encourage the pursuit of new passions.

Who Can Celebrate Beltane?

As mentioned at the beginning of this chapter, Beltane marks the arrival of summer, which is the time of year when flora and fauna thrive, and nature becomes more fertile and productive. This means that anyone can celebrate this holiday uniquely or according to their own neopagan beliefs. With so many different ways to welcome the summer, everyone can find a way to express their gratitude for the fertility this season brings. Whether you want to do this by giving special attention to your garden and animals so you can bring new life around or simply honoring the fertility god with symbols and decoration in hopes of making your work more productive, the choice is yours. You are free to share this celebration with your friends and family, or you can reach out to fellow pagans in your community. And while any celebration becomes more joyful when celebrated in a group, the rituals and preparations for Beltane can also be tailored to solitary practitioners. With some planning, you can organize your own Beltane celebration and focus on connecting with nature and drawing its energy to you, bringing fertility to your life.

Beltane is a special time in the Wheel of the Year, with a powerful magic everyone can sense and appreciate. Even those who aren't connected to their spiritual self or nature can notice the subtle changes around them. And it is not only the unfolding of nature that makes it hard to miss; it's the shift in energy that everyone can feel, empowering them around the 1st of May. It's no wonder that we become so productive around this time of the year. It's as if nature urges us to take action and fully enjoy our lives. It encourages us to spend time in nature, move our bodies and harness our potential to develop new ideas. Then it assures that when we connect with our spiritual self and our spiritual guides and do whatever we need to bring the fertile energy into motion, our endeavors will result in a favorable outcome. So, if you need a little encouragement to become more productive and increase the fertility of your actions, remember to honor nature at Beltane.

Being the largest fertility festival, Beltane is the best time of the year to create something. However, you shouldn't forget to give thanks for all the fruits you enjoy during the summer – be that *literally* or *through your work*. Nature's ability to create new life is a miracle to behold, and Beltane is the best time to acknowledge this. This can be done in so many ways, as all it counts is creating something new that brings joy to your life and to the life of those around you.

Today's Beltane customs are very similar to the way our ancestors celebrated this sabbat, from the fire to the Maypole dance to offerings made to the deities and protective spirits. The ancient and contemporary Beltane traditions will be discussed in more detail throughout the following chapters.

Chapter 2: Beltane Deities and Mythology

Beltane honors Earth's energies and the beauty of various seasons, especially spring and summer. The Earth radiates charm on all living beings with blooming fertility and new bustling life in nature. This is primarily what Beltane culture entails – new life and growth. It also focuses on self-esteem, self-development, and healthy boundaries for oneself. When you focus on yourself and practice self-love, you engage with all your senses and develop a self-protective instinct, a trait you must build to endure the long journey with ease.

As you already know, the word "Beltane" is associated with the Celtic deity, Bel, and refers to the "fires of Bel." Believers and worshippers celebrate the fire festival in honor of the Beltane deity and welcome the spring and summer seasons. They also believe that the new season is the epitome of fertility and growth, which is why believers prefer to organize important events like weddings and other special occasions during this period. This chapter observes some significant myths and deities associated with the Beltane tradition to decipher the beliefs in depth.

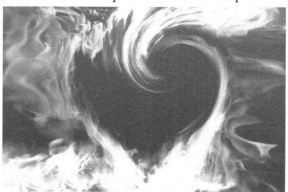

The Goddess of Beltane – Queen of the May

Popularly known as the Divine Lover and the Lady of the Heart's Blossoming, The Goddess of Beltane symbolizes fertility and full bloom. She represents femininity, sexuality, and the manifestation of growth. This deity's other popular names include the Goddess of Spring, the May Bride, and Flora. Devotees associate the woodland spirits with the May Queen as she represents the growth of natural elements and the earth. Since the goddess represents fertility and the onset of spring, her celebrations often overlap the rituals performed for the Blessed Virgin. It is believed that the May Queen's blessings bring good luck and success to believers celebrating momentous occasions during this phase.

According to tales, the May Queen is quite young – presumably around 13 years old – and is considered extremely pretty. This stuck with Beltane devotees in the past, which led to the advent of new traditions, like the Floralia celebrations in Rome. A new queen is elected every year, and the previous queen chooses the next leader in line. The May King accompanied the May Queen in the procession, followed by hundreds of people. Men with decorated poles followed the King and Queen. Another significant rite recognized in pagan rituals is the epic fight between the Queen of Winter and the May Queen. Men led the group as "supporters" who dressed as beautiful women to honor the queen. They enacted the fight where the May Queen emerged victorious against the Queen of Winter after capturing her.

This also symbolizes the onset of the spring season and the end of cold, dark days. In some regions, young boys carved a man doll out of straw and carried it while running around the town to banish winter. As they ran through the town, young girls followed them with flowers in their hands and sang softly to welcome spring. When summer ends, fall approaches with the grace of the Dark Mother, or Cailleach. She carries a scythe and a sickle and brings winter storms. During this period (presumably around six months), the Dark Mother is stronger and fiercer, which is why she wins the battle against the May Queen and brings winter. May Day festivals and May Fairs are common in several countries following Beltane traditions.

The May King – The Green Man

Essentially, the festival's significance can be traced from the Sacred Marriage between the May Queen and the May King, who is also referred to as the Green Man in some tales. While he has many other names, such as "Jack in the Green" or "The Oak King," he is better known as the May King—the God who fell in love with the Goddess of Spring and ultimately made her the May Queen. As the spring and summer season befalls on earth, the Green Man rises to power and reaches his full height, symbolizing growth and freshness. As winter arrives, he diminishes in size and in wisdom, only to grow back stronger during the next seasonal cycle.

The connection between the May King and the May Queen is divine. They thrive in symbiosis and share an intimate bond. This revered wedlock is a sacred symbol of marriage and togetherness imprinted in the Celtic culture and beliefs. It is known as "Hieros Gamos" or "the Sacred Marriage" and represents the merger of the Sky and Earth. The Green Man completes the May Queen's timelessness and transient perspective. She cannot complete the seasonal cycle without leaning on the May King.

Despite being symbolic to Beltane, the Green Man is perceived as the embodiment of growth and a new season across many cultures throughout the world. Naturally, his identity, characteristics, and personality change across every story and culture. However, his essence remains the same. As humans (along with other living species), we always feel the need to define our relationship or our connection with the natural entities or world. This need existed throughout the past and can still be felt today. The Green Man slyly connects the dots and elusively describes the relationship. This is probably one of the reasons he is still considered important in several cultures and redefined based on quintessential perceptions.

Throughout the festival, the Green Man is symbolized in the form of hidden silhouettes around dark corners or on church ceilings. Since the Green Man also represents growth and virility (next to the May Queen), his strong iconography thrived for many centuries. On Beltane Eve, the Stone Circle ritual calls the Green Man's spirit and seeks his blessings. This festival also celebrates how we interact with nature and thrive harmonically with non-living entities – another critical portrayal of the Green Man.

The Beltane Festival

As mentioned, fire, fertility, and growth are vital to Beltane. People celebrate the festival between the time of the Summer Solstice and the Spring Equinox, which is known as Beltane. Lughnasadh, Imbolc, and Samhain are three other popular Gaelic festivals celebrated to date. Psychics are active as they feel more powerful in contacting spirits from the underworld. This is when the layer between the underworld and our world becomes extremely thin, giving us the ability to connect with souls in other dimensions. Everything becomes surreal, and people become more joyful during this period. This also marks the start of the farming year when harvesters and farmers anticipate a fruitful yield throughout the rest of the year.

The Beltane festival oversaw many rituals that were carried out as protective measures for loved ones, crops, and even the cattle that would graze the pastures throughout the festivities. Mostly fire, smoke, and ashes were implemented in said rituals due to their inherent purification and cleansing effects against malevolent beings. Lighting bonfires and celebrating your existence around them became a common tradition. It is practiced to date with several variations – more on that in the upcoming chapter. Aos Si, a supernatural race, was honored with drinks and food during the celebration. Houses and cattle were decorated with yellow flowers and the ones that grew during the spring season – typically May flowers to trace the significance.

It was common practice to grow or even construct one's own May Bush (thorn bush), adorned with shells and ribbons, around one's home. People celebrating indoors extinguished the fire and relit it with the traditional and honorable Beltane bonfire to commence the festival. People even jumped or walked into the fire to honor the Beltane deity in the past. As mentioned, people still celebrate this festival today, but certain customs have vastly changed. Areas like the town of Peebles and Newfoundland have retained the traditional customs of attending the Beltane Fair and decorating the May Bush.

Sex and intimacy are also some intricate qualities represented by the Beltane customs as they are associated with the merger of the May Queen and the May King. Sexual imagery and fertility were implied during certain rituals, most of which are non-existent today. The Green Man is also honored during this period with paper mache masks and hawthorn blossoms with green leaves.

The Tradition of Handfasting

The popular lore of the Goddess and God's Great Wedding is vital to Beltane customs as it brings forth the famous tradition of Handfasting. In this tradition, a married couple commits to the sacred bond for a year and a day. This ritual symbolizes unity and association between two people through marriage and secular vows. It is often practiced in pagan weddings and Celtic rituals traced from ancient Ireland. The ritual can be dated back to 7000 BC, when people in love often took vows in the presence of a priest. The wedding was officiated after tying a ribbon or a cord over the couple's hands as both partners committed to staying engaged for at least a year.

The aforementioned Handfasting tradition is traced from the Sacred Marriage between the May Bride and the Green Man. They come together to unify the Sky and Earth, which brings abundant joy and manifests renewal. It is a time of glory, happiness, fertility, and prosperity. Since the spring and summer times are associated with the May Bride and the Sacred Marriage, believers prefer to conduct weddings and important events during this phase – which is between April to June. They believe that the prime time on the Wheel of the Year can help them fulfill their wishes and force desires into shape.

This ritual continues to date, and you can still spot modern couples following the Handfasting ceremony on their wedding day. Before commencing the sacred ritual, the officiant guides the couple by explaining its significance and coherence. The partners then entwine their hands in the form of an "8" shape, and a cord or a knot (typically a red ribbon) is securely tied around their hands. The vows are repeated, and the officiant chants the symbolism of commitment. After the officiant's words, the couple unties their hands, and this act symbolizes staying together but with freedom of mind and speech.

It is believed that this ritual brings the partners closer, and they symbolically enter a long-term, happy marriage that may last forever. Today, the couple can choose how long they want to stay together, and if they wish to separate after the predetermined time period, they can part ways without reprehension. Most couples still prefer performing this tradition as they believe it to be a "secret" of long-lasting relationships and a happy marriage. Traditionally, couples were tied together and had to "stay bonded" until midnight. Today, some ceremonies use this tradition as the main theme for the couple to exchange vows.

Another interesting ritual that follows the Handfasting tradition (not necessarily in all ceremonies) is "jumping the broomstick," in which a couple can get married in the eyes of their society by jumping over a broom on the floor. The broom represents a line or threshold that the couple must cross to enter a new phase of their lives. Typically, this ceremony was only performed by those who could not afford the wedding expenses or preferred not to pay.

Gods and Goddesses Associated with Beltane

Several gods and goddesses from various cultures represent Beltane ideals, which is why some devotees perceive them as Beltane deities. Even though some of them are more prominent in other cultures (mainly Greek, Roman, and Egyptian), Beltane believers still consider them significant and honor them as a part of their own culture.

Cernunnos: Celtic

Cernunnos represents vegetation and fertility due to his association with male animals. He is considered the best hunter and is personified as a shaggy, wild male with a long beard. Just like the Green Man, he also symbolizes greenery, vegetation, and forests. In some Wicca tales, he is known as the "Horned God" and is married to the mother goddess (traces from the sacred marriage between the Green Man and the May Queen). Despite being a positive embodiment of natural entities, his horns give him a devilish look, which is why some cultures compare him to Satan. However, in general, he is a compelling male figure with a lot of power and fertility.

Artemis: Greek

The daughter of Zeus and the moon's representative, Artemis is a Greek goddess honored during the spring season due to her association with forests. Apollo, the God of music, dance, and archery, is her twin brother. Due to her connection with nature, forests, and animals, she is also deemed to be a great huntress. During her time in the forest, she looks after young creatures and saplings, thereby maintaining the integrity of the forests. Even though she does not have any children, she is still considered the provider of infants and represents fertility, motherhood, and puberty.

Bacchus: Roman

One of the most significant deities of Beltane and Roman cultures, Bacchus symbolizes debauchery, wine, and grapes, thereby giving him the moniker "the Party God." "Bacchanalia," a series of secret ceremonies, were conducted on the Aventine Hill in ancient Rome, where women gathered to celebrate and be blessed with fertility and abundant growth. These ceremonies also commemorated Bacchus due to his association with the harvest. He is the liberator and the patron of beverages.

Bes: Egyptian

Bes is the protector of young children and mothers. Beset, his wife, represents fertility and is equally respected and worshiped. Couples struggling to conceive children often seek the blessing of Bes and Beset through a series of rituals and holy ceremonies. Bes is not only the ultimate "father" but also characterizes dancing, music, humor, and sexuality. The Ptolemaic Period witnessed a major rise in the deity's worshippers, resulting in "the cult of Bes." Steadily, the Romans and the Phoenicians also started worshiping him to fulfill their sexual and fertility needs.

Hera: Greek

Hera is the archetype of new brides and marriage. In some ancient tales, she is illustrated as the protector of nature and wildlife. She also takes care of young creatures and nurses them back to health. Juno, the Roman God, is considered the equivalent of Hera as both are the protectors of women. Worshippers wishing to conceive children often made offerings and paid tribute to Hera by presenting apples, paintings, votives, small statues, and other food items. "Heraia," an event conducted in her honor, took place in ancient Greece (around 6th century BCE), where a group of women competed for fitness and athletic motives.

Flora: Roman

As the name suggests, Flora is the mother of flowers, blossoms, nature, and spring. Ancient Romans celebrated a festival in her honor called "Floralia," where people performed in theaters and wore floral wreaths. It is believed that the festival first took place around 240 or 238 BC. Spectators also adorned bright robes to signify the onset of the spring season. The festival was held between April 28 to May 3, which aligns with the Beltane festival period. Devotees offered honey and milk to Flora and sought her blessings for success and growth while protecting the birth of new flora during spring and summer.

Pan: Greek

Another prominent Greek deity, Pan, is the god of agriculture and cattle. He is believed to be a wild shepherd roaming around green fields and pastures like a young boy in the countryside. He takes care of the flocks while enjoying his time in the wild. The pan flute's namesake derives from Pan himself, as he is often depicted carrying one, which he uses to play impromptu melodies as they come to him. Much like a faun, he has horns atop his head, as well as the legs of a goat. Known as the god of the wild, he presides over the forest and all its inhabitants.

Xochiquetzal: Aztec

Abundance, life, fruits, and fertility are the domains ruled by this Aztec Goddess. She is the epitome of the spring season and is associated with young blossoms. She also represents craftsmen and prostitutes due to her symbolism of household arts, sexual love, and beauty. Xochiquetzal is illustrated as a young and beautiful woman adorning a colorful outfit with flowers and vegetation. She is also believed to be the mediator between the gods and humans. Xochiquetzal is youthful and beautiful at all times because her powers do not let her age. Women worshiped her during the harvest season for fertility and growth.

Priapus: Greek

According to some tales, Priapus is Dionysus's son. However, some confer him to be Zeus's descendant. Priapus is known for his enormous phallus and is worshiped individually instead of being included in a cult. Ironically, his sexual frustration overshadows his desire for intimacy and lust. Devotees of the harvesting and agriculture backgrounds sought his blessings for fertility and protection against destructive forces. In some stories, he is depicted as a dwarf with a Phrygian cap and holding a basket of fruit. Other tales describe him as being impotent. A popular legend tells the story of Priapus raping goddess Hestia in her sleep – the entire attempt being unsuccessful as a braying donkey thwarts him midway, waking Hestia up along with her guests who chase Priapus away.

Kokopelli: Hopi

This god represents childbearing and marriage. He is famously known for the tale where he carries children on his back and gives them to women fit to bear offspring. He comes alive during spring and dances while playing his flute. According to one story, Kokopelli roams around playing the flute while turning the dark, cold winter days into pleasant springtime through his melodic notes. His music also provides a gateway toward abundant growth and harvest throughout the season. His back is hunched due to the heavy symbolic bag of seeds and his intense flute tunes. The notes from his flute melt all snow and pave the way for warmer, brighter days.

Apart from these main deities, other idols like Sheela-Na-Gig in Celtic culture and Mbaba Mwana Waresa in Zulu traditions also share certain traits with Beltane beliefs. As you can see, most of these deities represent fertility, motherhood, growth, agriculture, natural beings, or passion, which are quintessential to Beltane traditions. Beltane deities and ideals collectively project celebratory instincts and stress the importance of being happy. When you focus on the positives, you can attract success and growth. With the onset of the spring and summer seasons, the bright colors and blooming flowers make it easier for people to celebrate the new season and fulfill their desires.

Chapter 3: The Beltane Bonfire Ritual

The traditional Beltane bonfire is one of the most significant rituals held during this sabbat. Lighting the fire on the night before May 1st signifies entering into a new, fertile state with reinforced spiritual energy. According to the legends, by honoring the Sun with a bright fire, we ensure that it will nourish our crops and animals, providing a generous harvest and sustenance during the winter season. This magnificent force empowers nature, its spirits, and every creature that inhabits it, including the Celtic god Bel, who is also honored with the bonfire. The growing power of the sunlight presents an opportunity for cleansing after spending the winter months indoors, surrounded by darkness. As Bel sustains the fire, his help will also be needed to cleanse humans, animals, and crops from harmful energy through fire, smoke, and ashes. As you have learned from the previous chapters, Beltane is also the best time to communicate with spirits from the Otherworld. The flames and the offerings made to the spiritual guides we want to evoke will ensure the favors we may ask them are granted. If appeased, the benevolent spirits will all keep us on the right path, so their malevolent creatures won't impede our work.

Along with a feast, maypoles, and other nature-based traditions, the fire helps celebrate the beginning of summer, representing the peak of nature's fertility. According to pagan lore, Beltane festivities are also held to honor nature's most beautiful love story. In most pagan traditions, this sabbat is well-known as the Great Wedding between the Spring god (or the May King or the Green Man) and the maiden Goddess Flora. The fire helps their love come alive, while the maypole, with its colorful ribbons, depicts the feminine energy being wrapped around a male form. When this great love is set free, everything in the world becomes more beautiful as nature bubbles with fertility.

Modern Beltane Bonfires

Some elements of the ritual are rarely practiced anymore (like driving pastoral herds between two fire posts), while others are still kept alive in modern days. As in the past, Beltane bonfire rituals are held by a large group of people, gathered in merrymaking and embracing their fertility. The fire is lit by grinding two pieces of wood together until they start to spark, signifying the union of two powerful forces. Young people will still leap across the bonfire in hopes of ensuring fertility or finding the other part of their soul. In honor of the Great Wedding, couples often announce their engagement or celebrate a Handfasting around the bonfires.

The traditional colors are still used as the representation of this great sabbat. The color green symbolizes growth and fertility, red refers to strength and passion, while white indicates purity and clarification. These hues are incorporated into the decorations on the Maypole, May baskets, homes, and self-adornments alike.

The main reason why a group often holds this ritual is that it requires the participation of multiple people. There are roles assigned to each one of them, beginning with the May Queen and the Green Man. Depending on the relationship between the people in each role, fertility can be represented in many different ways. For example, family-oriented rituals may involve fun and games appropriate for all ages. On the other hand, if the participants are adult couples, more lust and passion are usually displayed.

Holding Your Own Beltane Bonfire

The beauty of this ritual lies in its simplistic and customizable nature, which allows anyone to transform a simple element like fire into something wonderful and unique. Whether you live in the countryside or in the middle of a city, you can always encounter a little piece of nature to light a pile of logs and a group of people gathering around the flames. The rest of the magic comes from within you, and you can bring it to life with music, dancing, and the creativity you put into the decorations.

You may use any nature-based traditional decoration and element in the ritual you want, including the maypole crafted from a piece of wood, ribbons, and crystals. If you are part of a group consisting of practitioners using altars or other sacred spaces while preparing for a ritual, you can all create a small maypole and place it on your altar besides all the other decorations. These elements should reflect your preferences when manifesting intentions. For example, if you want to meditate before the event and ask for guidance on how to prepare for the ritual, you will need crystals, candles, and symbols to help you relax and help your mind focus. Visualizing how your soul would look covered in fresh flower blossoms may help manifest your hidden desires. You may also ask for a specific favor from your spiritual guide. If you are looking to attract a lover during the event, you can burn a green or a purple candle to manifest a new relationship. After this, you will be ready to take the necessary actions to make your dreams a reality.

Preparing for the Ritual

Traditionally, the fire should be lit on the last night of April (May Eve) and burn until sundown on the following day. Here is what you need to prepare for the ritual:

- **Several types of wood:** Originally, there were nine different types used in one bundle, but feel free to use as much as you can find.

- **A space to light the fire:** In larger, open spaces, feel free to light a fire as everyone will be safe. Those who live in the city will need to contain their fire in heat-resistant containers or cauldrons.

- **Red, green, and white ribbons:** These will be needed to tie the bundles with and can be used for various other decorations you want to include.

- **Flowers, herbs, and seeds:** Representing nature's different sides. The colors you use for your flowers embody the same symbolism as the ribbons.

- **A person playing the May Queen:** Ideally, this should be a woman who has a committed partner and is within her childbearing years intending to conceive during the following months.

- **A person playing the Green Man:** This role should fall on the partner of the woman playing the Queen, but essentially, any adult man can play the role of her consort.

- **Green, red, and white clothes:** Several men and women should dress up in the traditional Beltane colors.

- **Flower crown and headdresses with antlers:** The flowers will adorn the female participant, whereas the males will wear the antlers.

- **Drums and other instruments:** Anything will do as long as you can make a loud noise with it.

- **A spokesperson:** They will welcome the season and introduce the main couple.

- **Crystals representing vitality and passion:** An optional choice depending on your beliefs.

- **Decorations for your sacred space:** This is for those requiring an altar or similar space to prepare for their rituals.

Initiating the Ritual

After preparing all the decorations and other elements of the ritual, one person should be chosen to light the fire. They will also be responsible for feeding it safely until the time comes to extinguish it. First, everyone should form a circle around the fireplace, with the Green Man and the May Queen being on opposite sides.

Then, one person should welcome the entire procession with this chant:

"The Great Beltane is here, making the earth alive and fertile.

As it was when our ancestors planted their crops come summer.

The earth that was cold for months is now warm, and it awaits.

For it now begs us to plant our seeds and feed our animals.

This is a season for love and passion for igniting.

We welcome this season with a fire set alight.

Now, the bonfire can be lit while the person continues their chant:

As this fire grows, it will light up the night

From this fire, we will grow stronger.

This fire of lust and passion,

Brings us the grift of fertility.

Tonight, the Green Man arrives from the forest
To reclaim his maiden, the May Queen.
She is the Goddess of nature and fertile fields
And he is the one who helps us sow our seeds."

As they are introduced to the rest of the group, the designated May Queen and Green Man should be slowly let into the middle of the circle near the fire, with everyone else surrounding them.

Those around the May Queen and the Green Man can start to chant the following blessing:

"Summer is here, and we welcome the fertility it brings.
We are happy to greet this new season of passion
and welcome it with open arms and hope in our hearts.
We came together at Beltane to create and celebrate life
and to honor the Great Wedding and the union
out of which all life comes.
With each new life nature creates, we shall grow and thrive.
So it is, and it shall be."

Traditional Courtship

This is the most important part of the ritual, as the May Queen has to be courted by her consort before their union can be officiated. First, the couple will begin chasing each other in the middle of the circle by traveling from east to west, following the sun's path. They should start slow, as a traditional courtship may take some time to yield its fruit. While doing so, they can wave to the other participants to make everything more fun for everyone. It will also make it more of a joyful courtship rather than one person simply running after another. From time to time, the Queen can allow her consort to get closer, pretending readiness for the union, and slip away just before he reaches her. They should make a full circle at least three times before ending the chase in front of the fire, which should be burning bright by now.

While the Green Man is busy pursuing his love, those around them can start making noise with drums and other instruments, including their hands. Chanting traditional pagan songs is also a great way to bring more merriment and bonding into the experience. Make sure you start slowing as well, following the rhythm of the main couple. Once he hastens his pursuit of her, so too does the tempo of the accompanying music. The chanting and the noise should slowly become louder and louder, culminating just before the couple has completed their chase.

When they have made their journey around the fire at least three times, the drumming and the chanting should stop at once.

Now, the main spokesperson should recite the following:

> *"Finally, love and life are brought together in fire and passion.*
>
> *Now, the May Queen may express her love to the Green Man:*
>
> *I come from the earth and carry the womb for all its creatures.*
>
> *Within me, new life will grow this summer.*
>
> *My blood will be the water; my breath will be the air, and my spirit the fire.*
>
> *My honor will sustain the life I now create with you.*
>
> *To which, the Green Man Replies:*
>
> *I am the oak growing in the forest.*
>
> *I bring the seed, the energy to this new life.*
>
> *My honor, too, will sustain the life I now create with you."*

If real-life partners play the couple, they may embrace and kiss and even fall to the ground, symbolizing their union. If not, a simple, platonic embrace will suffice. Now, all the masculine and the feminine spirits are united, and the great rite will very soon result in a much-desired conception.

Once the embrace of the main couple is broken, the spokesperson will declare the union completed by saying:

> *"Nature has once more life to give, and the earth will bring us sustenance! Our fertility will be potent this year, and we shall be blessed with everything we wish for in life."*

Closing the Ceremony

After ensuring the fertility everyone wishes for in their lives will be granted, it's time to cheer and clap as loud as you can. This last part of the ritual celebrates the success of the coming months by dancing around the bonfire and singing and chanting lively poems. Feel free to get inspired by the vivid colors around you and remember that in the same way nature comes alive, so will your creativity and fertility be renewed. Those in a committed relationship can focus on growing together, while those looking for a lover have an opportunity to find each other around the fire. Most importantly, each individual can find themselves revealing their true passion and desires. Whether it comes to professional or personal life, this is the best time to start on the right path and become the best version of yourself. This way, you will develop a much deeper appreciation for yourself and others. There is no better way to form strong bonds within a community than for each member to become the individuals they are meant to be. For this reason, everyone is encouraged to continue the ritual until they are ready to start their summer and put all their efforts into their endeavors.

Making Beltane Bonfires Unique

The experience you get from the Beltane bonfire ritual may vary depending on your spiritual beliefs, expectations, and your willingness to have as much fun as you can. You can organize a more peaceful and welcoming event or have a more chaotic atmosphere full of color, displaying your hedonistic side. The number of people representing each color can be adjusted according to your preferences. So, if your group wants a more natural display, you can always have more whites and greens, sprucing it up with a touch of red.

If your ritual is more work or spirituality-oriented, you may want to customize the entire procession to suit your needs. You may change the songs or adjust the role assignment. For example, if you are a group of friends looking to venture into a new endeavor together, the May Queen and her consort can even be played by two people belonging to the same gender. By fortifying their unity, the group can help all of you thrive, which will result in all of you achieving your dreams.

If the celebration is held near the participants' homes, everyone can take a piece of smoldering wood to their house after the ritual is finished. This will ensure fertility in all your endeavors during the coming months.

A Final Word

The Beltane Bonfire ritual has once been one of the largest festivities on the Celtic calendar. Under the pressure of Christianity, the celebrations have been reduced to only a few participants, who kept their ancient customers alive. Fortunately, in the past decades, the number of participants has been increasing steadily, slowly restoring this sabbat to its former glory. The fundamental elements, such as the Green Man's cycle of life or the procession of the May Queen around the bonfire, are kept alive for generations to come. However, as the dynamic within a community changes with the years, so do the minor details of the bonfire ritual. The various elements are often represented in different ways and are always tailored to the needs of the community.

No two Beltane bonfire rituals will be the same, which is exactly what makes this yearly event so unique and joyful. With the union of different cultures and belief systems, we are creating even more room for the interpretation of the bonfire. It's not solely about the age-old story of birth, rebirth, fertility anymore. The practice has become a way to form soul-deep connections and explore our differences. Year after year, massive bonfires in Scotland and Ireland welcome visitors from different cultural backgrounds. That said, everyone is free to organize their own ritual and make it as unique to them as they want it to be. No matter where you are located, if you have a piece of nature you can use to light a fire, you can have an immersive Beltane experience. All you need is a group of like-minded people and a little bit of creativity, and you can create a unique event for everyone to take part in. Nature and the atmosphere you cultivate will bring the community together and help overcome challenges.

Chapter 4: Beltane Customs, Then and Now

Due to the introduction of different religions and other outside pressures, even the most ancient traditions are bound to change. Beltane customs were no exception to this rule either, as Christianity and industrialization have definitely taken their toll on this earth-based tradition. While the druids were able to preserve the essence of the sabbat, over time, many new customs were introduced into the life of pagans. No longer feeling the need to rely on nature for survival, modern pagans have left behind their habit of celebrating the point when longer days have begun. That being said, in recent years, there have been significant efforts to revive these ancient traditions, and they have been quite successful. The most significant Beltane rituals will be discussed throughout the rest of the book. However, in this chapter, we cover how these customs have changed in general and how they are practiced now as opposed to their ancient roots.

Beltane Then

Due to the harsh winters in the Northern Hemisphere, ancient Celts were forced to spend the colder months in their homes, unable to feed themselves (or their animals) fresh food. The arrival of the warm weather represented such a joyous occasion that the Celts felt the need to express their gratitude in an elaborate yet natural way. First, they greeted the budding spring with Ostara. And when the soil was ready to nourish the seeds into crops, and the pastures were green enough to feed the livestock, the Celts welcomed summer with Beltane. The favorable change in weather conditions made them optimistic about a new beginning, and their Beltane customs are a true reflection of this.

One of the most noteworthy practices was the traditional Beltane bonfire, lit on the evening before May Day and left to burn until sundown on this day. While primarily organized in honor of the Celtic deity Belenus and the sun, several other practices, including cleansing rituals for humans, crops, and animals, were tied to the fire burning. Young unmarried people would jump over the fire in hopes of finding a partner in the coming period, while those already married wanted to fortify their bond. Cattle were driven over the bonfire smoke, and the ashes were spread onto the fields. People would bring food, drinks, and musical instruments to the bonfire and chant songs while dancing around the fire to the beat of drums. They adorned themselves and their homes in yellow May flowers and made gift baskets full of these, too. The blossoms of the May tree were also gathered, but these were used for much more than decorations. A delicious wine was made from them, which was always ready to be consumed at the next Beltane.

The ancient Celts also took advantage of the weakened barrier between the worlds and communicated with Aos Sí and other spirits living in the Otherworld. After providing them with generous offerings, people would ask these benevolent spirits for protection and guidance throughout the coming months.

The May Queen and the Green Man union was known to be of tremendous importance at Beltane celebrations. Handfasting ceremonies and betrothal announcements were often held to honor the Great Wedding and unite couples in love and passion. And while official weddings weren't customary, married couples often used this night to get inspired by nature and conceive a child. On May Day, large poles were erected, symbolizing the male form. The poles were adorned with colorful ribbons, representing the female form wrapped around its male counterpart.

During Beltane, even meals as simple as bread were prepared ritualistically, further honoring the well-being of the crops and the animals it took to create them. The druids were a well-educated class, able to journey between the worlds and heal those in need. They conducted some ceremonies on May Day and the night before. Other rituals were simply done with different people holding eminent positions within their tribe. Regardless of who was directing them, ancient Beltane festivities were closely associated with nature and its role in sustaining all life on Earth.

It's not entirely clear when the Maypole setting custom has become part of the Beltane celebrations, as it's mentioned far fewer times in Celtic tales than the traditional bonfire ritual. There are remarks about villagers erecting Maypoles, but its purpose wasn't entirely clear. Due to its phallic shape, it is theorized that the structure was a symbol of fertility, so it has been accepted as such in modern times. Initially, only young girls danced around the Maypole to attract a lover and increase their own fertility. Eventually, this tradition evolved and became much more elaborate, with all the different decorations being used; even the ribbons – having originally been one wreath – were shredded into pieces, and each piece tied in different colors. Around this time, villagers of all ages begin to participate in the ritual, using poles of different sizes. Some were shorter, while others were so tall, they needed to be embedded deeply into the ground. The completed Maypoles were usually left standing until the winter, but sometimes they remained until the following Beltane.

Beltane Now

Nowadays, May Day customs have a somewhat different take on the ancient Celtic Beltane festivals. For starters, save for a very few people who still earn a living cultivating crops and raising cattle, we don't have to hurry to work when the warm weather arrives. That being said, many people still feel the need to celebrate the day when spring turns into summer and life begins to show itself. In fact, many pagans, Wiccans, and druids recognize Beltane as one of the most meaningful spiritual times in their lives. They just celebrate it differently – by moving it into the cities and putting a modern twist on it. In Scotland and Ireland, large gatherings in villages around this time of the year are becoming increasingly common. However, those living in large cities are even more drawn to the lure of these earth-based holidays. So, they simply found a way to make room for Beltane celebrations close to their home. This allows for a more intimate gathering, which is often even more appreciated than participating in an event with thousands of other people.

People with Celtic roots around the world have opted to reignite the old fame of the festival by taking its essence and centering it around nature and community. While modern Beltane festivities are much more organized affairs, this doesn't mean they have lost their meaning entirely. They just allow for more creative freedom when incorporating the traditional elements, like the fire, the Maypole, or the flowers. The modern twists consist mostly of organized music events, such as choreographed dancing and outdoor theaters.

One of the essential features of Beltane that remains the same is the traditional bonfire. As it has been done in ancient times, the election of a May Queen and the Green Man. precede this elemental ritual However, the latter is sometimes left out due to alterations in the symbolism. Except in Pagan cultures, the magical union of the couple isn't considered necessary anymore for the fertility of nature. Rather than celebrating this during the bonfire, the emphasis is put on the fertility of the soul.

Those who still honor the Great Wedding and the unification of the masculine and feminine energies do it with the traditional Maypole. Once erected as a simple pole with a few ribbons and flowers around it, this structure has now become an essential part of the May Day celebrations. It can be anything from a tall plastic bar to a standing tree stripped of its lower branches – as long as the ribbons can be wrapped around it, the pole will serve its purpose – which is much more than being a symbol for fertility. In fact, some communities prefer to have a permanent fixture for the Maypole and will leave the decorated structure to serve as a reminder of vitality and fertility for the entire season.

In modern times, Maypoles are erected for people to dance around them while waving the colorful ribbons in an intricate pattern. Each participant will bring their own ribbon and secure it to the top of the pole. If a separate bar is used for the base, this is done before its placement in the ground. If living trees are used, one or two people will climb and tie the ribbons to the taller branches. Then everyone will take a ribbon and start moving around the pole in a circle. Some people move in a clockwise direction, while others will move counter-clockwise. Typically, the same number of people is required to move in both directions to get the traditional pattern, but this can be altered to the participant's preferences. The colors are alternated as the ribbons flail until the entire surface of the pole is covered with them, from top to bottom. Holding their ribbon in their hands, each person must pass the person closest to them from the left, then do the same with the person coming next from the right. They will also alternate between passing people from the outside and letting them pass under their ribbon – and passing them from the inside and going over the other person's color. They will repeat these steps until the pattern is completed. In the end, as the ribbons act as the female form around the base, they create a sheath symbolizing nature's womb enveloping the new life. At this point, the ribbons are tied in a knot to prevent them from unraveling and ruining the pattern. Creating the intricate pattern has the same purpose – the ribbons won't be able to unwind easily, and the sheath remains intact for as long as it needs to be.

This Maypole dance is also followed by chanting and drumming, and when the songs are over, everyone feels more free and ready to admire their creation. Men, women, and children of all ages participate in this elaborate ritual, which is another modern notion. Due to the sensual nature of ancient Celtic practices, children weren't allowed to take part in them. The custom of the Maypole setting and the dance that follows is focused on expressing creativity and having fun, so there is no need to exclude anyone from the community.

But this dance isn't the only activity that makes it easy for everyone to participate. Food and drinks are prepared for all ages and tastes. Apart from the traditional May wine produced from sweet woodruff, natural drinks are made from fresh, natural produce, including edible flowers and early summer veggies and fruit. At some modern Beltane feasts, the traditional bannock is still being offered. Once a staple part of the Celt's cuisine, this flatbread is one of the few recipes that managed to survive the test of time. It's still popular at all four major Celtic festivals, including Beltane. Typically prepared on the last day of April, it is served as breakfast on the 1st of May when people rise from their slumber after the bonfire ritual.

The Maypole dance has many variations, depending on the ritual's purpose or the pattern the participants want to achieve. It can be done in parts, with only men and women taking turns, or in teams where groups of people move past another group by dancing around them and waving their ribbons onto theirs. People often choose to flail different patterns to secure their ribbons or simply display their creativity. Apart from the ribbons, modern Maypoles also incorporate garland, flowers, and even gemstones sewed to the ribbons. When it comes to the music participants dance to while waving their pattern, it also depends on personal preferences. Some communities will stick to live music performed on traditional Celtic pipes and drums, while others will opt for modern bands or play pre-recorded music if it's their only option. After all, it's all about having as much fun as possible and enjoying nature's gifts.

Another modernized Beltane custom that has recently gained popularity is a-Maying. This term essentially refers to a group of activities, including young women and men who venture into nature to pick flowers and other greenery. These will become part of the home decorations, the headdresses, or attached to the ribbons of the Maypole. Apart from the traditional yellow, flowers in other colors are now used for these purposes. A-Maying may also include chanting songs and dancing freely on the fields while picking flowers or performing in the middle of the city. In Ireland and Scotland, there are larger events where people can participate in different a-Maying practices, including art, film, comedy, music, literature, and poetry. Or they can simply enjoy interacting with other community members while admiring handmade artisan products and other works of art. In some cultures, the young will feel free to give in to their lustful nature and find a lover during their a-Maying adventures.

The assimilation of the ancient Celtic beliefs into other cultures has had a great impact on the waning interest in the customs associated with this unique world. However, it wasn't the only reason for the massive changes Beltane and other celebrations have gone through. Industrialization and the recent rise of modern technology have made our lives far safer and much more convenient than ever before. But it has also had a negative effect on our relationship with the outside world – especially the living parts of it.

Since we are no longer confined indoors during winter and can have fresh food on our table any time we want, we have lost our connection to nature's rhythms. We can't appreciate the sun for nourishing life on earth, even though we still greatly depend on it. Due to our busy lives, we rarely spend time outside, which means we can't feel the powers of nature surrounding us and its spirits protecting us from harmful forces.

We have all felt the toll the modern world takes on our souls. Sometimes, we just wish to break free from this fast-paced society and turn our back on its superficial customs, even if it's just for a day or two. Celebrating Beltane can provide the perfect solution to fulfilling our needs to belong to a community based on real values. This was the reason why Beltane festivals experienced a magnificent revival throughout Europe – and this is why you should take part in or host one, as well. Whether you have Celtic roots or just feel the need to explore a culture that's calling to you, the May Day celebration can connect you to a unique community. In this society, you will find trust and a sense of belonging, regardless of your spiritual background. After all, modern Beltane customs represent the combination of ancient Celtic beliefs and individual experiences.

At the same time, they are also incorporating bits and pieces from other religions – in which everyone can find something fulfilling. When organizing a Beltane celebration with a group of like-minded people, everyone can put parts of themselves in it and still end up with festivities you can all enjoy. You can get as creative as you want to, and no one will judge you for it. After all, everyone will do the same – because that's the beauty of celebrating this vivacious time of year: everyone can participate in their own way.

Most importantly, by honoring this sabbat, you can reconnect with nature, and your own spiritual self, unveiling your hidden desires. Not only will you not have to sell your soul in exchange for perseverance, but through Beltane, you can get parts of it back. There is something incredibly freeing about enjoying nature and dancing around with colorful ribbons in your hand. Or you can simply feast yourself on traditional Celtic meals and drinks – they are much healthier than the commercial products we consume nowadays. Unlike other ancient festivals with a modern take, this one still remains nature-based and free of commercial spoils. The spirit of this festival will teach you to be more kind to yourself and listen to your intuition. Even if you are just visiting one, you will have a unique experience that leaves a lasting impact, and if you let the spirits in, they will change your life for the better.

Chapter 5: Preparing Your House and Altar

As you know, Beltane happens to be a fire festival and is centered around honoring life. It is an exciting time of year when every pagan celebrates the fertile magic of our mother earth. This spring festivity is focused on passion, new life, rebirth, and fire, and your decor should symbolize the same. The great thing about this holiday is that you can find creative ways to celebrate the magic of Beltane that's unique to you. This step-by-step guide will offer tips to prepare and decorate your altar and house, and you can pick and choose what appeals to you.

Decorating the Sacred Beltane Altar

There are many creative ideas to consider when decorating the altar for your Beltane celebrations, and, if you want, you may incorporate them all into the decor. However, the decision about which ones to use would heavily depend on the altar space you have. But we have plenty of options for you to choose from regardless of how spacious your area is. The next chapter has several recommendations and guidelines for crafts and plant ideas. But for now, we are going to focus on the decor basics for a perfect and devoted Beltane altar.

The Beltane Color Scheme

Around the Beltane festival celebrations, the earth happens to be green and beautiful. As a matter of fact, you are going to see a new grassy haven and trees reborn after surviving a long and dormant winter. So, it makes perfect sense to make use of green hues abundantly. You can also incorporate the brighter spring colors, including the yellow hues of dandelion daffodils and forsythia, or go with the purplish lilacs or perhaps the robin's egg. You can adorn your Beltane altar using all of these or perhaps just choose the one that speaks to you.

Honoring Masculine Energy

This pagan festival honors the masculine energy of God at its most vital and potent state. This potent masculine energy is often depicted through an erect and large phallus, although it is not exclusively the only symbol to depict the sacred masculine. Some other representations include acorns, antlers, seeds, and sticks. You can opt to include all the possible symbols because it is about showing your dedication and enthusiasm when celebrating this festival. A maypole would be an excellent choice as a centerpiece, given its naturally phallic shape that honors masculine energy in a very direct way.

Honoring Feminine Energy

Fertility plays a monumental role in Beltane, which is why its rituals highly revere the feminine energy, which is represented by the goddess, to mention one. The source of her fertility, much like mother earth, resides within her, which is why other symbols in honor of her include a cup/chalice – representative of a woman's womb – or certain circular items such as rings or wreaths that hint at the never-ending cycle of life. The goal is to put objects on the altar that closely represent the divine feminine and can be used in the Beltane celebrations.

Bringing in Some Faeries and Flowers

As mentioned, Beltane is a festival that celebrates the greenery of mother earth, and at this particular time of the year, the earth is in a way being reborn. The spring brings new life and blooming flowers, and green abundance can be seen everywhere. Flowers that grow during the months of spring, such as forsythia, tulips, daffodils, daisies, and hyacinths, are also common offerings placed at the altar during the Beltane festivities (more flower options are available in chapter 6). If you are quite crafty, you can make your own floral crowns for you and your family to wear during the celebrations. The same afore-mentioned floral options, in addition to fresh herbs, can be used for the Sabbat ritual and for cultures that have the Faerie realm ingrained within their traditions and folklore.

Honoring the Festival of Fire

There are four renowned fire festivals according to the modern traditions of Paganism, and Beltane is one of them. So, to honor the spirit of fire, you must incorporate the element of fire in your altar decorations. The most popular tradition is organizing a bonfire in an open field outside, but this may not be possible for everyone nowadays, especially those living in a city. Luckily, practicing pagans needn't worry, as there are creative ways to get around the obstacles of big city life. A practical alternative is to use candles on the altar – alternatively, one can also go with an indoor fire within a tabletop cauldron (make sure the cauldron is heat resistant and you have taken all the safety measures necessary before taking the celebrations inside).

Decorating Your House to Welcome Beltane

Now that your altar is decorated and embodies items that capture the Beltane spirit, it's time for you to welcome the Beltane energy in your house, too. There are plenty of cost-effective ways to fill your home with Beltane energy – and they're quick and easy to implement.

Welcoming the Energy of Fire

Since fire is one of the most significant elements in Beltane, it is appropriate to welcome it into your house as well. This means that you can take this amazing time to decorate your abode with some fire blessing – and by this, you don't have to start an indoor bonfire because *candles will work just fine*. As mentioned above, you can opt for a cauldron of cast iron and have a small fire.

Bring In the Flowery Nature

During Beltane, the gardens bloom with beautiful flowers, and the spirit of spring permeates everywhere. But around this time of the year, you will also see the early summer blooms, highlighting the fertile nature of mother earth. You can decorate your house with vases and bowls of all the spring and summer freshly cut flowers and potted blooms. Consider using the flowers with bits of grass, and you can also put flower petals in a water bowl or press flowers between glass frames. Again, you can always unleash your creativity by making floral crowns or making a May Day Floral Basket that you can hang up on the door.

Add Ribbons and Braids

In several countries and rural societies, ribbons are important in the Beltane festival. You can see ribbons appear around the Maypole, and young men and women would exchange ribbons as a token of love. It is also an intuitive and "Beltane-appropriate" idea to form some blessing braids with vibrant spring hues of yellow, blues, greens, and purples. These could be used to decorate the walls around your house. You can hang ribbons in your front yard or decorate the house from the inside with the same colorful ribbons.

Butterflies, Birds, and Bees

Spring is a time of excitement, not only for human beings but for the entire animal kingdom. You can see birds welcoming their newly born chicks, the bees buzzing around here and there with joy, and trying to pollinate the newly bloomed flowers. At the same time, butterflies would also be ready to escape their cocoons by this time and fly about in their full glory. To welcome some of your fluttery friends into your home, you can consider adding the plants that are known to attract these winged creatures. For indoor decor representing butterfly energy, you can add a few pieces of relevant artwork. Various cultures around the world associate the spirit realm and wisdom with bees. To ensure that you keep the doors to the other realms open for communication at the festival of Beltane, decorate with hives, honey, and bees as well.

Rituals and Prayers of Beltane

The time of Beltane brings along seedlings, sprouts, and grass. You see the wild forest breathing in a new life. You can say simple prayers to start the Beltane festivity and celebrate the rebirth of the earth. The traditions of Beltane are as diverse and colorful as the essence of this festive season itself.

The Goddess Ritual to Honor the Sacred Feminine

You have to be on the lookout for the arrival of the spring season because that is the time during which we can enjoy the full bloom of mother earth. It is the time when the earth will be exposing its magical fertility. This annual occurrence marks the universal celebration of the Sacred Feminine.

A pagan worshipper uses this annual occurrence as an opportunity to revel and give thanks to the mother goddess and celebrate all of those long departed who had found strength and solace in her power. Both men and women may participate in this celebration, with a strict focus on honoring the feminine energy. An important thing to keep in mind is to be open and receptive toward new energies from different deities pulling you to them. Should that occur, all that is needed is to adjust the attributes of your rituals as required.

The Bonfire Ritual of Beltane for Group Celebrations

Beltane being the fire ritual, one can celebrate it by combining a roaring bonfire along with love for the May Queen and forest Gods. It's a relatively simple ritual compared to others, as its requirements only include symbols that represent the May Queen and the Forest King's union (chapter 3 offers easy instructions to initiate the ritual as a group). This is a very playful ritual and, depending on the relationship between the group participants, it can grow to be a lusty one as well. However, if you conduct these celebrations within the family, you can keep things civil and age-appropriate.

The Ritual of Planting Rite

This particular ritual is meant for solitary practitioners. However, you can also perform this in a small group if you want. It is a very basic rite practice that is all about celebrating the fertility of the planting season. You will definitely need to perform this ritual outside. If you do not have access to a yard, you can use some soil pots and plant a garden in them.

Beltane Specific Symbolism

Modern Paganism uses various symbols, sigils, and runes in ritualistic celebrations, such as Beltane. One of the most important symbols for the Beltane festival is the fire element. The symbol is a simple triangle and is used for conducting the focused fire meditative ritual to harness the power of the volatile element. You can also use the sigil of "confidence" during the Beltane festival.

In Beltane celebrations, runes hold a very special place, and they serve as a symbolic representation of the pagan belief system. Runes hold a sacred spiritual meaning in Paganism and are a way to let go of infatuation with the individual – and instead, think about a *shared ritualistic performance.* While marking or being marked by a rune, the person has to focus hard on the core intention, and every time they see the rune, they get a reminder about that intention. The most commonly used runes are usually derived from Germanic sources and belong to Anglo-Saxon and Norse ancestry. Celtic Ogham symbols are used, and some groups create their own unique symbolism. One of the widely Germanic Algiz runes is associated with protection and is often painted at the forehead of the main person in the Beltane festival. You can use any of these symbols when decorating your home.

Dress Ideas for Beltane Festival

Once you have everything ready and set for the Beltane celebrations, one thing that must be on your mind is how to dress for it. It is definitely a pressing question and one that absolutely puzzles some modern pagans. But Beltane dressing options are quite a few, and you can incorporate your own modern style in the attire – think modern festival outfits we wear today. Some dress ideas are as follows:

1. You can go with the earthly mother dress options and add some hues of greens and other earthly colors that show abundance and nature.

2. Another option is to select a vibrantly colored kaftan. You can go for one that has butterfly stripes or some natural seasonal hues in print.

3. You can choose a Batik, a traditional dress decorated using dye and wax. It comes in eye-catching and inspiring designs. You can get this in a flowy frock or go for a blouse and skirt.

4. Since fairies are also a part of Beltane celebrations, you can opt to select dress styles that look similar to fairies or pixies.

5. An important accessory for the Beltane ritual is a flowery tiara or handmade flower headpiece.

For men, the dress ideas for Beltane revolve around earthly colors, and some select a Medieval tunic or Pirate style shirt. However, most men usually keep it simple with earthy hues. Although, you can always have some runes, sigils, or other symbols printed on the shirts.

With the many different and creative ways to decorate your altar and house in preparation for the Beltane festival, you can tailor these options to suit your preferences, as long as it connects to the core spirit of this festival. In this chapter are also some basic rituals for Beltane to help you get inspired when choosing your decor – note that there are many more rituals you can explore, which are covered throughout this book. Beltane decor and rituals make use of plants and crafts quite a lot, which is why we offer plenty of ideas that incorporate them.

Chapter 6: Beltane Trees, Plants, and Flowers

Now that we have covered the history, mythology, rituals, and costumes of Beltane, this chapter will discuss all of the plants associated with this festival, like sacred trees, flowers, and other plants.

Sacred Trees

You will find that most Wicca traditions usually include certain types of trees in their bonfire rituals. The sacred trees we cover in this chapter are the first nine trees in the Celtic tree calendar. The ancient Druids' power runs through the woods of these trees, and they are usually used in magic rituals and spiritual enlightenment.

The Birch Tree

The Birch, or Beithe, is the first of the nine sacred trees on the Celtic tree calendar. Traditionally speaking, it follows the Winter Solstice, and it is connected to Beith, the Ogham symbol. Whenever a forest burns, the Birch tree is usually the first one to grow back. For this reason, the tree is often connected to regeneration and rebirth. If you are working on achieving a goal in your life, the Brisch wood will add power and momentum to your new ventures. Additionally, this tree can be used in various spells related to creativity, fertility, protection, and healing. The birch branches are popular among many witches who often use them to make brooms which they use for magic. Branches can be incorporated into a number of rituals like enchantments, purification rituals, and renewals, such as new beginnings spells. The birch tree wood can help a person overcome their fears and become courageous, and it can also be used to ward off evil spirits.

The Rowan Tree

The Rowan tree is connected to success, power, and astral travel, and it is also connected to Brighid, the Celtic goddess of the hearth. The Celts called this tree Luis, which is an Ogham symbol. The Rowan tree can provide you with protective powers. For instance, you can create a talisman by carving a specific charm into a small rowan twig and wearing it to ward off any harm that may come your way. Ancient Norsemen would regularly create such talismans to protect them on their travels, hunts and daily life. Additionally, many North European traditions dictate the planting of Rowan trees in graveyards because they believed these trees would aid the dead in passing on from this realm to the next. Crosses made of rowan twigs were hung in homes and barns to further protect people from anything malevolent.

The rowan berries are also used in various spells. For instance, if you want to protect yourself and your family from the flu, then you will need to get a few dried rowan berries and a white or purple cloth. The berries should be placed in the cloth, which you will tie up with a white or purple ribbon. Hang it in your kitchen during the wintertime to prevent illness.

The Ash Tree

In Norse mythology, Odin, the ruler of the gods and Asgard, would hang himself from an ash tree for nine days and nights, believing it would bring him infinite wisdom. For this reason, this sacred tree has always been connected to knowledge and divination. According to the Celts, the Ash tree is also considered sacred to the Lugh god. This tree can be used in various rituals and spells as a result of its connection to knowledge and divinity. For instance, the Ash tree is used in prophetic dreams, ocean rituals, and spiritual journeys. You can also use it to make various magical tools which are considered very productive compared to tools made from other trees' wood. Some of the tools you can create are a wand, staff, or broom.

It is believed that the Ash tree bark and wood have healing powers and can protect people from drowning as well. Ash or bark shavings are great ingredients to add when making a witch bottle. It is believed that if you put Ash tree leaves under your pillow, you will have prophetic dreams, and if you put them in a bowl of water near your bed, they can protect you from diseases.

The Alder Tree

The Alder tree is often associated with divination and prophecy for many pagans, as it is believed to connect worshippers to their intuition, thereby helping them make better spiritual decisions. The Alder tree flower, along with its branches, has been historically used in charms that call upon Faerie magic. For example, flutes or small whistles were constructed from said branches to summon the ancient air spirits. So, if you are interested in playing a musical instrument like a flute or pipe, you can make one from Alder's wood. This wood has been traditionally used in charms or spells that protect the heart – and even more often constructed into wands with runes carved into them.

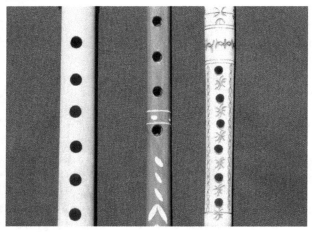

The Willow Tree

The Willow tree, according to Celtic legends, is revered by poets and druids. However, its significance for the Celts lies in its association with the creation story of their belief system. This tree is considered the tree of enchantment and dreams. It is believed that if you plant a Willow tree near your house, it will help protect it from natural disasters like earthquakes, floods, storms, and hurricanes. As a result of their protection powers, these trees are usually planted near cemeteries as well. The Willow tree wood is associated with knowledge, healing, and nurturing. Witches use the woods of this tree to make brooms that they can use when performing magic and spells. It is also used in spells that can help a person express their emotions and understand all matters of the heart, like love. This sacred tree can also be incorporated into spells that can help ease one's sadness.

You can soak Willow in water and wove it into bowls or baskets. Willow can also be used in love spells. For instance, if you want someone to love you, you will need three branches from a Willow tree, weave them together, and then tie them in a circle but make sure that it is loose, not tight. Put the finished product on a table near you and inside the circle, and add the picture or name of the person you love.

The Hawthorn

The Hawthorn tree symbolizes love and protection. It is usually used in various spells associated with masculinity and spells that can help a person advance in their career. If you are struggling with your professional life, you will find many Hawthorne tree spells that will help you to make better decisions for your career. You will find that this tree has a strong connection to the realm of the Faerie. According to legend, when a Hawthorn tree grows with an Ash and an Oak tree, it can attract a fairy. This tree also has cleansing and protection powers.

To protect your new bundle of joy from negative energy, place thrones from a Hawthorn tree under their crib. You can also protect your home from harm by tying a thorn with a red ribbon and hanging it over your door. You can use parts of this tree in protection spells by collecting a few thorns from the Hawthorn tree. Write the name of the person you want to be protected from on a piece of paper. Next, you will need to wrap the piece of paper around the thorns and bury them underground. It is recommended to bury them near the tree where you collected the thorns from, if possible.

The Oak Tree

The Oak tree is famous for its strength and power. It stands tall, and it is usually longer than all of the other trees around it. According to the ancient Celts, Oak trees were sacred. The Oak is called upon during rituals and spells to bring success, protection, fertility, good fortune, money, and strength. The wood of the Oak can be used to make various magical tools, while the leaves can be incorporated into spells and purification rituals.

Oak has protective powers, which is why some people would hang a twig from this tree in their homes to help protect and strengthen their families and ward off any negativity. You can also burn a bark or piece of wood from an oak tree for healing and good health. It is also known to bring fertility and good luck.

The Holly Tree

The Holly tree wood is believed to have shielding powers, so it is usually used in protection spells. It is also used in building weapons. To protect your family and to bring good luck, you can hang a twig from a Holly tree in your house. It can also be worn as a charm. The tree's leaves are utilized in the process of making holy water by soaking them in spring water overnight under a full moon. Since the Holly tree is believed to offer security, you can build a Holly tree hedge around your house to protect it from evil spirits.

Holly is used in spells to help turn your dreams into a reality. For this spell to work, you must gather nine leaves from a Holly on a Friday *after midnight*. Wrap them in a piece of white cloth and seal them with nine knots, then put them under your pillow. If done correctly, the belief dictates that it should make your dreams come true.

The Hazel Tree

The Hazel tree is connected to wisdom, knowledge, dream journeys, and divinations. In fact, the druids sought wisdom through Hazel trees. The tree is also part of Norse mythology and was called the Tree of Knowledge. Thor, the god of war and fertility, considered this tree to be sacred. Its wood is usually used in various spells. For instance, if you want to seek help from the faeries, bring a few hazelnuts, tie them onto a cord, and hang the cord up in your house. If you want to make a wish come true, make a crown using twigs from the hazel tree, put it on your head, and state your wish. Hazel Twigs can protect your house from lightning as well.

- These nine sacred trees are used to build the Beltane fire during the festival.
- You can also make a May Bush using a flowering branch from a Hawthorn tree, and you can decorate it with ribbons, tinsel, and colored eggshells.

Flowers, Flowers, Flowers

Trees aren't the only plants used to celebrate the Beltane festival; as explained in previous chapters, flowers are a big part of the celebrations, too. Flowers have always been associated with magic, and those blooming during Beltane are always incorporated into the festivities.

Tulips

Tulips are usually associated with prosperity and can be used in various spells as a result of their different colors. You can use white tulips for cleansing and purification by putting them in vases and placing them around your house during the spring. Yellow tulips should be planted near your house's front door to protect your family from harm, while red tulips are used in love spells. If you want to attract a lover, put a tulip bulb on your altar.

Forsythia

Forsythia is a yellow flower that is usually associated with the sun. This flower is typically used in spells that can make things happen for you, particularly something you have been yearning for. Just like the tulips, if you want to find love, cut off a few of the Forsythia flower's stems, put them in a jar filled with water, and place the jar on your altar. The moment the flowers bloom, your love life will too.

Violets

Violets represent tranquility and peace. This flower's petals are believed to be good luck charms, while its leaves can protect you from evil by sowing them into your pillows. Additionally, putting violet leaves in your *right shoe* can attract new love. Violet can also be used in healing spells too.

To perform a healing spell, you will need a white string, purple paper, a black pen, a purple candle, scissors, fresh violets, and a vase. You will first need to light the candle and then fill the vase with water. Put the violets in the vase and chant. At this time, only focus on the person you are trying to heal and their ailment. Using the scissors, cut a heart out of the purple piece of paper. On one side, you will write the name of the person you are trying to heal, and on the other side, write a sweet message wishing them a speedy recovery. Make a small hole and put the white string through the top right side of the heart-shaped paper. Tie the string around the vase or attach it to it and give it to the sick person.

Crocus

The Crocus flower blooms early in the spring, and it is usually used in spells that can bring new romance to your life. It can also be used to improve your visions and dreams. The flower is used in various spells; for instance, its incense is often used during divination to help you receive messages from the otherworld.

Dandelion

The Dandelion is connected to growth, transformation, and moving on. It is believed that associating your bad habits with a Dandelion's blowballs, then subsequently blowing them away, could help you rid yourself of them. The leaves of a Dandelion flower can be used for various rituals like purification, cleansing, and healing. To bring positive energy to your home, plant this flower in the northwest direction. They can also help eliminate negative energy and dark thoughts.

You can use the flowers we have mentioned here to make flower crowns to celebrate the Beltane festival. You will need flowers, ribbons, and green pipe cleaners. Make a circle using one pipe cleaner and make sure that it fits on your head. Now, get two green pipe cleaners and twist them to create a structure to add the flowers. Next, weave the flowers into the pipe cleaners. Cut the ribbons into different lengths and tie them to the back of your crown.

Other Beltane Plants

Magical Herbs

Beltane is clearly the perfect time of year to plant a herb garden. However, if you are going to use the herbs for magic, then you first need to be familiar with different herbs' magical properties. For instance, vanilla can make you irresistible if you put a bit of it behind your ears, and it can be used in rituals to help a person make new friends. If you put lavender under your pillow, you can have a good night's sleep, and it can aid you in your search to find love if you hang it in your home. Cinnamon can bring you courage when you tie a couple of cinnamon sticks and put them under your bed. Mistletoe can do more than just give you the chance to kiss your loved one under it. In fact, this plant can provide protection when you hang it over the windows or doors at your house. Apple blossoms can be a great ingredient to add when making a love spell, as you can add them to potpourri, incense, and tea.

If you have a falling out with a friend or your relationship is falling apart, then you can burn Sweet Annie, and it will help repair your relationship and bring you and your partner closer. Finally, plant rosemary in a pot and put it under your bed to give you a restful sleep.

- For a May bath, add mint, sage, or thyme to help you soak up energy.

- Use herbs like nettle, cleavers, and chickweed to get rid of winter blues.

Plants play a huge role in Beltane celebrations. The nine sacred trees' wood is used to help burn the Beltane bonfire that will kick start the festivities. The flowers can add color to the beautiful spring festival, and you can also use them to make a crown look and feel festive. Herbs can be beneficial all year long, but you can start planting them during the Beltane celebrations, and they can help you welcome the spring and summer as they will eliminate winter blues and sluggishness.

All the plants associated with Beltane can be incorporated into various spells and rituals since they all have connections to various mythologies. If this is your first time celebrating Beltane, use the tips we have mentioned here to make a beautiful flower crown or a May Bush so you can experience everything this festival has to offer.

Chapter 7: Beltane Family Activities

Since the Beltane festival is highlighted by fire and other mature elements, many parents want to find ways for their kids to take part in age-appropriate activities. Although the entire ritual is based on fire, and other parts of the ritual are based on fertility, which can be challenging to discuss with your youngsters, there are ways to include them in the festivities. This chapter looks at some family-friendly activities to turn this Beltane celebration into a family affair.

Traditional Beltane Celebrations

If you're based in Scotland, Ireland, or any locality where Beltane is publicly celebrated, you'll find there are quite a lot of things to do. For instance, in the city of Edinburgh, there is a big festival held at Calton Hill in which there is a procession that starts at the National Monument and then makes its way to Calton Hill, where the rest of the festival takes place. There is a lot of action and plenty of activities at this festival. The audience gets to see several entertaining and high-power stage performances, musical performances, dances, along with many fire-related performances as well. The main highlight of the event is the story of the May Queen and the Green Man, of course, and there are different performances specifically targeted toward this plot. There is plenty of food and music to enjoy, and those of legal age also indulge in copious amounts of alcohol. For this reason, it may be challenging for parents to include their kids in a celebratory event that involves adults who are drinking heavily. Along with this, while there are a lot of kid-friendly activities, it's a very hectic environment and can be quite tiring for them. It's also tough to enjoy the festivities as a parent when a rowdy crowd surrounds your children.

Beltane with the Family

When your children are relatively young, it may seem difficult to celebrate Beltane as a family, especially with the adult themes such as fertility, reproduction, and, in particular, the idea of humans reproducing. It can also be quite challenging to include your children in the experience and help them understand the festival in age-appropriate ways. Naturally, you want to find a way for your children to enjoy the festival without feeling insecure or embarrassed about the topics. As parents, it can be just as embarrassing and overwhelming to approach the situation when talking about the pagan Gods you are celebrating, especially when they are depicted without any clothes on and are flaunting their reproductive organs. Additionally, in many festivals and the various performances within those festivals, human sexuality is being celebrated. Of course, there is an age-appropriate time for children to learn the names and purposes of reproductive organs, so this can be tricky for parents to delve into. Also, some parents are simply not comfortable discussing these topics t with their children, and smaller children have primarily focused on the celebratory aspect of the occasion anyway.

Luckily, there is a way around the subject. You can educate your children on the meaning behind Beltane by focusing on the aspects of fertility and reproduction that aren't related to adult themes. Every living thing goes through a reproduction, fertility, and growth stage, whether that is plants, insects, animals, or even Mother Earth itself. In fact, there is no shade of sexuality in any of their reproductive cycles or in the way all these things grow in nature. There is nothing sexual about the way we look at plant growth or the development of a hive of bees though it represents all the same things that happen with human reproduction. This way, you can educate your children on the subject and keep the focus on celebrating the fertility of the earth and the vitality of life. For instance, if you and your family really enjoy fishing, why not celebrate how the fish in the ocean grows, how the seas and the rivers and oceans are home to thousands of different living things. All these creatures of the water grow and develop; even the oceans are in a constant state of growth and development. These are all wonderful ways to bring your children around to the fact that there is a continuous cycle of life that is going on and, as living things, we should all contribute to the community we are a part of.

There is no need to put yourself under a lot of pressure in this situation. A lot of parents are apprehensive about this approach because they are worried that they will receive criticism from friends and family that they aren't upholding traditions or following the "real" pagan values. Whereas in reality, the best values are those that work best for you and allow you to internalize the values and teachings of a culture in a way that you understand them. Moreover, just because you are celebrating the planet's growth doesn't mean you will never get around to celebrating human sexuality and growth; it's just a matter of time. In fact, when your children already understand the concepts of fertility, reproduction, and growth in the context of other things, they will most likely take the idea of human sexuality with a lot more maturity and a lot more respect for the entire process. Celebrating Beltane should be a humbling experience to help us realize how we develop as a species, and it should instill respect for both genders and their role in reproduction. Of course, older children can be taught how sexuality and intimacy are a meaningful part of human reproduction at a suitable age. Then, they'll be old enough to give the topic the respect and appreciation it deserves.

Now, let's shift our focus to turning this into a fun family event. After all, Beltane is about fun, gratitude, and positivity. Let's take a look at a few fun activities you can do with your children and some art and craft ideas that will be a great learning experience. Unleashing your creativity with crafts and playing games will help bring your family closer to the spirit of Beltane.

Beltane Activities

Family Abundance Ritual

You will need:

- A small flower pot for every member of the family
- Potting soil to go in the flower pot
- Some seeds of your favorite plant, any flower or herb, will do
- Some water
- A small fire
- A small piece of paper for each member of the family

Procedure:

1. The idea of this principle is to thank the Earth and the Pagan Gods for everything they have given us through the Earth in the form of food, shelter, security, family, and every other material and non-material item we have in our life. Generally, this process is broken down into three distinct steps: one person can go through all the steps together if they wish, and then the next person can do the entire procedure and so forth until everyone has done the entire process.

2. Ideally, you should have a small table or some kind of flat, elevated surface that you can use as the central point. Also, you will need to be out in the garden or in some open place for this procedure. Most people prefer to do this at night or in the early evening, just before dinner. It's a good idea to prepare a spring dinner before you go out for this. This meal could consist of fresh spring vegetables, fresh fruit, and bread. With your meal ready and all your items prepared, head out to the garden.

3. Light a small fire and let that burn while you go through the process. The eldest of the family should lead with this ritual. The first step is to go to the altar or the table and start off with a prayer thanking the Gods and welcoming spring. Talk about the abundance that this season brings, how it helps us grow crops and the many benefits we gain from it. Express your gratitude for the plants you are about to pot, the soil you have, the weather they will grow up in, and anything else that helps you cultivate a flourishing environment.

4. Every person should start by filling their pot with soil. You can either have a larger container of soil that is passed around so people can fill their smaller pots, or you can have the soil set up in one place, such as the altar, and have everyone go to the altar to fill their pot. Next, pass around the seeds and make sure that you say a prayer before you sow them into the soil. This time you can thank the Gods and the Universe for the seeds they have provided, the plants that grow from them, and the fruit they provide. Reiterate how these plants are a source of sustenance, health, and happiness for the family. I wish the plants luck for good growth in the future. With the prayer complete, everyone can push down their seeds and get ready for the third stage of pouring some water on the soil.

5. Before you pour in the water, you can say another prayer expressing your gratitude for water and its many benefits. Appreciate the fact that it is used for human consumption animal consumption and is also an invaluable resource for helping the plants grow. Then, you can pass around the cup of water, allowing everyone to pour as

much as necessary onto their seeds.

6. Last comes the pieces of paper you had prepared. Hand one piece of paper to every person in the family to write down something they deeply desire. This could be a physical thing, or maybe they just want success and happiness in their lives. It's. These desires can be literally anything. For instance, if the children want to wish for a pink unicorn, let them, as it's all about looking into yourself and coming out with something that helps you express your desires. Write this wish down on the piece of paper and cast this into the fire you have going. This way, you send your desires and wishes into the universe and let the Gods and greater energies take over. You are showing that you are grateful for them and trust their guidance.

Bonfire/Camp Night

The word "Beltane" can literally be translated to "Blazing fire," so a bonfire or camping night is certainly fitting. If you have access to an outdoor space, you can build your own bonfire and set up camp. You can host the bonfire with stories, songs, dances, and any other activities that bring you and your family joy and happiness. To reiterate, it is a time to celebrate and have fun. Of course, if your children are little, extra safety measures should be taken, such as having a smaller fire in a more controlled environment. An example of this includes switching your bonfire to a BBQ pit, or you can consider cutting the fire out altogether and simply spending time together outside as you partake in the activities.

A Nature Walk

The Beltane season is all about appreciating Spring and celebrating the many good things that come with this season. Children already enjoy being outdoors, and this can be a great opportunity for the entire family to go for a hike or a nature walk outside and explore the new plants that are coming to life as Spring approaches. You can use this time to talk to your children about the various plants that grow in the region, how they go through the life cycle and what kinds of things they are used for. It's a great way for them to explore their surroundings and connect with nature.

Be sure to offer them bags of some kind to collect cool items that they come across. This could be a strange rock, stick, colorful leaves, new wild fruit, or anything else that tickles their curiosity. After a cold winter, this is a great time for them to get some fresh air and enjoy the beautiful greenery.

Beltane Crafts

Maypole Altar Centerpiece

Not everyone celebrating Beltane is living in an area where they can connect with plenty of other pagans so having a full-sized maypole is not always feasible. Moreover, for people living in apartments and those living in city homes without a backyard, putting a 10-foot-tall maypole isn't possible either. However, you can still set up this major component of Beltane in your home, even indoors.

You will need:

- A 1-inch-thick dowel rod or any other kind of hollow rod that is at least 1 foot long
- A wooden base with a cutout that's the width of the rod. The wooden base can be 4-6 inches in diameter
- Multiple pieces of ribbons in different colors, each being 2 feet long
- A hot glue gun
- Any other decorations you would like to place on the maypole

Procedure:

1. The easiest way to connect the dowel rod to the base structure is to simply glue it in using the hot glue gun.
2. Coat one end of the rod with the glue and stick it into the base plate. If you use metal rods and plates, you can also weld these together.
3. You can also paint and decorate the dowel pole itself with paint or stickers or whatever else gets your creative juices flowing.
4. Then you can use the maypole on your altar as the centerpiece. Also, while using the hot glue gun, you can attach the ribbons to the pole, and later you can braid these with your friends and family.
5. If you have more room or are making a maypole for a larger gathering, you can always extend the length of the pole but be sure to also enlarge the size of the base to compensate for the height.
6. To add a bit more of the Beltane spirit to the maypole, you can decorate the base of the maypole with fresh flowers and colorful ornaments to keep the spirit of fertility and growth alive.

Floral Crowns

For any Beltane function, wearing flowers, especially spring flowers, *is a must*. Nothing says fertility and spring quite like a set of fresh flowers. Moreover, flowers are an excellent choice for the ladies to wear as it is another way to symbolize growth and fertility. It's a great piece of jewelry that will pair perfectly with anything you wear on that day – just make sure to match the color scheme of your attire (think warm spring colors and pretty pastels). Rather than buying premade floral crowns, you can very easily and inexpensively make these at home. It will be a fantastic activity for all the children to join in on, allowing them to get crafty.

You will need:

- Some pipe cleaning wires or any other kind of metal wire that will hold its shape well
- Some ribbons of various colors
- Plenty of fresh flowers with the stems on
- Some tape or glue

Procedure:

1. Using the metal wire, trace around your head to get an accurately sized ring.
2. This might take more than one pipe cleaner, so you can always twist the ends of the two together to create one large circle.
3. Once you have the ring ready, start building on it with more wires or pipe cleaners to give the crown its body and develop the base you will be putting the flowers in.
4. Once your crown is a good size, start lacing and braiding the flowers into the crown. Sometimes you might find that the flower itself is not facing the direction you want or that there isn't enough of a stem to give it proper support through the base in the crown.
5. In this case, you can use glue or tape to secure the flower in the position or space you want on the crown.
6. Make sure you do this with the crown of your head, as you don't want to get glue in your hair or glue the crown to it.
7. Lastly, cut the ribbons into various lengths and attach these to the rear side of the crown. If you have space in the crown itself, you can tie the ribbons directly to the wire or use tape or glue to stick the ribbons onto the crown. By using wires and cleaning pipes, you can ensure the crowns accurately match the size of each person's head.

That's it! Your crown is ready. Now you have a fantastic accessory to wear while you dance around the maypole and tie the braids.

Chapter 8: Cooking for Your Beltane Feast

For any festive celebration, there must be food. This is how it's always been, even in ancient times. Luckily, the same applies to Beltane, which has been around for centuries and has its own selection of tasty festive dishes. If this is your first time celebrating Beltane, you naturally want to impress your friends and family with your cooking skills. But this begs the question: what do people eat for Beltane? The ancient and modern Beltane celebrations have something in common – there is always a large feast. Traditionally, there should be a time set during celebrations solely for eating and drinking. It is considered a sign of respect for the Aos Si.

Certain dishes are usually associated with this festival. Oatcake is one of the most popular Beltane dishes. It is a Scottish dish with a strong connection to ancient legends that we will discuss later. This festival also features cow and goat meat and animal products like milk and butter. You can slow-roast a goat leg or make beef shish kabobs and spread garlic butter or fresh butter on bread to eat with your main dish. Rabbits, oysters, and goat meat should also be a part of the Beltane menu. To keep the traditions alive, it is recommended to have a glass of spice-infused warm milk with a dash of honey.

Spicy food is also served on this special occasion since Beltane is all about heat and fire, so serving spicy food would make sense, like hot stuffed mushrooms or adding a hot pepper spread to any type of dip you are making. When it comes to drinks, mead is a very popular Beltane beverage that the ancient Celts enjoyed. You can easily find mead in the wine aisle of any grocery store. During the celebrations, you can also choose to include beverages like ginger ale, lemonade, and honeyed wine.

You will find certain fruits that are usually incorporated in various Beltane recipes like lemons, figs, cherries, bananas, avocados, peaches, strawberries, pineapples, papayas, and vegetables like ginger garlic, mint, lettuce, radishes, rhubarb, and jalapeno peppers. Additionally, honey, mint, thyme, nutmeg, and almonds play a huge part in Beltane food as well. No feast is complete without bread; in addition to oatcake, banana bread goes great with the food served during this festival.

Beltane Food Recipes

In this part of the chapter, we give you some recipes that will help you prepare a large feast for your loved ones. You will be the star of this year's celebrations and crowned the top Beltane chef.

Beltane Oatcake

As previously mentioned, the Beltane oatcake is a Scottish dish. The ancients believed that eating a piece of oatcake on the morning of the Beltane would result in plentiful crops and healthy livestock.

Ingredients:

- 1 teaspoon of butter
- 1 ½ cups of oatmeal
- ¼ teaspoon of baking soda
- ⅛ teaspoon of salt
- ½ cup of hot water

Instructions:

1. Bring a bowl.
2. Mix the salt, baking soda, and oatmeal in the bowl.
3. Melt the butter.
4. Pour the butter over the oats.

5. Add water to the mix.

6. Next, stir the mixture until it hardens and forms a dough.

7. Take the dough out of the bowl.

8. Place it on a sheet of wax paper.

9. Knead the dough.

10. Split the dough into two equal halves.

11. Use a rolling pin to roll each of the halves into a ball.

12. Flatten it like a pancake with a ¼ thickness.

13. Prepare a frying pan.

14. Cook the oatmeal in the frying pan.

15. Turn the heat to medium-high.

16. Cook until they become golden-brown.

17. When it is done, cut it into quarters.

Tips

According to tradition, the Beltane oatcake is usually cooked using animal fat like bacon grease. Then, it is put on embers to be cooked over a low flame until both sides are golden. Once your oatcakes are fully cooked, you can eat them with eggs and milk. However, we opted for butter instead of animal fat in our recipe and chose to omit cooking over an open fire. So, if you prefer to use fats, just replace the butter with grease.

Green Man Cake

Our second recipe here is the green man cake. The Green Man is one of the most prominent figures in Celtic lore. He is also usually represented during the Beltane festivities. The Green man is the god of plant life and vegetation and is also considered the forest's spirit. He usually grows and becomes powerful during Beltane. For this reason, you should always honor him in your celebrations.

Ingredients:

- 3 eggs
- 2 teaspoons of cinnamon
- 2 cups of powdered sugar
- 2 packages of softened cream cheese
- 4 teaspoons of baking powder
- 2 cups of brown sugar, firmly packed
- 2 teaspoons of vanilla extract, pure

- 2 ½ cups of all-purpose flour
- 1 teaspoon of vanilla extract
- 1 cup of softened butter
- 1 cup of milk
- 1 package of white fondant
- ¼ cup of cornstarch
- ½ teaspoon of salt
- 1 teaspoon of ground nutmeg
- 1 teaspoon of ground cloves
- ½ teaspoon of extract, rum-flavored
- ½ cup of softened butter
- Leaf-shaped cutters
- Green food coloring

Instructions:

1. Preheat your oven to 350 degrees F and lightly flour and grease the pan.
2. Get a large bowl.
3. Combine all of the dry ingredients and mix them together in the large bowl.
4. Blend them together.
5. Get a second bowl.
6. Now mix the liquid ingredients together (the rum extracts, eggs, vanilla, and milk).
7. Next, add the butter to the flour mix.
8. Beat the mixture until it forms a dough-like texture.
9. Slowly add the liquid mixture.
10. Gently blend them together until both mixtures are combined.
11. Keep beating until the mixture becomes smooth.
12. Now, add the brown sugar.
13. Keep mixing for about 30 seconds.
14. Pour the mixture into the pan.
15. Spread it evenly.
16. Put the mixture in the preheated oven.
17. Let it bake for about 45 minutes.

18. Take it out of the oven.

19. Leave it to cool down.

20. After it cools, remove it from the pan.

21. Add the frosting.

Frosting

1. Get a bowl

2. Mix the butter and cream cheese in the bowl

3. Next, add the vanilla extract to the mixture

4. Add the powdered sugar and stir

5. Blend them all together

6. Now spread the frosting evenly over the cake

7. Leave it for an hour or more until it firms up

The Green Man Prep

1. Get the green fondant.

2. Roll the fondant into a ball.

3. Next, add a very small amount of the green food coloring.

4. Blend it in until it reaches the green shade you prefer.

5. Roll out the fondant until it reaches ⅛ of thickness.

6. Cut out the leaves into various sizes using a cookie cutter that is leaf-shaped.

7. Put the leaves on the cake and press on them.

8. Keep adding the leaves until you make it look like the Green Man.

9. To make the eyes, roll 2 pieces of the fondant, flatten them, and place them on top of the cake among the leaves.

Tips

- To make sure that the cake is baked, insert a toothpick. If it comes out clean, then it is ready.

- If this is your first time using fondant, you may find it a bit tricky. However, practice makes perfect, so the more you practice, the better you will get.

- Draw lines on the leaves to make them look more realistic

- It is better to work with small pieces of fondant at a time because it dries out quickly after you roll it out.

- If you have never baked before or prefer fast recipes, then you can buy any cake mix from the supermarket.

Early Summer Salad

If you plant your own fruits and vegetables, you know that your garden may not be blooming with the various fruits and vegetables during the Beltane. However, since the Beltane festival is a summer celebration, you can use any early summer fruits and vegetables available to honor this special day.

Ingredients:

- 2 hard-boiled sliced eggs
- 4 chopped green onions
- 2 cups of leafy greens (you can use arugula or baby spinach)
- 2 cloves of minced garlic
- 2 cups of washed and drained dandelion leaves
- 2 teaspoons of Dijon mustard
- 1 diced tomato
- 1 cup of dried cranberries, strawberries, or raspberries
- 1 tablespoon of honey
- ½ cup of diced cucumber
- Chopped leaves of basil
- Pinch of pepper and salt
- ½ cup of chopped nuts
- ½ cup of extra virgin olive oil
- ¼ cup of strawberry vinegar

Instructions:

1. Get a bowl.
2. Add all of the salad ingredients to the bowl.

3. Mix all of the dressing ingredients together.

4. Pour the dressing on the salad.

5. Serve the salad.

Tips

- All the ingredients you use in this recipe must be fresh

- If you or any of your guests are vegans, then you don't have to include the eggs, and you can use nectar instead of honey

- Remove the seeds from the cucumbers before adding them

- This salad pairs perfectly with buttered bread and a nice glass of wine.

Candied Flower Petals

We have stressed in previous chapters that flowers play a huge role in the Beltane celebrations. Everyone knows flowers look and smell great, but a little-known fact is that some flowers can make for a very tasty treat.

Ingredients:

- 1 beaten egg white

- Flower blossoms or petals (rinse and dry them first)

- Sugar

- Water

Directions:

1. Get a small bowl.

2. Add the egg white to the small bowl.

3. Sprinkle a small amount of water into the egg.

4. Beat them together using a whisk.

5. Dip the flower petals or blossoms into the mixture.

6. Sprinkle the sugar on the flower petals or blossoms.

7. Put the petals on wax paper and leave them to dry.

8. They will probably take from 12 hours to 2 days to dry out.

9. When dried, put them in an airtight container and use them whenever you want.

Tips

- Only use edible flowers like roses, violets, pansies, nasturtium, or lilac blossoms

- This recipe takes a long time to prepare, so plan it in advance

- Flowers are fragile, so handle them with care when adding them to the mixture

- If you are in a hurry and want to speed up the drying process, you can put them on a metal tray and leave them in the oven for a couple of hours. The oven should be heated to 150 degrees F

- Candied flowers can be added to salads, eaten as a snack, or used to decorate cookies and cakes

Asparagus and Cheese Quiche

Although asparagus is a very popular spring vegetable and a delicious one too, you will still be able to find it by the time of Beltane. This is a very easy and quick recipe, and if you follow the instructions, the asparagus will be cooked just right. It will be nice and firm instead of mushy.

Ingredients:

- 6 eggs
- 2 tablespoons of butter
- 1 pound of freshly chopped asparagus spears
- 1 medium diced onion
- ½ cup of sour cream
- 1 cup of goat cheese, crumbled
- 1 clove of minced garlic
- Pepper and salt
- ½ cup of cooked bacon or ham (this is optional)

Instructions:

1. Preheat the oven to 350 degrees F.

2. Get a pie plate (with non-stick cooking spray).

3. Add the pie crust to the plate (skip this step if you don't want to add crust).

4. Put the butter in a skillet.

5. Put it on low heat to melt.

6. Add the onion and garlic to be sautéed.

7. Next, add the asparagus.

8. Leave it to sauté for about five minutes.

9. Get a large bowl.

10. Add the goat cheese, sour cream, eggs, and salt and pepper, then mix them together.

11. Next, add the sautéed vegetables (asparagus, onions, and garlic) to the mixture.

12. Mix them all together.

13. Add ham or bacon (if you don't want to add ham or bacon, then skip this step).

14. Now, place the mixture on the pie plate.

15. Put it in the oven.

16. Leave it to bake for 40 minutes.

17. After it is done, take it out of the oven.

18. Leave it to cool down for about 10 minutes.

19. Cut it into slices before serving.

Tips

- Don't overcook the asparagus

- You can use any shredded cheese instead of goat cheese

- This is a gluten-free recipe. However, if you want to add pie crust, then put it on the plate first before adding the ingredients

- Insert a knife in its center to know if the quiche is baked. If the knife comes out clean, it is ready

- Prepare the ingredients in advance and place them in the fridge

Peppery Green Beans

We have mentioned that spicy food is a must in any Beltane feast, which will make this dish a great addition to your menu.

Ingredients:

- 1 pound of bacon
- 1 pound of green beans

- 1 chopped medium onion
- 1 tablespoon of pepper (you can add more if you like)
- ½ teaspoon of salt
- ½ cup of butter
- ½ cup of water

Instructions:

1. Cook the bacon (it should be crispy).
2. Crush the bacon into small pieces.
3. Prepare a large saucepan.
4. Add the butter and onion to the saucepan.
5. Leave them to sauté until browned.
6. Next, add the water and green beans.
7. Bring them to a boil.
8. Reduce the heat when the water starts to boil.
9. Cover the pan and let it stew for 15 minutes.
10. Next, drain the water.
11. Sprinkle the salt and pepper.

Tips

- You can use turkey bacon instead of pork bacon if you prefer a less fatty option
- This dish should be served hot
- You can prepare this dish in a slow cooker. You will just need to add 2 cups of water instead of one, and you will need to leave the beans to stew for 3 hours instead of 15 minutes

Beltane Bread

There isn't a Wiccan or a Pagan ritual that is complete without bread. If you love baking, then unleash your talent when preparing for the Beltane feast. However, this won't be a regular loaf of bread. Since this is the festival of fertility, there is no better way to honor it than to make phallus bread.

Ingredients:

- Melted butter
- A loaf of bread dough

Instructions:

1. Since this is a fertility bread, you will need to roll out the loaf appropriately to make the shape of a phallus.

2. Shape the dough like a tube.

3. Next, cut it into 3 pieces; 2 small round pieces and one long.

4. The round pieces will be the testes, while the long one will serve as the shaft.

5. Now, shape it to make it look like a penis.

6. Next, leave it in a warm place for a couple of hours to rise.

7. Put it in the oven and let it bake at 350 degrees F.

8. Leave it for 40 minutes until light brown.

9. Take it out of the oven.

10. Brush it with melted butter.

Tips

You can either prepare the bread dough at home or opt for frozen dough that you can buy from any grocery store

Beltane Berry Sangria

Now we need a delicious beverage to drink with our meal. Beltane berry sangria can be a great addition to your meal since the fruits we use in this recipe will be easy to find during Beltane.

Ingredients:

- 1 lemon

- Grape juice, white

- 2 bottles of any sweet wine that you prefer

- Your favorite in-season berries like strawberries, blueberries, raspberries, or blackberries

Instructions:

1. Get a pitcher.

2. Pour the wine bottles into the pitcher.

3. Now add the grape juice to fill the pitcher.

4. Squeeze the lemon in the pitcher.

5. Decorate it with the berries of your choice.

Tips

- You can add up to 3 bottles of wine
- You can experiment with the berries and use a different type each time

The recipes we have mentioned in this chapter are all perfect for a Beltane celebration feast. You can opt for a couple of dishes for a small gathering, but if you are a large group, then go big and try every recipe in the book. Most of the recipes here are quick and easy to make. However, as mentioned previously, a couple will take longer than usual and need to be prepared ahead of time.

All of these dishes have a connection to Beltane. Learning about this connection and its history will make a great topic of conversation to impress your guests with your knowledge.

Chapter 9: Beltane, the Druid Way

In this chapter, we explore how Druids used to celebrate the festival of Beltane. This celebration between the Summer Solstice and Spring Equinox (Ostara) is often linked with major events across Irish mythology. Some people like to call it "the first of summer" (or Cétshamhain). These festivals always took place during the summertime, which was the perfect time for farmers to drive their cattle to the sunny pasture lands.

Generally, pagan religions tend to follow the Wheel of the Year for the annual celebrations and may change the exact dates or names according to the cultural context. As a matter of fact, a total of eight festivals were celebrated by the pagans, and these festivities have been periodically spaced around the year, with a six or seven-week gap in between. This segmentation of festivals divides the "wheel" into eight exclusive segments. The four Celtic (or Druidic) festivals, Imbolc, Lughnasa, Beltane, and Samhain, have been long since practiced helping and guiding the followers in synchronizing with the rhythms of the natural life force.

The Festival of Samhain

This festival is celebrated on the 1st of November or the night of October 31st. It is considered one of the most important festivals in the Pagan religious calendar. Interestingly, for pagans, this festival marks the birth of a new year and the death of the previous year – some pagans use the festival of Imbolc to mark the beginning of their new year. Historically, this festival was celebrated with big feasts, and people would boast about their battle stories. After the Roman invasion, the festival of Samhain also included celebrations to honor Pomona, the goddess of tree fruits.

Even if "death" happens to be a central element of this festival, pagans did not consider this a morbid or gloomy event. Moreover, pagans did not regard death as something to be afraid of. In fact, according to the pagan belief system, death is simply a part of life and must be welcomed and embraced. Because of this conceptualization of death, they also regard old age as a time of great wisdom. The pagan practitioners performed the festival as a way of remembering the departed ones and inviting their spirits to join the festivities. The festival of Samhain often reflected some form of disorder and darkness. The modern-day practitioners of this festival regard it as that time of year when the boundaries of the spiritual world and earthly world are slim. Modern practitioners use rituals to connect with the dead.

A feast is still an important part of this celebration, but some practitioners keep it simple, while others opt for an extravagant dining experience.

The Festival of Lughnasadh

Frey Fest or Lughnassadh (pronounced as "loo'nass'ah") is celebrated on the first full moon when the first fruit of harvest appears – usually around the beginning of August. Historically, it was the festival of the god Lugh and was also commonly referred to as "Lammas" by many. This celebration was of great significance to the agricultural communities as it marked the beginning of the harvest for that year. This would be the time of year when the fields would bloom with ripe crops (corn), and the farmers would start reaping the harvest. The harvest not only begins at the start of the festival but usually continues until the festival of Samhain.

In the modern world, farming is not a part of everyone's life, and many modern-day pagan druidic practitioners are not farmers. However, regardless of their professions, Lughnasadh carries a lot of significance for them as a religious festival and still denotes the beginning of the harvest season.

The Festival of Imbolc

The festival of Imbolc has several names. Some call it Imbolc (pronounced "im'olk"), while others refer to it as Disfest, Oimelc, or Candlemas. It is linked with the return of life and light and was historically an important festival for the Druids. This festival was celebrated around the 1st or 2nd of February and denoted the success of a farming season. As the food reserves would start to decrease during winter, the Imbolc festival and its celebrations were organized. The rituals were primarily performed to ensure a steady supply of food over the next six months until harvest season.

The Imbolc festival is characterized by the lighting of holy fires in honor of the power of the sun that will gradually increase in presence over the following months. It was a celebration to honor and pray and hope for a warm, sunny season. Initially, the festival fires were primarily utilized to burn the discarded items or Yule decorations. The worshippers would walk around their communities' districts holding lit candles. The Imbolc celebration is dedicated to honoring the goddess Brigit, who is revered as the goddess of fertility, fire, and healing.

Imbolc is still a very special time of the year for pagan practitioners. Nowadays, more and more people recognize the importance of the natural life cycle. People are honoring life and death, heat and cold, and accepting the natural progression of humans and nature and why human actions must parallel nature's course. This festival is also a reminder that one should complete necessary tasks to prepare for the coming busy year ahead of them. There are many activities that are performed during such celebrations, like telling stories, sharing poetry, making candles, or planting flowers in preparation for the upcoming spring season.

The Festival of Beltane

As explained throughout this book, Beltane is celebrated across different regions with many cultures participating, so, naturally, Druids had their own spin on the celebration. Druid origins trace back to ancient Wales, and these were from the early Celtic religion. But the origin of Druidism has largely been shrouded with mystery, and Druids were also linked to Gaulish culture. Their primary role was to help people establish a connection with the deities, much like the priests of today. If you peruse through the history, you will find various references that Gaels were the ones who observed Beltane. These days, it is observed by Galician, Manx, Scottish, Wiccans, Irish, and Celtic neopagans.

Beltane has been – and continues to be – one of the most widely observed pagan festivals in recorded history. As previously mentioned, it happens to be among the four seasonal festivals in Gaelic traditions. Its importance is only matched by the remaining three; Lughnasadh, Samhain, and Imbolc.

Ancient Druidic Beltane Festivities

Like anyone who celebrates Beltane, druids would decorate their houses with flowers, visit holy wells, hold feasts, and light bonfires. The celebrations around Beltane always focused on casting a protective shield around the believers and had an enchanting effect. The typical Druid way to celebrate this festival involved bonfires, dancing, maypoles, and fertility rituals. As explained in the introduction to Beltane (Chapter 1), the festival name can be roughly translated as "the fires of Bel," and this referred to the Celtic sun god Belenus – although the literal translation is "bright light." The festivities involved lighting one fire for purification and the other for increasing fertility, which is one of the reasons why they drove their cattle between these two bonfires, believing that it purified the herd and enhanced their fertility as well. The practitioners also visited nearby Holy wells. It was common for people to hold a huge gathering and offer a sacrifice to the god, Beil.

Modern Era Druidic Beltane Festivities

In modern-day celebrations, the Druid way may not always be a commonly practiced ritual, and various modified versions can be found. But the Beltane bonfires are still practiced with the same enthusiasm. The maypole ritual is also commonly practiced, and followers wear flower-woven headbands, many of whom participate in dancing around the bonfire, which is thought to be a significant fertility ritual.

People celebrating the Beltane festival would also implore the Druid ritual of constructing "May baskets," which were filled with goodwill and flowers. These baskets are then given to those that are in need of a little good fortune. On the day of Beltane, it was also very common for people to douse all the house fires, and, during the celebration, they would re-light them from the Beltane bonfire. The festivities and rituals often involve a big feast with an abundance of food and drink.

Druidic Prayers and Songs of Beltane

While there are many songs and prayers for Beltane, one of the Beltane songs, *"Am BeannachadhBealltain (The Blessings of Beltane),"* comes from Gaelic customs dating back to the 19th century. This prayer is about honoring the Holy Trinity (i.e., The Father, Son, and The Holy Ghost). Check the two verses below.

"Bless, O Threefold true and bountiful,
Myself, my spouse, and my children,
My tender children and their beloved mother at their head,
On the fragrant plain, at the gay mountain sheiling,
On the fragrant plain, at the gay mountain sheiling,
Everything within my dwelling or in my possession,
All kine and crops, all flocks and corn,
From Hallow Eve to Beltane Eve,
With goodly progress and gentle blessing,
From sea to sea, and every river mouth,
From wave to wave, and base of a waterfall.
Be the Maiden, Mother, and Crone,
Taking possession of all to me belonging.
Be the Horned God, the Wild Spirit of the Forest,
Protecting me in truth and honor.
Satisfy my soul and shield my loved ones,
Blessing everything and everyone,
All my land and my surroundings.
Great gods who create and bring life to all,
I ask for your blessings on this day of the fire."

There are also several prayers dedicated to Cernunnos, the horned god who is associated with animals and masculine attributes. He also has links with fertility and vegetation. The depictions of Cernunnos are found around the British Isles and Western Europe. The following is a prayer used to pay homage to this animal god.

"God of the green,
Lord of the forest,
I offer you my sacrifice.
I ask you for your blessing.
You are the man in the trees,
the green man of the woods,
who brings life to the dawning spring.
You are the deer in rut,
mighty Horned One,
who roams the autumn woods,
the hunter circling round the oak,

the antlers of the wild stag,

and the lifeblood that spills upon

the ground each season."

In addition to this, the Druid Beltane festivities also involve paying tribute to the fertile mother earth; it does not matter whether you want to honor the sacred femininity of the goddesses or pay regard to the masculinity of the gods. The following prayer is recited as a way of offering gratitude to mother earth for her blessings:

"Great earth, mother!

We give you praise today

and ask for your blessing upon us.

As seeds spring forth

and the grass grows green

and winds blow gently

and the rivers flow

and the sun shines down

upon our land,

we offer thanks to you for your blessings

and your gifts of life each spring."

The people celebrating Beltane should observe the blessings of Flora or May Queen since she is viewed as the princess of Fae, the goddess of blooming flowers, and also a young bride. The May Queen is associated with fertile glory. The customary ritual to honor May Queen was always associated with singing the prayer below during the Beltane celebrations. The practitioners would also present a variety of gifts like honey, milk, and flowers.

"The leaves are budding across the land

on the ash and oak and hawthorn trees.

Magic rises around us in the forest, and the hedges are filled with laughter and love.

Dear lady, we offer you a gift,

a gathering of flowers picked by our hands,

woven into the circle of an endless life.

The bright colors of nature herself

blend together to honor you,

Queen of spring,

as we give you honor this day.

Spring is here, and the land is fertile,
ready to offer up gifts in your name.
We pay you tribute, our lady,
daughter of the Fae,
and ask your blessing this Beltane."

Celebrating the Vernal Equinox

The Celtics (Druids) or pagans also celebrated Vernal or Spring Equinox every year around 20th or 21st March. This time was primarily used to honor the renewal of life on Earth as the spring season started. This festival is a solar festival and has to be celebrated when the length of night and day are equal. This seasonal change was welcomed through different festivities in the ancient era. The predominant Celtic festival at this time was Ostara, which was celebrated to honor the season and the goddess Eostre (also known as Ostra).

Even nowadays, the festival of Ostara is celebrated in the Modern era to welcome the Spring season. The practitioners associate the changes happening in the world around them with the gradually increasing power of gods and goddesses. During the celebration of Spring Equinox, the goddess and god are usually portrayed as Mother Earth and the Green Man. According to the folklore associated with this festival, Mother Earth gives birth to the Green Man during harsh winters, and then he lives through the year to die at the time of the Samhain festival. Some pagan practitioners celebrate the Vernal Equinox by symbolically representing the courtship of the goddess and spring god. The celebrations involve activities like egg races, egg-eating, egg hunting, egg painting, and other common spiritual rituals that were often held during this period.

How to Celebrate Summer Solstice

The celebrations of this festival usually took place between the 21st and 24th of June during the second half of the summer season, when the movement of the sun remains at an all-time low—the summer solstice; the longest day of the year when the sun is at its peak elevation point. This festival was celebrated and welcomed with bonfires, serving as a ritualistic practice to add to the energy and power of the glorious sun. This time of year holds a very sacred and unique significance for practitioners because, according to them, the goddess happens to be at the strongest and most powerful point in her fertility and power. For some pagans, the summer solstice depicts the marriage of the goddess and god. Their reunion is the force that creates the fruits of the harvest. This festival symbolizes life and growth for the pagan believers.

Celebrations of the Mabon

The Mabon or Autumn Equinox festival, also known as "Fallfest, Harvest Home," is celebrated every year on the 20th or 21st of September. Like the "Vernal Equinox," Mabon is also celebrated on the day when night and day-time are of equivalent durations before the duration of darkness starts to expand gradually – as winter approaches. As summer draws to a close and the celebrations associated with it begin to decrease, the upcoming season of winter is characterized by a time of hibernation and earthly rest. Therefore, fruits and other forms of sustenance are collected in preparation, and pagans will utilize this time of stillness to revisit their past and reflect on their successes.

This time is marked by observing and acknowledging the changes that have taken place, which ultimately result in the final turning of the wheel.

It also marks the end of the summer season for said year. For pagans, this happens to be one of the less celebrated festivals compared to others. But people may celebrate the harvest festival to show gratitude to the goddess for blessing them with food and water for the winter season.

Celebrations of Yule

This festival is the Winter Solstice and is a celebration of the return of light. It is the point when the sun starts to regain its strength and marks the return of the summer season. It is a time of great joy for pagan believers because it depicts a turn from the dark time in a year to the path towards the light. The Yule or Winter Solstice festival – celebrated around the 20th or 21st of December – was a symbolic guarantee of warmth and the Spring season. It denotes that the season of growth happens to be just around the corner, and there is hope. The Druidic belief states that this was the period when the Queen of Heaven, also known as the *Great Mother*, conceived the Son of Light. Worshippers and attendees rejoice by lighting fires as a sign of the summer and the sun's triumph over the darkness and cold of winter.

In essence, the Druid way of celebrating various festivals has long been embedded in the seasonal cycles. It is full of colorful rituals, energizing chants, and a deep honor for the forces of nature at play. The historical practices are rich. However, the modern era practices have been modified to accommodate the modern-day Druids' evolution of the lifestyle.

Chapter 10: Beltane Spells, Charms, and Baths

This chapter delves into the types of spells and rituals that go well with the Beltane festivities, such as fertility, prosperity, creativity, and love spells. Here, we recommend the charm, spell, or bath that can be used for each ritual. We also provide more details concerning the instructions, tips, and tricks for using each charm, spell, and bath.

Fertility

Since Beltane represents fertility and fire, this is often represented by the magic performed during this period. Those who may not need to wish for their own fertility can still show their appreciation for the fertility and vitality of the earth. One way you can do this is to plant seeds into the ground and nurture them as they grow. If you'd like to plant a garden, Beltane is the appropriate time to perform some fertility magic to have abundant crops during harvest time. The following methods can be incorporated into your rituals to ensure fertility.

Fertility Spell

During Beltane, fertility is a common theme, and there are different places where young people can go before the onset of the ceremony. They will spend the night in the forest and return with signs of nature, such as flowers and branches, which will be used to decorate their town the next day in honor of springtime. These escapades can be carried out during the wedding ceremony. In this context, it is referred to as "handfasting." As mentioned in previous chapters, handfasting is where the couple's hands are bound together during the ceremony. Even married couples can also undertake this spell to enhance fertility if they are interested in conceiving.

Beltane Bath

You can take a luxurious Beltane bath to relax, and this can also be a good time to meditate. To prepare your bath, you'll need milk and honey as the major ingredients you will use to make an offering to Flora, the Goddess of flowers. The mixture is also used to enhance fertility, and including roses helps to provide a feeling of emotional healing and self-love. During this bath, make sure you take the time to connect with the Earth Goddess and evoke the spirits to give you fertility and love. Focus on what you want to achieve when you begin meditation.

You will need:

- 2 cups milk
- ½ cup honey
- Rose petals
- 1 cup salt

Directions:

1. First, run warm bathwater.
2. Add salt, honey, and milk to a jar.
3. Seal the jar and shake the contents.
4. Pour the mixture into the bath.
5. Add rose petals.
6. Soak yourself in the bath and gently rub your skin.
7. Lie back and relax, allowing your skin to absorb the contents.

Birth Charms

You can consider different birth charms as part of your Beltane fertility ritual. You can wear different charms such as the Rose Quartz tipple moon Wiccan jewelry, green witch clothing, and a Beltane pagan fertility necklace. Traditionally speaking, weaving is the process of joining two substances to create a third one, which is why it's significant for birth charms. You can also make a small charm token you should place within the circle of stones symbolizing the altar.

Carvings, mandala flowers, honeysuckle flowers, crystals including quartz, aquamarine, copper, or citrine can also be used for this purpose. Light your candle representing the God of the Sun and close your eyes. You must start visualizing the image of the flame beginning to grow bigger. As the flame grows, you should also visualize your dreams and aspirations growing bigger simultaneously.

Beltane Love Potion Ritual

As we briefly touched on in chapter 6, you can also use Beltane charms, spells, and baths to perform love rituals. The following are good examples that can help you achieve your love goals.

Love Charm

If you are experiencing problems in your relationship and you want to find a solution with your partner, you can share a cup consisting of the following ingredients.

- 1 cup pomegranate juice
- 1 cup apple juice
- 2 tablespoons honey
- ½ cup rosehip tea
- 3 basil leaves
- 1 sprig of rosemary

You must add the juice to a non-reactive pot and bring it to a simmer. Add each ingredient, and make sure you stir nine times in the clockwise direction every time you add something. Turn off the heat and let the mixture sit for about 10 minutes. You can drink the solution immediately or leave it to chill for a bit. You can keep it in the fridge if you want to save it for another day, but it should not exceed 5 days.

Love Spell

To perform a love spell, you must follow the steps below.

1. Think about what you wish and desire from a partner. Write it in a column on a piece of paper.

2. Then, in the other column, write the qualities you are willing to offer

3. Cast a circle, and you can begin by cleansing your mind. Imagine the universe's energy mixing with your energy, and imagine it all turning orange or purple. Face towards the North and use your finger, wand, or athame to point to the ground as you feel the energy flowing out. Start moving clockwise around the circle's circumference and imagine it forming inside you.

4. Sit inside the circle, light two pink or red candles, and set them apart.

5. Read the first word on the first column and move the candle on your right toward the one on the left. Repeat the same steps as you read from the second column, and move the candle on the left to the right.

6. Continue reading from your columns all the way down to the last word until the candles finally touch each other. Blow them out and close the circle by using your finger or picking your wand, athame, or any other thing you used to draw the circle.

7. While pointing at the circle's boundary, begin to move counter-clockwise until you complete it. You will begin to feel the energy flowing back while simultaneously visualizing the circle disappearing.

Beltane Love Bath

Beltane is famous for its association with attraction, love, and the power of feminine charm. You can use ritual baths to cleanse your spirit and draw out your inner beauty. Create your little Beltane bath altar by getting candles and a bouquet of fresh flowers, seashells, lavender candles, and mirrors to honor Aphrodite. It is said to be born from the sea. You also need to include wildflowers in your bath. However, the following flowers, Wisteria, Dandelion, Cherry Blossoms, and Garden Roses, all symbolize grace, beauty, and confidence, which is why they are highly recommended too. Last, consider including sea salt for cleansing before undertaking your bath.

Beltane Creative Transformation Ritual

About six or more people can present the Beltane transformational ritual. The tools and materials required include the following: colored ribbons, chalk, cue cards, scissors, cardboard chips, and egg shakers that both match the color of the ribbons you choose, baskets for the egg shakers, and a small altar to hold a red pillar candle, a plate of buns, athame, and incense.

The maypoles must be set up in the center of the space, in the middle of two circles drawn with chalk. Mark the inner circle with a counter-clockwise arrow and include the words "air" and "water." The outer circle is then marked with a clockwise arrow and the words "earth" and "fire." The altar must face north and should be situated under the stars – so, *outdoors*. Other elements like cardboard chips, scissors, and egg shakers should be under the altar.

To begin the ritual, the members will sing the following song:

> *"I love the oxygen.*
> *I love the Eastern winds.*
> *I love the breezes.*
> *I love the winged things.*

I love the whole world;
It's such a brilliant place.
I love the bright sun.
I love the Southern flames.
I love the campfire.
I love the passion's flames.
I love the whole world;
It's such a brilliant place.
Boom dee ah dah. Boom dee ah dah. (x4)
I love the ocean.
I love the Western fish.
I love the clear brooks.
I love the surge and swish.
I love the whole world;
It's such a brilliant place.
Boom dee ah dah. Boom dee ah dah. (x4)
I love the mountains.
I love the Northern hills.
I love the soil.
I love the daffodils.
I love the whole world;
It's such a brilliant place.
Boom dee ah dah. Boom dee ah dah. (to fade)"

Every person who wants to participate in the maypole can do so, as this is the time to celebrate the earth and every living thing on it. The participants will select a shaker from the basket to reflect the color of their ribbon and arrange themselves accordingly. This is followed by the food and drink session, where everything is moved clockwise. The ritual is closed by giving thanks for the blessings.

Spell Meditation

Aside from fertility, you can also meditate on other elements you want to manifest in your life. This can be positive energy or creativity, for instance. All you need is a quiet place where you can comfortably and uninterruptedly meditate. Verbally express everything you want to achieve, and express your desire for the wisdom you need to be creative in whatever you do.

Creativity Bath

You can take the Beltane creativity bath to cleanse, create famine power, and bring balance to your life. Use different herbs like Mugwort for protection, frankincense for purification, and rosemary for healing. While taking a bath, you should really feel the water on your body. It is important to listen to guidance from your higher self. Utilize citrine or Carnelian crystals to create a balance in your sacral chakra. Carnelian is very good for you since it helps you connect with yourself and find what you want to improve upon.

Beltane Prosperity Spells, Charms, and Baths

If you want to prosper in any particular aspect of your life, fire is the most important component to use for the ritual. If you don't have sufficient space to make a bonfire, you can use candles instead. During a ritual, the colors should include red for passion, purple for spirituality, green for prosperity, yellow for happiness, and white for harmony. Remember, the most crucial aspect of your ritual is your intention, so keep your goals or dreams in mind during the entire process.

A surefire way to manifest your intention in a prosperous way is to write your intentions on a leaf of a bay. Cast the spell at dawn over the flame of the candles and visualize a wish that you want. For instance, a wish you want may involve success or fame or good health, and you can wish for whatever as long as it is your true desire.

Beltane Prosperity Bath

Using a prosperity bath kit can aid your spells of good luck and money drawing. If you fail to get a prepared solution for your bath, you can use crystals of your choice and add them to the water. You can consider different stones, but make sure they align with your intention. Don't forget to say your intention before taking a bath. Then, all that's left to do is relax in the water and feel your body absorbing it slowly. Just make sure you avoid soaking in the bath for longer than a couple of minutes.

Beltane Prosperity Charm

It is of the utmost importance to reflect and be mindful of the wishes you hope to fulfill before you perform this ritual. Generally, white eggs are used for wishes involving plants and people, whereas brown eggs are the norm for wishes that involve animals. Use a needle to pierce two holes at each end of the egg. Then, carefully, remove the yolk from the egg. When the inside is clear, paint your Talisman, and you'll be ready to perform your charm.

Select a symbol that represents your wish, such as a coin for prosperity, a heart for love, a candle for wisdom, or any other meaningful symbol to you. Depending on your intention, you can also paint the whole egg with your preferred color. When the egg is ready, find a suitable place to hang it using a thread. You can use thin wool or embroidery thread which should pass through the two holes on both ends. Secure the egg with something to keep it stable. The next thing is to clear your mind and focus on your intention and desire for fruitfulness in your life. Ask for blessings as part of the charm made from the shell. Remember to use words you are comfortable with since the charm is all about your intention.

Having explored different Beltane spells, charms, and baths, you can now choose the ones that appeal to you and your desires when performing your rituals. Like any other ritual, you must have a clear intention and make sure you have everything you need before getting started. And last but definitely not least, you must understand all the tips and tricks required to perform each ritual.

Beltane Quick Reference Sheet

There are many terms and symbols you must learn about when it comes to Wiccan, Druid, and pagan celebrations. This is why you may find it hard to keep up with the plethora of information mentioned in the book, especially if this is your first time learning about Beltane and how this May Day is celebrated. This book is very easy to keep up with and is perfect for beginners and experts alike. However, you will undoubtedly benefit from having a quick reference sheet that you can refer to whenever you need to touch upon all the knowledge you obtained.

Here, you will find a summary of all the important details and main information points on preparing and celebrating Beltane.

What Is Beltane? (Chapter 1)

The Beltane fire festival is a Celtic ritual celebrated since the Iron Age and is among the greatest of its kind. Although it had died out throughout the years, it was brought to life once again in 1988, becoming one of the most important events in the Wiccan and pagan community. Beltane brings people together each year, allowing them to celebrate the changing seasons and the fertile land.

According to Celtic traditions, there are four quarter-day festivals, of which Beltane is one. The fire festival celebrates the return of summer, fertility of the land, and the reappearance of livestock on the pastures. The term Beltane could be somewhat translated into "bright fire." It remains among the most important rituals and is typically associated with the Beltane bonfire's lightning. Ancient Celtic beliefs suggested that fire was a healing and purifying element. People used to dance, walk, and even jump over it to benefit from its powers. Farmers also used to take their cattle past the bonfires to protect and cleanse them before they were led onto the pastures.

They also used to put out hearth fires and lit up a new Neid fire (a sacred Beltane fire), connecting all the community members. It was a central practice that brought everyone together. Courtship rituals were also popularly conducted during Beltane. The festival was all about warding off the darkness and welcoming the light.

The ancient Gaelic Beltane festival was what gave rise to the Beltane Fire Festival that we know today. The Gaelic celebration started in the evening prior to the beginning of May, signifying the start of summertime. The modern Fire Festival first came about in 1988, when a group of aficionados started it. The festival, which takes place on Calton Hill, located in central Edinburgh, Scotland, has grown in popularity. As of 2013, more than 300 performers and collaborators have made it there to celebrate.

The Witch's Wheel of the Year (Chapter 1)

Prominent Celtic festivals, specifically the eight Sabbats, are represented through the Neo-pagan and Wiccan Wheel of the Year. This wheel encompasses four solar and four seasonal festivals. Winter solstice, Summer Solstice, Spring Equinox, and Fall Equinox are the four solar festivals, while the four seasonal festivals are representative of the major seasonal changes. Many present-day Wiccans believe that an ancient Wheel of the Year presents the seasons and the passage of time. While there is no evidence suggesting this seasonal model existed in the past, the Celts celebrated these festivals, which were highlighted on the wheel thousands of years ago. It is possible, however, that the festivals were named differently.

Ancient Celts believed the nature of time to be cyclical. While everything comes to an end, such as the seasons and life itself, nothing in the world is truly lost because it eventually returns again somehow – the seasons change, and people are born. This means that the natural cycle is always in action, even when it doesn't seem like it. Modern science has proven time to be linear, but we still can't deny the cyclical essence of life.

Jacob Grimm, who's a mythologist and scholar, was the one who initially suggested the present-day Wheel of the Year around 1835 CE. The wheel represents the following eight major events. The exact dates for most of them typically change from one year to the other. However, the range remains fixed.

Samhain	Samhain falls on the 31st of October and signifies the beginning of a new year cycle. You can think of it as the Wiccan version of New Year's. The word *Samhain* means the end of summer, representing the end of the light season and the beginning of darkness. The main point behind Samhain is not to associate darkness with grieving or evil but to highlight it as a natural part of life.

	Darkness has to come so there can be light.
Yule	Yule typically falls between the 20th and 25th of December and celebrates the Winter Solstice. Winter Solstice is the shortest day of the year, and from that point forward, the days begin to grow longer while the nights fall shorter. Ancient Celts believed trees to be the homes of spirits and deities, which deemed them sacred. Every Yule, Celts would make sacrifices and decorate a tree outside to honor the sun god's birth.
Imbolc	Imbolc occurs on the 1st or 2nd of February and is Old Irish for *"In the belly,"* which references pregnant sheep. Imbolc falls halfway between Winter Solstice and Spring Equinox. It is a symbol of purification and rebirth. Since the festival is associated with pregnancy, it represents future promises, hope, and fertility.
Ostara	Ostara falls between the 20th and the 23rd of March. Ostara fulfills Imbolc's promises and is celebratory of the Spring Equinox. Although it is a long-standing holiday, there is a lot of uncertainty when it comes to ancient Ostara practices and celebrations. However, it is strongly linked to Easter because of symbols like the egg and the rabbit and activities like the Easter egg hunt.
Beltane	Beltane celebrates May Day and is held between 30th April and the 1st of May. Beltane is celebrated because it signifies fertility, light, and the start of summer. Many people believe that its name is associated with the phrase "Bel's Fire," alluding to the Celtic sun god Bel. However, as explained above, the term means "bright fire." Bonfires were a significant aspect of Beltane, as they are with many other festivals. Fire, in this case, corresponded to passion. It encouraged individuals to let go of their inhibitions and follow their desires. Dancing, which was often done around a tree, was also a very important aspect of the celebration. This act transformed into the "Maypole" symbol, which involved the decoration of a tree with long ribbon strands for people to hold onto and wave around as they danced.

Litha	Litha takes place between the 20th and the 22nd of June. Many people suggest that the word *Litha* is the Anglo-Saxon word for June. Litha celebrates the Summer Solstice, the longest day of the year. The Celts believed that this was when the Oak King gave up his throne to the Holly King, his brother, which is why it's considered the turning point of the year's cycle. It also marks the day when the days would shorten, and the nights would become longer. Fresh fruits, dancing, honey cakes, and bonfires are important aspects of the festival.
Lughnasadh	Lughnasadh falls on the 1st of August and is named after Lugh, the Celtic hero-god. This deity is associated with truth, righteousness, and order. This festival marks the end of summer and the beginning of autumn. The Celts used to offer their deities the first harvests of fruits.
Mabon	Mabon falls on the 20th to the 23rd of September and celebrates the Autumn Equinox. It is regarded as an opportunity to reflect on everything that has been lost and gained throughout the year.

The Bonfire Ritual (Chapter 3)

The Beltane bonfire is a long-standing tradition that has been practiced for centuries. It was not the average bonfire, consisting of a few logs and fire. The nature of the festival was to involve the whole community in a string of celebratory festivities where they collectively engaged in music, lovemaking, and dancing. The fire, traditionally, is lit up on the last night of April or May Eve. Ancient Celts would leave the fire to burn until sunset on the 1st of May. A bundle that consisted of nine types of wood was wrapped up in colorful ribbons that were used to light the bonfire. Each family in the village would return home with a piece of wood to guarantee fertility throughout the season. It's not very practical to hold a huge bonfire or participate in Maypole dancing in the modern-day world, and that's totally fine. It doesn't mean you can't celebrate Beltane just the same. To conduct the ritual, you can use a tabletop brazier, a small fire bowl, a heat-resistant bowl, or a small cauldron.

Key Preparations:

- Set up a bonfire beforehand and make sure that you have someone to light and tend to it

- A woman of childbearing age to be the May Queen. If you have someone trying to conceive, she would be the best choice.
- An adult man (ideally, someone who had partnered with the May Queen) to play the part of the King of the Forest. However, any adult man will suffice as the Green Man
- Drums and other sources of noise
- Optional: flower crowns for all females and antler headdresses for all males

Note that you can have two May Queens or two Kings of the Forest if you wish to include a same-sex couple in the ritual.

Key Activities:

To celebrate:

- Everyone should circle around the fire. The King of the Forest and the May Queen should stand on opposite sides.
- The High Priest or High Priestess should welcome the attendees with a chant.
- The fire started should light the bonfire while the person continues their chant.

Check the chapter for the full chant.

The Courtship:

- The May Queen and the King of the Forest should move according to the sun (clockwise) around the circle three times before stopping in front of the bonfire, where the King's pursuit of the queen ends. They should weave in and out of the attendees. The chase should be fun and joyful.
- Everyone should be drumming (start slow and then raise the tempo as the couple speeds up.
- The High Priest will declare their union with a chant.
- Closing the Ceremony
- Everyone should clap, sing, dance, and even recite poems.

Please check the chapter for the chants and detailed step-by-step instructions on the ritual.

Setting Up a Beltane Altar (Chapter 5)

Colors of Beltane

Color	Symbols
Red	• Passion • Vitality • Strength • Vibrancy
White/Silver	• Cleansing • Clearing • Dispersing negativity
Green	• Growth • Fertility • Abundance

Beltane's other colors are vibrant spring hues of yellows, blues, greens, and purples.

Beltane Specific Symbolism

Symbol	Fire
	• A simple triangle is used to conduct the meditative fire ritual.
Sigil	Confidence
Rune	• Often painted on the forehead. • The person should focus on the core intention while getting the rune. • It is usually associated with protection.

	• Celtic Ogham symbols can be used to create unique symbolism.

Fertility Symbols

Masculine Energy	• Antlers • Seeds • Sticks • Maypole
Feminine Energy	• Cup • Statue • Cauldron • Ring • Wreath

Other Symbols

Flowers	The most popular Beltane-related flowers include: • Forsythia • Tulips • Daffodils • Daisies • Hyacinth
Faeries	Faeries are honored in Celtic folklore, which is why you can leave them gifts and offerings on the altar.
Butterflies Birds Bees	• Decorate with outdoor plants that attract these creatures. • Decorate with hives and honey.

Clothes

- Wear dresses in earthly colors like green.
- Wear a kaftan in earthly colors or prints.
- Wear a Batik (traditionally decorated dress).
- Dress like pixies or fairies.
- Wear flower crowns or headpieces.

Trees (Chapter 6)

The Birch Tree	Birch trees are very strong and are among the first to grow their leaves and restore their vibrant green color when spring returns. They are also quick to regrow after forest fires, making them symbols of regeneration and rebirth. They can add momentum to new beginnings and are used in magical work for fertility, protection, creativity, and healing. This tree grows up straight, which is why it was commonly used to make Maypoles. If you find them lying around, you can use birch barks to write your spellwork.
The Rowan Tree	The Rowan tree is a symbol of astral travel, power, and success. It is also associated with the Celtic goddess of the heart, Brighid. The Celts used to name this tree after an Ogham symbol called Luis. It is believed that this tree holds protective powers, which is why you may want to carve out a charm from a Rowan tree to bring and wear as a necklace or bracelet. Many cultures believe that planting Rowan trees near graveyards would ease the passage of the dead. Many people also made crosses out of twigs for protection from enchantments. You can incorporate Rowan berries into your spells as well.
The Ash Tree	Odin, who is the god of war in Norse mythology, used to hang ash trees for nine days and nights because he thought it would make him wiser. Since then, the tree has been associated with divination, wisdom, and knowledge. As a result, the Ash Tree can be incorporated into numerous spells and

	rituals. For example, its use is significant in ocean rituals, taken on spiritual journeys, and used to summon prophetic dreams. It can also be used to make brooms, staff, wands, etc... The Celts also believed that it was sacred to the god Lugh. The tree is believed to hold healing properties and can protect people from drowning or diseases.
The Alder Tree	The Alder tree is commonly associated with spells that have to do with prophecy and divination. This is because they can heighten the intuition of individuals, making them capable of improving their spiritual decisions. The flowers and twigs of this tree work as charms and can be used in faerie magic and spells. For instance, it works as a protector of the heart in spells. This tree can be used as a musical instrument, as it was once used to make whistles. You can also use it to make wands.
The Willow Tree	This tree is associated with dreams and enchantment. It is thought that planting the Willow tree can help protect us from natural disasters like storms, earthquakes, floods, and hurricanes. These trees are symbols of nurturing, healing, and knowledge and are often used to make brooms that are used to perform spells and magic. These spells are typically associated with love and the expression of emotions.
The Hawthorn	The Hawthorn tree is a symbol of love and protection and is typically used in spells that have to do with masculinity and career advancements. For example, they can aid in professional networking and improve business decision-making. It is also strongly connected to the Faerie realm. Legend says that planting this tree can attract a faerie. It also has protection and cleansing powers.
The Oak Tree	The Oak tree typically stands taller than all the others around it. It is renowned for its power and strength. Oak trees are considered to be sacred by

	the Druids. They are also used in numerous spells, especially those intended to bring fertility, success, good fortune, financial abundance, strength, and protection. Oak trees are also included in purification rituals.
The Holly Tree	The Holly tree is incorporated into protection spells because it is thought to hold protection powers. You can hang a twig around in your house or wear it as a charm. Many people also use it to make holy water and use it in spells to make their dreams come true.
The Hazel Tree	The Hazel tree is correspondent to dream journeys, knowledge, wisdom, and divination. The Druids used it to seek wisdom, and it was also named the Tree of Knowledge in Norse mythology.

Flowers Chapter 6

Flower	Symbol
Tulips	• Prosperity • White tulips – cleansing and purification. • Yellow tulips – protection • Red tulips – love
Forsythia	• Sun • Anticipation • Used in divination workings
Violets	• Tranquility and peace • Can protect from the evil • Luck

	• Magic enhancement
Crocus	• New love • Vision enhancements • Intuitive dreams
Dandelion	• Growth • Transformation • Moving on • Ritual cleansing • Healing • Purification

Family Activities and Crafts (Chapter 7)

- Family Abundance Ritual
- Bonfire or camp night
- A nature walk
- Make a Maypole altar centerpiece
- Make flower crowns

Beltane Feast (Chapter 8)

Popular recipes include:

- Beltane Oatcake
- Green Man Cake
- Early Summer Salad
- Candied Flower Petals
- Asparagus and Cheese Quiche
- Peppery Green Beans
- Beltane Bread
- Beltane Berry Sangria
-

Beltane Spells, Charms and Baths Chapter 10

Fertility	• Fertility Spell • Beltane Bath • Birth Charms
Beltane Love Potion Ritual	• Love Charm • Love Spell • Beltane Love Bath
Beltane Creative Transformation Ritual	• Spell Meditation • Beltane Creativity Bath
Beltane Prosperity	• Beltane Prosperity Bath • Beltane Prosperity Charm

Conclusion

The Beltane festival has stood the test of time and has continued to remain a significant time of the year when all pagans can come together. Even though other elements overlap between the different cultures, there is something special about the Beltane festival that is unique and vibrant. It has an energy about it that attracts all kinds of people from all walks of life. Even people who do not typically participate in the pagan culture can become a part of this unique festival.

Over the course of this book, we have covered in-depth the religious and cultural background of the Beltane festival and what makes this such an important time for all living things. Even those who are new to the pagan culture can't help but notice the change in the energy of the Earth at this time of year. It is as if the universe evokes positive vibes to create an atmosphere of prosperity and plenteousness.

Throughout the ages, the time of Beltane has been an important one, especially in the Northern Hemisphere, where the winter season can be extremely harsh. Something about the long, dark winter season seems to diminish that inner flame of happiness and liveliness. People seem gloomier, ordinary tasks can become more challenging, and life doesn't flourish as well as it does during the warmer months. Even though the traditions, festivities, and practices around the day of Beltane have changed, the spirit has remained the same. With the different perspectives that we have covered in this book, you will have found something that resonates with you that you will enjoy with your family and friends.

Life in the modern world is a bit like an ongoing winter. We are constantly struggling to get things done in this fast-paced society. There seems to be a never-ending list of chores. People are isolated in their own lives and obligations; communication is not as frequent as it used to be, even though technology has granted us access to people around the world. There is a general feeling of disconnect and even isolation. With the recent pandemic, this has only increased – and although people have had the time to reconnect with their friends and family, as soon as the world opened up, people very quickly went back to their old way of life. There's no doubt that things are a bit different today than they were in the past, from the way we live to the way we interact, but we do not value human connection the way we once did a few hundred years ago. Although communities were much smaller then, they were more interconnected. People understood the importance of having that community feel and how it impacts every living thing.

In this book, we have covered several ways you can bring this celebration to your home and how it can serve as a wonderful way for you to connect with your loved ones. Whether or not you were initially familiar with Beltane, you now have all the information necessary to establish your own rituals and celebrations. This time of year is about acknowledging just how important it is to enjoy the time that we have with the people that we love and care for our community to ensure its growth and prosperity.

Part 5: Midsummer

The Ultimate Guide to Litha or the Summer Solstice and How It's Celebrated in Wicca, Druidry, and Paganism

Introduction

Litha or Midsummer is a very powerful and important time to celebrate the abundance of life and all the good things that the glorious sun brings to one and all. Since the dawn of time, we've been acutely aware of the importance of the sun and how its power is responsible for life. Every culture has celebrated the power of the sun in its own way, and in this book, you'll learn all how Wiccans, Druids, and Pagans pay homage to the sun.

You'll find out all about the various deities, celebrations, and rituals that you can participate in, as an individual or with friends and family. Unlike other books out there, you'll find this a very easy and informative read, chock full of insight and ways that you can honor the period of Litha in line with the old ways, even in this modern world.

The rituals and charms here are simple, easy to understand, and you'll find hands-on instructions to make your own with no stress or fuss. Another great thing about this book to look forward to are the delicious recipes for meals that represent the spirit of Litha so that you can truly celebrate in spirit and authenticity.

If you've always felt pulled toward Litha but have never known where to begin, then you've made a brilliant decision picking this book as your starting point. Even if you're already familiar with the origins and ways of Litha, this book will give you even more insight into the deep mysteries of this festivity. If you're ready to reconnect with your roots or find your connection to nature once more, don't waste any time. Let's get right into chapter one!

Chapter 1: Introduction to Midsummer

Midsummer, or Litha, is a pagan festival celebrated on the summer solstice in many European and Scandinavian countries. It is also known as Litha Day, Midsummer Eve, Summer Solstice Eve, or just summer solstice. It marks an important turning point in the year; when it falls between June 20th and 23rd in the northern hemisphere and December 20th and 23rd in the southern hemisphere, it marks the longest day of the year and is an important marker for tracking the seasons.

Etymology

The name "Midsummer" comes from Old English "mid-sumor," which means "middle of summer." The name was used to signify that they were halfway through their summer season (Jun 24th). Many other Germanic languages have similar terms, such as the Saxon term Midsummersdaeg, which is known in English and Swedish, Danish, and Norwegian. Litha appears to be of Old English derivation (derived from the Goddess called Lith), and it is an Anglo-Saxon word used to signify a fire festival.

The solstice also marks an important turning point in many other pagan festivals such as Yule, Ostara, and Mabon. The importance of this turning point relates to astrological beliefs that the sun's power either grows or dwindles over time. It is believed that during the summer solstice, the sun reaches its peak of power then will continue to wane towards December 21st, where it reaches its least amount of power. The opposite is true for the winter solstice, where the sun grows to its most powerful stage before gradually waning as we near June 21st of the next year. Scholars believe that many pagan festivals such as Yule and Midsummer are directly linked to seasonal changes, with many held at specific times of year relating to the Sun's movement in relation to Earth.

Across Cultures and Time

Midsummer has been an important festival for hundreds of years for people living around Northern Europe, and there is ample evidence that predates Christianity. In the year 98 AD, for example, scholars found an account of the reign of emperor Domitian (81-96 AD) in Rome where a pagan festival that was held on December 22nd is described to involve "sacrificing a sow in the temple of Minerva" (which is a goddess from Roman mythology). The celebrations also involved drinking, singing, dancing, and merriment. The Romans were often tolerant of other religions, such as those who adhered to paganism. It may be that they continued to hold celebrations at specific times of the year that reflected their own traditions.

However, religious tolerance did not continue as Emperor Constantine I converted to Christianity in the 4th century. Constantine established the first Christian Church and saw pagan practices as a threat to Christianity. It is said that Constantine even attempted to restructure the Roman calendar and removed pagan rituals and celebrations from it to consolidate power and rid Roman society of pagan influence. In the 8th century, there was a revival of interest in all things pagan; however, Anglo-Saxons broke away from Catholicism, bringing new traditions, including celebrating summer solstice (as well as winter solstice) on Midsummer's Eve.

According to several sources, the summer solstice celebration did not really become widespread again until the 19th century. After the Second World War and with the onset of industrialization, many Pagans felt that they were losing their culture and decided to hold on to what they could. This was a time when paganism was becoming increasingly popular, with many people preferring to practice a form of nature worship as opposed to mainstream Christianity

Pagans and Midsummer

Midsummer is often celebrated by Pagans who worship the sun God "Sol" or "Sol Invictus." It is common for Midsummer celebrations to involve bonfires. It is believed that this originated from the ancient Norse tradition where fires were used to scare away evil spirits who dwelt in darkness. Bonfires are still commonly used at festivals such as Beltane, which is another pagan festival that is often held on May 1st. However, in Scotland and Ireland, the bonfire tradition was different from that of the Norse. It was believed to be guarded by Druids, who were often associated with witchcraft.

The Druids believed that fire could cleanse not only a person of their sins but also avert disaster. These Druids built bonfires to purify crops and animals, protect livestock, and celebrate key events in their lives (such as marriages). It was also believed that the Druids could guide people's souls after death, and they would release them from their bodies by burning a fire in the center of a circle. A bonfire is still a common sight at many festivals, and it is believed that bonfires continue to carry on many Celtic traditions.

Midsummer across the World

In Sweden, Midsummer is no longer celebrated as widely as it once was. It is thought that this may be because it has become more "mainstream," with many people no longer following Pagan beliefs but instead following other religions such as Christianity or Islam. Whatever the reason, many Swedes still celebrate a version of Midsummer on or around June 24th, and it is still a national holiday.

Many Swedish traditions are similar to those that are celebrated in other countries. They decorate doorways with wreaths made of greenery, bright flowers, and ribbons as an omen for good luck. They also light bonfires on June 23rd (St John's Eve) at nighttime. The fires often burn throughout the whole night, and there is usually music, singing, and dancing around them. In some areas, bonfires are even used to light the fields, a practice that continues today.

In Iceland, Midsummer celebrations are quite different from those in other countries. Instead of celebrating by lighting boats with torches, Iceland has its own traditions, which are more akin to Nordic festivities. In Iceland, however, there is no wave starting on Midsummer's Eve, and instead, the people celebrate at Sun Festival on June 23rd. The festival begins with a procession of horses across the island followed by many rituals, followed by the Althingi (which is the parliament of Iceland) meetings at noontime, which lasts for several hours.

In some parts of England, it is customary to celebrate Midsummer by lighting a candle at every window on June 24th. This is believed to have originated from the old Norse tradition of lighting candles on St John's Eve.

In Lincolnshire, people celebrate Midsummer's Day also on June 24th, and it is said that a man known as "Jack-in-the-Green" leads processions through the streets (or used to at least). Jack would wear a leafy crown on his head, and the procession would contain several people carrying torches and lanterns. The festivities were also said to be accompanied by very strict guidelines, with one disobeying them, leading to being severely punished. Apart from lighting bonfires and wreaths, most of the celebrations today are very similar to those elsewhere in the country.

In other parts of England, Midsummer is celebrated on June 23rd. This could be linked to old pagan customs that were practiced in Scandinavia, where it was customary for May Day (which falls on May 1st) to be followed Midsummer. The celebrations that occur on June 23rd tend to be grass festivals, and there is a tradition of people jumping over fires while wearing flowers.

In Cornwall, Midsummer's Eve celebrations are held at nighttime as opposed to daylight hours which was typical everywhere else. Many people take to the streets and carry flaming torches, while many fire rituals occur around the county. Another Cornish tradition was the lighting of lanterns that would be carried through streets. However, in 1881 this tradition was sadly banned until 2000 when it resumed once again.

In Scotland, Midsummer is also known as "the night of the witches" or "Halloween," as it is called in English, but in Gaelic, it is referred to as Latha na Caillich ("Nuadh na gCaorach"). In Scotland, midsummer was traditionally celebrated by lighting bonfires, dancing around them, and jumping through them (which was also customary in Finland). The tradition of fire leaping is linked to the Celtic druids, who were often referred to as "fire-worshippers."

There's also a custom in Yorkshire where people dip their hands in water before dipping them into the fire ashes, which is believed to bring good luck. However, in Dumfriesshire, this tradition is more of a rural celebration and is known as the "Highland Games." Dancing around bonfires and jumping through them was said to be very dangerous for young people, but adults still participated in these celebrations.

In Scotland, it was once customary for men to go from house to house asking for a game of Old Mother Hubbard which was based on guessing how many beans they had in their pockets. If the person guessed correctly, they would have to pay a penny. However, if they failed, they would have to do something violent or foolish such as clapping their hands or slapping themselves on the forehead with a wetted handkerchief. In some parts of Scotland, it is also customary to dress up as a famous person in history. It was believed that these so-called "superstitions" would bring good luck, and if they were followed throughout the year, they could bring a lot of wealth.

In Wales, Midsummer celebrations are known as "Y Gogledd Iau Cymreig," which means "the night of the assembly at the church." This tradition has been held since the late Middle Ages, and nowadays, it involves going from house to house singing traditional hymns while carrying a candle. People also use a decorated bucket to collect money for charity. In Wales, it is believed that the overnight stay in church on Midsummer's Eve would mess with one's mind, and as a result, people would experience very vivid dreams. Midsummer's eve was once known as "Y Bryn Awst," which means "the night of the milk." This was said to be a tradition borrowed from Ireland. The milk was used as part of a charm that could bring good luck and prosperity to the individual who drank it. In Scotland, however, many superstitions surrounding Midsummer are carried out by men who do not want their wives to know about their true identities. In this country, it was believed that the person who spilled water on Midsummer's Eve would die the following year; this was a very common belief.

Also, in Wales, it is traditional to eat Ymert on Midsummer's Eve, and this is supposed to bring good luck to the individual who eats it. In some parts of England, people were once required to carry around a "bewitched" coin to bring good luck to anyone who wore it. The tradition was said to have originated from when Druids wore bewitched coins to perform magic for their followers. In Cornwall, it is believed that if a girl lights a sparkler on Midsummer's Eve, she will become pregnant. In the past, people believed that witches would fly over the fields on Midsummer's Eve, and this is an old superstition from the Middle Ages. In some parts of Wales, it was once customary for people to dress in black and hold parties under the moonlight or in barns. Many of these parties were also conducted in conjunction with customs such as "Black Dog," "Barley-Wig," and "Bean-stealing." It was once said that people would cut out the image of St. John's head from a coin and throw it in the water to get rid of evil spirits and protect against evil. St. John's Day is also celebrated on June 23rd, which could be linked to

Midsummer celebrations.

In England, there was once a custom where people would jump through straw targets while wearing a red hood or cap and carrying a cow's skull or a black cat's head and food or coins. It was said that if the person jumping fell into the water and drowned, they would become a ghost for three days afterward (which are known as "Bubbling Wells").

In Lancashire, there are many superstitions, such as those involving the moon. Many people would go to where the full moon rises, hoping that this would bring some sort of luck for them or their crops in the following year. In parts of Ireland, people believe that if they drink water from a lake on Midsummer's Eve, they would be able to see a white horse with a black man sitting on its back. Across Europe, Midsummer celebrations stemmed from pagan traditions dating back to Neolithic times. Today, it is still common to see people dancing around bonfires and dressing up as "old men" who have been reborn in the new year.

The Essence of Litha

In the cold of winter, the Solar God is born. He is the Oak King, who rules the light. At this time, people light candles and feast, and they place evergreen plants in their homes to remind them that after winter must come summer and light. The Holly King who rules winter must eventually give way to the Oak King's arrival. It's all about the battle of power between these two kings, who continue to conquer each other in their due season. Think of this as a metaphor for life's natural pendulum swing. Light to dark, good to bad, high to low, birth to death and back. It's a celebration of the cycles of nature.

No matter who you're or where you're in the world, you can celebrate this holiday in a way that's authentic to the roots of the festivities, as well as your intuition and personal neopagan beliefs.

Chapter 2: Litha Deities and Mythology

It is believed that the Gods and Goddesses in the Litha ritual are the deities of love and fertility. The lore of Litha refers to their mythology and rites in three ways:

1. As a time for marriages.

2. As a time for the gods to come down to earth.

3. As a mark that the light was beginning its struggle against darkness.

Litha deities are ancient Celtic deities that typically represent fertility. Ancient peoples called upon these gods during times when they needed help with impregnation or cultivating crops. The lore of these deities can be found referencing them both as agents of love and agents of agriculture.

Litha

Litha, a Gaelic word that means "Summer," is the ancient Celtic goddess of love and fertility. The best-known stories of her begin with her as a crow who would steal the breath from everyone's mouths while they slept, and she or her children would put out fires. As time went on, she was given several different attributes. She was sometimes depicted as a woman with a dog who helped keep the fields fertile by drinking milk from them. She also taught women how to make cheese. In some versions of the myth, she would shape the cheese into babies for people who wanted some extra help caring for them before they were born. In other versions, she would turn into a cat and trick people into throwing their babies for her to eat. You can offer Litha ginger root, earth, honey, cauldrons, divination tools, handmade potpourri, white candles, white flowers, and incense.

Cernunnos

Cernunnos is the Celtic God of Nature, often portrayed with antlers. He is known to have been the most widely worshiped God in Britain and Gaul before Christianity. He was also said to be the God who watched over animal herds, protecting them from harm. The Romans believed that he was part human and part stag, which is what earned him his crown with antlers. Cernunnos was followed by many Druid priests who worshiped him for his powers related to nature and fertility. It is said that he had three wives, all of which were Goddesses

To honor the Celtic deity Cernunnos, a popular figure of the Neopagan religion of Wicca, it is customary in many regions to offer him a sheaf of wheat or food-related items during the spring festival. He may also be given ribbons, green mistletoe branches, or flowers. Certain offerings are more common in some areas than others; for example, apples and pomegranates are very popular with followers in San Francisco, while wine is common among those who worship Cernunnos in Central Europe. This tradition traces its roots as far back as ancient Roman times.

Gwydion

Gwydion is a Celtic God who was known for his powers of magic and Druidry. He was the son of Don and the brother of Arianrhod, another Great Goddess. Because of his divine parentage, his magical powers were strong, being able to conjure up whatever he wanted with just a word. In one legend, Gwydion disguised himself as a stag and seduced Arianrhod's virgin form to create a son called Lleu. In another story, Gwydion is credited with creating Oengus by carving him out of the side of a great oak tree.

This ancient Celtic holiday called Beltane celebrates the end of winter and the beginning of summer by honoring Gwydion, God of light and fertility. He sneaks up on his wife with a sudden kiss to awaken her from her cold winter slumber. All around them, greenery starts springing up from the bare ground in an explosion of bluebells—symbolic of everything that will grow in this new season. Here are offerings you can make to Gwydion during Beltane: A warm meal of soup or stew, a loaf of bread, a mug of ale or beer, and a candle to light the way.

Lleu

Lleu, also Lugh, is a powerful god, warrior, and magician. His mother, Arianrhod, tried to make him immortal by sewing his body into four suits of armor, but his uncle Gwydion set him free once more, and he took his human form. Because Arianrhod found his human form too beautiful for her liking, she put three curses on him. The first was he would bear no other name unless she gave him one. The second was he'd bear no arms unless she let him, and the final curse was he'd have no wife of any of the races on Earth. However, Gwydion saved Lleu by turning him into a stag, a sow, then a wolf. Once Lleu was free from Arianrhod's grasp, he became human again and successfully won his mother's love.

You can offer Lleu a couple of eggs, a pot of milk and honey, fresh (or dried) flowers like lavender, violets, hawthorn blossom, honeysuckle, hazelnuts, and gold coins. The hazelnuts should not be eaten until the end of the ritual; instead, you should bury them in the earth before going to bed on Beltane Eve to ensure fertility in your home for the next year. You can also offer a wand made from a willow branch, with its leaves still attached, and has been stripped from its bark when it was cut down for this purpose, and branches from an ash tree so that he can carry it back to Annwn in triumph over winter's defeat.

Merlin

Merlin is one of the most well-known characters in Arthurian legends. He was said to be the half-brother of Morgan le Fay, and it is believed that he lived around the 5th or 6th century A.D. Merlin was said to be an amazing enchanter who helped Uther Pendragon win over Igraine. He also helped Arthur by teaching him to be a good king, and in some stories, he is even said to have created Excalibur for Arthur.

Merlin is a mythical figure who represents the element of fire, and in Britain, he's associated with the three left-handed cauldrons. In other words, he's seen as a magical being who helps people and animals on their journey across life's path. According to some legends, he also has power over weather patterns and volcanoes, so you can give him gifts like candles or incense.

The Battle for Power between the Holly King and Oak King

The Holly King and the Oak King are opposite deities in the Pagan tradition. The battle between them is an integral part of the Litha celebration, representing many things to different people. It is a celebration of the duality of life and death, a battle between light and darkness, or summer and winter.

As with any other "battle" mythology, this one is not quite what it seems.

The Litha celebration is a three-day festival that occurs in the middle of summer, around the time of the Vernal Equinox. The first two days are called Ostara and Beltane, and the third day takes its name from Litha (meaning "day of light").

In its most basic form (as per tradition), the battle between the Holly King and Oak King happens during Litha. Whoever wins the battle gets to decide what to do with their power for one whole year. If you win, you can choose your destiny. If you lose, then your fate is chosen for you.

In one interpretation, this battle is between the god of fertility (Oak King) and the god of death (Holly King). The Oak King represents the power of the past, and the Holly King represents renewal and growth. In essence, it is a conflict between life and death.

This battle isn't really a physical one: rather, it's symbolic of the ongoing struggle between light and darkness, creation, and destruction. Some may view life as a never-ending struggle or war; instead of victory or defeat in any one instance, it is a continuous victory over darkness whenever you choose to do good in this world.

In another interpretation, Litha can represent choice versus destiny. "Light" can refer to the power of choice and free will, while "darkness" can signify destiny, fate, and predestination.

This "destiny versus free will" theme is especially prevalent during Litha; it's a time when the boundaries are thin between our world and the spirit realms. It's a time when you're meant to be aware of your own mortality, your own choices, as well as your spiritual destiny.

On the third day of Litha, there is a ritual called "crossing the bridge." This ritual is about crossing into your own personal afterlife (either literally or figuratively). You can apply a dual meaning to that idea, symbolizing the passage from one side of life to the other.

Many Pagans choose to emphasize the light and dark aspects of Litha through their personal actions and lifestyles. They might choose to be more light-hearted or romantic during the festival, or they may make a special effort at completing their bucket list or work on achieving some other goal that was on hold for most of the year.

Many Pagans also choose to mix up their daily meals with herbal fertilizers just before they eat them (since this time represents spring when all kinds of plants are sprouting and growing). They may also grow plants themselves if they have room in their gardens.

During the festival of Litha, Pagans may especially honor their deities. They may choose to wear costumes based on the Sumerian King and Queen Gods, Inanna and Utu.

The final interpretation of the battle between Oak King and Holly King can be summed up as "the good fight" or simply "the struggle." It's a symbolic representation of what it means to be alive in general.

Litha is a time when you can reflect on the balance of light and dark, life and death. It's a time when you can live in the moment and enjoy your life. It's also a time you can use to set powerful intentions, especially if you feel that your destiny has been chosen for you. It's easy to get caught up in the all-consuming chaos of our daily lives. Sometimes it's hard to see why we're still fighting every single day or why we're here at all. It might seem as if we have no choices. Realize that you do have choices, even if your life may seem like you're on autopilot sometimes. This is a time to listen to your intuition and trust your instincts.

Acknowledge the good things you do and focus on the lessons learned, and use this time as an opportunity to set your intentions for the year to come, no matter what happens during Litha. Keep in mind that if you win, your destiny is chosen for you; if you lose, then your fate is chosen for you. Having said that, Litha is a time for many to realize that they can't just give up or give in and accept death every time they brush up against it. It's not like we're being defeated in every instance of friction; we can win battles all the time, even if we don't see them as such right away. It is an opportunity to reflect on what you've done, learn from it, and plan the rest of your year. There's always another battle to be fought and won.

Wicca, Litha, the God, and Goddess

To the average citizen, Wicca and Litha may seem completely unrelated. To a group of people who follow Wicca beliefs, however, Litha is one of the holiest days in their year. It is a day where they welcome back their Sun God and celebrate with festivals and ceremonies to honor Him. So, this has everything to do with the way Wiccans see themselves as children of nature.

They worship many Gods, including the Goddesses represented by Gaia (Earth), Artemis (the Moon), Diana (the huntress), Hecate (wisdom), and Selene (the moon). These Goddesses, who embody the qualities that make humans human, are in Wicca called "The Five Grandmothers" or "The Sisters." The five elements of Earth, Fire, Water, Air, and Spirit also represent these Goddesses.

To people who follow Wicca's beliefs, it is important to be aware of their environment to understand their role as a child of nature. Especially when it comes to Wicca festivals such as Litha (Lith=LIGHT), therefore Litha is a time for Wiccans to remember the God and Goddess. As children of nature, Wiccans believe the Sun God is a very important deity whose role as the provider of all things is felt strongly by them. This belief caused the Celts to believe in their sun-God, named "Litha," because he represented light and knowledge.

The main festival of Wicca is held on the Summer Solstice. This is because it is the day that symbolizes the highest point in light, knowledge, and power. It is also on this day that Litha was born as a God. This celebration represents one of the few times when Wiccans can truly lose themselves in dance with others in their community to honor their deity, who they see as a beautiful man with long golden hair, wearing gleaming armor. This time is also a period to celebrate fertility in all its natural forms.

Wicca follows the Wheel of the Year cycle, where 8 celebrations are held throughout the year. These celebrations focus mostly on Litha in the summer when Wiccans celebrate God. The longer days make it possible for Wiccans to prepare for their faith by cleaning and purifying their homes and themselves.

Generally, during Litha, Wiccans will gather for outdoor rituals. In preparation for this event, many will take part in a fast and only eat raw fruits and vegetables. This is done to cleanse the body and get closer to the God who possesses amazing powers, including night vision. It is said that during this time, His ability to see in darkness allows him to see inside you as well.

As mentioned, Litha represents the birth of the Wiccan God. His arrival into the world is in the form of a child -- Cronos. The great god Jupiter sent his son Saturn to represent the Wicca. Today, they celebrate this day on December 21st according to their belief.

In honoring their God, festivals are held with bonfires and songs of praise to celebrate His return and give thanks to Him for still being with them. There are many candles and lights in the houses of Wiccans to symbolize their God's return. During Litha, the Goddess is at the height of her fertility, and the God is at his most virile.

Wiccans also hold festivities for Litha in the form of birthdays and weddings. This shows that God does not differentiate between the rich and poor and that all are equal in His eyes.

There are also many rituals held on this day, one being where Wiccans take a bath as a symbol of purification, renewal, and immortality. The bath is completed in a westerly direction to indicate the coming of the Sun God.

The celebration of Litha is one of the most joyous celebrations for Wiccans as it represents the light and knowledge that is re-awakened when their God returns from his Winter sleep. This marks the beginning of a harvest period where their Goddess grows ripened grain and fruit for them to enjoy. Like all other celebrations, all Wiccans are encouraged to be always in tune with nature to recognize their role as children of nature. Only in this way can they fully understand what it means to be a part of something much bigger than themselves, which can seem limitless.

Beltane Deities

Every pagan is familiar with the major festivals of Beltane and Litha when the ancient Celtic and Gaelic people would celebrate spring's arrival by engaging in a celebration of fertility and hope. These are two important holidays within the standard Wiccan season that we can easily overlook in our modern-day life. But as we shall see, there is much more to know about these festivals than just the usual get-to-know-you that many Wiccans provide. Let's explore these holidays and discover why they are so vital to our modern pagan path.

Beltane was one of the four great fire festivals of ancient Celtic traditions based upon the Gaelic calendar. Beltane marks the beginning of summer, when livestock and crops were supposed to feed by themselves and when animals would stop hibernating. This was a time when it was believed that supernatural beings were most likely to meet people, so it was a good time for divination or other rituals that involved contacting spirits or deities. It was a time when people cleaned up their homes, organized the yearly festival feast, and prepared for the coming of summer.

It is still remembered as one of the four significant fire festivals of Celtic traditions, along with Lughnasadh (Litha), Samhain (Halloween), and Imbolc (Candlemass).

Beltane marks the time to celebrate and brighten up your home for the months ahead. The festivities always include May Day, Maypole dancing, and other merry-making such as fireworks, bonfires, and ritualistic offerings to the moon goddess. But more than that, it is a festival in which the deities of ancient Celtic traditions are honored, the major deity being Bile, the sun god, and the deity of harvest.

Bile

According to Celtic lore, Bile began his reign over the year on Beltane and would continue to rule until Samhain. Bile was worshiped as a god who could bring prosperity and growth to the lands, although he was also associated with fire. He was a benevolent deity who rewarded those who honored him with good fortune. Part of his duty included keeping famine at bay and ensuring that people worked hard to gain prosperity through his blessings. He also kept evil spirits from harming people, and in fact, he was a figure who helped priests in enacting rituals to banish evil spirits.

In many countries, bouquets of flowers are offered to Bile (or fertility) instead of food offerings like cakes or bread because their scent blooms with life late into the dark days of winter. It's an easy way to make the transition from cakes and bread to flowers. Bile prefers this offering because it leaves him with more energy by the time Beltane is over. Flowers that grow in spring are especially loved.

On Beltane, the festival of Bile would be celebrated with bonfires, divination, and other rituals to the sun god. People would try to contact him through various magical techniques such as divination or casting spells. They would give him food and drink as sacrifices to ensure that he would continue to watch over them through the coming autumn months that were considered barren for many folk's needs. In return, they received blessings of good health and prosperity during the coming year.

Beltane was seen as a time to pull together the community and celebrate their good fortune. Folk would carry out rituals involving May Day and ritual dances such as the maypole dance, where they would pray for a bountiful harvest for their crops. They would make food and drink offerings to Bile and other gods and spirits of nature such as plants, animals, stones, and wind. Although Bile is not one of these deities that we worship at this time, he is important enough to qualify him as one of the major deities within our modern traditions based upon Celtic traditions.

Amaterasu

Amaterasu is still revered as a deity in Japan, 6,000 years after her death. The Japanese see this as another example of Beltane's influence from ancient Europe and think of her as their own goddess who comes alive again in Springtime when everything blossoms and new life starts. They believe she is the most important of all Shinto gods and was the first to rule over Nippon.

Amaterasu is depicted in art as a beautiful woman with long, black hair flowing over her shoulders. She has three faces that represent her ability to see in all directions. She is normally shown with two white dogs who are said to be able to find anything when lost or stolen — even missing socks. It is believed Amaterasu never really died and has always been here watching over us. We should worship her more often, especially on Beltane.

Amaterasu offerings are usually gifts made of wood. This is because wood is sacred to the goddess of the sun, who drives away the darkness. She will be happy with any object that has been crafted from this natural material, including small mementos or potion bottles. The goddess may have high expectations for the quality of her offerings during Beltane, so do not disappoint her by giving her something she would not enjoy. One potential gift would be a painted wooden tile with a quote from Mother Earth on it.

Apollo

As mentioned, Beltane is a Gaelic celebration of life and the driving out of winter. It is also known as the "Festival of Healthy Life." Possibly one of the most important mythological deities in Beltane lore is Apollo. The connection between Beltane and Apollo goes beyond just mythology, though. There is an underlying connection to this Greco-Roman god through various festivals, traditions, and games played during Beltane celebrations for centuries.

Beltane was a significant festival for the Celts, especially in Ireland. Apollo, a deity who symbolized light and the sun, was celebrated. He is also known as Apollo Dactylus to signify his connection with the two-fingered hand gesture that represents him. According to Greek mythology, this god had two fingers because once, as a baby, he held out his hand towards Zeus, who cut off one of them so that he would never be able to point or hold objects away from himself ever again.

This god also has an association with bunnies. Apollo was a god that favored the Greek god Pan, and to honor his counterpart from Ireland, the Celts would take young bunnies at this time of year as though they were heralds for the king. They would then be sacrificed on a high hill during Beltane, where Druid priests would make offerings to Apollo in remembrance of his godly nature.

Offerings that are appropriate for Apollo include cowry shells (which are small sea snails), jewels made of precious metals (gold, silver, brass, and copper coins), as well as gems (quartz crystal balls such as amethyst or rock crystals like turquoise). It's important to know that Apollo is the god of music, prophecy, poetry, and healing. So, offering appropriate gifts is important because they will help you in your life and work.

One point to remember when offering a gift is that it must be considered, first and foremost, a representation of yourself. It should not be something you don't really want yourself, but something that would please you.

Horus

It is often assumed that Horus's connection to the May 1st festival of Beltane has something to do with his role as a God of Spring. More specifically, it is believed that his role as God of Morning and Daytime may have contributed to him being worshiped in conjunction with the Celtic springtime festival.

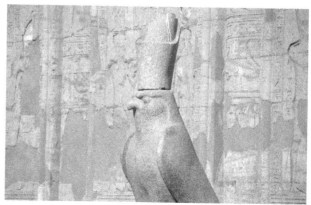

Other theories support this, like the idea that Horus was feared by both Greeks and Romans, who might have seen his resurgence in their own traditions during Beltane. The Ancient Egyptians who worshipped Horus saw their god as a god of both light and dark, which could be seen paralleling the wild revelry at Beltane as well. In this view, Horus was the God of Morning, and the world would be reborn with him.

The reason Horus seems associated with Beltane has more to do with his connection to Spring than anything else. It wasn't until later in history that he was equated with Phanes, who was also worshiped at Beltane because of his role as a fertility deity.

The argument for associating springtime festivals with Horus and early Christianity, in turn, associates the two religions, at least partly since both were syncretized from their earlier forms of worship. Thus, Horus might have had a connection with Beltane, but he was also the God of War and hunting who would have been seen as a Sun God at times. Some people offer the god Horus flowers, wine, or incense. They may also offer him a sistrum or Hathor.

Chapter 3: Midsummer Customs: Then and Now

Picture this: Above you, the glorious sun burns brightly. All around you're very happy witches dancing around a bonfire. They feast on vegetables and fruits that they've gotten fresh from the harvest. You hear laughter and turn your head to notice the children playing as they roll around on wheels that represent the sun. The children run about chasing bubbles in the air, which float and remind you of fairies. Everything and everyone around you pulsates with a glorious light that seems to come from within. This is the picture of the summer solstice, also called Litha or Midsummer.

This happens to be the longest day in the year, and it also has the shortest night. Currently, the sun arrives at the zenith, reaching the height of its power physically and spiritually as well. Once this day is over, the days to come will become shorter and shorter as we move on to the darker portion of the year. Come the Winter Solstice; we have the reverse of the entire process as we journey back to the abundant light and fertility of Midsummer.

In December, it goes into Capricorn if you happen to be in the southern areas of the world. In the past, Pagans celebrated fire, the sun, and the land's fertility at the time. There's not a single culture that hasn't celebrated this time in some way, whether it's the Jews, Romans, Norse, Celts, or Greeks. Regardless of the differences in how they celebrated, there were always common themes that cut across cultures.

Midsummer is usually celebrated as a fire or solar festival or both. While many cultures incorporated the element of water, making pilgrimages to wells considered sacred and other powerful bodies of water, as explained earlier, bonfires were more common across all of them. It was also standard practice to have vigils that would be held from dawn on the day of Midsummer until sunrise the next day.

Three sabbats come after Midsummer, and those are harvest festivals. Midsomer itself is not a harvest festival, but it's all about celebrating growing things in every aspect of life. It's a celebration of the crops that grow in the field and all of nature. This holiday is all about prosperity, abundance, fertility, good fortune, and success.

During Midsummer, the ancient druids would gather sacred herbs, and even today, this is still a practice. These plants are meant to be used in the preparation of food, healing, as well as magickal works. There are many Midsummer rituals that we perform today that can be traced back to the rites and rituals that earlier pagans held.

Across cultures on the planet, it was the norm to light bonfires on hilltops so everyone miles away could see them. Those close enough would dance around the flames, or they would light wheels on fire and roll them down the hill.

Back then, it was a time to get in touch with the faerie people, also called the Fae. It was considered much easier to connect with them in the time between times, which is the point of transition from summer to winter. These magical beings love flowers with sweet smells, nectar, and honey, as well as other elements that are only available at this time of year. Even the late Shakespeare wrote about the fae in his play, A Midsummer Night's Dream, as they caused mischief during the festivities.

In June, the full moon is also called the Honeymoon, a time for many to get married. It was strongly believed that May marriages wouldn't work out well, especially as the god and goddess would have their own rites at this time.

Ancient Greeks believed that this was the time the Titan Prometheus had given humans fire as a gift, which helped us all become civilized. Athena was a goddess with attributes of the sun, and the people would celebrate the Panathenaia to honor her. They would pray to her to allow the rains to fall for a bountiful harvest.

Ancient Romans would celebrate this time in honor of Juno, the Roman counterpart to Hera, who was wedded to the king of the gods, Jupiter. Juno oversaw marriages; the month of June is named after her and is considered a great time to get married. Women who were married would celebrate Vesta, the goddess who was in charge of the home and hearth fires, during the Vestalia festival.

Ancient Chinese saw the summer solstice as a female season, the Yin to its Yang counterpart, the winter solstice. Their celebrations were all about the earth's renewal and fertility, and they would burn offerings and say prayers borne on the smoke of the offerings up to the gods in the heavens.

For the ancient Saxons, the middle of the year was Midsummer, and their year started with the winter solstice. They would celebrate the god of thunder, Thor, as he was the one who brought the rains that made earth fruitful. When the Christians came around, they syncretized this holiday to become the Feast of St. John, also called John's night or Johannisnacht. Those in Finland call this time Juhannus, and it's a time of joy because, at last, the light shines after many days of darkness.

Most pagans today associate the summer solstice with Midsummer, but the word does not appear in any pre-Christian pagan customs or descriptions of the holiday. Early Christian holidays are also associated with specific days of the solar year, but it is unlikely that Midsummer was celebrated because it is a time when in northern regions, night turns into day, and there are no hours of daylight.

According to archeological evidence, some people have tried to reconstruct ancient pagan solstice celebrations. On the evening before Midsummer, they followed a pattern of dancing around the maypole and holding bonfires on rooftops or hilltops throughout Britain. In the morning of June 21, people would gather at the high place for a Maypole dance, which represents the Midsummer night dance.

In Germany and Scandinavia, Midsummer fires were lit as part of a midsummer celebration which included great feasts with pig roasts. Because most extant ancient Germanic material has been found on sites related to Christianity, it is not known precisely what forms these old celebrations took in pre-Christian times. In addition to the dancing of circles around maypoles, several other rituals have been interpreted as ritual purification.

Litha's association with wassailing derives from an ancient tradition where people would drink mead or cider around a tree to ensure a fruitful growing season for apples or other fruit. The custom of wassailing descended from the Norse "Veslinga," which was a drinking party for the gods, held at Yule. Increasing urbanization between 1900 and 1950 led more and more people to absent themselves from traditional Litha events in favor of indoor festivities, such as New Year's Eve parties.

The original Icelandic words were "Litha" "Litthæn" (lit-thēn), which means "fire festival" or "sun feast." The Old Norse name was "Veslingr." In Sweden, it was called "Lithasången."

In the old days, Midsummer was marked with various customs and traditions. Lamps were lit to guide weary travelers' home from distant places. Some people made bonfires to keep witches at bay. Others wore flowers in their hair or carried flowering branches for luck or fertility. The young maidens would swim naked in the ponds and rivers, waiting for the first frog to come along so they could kiss it for good luck.

It is also said that Midsummer was the time when many rituals and customs involving "the removal of harmful influences" took place. It was an effort to remove the darkness, negativity, and stagnation from individuals, communities, and the world at large. Many cultures performed rituals to protect themselves from evil spirits. In parts of Ireland, it was believed that singing a specific type of song would drive away all evil spirits from a house. In parts of Europe, people wore flowers in their hair or carried flowers to protect themselves from plagues and infections while outdoors during this time.

When it was believed that the night lasted all day, no one wanted to wait around until evening before they were wed. As soon as the sun was high in the sky and there was plenty of daylight left, they would tie the knot, knowing that they'd get a good portion of their "honeymoon" after sunset.

Midsummer Now: Return to the Origins

Midsummer today is mostly seen as an excuse to have fun outdoors. Therefore, people everywhere are invited to throw water balloons at each other and light fireworks even though it's not a national holiday. And why do we get laden with food treats for no good reason at all?

So why does Litha have an ancient meaning? Because it was originally a festival to celebrate the spring equinox, which marks when day and night are equal lengths. It also marks the first day of summer in the Northern hemisphere – when crops are ready to harvest and people wear short sleeves. It is thought that this winter solstice festival was connected to fertility and love, making it perfect for celebrating weddings and family members.

With its humble origins as a celebration of life itself, Litha has grown into one of the most popular holidays on our calendar – a holiday we do not take seriously despite how important it is. We now celebrate celebrations like St. Valentine's Day and Father's Day and forget that Litha used to be celebrated with a sense of wonder and awe. To this day, people continue to celebrate it as if it were Christmas, decking out their lawns with decorations, setting up countless inflatables in parks, and buying tons of fall and winter decorations to display. It's as if they've forgotten that we're celebrating a time when summer is coming – bringing great things like rainbows and blooming flowers instead of snow and cold.

The winter solstice has been around for thousands of years, but it didn't get its modern holiday status until well after Christianity was established. However, we don't know why the winter solstice was changed to Midsummer. Some assume it's because the Christian church wanted to take a popular pagan holiday and make it their own. Others assume it's because people who followed Jesus wanted to celebrate the summer solstice too. We do know that if Christians had tried to convert pagans by taking away a solstice festival, they would have been out of luck because pagans celebrated both the winter and summer solstices for thousands of years before the birth of Christ.

By changing Litha from an equinox marking the end of winter into a summer festival celebrating fertility, you'd think that Christian missionaries would have no problem with it. But they did. They despised it. They made their disdain clear by leaving the name "Litha" in place but attaching a saint's name to it: St. John's Day on 24 June and St. Peter's Midsummer on 29 June. Carnaval (Shrove Tuesday) was also given a Christian name, calling it Mardi Gras before it became known as the eve of Lent.

We don't know much about Saints John or Peter except for the fact that their feast days were celebrated by lighting bonfires and lanterns on hillsides and beaches. As for St. John's Day, it was commonly celebrated by lighting faggots or bundles of firewood on the beach or near a river and throwing them into the water so they would burn while floating on the surface. The fires were not just beautiful to look at but had healing qualities, as people believed that St. John's fire helped to purify a place and make it suitable for crops to grow.

Midsummer has also become a holiday known for the drunken antics of young people drinking and getting silly. And therefore – because we've forgotten its deep roots in nature and the earth, we have no idea what it was originally about. But if you're looking to get decked out in your best summer attire and throw a fire-filled party on Saturday night, go right ahead. Just remember that this day holds deeper meaning than beer pong and water balloon fights. Something about the present-day has us very disconnected from nature, and so this festival is a great opportunity to honor the connection we all have to Mother Nature and rediscover our natural rhythms.

If you want to celebrate Midsummer properly, take a moment to look back in history and remember the meaning behind it. It's a celebration of the beginning of summer – a time when the nights are usually filled with joy and laughter while the days hold great promise. So, face east on Saturday night, when darkness falls, because that's where the sun rises, and its light brings renewal, hope, and growth. As you watch that last sliver of sunlight disappear, say goodbye to short sleeves, t-shirts, and flip flops – a token of summer's end. And as you watch the Sun come up the next day on Sunday, say hello to the end of summer – a time when you can break out all your fall and winter clothes.

Chapter 4: Your Clothes, House, and Altar

How to Set Up a Litha Altar

A Litha altar is a small table or space dedicated to celebrating the Earth's bounty during the summer solstice. This holiday offers an excellent opportunity to create an engrossing altar that will help you connect with your environment by honoring natural concepts like growth and renewal. It is also the best time to honor the gods and goddesses of fertility, prosperity, and nature.

This chapter will introduce you to some simple steps for creating a beautiful altar that incorporates a theme of growth and renewal. You don't have to be an experienced altar maker – just follow the instructions for making Litha altars below to create this great spiritual symbol. As you'll see, even if you're a beginner, it's easy to set up an altar that will help everyone in the house reconnect with nature.

Creating Your Litha Altar

Your Litha altar can be as elaborate or simple as your time and budget allow. It will be a great focal point for showing off your personal style, giving you an easy way to reconnect with nature during the summer. Use these steps to create a beautiful altar that will bring back memories of the summer solstice for years to come.

Step 1: Gather Your Supplies

Begin by gathering all the items you'll need to create your altar. It's easier to focus on working if you have everything laid out in front of you. You need to gather the following:

- A small-scale festival altar (for a group of people or a small celebration).

- Any rocks, plants, or natural elements you want to exhibit on your altar.

- A cord or string – at least 50 feet.

- A sun and moon symbol about 4 inches long and 5 inches wide, cut from paper or cardboard.

- 1 – 3 plastic eggs (white is best).

- A small piece of Day-Glo paint (optional).

- Any materials you want to use to decorate your altar, like candles, incense burners, flowers, etc. (optional).

- A set of hand tools – hammer and nails, saw, screwdriver (if making wheels), cutting wheel, sandpaper, etc.

Step 2: Decorate Your Altar

Next, it's time to begin decorating your altar. If you're following a sun-and-moon theme, begin by displaying the sun symbol on the top of your altar. This is easy to do by placing the symbol in a bag with a string and hanging it from an overhead hook. The moon should be placed on the bottom portion of the altar.

If you don't want to follow the sun and moon theme, you can focus on displaying spring plants on the top portion of your altar. Make sure you display them so that they are facing the sunlight. Place your torches or candles in a way that lets you put out fires quickly if needed. You'll want to maintain good control of any flames on your altar during Litha.

Place any tools or other objects in a deep bowl or bucket to hide them from view. If they are displayed directly on your altar, they may draw unwanted attention.

Step 3: Set Up the Base

Next, set up your base. This should be a flat, stable space on the ground, with a minimum of two feet clearance off the floor. It can be any size you choose, but at least 8 x 10 is optimal. You can set up your altar on the ground or on a table – either way works fine so long as all your other items are placed securely on the base in advance.

Step 4: Create Your Altar Structure

Now that you've set up your base, it's time to build your altar structure. Start by building an A-frame from your boards and windowsill. The top of the A-frame should look like a pyramid, hence its name. You can use either a nail gun or a hammer to secure the pieces in place. Position the A-frame to where you want it – place it on a dresser or sturdy table so that you can move it easily as needed without damaging the floor or other items on top of it.

Next, begin securing your supplies onto the A-frame until you have completed one layer of your structure. You can use forceps or clips to hold things in place – if you choose to use clips, make sure nobody will be able to reach the attached cord by accident. Keep adding layers until you have completed your altar structure.

Step 5: Add the Wheels (Optional)

If you want your altar structure or top layer to be mobile, they must be properly attached to a base. You can build a sturdy platform from scrap lumber, but it's often easiest just to add wheels so that everything moves with one turn of the hand. Select wheels that are the right length to hold the weight of your structure and secure them wherever you like. Some people prefer to place the wheels at the back of their altar, while others prefer to set them up in front.

Step 6: Place Your Altar Items

Now that your base is secure and your structure is built, it's time to place your items on top. Start by arranging things like incense burners, candles, and other accessories on any horizontal surfaces within reach of a hand. Then move onto your vertical pieces – things such as candles or small wooden statues should be placed at eye level.

Step 7: Set Up Your Sun and Moon

The sun and moon are an important part of any Litha altar. If you can, set them up on opposite sides of your altar, as if they were in opposition to each other. You don't have to set up a special area for them or put them on special pedestals – just make sure that you have easy access to them throughout the day. People often like to keep their altars by a window so that there is plenty of sunlight to help charge the altars.

You can go all out with your sun and moon altar decorations – you don't have to use actual pieces from nature. You can use an old sundial you find at a thrift store or flea market – just be sure to clean it up and give it a fresh coat of paint. If you're setting up your altar inside, keep in mind that adornments like incense burners and paper flowers don't require a lot of "sunlight" to work properly.

Step 8: Place Your Offerings

Now that your altar is complete, it's time to start adding things to make the area look more pleasant. First, add seasonings onto the top part of your altars, such as salt, pepper, and cinnamon sticks. Then add things like flowers, small candles, and twine. You don't have to have a full altar from the beginning – you can create a smaller altar later if you decide to hold another celebration in the future.

Step 9: Celebrate Litha Differently

Litha celebrations are often held outdoors at night, but you can celebrate at home during daytime hours as well. If your household is too small for an outdoor celebration, the main things you'll need will be your base and structure, along with some special Litha preparations in advance, such as incense burners, salt, and sage.

You can begin each Litha celebration with a simple blessing. Hold a ritual in which each person prays for protection and guidance. You'll also want to gather flowers or herbs for Litha so that you have some fresh things to rely on during the celebration. Place the herbs on top of your altar, scatter them around or use them in drinks and foods. Carry a small bag of these flowers with you throughout the day so that you have something beautiful to offer people who come by to celebrate Litha with you.

If you have enough space for an outdoor celebration, remember to clear your area of stray branches and leaves so that the outdoors is clear. If you don't have enough room for an outdoor Litha celebration, you can use special lighting techniques indoors to make your altar glow and shine. You won't need many lights, but you should have candle lights or other flames with bright white light. You can set them up along the walls of your home or outside on top of your altar structure.

Step 10: Offer Your Intention to the Universe

As the sun begins to set, you must offer your intentions up to the universe in the form of prayer. Hold a ritual in which you both offer your intentions and pray for the other person's intentions to be answered. You don't need to make specific promises or sign anything to the universe – simply pray that those you ask will be blessed with good health, happiness, and success.

Step 11: Celebrate the Night (The Rest of the Day Is Your Own)

Once it's dark, you can have fun with your friends without worrying about being bothered by unwanted guests. Bring out food and drinks and enjoy some good music as you celebrate Litha together. It may be fun to dress up in costumes or to use old-fashioned games such as dreidel spinning to recreate old traditions. Be sure to say goodbye to the sun before it disappears behind the horizon. This is a good time to tell your ancestors, friends, and loved ones that you're glad they're in your life and that you know they'll be back again soon.

Step 12: Give Yourself a Break from the Altar

To keep your Litha altar running smoothly, it's important to give yourself plenty of regular breaks away from it. It can be very tempting just to leave your altar out in the open until the next major holiday comes along, but this could invite unwanted spirits without a proper invitation. Instead, use the space around your altar as a storage area in which you keep things you don't need all the time. Keep the area clear of clutter and then spend ten minutes every few weeks clearing it and arranging the items in better order. If you put off this process until next year, you'll likely find that your altar isn't up to date during Litha.

Step 13: Remove All Altar Items on the Last Night of Litha

Once Litha is over, take all your altar items outside and burn them so that they do not interfere with future celebrations. If the burning is during daylight hours, it should be safe enough for children to see what is happening. You can also bury your items in the ground if you desire. Just make sure that they are buried deep enough so that they won't resurface during the next celebration.

Step 14: Be Grateful for Your Altar Space

Once Litha is over, you don't have to worry about cleaning up your altar – it can go back to being a storage area for things you don't need. If you do decide to use it again in the future, clean it thoroughly with hot water and soap so that nobody can walk on your altar or leave their mark on it.

Concluding Altar Affairs

You can do things differently if you use your own creativity and ingenuity. You don't have to follow these steps; instead, you can come up with a system that works best for you. If you have time, create a photorealistic altar that has plenty of space for candles and flowers. If you're short on time and money, consider making an altar out of recycled materials – just be sure to clean off any stains and give it a fresh coat of paint before using it.

As long as your altar is open to the sun, it will work well every day of the year. You'll likely want to rearrange your altar items so that you can see the sunlight on them, but this should only take a few minutes once every few months. You will want to place your altar in the best location possible to get plenty of sun – out on your porch or patio might work best if you have a nice view of the sky. Otherwise, set it up in a room that gets plenty of sunlight on a daily basis.

Remember to give thanks to every aspect of your altar space, from its perfect view of the sun to its ability to keep bugs and clutter out of your home. It's amazing how something that used to be your worst nightmare can become one of your best friends once you find the right ways to use it. Litha is a great time to start a new altar, and you'll soon find that it doesn't take as much work as you thought it would.

Dressing for Litha

What to Wear to the Ceremony: The ceremony is focused on honoring the sun, so we need lighter colors. Silks, pastels, and whites are all good choices. Natural fibers are not only more comfortable in the heat, but they are also more period-accurate.

For men, a tunic of silk or linen works nicely. If you have a cotehardie, try it without anything under it and let the daylight paint the colors on your shoulders. A silk doublet looks good with a hose, but if you don't have a hose to match, go for a pair of white cotton leggings. You can wear silken belts and jewelry to complete your outfit if you like.

You can also wear a shirt with long sleeves under your tunic. If you're going to dance, wear your best shirt and hose or doublet. Wear something over the shirt if you will be dancing. To hide sweat marks, use linen overcharge that is dyed a pale gold-brown shade. If you want to take your outfit up a notch, wear a fancy hat. If you're not dancing, you can wear a tunic with an overdress.

Choose your shoes carefully. Remember that your feet are still tender after celebrating Beltane with other sacred fires. You can make them harder by wearing leather boots (which last a very long time and are relatively inexpensive to replace) or softer by wearing soft (white) velvet boots. A pair of leather cross-over booties on top of shoes is also a very nice touch.

What to Wear at the Dance: If you have something regal on already, keep it on. Otherwise, first, change into a doublet under your fancy tunic. This will be more comfortable than bare skin if you will be dancing later in the evening, and the doublet can be removed after the social dances have concluded. Remember to put it back on before you leave.

Hose are not period-accurate for this time, but if you want them for comfort, go ahead and wear them. You can also wear them over an undershirt. For shoes, wear tall black boots or soft leather cross-over booties. You can also find some renaissance boots on eBay that are affordable and look decent (but will not last as long as leather boots). If you have a pair of period-accurate shoes, then, by all means, wear them. Otherwise, avoid the flats and go for something with a little heft to it. If you need inspiration for your outfit, there are plenty of Renaissance Fashion images online that you can look at.

How to Decorate Your House

Litha is often a joyous time to rejoice in nature's rebirth with family and friends. Decorating your house is a wonderful way to make this joyous season even more special. A great way to decorate your house is by making garlands or wreaths out of different natural materials. Examples include flowers, herbs, grasses, berries, and pinecones. You can also use corn husks and milkweed pods for this purpose.

To make a wreath using milkweed pods (which I highly recommend as it's so much easier than you'd think), all you must do is fill up the pods with rice (or other grains) and tie them together with string. Then, simply tie them to your door or a window for everyone to see.

Another thing you can make is a small place setting for each person that's coming over. You can customize them based on their favorite season and color. A simple example would be having a yellow theme for fire sign friends. You can include yellow candles, yellow flowers, and brass decor (such as candle holders, plates, cups).

While you're at it, why not make some flowers? Most of the recipes for flower petals call for arrowroot powder (to give the petals stiffness), cornstarch (to keep them from sticking together), and Epsom salt (to give the flowers their blossom scent). You can easily make this by taking 1 cup of arrowroot powder, 1/3 cup of cornstarch, and 2 tablespoons of Epsom salt and mixing them together in a bowl. Then, simply add 5 drops of your favorite essential oil to the bowl. If you're feeling particularly crafty, you can also make decorative sunflowers out of popcorn kernels. All you must do is pop a kernel until the piece pops up about 1/4th into the air. Then, use a toothpick or something similar to push a seed onto the top of it so that it looks like sunflower petals.

If all else fails, you can always make a bunch of spiders out of clay (simple spider figurines are also a good addition if you have children at home). You can also make other spider-related decorations such as spider web garlands or even chocolate spiders (a unique way to celebrate this time of year).

Finally, if you can't find any natural materials in your house or on your property, there are still plenty of ways to decorate your house during this time. You'll just have to think outside the box a little. Try making the walls blue and accented with gold instead (think about how wonderful the colors will look against the sunset). Or why not use white paint and decorate the walls with gold ribbon? In the next chapter, we'll talk about more crafts and plants that fit Midsummer.

Crystals

Crystals are a natural element that can also be used during Litha. Use crystals from the Beryl and Amethyst families, along with Aventurine, Bloodstone, Quartz, Sodalite, and Rose Quartz. Place the crystals in water in a circle around an image of the Goddess or another symbol of power such as a Moon Bear or a Raven. You can also place them on your altar and within the sacred space in your home. You can also place them on your solar plexus, heart, or throat chakra for a few minutes while meditating.

Runes

Litha is the first full moon in winter, so you can use runes related to this season. To determine what you need to draw, consult your personal rune advisor. Generally speaking, runes related to growth and renewal are appropriate at this time of year. These include symbols such as the symbol for earth (Othila), the symbol for mother fostering growth in children (Berkana), and perhaps other simple, life-giving runes as well. Your personal rune advisor will also be able to tell you about any specific needs that might exist during this time of year in the realm of Wicca practice or any other spiritual work being done at your home circle.

Incense

- **Borax:** This ingredient is used in many different herbal remedies for relaxation. Some people find that it creates feelings of euphoria and comfort, which may help alleviate stress or help them relax during rituals. It is widely used in homes and bathhouses to help soothe respiratory ailments.

- **Lavender:** This is one of the most widely used herbs, especially for incense. It's believed to create feelings of peace, tranquility, and relaxation, which may help alleviate stress or help people relax during rituals. Make sure you choose lavender essential oil and not lavender buds, as this will burn hotter and may cause skin irritation.

- **Juniper:** Fiddly-finger Juniper is a popular incense in the Pagan community today; however, it can be quite expensive; a fiddly-finger Juniper typically costs around $10 – $15 a block. In general, the scent of Juniper is pleasing and relaxing.

- **Myrrh:** Myrrh incense (or resin) is an alternative to frankincense and myrrh combined in incenses. Like resins, myrrh has a pleasant aroma and a warm and comforting effect on the body. It has a distinct spicy smell like nutmeg or cinnamon. There are many different types of Myrrh incense, including attars that have been scented with natural oils, figs, or even myrrh cones infused with oil and dried out for use.

- **Pine:** Pine is a popular incense in the Pagan community, though it's also quite expensive. There are three different types of pines: camphor, cedar, and frankincense. Camphor pine is the most expensive and aromatic during rituals, while cedar pine is next on the list. Frankincense is typically the least expensive and least aromatic of these types of pine trees that might be used as incense.

- **Rose:** Rose essential oil has a sweet scent that can be used to help relax or create feelings of peace and tranquility during rituals. It can also help with positive energy healing as it helps in creating positive energy situations/emotions within people.

As you celebrate Litha, it's always important to stay safe during the festivities. Always follow all safety precautions when burning incense and never leave the area unattended.

Sigils

The summer solstice is a time of focus on manifestations of light and abundance. It is especially appropriate to use sigils that represent these things at Litha – such as sigils for beauty, healing, health, and joy. So how do you use sigils for wealth and abundance?

Sigils for prosperity during the month of Litha take the form of gold or yellow circles or simply objects symbolizing gold and riches. Of course, it's in your best interest to be making a lot of money all year round, but if you're struggling now, you can use this time to focus on your financial situation. Write out a sigil that represents what you want. You can create sigils just by taking a word that represents what you want and writing each letter on the other stylistically. Remove the vowels and use the consonants only. You can make up two or more sigils if you want to increase the chances of attracting them into your life.

Chapter 5: Midsummer Trees, Plants, and Flowers

Sacred Trees

Ash Tree

Ash trees are significant in Wicca and represent the Goddess, and we, therefore, tend to find them in the Litha season. This is because ash leaves and bark produce a blue dye that can be used for dying fabrics, including ritual robes – it's traditionally considered unlucky to make any type of new garment at this time. The goddess may wear an outfit of sky-blue when celebrating Litha with her children.

Litha, being summertime's longest day, may also be seen as a time when life is abundant and everything flourishes – just like an ash tree – so these trees often have positive associations with prosperity. In some parts of Europe, ash trees were also associated with miraculous events. The Knights Templar were said to have used ash leaves in magic potions.

While older traditions interpret the bright blue dye produced by ash as an indication of good fortune and prosperity, the modern folklorist Harrison describes a more ambivalent association with the wood of this tree. He references superstitions that believe it may cause headaches or melancholy and its association with sickness, misfortune, and tragedy.

The most famous legend surrounding the ash tree concerns St. Nicholas, the "Father of Christmas," who, it is said, once gave a sack of gold coins to a poor man who was not supposed to find it until later in the year – December 6th. Finding these coins was supposed to bring good fortune for the household for many years after.

The Ygdrassil Tree is a mythical, sacred ash tree in Norse mythology. The tree is central in Norse cosmology and known as the world tree. The name of the tree alludes to its great size, spanning nine worlds with its roots resting in three realms. Ygdrassil symbolizes life's all-encompassing universal forces, including fertility and growth.

Ash Tree Love Ritual

The mid-summer ritual is a pagan spell that can be performed to help you find your true love. This ritual is said to have been created by the French poet, adventurer, and occultist, Robert Ambelain in the 1920s.

You'll need:

- Ash tree bark
- Dried nettle
- A black hen (or picture of a black hen, or a cat, or any other bird)
- A white candle (could be shaped like a bird in the absence of a picture)

The basic ritual involves tying three knots with strips of ash tree bark to form a triangle and then placing dried nettles at each triangle point. A black hen was originally used as an ingredient in this spell because they are believed to be fairies who love birds and eggs. However, that may not be very practical in these times, nor is it fair to just let an animal roam around on its own.

When performed to help find true love, this midsummer ritual is meant to leave the birds with an eternal link to your lover. The symbolism of the bird is also used because it represents fertility and rebirth.

Nowadays, it can be replaced with any sacred or lucky animal (i.e., a cat or crow) that has never been hurt by humans before. You don't have to use a live animal for this ritual. You can use a picture of one instead, or even better, you can use a white candle shaped like a bird.

Directions:

1. Approach the tree and bow down towards it.
2. Start by tying three knots with strips of ash tree bark in a triangle. As you tie each knot, say the name of your love.
3. For each knot, place a strip of dried nettle under the bark at that point of the triangle.
4. After completing the knots, place a black hen (or a picture of one or the animal you've chosen) in the center of the triangle on top of the nettles.
5. Light a white candle, preferably made from beeswax, and place it at the top point of the triangle.
6. Pray to Lady Midsummer until you feel a sense of completion, as though your prayers are answered. (Use the prayer after the directions here if you wish.) You could also sit in quiet contemplation of your love until the candle goes out or the wind carries the picture away if you're outdoors.
7. Thank Lady Mid-summer for honoring you and your request.

Note:

The old French poet Robert Ambelain, who created this ritual in the 1920s, believed that those who performed it would achieve great power. This ritual is said to have been inspired by an ancient druid mid-summer ritual that many believe was written about in one of Horace's poems. The main idea is that you perform these rituals with your true love in mind who you wish to meet soon. You find the best spot for this ritual, which may be in a place where you and your love have been alone together before.

It is said that once you have tied the third knot, a romantic event will occur in your favor. If something or someone ruined your relationship with your soulmate, but they're supposed to be with you, doing this ritual will bring them back to you. If they haven't been able to find happiness in their present relationship with someone else, the spell is likely going to help them find their way back to you. Make sure that your thoughts are focused on the one you love and intend to be with as you tie the knots.

The ritual can be performed at any time of year by yourself or with a group. When performed in a group fashion, everyone should be standing around the circle and keep their eyes closed while verbally concentrating on their thoughts or intents.

Rowan Tree

The Rowan tree, in ancient times, symbolized life and rebirth. It is the tree of life and death in Celtic culture to this day. The Druids performed blood sacrifices on its branches, and kings were often crowned beneath its shade.

In the folklore of many countries, the Rowan tree is said to be a magical one whose wood can change into whatever kind of wood an individual needs (the Irish call it "the wood from which all special magic tools are made"). The custom was to carve a knife or other tool out of an oak root, but you would have your tool for good if you used a Rowan root.

The Druids used the Rowan tree for many traditional practices, such as divination and healing. They also used their leaves to create amulets with protective powers. There are several beautiful examples of this on display at the National Museum of Ireland.

The tree has a special connection to the Roman Goddess Hebe, known as the goddess of youth. According to Roman mythology, the goddess misplaced her chalice of youth, but thankfully she recovered it with the help of an eagle who had to fight on her behalf. It is said that the Rowan tree would spring up at every spot where the eagle lost a feather or shed some of its blood in battle. Rowan trees are believed to ward off evil spirits, and that's why you find loads of them growing around old Celtic burial sites.

Rowan Tree Ritual

When it comes to this ritual, it's important that you keep in mind the significance of the tree, which is not only abundance and youth but protection from evil enchantment and witchcraft as well. The ritual takes place in the early morning. You'll need to harvest the rowan berries and some evergreen tree trimmings.

You'll need:

- Rowan Tree
- Dried Moss
- Evergreen Tree Sprays
- Aquamarine

Directions:

1. Gather in a circle around a Rowan tree with berries hanging from it.

2. Pick some berries and pass them around so that everyone can take a handful and fill their pockets with them. Dried moss is also gathered to place over your eyes for protection against evil spirits. Varying amounts of dried moss are used depending on your own tolerance for discomfort inflicted by texture.

3. Sprinkle dried moss over each person in silence until everyone is blindfolded, then pass around evergreen branches, making sure everyone has at least one branch to touch and smell.

4. Once everyone has everything they need, each person will touch the Rowan berries, then place them on their heads to represent crowns. This is to honor the Rowan King, who guards our land and keeps us safe from evil spirits.

5. After a few moments of meditation, take your evergreen tree branch from your pocket and inhale deeply from it. The scent will protect you from evil forces as you go about your daily business.

6. Hold the branch up above your head with both hands while you say, "By the power of Rowan."

7. Then, walk around the circle three times in a counter-clockwise direction so that everyone can see you.

8. As you reach each person, say "By the power of Rowan." before placing the branch on their forehead.

9. Each person makes three passes around the circle, then places their branch back in their pocket and repeats the entire ritual with the next branch.

10. Before returning to your place, clear your eyes and exhale deeply from your bough. This is a protection against evil spirits and should protect you from any that may be lingering, causing you anxiety or distress.

11. Once everyone has returned to their original spots, take off your crown and place it on one of the last remaining branches. You're now ready to enter a period of meditation just before sunrise.

12. The leaders of the ceremony will say a prayer that leads you into a period of deep thought. It's best if you keep your eyes open so you can see the full moon, or you can close them to focus strongly on your thoughts. You may also focus on nature in your mind's eye or your surroundings. Take whatever time feels right and set it aside.

13. As the sun rises, everyone will open their eyes as they enter another period of meditation while they wait for sunrise.

14. Afterward, stand and recite the last petition of your group: "By the power of Rowan, for so mote it be." Then leave the circle.

Hawthorn Tree

Hawthorn goes by folk names, some of them being hawberry, mayblossom, whitethorn, thornapple, and bread and cheese tree. The great thing about this tree is that it grows rather quickly, and it's known for its protective attributes because of its ability to form a hedge. No matter what species of this tree you're dealing with, they all have thorns, which are an intrinsic part of their magic. If you've ever heard the term "hedge witch,'" it's thanks to those who learned to work magic and get medicine from this lovely tree.

This tree is also known as the may tree, it is a faery tree that the Druids hold in high regard. They use this tree for sacred heart medicine and in rituals as well. It is common for this tree to be found near ancient sites where Druids worshiped or around sacred waters, such as lakes or springs, growing alongside the rowan and oak trees. The legend goes that if you see a hawthorn tree, it means that you're closer than you realize to the fae folk, who are magical beings that you can sense if you're spiritually aware and in touch with your psychic senses. You can also bring their presence into your space by gathering its berries, leaves, bark, and branches. This tree can also be used to foretell the future through rune casting during Litha rituals. The hawthorn tree is an extremely special tree to Druid priests and shamans as it was both sacred and magical.

Hawthorn is a very magical tree, also called the tree of Mars. It is said that when the liquid from the flowers is distilled, it can help with getting rid of splinters and thorns as well as prevent leprosy. The ancients would also boil its crushed seeds in wine to treat bodily pain.

It's always been known that this tree has the ability to heal the heart, not just emotionally but physically as well. This is because it does wonders for your circulation, so your heart can do its job better. Even its berries are lovely for health as it possesses antioxidant and anti-inflammatory properties. When it comes to emotions and spiritual matters, this herb can bring wholeness to you. Say your feelings have been hurt and your heart is broken, making it hard for you to feel like you can open up. With hawthorn, you can find healing from your emotional damage, because energetically speaking this plant is a protective one that will set up an energetic hedge of protection around your heart. This way, you can explore love and life again with no worries of being hurt. Celtic lore holds that hawthorn happens to be the passage way to the otherworld, allowing you access to the mystical so you can draw on the power of the fae to bring you that which you desire. On that note, let's get into a great abundance ritual you can do with this tree.

Abundance Ritual

A midsummer ritual will imbue your days with a potent abundance of energy. It's best to do it when the Sun is in Gemini so you can reap the full benefit of their mercurial energies, but if you can't wait until then, this recipe should work well in any season. If the ritual is done indoors, light a fire or a candle next to the ritual space.

You'll need:

- Hawthorn bark
- Strawberry leaves
- Oak bark
- An object that represents wealth

Directions:

1. Starting at sunrise, place one hand on an object that restricts wealth and one hand on something that represents wealth. Like a wallet and a gold coin. Or a credit card and some fifty-dollar bills.

2. Shake hands with the Sun, thanking it for its abundant love, and then move your hands apart while keeping them pointed towards the Sun.

3. Next, imagine you're pulling in the energy of the Sun into yourself. As you do this, focus your thoughts on attracting wealth into your life and your business.

4. As soon as you feel like there's enough energy to work with, light a candle if you're indoors or start a fire outside in a windless area that isn't affected by smoke from wildfires. Be aware that this will attract unwanted energy, so it's important to clear the space before you start working.

5. Burn the strawberry leaves, oak bark, and hawthorn bark in your fire or candle flame.

6. When they are completely burned, scatter your burned materials in a circle around yourself and keep doing this as long as you feel comforted by the energies of wealth flowing through you. If it's not enough to do it outdoors, do it indoors where all you need is a candle or small fire.

7. The next step depends on how much time you've got. If you're able to spend about an hour each day, continue doing the ritual for seven days straight and concentrate on attracting more money into your life. You can do this at any time of the day, though the best time is between noon and three o'clock.

8. If you're short on time but still want to do this ritual for a few days, you'll need to devote about fifteen minutes each day throughout the following week. As you sit there and hold your hands out towards a flame or fire, it's suggested that you concentrate on what your life would be like if money were no issue. What would you do with all that extra time?

9. Afterward, be sure to cleanse yourself before you go to sleep. This can be done in any way that you feel works for you. For example, if you're an energy worker, then it's suggested to chant or say something positive like "I am a powerful healer, and I am safe." If you're not an energy worker, just focus on purifying yourself. Light a candle and say some form of forgiveness prayer.

Beech Tree

The beech tree has been a fixture of the landscape in many cultures. The ancient Greeks revered it, and it was reintroduced to England in a more contemporary form by the Romans. While deforestation has reduced its size and population over time, its presence can still be felt today in many parts of England. With its leaves turning gold, this tree is said to represent growth, renewal, rebirth, and light shining through darkness during Litha.

The beech tree's leaves turn red in Litha, which symbolizes the following:

- The spring and rebirth of creation after Winter has passed.
- The blood-red of the sun at sunrise.
- The fluidity of water, often associated with the moon.
- It is said to represent new life, often associated with rebirth and sexuality – which plays into the themes of Litha's fertility and sexuality and its connection to both creation/rebirth and to the moon (dawn).
- Fire, due to its association with the sun and its use in religious practices to symbolize the deity
- The life-giving properties of blood
- The red of menstruation – hence why it is associated with sexuality, too.

The beech tree is also associated with fairies and elves due to the popular belief that they lived in it. As Wiccans embrace nature and believe that such creatures do exist, this may be part of their reasoning for using beech trees in Litha rituals.

Beech Tree Ritual

You'll need:

- Beech Tree (or just four beech tree branches)
- Four Bowls
- Water

Directions:

1. First, go to a beech tree in the forest and cut a branch off.
2. Fill a bowl with water, then place the beech branch in the bowl.
3. Place three bowls in a row. Put one side of the branch in each bowl.
4. Then, pour water from one bowl into the next until all four bowls have been filled with water from the first.
5. Stand behind or to the side of one of them and pour your power onto it while chanting:

> *As I move this branch from east to west,*
>
> *I break my own mental barriers today*
>
> *And walk towards my goals with newfound strength.*
>
> *In light and love, I take my place on earth.*

6. Repeat this process for all four branches, taking care to swap them so the power flows equally. Once you've finished, bury the bowls in the forest or leave them somewhere and walk away.

Rumor has it that this ritual works best when performed near an actual beech tree, but I think it's very effective regardless of where you do it. You can simply cut some of the branches off the tree and perform the ritual at home, then bury them in your backyard or take them back to the forest and leave them there. This ritual is a great way to strengthen your connection with nature and ensure your intentions are carried out. Perform according to your own beliefs, but keep in mind that it is in your best interests to perform other rituals to help your intentions remain clear and give them the power they need to manifest.

Hazelnut Tree

The hazelnut tree is one of the most worshiped trees in Litha. The hazelnut tree is believed to have been given to early human civilization by the Phoenicians. The legend says that a Phoenician trader found an abandoned baby, named him Thoth, raised him as his own son, and taught him all his trade secrets, including how to grow the hazelnut tree. As soon as he grew up, Thoth returned home and planted a seedling under his father's fig tree. Whenever people pluck figs from the tree, they would find seeds on it which can be used for cultivation purposes. With this new knowledge – or at least ancient knowledge – people started cultivating hazelnuts as well and kept them until the present time. Hazelnut trees are traditionally planted on Litha. In Lithuania, children plant hazelnut trees with the help of adults, though they must take care of their new tree for 10 years until it is mature enough to produce nuts. In other regions, people plant hazelnuts and walnuts in Litha.

Hazelnut tree branches are sometimes put on the roof to keep witches from getting into the house. Hazelnuts are also believed to have aphrodisiac properties and can be used to treat snake bites or open wounds.

Pelasgians believed that hazelnuts were sacred as they would sometimes mark a crossroads where one must choose between two paths; therefore, they have become a representation of life choices or divine destiny in Celtic folklore. The Druids used them in their ritual ceremonies, including healing and divination. They also believed that hazelnuts were the fruit of the Dé Danaan, who were a tribe of supernatural beings who inhabited Ireland before the arrival of humans. The Druids would eat the nuts in soup or baked into a pie to honor their presence in religious ceremonies. Additionally, they would use hazelnuts to find hidden treasures and hidden springs by burning them on an altar placed at De Danaan tombs. Hazelnuts were a form of currency among pre-Christian Celts; however, they only had worth when exchanged with another person or used as payment for services rendered. This way, the hazelnut tree's natural worth was not devalued as much. Hazelnuts were seeds of the sacred hazelnut tree often depicted on Celtic crosses, symbolizing fertility and knowledge.

Hazelnut Ritual

You'll need:

- Hazelnut oil
- Basil
- Cinnamon sticks or Lavender flowers
- White sage

Directions:

1. Pour a small amount of hazelnut oil into a bowl and add one tablespoon of either cinnamon sticks or lavender flowers.
2. As you stir the oil, make sure to wear protective gloves.
3. Breathe deeply as you stir.
4. Laugh as much as possible. Do this until your laughter turns into tears, and then dry your eyes on the fabric that's around the heart space. You should then feel healed, if not completely whole, once again.

Elderberry Bush

The Elderberry Bush is a sacred plant of the old Gods of Europe. Associated with midsummer, this plant celebrates the turning of the Wheel of the Year to Litha, the season ruled by Father Sun.

As flowers are traditionally associated with Mother Earth, our thoughts should turn to her when celebrating Litha. The Elder has many associations with earthen fertility and is thought to represent Mother Earth giving birth to Father Sun in early spring. In Litha, she may give birth again as another year turns over into autumn, beginning its descent into winter.

Popular folklore refers to the elder tree or bush as the home of elves and fairies in the European tradition. Well-regarded Elder trees were often considered a source of healing and were thought to be inhabited by spirits of the dead. The two were often linked together, one belief being that one would not die until their name was sung by a bird sitting on an elder tree. A similar belief more prevalent in Great Britain is that the souls of the restless dead inhabit elder trees and can be heard at night banging on hollow trunks or branches to let people know they are there. It is said that these spirits can become angered if their tree is cut down.

This Elder tree is well-known in our own culture as a sacred plant of the woods, often used in ceremonial rituals by Native Americans. It is said to have been heavily utilized in early Celtic practices. Although being described as "nature's gift," this tree was also a metaphor for life and death, representing almost every aspect of growth and decay. The unripe fruit was used to represent youth and immortality before they reached their full maturity.

Elderberry Ritual

You'll need:

- Elderberry bush
- Berries
- Rosemary
- Green clothes

Directions:

1. After sunset, go up to the elderberry bush and show it a small offering of a handful of berries.

2. Gently take leaves from the rosemary and say a prayer under the moonlight.

3. Hang out with your friends in green clothing for as long as you want to celebrate.

4. Bring gifts for everyone because generosity is part of the growth that stems from midsummer rituals

The Yew Tree

The significance of the Yew tree in Litha has been handed down through the generations. The yew tree is believed to be a powerful pagan and Druidic symbol, but its allure extends beyond these beliefs. For example, it was thought that Druids used to tie consecrated cakes at its topmost branches during sacred celebrations, while others used the bark of the Yew Tree as an antidote against poisoning in humans. As you can see, there are many things that this very special tree can do for us. But what makes it such an influential symbol? The answer lies in its deep connection with death and immortality, both of which seem to be forever intertwined with the power of this ancient tree.

The Yew Tree is not just some common, old tree. It stands for something much greater than what we may think. This seemingly insignificant tree still has a mysterious meaning, making it a vital part of our lives. So, what is the purpose of the yew tree? What can we learn from this great old symbol of wisdom? As with most things in nature and spirituality, you cannot help but be impressed by its beauty and grandness all throughout the summer season. But there seems to be more to it than meets the eye, at least if you take a closer look at it.

The Yew Tree is perhaps one of the most powerful trees known to mankind. The Druids and other Pagan groups believed that a yew tree would instantly turn into a dark green shade when an elder of their group passed away as if mourning over the loss in its own way. The yew tree has some interesting properties that one should not ignore.

The yew tree is also associated with the fairy world, and it often replaces the mistletoe as a symbol of marriage. The red berries of the yew were particularly sacred to the ancient Druids, who used them to brew ritual beer. Many people still use the yew tree for making sacred wine in their ceremonies.

That said, I think it's safe to say that some part of Litha or Midsummer is meant to celebrate life. The fact that we do not typically see any other trees besides these listed points directly *to life* being involved in this festival. The fact that there are some trees listed and berries should be more than enough to convince anyone to add Litha or Midsurhime decorations to their home. At the very least, you should have a red candle and an offering bowl on hand.

Yew Tree Ritual
You'll need:

- Yew tree bough
- Honey
- A sharp knife

(There's a lot of debate about whether you should cut yew, so do what you think is best.)

Directions:

1. Cut the yew tree bough into pieces.
2. Put honey on it liberally and allow it to saturate into the pieces of wood.
3. Place the wet bark pieces in a small container or jar that will hold them snugly, then seal it tightly shut.
4. Carve your name into the bark.
5. Stuff a piece of paper with a list of things you wish to accomplish.
6. If you're using a jar, stuff it in there too and seal it up. If not, place the bark back under the yew tree for about 10 days.
7. Then put it in your room somewhere that is safe from harm and where no one else will be able to find it easily.
8. After 10 or 11 days, take out a piece of bark and carve your name into it again.
9. Now, you can do one additional task on the list so that the items are under your control.
10. Replace this piece of bark under the tree or in your room.

11. After another 10-11 days, repeat this step; you may add another item to your list each time you repeat it.

12. Continue to do this until all items are done, then burn the bark and paper. If you're using a jar, empty out what is left inside if there's still bark in there and peel it off before burning everything.

13. When you're finished, your wish is granted.

If you don't have the time to wait about 11 days for each item, try doing it every 2 or 3 days. If you don't even have time for that, do it every day until all items are complete. Don't skip a day in between each step.

Flowers

- **Sunflower:** One of the most popular flowers for Litha. It can be displayed as a bouquet or planted outside in your garden. They're also very easy to grow and make great cut arrangements (perfect for any occasion).

- **Sweet Peas:** The sweet-smelling pea is another popular flower during this time of year. You can put them in a vase or just enjoy their scent by letting the vine run throughout your home.

- **White Roses:** As a gift, it's said that white roses symbolize purity and love. You can present them to someone as a gift or incorporate them into your Litha decorations.

- **Tulips:** Tulips are also great to give as gifts or incorporate into home decorations. They come in many colors, so you can find one that best matches your theme.

- **Red Roses:** Red roses symbolize passion, desire, and love. They make great gifts, so be sure to have some on hand if you need to bring something to a party or gathering.

- **Orchids:** Orchids are perfect for any time of the year, but they're especially beautiful during the Summer. They're also very popular at this time of year, so you can easily find a bouquet in your favorite color.

- **English Roses:** Also known as Rosa "English Romantic," these flowers are bright and beautiful. You can either give them as gifts or incorporate them into your home decorations for Litha.

- **Pink Gerbera Daisies:** Gerbera Daisies are perfect for any occasion, especially Litha. They're known for being bright and beautiful, so be sure to pick up a bouquet.

- **Hydrangeas:** Hydrangeas are very large and full of flowers. They're also very common at this time of year. Gif them or use them in your home decorations.

- **Red Tulips:** They're a tribute to the Holly King, which is fitting for the Summer Solstice. Give away as a gift or decorate your home with them.

- **Purple Hyacinths:** Hyacinths are perfect for this time of year because they're very prominent in the floral world. You can give them as gifts or incorporate them into your home decorations.

- **Blue Roses:** If you want to give your gift a pop of color, then consider buying blue roses. They're especially beautiful during this time of year and make great gifts.

Other Plants of Beltane

- **Yarrow:** Yarrow flowers are associated with good luck, healing, love, and lust. They also represent selfless love or true love. Yarrow is also said to bring victory in any fight or challenge.

- **Venus Fly Traps:** Venus fly traps grow on the flesh of animals such as beetles and crickets, taking nourishment from these insects as they die in their jaws. In contrast, flowering plants live solely on water and sunlight; they do not grow on anything else. This living nature of the Venus fly trap's body parts means it can revive and transform itself as it grows larger throughout the seasons. In the same way, our Lady is the Goddess of death, rebirth, and regeneration. Her very nature is change and transformation. Like the Venus fly trap, she can take nourishment from those things that others deem useless and, in turn, fill their life with purpose as she grows within them. Litha is a time when we celebrate the cycle of death, rebirth, and transformation. In Litha, we are reborn as full-fledged children of the Goddess. This festival, in which she was reborn from what others cast aside, nourishes us with her strength. In the same way as the Venus fly trap grows in size, so too does our Lady grow within us. Our Lady is not stagnant like a flower that lives only on water, but she is ever-changing, ever-growing. She does not live on what she absorbs from others; rather, it is her nature to transform those things around her into something greater than before.

- **Dandelions**: Dandelion seeds blow away from their stems in the wind. All over Europe and North America, children love blowing on a dandelion until all its seeds have left and danced away in the wind like little parachutes.

- **Lily of the Valley:** Lilies are often used to represent death and funerals. In some cultures, they are funeral flowers and have a long tradition of being used on graves.

- **Maypole:** A maypole is a tall wooden pole erected on St. John's Day, which serves various purposes, from fertility ritual to dancing around it (hence "Maying") to having its tip cut off at the end of July for harvest. Among the Celts, the Mayday festival was celebrated on Beltane.

- **Mistletoe:** Many plants have a sexual meaning (such as daffodils), so it is not surprising that mistletoe is also considered to be symbolic of love, especially when grown on an oak. It is said that lovers who kissed under the mistletoe were ill-fated or would later die, but those who abstained from kissing under it were destined to be happy.

- **Passionflower:** A passionflower can be used to mark a funeral or mourning period.

- **Rosemary (Rosemary Flowers)**: Rosemary flowers are associated with good luck, healing, love, and lust. They also represent selfless love or true love. Rosemary is also said to bring victory in any fight or challenge.

- **Red Poppy:** Red flowers traditionally were used for decoration at this time. The red poppy is one of the most common flowers of Litha, as it is considered a symbol of fertility and love. Red represents both love and violence and fertility and hope for men and women everywhere. In pagan tradition, red is a color used to represent life, love, compassion, death, and health. It is often associated with fire—the main source of heat and light for people since ancient times. Fire also represents the light and life of the sun—the most powerful natural resource on earth. Furthermore, it is believed that red is a symbol of passion and valor. During Litha, many people use red to express hope or attract renewal. Litha and Samhain are often associated with death, but they are also associated with life—with the cycle of death and rebirth that we experience throughout our lives.

- **Vervain:** A plant sacred to the Gauls, it is reputedly used in the preparation of love potions.
- **Witch Hazel:** The hazel leaf is associated with wisdom, learned people, and witches.

Chapter 6: Celebrate the Sun and Jump over Fire

Importance of the Sun in Litha

As you have gathered by now, the Sun has great importance during Litha since it is at the peak of its power. The sun represents strength and power, made only possible because of its energy. As a result, Litha celebrates this solar deity's existence and power by focusing on light and color, allowing for transformation. This gives way to an atmosphere within a society filled with optimism and warmth to help carry us through the difficult times ahead. For you see, the dark half of the year does not have a spirit animal to help carry us through. Winter Solstice, the darkest point in the year, is considered the death of the Druid year. The Druids consider this day as one to reflect on past mistakes and create resolutions for a future filled with hope and light. What one sabbat represents is very different from those of others.

Sun Gods typically represent masculine energy which is extremely relevant during Litha because society celebrates his existence during this time. During Litha, we celebrate the Sun god's positive masculine traits like strength and power, which are crucial to recovery from our feelings of helplessness.

Celebrating the Sun

Sun Meditation: A sun meditation is a special type of meditation that honors the power of the Sun. It involves imagining the sun being brought back to life through meditations, prayers, and ritualistic sunbaths. The term "sun meditation" comes from the idea that people are giving their energy to the Sun. They visualize themselves giving their life force to the sun, and in return, the powerful light from the sun will be able to be used to help their physical body heal itself over time.

Sun meditations can be done from the ground up or from atop a mountain. The basic goal is to bring the power of the sun back for its people to be able to make use of it again during the upcoming months. If done properly, the Sun is supposed to bring power and glory back to its people, and on a personal level, there is also healing and protection that can be achieved through these special sun meditations.

While some people may simply do a sun meditation at home, one should, instead, do this meditation in full public view where others can see them. This way, they feel that they are being watched as they give their energy to the Sun again. This will bring about the manifestation of the Sun's divine power quicker than if it were being done in a private area.

These meditations can be done at any time during Litha, but they should be performed during the day to benefit from the sun's energies. It is best to do a morning meditation before noon because once it hits midday, there will be too much glare due to light reflecting off everything underneath it. If you're simply doing a prayer, then this time of day will suffice; otherwise, make sure you perform your rituals right after dawn. The main idea behind these sun meditations is to make sure the Sun is full of energy again to be lit up like a candle flame during Litha.

The sun meditations can take a long time, and you should be patient with yourself as you prepare for this ritual. It is best to dedicate at least an hour or so before your desired ceremony time. The more time you put into practicing these rituals, the more powerful and effective they will become over time. You will also find that the number of thoughts you give to the Sun during your daily practice will increase, and often days or weeks go by where no ideas are given about what to do as it becomes second nature for you to perform this ritual every day.

It is also a good idea to maintain the proper mindset during your rituals because if you think negatively, this will cause negativity to rise from the physical plane, and it will be hard to undo this effect.

What to Do for a Sun Meditation Session

These sun meditations require some preparation to be sure you will have everything needed at hand. This includes everything you feel is vital to get the most out of your meditation:

You'll need:

- Your sunbelt
- Incense
- Candles
- Water
- Essential oils

Eyes are closed throughout this practice, so it feels very natural. You may, however, want to consider wearing sunglasses or eye protection in case of headaches or discomfort that occurs during these exercises. Spending this time in complete darkness will help your body to stay focused on the light of the sun and not let any other thoughts or things distract you.

Directions:

1. The first step is to put on your belt (sunbelt), a sacred item used for healing in ancient times. It must be made from a natural material that feels good against your skin, so you could opt for one made of leather, cotton, or hemp. Put your belt on and look where it hangs from your body to be sure it fits right and feels comfortable.

2. Now, you'll say a prayer that has been previously adapted for the Celts. It is usually something along the lines of *"I honor Litha, God of Life, Love and Light. Help me manifest my spiritual awareness. Let it be done as I will it."* You can also chant this as if you're attempting to awaken something.

3. Next, you will need to put a few drops of essential oils into your incense, such as Lavender, Frankincense, and Pine. Incense should

be burned afresh every time, so you will need to have some more incense for this ritual to work properly.

4. Afterward, you will need to say a prayer asking the Gods and Goddesses to help your energy reach the Sun God. This involves making your body feel as if it is full of light and will get you into a hypnotic state that will allow the power of the sun to awaken within you.

5. Once this feeling is achieved, you're ready to move on to the next step, which is visualizing yourself standing near a pond. Imagine yourself being under a waterfall or by a lake. The more water present in your visualization, the more effective this ritual will become.

6. When you're in complete darkness, you will then request the Sun to be lit up like a candle through the power of your sunbelt. This will then bring about the manifestation of your energy that is soaking into your consciousness so that it can be passed onto the light that is around you. From there, all this energy is absorbed into your body, radiating from you to fill up all of space with light.

You may feel as if you're being consumed by this light at first, but do not worry. The Sun's power, God's Fire, and Divine Consciousness will guide all this energy into the correct direction, into your body, and it will start to heal everything that is needed to be restored. It will promote your health, vitality, and growth into a higher state of being.

Once you complete this practice, you can then take a break before you continue to do another one with the same intentions for the night. You can also do this ritual to gain more insight or develop your spiritual abilities. It is a fast way to gain enlightenment, and the changes that come about because of this technique can be felt very quickly. Therefore, it is important to have patience when performing these techniques because they may seem strange in the beginning until they become natural over time.

Making Sun Jars

Making a sun jar is not difficult, and it's easy to get started with just one jar. Here are the supplies.

You'll need:

- **Jars** — You can use any clear glass jar. It can be round or square but should be a size that's easy to handle. A mason jar works well, as does a jelly jar. If you have a basket to hold your collection of jars, that's great. Or you can put them in boxes as I do.

- **Sand** — Be sure it is white or dark-colored non-toxic sand from the craft store or home improvements store. You may want to buy more than one bag of sand to keep on hand since you want your jar to fill the jar, leaving about 1/2 an inch of space from the top of the jar.

Directions:

1. Fill the jar about 3-4 inches from the top and let it dry.

2. Carefully seal your jar with the lids – you're just following the directions of a sealer.

3. Use your intention to charge your jars with power.

4. Once they're sealed and dry, place them on a windowsill in direct sunlight to charge them up.

5. Put them away until you're ready to use them

Sun jars last for quite some time before they need recharging again. You can leave the jar out overnight to get a full charge and place it on your altar. When you're ready to use the jar, place it nearby you as you do your meditations or spells, and imagine the powerful rays of the Sun deep in the glass, warming your aura like a portable heater.

You can also place your sun jars in cupboards or on lower shelves of closets for added power. You can even keep them in a basket near your front door so that they transfer their energy every time someone enters or leaves the house. Sun jars are especially good at protecting your home during the cold months.

Sun Salutation

Sun salutations are a series of flowing yoga poses that can be practiced individually or in sequence. The sequence of movements is designed to warm the body with the sun's energy, and they are often done outdoors during sunrise or sunset. This is an excellent way for Litha celebrants to tune into this beautiful time of year by connecting with both the divine masculine (solstice) and divine feminine (nature).

Physiologically, sun salutation exercises are designed to be gentle and restorative. They were originally intended as a healing practice for the troops during times of war when the body was weakened by stress. Over time, sun salutations have become a healthy way to warm the body and clear blockages from the flow of chi or life energy in the body. Here's a sequence of poses you can use:

Mountain Pose: Stand straight and make sure your big toes are touching each other. Raise all toes, loosen them up by fanning them out, then drop them back down so they grip the floor. Separate both heels a bit if your ankles are touching and causing some pain. Feel your feet and calves connect with the floor. Think of them as roots if that helps. Engage your quads (front thigh muscles), pulling them up so your kneecaps rise. Turn your thighs inward so your sit bones get wider, but make sure your spine remains in its naturally curved position. Draw your belly in slightly, stretch your collarbones and ensure both shoulders are right in line with your pelvis. Give them a shrug, bringing them to your ears, then roll both backward to relax your shoulder blades. Both arms should hang loose, and there should be a slight bend in your elbows as your palms face forward. Keep your neck long, your chin in a neutral position (not lifted or tucked in), and feel the crown of your head connect with the sky. Remain in this position for 5 to 10 breaths.

Standing Backbend: Now, put your palms on your sacrum or lower back and let your fingers point down. Press both feet into the floor, engage your quads to raise your kneecaps, and squeeze your buttocks and thighs. Push your hips forward and begin arching your torso backward, making sure you look straight ahead, or you drop your head all the way back. Let your arms support you, and make sure your buttocks and legs remain engaged. Hold this position for 3 to 7 breaths. To get out of this, keep your arms and buttocks strong as you slowly breathe and come up, with your neck being the last to get back in starting position in mountain pose.

Standing Forward Bend: From mountain pose, bend both knees a bit, hinge from the hips as you fold over, bringing your torso to your legs. Make sure you use your hips, not your lower back. Breathe in and stretch your chest so your spine grows longer. Breathe out and gently straighten your legs, taking care not to hyperextend them. Lift your kneecaps and spiral your inner, upper thighs back as gently as you can. When you breathe out, extend the torso downwards, making sure you don't round your back. Allow your neck to grow longer as the crown of your head reaches for the earth. Draw your shoulders back and down toward both hips. Allow yourself to gently unfold from this position when you're ready.

Runner's Lunge: Get on all fours, toes and knees flexed and touching the earth, hips over knees, hands a bit wider than shoulders, and shoulder blades away from the spine. With your hand, grip the earth and turn both shoulders outwards. This engages your lats. Straighten both legs so your knees go off the ground, and you're now in plank position. Check your legs to make sure they're hip-width apart. Flex your hips and shoulders, engage your core, make sure your ribs are down, and there's a slight tuck in your pelvis. Keep your chin tucked all through this move. Now, squeeze your glutes and quads, bring the right foot between both hands, making sure the right knee forms a 90-degree angle and the right foot is firm and flat on the floor. You can have the left leg fully extended (with no hyperextension) or slightly bent at the knee. Flex the left glute while you make sure your weight is properly distributed along the ball of the foot. Remain in this position for 10 to 20 seconds. When you're done, go back into plank position.

Chaturanga: From plank, bend both elbows and lower both shoulders. You want them all at the same height. Squeeze both elbows inward. Make sure your legs and upper body are above the floor only by a few inches. You can gaze slightly ahead or down at the floor. Broaden the upper back and chest. As you breathe out, come into plank position again. If you need to rest, you can drop your knees and push back on your heels, stretching your arms out in front of you with your fingers splayed on the ground. This is Child's Pose.

Upward Dog: Lie on your belly and extend your legs behind you. Put both hands on the floor, palms down, forearms perpendicular to the earth. Press into your hands and straighten both arms to help you light your torso off the floor, bringing you onto the tops of both feet. Make sure your elbows have a slight bend in them as you flex your abs, arms, and thighs. Keep the shoulder blades and buttocks firm and your eyes fixed ahead of you. Hold this pose for 15 to 30 seconds, then come down to your hands and knees.

Downward Dog: Push both hands down into the earth as you raise your hips to the sky. Keep a slight bend in both knees while pressing into the ground with your feet too. Make sure your spine is straight and your shoulders are flexed with your head angled toward both feet. Remain here for a minute.

Final Steps: Repeat the runner's lunge on the other side of your body. Do the standing forward bend again, then the standing backbend, and wrap up with the mountain pose.

Jumping over the Bonfire for Litha

The most important event of Litha is the ritualized act of jumping over the bonfire. It was performed in ancient times to celebrate the rising Sun, and nowadays, it is done in remembrance of our ancestors. The bonfires were built by women (who also made sure they had enough fuel), and they were seen as a symbol for the womb, which became fertile when lit by fire.

This celebration has been followed for ages, not only during Litha but all year round in some parts of Europe. The ritual first involves constructing a bonfire, which can be done over three weeks. After it is ready, a festival begins, either on June 21st (the summer solstice) or on the next full moon.

The fire is built to call upon the spirits and to help them reunite with their loved ones. A bonfire is also considered a symbol of unity and togetherness since people gather around and jump over it together to connect with their ancestors' spirits. Many pagan communities have kept this tradition alive by building large fires in public parks and jumping over them on midsummer nights.

Some communities still perform these rituals privately in their own neighborhoods, while others go out into nature in groups. On the day of the celebration, after the fire is lit, everyone gathers around it. When everyone is ready to start, one of them begins to chant an incantation to ask for blessings and guidance from the spirits. They then open a way to allow spirits to enter the circle. The chanting stops, and everybody jumps over the flames with joyful cries.

The jumping over bonfires was once a very important event that was performed at midsummer before eventually turning into our most popular bonfire tradition. Regardless of how it was done in ancient times, we can still experience this as an enchanting celebration combined with ancestral wisdom that helps us mend relationships with our loved ones who have passed away or simply feel closer to them.

Conducting a Midsummer Fire Ritual

Before the midsummer fire, it is important to get things in order. Cleanliness is vital for any good ritual, and a cleansing bath can be taken beforehand. Additionally, it would be beneficial to assemble the tools that will be used throughout the ritual.

These include items such as salt and incense and elements of various plants or wood. The ritual itself may also involve dancing around and kindling "the fire" with a piece of wood or a tapering flame on some type of vessel.

You'll need:

- A candle
- A piece of cord or twine
- A stick from an oak tree (or any living or dead vegetation)
- Any incense
- Salt (or ground black pepper or cayenne pepper)
- Knife
- Knife sharpener (or stone)

Directions:

1. Prepare: finish up last-minute preparations (i.e., clean up your work area, gather water, etc.)
2. Gather the materials that you will need for the fire.
3. Take a cleansing bath (i.e., take a shower)
4. Dress for success. Make sure you're wearing all or most of your ritual clothing (vest, hat, etc.). You might also want to put on a crown made from any type of tree or plant, especially if you're using one in the ritual itself.

Saltwater Bath Ritual

This ritual can be performed before or after the ritual around the fire. It is just your basic cleansing bath, only with sea salt and water drawn from a running stream added to it. If you do not have any sea salt available, regular table salt will do.

You'll need:

- A bathtub or large washtub
- Sea salt or table salt
- Water from a running stream (if not available, just regular water will work)
- A knife and/or stone to carve with if you wear a crown made from the wood of a tree; otherwise, this is optional
- A candle (about 2 inches tall)
- A piece of cord or twine, preferably red and black, but any will do so long as it's strong and flexible and won't break easily
- A stick from any kind of vegetation (i.e., any tree or plant)
- A taper (a bit of dry, living plant that can easily be broken and points to the top or ends of a candle will work)
- A piece of chalk (in case of a burn)
- A match or lighter
- A small mirror
- A sharpening stone
- Hat and Gloves

Directions:

1. In your bath, add 12-16 drops of incense into the water, as well as a few pinches of sea salt or table salt.

2. Take the time to enjoy your bath and relax while you prepare yourself for the ritual.

3. Also, take care not to let your skin get too dry while taking this bath; taking a shower afterward could make things easier.

4. As soon as you're done with your bath, take your candle, the taper, and the cord or twine, and dress appropriately. If you're using a crown or a headdress to wear, then you will want to put it on as soon as possible.

Set Your Working Space: Assemble the materials that you will use in the ritual by setting them around you in a circle or as close to a circle as possible. If you use twine or cord, then use it according to the directions on the package or advertisement that it came on so that it doesn't break while you perform your fire ritual. If you're using a taper, then make sure that the chimney is large enough for the candle and stick of vegetation to fit into.

Bury your tools or hide them in the ground (if they are not already hidden) and put on your crown, hat, and gloves. Once you have all of this on, stand facing the working space (unless you're making the ritual a group event, then everyone should stand facing the same direction).

Light up. Now that everything is set up, light up your candle using your taper. If you use a cord, tie the ends off it with a knot that won't come untied. If you're using twine or cord, then cut it into four pieces and wrap each piece around the stick that is used for this ritual. If your twine or rope is too long, just tie it back together so it won't get in the way. This takes some practice, and you may need to look at your twine or cord before performing the ritual to make sure that it won't break while you perform it. Now light up your candle by lighting the taper on top of the candle. Once both are lit, say, "I bless all the life that will exist after this fire dies," and blow out your candle by blowing lightly into it.

Now get your knife ready. Make an incision in the twine or cord around the stick. If you cut straight down, it should be a single strand. If you cut diagonally, it will be a double strand. If you accidentally cut the cord or twine in half because it's too long, then just use one half. If you would like to draw a circle on the ground, get your chalk and draw a rough circle at least 7 feet across. If you're making a ring of incense around your working area, then make this into a ring large enough for you to move around in it comfortably.

When all of this is done, light up your fire using your match or lighter and say, *"I bless thee with all life"* while doing so (if you choose not to use incense, then skip this). This part of the ritual aims to get the fire started and impart energy into your tools and working area. To do this, you must draw a circle with your stick in the dirt around yourself. When you're done, draw a smaller circle inside of that one about 1 foot in diameter (i.e., it will be about

6 inches across). Do not step outside of the larger circle or scatter any of the embers or ash.

If you're using incense (if not, skip this part), then do so while saying *"I bless thee with all life"* while lighting up your incense. Each piece should be about 1-2 inches in diameter and laid down with the top of it facing towards you. Each piece should also be placed on top of a small rock or pebble so they don't move around while burning (if they do, then just lean your stick on them). Once all of this is done, say, "I bless thee with all life," while blowing into the embers.

Now that your tools and fire have been blessed, carve the word "life" in big letters and "hope" in smaller letters with your knife into the twine or cord. Now that you have done this, blow out your candle, and if you used incense, put it away.

Get a stick from either outside or inside the circle and burn it while saying "I bless thee with all life" over it. Once burned, throw it into the fire. If it doesn't catch on fire right away, just place some wood pieces on top of it until they catch. Once the last piece of your twine or cord has burned completely, then say, "I bless thee with all life" while lighting up your incense.

Now that the fire is lit, everyone can start to leave. If this ritual is being done as part of a group ritual, everyone can form a line and follow each other out of the circle one by one without stepping outside it. If this ritual is done by yourself, then you should just walk out of the circle while bending down and keeping your hand on the small rock or pebble that you placed at the entrance of your circle. This is not necessary for you to do if this ritual is being done for personal reasons.

The purpose of this ritual is to bring about change and get yourself ready for what's to come (i.e., a spell or ritual). By doing so, everything that occurs in your life will be working towards your goal (your goal could be anything). The symbols of life and hope will help you reach your goal. Remember that you can use this ritual for any prayer or spell that you want to perform, and you don't have to stick with this charm if you don't want to (you can make up anything meaningful to you).

Chapter 7: Family Activities and Crafts

Family-Friendly Midsummer Activities

Now let's learn about some activities you could do with your family on Litha.

Make Sun Paintings: All you'll need are some different colors of paint and paper plates to create these beautiful sun paintings. And if you're feeling creative, print out an outline of a sun's rays and use markers or crayons to fill them in.

Go Sunbathing: Make your own sunbathing "beach" at a park near your house or at a nearby field. If you're feeling ambitious, decorate the area with colorful flowers and bring some cool drinks to keep everyone sweet and hydrated.

Beach Day: Who doesn't love the beach? It's hot, it's sandy, and there's always something to do. Why not take the opportunity to visit a local beach during Litha? Remember to bring water, sunscreen, and towels.

Rock Painting: Litha is an excellent time for art projects because you'll have all the time in the world to be creative. If you're feeling creative, why not make a big rock painting of one or several gods and goddesses you resonate with? This kind of project doesn't have to be difficult if you practice beforehand and have some old magazines for reference.

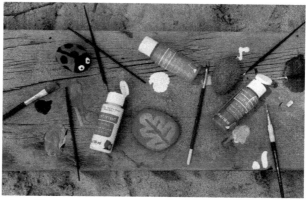

Summer Art Classes: There are many summers camp classes that you can take. Do you want to learn how to preserve fruits and vegetables? How about painting drums or pottery? Your local arts and crafts store will be happy to help you find the appropriate course for your family.

Go Camping: It's fun to go camping during the summer. You can make a temporary campfire, set up tents, play games, cook delicious meals, and go swimming. While you're at it, why not take a photo of your family that looks like it was just taken from the lake?

Go to the Beach: You don't have to visit an actual beach if you live in a city. You can collect some sand or sprinkle some ocean water into your backyard. Just keep in mind that whatever you do, keep in mind that Litha is only around 2 weeks long.

Make a Solar System Out of Paper: Did you know that the solar system is made of planets? Planets orbit the sun in a circular motion. You can use construction paper to create your own solar system. Make sure to put the sun in the middle.

Cook Delicious Solar Treats: Plan a tea party or cookout. Invite your family and friends to sample some delicious treats such as pizza, burritos, sandwiches, and other hot foods. These foods will remind you of the Sun's powerful heat.

Go to a Bakery: If you ever want to eat some delicious and cheap treats, then going to a bakery is a great idea. You could even make your own if you have the time and the ingredients.

Make Your Own Cactus Garden: Cacti are one of the defining symbols of Litha. They're just like the sun in that they contain almost everything needed for life, but they don't always get enough attention or care. Create your own cactus garden in a pot or a planter box.

Go for a Walk: Go for a walk in the woods, the mountains, or even outside your neighborhood. You could even just go for an afternoon walk around your neighborhood. You never know what you're going to find.

Visit a Museum: Museums are great places to visit because they contain so much knowledge and history that you might not learn anywhere else. And if you want to become more familiar with some sun gods like Ra and Apollo, then this is the place to start.

Read a Good Book: Why not read a good book to check out the full potential of this beautiful season? Being able to read is one of the most important abilities that you can have as a person.

Learn Something New: Reading and learning are two skills that will serve you throughout your entire life. The more you go out on adventures, the more you will be able to learn.

Listen to Music: Midsummer is the perfect time to listen to some music. A good mix of rock and classical music might help you relax and relax at least temporarily.

Take Family Photos: What better time to take family photos than during a beautiful, warm summer day? The only way to make sure that your photos look fabulous is by having a good photographer. If you don't have the time or energy to do it yourself, then find a local photographer who can help you out.

Visit an Aquarium: Aquariums can be so full of life, color, and beauty that they will take your breath away. You'll be able to see thousands of different kinds of sea life in one place. This is perfect for anyone who's ever dreamed of being a marine biologist.

Take a Day Trip to a Park: Parks can also be full of life and color. There's no end to the kind of activities that you can do at a park. Hiking, picnicking, swimming, or even just reading a book would be perfect.

Take the Kids on a Walk: A good walk will do wonders for kids' minds and bodies. The fresh air and the fresh air will really help them feel relaxed. Plus, it's great for bonding with your family.

Make Midsummer Bonfires: Bonfires are something that everyone should experience in their lifetime. These bonfires are very spiritual and can help you to relax after a long day.

Go Swimming: Swimming is a good way to cool off on a hot, sunny day. Whether you like pool swimming or the beach, it's something that you should do at least once in your life.

Go on a Picnic: Picnics are perfect for Midsummer, especially if you don't want to sit inside and watch TV all day. If you want to feel the full effect of this season and its warmth, then sitting outside as the sun goes down is the best way.

Go Canoeing or Kayaking: If you have water nearby, then going canoeing or kayaking is a great way to spend time with your family. You can go on a trip for miles and still be in the same place. This will help to clear your mind and give you some time to relax.

Midsummer Crafts

The Blessing Besom

Most people make midsummer blessings using flowers and herbs. However, in most countries around the world, midsummer is also a time when witches and other practitioners of the magical arts gather to work together at their magic tables. For this reason, witch blessings are known as blessing besoms that are made with leaves, twigs, and more natural items.

You'll need:

- Holly bushes or oak leaves (fresh)
- Sharp knife
- Acrylic or watercolor paint (orange, red, pink, blue/green)
- Pins

Directions:

1. First, choose your materials. The best type of plant for a witch's blessing besom is oak leaves or holly bushes that can be found throughout the summer months. When it is time to pick the materials for your blessing, always choose only fresh leaves.

2. Clean the leaves at least 24 hours before use. To keep its potency, you should always wash off all sprigs of plants before making a blessing besom.

3. Cut the material at an angle. You can cut your leaves at an angle using a straight edge such as a ruler. When cutting your material, make sure that the cuts are not larger than ¼ inch wide.

4. Paint the leaves. After cutting your material, you should immediately paint them with any type of watercolor or acrylic paint to preserve their color. Add blue-green colors for the High Priestess, orange colors for the King, red colors for the Queen, and pink for the Priestess.

5. Next, cut your leaves into three pieces and fold them twice at the bottom and top with spaces in between to create a triangle.

6. Pin them on green paper. Next, you will pin your witch's blessing besoms onto a piece of green paper. This will help the leaves maintain their color. When pinning them onto your besom, you should make sure that your pins are not too close together as this will make them hard to work with.

7. Let the leaves dry for at least 24 hours to get a tacky feel on the paper. Once they are dried, you can fold the paper to resemble a fan.

Lavender Dream Pillow

The Sun has great importance during Litha since he is at the peak of his power. He brings life and warmth to our world, so it is appropriate that we honor him on this special day.

A bed is one of the most personal and private places in our home, so it's only fitting that we show some love for the sun by making one for ourselves. Many methods and processes can be used to make one's own lavender dream pillow, but I've done mine a bit differently.

You'll need:

- One small lavender flower (or two for larger pillows) with its center attached

- Fresh Viola flowers (4 to 6 per pillow). Do NOT use viola flowers from a florist, as these have been sprayed or plated in plastic or glue. You can find these in the organic section of a grocery store).

- Fabric (any color or material). Use a measurement is of your choosing, but I suggest an amount that is enough for it to be folded over on itself

- Needle and thread

- Optional: Lavender scented oil (this could also be used in place of the flowers altogether).

You should use only pure lavender for this project, not a combination of different herbs.

Directions:

1. If using oil: Put several drops on a cotton ball and put it between the two pieces of fabric to form your pillow. If using the lavender flower: Simply insert the flower directly into your fabric and tie it off with a secure knot.

2. After choosing your preferred method, fold your pillow over so it looks like a normal pillow, making sure that all ends are secure.

3. Then, cut a small slit for the ribbon loop to slip through later. This is preferred rather than trying to sew in the loop onto your pillow because

there won't be any stitching that could rip out in the future.

The Dreaming Ritual: Do this on an evening of a full moon to ensure that you get maximum energy from this process and draw from both the moon's and sun's power.

1. Lay on your pillow and close your eyes.

2. Visualize the sun coming into focus and shining down upon you through the slit in your pillow. You might even see it rising from behind a tree or other object.

3. Repeat this visualization until you feel it becoming a reality or until you become tired of it.

   If done correctly, your pillow will now start to glow with the light of the sun when you lift the top corner of your pillow to look at its current state: glowing.

Litha Herb Pouch

You'll need:

- Sage to give you wisdom
- Mint for clarity
- Rosemary to improve remembrance
- Thyme to develop your psychic powers
- Basil to have the good fortune
- Lavender for peace and calmness
- Hyssop for purification and cleansing
- Mugwort for dreams and divination
- Peppermint for love and passion
- Yarrow to boost healing
- Tea towel
- A strainer
- A small pot
- Fresh water

Directions:

1. Fill a small pot with 1 inch of fresh water and bring it to a boil.

2. Add one cup of dried herbs. You can either choose the herbs you prefer from the list provided or mix all of them in equal parts into a cup and use that instead.

3. Reduce the heat to medium-low and simmer for about 10 minutes or until the water is infused with its flavor.

4. Strain in a clean tea towel over a bowl for a refreshing summertime herbal infusion.

How to Make a Sunflower Candle Ring
You'll need:

- A big, empty can (an old pickle jar will do)
- A pair of scissors
- A white sunflower
- Brown yarn

Directions:

1. Use scissors to cut half of the petals off a white sunflower head. For this project, we used an heirloom sunflower.

2. The petals will be very pointy, so you want to go ahead and pinch them down with your fingers and smooth them out as much as you can while they're still attached to the flower.

3. Take the flower apart and place all the petals around the jar's top edge. Tuck them in wherever you can to make a full circle. Make sure that you have enough overlapping petals to completely cover the glass when they are placed on top of one another.

4. Next, cut a 6" piece of brown yarn and tie it around the bottom center of your sunflower ring.

5. Shove your candle wax into your empty pickle jar until it is about a third full. Then, tie your sunflower ring to the middle of your candle wax using more brown yarn. This will keep it steady while it is being burned.

6. After it has burned for a while, pull out petals that might be stuck inside your jar. This will allow you to use the jar for other things if you want to.

Chapter 8: Midsummer Foods

What to Eat for Litha?

One custom during Litha is to eat foods that will help you with your inner health during these transitional times. Foods like fruits and vegetables with properties that reduce inflammation and increase circulation are important around this time because we are about to prepare for a new cycle in life.

Some examples of good foods during this time are cherries, plums, raspberries, elderberries, black currants, goji berries, and all berries in general, which help eliminate uric acid, have antioxidants, and increase your energy. In addition to eating all the fruits and vegetables available at this bountiful time of year, it is also helpful to add some roots (e.g., ginger) and grains (e.g., quinoa, amaranth) to your diet. These help aid digestion and give your body an abundance of strength.

Some foods associated with Midsummer are brawn, fruit, cheese in Yule-seasoned bread, and hard-boiled eggs with horseradish mayonnaise. Some traditional beverages for this time are cider, dandelion tea, and elderflower cordial.

Brawn, also known as head cheese, is a meat dish made of a pig's or sheep's head cut off just above the eyes. It is cured until all parts are edible, then boiled and served cold with cider vinegar on it. Usually, brawn would be served at special occasions such as weddings and Midsummer.

Cider is a popular drink in Britain as it originated in England and France. It is usually made from apples and is served topped with yeast. There are many different types of cider, and someone from Britain might not recognize a cider from elsewhere.

Dandelion tea is an herb that has been common in Britain for many years. It is used to make tea or a tisane, typically by adding some leaves to cold water in a teapot where the water and leaves are simmered and steeped until the desired strength. It can also be used to cook things like syrup, jam, or jelly. Dandelion is a versatile herb, as it can be eaten raw and can also be used in salads or sandwiches.

Elderflower cordial or elderflower champagne is a sweet drink that has been used since the Middle Ages in Britain. It is made from elderflowers which are picked from elder trees and then steeped in water for several days. The result is a gluten-free and low-sugar beverage with a natural sparkling effect.

Hard-boiled eggs with horseradish mayonnaise are popular at Midsummer as they represent the sun. The yolk symbolizes the sun's yellow light, while the white symbolizes its life-giving energy. The mayonnaise represents the sun's ability to sustain the earth.

Many other foods are associated with Midsummer celebrations. Brawn, hard-boiled eggs with horseradish mayonnaise, and cider are all typical foods that are eaten at Midsummer celebrations. All these foods were also eaten at Easter and Christmas traditions as well.

The most famous traditional Midsummer food is eggs, which were said to have been introduced by King Arthur on his return from Brittany in 442 AD. The custom of eating eggs on Midsummer dates back as far as the early Middle Ages. The custom was to take an egg and roll it in flour, dip it in sugar, then roll it again in breadcrumbs, and finally dip the breadcrumbs again in sugar.

Eggs were used at the time because they symbolized fertility and abundance. They are also associated with daybreak because an egg, when broken, will have a visible yolk that looks like a rising sun. Eggs, especially free-range organic ones, are high in lecithin, a fat produced by the liver that aids in the production of neurotransmitters that affect moods. They also contain choline, another brain nutrient that helps with memory and learning ability during these times of change. All these things are important because as we undergo changes during the summer solstice, it is good to bolster our minds with positive thoughts (e.g., imagination, creativity) and our bodies (e.g., energy).

The tradition of hiding Easter eggs on Easter Day is thought to have originated in England during the Middle Ages. According to legend, the tradition started out as a way of hiding eggs from the Midsummer fairies that were thought to be evil creatures.

In some parts of Britain, it is considered bad luck to find an egg, which is why they are often hidden. In 19th century Sussex, the custom was to take a white egg and break it on Easter Sunday morning. The belief was that although people would not eat the egg, doing so would prevent them from finding another one until after Easter Sunday. In Welsh mythology, if you ate an egg on Midsummer's Eve, you might turn into a goose and never be able to become human again.

We have gathered some Midsummer recipes that you can make in your own home to best celebrate Litha or the Winter Solstice with your family and friends.

Midsummer Oatcake

Here's the recipe for oatcake:

- 3 cups of flour
- 1 cup of cooked oats
- 1/4 cup of baking soda
- 1 tsp. salt

Directions:

1. Mix all ingredients together and put them into a small oven dish.
2. Place the oven dish into a casserole dish filled with water.
3. The cooking time is approximately 30 minutes at 350 degrees Fahrenheit, after which the oatcake is browned and crispy.
4. You can top your freshly baked oatcake with honey and enjoy it as a delicious treat.

Herbal Lemon Cookies

The following recipe for herbal lemon cookies is easy to make and can help bring some positive thoughts throughout your day.

Ingredients:

- 1 stick butter
- 2 cups sugar
- 2 eggs
- 1/4 cup flour
- 1/4 teaspoon salt
- 1 tablespoon baking powder
- 2 tablespoons chopped fresh lemon zest
- 3 tablespoons fresh lemon juice

For the filling:

- 1 (3 oz.) package cream cheese, softened and divided into two 8-inch squares
- 8 oz. whipped topping

For the frosting:

- 4 oz. softened cream cheese
- 1 stick butter, softened (1/2 cup)
- 2 cups confectioners' sugar
- 3 tablespoons milk

Directions:

1. Whip cream cheese, butter, and milk together until fluffy.
2. Add sugar and beat until smooth.

For cookies:

1. Cream butter and sugar together in a large bowl.
2. Beat in eggs; beat well.
3. Stir flour, salt, and baking powder together; add to creamed mixture.
4. Stir in lemon zest, lemon juice, and one of the squares of cream cheese; mix well.
5. Drop teaspoons of batter onto a lightly greased cookie sheet.
6. Bake at 350 degrees for 10 to 12 minutes.

For filling:

1. In a small bowl, combine 2 oz. of the whipped topping and 2 oz. of the cream cheese; set aside.

2. Place the remaining whipped topping in a large bowl and beat until creamy.

3. Top each cookie with one square of cream cheese filling; top dough with another cookie, set on top, and press down gently.

4. Top with the remaining cream cheese-whipped topping and press down gently.

5. Drizzle 2 oz. of the cream cheese mixture over top and frost with remaining whipped topping.

6. Cut into wedges to serve.

Tip: If you want a variation on this recipe, try adding 1/2 cup of chopped nuts.

Midsummer Mead

Ingredients:

- Tea made of Chamomile, Lavender, and Hops
- One gallon of raw apple cider
- One-quart honey
- Two cloves
- A pinch each of Nutmeg, Allspice, Cinnamon, and Ginger

Directions:

1. Mix all the ingredients into a pot and simmer for five minutes. Let it cool.

2. Add lemon juice if needed.

3. Pour into gallon glass jars with tight lids or crocks.

4. Keep in the refrigerator or cool cellar for three weeks at least before you drink it.

5. If you want to sweeten the mead after these weeks, strain out the spices and pour half a pint of honey syrup (honey mixed with water) through a coffee filter into the jar with the mead so that no unwanted debris is left behind.

6. Leave the mead at room temperature in a dark, cool place for another two or three weeks.

Tips: Dead yeast cells will be left in your strainer. These become wine yeast, and these are what can be used to make future batches of mead.

If you do not have an extra gallon of fresh raw apple cider, almond extract can be added to give a flavor like apple, especially if you decide to sweeten it with honey syrup instead.

Fiery Grilled Salmon

This is a Midsummer favorite that your friends and family are sure to enjoy. Let the fiery taste of this meal remind you of the warmth of the sun and how it generously touches one and all with light and hope. The salmon is a symbol of the sun and thus is an important part of the summer solstice. The honey represents sweet times ahead, while the lemon juice stands for the bitter times in between. (Ironic since they are sour). The onion powder adds zest to this dish.

Ingredients:

- 3 fillets of salmon, fresh or frozen
- salt and pepper as per your own taste
- 1 tablespoon honey
- 1/4 cup lemon juice
- sprinkle of onion powder to taste

Directions:

1. Prepare charcoal for your grill cooking.
2. When the grill's nice and hot, place each salmon brick onto the grill and cook until done.
3. Mix lemon juice with honey until combined well.
4. Apply lemon-honey sauce onto cooked salmon with a pastry brush or spoon.
5. Sprinkle onion powder onto the cooked salmon flesh.

6. Serve hot, cold, or room temperature.

Tip: Try serving over a bed of white rice and pour the liquid over the top or serve on a bed of salad.

Midsummer Fruit Salad

The Sun has great importance during Litha since he is at the peak of his power. If you haven't been outside in the last 30 days, you shouldn't be cooking food on that day because you risk ruining your harvest and getting sick in general. So, you can opt for a delicious fruit salad instead.

Ingredients:

- 1/2 cup raisins
- 1/2 cup currants
- 1/2 cup red seedless grapes
- 1 banana, sliced and cut into bite-size pieces
- 1 apple, peeled, cored, and chopped
- 1 orange, peeled and sliced into bite-size pieces
- Bunch of grapes (enough to cover the bottom of the bowl)

For the Dressing:

- 2 tablespoons of honey
- 2 tablespoons apple cider vinegar or lemon juice
- 1 tablespoon olive oil
- 1 teaspoon ground cinnamon
- 2 tablespoons water

Directions:

1. Place everything except the grapes in a large serving bowl.
2. Toss gently to mix.
3. Place the grapes on top, then pour the dressing mixture over everything.
4. Mix lightly to coat everything in the dressing.
5. Serve cold.

Tip: When using fruit, remember that they all have different sweetness, acidity, and bitterness levels. So, you should mix them in your salads with the right balance.

Snack Wraps

If you're looking for a quick and easy summer snack, try these snacks-wraps. They'll keep your hands free and your space tidy.

Ingredients:

- 1 whole wheat wrap (or tortilla)
- 1/2 teaspoon olive oil or melted butter
- 1/4 cup olives, sliced into rounds
- 1 tomato slice (you can use Roma)
- 1 leaf of lettuce
- 3 slices of cucumber
- 2 tablespoons hummus or guacamole
- Cucumbers for garnish (optional)

Directions:

1. Spread the wrap with hummus or guacamole.
2. Top with cabbage leaves, olives, cucumbers, tomatoes, and lettuce.
3. Roll the wrap-up and cut it into 1-inch (2.5 cm) pieces.
4. Garnish with cucumbers and serve.

Tips: Try adding cheese or meat to make the wraps more filling. You can use any kind of edible wraps, such as a tortilla, naan bread, or lettuce leaves. If you're not into veggies, replace the lettuce with another kind of leafy green. Cilantro is delicious, so definitely try that. You could also add fresh herbs like oregano, basil, or chives. This recipe is especially great for families with kids who might not like olives and cucumbers. You can also use a paring knife to cut the wraps into smaller pieces. Again, cut them as you wish, but keep the shape consistent.

For a super filling treat, add some crumbled goat or feta cheese (or both). You could also add red pepper flakes or a sprinkle of your favorite spice like chili powder, paprika, or salt.

Instead of tortillas or wraps, you could also try making pizzas with these same ingredients: whole wheat flour, vegetable oil spread (1/2 teaspoon), and yeast. Make sure that the dough is soft and pliable before using it to stretch over your rolled-up veggies.

Chapter 9: Midsummer, the Druid Way

How Druids Celebrate Midsummer

On Midsummer's Day, Druids light bonfires and celebrate the longest night of the year. The fire symbolizes the sun god, and traveling around them is a spiritual act to meditate on all that they represent. They call Midsummer Alban Hefin (pronounced AHL-Bahn HALF-fin), which means "holy eternal light."

Druids would gather in large groups at stone monuments called megaliths during midsummer. These stones are known by several names, including menhir, dolmen, and cairn. The original purpose of these megaliths is not known, but many believe that they were used for religious ceremonies. Similarly, it is said that Stonehenge is a place where the veil between life and death is thin, and many people visit this area to meditate on the cycles of life.

Today, many people in the UK celebrate midsummer by visiting Stonehenge. This ancient monument is over five thousand years old and is believed to have been used as a burial ground for many centuries before it became a place of worship around 3100 BC. During the gathering at Stonehenge, people wear white clothing and ride on horseback to celebrate midsummer. The Druids held meetings in stone circles to pray for healing, abundance, peace, and to honor Mother Earth. To this day, Stonehenge remains one of the most popular places to celebrate midsummer.

Druids celebrate Midsummer by choosing a beautiful tree and decorating it with flowers. They believe that trees are a symbol of growth and hope for nature. Druids also decorate their homes, gardens, temples, and other buildings with flower wreaths during midsummer to represent the circle of life.

During midsummer, Druids enjoy various fruits and vegetables to celebrate the harvest season. Many prepare a traditional feast of food from their local lands, including lamb, cabbage, and cakes made from wheat grain.

Differences between Wiccan Midsummer and Druidic Midsummer

Wiccan Midsummer represents the time when the Goddess separates light from dark and gives us the gift of life. The stage for this event is set by astronomical changes in both solar and lunar movements, which create opportunities for new beginnings on a personal and spiritual level.

However, Druidic Midsummer is more rooted in ancient Celtic beliefs. Litha is celebrated as sacred in this tradition because he represents rebirth, summer's final harvest, change from cold to warm weather, and masculine evolution into feminine energy that continues throughout the year; it's never too late to start anew.

The most important date in this season is June 21, the summer solstice, which marks the beginning of the Celtic new year. This day was always considered magical and is still celebrated with a variety of celebrations around the world; many Wiccans call it Wiccan Midsummer. Here are a few major differences and similarities between Wiccan Midsummer and Druidic Midsummer:

- Wiccan Midsummer does not celebrate the solstice, which is the darkest day of the year, unlike the Druidic Midsummer.

- Wiccan Midsummer celebrates only the first day of Litha. Druidic Midsummer has a 14-day period characterized by increased spiritual power and the use of more elaborate, more powerful, and more intense rituals. However, it is a very important period in both practices because it marks the beginning of summer and a sharp increase in fertility.

- Druidic Midsummer is more complex as physical and mental aspects are considered, whereas Wiccan practices relate to purely spiritual energy.
- Both Wiccan and Druidic Midsummer will include rituals, spells, and activities.
- Both will have a new moon and a full moon.
- The time frame of both celebrations is around the same.
- Tools and symbols used could be similar, although not identical in any way. However, there is also a huge difference between the use of stones, shells, and animals in Wicca compared to Druids.

Celebrating Alban Hefin

Many ancient cultures celebrated the start of the summer solstice and how it marks the coming of light by marking the day with rituals and festivities. Of course, druids were no exception to this rule. The Druids were known for having great respect for nature, which is why they believed that Litha starts when the Sun God strengthens his golden rays, and they are bright on all four seasons of the year. Litha is most important in Alban Hefin because it marks one of three high points in the druid's calendar: Midsummer (when Hefin dies) and Samhain (when he becomes reborn).

Since the Druids never celebrated any other holidays all year round, Litha always went through a great festivity. The celebrations may have varied from one place to the other, but a certain pattern continued into modern times. An oak branch would be lit on fire and burned until it all that was left was ashes. The ashes were then thrown far away, and another oak branch placed on top, ready to start the whole process again. As Litha was a holy day for druids, they wanted to show their respect for the sun by staying inside most of the time and fasting. They would also wear white clothes and a golden sickle.

There were some celebrations throughout the day, but the most important one took place in the evening. During that time, the druids formed a large circle where they would sing together. They would use a sort of cauldron as their instrument to announce the arrival of Litha. The songs were then followed by dances and magical rituals, during which they would try to contact the goddess of nature or her son, Arianrhod's child. It is believed that these two were responsible for giving life to plants and animals.

After all the rituals were performed, the Sun God would be sacrificed, and some of his blood used to water the earth. The gathered people then rejoiced and celebrated the fertility of nature. This celebration was common until the arrival of Christianity, when Christian priests managed to destroy this practice. Litha is not celebrated at all in many places today, or it has lost its original meaning.

Litha was one of the most important holidays for druids, but it is also one of the most important ones in modern times. The ancient ways were abandoned, but the idea that we should have a moment of reflection and enjoy nature's gifts can still be found in modern celebrations.

Alban Hefin Rituals

The sun is the ultimate source of life in Alban Hefin or Alban Hefin week. During this time, all who venerate The Great Mother will do what they can to make sure that she does not forget who created her and her duties. It's safe to say that these tasks are for one sole purpose: to honor and please the divine mother – The Sun, the giver of all life.

This list includes rituals for sunrise and sunset and a few important day-to-day tasks that take place throughout this week.

Sunrise/Sunset Meals

Bringing food to your ancestors is a daily ritual in Alban Hefin. Each day, either you or a family member will make sure they will bring food to the ancestors' mound. This ritual is done at the end of each day.

Once again, once the sun has risen and reaches its zenith, you will bring food to our ancestors. The exact rituals vary from household to household, but in general, it goes like this: You may either dig a small hole in the ground, put some soil down, and place a small amount of bread and water into it. Then you place a few coins in the middle. Then lay some food and water on top of this before finally covering it back up with earth.

While some believe that this ritual honors the ancestor spirits, others believe that these food offerings will nourish them and keep them alive if they don't consume them. Therefore, it's thought that if they refuse to eat it or do not return home, then they must be sad and lonely because of death in the family.

Sunrise/Sunset Fast

This is a very simple ritual that should only take a couple of minutes but can have massive impacts on someone's life if done wrong. This is because the Sun God has easy access to those who lie.

Throughout the morning and throughout the evening, the sun will shine down on us and ask if we have been able to fast from all meat and meat products. This must be done for a full week during Litha – or until you or a family member can complete this ritual. One must never lie while answering this question, as they will be cursed forever by their ancestors and the Sun god.

The Rite of Peace

This rite is almost identical to when we greet the sun at dawn, but it takes place at sunset and lasts until sunrise. This ritual is the start of Litha and marks the beginning of summer. It's a time to honor The Sun and all it brings with it, such as warmth and light.

At dusk, you'll greet the sun as you do at dawn. Then after sunset, you'll sit down and light a fire. Once you have done this, it's time to recite the Rite of Peace:

The sun has set and rose again, blessed be his life.

Our thanks for his gifts last night and this morning;

our thanks for life itself.

Our thanks for clear eyes to see the beauty he has given us.

Our thanks for health, which we now offer back to him;

our bodies in return for his bounty.

You may or may not cleanse yourself before you move on to the Fast of the Sun. It all depends on what you or your family believes.

Sunrise to Sunset Fasting

Like the Rite of Peace at dawn, this ritual is perfect for anyone who sits and watches over their ancestors' mound from sunset to sunrise. This ritual must be done during a full moon day in Litha. The best would be a Friday or Saturday during the full moon (the first or third one).

Rituals can be difficult for some, so this method is perfect for those uncomfortable with complex rituals. At sunset, as you would typically do when greeting The Sun, you simply get on your knees and say the following prayer:

Sun Father, may I have the courage to be honest with myself in all things.

May I have the strength to avoid harmful substances

and to pursue those things that will help me grow.

As I give of myself today,

please accept my sacrifice

and grant me your protection in my life.

All you really need to do is ask yourself if you have been able to fast from food or not. If so, then go ahead and wash before moving on to the next ritual. However, if not, and if a family member has completed it, then your ritual is done.

Sunrise/Sunset Offering

This ritual is like when you greet the sun at sunrise/sunset. During this ritual, you're simply making sure that the ancestors are fed, for it is their duty to protect you and your family. They will not do this if they are hungry or if they feel like they're being forgotten, so make sure that they are fed each night. This is done at sunset time. However, before you offer them food (which must be done on the evening of a full moon during Litha), be sure that your surroundings are arranged. They should be nice and clean as well as safe and protected from vandals of any form.

Ritual to Release Negativity during Alban Hefin

In this spell, you will make a great bonfire to prepare for the significant energy of Litha or Beltane. You will also make a fire to release unwanted thoughts and emotions.

This spell can be performed on all four quarters of the year with the use of a green branch such as oak, hazel, birch, or willow. You can choose to use other materials, but these are the ones most used by Druids in association with Litha.

You'll need:

- Green branch/firewood
- Cauldron or large fireproof bowl (either one will work, just be sure it's big enough to burn the branch)
- Water with sea salt or fresh water—it's up to you.
- The witch's tool of choices such as Athame, wand, sword, or staff (if you do not have a tool, you can simply use your hand)

Directions:

1. **With the Athame or Sword:** Hold the athame with both hands and slowly point it straight out in front of you, about 2 feet away from the bonfire. Then slowly raise it up to about 8 inches or one foot above the top of the fire. Repeat the following incantation (if using a sword, replace all the words that are in italics with either a few words or a phrase of your choosing): *Ahimsa, ahimsa, ahimsa.* This is repeated three times, after which you will bring the athame down and repeat *"So mote it be"* while lowering it into the fire.

2. **With the Staff or Wand**: Hold your staff with both hands and slowly move your staff above to just above eye level, as if you're brushing away negative energy with it. Then you will spin it sideways while

saying, *"By air and earth, by fire and water, sword and staff."* The words *"by sword and staff"* should be said while bringing your staff down sharply as if to cut through the negative thoughts and emotions. Repeat this three times while placing your hand above the bonfire.

3. **With Water or a Cauldron:** Hold a glass of water in your right hand or dip your right index finger into the water. Then with your left-hand point at the fire with that finger. This represents the element of fire being consumed by the element of air (water), which is done in respect of the Sun, which is at high wattage during this time of year. Afterward, place your right hand above the fire while saying, *"So mote it be."* Then pour a bit of the water into the fire and repeat *"So mote it be"* three times.

4. **Using the Green Branch or Firewood:** Once you've finished with any one of those three methods, place your green branch or firewood into the fire and repeat the following incantation: *"Earth and sky, air and sea, burn up all my strife. By witch's will, so mote it be."*

5. Then, you may sit back and bask in the warmth of the fire, or if you have a bonfire on your property, enjoy it from a distance.

Tips: If you're not using a bonfire outside, light your fireplace and place a green branch or firewood into it. Do not use flammable materials for this spell. Green branches are used because they contain negative emotions and thoughts that will be burned away by the fire. You want all those feelings to be released on this night so that you can become whole once again. Feel free to sit next to the fireplace or insert yourself into it while doing this spell if possible.

Do not use branches from the Yew tree for this or any other spell, as it is a poisonous tree. However, burning branches from the birch tree are said to be good for protection against psychic attacks.

Chapter 10: Midsummer Spells, Charms, and Rituals

Litha Love Spell

If you use this spell on Litha, you will be involved in a romantic relationship with someone who is already attracted to you, and that person will be a good match for you. You will both be strongly drawn to one another, and if everything else goes right, your relationship will flourish with passion and love.

You'll need:

- A tall urn (can be small like a vase if you prefer)
- Fresh flowers (whatever blooms in the season of Litha)
- honey

Directions:

1. An hour before sunset on Litha, fill your urn with fresh water and set it outside to catch the sun's rays, then pour out the water.
2. Place your flowers next to it.
3. An hour later, fill up your urn again with fresh water and place it in the center of your flower arrangement.

4. Add a tablespoon of honey to your urn (it acts as an offering to the Gods).

5. Pour out the water again and let it sit. Put flowers in the urn. You must do this ritual on the night of Litha since it involves sun magic, but it would still be nice to keep your urn with flowers and water in after Litha is over so you can use it as an offering during any other full moon or sabbat.

Tips: This spell is best performed at night and on a full moon or sabbat of summer. It is important to have the same intention each time, so make sure you have a clear intention of what you want to happen between you and the person of your desire. It is important to evaluate your own intentions and motivations before performing this love spell and that you can make sure there are no negative feelings involved. For example, if you're extremely jealous and controlling of the other person, it can backfire, and again, if you use dark magic to power your love spell, it will backfire.

Litha Love Rekindling Spell

The love rekindling spell can be done on Litha for any type of love.

You'll need:

- A small handful of dried love grass
- A red ribbon
- One small candle lit in your altar space
- Purple carnations (optional)

Directions:

1. Light the candle and utter these words: "Love, I call to you. As I kindle this flame, may my love burn brightly once more."

2. Gather the dried grass into a pile on your altar space.

3. Place the red ribbon over it and knot it at one end to form a ceremonial wreath, then wind around until you have made a complete circle with it.

4. Light the candle and place it in the center of the wreath.

5. Allow the flame to consume it.

6. When you're finished, toss your wreath's smoldering remains into a fire or out at sea as an offering to Gaia.

Tips: You may enjoy this spell with a meal of freshly brewed love potion tea. Add one teaspoon of crumbled dried love grass to a cup of water and steep for five minutes, then drink up to three cups daily (one cup before bedtime, one in the morning, and another early in the day).

Litha Healing Spell

Use this spell when you're feeling a little unwell or if someone else doesn't feel so good. To be clear, this is not a replacement for seeing a medical professional.

You'll need:

- One quartz stone
- One copper wire
- Six small cotton balls soaked in sage oil
- Two drops of bergamot essential oil or flowers (rose, lavender)
- 1/4 teaspoon dried blueberries or cinnamon sticks.

Directions:

1. At dusk on the night of the full moon, ground your first stone into a fine powder using a mortar and pestle. You can also use a blender to crush it up if you want it in pow
2. der form.
3. In one part of the powder, mix two drops of bergamot with two drops of sage oil. In another area of the powder, mix in the blueberries and cinnamon.
4. Separate six cotton balls and dip each one into sage oil for one second. Then place a small amount of your ground stone mixture into the center of each cotton ball. Lay them out on a piece of parchment paper and let them dry overnight.
5. Cut a small piece off the copper wire, then roll it around itself and form it into a circle.
6. Create a small hole at the top of the circle about two inches above the cotton balls. Thread your wire through and knot it at the bottom. Leave your healing circle out until the next morning, when you can take it in to add to your Litha altar.
7. To use your healing circle, hold both ends of the wire in one hand and place your other hand over the hole at the top. Ground yourself, then call upon the energies of Litha to work their magic and join you in this healing circle.
8. Once you're finished with your spell, wrap it back up in the parchment paper to store it until next year. Replace the cotton balls with fresh ones every night during Litha.

Litha Money Spell

You'll need:

- A white candle
- A red candle
- A green candle
- Myrrh oil with your favorite incense (optional)
- Money to represent your desires

Directions:

1. Think about their needs, obstacles, passions, and how you can make them more prosperous.

2. Visualize yourself as a powerful being who is using divination tools to bring success and good fortune into their lives.

3. Light the red candle, and as you do, imagine the power of Litha radiating from it to empower your spell work.

4. Look at the white candle. Imagine your best desire coming true as you light it with the red candle, representing the merging of your energy with your desire's energy.

5. Light the green candle with the red candle and feel the abundance of nature flowing into your life. Feel appreciation for the good to come your way as if it's already happened.

6. Align yourself with the powers of divination by putting a bit of myrrh on the coal in the incense burner.

7. Take the white candle in your hand. Visualize white energy flowing into, out of, and around you as you say: *"I open myself to all who circle me. I ask for protection from those who would wish me harm and invite prosperity from those who can give it."*

8. Take a deep breath, then say: *"Litha is upon me now! The seasons turn, and winter grows old! I welcome in new beginnings and seek out my success!"*

9. Take the green candle in your hands. Visualize green energy flowing out of, into, and around you as you say: *"Green candle, I set thee to burn for me! May it bring success and prosperity this coming year, especially for my deepest secret wish."*

10. Now take the red candle, visualize powerful red energy flowing all over you, into you, and out of you. Understand that this power will attract prosperity and success into your life. Feel it within you and visualize the red energy mingling with the green and white.

11. Don't forget to visualize yourself being successful in the end to get what you want. For example, if you wish for a promotion at work or to find a great new job, visualize being a manager or signing that big contract for your business.

12. Set the red candle down and hold your hands over the flames at a safe distance, receiving the power of the flames and imbuing them with your intent, saying: *"Litha is my guide, and I am now open to all the goodness and abundance she has to offer me."*

Use this ritual several days in a row to help make your wishes come true.

Litha Protection Charm

You'll need:

- A packet of salt
- Water
- An item for your power (Sword, wand, staff, etc.)
- Matches or a lighter

Directions:

1. Pour the packet of salt into the water to dissolve it and then carry that water outs
2. ide.
3. Erect a circle around yourself that you will not step out from until the ritual is complete.
4. Bring the item you want to magnetize to your center.
5. As you say the incantations, draw the item to yourself.
6. After you have done this several times, let go of the item and allow it to return to its natural location or continue moving in whatever direction it desires outside your circle.

The spell will only work if you follow all these steps with exactness and is moderately difficult.

Litha Charms

Protection Charm

The spell should be cast during either sunrise or sunset but no later than 4 pm.

You'll need:

- 1 White Widow Spider
- 1 White Rose Petal

- 3 Dried coriander Seeds, tied together with a red ribbon
- 3 Dried sunflower Seeds, tied together with a yellow ribbon
- Thyme minced and mixed with olive oil

Directions:

1. Find a sunny spot to set up the altar and prepare the charm by placing the seeds on your altar.

2. Place the spider so it faces the seeds with its body while being held by its legs close to your chest or neck. This helps you absorb its power while you're casting the spell:

   Sun King, I call you in

   While thy light doeth shine so bright

   Let my heart be neat and pure

   Sun King, I call thee in!

Litha, Good Luck Charm

You'll need:

- A sprig of yarrow
- A piece of white cloth
- A picture or a representation of the sun (gold paper, a small urn, etc.)
- A length of red thread or ribbon
- A jar with an airtight lid

Directions

1. Prepare the cloth by folding it over and cutting it three times with scissors so that there are six pieces.

2. Fold these pieces in half, then fold them again in half so that it's three strips.

3. Fold the outer edges of all three strips under. After that, you'll be left with a circle with straight edges.

4. Place the pieces of cloth inside so that their length is just below the rim of your jar (or whatever you're using to store your charm).

5. Put a piece of yarrow on top, covering the circles, and make sure they are touching.

6. Add the sun's picture or representation, making sure that it is visible by placing it in such a way that you can see most of it through the space provided above and between the cloth pieces.

7. Tie your charm with a piece of red thread or ribbon so that you can pull on it to remove the charm when you wish to use it.

8. Then, fill your jar with salt water until the cloth pieces sit below the rim, and then seal it with a lid. The lid should be put on tightly enough for no water to leak out but not too hard to break the jar. If any water leaks out, just wipe it up with a dry cloth or replace the lid with another one from an unused jar.

Tips: Use this charm on the first Saturday of Litha to take the sun's picture outside for good fortune and for protection against evil. You can also use this on Christmas Eve to bring wealth and happiness into your life. Your wish will come true if you use it during Litha and every day with a red thread tied around it. The red ribbon is to bring money into people's lives and to help them in their financial dealings during the coming year.

Litha Solar Plexus Bath

This bath will make you feel powerful as the energy from the Sun radiates through your body in this ebb and flow. Do this bath every morning for a few weeks before Litha to help your Solar Plexus Chakra.

You'll need:

- 2 pounds Epsom salt
- 1 tablespoon each of lemon, lime, and grapefruit peel
- ⅔ cup baking soda
- 3 tbsp lavender flowers or rosemary leaves
- 10 drops lemon essential oil
- 1 tablespoon mint extract (or to taste)
- ½ pint honey or maple syrup
- Other herbs of your choosing (basil, bay, bergamot, cedar, clary sage, and frankincense)

Directions:

1. Mix the Epsom salt and baking soda in a bowl, then stir in the other essential oils.

2. Then sprinkle the bath with the fruits, flowers, and herbs.

3. Pour some honey or maple syrup into your bath, and then sit for at least 15 minutes. Or you can simply pour in as much as your body will absorb.

4. When you're done, dry yourself with your towel. Then grab another one and pat down your entire body to get the extra oil off, but don't rub it into your skin.

Litha Spiritual Awakening Bath

You'll need:

- 1-quart size jar
- 2 cloves
- 6 cloves of garlic
- ¼ teaspoon salt
- 3 tablespoons dried thyme
- 3 tablespoons dried basil flakes
- 4 tablespoons extra virgin olive oil
- 4 cups of boiling water
- 12 drops of lavender essential oil

Directions:

1. Fill the jar with herbs and spices.
2. Add the salt, garlic, and thyme to the jar.
3. Then add 1/4 cup of olive oil.
4. Pour in 3 quarts of boiling water into the jar, then top it off with 6 drops of lavender essential oil.
5. Place this lid on top and shake well until all ingredients are mixed.
6. Let sit in a cool dark place for 24 hours before using.

Tips: It is advised to change the water of the herbal mixture once every week or two.

This mixture can be added to your bath to soak in it, or you can add it to your natural bath salts. Unbreakable glass jars are highly recommended for long-term storage as they are sturdy and less apt to break compared to plastic. This mixture can be stored for about 4 months.

Midsummer Quick Reference Sheet
The Gods and Goddesses of Litha

Though there are many more – here are a few gods/goddesses of Litha:

- Apollo
- Pan
- Diana/Artemis (depending on which you think is the serpent)
- Hecate or Juno Lucina (depends on whether you consider them goddesses of fertility, childbirth, or sunset)

- Pales (a goat-god who watches over herds and flocks – also a personification of shepherds and shepherding)
- Sylvanus or Silvanus (identifying the oak tree with the god of wild nature)
- Mercurius (pertaining to Mercury)

The Colors of Litha

- **Blue:** A cool color, like ice. It can also be associated with water and birth. Some people associate blue with tranquility, peace, serenity, etc.
- **Green:** Represents life and growth. Nature's symbols include green plants such as trees, grasses, and flowers.
- **Yellow:** Represents happiness and lightness in many cultures around the world; however, not all cultures use yellow for this purpose (for example, America). It can be considered a golden hue like sunshine or amber that some see as comforting in contrast to dark colors that tend to be depressing or sad in nature (black).
- **Red:** A high-energy color representing danger and aggression in many cultures. However, in America, it represents love, and in China, it represents happiness.

Litha Symbols and Correspondences

- Alchemical Planet: Sun
- Element: Magick
- Fire Astrological Signs: Leo, Aries

Litha Trees

Aspen, birch, cedar, chestnut, cypress, hazelnut, holly, hornbeam, juniper, maple, oak, pecan, pin, post, oak, willow, witch hazel, yucca.

Litha Plants and Flowers

Elderflowers, lilies of the Valleys, white-flowered vetchling (Vicia alba), bronze-leafed vetchling (Vicia ursina), violet plume or violet head (Verbascum phoeniceum).

Part 6: Lammas

The Ultimate Guide to Lughnasadh and How It's Celebrated in Wicca, Druidry, and Celtic Paganism

MARI SILVA

LAMMAS

BLESSED LAMMAS!

THE ULTIMATE GUIDE TO
LUGHNASADH AND HOW IT'S
CELEBRATED IN WICCA,
DRUIDRY, AND CELTIC PAGANISM

Introduction

There is a rich and intricate history to the pagan lore encompassing the Wiccan, Druidic, and Celtic religions. They all stem from the same Gaelic roots, originating in Ireland, Scotland, and various other parts of the British Isles. These religions predate Christianity, which eventually spread across Europe, supplanting the native traditions with their versions of the rituals, ceremonies, and mythology practiced there. The festival of Lughnasadh was one such holiday that was absorbed and adapted by the Christians into Lammas.

For anyone interested in the modern-day pagan religions, this book can serve as a fantastic guide as you delve deeper into practicing the celebrations of their important festivals – Lughnasadh in particular. While it can seem overwhelming to get all the preparations and rites for proper observation of Lughnasadh correct, you will find that once everything has been broken down into its individual components, it will be much easier to comprehend.

To understand this guide, you don't need to be an expert in Wicca, Druidry, or Celtic paganism. It will provide all the necessary information concerning Lughnasadh and Lammas, including a comprehensive background to help you grasp what it is and why it's so important to these pagan religions. You must respect their beliefs when attempting to celebrate these rituals on your own. Doing it right isn't so much a matter of success or failure but more following the traditions as practitioners have done for centuries.

One of the best parts about Wicca, Druidry, and Celtic paganism is the DIY ethos encompassing their practices. You don't need to spend a lot of money to carry out their rituals, and finding or creating the necessary materials for spells and charms is highly encouraged. Much of the religion involves personalization, meaning the involvement of objects or prayers tailored specifically to you. The power of nature is a major aspect of their belief system, so instead of worshiping a single, omnipotent deity, you will invoke the spirits of the earth itself.

Unlike other guides, this one offers step-by-step instructions on carrying out the rites associated with Lughnasadh and Lammas. Learning the basics about a ritual isn't enough to participate – you need to be able to perform them. From the reagents required and constructing your altar to the specific prayers and blessings, you'll receive a complete education on celebrating these feasts and holidays.

The beliefs held by pagans permeate their physical, mental, emotional, and spiritual beings, helping to create a very well-rounded person. Every aspect of your life can be directed by the ideals of living in harmony with nature, tapping into a power deep within yourself. Magic is about enacting change, both internally and externally, so you must be willing to work on both to keep everything in balance. As you delve into your exploration of paganism, you will find that it offers many benefits in the short-term and long-term.

Celebrating Lughnasadh and Lammas means taking your first steps into a world of an ancient culture that has existed longer than many other religious traditions. Its popularity has spread far beyond the scope of its origins, greatly enhanced by the advent of the internet and the ease with which information can be shared. The barrier of entry for Wiccan, Druidry, and Celtic paganism is very low – so long as you have the desire to participate and sincere respect for the culture, you will be welcomed with open arms.

Chapter 1: Introduction to Lughnasadh and Lammas

Before we begin our exploration of the beliefs, traditions, and celebrations of Lughnasadh, it will be beneficial to have a clear understanding of what each neopagan religion is about. There can be similarities between the religions, but they are different enough to all stand in their own right. We're focused on three: Wicca, Druidry, and Celtic paganism.

Defining Wicca

The traditions of Wicca – as they are today – were first established in the middle of the 20th century. It is a duo-theistic religion, venerating various aspects of the Triple Goddess and the Horned God. Those who practice Wicca heavily emphasize the cycles of the moon and the sun. Themes involving the moon and sun play a part in the ritual magic performed by followers of Wicca, with the interplay between darkness and light, or night and day, being a core concept.

Wicca is a duo-theistic religion.
https://unsplash.com/photos/-AfRBlhuaHE

The cycle of life, death, and rebirth is another facet of Wicca that many practitioners focus on. The dominant view is that people will be reincarnated after they die, rather than moving on to an afterlife or plane of existence espoused by religions such as Christianity, Norse paganism, or Greek paganism. Such cycles are often seen on micro and macro levels, like a plant's lifespan or the ever-changing seasons.

Many Wiccans follow an ideal known as the "Wiccan Rede," which states: "An ye harm none, do what ye will." In the context of Wicca, it means that if whatever you wish to do won't bring harm upon anyone, you're free to do as you please. Another prevailing concept is that of the "Threefold Return." This claims that whatever energy you put out into the world will be returned to you with three times the power. Outside of these basic ideas, there are no governing principles within Wicca. There is no firm hierarchy to the religion, and anyone is welcome to join.

Defining Druidry

Druidry is a religion that focuses on protecting, preserving, and restoring the natural world. They seek to spark creativity, acquire great wisdom, and live in harmony with the earth. To personify these desires, druids have three figures: the Singer, the Sage, and the Shaman. Every druid should strive to encompass all three aspects, bringing them together to work hand in hand toward a better future for everyone. Philanthropic causes and fraternal bonds are major facets of their religion.

Since Druidry predates Christianity, its practitioners have existed for many centuries. However, with the advent of Christian missions to the British Isles, most druids were driven underground by the end of the 7th century. It wasn't until the early-1700s that it began to make a popular comeback. The foundations of modern Druidry were established by those who felt disenchanted by other organized religions. Its resurgence is owed to scholars delving deeper into the history of druids and paganism and a greater general awareness of the finite nature of the Earth's resources. Anyone who desires to live in balance with the natural world might find that Druidry suits them.

Defining Celtic Paganism

Celtic paganism has similar roots to Druidry, established by the ancient Gaelic and Celtic tribes who resided in Britain, Scotland, and Ireland before the 3rd century. Druidry and modern Celtic paganism differ in how closely practitioners attempt to recreate the rituals and traditions of the ancient religion. Druidry is more concerned with working in the present and safeguarding the future, while Celtic pagans deeply respect the past.

The number three is very important to Celtic paganism. Many deities are assigned three faces or three aspects. Animals and agriculture are common components of the religion, and the ancient Celtic pagans practiced animal sacrifices. The modern revivals typically replace living animals with effigies to perform sacrificial rituals. Most rites involving food offerings or sacrifices continue to be used, especially during the Sabbats, like Lughnasadh.

The Celtic pagan afterlife consists of two parts: the Otherworld and transmigration. The Otherworld is a realm of fairy folk, elves, and other supernatural beings. The gods worshiped are generally believed to come from the Otherworld. Transmigration involves the energy of a person, usually represented by the soul, being recycled to create new life. It is similar to reincarnation, except rather than the same soul inhabiting a new physical body, the abstract matter is broken apart and reformed into an entirely new soul.

Lughnasadh, Lammas, and the Sabbats

Eight major festivals, also known as "Sabbats," are celebrated in the pagan religions that coincide with specific seasonal events meant to mark important milestones throughout the year. Together, these festivals are known as the Wheel of the Year. These include Litha, Imbolc, Yule Beltaine, Lughnasadh, Ostara, Samhain, and Mabon. The one this guide will focus on is Lughnasadh, as well as its Christian counterpart, Lammas.

Lughnasadh starts off the three main festivals celebrated by Wiccans. The other two are Mabon and Samhain, both falling within the autumn section of the Wheel of the Year. This is a cyclical system, and each festival has a corresponding opposite. For Lughnasadh, that is Imbolc, which denotes the start of the spring and sowing season. Just like human beings, the seasons follow the natural path of birth, maturity, and death. Where Imbolc symbolizes birth, and Beltane maturity, the act of reaping fully-grown crops makes Lughnasadh akin to death.

The second Wiccan festival is Mabon, which coincides with the autumnal equinox – the midpoint between the three festivals. This is generally between September 21st-24th. It's a Thanksgiving feast, where Wiccans make offerings to the gods to bless them for the winter. If Lughnasadh represents a physical death, Mabon symbolizes the period of mourning, when a person's spirit has left its corporeal form but lingers on as a spirit.

Samhain is the third of the Wiccan festivals, celebrated on November 1st. Due to its proximity to Halloween, many people conflate the two, but in practice, it's closer to the Christian holiday of All Saints' Day. On Samhain, practitioners venerate those that have passed on, including their ancestors, family, friends, pets, and elders. This is done to help those who have died pass on to the afterlife. As a major pagan festival, it is also considered a day of darkness, set directly opposite the Wheel of the Year to Beltane, which is a day of light.

What Is Lughnasadh?

Lughnasadh is the first of the autumnal festivals, usually celebrated on or around August 1st. It marks the beginning of the harvest season, occurring at the midpoint between the summer solstice and the autumnal equinox. The Celtic pagans began celebrating Lughnasadh as far back as at least the 15th century, with the festival being mentioned in Irish literature dated from around that time. A tale in the Ulster Cycle known as Tochmarc Emire, or the Wooing of Emir, describes the festival as a celebration of a wedding feast in honor of the pagan god, Lugh.

Lugh is one of the Tuatha Dé Danann, a race of supernatural beings that can be considered the Celtic pantheon. He is the patron god of warriors and artisans, revered for his skill as a fighter and craftsman. Lugh also is often viewed as the protector of sworn oaths and contracts. If one were to break their word, it would be Lugh's wrath that they would face. Lughnasadh is named after him, meaning "Lugh's assembly."

It is believed that the festival originated as either a wedding feast for Lugh himself or a funeral feast for his foster mother, Tailtiu. During Lughnasadh, an athletic competition may be held similar to the games described in the Iliad when Achilles holds them in honor of the fallen Patroclus to ensure his spirit can move on to the afterlife. They were known as the Tailteann Games and usually held in Tailtin, now called Teltown, in County Meath.

What Is Lammas?

Lammas, also called Lammas Day and Loaf Mass Day, is the Christian equivalent of Lughnasadh. Like its counterpart, Lammas celebrates the start of the harvest season, or the "First Fruits of Harvest," as it's called on the liturgical calendar. This refers to the loaf of bread used during the rite of Holy Communion, where church members receive the Eucharist or the body of Christ. Modern pagans tend to use the names Lughnasadh and Lammas interchangeably.

The concept of Lammas was that Christians would bring a loaf of bread that was made with the newly-harvested wheat crop to the church, where the priests would bless it. This was meant to help ensure a bountiful harvest season for those who brought in a loaf. It is unclear when the traditional celebration of Lammas began, but there are accounts from the 16th century where it is mentioned in reference to the start of the harvest season. In William Shakespeare's Romeo and Juliet, Juliet Capulet is said to have been born on Lammas Eve.

In the Norse pagan religion of Asatru, a festival celebrated on July 31st or August 1st is called Freysblot, or the Freyfest. Similar to Lammas Day in Christianity, it involves the first grains harvested and loaves of bread made from these grains, which were then sacrificed to the gods to receive their blessing. The Freyfest is also one of eight festivals, as with Lughnasadh, and includes a wheel to represent the cycle of the changing seasons throughout the year.

Lughnasadh and Lammas Then

During the early days of Celtic paganism, Lughnasadh celebrations were depicted as a struggle between the god Crom Dubh, who sought to protect the grain from being harvested, and Lugh, who fought to bring the grain to his followers so they could stay fed throughout the winter. Some of the rituals practiced by the pagans included singing, dancing, eating, drinking, playing folk music, encouraging coupling, and making a journey up one of Ireland or Scotland's vast mountains. Sporting contests were also very popular, with games like horse racing, weight throwing, caber tossing, and hurling.

When the pagans celebrated, Lughnasadh would climb a mountain and would often wear flowers themselves. Once they reached the top, they would bury the flowers, signifying the end of summer and the start of autumn, when the plant life would start to wilt and die. Sparring was another favorite activity during this festival, although they usually fought with sticks instead of battlefield weaponry.

Some pagans would also pay a visit to holy wells, dropping coins into them and praying for their good health, their loved ones, and their crops. This and the trek up the mountains transformed into the idea of pilgrimages when Christianity rose to prominence. This supplanted the celebration of the pagan gods in favor of Christian martyrs and saints. However, the pagans continued to hold the Lughnasadh festivals, maintaining their original traditions.

The feasts during Lughnasadh would include food prepared with the freshly-harvested crops, which the pagans believed would confer a blessing from the gods upon their households. In Scotland, this took the form of the lunastain, a special cake used as an offering. This practice was later adopted by the Christians and other pagans, which is why the names "Lughnasadh", and "Lammas" are used interchangeably by modern pagans.

One ritual for preparing the bread and cakes for the feast involved a meticulously decorated altar adorned with symbols of the harvest season: scythes used for reaping, corn, apples, grapes, or other foods gathered at this time of year, and leaves changing color. After the altar was completed, a circle would be drawn around it, and a blessing given to thank the earth.

Once the ritual was over, the people would break bread with one another, initiating the feast to come.

Lughnasadh and Lammas Now

The modern-day celebration of Lughnasadh is similar to that of the older traditions, with singing, dancing, traditional folk music, eating, and drinking. Where it differs is in the use of animals. While a traditional festival queen is chosen from the local girls, a goat takes the crown as king. There will also be other celebrations: fairs, parades, markets, and more. The festivities commence as soon as the sun goes down the night before Lughnasadh.

Many neopagans incorporate aspects from other festivals that occur around the same time in other religions, like Christianity and Asatru. This has widened the scope of what is celebrated, from honoring Lugh and the upcoming harvest to a more general day of giving thanks and seeking blessings for the winter to come. Wiccans, Druids, and Celtic pagans each have their own variation of the modern celebration as well.

In Wicca, both names for the festival are used for the same day in their calendar. It is considered a major period for the act of betrothal in their religion, which is called handfasting. They will also make a figure out of baked bread that is known as the corn god. It is sacrificed and consumed ceremonially to gain the blessing of this god for a successful harvest.

Druids celebrate Lughnasadh and Lammas as one of their four fire festivals, the others being Imbolc, Beltaine, and Samhain. This is based on the story of Cú Chulainn, a demigod from the Ulster Cycle, attempting to woo Emer. She tells him that to win her favor, he must remain awake for an entire year. Instead of choosing dates like the solstices or equinoxes, she lists these four festivals, each corresponding to the beginning of the four seasons. They often strive to recreate the traditional celebratory activities as closely as possible.

Some neopagans have attempted to strip away the influences of Christianity, returning their practices to the traditions of the old Celtic pagans. They have reconstructed the rituals and beliefs based on historical accounts and the facets of Gaelic celebrations known to have been used since pre-Christianity. Unfortunately, written sources are not easy to come by, so there is no way to gauge the accuracy of their reconstructions. Most neopagans strive to honor the spirit of the traditions, even if they cannot reenact the celebrations precisely.

Materials of the Lughnasadh Festival

One of the most important aspects of Lughnasadh and Lammas is the various trappings and accouterments involved in the celebrations. Symbols are given high regard in the pagan religions, stemming from the fact that many of their members in the pre-Christian era were not literate. To understand the rituals and beliefs, symbols needed to be used as a way to communicate across many tribes, clans, and cultures. When groups often spoke widely different dialects of the Gaelic languages, they could still use universal symbology to correspond with one another.

Incense, herbs, and other plants were employed in the rituals and blessings during the festival, as this was a common part of paganism in general. Certain herbs and plants are believed to confer a particular outcome for different needs. Incense is meant to help purify the soul and ward off evil spirits, which is necessary when performing a protection spell or asking for a blessing. Pagans lived an agrarian and agricultural lifestyle, so plants and crops were always a major aspect of their daily lives.

The tools of Lughnasadh include candles, stones, and crystals. These comprise a significant portion of the celebrations, as these tools are imbued with meaning in their implementation. Animals play a large role in the rituals as well. Like most pre-industrial societies, the pagans utilized animals for many reasons, from transportation and moving goods to aid in tending their crops. They also provided food, such as eggs, milk, and meat, and their pelts would be crafted into items like clothing and tents.

Chapter 2: Lammas Deities and Lore

Lugh is the primary deity honored during Lughnasadh and Lammas, but he is not the only one. There is also his foster mother, Tailtiu, whose funeral is sometimes cited as the origin of Lughnasadh; Crom Dubh, who protected the grains from mortal hands; and the Grain Mother. Neopagans have also adopted Brighid as part of those worshiped during Lughnasadh. As with most religions, the pagan deities play an important role in their culture and faith. The gods are believed to be able to grant blessings to those who venerate them, and the myths associated with them offer morals and lessons that help shape the way people are expected to conduct themselves.

Many of the stories involving these gods conform to the universal archetypes found throughout most religions around the world, which made it easier for other cultures to transplant aspects of their own gods onto the pagan deities. When the ancient Romans invaded the British Isles, they projected their pantheon, largely adopted from the ancient Greek pantheon, onto those worshiped by the pagans. They found common traits shared between gods – or adjusted certain pagan gods to fit with their Roman counterparts based on their societal role.

The deities and lore are important.
https://picryl.com/media/ivan-bilibin-114-74a938

A conquering culture associating their own deities and lore with that of those they conquered was a common tactic to encourage a smoother transition between independence and subjugation. When a monotheistic culture such as Christianity spread to the pagan world, they chose to supplant some of the gods with saints, while others had their role in society diminished or were simply eliminated. In the case of Christianity's rise in the Gaelic regions of Great Britain and Ireland, they often adopted the festivals associated with pagan deities into holidays that celebrated a saint and the general beliefs but removed any association to the pantheon.

Due to the archetypal nature of many religious stories and iconography, these facets could be incorporated into the new religion. This sometimes resulted in an evolution of traditions that conflated both pagan and monotheistic beliefs into an amalgamation of ideas. Further obfuscating the matter is the fact that written records of pre-Christian paganism are rare, so there are only bits and pieces of the original traditions available today. In some cases, even these were documented many years, sometimes centuries, after the practices were commonplace.

A major source of the geography and ethnography in the pre-Christian Gaelic regions comes from the Agricola, written by the Roman historian Tacitus over half a century after the Roman conquest of Britain. He never set foot on the British Isles, basing his descriptions on the accounts related to him by his father-in-law, Agricola, who was an important general during the Roman campaign to subjugate the Britons. As this information came second-hand from a non-Gaelic source, many years after his time in the region, it is impossible to verify the accuracy of the depictions within this work, but it is still the best look available at Celtic paganism during that period.

Since it is difficult to determine which parts of the recorded traditions came from the original pagan religion and which have been corrupted by conquering societies, historians tend to rely on deduction techniques to reconcile the two. They will look at the oldest accounts describing parts of a particular myth or tradition, comparing them with the later versions that had been merged with other cultural depictions, and filter out the non-pagan influences to the best of their ability. Unfortunately, so much has been lost to time, but the snippets of pagan lore that have survived paint a vivid picture of a people who held strong ideals, valuing their families, ancestors, and nature.

Lugh

As the King of the Tuatha Dé Danann, he holds an incredibly important position within the pagan religions. In his youth, he was said to be a skilled warrior, using his large size and talent for wielding a spear on horseback to decimate his enemies. Lugh has also been described as exceptionally beautiful, owing to his ethereal nature. One source states that he had curly yellow hair and white skin, often appearing garbed in a green cloak fastened by a silver brooch. After becoming king, he added royal regalia to his dress.

Although he was born to Cian, a member of the Tuatha Dé Danann, he was given to Tailtiu, who was the Queen of the Fir Bolg, for her to foster him as part of an alliance between two dynastic powers. Lugh was raised among the Fir Bolg, where he developed his prowess as a warrior. However, he longed to return home and take his place as one of the Tuatha Dé Danann, so he made the journey to the Hill of Tara, where King Nuada was holding court.

The only way the sentry guarding the gates of Tara would allow Lugh to enter was if he possessed some skill that would benefit the king. He took up the challenge, offering his sword-fighting, smithing, magic, musical, and historical skills, among many others. Since the Tuatha Dé Danann already had members capable of these things, Lugh was denied entry. It was only when he pointed out that the Tuatha Dé Danann might have people who could do one of each skill they lacked, an individual who excelled at them all. This won over the sentry, and Lugh was granted access to the king.

At some point, Lugh acquired his most famous weapon: the Spear of Assal. It was made of yew and imbued with an enchantment allowing him to always hit his mark and return to his hand on command. By some accounts, it was claimed whoever wielded the spear could never be defeated in battle. One story states that the tip of Lugh's spear needed to remain submerged in water when not in use; otherwise, it would burst into flames. This presumably meant that when fighting in battles, his weapon would ignite, allowing him to wield fire against his foes.

The importance of animals in pagan traditions is reflected in Lugh's horse and hound. His horse was named Aenbharr, given to him as a gift by Manannán mac Lir, the Tuatha Dé Danann god of the sea. Aenbharr could travel over both the land and water at great speeds. Lugh's hound, Failinis, was an invincible beast on the battlefield and never failed to catch its quarry during a hunt. It was also said that Failinis could transform water into wine by bathing in it.

Lugh is also famous for being the father of the demigod hero Cú Chulainn, a major character and hero in the Ulster Cycle mythos. Cú Chulainn inherited his sire's skill as a warrior, spending much of his life vying against the enemies of the King of Ulster, Conchobar mac Nessa. Cú Chulainn also used a formidable spear in battle, and when the king and all his warriors had a curse placed on them, making them unable to fight against the invading forces of Queen Medb, it was Cú Chulainn alone who fended them off.

During the Roman conquest of Britain, Julius Caesar compared Lugh to the Roman god Mercury due to their shared association with crafting and the arts. Others conflated him with Mars, the Roman god of war. Christianity supplanted him with St. Mologa, an Irish saint who supposedly lived during the 7th century and was noted to possess healing powers beyond those of the druids. Other religions have also made comparisons to their own deities, such as Lleu Llaw Gyffes from Welsh mythology or the Norse gods Thor, Loki, and Baldr.

Tailtiu

Tailtiu was noted as the wife of Eochaid mac Eirc, the last of the Fir Bolg High Kings of Ireland. The capital of Eochaid's kingdom was named Teltown in her honor and remains there to this day. When the Tuatha Dé Danann sought an alliance with the Fir Bolg, they offered Lugh to Tailtiu as a foster son, allowing him to grow up immersed in Fir Bolg culture. He came to love her dearly, viewing her as his real mother. Tailtiu is associated with agricultural prosperity, connecting her directly to the festival of Lughnasadh.

One tale recounting the origin of Lughnasadh shows Tailtiu clearing out the fields of Ireland to grant mortals a place to plant and grow their crops. She expends all of her energy during this task, eventually dying from exhaustion. This event triggered Lugh to establish a harvest feast and funeral celebration in her honor, later transforming into the traditional festival of Lughnasadh. This is why the Tailtin Fair, a festival of games and competitions, was held at Teltown in pre-Christian times and later resurrected by neopagans in the 20th century.

There are several important "mother goddesses" in the Celtic pagan religions, and Tailtiu is considered one of them. Most mother goddesses are characterized by their association with the earth and nature, which Tailtiu qualified for through her agricultural efforts. She can also be viewed as one aspect of the Triple Goddess, known in Irish mythology as the Morrígan. There are three components: Mother, Maiden, and Crone – representing the three ages of a woman's life. Tailtiu is most commonly connected to the Mother aspect, particularly in her rearing of Lugh.

Although there aren't any definitive non-pagan deities conflated with Tailtiu, certain facets of her story are shared with figures from other mythologies. The Norse goddess Freya is considered an agricultural and fertility deity, and she also has a harvest festival that takes place around the same time as Lughnasadh. She is the wife of Odin and mother of Thor, giving her a similar role to Tailtiu in her importance in raising a chief hero in their respective religions. Persephone of the Greek pantheon shares Tailtiu's position as a goddess of agriculture, but where Tailtiu is most often depicted as a mother, Persephone is considered a maiden.

Crom Dubh

Crom Dubh is an interesting member of the pagan pantheon, as he is shown to be both a positive and negative figure throughout the mythos. His name means the "black, crooked one," and he was the god of sacrifice. Regarding his conflict with Lugh, he is firmly established as an antagonist, striving to prevent mortals from gaining the ability to produce their own grain, and is thwarted by Lugh. Other traditions maintain that Crom Dubh would provide milk and grain to his followers in exchange for the sacrifice of a firstborn child. However, he was also considered extremely wise, and kings would seek out his counsel.

After the arrival of Christianity, Crom Dubh became closely associated with St. Patrick. There are various accounts of the pair as both friends and enemies. One story describes how he aided St. Patrick in gathering firewood and cooking food for the needy, while others have him attempting to kill St. Patrick. Another tale describes a time when demons attempted to claim Crom Dubh's soul, but St. Patrick and a host of angels defeated them in battle and turned them away, stating that Crom Dubh's good deeds outweighed his sins, and he was bound for Heaven.

Some pagan cultures celebrate a festival dedicated to Crom Dubh on the last Sunday in July or the first Sunday in August, falling in the vicinity of Lughnasadh. This day is known as Crom Dubh Sunday or Lammas Sunday, and a feast is held for anyone unable to provide for their family. Participants bring food prepared from their recently harvested crops, including fruit, grains, potatoes, cabbage, and bacon. They would also leave flowers upon his altar as a sacrifice to gain his blessing.

There will be singing, dancing, feasts, sports, competitions, and much drinking on Crom Dubh Sunday. Christians later replaced this festival with a holiday dedicated to St. Muchan, using a holy well originally associated with Crom Dubh as a place of veneration. This, too, ended in the 19th century, after the well was destroyed and a wall erected in its place. Select neopagans continue to worship Crom Dubh, but he is generally viewed only as a part of Lugh's story now, rather than a deity to be honored in his own right.

The Grain Mother

The Grain Mother is an aspect of the mother goddess who propagates a bountiful harvest each season. She appears in the spring to sow the seeds for the grain that will be grown throughout the summer and then returns in the autumn when it comes time to harvest the crops. The Grain Mother is also depicted as a fertility goddess; as is the case in many cultures, agriculture is often associated with fertility.

The traditions connected to the Grain Mother include depicting her as becoming pregnant while the seeds are sown, carrying the child during the growing season, and giving birth during the harvest time. Just as harvested grain begets the seeds to plant the following season, the child will grow into a woman and have a child of her own, continuing the cycle of birth, growth, death, and rebirth. This is a core facet of neopagan beliefs, as rebirth and renewal are often shown to synchronize human experience with nature.

Mother Earth

Mother Earth is the personification of nature itself, sometimes depicted as a matronly woman with a crown of thistle and holly. Many prayers and blessings within the pagan religions address Mother Earth in place of any other specific deity. She is often regarded as a separate being to Tailtiu, the Grain Mother, Brighid, and the Triple Goddess. The flora, fauna, and elements are all considered part of her domain. Concerning the harvest, she controls the wind that carries seeds to new soil, the rain that nourishes the seeds, and the earth itself that yields the crops after they've grown.

In some pagan traditions, a connection between Mother Earth and Lugh is made, where Lugh represents the sun that shines its light upon the earth. This is especially true during Lughnasadh, as the sun is honored for its role in bringing the harvest to bear. However, Mother Earth is rarely identified as having any association with the goddesses in myths concerning Lugh's personal history. Anytime a personification of the natural world appears, it is usually as a disembodied voice or a symbolic role to help guide Lugh along in his journeys.

Brighid

Brighid is a member of the Tuatha Dé Danann. She is a wise and fair goddess, one who protects, heals, cares for animals, and will inspire poems. Many of these aspects overlap with that of Lugh, so in certain neopagan religions, Brighid is honored alongside him during the festival of Lughnasadh. Her name translates to "the exalted one" in the proto-Celtic language, and some believe she has a connection to the ancient British goddess known as Brigantia.

Prior to the neopagan revivals, Brighid was originally associated with the festival of Imbolc, which is celebrated at the beginning of spring. Christianity adopted this holiday for their own St. Brigid, who has a connection to the eternal sacred flame. Neopagans also consider her a triple goddess, usually emphasizing the aspects of wisdom, healing, and protection. The healer is considered the Maiden; the protector is the Mother, and the sage is the Crone. The practice of making corn dollies can be traced back to Brighid, as these were often created in her image: that of a bride.

The Tuatha Dé Danann and Fir Bolg

The Tuatha Dé Danann are alternatively known as the "Folk of the Goddess Danu," and they serve as the pantheon in Celtic mythology. Their rivals are known as the Fomorians, who are shown to encompass nature's darker, destructive side. The Fomorians conquered and subjugated the other peoples of Ireland, including the Tuatha Dé Danann. After a long war where they fought tooth and nail for their freedom, the Tuatha Dé Danann finally defeated their enemies at the Battle of Mag Tuired, after Lugh slew their leader, Balor.

The Fir Bolg were considered the descendants of a group of native Irish people who had migrated to Europe. Those that dwelled in Greece became the Fir Bolg and eventually returned to Ireland, which had remained empty since its abandonment. They ruled over Ireland for a time, dividing it up into smaller provinces. When the Tuatha Dé Danann arrived, the two groups fought for power, with the Tuatha Dé Danann winning out in the end. Lugh's fostering by Tailtiu among the Fir Bolg was an attempt to make peace and ally with their former enemies against the greater threat of the Fomorians.

Alderiann

The god known as Alderiann is relatively obscure, but he is believed to be connected to the harvest and Lughnasadh through a particular tale involving Lugh. In it, Alderiann is described as a trickster, similar to Loki in Norse mythology, and Lugh encountered him while out hunting one day. Having heard about Lugh's many talents, especially his hunting prowess, Alderiann made a bet with him that he would not be able to track and kill the Great Red Bull before sundown. Confident in his skills, Lugh agreed to the wager, putting up the Spear of Assal as collateral. If Lugh succeeded, Alderiann promised to serve as his messenger for the next fifty years.

Lugh scoured the land in search of the Great Red Bull, but after many hours, he could only find a handful of tracks. Even then, the tracks made no sense, as they never led anywhere and simply seemed to disappear into thin air. Fortunately, a raven had been watching Lugh struggle in his hunt and flew down to tell the god a secret: the Great Red Bull was actually Alderiann, and he had given himself wings to remain hidden behind the clouds. The raven was tired of Alderiann always stealing his food, so he saw this as the perfect opportunity to get rid of the troublesome trickster.

Just as the sun began its descent beneath the horizon, Alderiann emerged from the clouds, confident that he had already won. To his horror, a massive spear soared through the air and skewered him, sending him plummeting to the earth. Lugh retrieved his weapon, and as he loomed over

Alderiann, ready to strike the killing blow, the trickster begged for mercy. Lugh relented, but only on the condition that Alderiann serves as his messenger and as his steed for the next fifty years. Not seeing another way out of being killed, Alderiann agreed.

Since Alderiann had the power to transform his body into many different shapes, Lugh found him to be incredibly useful. He could command Alderiann to change into various unassuming animals, allowing him to carry messages undetected by Lugh's enemies. When going into battle, Lugh often mounted Alderiann in his flying Great Red Bull form, and once they engaged their foes, the trickster transformed into a massive wolf or bear to help eviscerate rival armies. The sight of Lugh towering over his enemies, the Spear of Assal in his hand, and the beast, Alderiann, at his side became a common occurrence on the battlefield.

With three years left on his service to Lugh, Alderiann attempted a ploy to free himself early. There was a regular tradition for Lugh's people to sacrifice a bull during Lughnasadh, and Alderiann made himself look like a normal bull, melding into the group from which that year's offering would be selected. His intention was to remain there just long enough to make his escape, but he hadn't anticipated the pagans locking him to another bull with a yoke made from elder wood. This prevented him from transforming into any other shapes, and when the time came for a bull to be sacrificed, he was chosen.

After being stabbed with several spears, the people removed the yoke and carried the bull to their feast. Only after Lugh arrived was Alderiann able to change back into his natural form. With his final breath, he gloated that he had finally tricked Lugh, leaving the god's service three years early. That year's festival was dedicated to Alderiann, and it was said that the ravens came out in droves to help pick clean the carcass of their old foe. In some traditions, the practice of sacrificing a bull was outlawed due to this tale out of fear that they might accidentally kill one of the gods instead.

The Triple Goddess

The Triple Goddess, also known as the Morrígan, is one of the two primary deities in Wicca. She represents the feminine half of the duotheistic system and contains three aspects: the Maiden, the Mother, and the Crone. The Triple Goddess is sometimes identified as Hecate, Persephone, or Artemis/Diana from the Greco-Roman pantheon. In regard to Artemis/Diana, her specific aspects are given as the Huntress, the Moon, and the Underworld. There are many variations on who the Triple Goddess really is, but every tradition encompasses three phases of life.

Sometimes, the Triple Goddess is associated with the Seasons, the Fates, and the Graces. This is a broader interpretation, with each of the three facets representing an idea or concept. The Seasons are cyclical and transitory, constantly bringing about life, death, and rebirth. The Fates use a loom on which they weave the destinies of every mortal, which spans from birth to death. The Graces are three goddesses that personify beauty, charm, and grace, which are traits often connected to young women.

The Horned God

In Wicca, the male is represented by the Horned God. He is associated with the wilds, nature, hunting, and the cycle of life. Typically, the Horned God contains a duality that mimics both aspects of the world: light and dark, day and night, life and death, or summer and winter. Each of his two horns will be depicted in connection to one-half of these concepts. He also has three facets in certain traditions, like the Triple Goddess: the Warrior, the Father, and the Sage.

The Horned God might have been born during the cold, giving a child to the Triple Goddess in the warmer months before succumbing to death at Lughnasadh. He is once more reborn from the Triple Goddess in the winter, starting the cycle anew. At times, the Horned God is named Cernunnos, a Gallo-Roman god associated with stags and bulls. Others identify him as Janicot, Karnayna, Atho, or Herne. Due to similarities with deities from other religions depicted with horns and as great hunters, he is sometimes connected to the Wild Hunt of Norse mythology.

Gods of the Harvest

In addition to the gods associated with the likes of Lugh, Tailtiu, and the Grain Mother, many other cultures also have gods of the harvest in their own mythologies. Some of the stories and traditions have permeated others, as the ancient peoples migrated or conducted trade with contemporary cultures. At times, it can be difficult to discern which common aspects are due to parallel thinking and which were adopted from foreign influences. A selection of harvest deities include:

- Cronus, Demeter, Persephone, Hermes, Attis, Philomelus, and Palaemon in Greek mythology

- Saturn, Mercury, Adonis, Ceres, Proserpina, and Portunus in Roman mythology

- Isis, Osiris, Neper, and Shezmu in Egyptian mythology

- Freya in Norse mythology

- Jarilo, Radegast, and Veles in Slavic mythology

- Emesh, Kus, Lahar, Enbilulu, Tammuz, Sumugan, Enkimdu, Ninurta, Enten, and Nisroch in Mesopotamian mythology

- Balarama and Mahākāla in Hindu mythology
- Daikokuten, Ōkuninushi, Hoori, and Takeminakata in Japanese mythology
- Äkräs, Ukko, and Peko in Finnish mythology
- Shennong, Pa-cha, and Houji in Chinese mythology
- Ixtlilton, Patecatl, Xōchipilli, and Xipe Totec in Aztec mythology
- Dagon in Canaanite mythology
- Maris in Etruscan mythology

Chapter 3: The Sacred Grains and Other Plants

As a harvest festival, grains and other crops grown by pagans are a crucial aspect of Lughnasadh. There is a sacredness imbued within the plants that are harvested. They don't simply provide sustenance – they also bring spiritual power and divine blessings. Among the pagan traditions, there is a difference in the meaning and rituals associated with the various kinds of grain versus other types of plants.

Sacred Grains

The sacred grains in paganism are oats, barley, and rye. Each type has its own symbolism associated with it. There are various interpretations of their true meaning, but most scholars and historians can agree on a few. Some of the most popular interpretations have spread to other religions as well, especially Christianity. The church recognized the importance of grains and established liturgical celebrations that use grains in a few of their rituals.

Oats

Oats represent health, nutrition, kindness, and prosperity. With so many foods made with oats, this symbolism can be seen as something spread throughout the entirety of pagan society. They hold these values dear and want their people to follow these ideals in their daily lives.

Oats.
https://pixabay.com/es/photos/avena-cereales-campo-comida-grano-3717095/

Since you cannot make any food with only a single oat, there is a symbolic meaning to oats as a collective. They work best when a large number of oats are banded together for a single goal, and this unity should be reflected in your own communities. There are few times where acting on your own instead of with a group will net you better results.

Barley

Barley is symbolic of fertility. It is an incredibly resilient crop, able to be grown in nearly any climate. The rapid and widespread propagation barely helps it thrive. It can be cultivated throughout the winter, which helps offset the lack of other grains that cannot be replanted until the spring. The plants have brittle spikelets that will break off, assisting with their seed distribution.

Wheat

Wheat is believed to symbolize fertility, life, and abundance. Women have a close association with wheat, as it feeds them, allowing them to reproduce and, in turn, feeding their families. The wheat production has been increasing exponentially in recent years, so it is even more widespread now than it was for the ancient pagans. However, we all share the commonality of using wheat to create flour, bake bread, and make other bread-like foods.

Rye

Rye is a lower quality crop than oats or barley. The ancient Romans claimed that it was only fit to feed the poor, offering a limited amount of sustenance. However, it is a versatile plant used for things like rye bread and pumpernickel. It can also serve as an ingredient to make alcohol, such as rye beer or rye whiskey. There are also some medicinal properties to the plant, and herbalists will use rye extract to help heal patients.

More Sacred Plants

In addition to the sacred grains, pagans held some other plants in equally high regard. The connection between man and nature has a long history that goes back to millennia, and the crops grown by those within pagan society continue the traditions set forth by their ancient ancestors.

Corn

Corn is a peculiar example of the beliefs held by pagans concerning the crops they harvested. They maintained that a spirit of nature resided within the corn, so the act of reaping them resulted in the spirits having nowhere to go. The way pagans remedied this ill was by constructing corn dollies. These were made from dried rush or grains and meant to give the spirits a place to live until the following year's crops had grown. When the sowing season returns, the corn dolly is buried in the soil before the first seeds are planted, which is meant to release the spirit back into the corn as it sprouts.

Meadowsweet

Meadowsweet represents courtship and matrimony, although the reasons behind this are unknown. Some have theorized that this symbolism stems from the fact that meadowsweet flowers give off a different aroma before and after they bruise.

Meadowsweet.

Rosser1954, CC BY-SA 4.0 <https://creativecommons.org/licenses/by-sa/4.0>, via Wikimedia Commons https://commons.wikimedia.org/wiki/File:Meadowsweet_(Filipendula_ulmaria)_-_Shewalton.JPG

This is intended to echo the common trope that men and women undergo a complete change in behavior from the time they are dating to the time following their marriage. However, it also has medicinal properties, so the meaning behind the symbolism could be seen as relationships acting as a balm for a lonely soul.

Sunflowers

Sunflowers are seen as a sign of loyalty, adoration, luck, and the harvest. They can also symbolize vitality and intellect, traits often valued and respected in a pagan society. Due to their resemblance to the sun, the fact that they wilt and die when autumn approaches, like the sun disappearing earlier in the evening in the cooler months, can signal the beginning of the harvest season. Their vibrant yellow color makes them popular for expressing admiration for another person.

Mint

Mint symbolizes virtue, wisdom, protection, hospitality, willpower, and rejuvenation. The distinctive smell of mint plants has made it a favorite option as a housewarming gift. It has medicinal uses that include removing congestion in the lungs, throat, nose, and bronchi and encouraging mucus and cilia production. Some believe it can help ease the symptoms of morning sickness in pregnant women.

Calendula

Calendula flowers, also known as marigolds, are emblematic of warmth, success, creativity, and open communication. They have been used as part of bouquets during both weddings and funerals. Calendula flowers also have a connection to autumn, fitting in nicely with the festival of Lughnasadh. Some believe it represents the sun's journey across the sky, serving as a reminder of the warm summer light during the long, cold winter.

Ginger

Ginger represents strength, beauty, and vibrancy. Many pagan rituals and spells call for the use of ginger, and it is believed to have medicinal properties. It gives off a unique fragrance and is often utilized as a spice for cooking or to flavor candy, soda, pickles, or alcoholic beverages. Gingerbread, cookies, crackers, ginger ale, and ginger beer are all popular products created with this herb.

Cinnamon

Cinnamon is a spice derived from the inner bark of trees in the Cinnamomum genus. It has been used since at least 2000 BCE and was considered a gift worthy of kings and queens. The essential oil extracted from it is a popular choice for pagans, and the spice itself is considered to encourage abundance and good fortune. Whiskey, brandy, and cinnamon-flavored liqueur are common alcoholic beverages made with cinnamon.

Allspice

Allspice originated in South America and the Caribbean, but it has spread all across the world, becoming a popular spice used in cooking and magical spells. It is made from the dried berries of the plant Pimenta dioica, which is part of the myrtle family. In addition to the various cuisines that use allspice, it possesses innate characteristics that make it ideal for blessings or spells to encourage healing and good fortune.

Basil

Basil is a culinary and ritual herb whose name means "royal plant." It is native to India and tropical regions in Southeast Asia and Africa but is able to grow just about anywhere around the world. Besides its use in cooking, basil is often utilized as a folk medicine held by many practitioners to contain therapeutic benefits. It is also a great herb to plant in your garden since basil is known to serve as an insect repellent, including being potentially toxic to mosquitos.

Chapter 4: Crafts and Decorations

As Lugh is a god of craftsmanship, making your own crafts and decorations is a great way to honor him. There are many materials and supplies you can find around the house or for very cheap at a craft store, and you can even use parts of the ingredients used in the food for the harvest feast. Most can be completed in a relatively short amount of time while still giving you satisfying results. If you have children who need something to do while you're preparing for Lughnasadh, giving them one or more projects can occupy their attention. You can really let your creativity run wild with these crafts and decorations, but if you need a place to start, here are a handful of ideas that you can try.

Crafts

The types of crafts you can do to get into the spirit of Lughnasadh vary widely, from traditional corn dollies to rain collection barrels. The main thing to remember when finding a crafting project is that it should connect to the festival or the celebrated themes and ideas, such as the harvest and nature. Generally, you'll want your crafts to have some sort of functionality; otherwise, they would be considered decorations instead.

Corn Dolly

Pagans have used corn dollies during Lughnasadh for a long time, and there are plenty of variations on how they can be made. Some create a corn dolly in the image of the goddess Brighid as a bride, while others craft them to depict Lugh in his warrior form. These don't have to be too ornate; you can make a corn dolly with a basic human shape with no definitive features.

Corn dolly of a goddess.

In the past, corn dollies were made to house spirits believed to reside in corn after harvesting. They would then be buried in the field before sowing season the following spring. Neopagans will sometimes save their Lughnasadh corn dolly to reuse during Imbolc, where they are hung over the hearth to invite the goddess Brighid into their home.

Making a corn dolly is fairly simple. The materials required include:

- Several husks of corn
- Yarn or ribbon
- Cotton balls

Once you have your materials together, let the corn husks soak for a few hours to make them pliable; otherwise, they will snap while trying to shape them. When they are ready, take a strip of the corn husk and fold it in half. In the center, place two or three cotton balls to help the dolly hold its shape. Give the husk a few twists before using ribbon to secure it – and you have a head.

Take a couple of corn husks and fold them, tying them too to turn them into arms and hands. You can attach them to the body by sliding them in. Fold two more husks in half and place them at the bottom of the torso to give your dolly legs. Tie some yarn or ribbon at the waist to hold everything in place.

Brighid is a popular choice when making dolls; you can distinguish that by adding clothing she might wear. A skirt can be created by using more husks, tying them down in any way you like. You can also trim the skirt when it is in place if you want it to be shorter.

Allow the corn dolly to dry before decorating its face or adding additional flourishes to make it more personal. You can use any extra yard to give it hair or get a paint set to paint on the eyes, nose, and mouth. If you are feeling especially creative, you can add different decorations, customize clothing, or craft little items for it to hold. However, this isn't necessary to do. You can leave it plain, and it will still serve as a functional corn dolly.

Lammas Rebirth Incense

Incense can aid you in cleansing the spirit and reinforcing positive energy. When the harvesting season comes around, any herbs you've been growing will begin to dry out, so it's the perfect time to pick them and use them to make incense. Incense comes in many forms, so think about what type you want before you start. There is a big difference between loose incense and sticks. Both will work, but loose can be easier to work with depending on your fuel source.

A typical recipe for loose incense requires:

- 2 parts goldenrod
- 2 parts Sweet Annie or dried apple blossoms
- 1 part basil
- 1 part coriander
- 1 part heather
- 1 part yarrow
- ½ part cinnamon bark
- ½ part rosemary

Begin by placing your herbs into a mixing bowl one at a time. Grind up the leaves and petals so they can be fully incorporated into the recipe. When you start to blend your herbs, announce your intention to use the incense. This is meant to help focus the purification energy and help it be more effective. You can also charge your incense with an incantation that both states your intention and focuses your energy on a single spell.

An example of one such incantation is:

"Today, we give thanks to the cycle of rebirth

For the grains, corn, and fruit that we pluck from the earth

To those who carry with them the seed of new life

That we reap during harvest with the basket and scythe

We give thanks for the blessings upon fertile ground

That keeps us fed and hale all the year-'round

Everything that is and all that has been

Carried forth by faithful servants within

A blessing unto nature and the goddess of three

Ever sacred is your will that is worked through me."

Smudge Sticks

Smudge sticks allow you to cleanse a sacred space of negative energy, which is particularly useful when you are asking for blessings from the gods. The most popular materials to create smudge sticks from are sage or sweetgrass. These are fairly inexpensive and easy to find in most commercial retailers, but you can also construct your own if you desire. You can use herbs grown in your garden or forage for them in the wild.

The materials needed to craft your own smudge sticks include:

- Sage, sweetgrass, mugwort, lavender, juniper, or rosemary
- Scissors or garden clippers
- Cotton string

First, cut off 6 to 10-inch length pieces of the plants. You can use shorter pieces if you want, but the longer pieces are easier to work with, and you don't require as many leaves. Next, you need to make a bundle out of your herbs. Take a long piece of string (it is better to have too much that you can cut later); about six feet is fine. Loop the string around the herbs and plants, starting down at the cut end, keeping the strong tight.

Take the remaining string and wrap it around the base of the plant bundle, securing it in place, then wind it around toward the leafy end. After reaching this part, work your way back to the stem. The result should be a pattern that is crisscrossed. It must be tight enough that none of the plants will fall out but not so tight that it breaks them. Once you have reached the stem with this string, use that 2-inch bit of loose string from the first part to tie them together. Use the scissors or garden clippers to trim the ends of your bundle, so everything is even.

Now, you need to let your bundle dry. You can do this by placing it outside in a sunlit area or hanging it up in your home in a place where moisture cannot get to it. Depending on the humidity, it can take two days to a week for the bundle to completely dry out. After it has completely dried, place them in a bag or a dark storage space until you are ready to use them. Performing the smudging ritual is easy: simply burn one end of the bundle, allowing it to cleanse the area.

Berry Bracelet

In Ireland, there is a tradition to collect berries in a bucket at the beginning of August called Bilberry Sunday. If you ended up gathering a large number of berries, it signified a bountiful harvest that season. The best of these berries would be consumed during Lughnasadh as part of the First Fruit celebrations. Another part of this tradition involved using the remaining berries to craft a crown or bracelet that could be given to someone to signify your interest in them.

To make a berry bracelet of your own, you'll need:

- A bundle of berries (15 to 25, depending on their size)
- Sturdy cotton thread
- A needle

The best kind of berries to use for a bracelet are ones that are firm and have their stems still attached. Pick them as close to crafting time as possible, so they won't lose their solidity and start to rot. These berries shouldn't be too juicy, as once you start threading them together, juicier berries can burst and make a mess for those making or wearing the bracelet.

Crafting a berry bracelet is a very simple process. Measure out a length of cotton thread that is long enough to wear around the wrist. Take the needle and secure the thread through its eye. Then, pierce the berries through their stems, binding them all together. You can add in other flourishes, such as nuts or seeds, to serve as spacers between berries. Once you've finished adding the berries and other pieces, give it as a gift to a loved one to wear as a token during Lughnasadh.

Rain Collection Barrel

A major aspect of paganism is the respect for the earth and utilization of natural resources instead of artificial materials that create unnecessary waste. Since Lughnasadh takes place near the end of the summer, if you live somewhere that is particularly hot or dry, you might encounter the need to ration your water. Anytime there is a drought, there are certain things you can't forgo using clean, filtered water for, like drinking, cooking, or hygiene purposes.

However, other purposes, such as watering plants, washing your car, or cleaning the exterior of your house, might only be available for very limited periods. To offset the potential consequences of being unable to do these things completely, you can create rain collection barrels to store precipitation water during the rest of the year, allowing you to use it for any non-essential needs around your home.

While there are commercially-available rain collection barrels you can purchase, these will typically cost anywhere between $150 to $250.

However, you can craft your own version at home with supplies of no more than about $20. The material required for this include:

- A 50-gallon barrel (plastic, food-grade)
- 90-degree elbow CPVC fitting (¾ inch diameter)
- 6-inch length CPVC straight pipe (¾ inch diameter)
- CPVC T-Connector with a spigot on top (¾ inch diameter)
- Clear PVC glue
- A ¾-inch brass hose fitting

You will start with your barrel right side up, so the removable cap is at the top, but at the end of the build, it will be flipped over, so the cap is on the bottom. Using the PVC glue as a fastener, attach the fittings together to have a 2-inch drop out of the bottom. Use the CPVC elbow and more pipe to take the pipe beyond the edge of the barrel. Install the T-Connector to the removable top. This will serve as the spout from which you distribute the water.

When everything has been attached to the barrel, invert it so that the end of the PVC pipe faces downward. You must place the barrel on an elevated platform to allow gravity to move the water through the collector. A pile of cinder blocks or lumber will work so long as it can handle the weight of the filled container. At maximum capacity, it can get up to about 400 pounds.

The best method of getting the water into your barrel is via your house's gutters. Attach the downspout to your barrel by cutting a hole in the top and threading it through. This is ideal, as it directs the water that collects on your roof into your collector. If you don't have a downspout, you can cut away a portion of the top and attach a screen over the hole. This will prevent bugs and debris from getting into the barrel and contaminating your water.

The final step is to drill a hole near the top of the barrel. In the event of overflow, this hole will prevent any excess water from spilling out, potentially causing damage to your gutters or the exterior of your home. The final piece is the brass hose fitting. Attach that to the end of the pipe so a hose can be attached. When you need to access this water, all you'll need to do is turn the spigot. You can also use it without a hose like a spout, turning the spigot on and off to fill up buckets or water cans when necessary. You've now got an eco-friendly solution to any water limitations you might encounter during the harvest season.

Decorations

Part of getting into the spirit of a celebration is decorating your home with ornaments appropriate for the holiday. These decorations can be made to help enhance the atmosphere around your house for Lughnasadh. You can make them all yourself from cheap and easy-to-find items, making them a great choice for DIY enthusiasts. They can be a fun activity to do with your family or friends as you get ready to celebrate the harvest festival.

Fruit or Vegetable Candleholder

Candles are an important part of any pagan Sabbat, as they are often used in rituals around the altar. Creating a candleholder out of one of the traditional fruits or vegetables associated with Lughnasadh is a fantastic way to spend an afternoon and tie it into the festival's themes. You can use apples, acorn squash, eggplants, or any other firm fruit or vegetable.

The materials you'll need to make a candleholder include:

- A piece of fruit or a vegetable
- Cloth made of soft fabric
- A knife or corer
- Lemon juice
- Fresh herbs
- A tapered candle

The fruit or vegetable must be cleaned before it is ready to use. Once clean, use the cloth to wipe the fruit down and restore its natural shine. Use your knife to remove the top half of the core. You can cut down at an angle and clean up the hole once you pull the part of the core out. The candle should stand unsupported in the fruit, so it is better to err on the side of caution when cutting the core, and you can always scoop more out.

Rub some lemon juice into the hole to stop the fruit from browning. The citric acid will also keep the fruit firmer for longer, keeping your candle supported. You can drain any excess juice after ten minutes. Take whatever herbs you have chosen and press them into the cavity. You can light the candle and drip some wax into the base to better secure the candle, but try the hole first without. Now, you have an on-theme decoration that can double as the candle for any rituals or blessings performed during Lughnasadh.

Grapevine Pentacle Wreath

Pentacles are a common type of talisman used for magical evocations, particularly in neopagan religions such as Wicca. They can be made from different materials, like metal, paper, cloth, or parchment, but if you want to make one specifically for Lughnasadh, you can use a grapevine to make a pentacle wreath. This can serve as both a decoration and a component for rituals, blessings, or spells.

You will need the following materials for this project:

- Freshly picked grapevines
- A bucket of water
- Florist wire

Remember that you'll be bending and shaping the grapevine after picking, so you want them to be strong enough not to break but not so strong that they are not easy to handle. You should aim for 22 feet of grapevine so you can have some discards if needed. Soak your vines for 12-24 hours to soften them before shaping.

Use the grapevines while they are still wet – they will be easier to shape and will retain their form better as they dry. Start with the longest, and cut off the extra leaves and stems as you work. Shape the first vine into an 18"-diameter circle, tucking the vine into itself as it loops around. Do this with another six vines (adding more if you feel it needs it).

Next, cut 5 vines of equal length, each measuring about 20 inches. You'll use these to create the pentacle within your wreath. Use the first piece and string it across the circle, tucking it into the outside of the wreath and wrapping it to keep it in place. Repeat this process until you have the pentacle star pattern completed. You can use the florist wire to ensure everything remains taut and secure. Finally, use a bit of wire to fashion a loop from which you can hang it on a door or wall.

Cornhusk Chain

Since corn is one of the major foods consumed during Lughnasadh, you can make a cornhusk chain from the leftover husks. It's better to do this craft while the husks are still fresh, but you can use dried husks if you let them soak for 10 to 15 minutes in water. Blot them with paper towels once they've been hydrated, so they aren't too wet to work with. The process is very simple, almost identical to the construction paper chains children make in grade school.

What you'll need for your cornhusk chain includes:

- Fresh or rehydrated cornhusks
- A stapler or crafting glue

Start by tearing the husks lengthwise into 1-inch-wide strips. If they are fresh or have been soaked properly, they will rip on their own without any trouble. Make the first link in the chain by looping the cornhusk into a circle. Use your stapler of the glue to seal the loop. Repeat the process with the next link, but be sure to loop it through the first link. Keep making loops to lengthen your chain, using the glue or staples to hold the husks in lops.

You can hang your creation over any opening in your home or use it to decorate a tree or a shrine. The cornhusks can serve as a wonderful season-appropriate ornament. You can also utilize the chain as a calendar, tearing off a link each day to count down the time until Lughnasadh. Some pagans will incorporate cornhusk chains into their spellwork and prayer rituals, tracking specific aspects through the use of the links.

Sunflower Bouquets

A bouquet of sunflowers is very easy to create and has a variety of applications as the festival of Lughnasadh approaches. All you need to do to make one is pick and gather enough sunflowers to bundle together, using as many as desired. Tie them together with some string, ribbon, or twine. You can add other plants or herbs to help accentuate the bright yellow color of the flowers, such as sprigs of lavender or pieces of wheat. Once you've finished your bouquet, you can keep them in a vase or wrap a bit of lace around the stems and place them as the centerpiece at your feast.

The petals or seeds of sunflowers can be added to a charm bag for prosperity, or you can use the seeds to feed the birds. Sunflower oil is a good alternative to vegetable oil when cooking your Lughnasadh dishes. With the beauty and symbolism of sunflowers, they can make a great token of affection for your loved ones or be given to someone you're interested in courting. As Lughnasadh marks the end of the warm summer months, it may be the last time you'll get to see sunflowers, so they can help mark the occasion and give your home a warm, decorative feeling.

Chapter 5: Setting Up Your Lammas Altar

Not all pagans place the same amount of importance on their altars, but it is beneficial to know how to set them up properly for those that do. They should represent the sacred aspects of Lughnasadh, such as the harvest and the changing seasons. You want to honor the gods with your altar to receive their blessings. The best way to do this is to ensure you follow the neopagan religions' customs.

Lammas altar.

Bart Everson, CC BY 2.0 <https://creativecommons.org/licenses/by/2.0>, via Wikimedia Commons https://commons.wikimedia.org/wiki/File:Lammas_Altar_New_Orleans_2019.jpg

A Lughnasadh altar will differ from a normal altar by the types of items used on it. Everything will be related to the harvest or the god Lugh specifically. This can include sacrifices from your crops or autumnal plants, leaving grains, corn, or sunflowers. Items such as craftsmen or artisan materials should also be placed on your altar. You can add these symbolically through offerings like paints, pens, notebooks, or hammers.

Having an altar dedicated to Lughnasadh can aid you in harnessing your energy and expressing your intentions when reciting incantations or asking for blessings. Pagan altars, in general, will venerate the pantheon of gods and honor the relationship between the natural world and human beings. For Lughnasadh, this should be focused on harvesting the first crops and giving thanks for the bounty provided to you.

Location

The specific location of your altar isn't as important as placing it somewhere with meaning to you. It should be in a significant spot, such as your bedroom or a common area where you spend a lot of time. You can put it near the hearth to honor Lugh and the Grain Mother, as that is symbolic of welcoming the gods into your home. Ultimately, the best location for your altar is wherever you can access it easily and pay your respects on a daily basis.

Decorations

How you decorate your altar can give it flair and add to the ambiance of the harvest festival. Many pagans will drape a cloth over their altar, giving it a more ritualistic appearance and preventing any of the items placed upon it from scuffing up its surface. You can put candles, cornhusk chains, bouquets of flowers, or wreaths on or around the altar to bring out the seasonal atmosphere. Suppose you want to make it feel more reverent. In that case, you can decorate it with pagan symbols, such as a pentacle, ankh, Celtic shield knot, triskelion, or triquetra.

Offerings

The types of offerings you should make on your altar for Lughnasadh should all directly relate to the harvest, or the gods honored during the festival. A common offering is a loaf of bread baked with the first grains harvested that season. Any other crops that have been picked, like wheat, oats, barley, corn, potatoes, apples, onions, carrots, squash, or grapes, can be added on their own. In addition to the bread, you can offer wine made from the first grapes harvested or honey collected from bees in the late summer.

Other items gathered from nature, such as acorns, nuts, sunflowers, straws, or herbs, can be used to ask for blessings from the gods. If you make a corn dolly, that should also be placed on the altar. This will sustain the spirit within until it can be planted with next year's crops. Anything crafted specifically for Lughnasadh can be a good supplement to the typical offerings of food or symbolic items. You can also arrange everything in a basket to prevent the surface of your altar from becoming too messy.

When using tools or weapons as offerings, be careful while handling them. Anything with a sharp-edged or piercing blade can cause serious injuries if you aren't careful. Iron is often associated with protection magic in paganism, and the harvest season is the perfect time to invoke such spells. Scythes, sickles, hammers, whittling knives, or themes can all make satisfactory offerings for different types of spells and blessings. Since Lugh was both a warrior and a craftsman, using iron-wrought items can provide a strong connection to him.

Item Placement

Any items placed upon your altar should be positioned as close to the center as possible. When making offerings of multiple items, position them in a triangular shape around the middle of the altar, with the top angle pointing north. You can also choose a circular arrangement, representing the repeating cycle of the seasons. If you have five or six items, you can use each one as a point in a pentacle, placing them in a star alignment, with five offerings for each point and a six in the center. Another option is to make a spiral with the items, starting in the middle and swirling outward until you reach the edge of the altar.

Caring for Your Altar

You should keep your altar clean, removing any offerings with organic material once they go bad and begin to rot. Make sure to clear away any bits of debris that might fall off the items you've placed there. If you use a cloth to cover the altar, you can simply remove it and shake away the remains or wash it for a more thorough cleansing. Using candles on your altar may result in bits of wax dripping off, so make sure you have a candle holder or basin beneath it to prevent it from harming the cloth covering or the altar's surface.

What to Avoid

When setting up your altar, be sure to avoid cluttering it with too many items or decorations. There should be a sense of order to their arrangement. Overcrowding an altar could result in a discordant invocation, which may either cause them to fail or have negative consequences. The organization is important for both your altar and your mind. As your altar is a reflection of your spirit, too much clutter can make it difficult to get into the proper headspace to make your intentions clear when speaking an invocation or requesting a blessing.

Don't leave rotting food on it for too long. Rotten food isn't appealing to the gods and is a health hazard for you. It can attract insects that will fester and lay eggs within the food, causing a serious pest problem. Mold might also be an issue and can release harmful spores into the air. Should you inhale these spores, it could become hard to breathe or trigger an allergic reaction. Dispose of them at the first sign of rot in your organic offerings.

Since the altar you're making is dedicated to Lughnasadh, avoid using items or decorations meant for other festivals or don't connect with the harvest theme. It can be taken as a sign of disrespect if you don't follow the traditions of the religion whose holiday you are celebrating. There are still plenty of options to make your observance of Lughnasadh personal to you while remaining respectful of the pagan and neopagan beliefs.

After the Festival

When Lughnasadh is over, you have a few options for what to do with your altar. The next Sabbat is Mabon, which takes place on the autumnal equinox between September 21st and 27th. Mabon is the second of the three harvest festivals, the third being Samhain. Because of this, some of your decorations can be reused during Mabon, and you can leave them up throughout the harvest season. However, this mainly applies to those made with non-organic materials. Anything that will rot will need to be replaced before Mabon. Something like a cornhusk chain can survive long enough to be reused, but it will change color and size before then.

Offerings should always be removed following the festival, as any spells created (or blessings gained from them) have been expended. An offering represents a sacrifice to the gods or nature, so using the same one again will offend these powers and result in a failure to attain your desired outcome the next time. It can also bring bad luck and misfortune upon you, so taking such a risk is not a good idea. The meaning behind the offerings during Lughnasadh includes that the items or materials come from the first plants harvested. The offerings during Mabon should represent the second harvest of the season.

Your altar itself should be cleaned and maintained during the period between festivals. Make sure you get rid of any refuse and scrub away potentially-harmful pathogens with soap and water or surface cleansers. If you use a cloth draped over it, wash it properly or replace it with a fresh one. Your candles will most likely need to be replaced as well since they will be significantly burned down by the time the festival is over. During the interregnum between Lughnasadh and Mabon, feel free to use your altar for common pagan rituals and blessings. As long as you follow the traditions respectfully, there is no harm in giving thanks and venerating the gods and natures more often.

Chapter 6: Recipes for a Lammas Feast

No festival or holiday can be celebrated without great food specifically associated with it. Lughnasadh is no different. Like every Sabbat, it involves a ritualized feast filled with traditional meals. Many recipes are handed down through the generations of pagans, and others have been recreated based on historical accounts of the food found at the ancient Lughnasadh feasts. Here are some of the recipes that you can use for your own celebrations:

Grain-Based Recipes

The grain-based recipes include anything made with wheat, oats, or barley. They account for many of the most well-known traditional Lughnasadh meals. The importance of the grains gathered during the harvest confers a special meaning and power upon those who create and consume them.

Lammas Bread

A traditional Lughnasadh feast needs a loaf of Lammas bread, as it is a major feature of the festival. You can either eat the bread that has been made with the first grains of the harvest or crumble it up into four pieces and bury it around the barn, where you will store your grains to serve as a protective blessing. If you want to bake two loaves of Lammas bread, you can use them for both purposes.

Lammas owl loaf.

Ingredients:

- 2 cups of flour (whole wheat)
- 2 cups of bread flour
- 2 cups of scalded milk
- 2 tbsp of active dry yeast
- ¼ cup of toasted sesame seeds
- 3 tbsp of honey
- 3 tbsp of peanut butter
- 2 ½ teaspoons of salt

Cooking Directions:

1. Mix the dry ingredients into a bowl.
2. Mix peanut butter and honey into the cup of scalded milk and stir.
3. Cool the milk, peanut butter, and honey to 115 degrees Fahrenheit.
4. Stir the milk, peanut butter, and honey mix into the dry ingredients bowl, creating your dough.
5. Take the dough and knead it with your palms for 10-20 minutes until the fibers become more elastic.
6. Cover the dough with oil.

7. Place a cramp cloth over the dough.

8. Place the dough in a warm spot and let it rise until double.

9. Punch down the dough and make 1 large wreath or 2 rectangular loaves.

10. Allow the dough to rise again until double.

11. Bake at 375 degrees Fahrenheit until golden brown.

You will know your Lammas Bread is done if it sounds hollow when you tap it.

Lammas Cake

Although the word "cake" generally means a soft, sweet baked food made with flour, sugar, shortening, and eggs, it used to mean anything created with grains. A Lammas Cake is more of a fry bread than a modern cake and can be either sweet or savory.

Ingredients:
- 2 cups of all-purpose flour
- 1 ½ cups of cold water
- ½ cup of oats
- ½ cup of golden flaxseed meal
- ½ cup of chilled and cubed butter
- 1 teaspoon of baking soda
- 1 teaspoon of baking powder
- 1 teaspoon of xanthan gum
- ½ teaspoon of salt
- Oil for frying

Cooking Directions:
1. Add dry ingredients into a bowl and mix well

2. Add butter

3. Mix in the cold water

4. Blend together until you get a thick, stuffed dough

5. Roll the dough into a ball and place it in the refrigerator for 30 minutes

6. Heat up the oil in a skillet

7. Cut the dough into 6 pieces.

8. Roll each portion of dough in flour and flatten them

9. Add one of the six cakes into the skillet with heated oil

10. Fry until the cake is golden-brown on the bottom

11. Flip the cake over and repeat for the other side

Once the cake is golden-brown on both sides and becomes a bit puffy, remove it from the skillet and place it on a paper towel to cool. Repeat these steps for the rest of your cakes, and then garnish with sweet buttercream. Now your Lammas Cake is ready to be served at your feast.

Barley Mushroom Soup

One of the sacred grains honored during Lughnasadh is barley. It represents fertility and is also emblematic of a culture's ability to feed its poorest members. Barley is often considered a lower grade of grain than wheat or oats, but it is also cheaper and easy to grow in large quantities. You can start making Barley Mushroom Soup early in the day, giving it plenty of time to cook, or you can make it right before you're ready to serve your meal.

Ingredients:

- 5 cups of vegetable broth
- 1 cup of uncooked barley
- ½ cup of fresh chopped carrots
- ½ cup of diced onions
- ½ cup of chopped celery
- ½ pound of mushrooms (you can use enoki or morsels to get a more earthy flavor)
- 2 cloves of fresh minced garlic
- Salt and pepper

Cooking Directions:

1. Bring the vegetable broth to a boil

2. Reduce the heat

3. Add carrots, onions, celery, and mushrooms

4. Let the soup simmer for ten minutes

5. Add barley and garlic

6. Cover soup and let it simmer for at least an hour

7. Add salt and pepper

Barley Mushroom Soup can be served as a side dish during your Lughnasadh feast. Pair it with a piece of buttered bread for a heartier experience.

Grian Risers

A Grian Riser is a type of pancake that is puffy, eggy, and baked in the oven. In Irish mythology, Grian is the name of the sun, and these pancakes were named for their resemblance to the rising sun. You can top it with just about anything, making it as sweet or savory as you want. Possible toppings include fruit, honey, butter cream, or powdered sugar.

Ingredients:

- ½ cup of all-purpose flour
- 2 eggs
- ½ cup of milk
- 4 tablespoons of unsalted butter
- 2 tablespoons of sugar
- ¼ teaspoon of salt
- 1 teaspoon of vanilla extract

Cooking Directions:

1. Preheat your stove (400 F)
2. Add butter to a cast-iron pan and melt in the oven
3. Mix the dry ingredients
4. Beat the wet ingredients in a separate bowl
5. Combine wet and dry ingredients and mix well
6. Remove your skillet from the oven with an oven mitt or pot holder
7. Pour the mixed batter into the skillet
8. Place the skillet back into the oven and let it bake for 20 minutes until it is golden brown

Remove the skillet from the oven and slice the Grian Risers into small wedges. You can then add your preferred topping and serve.

Chocolate Chip Bread Pudding

This is a more modern variation of the traditional bread pudding made by pagans during Lughnasadh. Pudding is often seen as a symbol of unity, especially throughout the British Isles. Since this dish can be made using stale bread, it's a good way to use any leftover bread from your harvest and avoid wasting any of it. The addition of chocolate chips is a twist that would've been unavailable in the pre-Christian era.

Ingredients:

- 1 cup of torn or cut-up stale bread
- 2 cups of whole milk
- ¼ cup of brown sugar
- ½ cup of chocolate chips
- ½ cup of heavy cream
- 3 eggs
- 2 tablespoons of Kahlua

Cooking Directions:

1. Preheat stove (350 F)
2. Prepare a baking pan by covering it with a thin layer of oil
3. Place stale bread pieces into the pan and add chocolate chips on top
4. Whisk together the eggs, whole milk, brown sugar, heavy cream, and Kahlua in a small bowl
5. Pour the mixture over the bread, pressing down to make sure it absorbs the mixture
6. Let the bread soak for 20 minutes
7. Bake the bread pudding for 40 minutes, until it has set
8. Remove bread pudding from the oven and allow it to cool

You can add whipped cream on top and serve the Chocolate Chip Bread Pudding while it's still warm. Any leftovers can be covered by plastic and kept in the refrigerator for a few days. Reheat it in the microwave before eating.

Corn-Based Recipes

Outside of grains, corn is the next most important crop harvested around Lughnasadh. The pre-Christianity pagans believed that corn had a spirit dwelling within it, so harvesting the crop meant these spirits had nowhere to go. To remedy this, they would create corn dollies for the spirits to reside, while they used the harvested corn in recipes for their celebratory feasts.

Lammas Cornbread

Cornbread made during the Lughnasadh is a tradition that dates back as far as the festival itself. Combining the first corn harvested with the first grains resulted in tasty food for the feast while also honoring the gods.

Ingredients:

- 1 cup of all-purpose flour
- 1 cup of cornmeal
- 1 ¼ cups of milk
- ⅓ cup of white sugar
- 4 teaspoons of baking powder
- 3 teaspoons of dried sage
- 3 ½ tablespoons of vegetable shortening
- 1 teaspoon of salt
- 1 egg

Cooking Directions:

1. Combine all ingredients into a large bowl
2. Use a hand beater to mix the ingredients together for less than a minute
3. Pour mixture into a muffin pan with 12 individual molds
4. Bake at 350 degrees Fahrenheit for 15 to 20 minutes

Take the cornbread out of the oven and let it cool for 10 to 15 minutes. You can serve it plain or add a topping of your choice.

Chicken Corn Chowder

Chicken Corn Chowder is a great way to pack in some protein to replenish the calories burned after a long day of harvesting. The combination of ingredients can return your depleted energy, allowing you to finish off the day without becoming lethargic.

Ingredients:

- 6 slices of chopped bacon
- 8 chopped green onions, dividing the whites and greens
- 2 tablespoons of all-purpose flour
- 3 chopped medium-sized Yukon Gold potatoes
- 2 cups of chicken stock
- 3 cups of whole milk
- ½ teaspoon of mustard powder
- ½ teaspoon of dried thyme
- ½ teaspoon of ground allspice

- ½ teaspoon of ground cayenne
- ½ teaspoon of paprika
- 2 cans of drained whole kernel corn
- 1 can of creamed corn
- 2 cups of chopped or shredded cooked chicken
- 1 4-ounce can have diced green chili peppers
- Cheddar cheese and salt and pepper to garnish

Cooking Directions:

1. Fry bacon until crispy.
2. Lay bacon on a paper towel to soak up some of the grease.
3. Combine the potatoes, onions, and bacon fat in the pan.
4. Fry for 2-3 minutes, stirring as the onions soften.
5. Sprinkle a thin layer of flour into the pot and stir continuously for 1 minute, until the potatoes are covered with flour.
6. Stir the chicken stock, milk, and seasonings into the pot.
7. When the liquid starts to boil, reduce the heat to a simmer for 12-16 minutes.
8. Stir in the corn, creamed corn, green chili peppers, and chicken.
9. Allow it to simmer for another five minutes.
10. Remove the pot from the fire.

Distribute the Chicken Corn Chowder into individual bowls and serve them with the bacon, leftover onions, and cheese. You can save this meal for up to a week when stored in a refrigerator.

Cheddar Corn Succotash

Succotash is a great meal to have on the waning days of the summer and the beginning of autumn. Utilizing the newly-harvested corn in this dish to help celebrate Lughnasadh is part of the process of gaining blessings for a bountiful harvest to get you through the winter.

Ingredients:

- 4 cups of fresh corn kernels
- 1 cup of chopped white onion
- ½ pound of sliced bacon
- 4 tablespoons of unsalted butter
- ⅓ teaspoon of ground black pepper

- 1 ¼ teaspoon of salt
- 1 cup of sliced cherry tomatoes
- 1 teaspoon of diced garlic clove
- 2 ounces of fresh okra
- ¼ cup of fresh sliced basil
- ¾ ounces of shredded cheddar cheese

Cooking Directions:

1. Add bacon slices to a medium-sized saucepan.
2. Fry bacon on medium-low heat for 7 minutes, then flip and fry the other side for 5 minutes.
3. Place bacon pieces on a plate covered with a paper towel.
4. Break up the bacon into smaller crumbs.
5. Cook okra, garlic, and onion in the saucepan for six minutes.
6. Stir in corn, salt, and pepper for 5 to 6 minutes, until the corn is bright yellow.
7. Incorporate the butter, ensuring it all melts.
8. Stir in cherry tomatoes and basil.
9. Layer shredded cheese over the succotash.
10. Sprinkle bacon bits on top.

Serve the Cheddar Corn Succotash in bowls while hot. You can preserve leftovers for a week by covering them with plastic and refrigerating them.

Fruit-Based Recipes

Part of the festival of Lughnasadh, particularly in the circles that celebrate it as Lammas, is the tradition of the First Fruit. This is similar to the idea of making food out of the first grains or corn harvested, except it's more closely associated with post-Christianity iterations of paganism. The plucking of the First Fruit sometimes has a negative connotation with that of the forbidden Fruit of Knowledge of Good and Evil taken by Eve in the Garden of Eden. However, pagans generally view it in a more positive light.

Apple Butter

Apples in Celtic paganism are believed to imbue those who consume them with power, sometimes even immortality. Druid's wands are traditionally held to have been made from either yew or the wood from an apple tree. Although apples are more important in other pagan festivals than Lughnasadh, they still hold significance during the harvest season.

Ingredients:

- 1 ½ pound of cored, chopped apples (5 apples)
- ¼ cup of caster sugar
- 2 tablespoons of lemon juice
- ¼ teaspoon of ground cinnamon
- ⅓ cup of brown sugar
- ½ cup of water
- Pinch of salt
- Pinch of ground clove

Cooking Directions:

1. Add the apple chunks and cores into a medium-sized saucepan.
2. Stir in water, lemon juice, and caster sugar.
3. Bring the contents of the saucepan to a simmer for 20 to 25 minutes.
4. Remove the apples from the heat and throw out the cores.
5. Pour the mixture into a food processor and blend until it becomes smooth.
6. Add the pureed mixture back into the saucepan.
7. Stir in the brown sugar, salt, and spices, cooking over medium heat until it begins to simmer.
8. Reduce the heat to low and wait for 5 to 10 minutes until it has been slightly reduced and thickened.
9. Pour the apple butter mixture into pressure-sealed jars. Wait until they have cooled to use them, or store them in the refrigerator for as long as 3 weeks.

Blackberry Tarts

Food can often connect you to certain memories from the distant past, like picking blackberries with your family during the latter days of summer. These memories are a window into your own personal history, and reflecting upon them is a healthy way to process aspects of your present and future. As Lughnasadh was established to honor the memory of Lugh's beloved foster mother, you can use this festival as a chance to honor the memory of your own loved ones.

Ingredients:

- 1 double-crust pastry
- 6 cups of fresh blueberries that have been rinsed, drained, and divided

- ¼ cup of cornstarch
- 1 tablespoon of whole milk
- ½ teaspoon of lemon juice
- ⅔ cup of granulated sugar
- 1 jumbo egg
- 6 tart pans

Cooking Directions:

1. Preheat your stove (400 F).
2. Place a layer of baking foil on a baking tray.
3. Press and mash the blackberries in a bowl with a fork to release the juices.
4. Mix the sugar and cornstarch together in a measuring cup.
5. Pour the sugar and cornstarch mixture into the bowl with the berries.
6. Add the remaining 3 cups of blackberries.
7. Add the lemon juice.
8. Combine the mixture by folding it with a spatula.
9. Roll the dough from the bowl onto a surface that has been dusted with flour.
10. Cut 4 rounds that are about 1 inch bigger than your tart pans.
11. Carefully press the pastry into the bottom and sides of the pans.
12. Roll the dough again, cutting out two more rounds for the last 2 pans.
13. Distribute the mixture equally into the 6 tart pans.
14. Cut a top for the tarts from the extra pastry and secure them in place.
15. Dip your finger in water and moisten the top edges of the tarts.
16. Whisk the milk and egg together, using a brush to cover the tops of the tarts.
17. Sprinkle on any extra sugar.
18. Bake the tarts on the baking sheet.
19. Bake for 15 minutes at 400 degrees Fahrenheit.
20. Reduce heat to 350 degrees Fahrenheit and bake for another 15 minutes until the pastry is golden-brown and the filling is bubbling

Serve the tarts while they're still hot or warm. You can add a scoop of vanilla ice cream on top to make the dessert a little sweeter. Leftovers must be stored in an airtight container, and they will usually go bad after two days.

Cherry Pie

No late summer festivities can be complete without a cherry pie. Cherries themselves are a symbol of new life and regeneration. Just as the Grain Mother gives birth in the autumn, starting the cycle of the next generation, who will carry the seeds in the spring, cherries represent this beginning for the pagans. They are also a tasty fruit you can bake into a pie, combining the first cherries picked and the first grains harvested into a single dish.

Ingredients:

- 2 ½ cups of all-purpose flour
- 1 teaspoon of salt
- ⅔ cup of chilled vegetable shortening
- ½ cup of ice water
- 4 ½ cups of pitted cherries (half of them halved, the other half quartered)
- ⅔ cup of granulated sugar
- ¼ cup of cornstarch
- 7 tablespoons of cold unsalted butter cut into cubes
- 1 tablespoon of lemon juice
- 1 teaspoon of pure vanilla extract
- ¼ teaspoon of almond extract
- 1 jumbo egg beaten with 1 tablespoon of milk into an egg wash

Cooking Directions:

1. Combine the flour and salt.
2. Add in the shortening.
3. Use a knife to cut the shortening into the flour mixture.
4. The result should be small, coarse pieces.
5. Combine the ice and water separately.
6. Reduce the water level to a half cup.
7. Dose the water into the pastry mix a little at a time, stirring with your hands to incorporate it.
8. You want to end with large pieces of dough that clump together.
9. Add flour to your hands and a flat surface, ready to work the dough.
10. Knead the dough until it becomes more elastic.
11. Roll into a ball and separate into two halves.

12. Flatten the halves.

13. Cover in plastic wrap and chill the dough.

14. Stir the cherries, lemon juice, cornstarch, vanilla, and almond extracts in a large bowl until completely blended to make your filling.

15. Cover the bowl of filling and place it in the refrigerator for up to 24 hours, depending on how solid you want it.

16. Roll out one of the chilled discs of dough on a floured surface.

17. Rotate the dough 90 degrees after two or three rolls until your dough is in a circle with a 12-inch diameter.

18. Press the dough into a disposable aluminum pie dish, using your fingers to tuck it in and make it smooth.

19. Using a slotted spoon, spread the cherries into the pie crust, saving the cherry juice for later.

20. Store the pie in the refrigerator without covering it.

21. Pour the leftover cherry juice into a small saucepan.

22. On low heat, simmer for 5 minutes or until the lighted has thickened.

23. Cool the juices for 5 minutes, then pour them over the cherry filling.

24. Toss the filling gently to spread the juices around it.

25. Place the remaining 1 tablespoon of butter around on top of the filling

26. Preheat the oven to 400 degrees Fahrenheit.

27. Take the second disc of dough and pie out of the refrigerator and place it on the floured surface.

28. Using a pastry cutter or knife, begin cutting the dough into 4 strips that are 2-inches wide and 2 strips that are 1-inch wide.

29. Thread the strips on top of the pie, weaving them over and under at every other contact point.

30. Trim off any extra dough and use a fork to crimp the edges.

31. Brush the top of the pie with the egg wash.

32. Bake on a baking tray for 20 minutes.

33. Reduce the temperature to 375 F

34. Bake the pie for 30 to 40 more minutes until the crust on top is golden-brown and the filling has been bubbling for five minutes.

35. Cool the pie on a rack for 2-5 hours, or until cool, in the center.

36. Once the pie has cooled, slice and serve it at your feast. Store any remaining pie in the fridge for 4-6 days.

How to Imbue Your Food with Magic

Part of Lughnasadh involves blessing your food and imbuing it with magic. There are two ways to go about this: using an altar and a specific prayer or performing a ritual invoking the power of the gods while offering them a sacrifice. The main difference between these two modes of asking for a blessing is that the first requires a more precise construction and placement of your altar, while with the second type, you can perform the ritual just about anywhere.

Before the ritual, you must know what type of blessing you desire. Do you want to have a bountiful harvest? Are you honoring your family, friends, elders, or pets? Maybe you just want to thank the gods and leave them a place at your table. Whatever the motivation behind your blessing request, you have to focus on the reason you chose. Magic is more than rituals and incantations. Your intent behind the rituals matters just as much, if not more, than these things.

Harmonizing your rituals and intent begins even before you get to the blessings. While preparing your food, purge yourself of negative emotions. So long as you are only carrying positive energy within your aura, your intentions for the food will be imbued within it while you cook. The benefits of doing this can be felt when the food is consumed, passing along the positive energy and strengthening the power of your blessings.

Chapter 7: Family and Group Activities

Lughnasadh is a time to celebrate togetherness, especially with your family and community. The whole concept of a feast itself is about bringing people together, sharing in your good fortune, and strengthening the bonds between everyone. There are many activities you can participate in as a group. Something like baking Lammas Bread with the first grains harvested during Lughnasadh can be a great task to do with your family. You can give everyone a specific assignment, such as gathering the ingredients, kneading the dough, or mixing everything together.

Games and Competitions

The traditional first Lughnasadh celebration included funeral games put on in honor of Tailtiu. This involved many events, including foot races, horse races, chariot races, long jumps, high jumps, boxing matches, wrestling, spear throwing, hurling, swimming, sword fighting, and archery. The purpose of these competitions wasn't just for the veneration of the fallen goddess, though. They also brought the people together to proclaim new laws and provide them with entertainment.

More modern versions of the Tailteann Games carry over some of the original competitions but also add in chess, sailing, motor boat racing, bicycling, motorcycling, and shooting. As new technologies emerge and people find leisure applications for them, fresh or updated games are included alongside the older ones. While many organizers attempt to remain true to the spirit of the original games, they are done much safer, particularly where weaponry is concerned.

Even if you don't live somewhere that stages an official set of competitions, you can hold your own games with your family or community. Fun ideas include potato sack races, horseshoes, lawn darts, or tag football.

Make a piñata in the shape of something connected to the harvest, like a corn-on-the-cob, apple, or sunflower. A group game that doesn't involve much physical activity, such as chess, checkers, or bingo, can allow the older folk time to rest and keep them entertained. As long as you're enjoying yourself during the celebrations, anything can be a worthwhile addition to your festival.

Parades

As with many other holidays, Lughnasadh can involve a parade in honor of the traditions maintained throughout paganism. However, these generally aren't the types of parades normally associated with holidays, particularly in the secular world. There aren't any decorated floats or massive balloons involved. One of the older traditional parades is a pilgrimage up a mountain. Participants will carry a bundle of flowers with them, leaving one at different intervals along the way. This is meant to signify the end of the summer and the beginning of the harvest season.

Another form of the parade is the ritualistic journey taken around a series of wells, mimicking the one taken by Lugh during his foster mother's funeral. Participants move clockwise around the wells, stopping to pray at each one and make an offering to the gods, typically a coin or a small ribbon known as a clootie that is tied around a nearby tree. It is considered good luck to do this and is believed to confer blessings of health and protection for those who make the trek.

One of the stranger parades includes choosing a local schoolgirl to serve as the "Queen of Puck," crowning a goat as "King Puck." The goat is usually lured down from the mountains, and the ceremony is performed in a public area, like a village square or park. After being crowned, the goat is paraded through town, accompanied by street performers, people in costumes, and many of the "king's" other "subjects." Vendors will set up their stalls along the parade route to sell their goods to the participants and onlookers.

Music and Dancing

Music and dancing are important aspects of traditional Lughnasadh celebrations. Like with many festivals, these activities are often performed together, with musicians playing traditional folk songs as people gather and dance around them. This has long been a great way for a community to share their culture and honor the gods, with many revelries often lasting well into the early hours of the following morning. Music and dancing are also tried and true methods of artistic expression, allowing individuals to easily communicate their feelings and emotions to an assembled crowd.

Traditional Folk Music

The ancient Celtic pagans played music tailored to the instruments available during that period. The carnyx is one of the oldest known to have been popular between 200 BCE and 200 AD. It is a bronze horn-like instrument shaped like an elongated "S," with a mouthpiece on one end and a bell on the other. A carnyx is played by holding the middle portion and blowing on the mouthpiece, resulting in a sound from the bell facing the opposite direction. These bells were often crafted in the image of an animal head, such as a bird, wolf, or boar.

Other instruments favored by the Celts include horns, trumpets, flutes, and rattles. Lyres are believed to have originated with the pagans and were later imported to foreign lands, particularly within the Roman Empire. The types of music played on these instruments can be considered folk music, with very simple, easy-to-learn compositions and chanting or singing accompanying such performance pieces. Most of these songs were passed down orally, so there aren't many written accounts of music from the early days of Celtic paganism.

Neopagans have attempted to recreate the general style that would've been heard in pre-Christianity Scotland and Ireland. During modern-day festivals, musicians will play both traditional instruments and their current counterparts, adding guitars, pianos, violins, and drum kits. Genres like neofolk, Euro-pagan, and heavy metal all take influence from traditional Celtic music, updated with the sensibilities of popular culture. During Lughnasadh, musicians often play songs with themes centered on the harvest season or the god Lugh and the many folktales surrounding his life.

Celtic Dances

The music in the old Celtic traditions was often made specifically to be accompanied by dancing. This is why much of it possesses a very rhythmic quality. Handbells known as crotales, rattles, and other percussion instruments meant to be used during dances were inspired by the noises made by weapons banging against shields that ancient Celtic warriors made before battlefield engagements. Dancing and combat have been intertwined for ages. The physical prowess and agility displayed while dancing is believed to express a similar martial mastery in wartime.

A popular performative dance put on during Lughnasadh involves the god Lugh striving against Crom Dubh for dominion over the grain fields, as Lugh provided humanity with the ability to sow and harvest these crops. Another depicts him battling an evil force, represented by a large stone head installed on a hilltop or mountainside. Sometimes, it is a goddess whose fate is in question, ultimately saved by an actor playing Lugh during a choreographed dance battle.

One of the common traditions associated with dances during Lughnasadh is that of a courting ritual. Young men and women can express their affection for one another by presenting their intended mates with a flower or token of favor and engaging each other as dance partners. By proving capable of an extended, physically-demanding activity like dancing, young men and women can show their viability as strong, healthy mates. It is also an enjoyable way to work off any calories packed during the feast, offering both entertainment and fitness value to participants.

Arts and Crafts

Arts and crafts are a great way to spend time with your family or friends during the lead-up to and during Lughnasadh. Creating decorations to display around your home can get everyone into the spirit of the harvest festival. Making different arts and crafts projects can give you a stimulating activity to undertake while having conversations with your loved ones, especially if the task isn't very labor-intensive but takes a fair amount of time to complete. Try using a themed project to help initiate a dialogue concerning Lughnasadh and the holiday traditions to pass this knowledge to the younger generations.

Learn a New Skill

Expanding your mind and acquiring a new skill is never a bad idea. During Lughnasadh, you can try to pick up something related to paganism in general or the harvest in particular. Baking or cooking is a major part of the holiday, so if you don't already know how to do it, you can assist others in the kitchen, learning the craft for yourself. Magical subjects and spellcasting are also very important for pagan rituals and blessings, making this the perfect opportunity to gain familiarity with them before attempting an invocation on your own.

Divination

Divination is the art of predicting the future, often through external aid. Unlike fortune-telling, divination normally has a ritualistic component, such as reading tea leaves or tarot cards. Having the ability to foretell certain events is very useful, especially when it comes to growing crops. Suppose you know ahead of time what plants will thrive that season, where the best location to grow them is, or what type of weather you need to prepare for. In that case, your resultant bounty yields favorable results during the harvest.

Learning the craft of divination can take time to master, and having plenty of patience is required. It can take some people years or even decades before they're able to make consistently accurate predictions. It is believed that when the gods are more active, they are more likely to give powerful omens to their followers. Knowing how to interpret them properly can avoid being taken by surprise, especially when there are readily available warnings beforehand.

Astrology

Similar to divination, astrology is a method of forecasting future events by reading the characteristics of various celestial bodies. Ancient druids practiced a version of this as far back as 1000 BCE, using the Ogham, or the Celtic shamanistic alphabet, as a basis for their system. They organized their calendar into 13 lunar months and 28 days to a month. Each month had a specific symbol from the Ogham assigned to it, as well as a corresponding type of tree, guardian animal, and gemstone. These include:

Dates	Nickname	Tree	Animal	Gemstone	Traits
Jan 21-Feb 17	The Thinker	Rowan	Green Dragon	Peridot	Progressive, creative, moral
Feb 18-Mar 17	The Enchanter	Ash	Seal, Seagull, Seahorse	Coral	Creative, intuitive, spontaneous
Mar 18-Apr 14	The Trailblazer	Alder	Bear, Fox, Hawk	Ruby	Inventor, pioneer, discoverer
Apr 15-May 12	The Observer	Willow	Hare, Adder, Sea Serpent	Moonstone	Intelligent, curious, observant
May 13-Jun 9	The Illusionist	Hawthorn	Bee, Owl	Topaz	Compassionate, calm, curios
Jun 10-Jul 7	The Stabilizer	Oak	White horse, otter, wren	Diamond	Positivity, justice, confident
Jul 8-Aug 4	The Ruler	Holly	Cat, unicorn	Carnelian	Noble, successful, brave
Au 5-Sep 1	The Knower	Hazel	Crane, salmon	Amethyst	Knowledgeable, intelligent, curious

Sep 2-Sep 29	The Equalizer	Vine	White swan, hound, lizard	Emerald	Adaptive, strong-willed, unpredictable
Sep 30-Oct 27	The Survivor	Ivy	Butterfly, Goose, Boar	Opal	Charismatic, restless, optimism
Oct 28-Nov 24	The Leader	Reed	Hound, owl	Jasper	Willpower, learner, historian
Nov 25-Dec 23	The Scholar	Elder	Badger, raven, black horse	Jet	Resilient, confident, free-willed
Dec 24-Jan 20	The Achiever	Birch	White stag, golden eagle	Rock crystal	Motivated, ambitious, passionate

Alchemy

Alchemy pertains to pagan beliefs and is a bit different than the traditional practice, being more akin to herbalism and holistic healing. The primary goal of the original alchemists was to turn base metals, such as lead, into noble metals, like gold or silver. The modern paganism practice of alchemy seeks to transform the spirit or soul of a person rather than changing the chemical structure of objects. Herbs are typically used to make alchemical potions, some of which are purported to contain medicinal and healing properties.

Learning alchemy alongside other magical practices is a great way to enhance your knowledge of the natural world. You must become familiar with many different types of herbs and plants, including any benefits or harmful effects they might possess. Although it is considered a pseudoscience, many alchemists will use the scientific method to determine what results in their concoctions offer. During Lughnasadh, focusing on potions that can provide energy or increase concentration is especially useful, as harvesting crops can be exhausting.

Bonfires

Staging a bonfire during Lughnasadh conjures up the traditional depiction of Tailtiu's funeral pyre. It can also serve as a beacon in the dark for weary travelers, assuring them that their destination is near. Many bonfires built during the harvest festival will include offerings to the gods, such as sacrificial loaves of Lammas bread, goods created from the start of the harvest, or crafted representations of animals, particularly livestock. Bonfires typically burn from sundown on Lughnasadh to sunrise the next morning, and the ash and soot remain collected by the community to be used as spell reagents for the following harvest festivals.

Foraging

Making a day of taking your family or a group of fellow pagans out to go foraging is a good activity to help supplement your supply of foods and ingredients for the Lughnasadh feast. Items found in the wilds can also be used to decorate your altars, and many flowers and berries make wonderful accents for ornamentation. Nuts, acorns, fruit from trees, and other foraged goods are often edible, so you can mix up your own snacks to share with others during the harvest festival.

Gardening

In addition to growing crops, maintaining a garden is a way to increase your connection to the natural world. You can plant flowers for their pleasing aromas and aesthetic appeal or try growing herbs and spices for medicinal and cooking purposes. Different types of flowers and plants can offer benefits to your home, like marigolds being able to repel insects or peace lilies helping to improve the air quality of their surroundings. Having your family aid in the garden can bring you closer together, as hard work and caring for living things are fantastic bonding activities.

Harvesting

From the earliest days of agriculture through the present, farmers tended to their crops with the assistance of others. These were often their immediate family members, as anyone raised on a farm was expected to help with the labor and chores. Although harvesting crops may not seem like an amusing activity, you can make it more fun by involving your family or friends. The more people that participate in harvesting crops, the sooner you'll be able to turn them into great food for your Lughnasadh feast. You can make a game of it to entertain your children, having a contest to see who can harvest the most in a select period of time. Offer a prize, like an extra slice of pie or cake for whoever wins.

Activities for Children

When you want to include your children in any Lughnasadh activities, finding something entertaining enough to hold their attention is useful. Hiking is a very low-cost diversion, and you can bring along butterfly nets or birdwatching guides to interact with the wonders of nature along the way. Taking the opportunity to share a love of flora and fauna encountered in the wilds can help children understand what makes these things so important. Modern children are so inundated with electronics and technology that giving them a break to slow down and experience nature while exercising benefits their mental and physical health.

Find activities that children can enjoy as a bonding experience. Strengthen their interest in paganism by encouraging them to explore every aspect of the religion. You can guide their endeavors by setting up basic rituals and aiding them in making their own altars to celebrate Lughnasadh with the rest of your family. It's a good idea to start off with simple rites and spells, gradually introducing them to more complicated concepts. You don't want to overwhelm them, but children's minds are like sponges, and they can absorb a significant amount of information if it's presented easily.

Chapter 8: Lammas Rituals and Ceremonies

Carrying out the rituals and ceremonies associated with Lughnasadh is an aspect you must take very seriously. This part of the festival's traditions is where you interact most with the gods and nature, so you must get them right. There are many ways to honor the powers surrounding Lughnasadh, so choose the ones you are the most comfortable doing, and provide you with the types of benefits you seek. You don't have to be an expert in every facet of pagan beliefs, but you should pick one or two and study them until you know them inside and out.

As with any ritual or ceremony in paganism, you must make your intentions clear while performing them. Try to avoid selfish or greedy motivations, as that can bring too much negative energy into your space. While it's okay to attempt a ritual or ceremony with the intention of gaining a plentiful yield during the upcoming harvest, this shouldn't exceed more than you need to survive. Attempting to use pagan rites to enrich yourself beyond what's necessary may lead to failure and undesired consequences. It's up to you whether to perform these rituals and ceremonies alone or with others. The following examples are some of the most popular options.

Ancestral Meditation Ritual

Meditating on the wisdom and strength of those who came before is a powerful ritual to perform during Lughnasadh. It cannot be overstated how important the knowledge accumulated by previous generations is, helping you to overcome obstacles by learning from the past. To perform this ritual, you'll need:

- Your altar
- A candle

- A handful of incense or smudge sticks
- An item connected to a loved one who has passed
- Petals from sunflowers or leaves from an oak tree
- A mortar and pestle

To begin the ritual, light the candle on your altar, and then light your incense or smudge sticks from the flame of that candle. Crush the sunflower petals or oak tree leaves in the mortar and pestle until you have turned them into tiny bits. As you do this, say:

"From blood to ash, I ask for the wisdom of [insert loved one's name here]. Grant me the will to survive any hardship, and grant me the strength to carry any burden."

When you've finished crushing the petals or leaves, sprinkle them around the object connected to your loved one, creating a full circle. If you have anything left over, spread it across the front of your altar, from left to right. Close your eyes and repeat this prayer:

"I beseech my beloved [insert name of loved one here] to light the path ahead. Let me bask in your warmth and take refuge within your tireless arms. I ask that you keep my family safe and provide us with that which we need to survive."

After finishing the prayer, open your eyes and pick up one of the incense or smudge sticks. Move it in the shape of a five-point star, and then hold it out in your hands, saying:

"I thank you for your comfort and blessings. May we continue to walk in the light of your wisdom and look upon you as a shining beacon in the dark. I thank you for the love you offer and for the joy you share. *Please let me have the strength to pass on your knowledge and share your love with those who come after."*

Once you have completed the ritual, put out the candle and the incense or smudge sticks. Clean up your altar, but leave the item connected to your loved one in place. You can also remain and meditate for as long as you'd like, and when you are ready, thank your ancestors with a respectful prayer of your own.

Honoring Lugh

Since Lugh is one of the primary gods associated with Lughnasadh, performing a ritual to honor him is something many pagans choose to do. To do this, you should have:

- Your altar
- A candle

- An offering to Lugh (food or item)

Initiate this ritual by placing the offering alongside a candle on your altar. Light the candle and speak the following words:

"Blessed Lugh, whose magnificence we honor on this day, please keep watch over our family as we start the harvest. With your guiding hand, lead us to the bounty, that we might make more offerings unto you. By your spear, protect us; by your hammer, build us shelter; by your heart, save us from starvation. Blessed Lugh, embrace us so that we may honor you."

This invocation will call upon the different aspects of Lugh to grant aid, sustenance, and protection. His station as the King of the Tuatha Dé Danann sets him above the other gods and goddesses, so appealing directly to him for a blessing can bring immense benefits. For the offering, state:

"Blessed Lugh, we give thee an offering so that you may know our gratitude for giving us succor. Our good fortune is your good fortune, the fruits of our harvest made possible through your power. We thank you for your blessing and pray that you are satisfied with this meager token of our appreciation."

After you've finished the ritual, snuff out the flame of the candle and take your offering outside. Break it up and bury the pieces in four holes, each representing one of the cardinal directions: north, south, east, and west. Say the following once the pieces are buried:

"Blessed Lugh, thank you for your gifts. We return a small measure of our good fortune to you through Mother Earth, on whom we depend for our sustenance. If you should find this offering acceptable, please keep us safe in the days to come."

Harvest Ritual

A common harvest ritual invokes nature's power and thanks Mother Earth for her bounties. What you'll need to perform this ritual is:

- Your altar
- A candle
- A feather
- Food offerings (like Lammas bread)

The first thing you must do is cast a circle to raise the energy of your ceremonial space. Light the candle on your altar and recite:

"Here I am on the season's first harvest, the sacred festival of Lughnasadh. I seek to understand the cycle of life, death, and rebirth, and I wish to honor those who have endured each. Lord and Lady, grant me insight."

Once you have spoken these words, take the time to reflect in silence on the harvest, life, and Mother Earth. Do this for 10-15 minutes, remaining focused on your intentions and your musings. Next, place the offering of food upon your altar and say:

"Thanks be to Mother Earth, who brings us this bounty. Thanks be to the gods and goddesses who guide and protect us. As the goddess matures and her pregnant belly expands, the Sun is waning. Yet his energy still warms my bones and strengthens my mind. I offer unto both of you a token of my thanks, the first fruits of my harvest."

Following this, take a colorful feather from a peacock or a shimmering black feather from a magpie and lightly brush it across your cheek. Smile as you do this and repeat:

"Lord Lugh and Lady Gaia, I ask that you come to me. Help me see the joy in all things. Let me feel the warmth of the sun and a full belly from the feast. Rid me of my worries for at least one day so that I may honor thee with a lightened heart."

Use this time to visualize any friends or family members who might need their spirits lifted. Picture brushing the feather across their cheek and making them laugh. This can help to bring them joy during a difficult time in their life. After this, close your sacred space by snuffing out the candle's flame.

Bread Sacrifices

Performing a bread sacrifice is one of the more common rituals for Lughnasadh, as Lammas bread made with the first grains harvested is often baked as part of the festival celebrations. Once you are ready to begin the ritual, you'll need:

- Your altar
- An unsliced loaf of Lammas bread
- A candle (red, orange, or yellow)
- A few stalks of wheat
- A goblet of ritual wine or apple cider

You can initiate the ritual by casting a circle, but this part isn't a *necessity*. Light your candle, choosing the color representing the autumn season, mimicking the changing leaves. When lit, chant:

"The Wheel is turning, and what we have sown is ready to reap. We thank you for the food on our table during our celebration of Lammas. The soil is fertile; the earth yields us its gifts. We are grateful for all that your spirit uplifts. We thank you, Mother Earth, for granting us your boon. We thank you for the stars, the sun, and the moon."

The next step in the ritual involves holding the stalks of wheat in front of you and focusing on what they symbolize. They represent the power of nature and the coming winter. You must plan ahead to ensure you are prepared to survive until the spring. Be sure to offer up a sacrifice for the gift you have received. Make your intentions for the ritual known by stating your wishes for the oncoming harvest and the winter beyond.

Now, rub the ends of the stalks of wheat between your fingers. Allow the grain to be sprinkled atop your altar. If you are performing the ritual indoors, leave them on the altar for the time being. If you are outdoors, you can spread the grain upon the earth. Recite the following after the wheat has been removed from its stalks:

"The power of the harvest is within my soul. The seed falls to earth, where it shall be reborn whole. As the seasons change, so must I. Like the wheat in the fields, I grow and must die. Like the cycle of death and rebirth, I sow new seeds to take root in the earth. Seeds and small, but they create massive growth. This blessing is a key; your secrets it unlocks. I put aside this wheat, for you know the reason. I ask for your blessing through the coming winter season."

Take a piece of the Lammas bread you have prepared. If you have others with you, give the loaf to the person on your right-hand side. They should also take a piece. The bread should move around your group, with each person taking some. Use these words:

"This gift is given to you from the harvest."

After everyone participating in the ritual has torn off a piece of bread, everyone will say:

"This bounty has been given to all of us. We take this blessing and give you our thanks."

Everyone should eat their piece of bread as a symbolic gesture. Pass around the goblet of wine or apple cider, and allow each participant to take a sip. Use this time as an opportunity to reflect on the cycle of growth, death, and rebirth, particularly in how it pertains to your life. Consider the ways it affects you spiritually, emotionally, and physically. When everyone finishes the ritual, close the circle, and snuff out the candle. If you are performing the ceremony indoors, take the grains from the wheat stalks outside to spread them across the earth.

Bonfire Ceremony

You can perform a ceremony when building a bonfire for your Lughnasadh celebrations. This is reminiscent of similar sacrificial rituals performed by ancient pagans, but without burning any living animals as offerings.

Bonfire ceremony.
https://pxhere.com/en/photo/1633209

The materials required for this ceremony include:

- Sticks, timber, or wood
- Bricks or stones
- Matches, flint, and steel, or a grill lighter
- Doll or effigy of an animal (bull, goat, pig, or cow)
- Salt

Build the main structure of the bonfire in a safe location. Surround it with a circle made from bricks or stones to help keep the blaze contained. Use your preferred method of lighting the fire, and recite the following:

"By the cleansing flame on this very night, to the gods and goddesses, we offer this light."

Allow the fire to engulf the tinder and reach its full size. During this time, close your eyes and focus on your intentions for the ritual. You can hold hands with anyone else present to boost the energy given off, but remember to keep it positive. After the bonfire is roaring, create a ring around it and any participants with the salt. Be sure everyone remains within this circle for the duration of the ceremony. Next, speak these words, taking turns with any other participants for each line:

"As our bounty during this harvest has given us plenty, we wish to offer something in return.

A sacrifice made to Mother Earth, a sacrifice to the grace of the gods.

Here we give thanks for our good fortune and for the blessings of grain.

We also offer you this gift from our flock, proof of devotion from your supplicants."

Toss the dolls or effigies of the animals into the bonfire. In the time of ancient pagans, a bull would often be sacrificed before the Lughnasadh feast as a sign of appreciation for the favor of Lugh. Using similar imagery, albeit with inanimate imitations, can have the same effect. The idea is that taking the time and effort to perform the ceremony is itself an act of devotion rather than sacrificing a living being. Most modern pagans are against animal cruelty of any kind, so it is acceptable to use a doll or effigy in their place. Once these have been placed in the bonfire, say:

"To you, we freely give the fruits of our labor. We thank you for everything we have and choose to make this sacrifice because we would not have this bounty without your blessings. Thank you, Mother Earth. Thank you, Lord Lugh. We shall keep you in our hearts from now until the soil has thawed in the spring."

If you want to add any small personal prayers of thanks, this is the time to make them. Thank the gods and goddesses for any good fortune you've experienced that year. Help to focus this positive energy during the personal prayers of the other participants as well. When you have finished, a state in unison:

"We thank you for everything you've given and all you shall grant to us in the coming days."

With the ceremony complete, you can break the circle and initiate any other celebrations you wish, such as singing and dancing, feasting, or a parade. The bonfire can serve as a centerpiece to the festival, marking the night with a spectacular fiery display. As much as these rituals are about giving thanks to the gods and receiving their blessings, they are also about strengthening the bond within your family or community. Performing them together is a great way to build upon the connection you already share, reinforcing your relationship between each other and your religion.

Chapter 9: Spells, Charms, and Baths

There are two distinct phases when performing spells, charms, or baths: gathering power and energy and releasing it. This is often signified by a change in the tense used by the language of the incantations. During the gathering phase, you'll use the future tense, indicating the potential of the spell you seek to recite. When you switch to the release phase, the language will shift to the present tense to show that you are currently in the process of casting them. Unlike the magic from fantasy-genre stories, the kind practiced by pagans is primarily concerned with an individual's ability to enact change in their lives through esoteric, hidden knowledge.

Most spells, charms, and baths require herbs and other items to augment the spoken incantations. These help you focus your power and channel your energy. As with the rituals and blessings performed during Lughnasadh, the intent is a major factor in the success of any spell, charm, or bath. Although you can cast them anywhere, using your altar can help you keep your attention on the task. Remember the principle of "threefold return," meaning that any energy you put into the world will come back to you three times as powerful. Therefore, you mustn't attempt magic with ill intent, lest you become a victim of your own negative energy.

Understanding magic needs knowledge of what's known as the "doctrine of signatures." This philosophy claims that ailments affecting different parts of the human body can be treated through herbs and plants that resemble the afflicted areas. Many of these contain the name of the body part they're associated with, such as eyebright (eyes), toothwort (teeth), lungwort (lungs), liverwort (liver), and spleenwort (spleen). The hedge woundwort plant can be applied to any lesions or other physical maladies on the body, as it's believed to have antiseptic properties.

Choosing a location to perform any spells, charms, or baths is entirely up to you, but consider the fact that things like doors, windows, cracked surfaces, and other thresholds are viewed as portals to the space between worlds. Performing magic during transitionary periods, like between night and day, or the changing of the seasons, is also believed to affect the potency of your spells. While you are by no means limited to only using the examples provided, these are a great place to start. As you gain experience, you can begin to work out more complicated spells or even concoct your own.

Healing Spells

Having a working knowledge of healing spells can be hugely beneficial when you must exert yourself physically during the harvest. The mind can be a powerful tool wielded in the fight against pain, and strengthening it through the use of magic can help you overcome injuries to your body. You can cast these spells on yourself or someone else to ease the pain. Most healing spells require herbs to perform, and each type of herb provides a specific benefit, so pairing the right ones together will have the best possible outcome.

Healing Muscle Aches

For a spell to help heal muscle aches and pains, you can use herbs like turmeric, ginger, bromelain, devil's claw, or arnica. You can either burn them over charcoal or consume them while casting the spell. During the gathering phase, recite the following:

"Mind over matter, I will no longer suffer. Let the power flow through me and strengthen my body. When I have been healed, I will give thanks."

During this time, concentrate on visualizing your injuries being mended. Once you have built up enough positive energy, release it with these words:

"Mind over matter, my [state type of injury, i.e., sore back, torn ligament, pulled neck, etc.] pains me no more. I am whole and hale. Thank you for granting me this gift."

Repeat the spell as often as you need to return to full health. Allow yourself to rest for at least an hour between attempts so as not to overexert your energy, as this can make it more difficult to succeed.

Illness Recovery

The time around Lughnasadh is the beginning of the cold and flu seasons. Spending so much time outdoors, especially if it's particularly cool and rainy, can result in viruses or infections that may sideline you from participating in group activities. To combat this, you can perform a spell meant to speed up how long it takes to recover. Plants meant to aid in this process include garden thyme, honeysuckle, yarrow, peppermint leaves, green chiretta, and marigolds. To help with expectoration, you can use snakeroot, licorice root, tulsi, cloves, sage leaves, slippery elm root, or marshmallow osha root.

To perform a spell that encourages a speedier recovery, burn, or consume one or more of the first group of plants listed above. During the gathering phase, you will recite:

"I seek to restore my health. Through the power of nature, I shall recover. In all her blessings, I can find strength. In all her wonders, I can find wisdom."

This makes your intentions clear and allows you to focus your energy on the task of recovery. When you are ready to move to the release phase, say:

"I can feel the power of nature infuse my body. I am expelling the illness and breathing in clean air. As I humbly ask for your strength, I feel it flowing through me. As I humbly ask for your wisdom, it sharpens my mind."

After you have completed the spell, you can chew on one of the plants from the second group. This is for the practical purpose of helping clear out any mucus that might have built up in your throat or nasal passages, allowing you to breathe more easily. By combining magical incantation and herbal remedies, you can rid yourself of your illness without ever needing to take chemically-created drugs or medicines.

Migraine Remedy

It can be incredibly difficult to perform many tasks when you have a migraine headache. These can come about for many reasons, including exhaustion, stress, allergies, or light sensitivity. You can use feverfew, ginger, peppermint, butterbur, coriander seeds, rosemary, and lavender oil to aid in ridding yourself of a migraine. While gathering your energy for the spell, speak these words:

"My head is in pain, but I will not let it stop me. I trust in the power of the gods and goddesses to get me through this. As Mother Earth has given these herbs the power to heal, I will accept her boon and let them rid me of my pain."

You can choose to either dry the leaves or consume them raw. Their medicinal properties can relieve even the worst migraines, and casting the spell boosts its power. When you are ready to release the energy, state:

"From the earth to my body, the gifts of nature heal my ills. I am no longer in pain. I release the tension from my head and cast it aside. I can think clearly and breathe easier. Thank you for releasing me from this pain."

Take a few moments to relax and meditate after speaking the incantation. If the migraine was caused partly by stress, focus on every muscle in your body and consciously uncoil them. After you have felt yourself release the tension, you may start to feel better almost immediately. Continue to use the herbs as needed until your migraine is gone.

Divination

Divination allows you to glimpse what the future may hold. To perform a divination spell, you'll need an empty bowl, preferably made of wood, and a satchel of charms, such as tiles, feathers, glass marbles, or small, smooth stones. You should have at least a dozen individual pieces with 3 distinct shapes, sizes, or colors that are evenly split across them all. If you have twelve marbles, there should be four of each color.

Begin the spell by focusing on a question you want to know. This can be anything, from "will I stay healthy through the winter?" to "when is the best time to repaint my kitchen?" Ideally, you'll be able to discern the answer to any query, but if you're still a beginner, it can be easier to simply ask "yes or no" questions. This prevents you from deciphering the results, as interpreting a binary choice doesn't need much experience properly.

To begin the spell, place the bowl in front of you, on the ground, or on top of your altar. You will initiate your divination by saying:

"I wish to ask the gods and goddesses for their wisdom and knowledge. This question is for you, and you are alone. I understand that you are merely a conduit, and I will not get angry if your answers are not to my liking. I shall heed what you tell me and conduct myself as befits one of your loyal followers."

This will assure the powers granting you a response that you won't attempt to thwart their omens or ignore their advice. Take a deep breath to help you focus on your question, and ask it aloud. If you are asking a "yes or no" question, reach into your satchel and take out three individual charms once you have finished speaking. Place them into the bowl and state:

"This is the answer to the question I seek: yes or no."

Take a look at the charms in the bowl. If 2 or more are the same shape, size, or color, the answer to the question is "yes." If they are all different shapes, sizes, or colors, the answer is "no." Make sure that you do not get angry or upset, no matter what you see. Negative energy can be incredibly dangerous, and never more so than while casting a spell. To remain calm, it's a good idea to immediately thank the gods and goddesses, even if you are disappointed by the results. This can be something as simple as:

"I thank you for your wisdom and guidance. I shall heed your advice in this matter."

If you are asking a more complicated question, you'll dump the entire satchel of charms into the bowl. As you do this, you will say:

"I now seek an answer to my question. Through your guidance, I shall gain insight. Through your experience, I shall gain knowledge."

Interpreting the results is a bit trickier with an open-ended question. You need to be able to find patterns in the way the charms are laid out or how they're grouped together. For example, if you want to know what month you should start looking for a new job, you might find a letter or symbol that can represent a specific month. It could also be determined by the number of charms with the same shape, size, or color that are touching one another. Perfecting the art of divination in this manner takes time and experience, so if you make a mistake, don't get discouraged. Eventually, you'll be able to understand the omens as if they were second nature.

Protection Charms and Baths

Casting a protective charm or making a protective bath can help keep you safe and prevent injury or ailments from befalling you. This is optimal if you are worried about getting sick or hurt in the near future, possibly wanting to avoid missing out on something important. Instead of casting a spell using energy gathered and released, these work by gathering energy and infusing it within yourself or a specific area.

Protection Charm Ritual

A standard protection charm will create a field of energy surrounding your chosen space, such as your room, home, or property. The larger the area, the more energy is needed to keep them active. To cast this charm, you'll require:

- 3-5 candles
- A doll or effigy
- Chamomile petals
- Pen and paper
- Matches or lighter
- Flame-resistant bowl or ashtray

Start of by writing the following on the piece of paper:

"Please protect [insert name of the area you wish protected, i.e., your bedroom, your house, etc.] from all harm. I trust in the power of the gods and goddesses, and I will not allow negative energy to invade my space. Once this charm has been cast, it will protect [name of area] for three times three days."

When you have finished writing, fold the paper up and place it in the bowl or ashtray. Now you must set the candles up around the perimeter of the area you wish to protect. This can be in the shape of a triangle, square, rectangle, circle, or five-point star. After you set the candle down, light it and say the following:

"I light this flame to ward off any evil that seeks to invade my space. So long as it burns, no darkness will seep through its barrier."

Repeat this for each candle, and then return to the bowl with the paper in it. Place the doll or effigy in front of it. This will represent the power of the charm, as you will channel the protective energy into it. Sprinkle the chamomile petals into the bowl, then set the paper aflame. As it burns, focus on visualizing a protective layer of energy surrounding your chosen area. After the fire is out, hold your doll or effigy in your hand and speak these words:

"This power now protects [name of area] from all harm. I have nothing to fear from anything outside it. Thank you for delivering me from the darkness and into the light."

It is now safe to snuff out the candles, as the protection charm is being fueled by the energy you put into the doll or effigy. It must remain within the protected area to work. Taking it beyond the perimeter you've established will cause it to lose its effect and leave you vulnerable to harm. After nine days, you can burn or bury the doll or effigy, as its power has been spent. You can repeat the charming ritual if you desire to maintain the protection magic keeping you safe.

Protective Bath

A protective bath utilizes a similar concept to the protection charm, except you will be infusing your own body with the power instead of a limited area. To create a magical bath, you'll need:

- A bathtub
- Crystals or stones that can be submerged in water
- Non-toxic herbs
- Essential oils
- Salt

Begin by drawing a bath, but do not step into it yet. Hold your hand over the water and focus on your intentions, namely protection against injury or illness. This will charge the water with the positive energy required for the bath to work. Add in the herbs, salt, and essential oils to help you charge the water. Speak your intent out loud, saying something like:

"I seek to protect myself from any harm by infusing my body with the power contained in this water."

Step into the bath and move the water around you clockwise. Try to feel the energy absorbed into your skin and spread around you from head to toe. Soak in the tub and meditate on any worries you might have, as this will help you focus the protective energy on yourself. Next, submerge the crystals or stones in the water with you. These will be used to extract negative energy from your body. You can recite this as you do:

"I release the negative, stagnant energy from my body. I release the negative, stagnant energy from my mind."

You can repeat this process until you feel yourself becoming unburdened by tension, stress, and anxiety. The crystals or stones should absorb any unwanted energy, trapping it within them. You can also gently massage yourself to assist in releasing these toxins from your body and mind. After you are satisfied that you've cleansed yourself and become protected, you can drain the water from the tub. Remove the crystals or stones to a safe place outdoors, and allow the light from the sun and the moon to expel the negative energy they hold. This process will take about a week. When they've been purified, you can use them again in your next bath.

Essential Oil Crystal Baths

You can pair herbs and essential oils with ritual crystals to infuse your bath with powerful manifestations. The crystals serve as a catalyst and augmentation for the herbs or essential oils, magnifying the results far beyond what they'd be on their own. For each one, you'll need:

- A crystal
- Vial of essential oils
- Herbs
- Fireproof dish
- Bath

Rose Quartz

Rose quartz crystals have a soft pink hue, reminiscent of the symbol of love: a heart. They can help you heal your heart, especially after it's been broken. Place the crystal into your bath and add 3 drops of rose geranium, 2 drops of patchouli, and 1 drop of ylang-ylang. Burn rose petals or peppermint in your dish, and speak your intentions, stating:

"I seek to heal my broken heart."

Soak in the tub for at least 15 minutes, allowing the essential oils to infuse your body with emotional healing energy. When you are done, drain the water out and retrieve the crystal.

Obsidian

Forged in volcanoes, this stone is jet black. It contains properties that will help shield you against negative energy. Place the crystal in your bath and add 1 drop of sandalwood, 1 drop of cedarwood, and 1 drop of frankincense. Burn lavender or sweet marjoram and speak your intentions:

"I seek to protect myself from negativity and negative energy."

Breathe in the aroma of the herbs and essential oils for 10-12 minutes. Once you have been imbued with the shield, drain the water from the tub and retrieve the obsidian.

Citrine

Citrine is a shining yellow crystal, invoking the image of a bright sun. It can boost your creativity and encourage success in your life. Place the citrine in your bath and add 10 drops of lemon, 10 drops of yuzu, 10 drops of tangerine, and 100ml of rose water. Burn rosemary or sage and recite these words to let your intentions be known:

"I seek to stimulate my creative mind and achieve great success."

Inhale the fragrance of the herbs and soak for 15 minutes. You should be able to feel the effect on your mind, offering clarity and new ideas to come rushing in. When you're finished, drain the bath, and retrieve the citrine.

Amethyst

Amethyst is a vivid purple crystal that is semi-translucent. It can protect you against anger, guilt, fear, anxiety, and negative energy. Place the amethyst in the tub and add 3 drops of bergamot, 2 drops of cedarwood, and 1 drop of sage. Burn cypress or sage and state your intentions:

"I seek to rid myself and protect against anger, fear, guilt, anxiety, and any other negative emotions."

Remain in the bath for 15 minutes until you have soaked in the power of the amethyst. After you're done, let the water drain out of the tub and retrieve the amethyst crystal.

Moonstone

Moonstone has a shimmering blue-white hue, evoking the image of the moon. It can help you to harness your intuition, tapping into your inner strength and willpower. Place the moonstone in your bath water and add 3 drops of geranium, 2 drops of myrrh, and 1 drop of clary sage. Burn some frankincense or rose petals and vocalize your intent:

"I seek to sharpen my intuition, enhance my inner strength, and fortify my will."

Soak in the tub for 10 minutes, letting the herbs and essential oils permeate every inch of your body. Once you've finished, empty your bath water, and retrieve the moonstone.

Amazonite

Amazonite is a teal-green crystal that comes from the Amazon River. It can allow you to release trauma and find strength within yourself. Place the amazonite into the tub and add 1 drop of rose, 1 drop of clary sage, and 1 drop of chamomile. Let this soak overnight, and if possible, allow the light from the moon to infuse your bath water. During this process, charge the bath with your intent, saying:

"I seek to unburden myself of past trauma and strengthen my inner being."

The next day, return to the tub and burn rose petals, chamomile, or valerian. Get into the water and let it wash away the pain from your past. Remain there for at least 20 minutes. Visualize the trauma melting away and your body absorbing renewed strength. When you feel lighter, empty the bath, and retrieve the amazonite.

Abundance Spells

Casting a spell to encourage abundance in your life requires your altar, a bowl, a candle, and plants and herbs such as basil, spearmint, marigolds, honeysuckle, nettle, dandelions, or lemongrass. You can begin by placing the plants or herbs in the bowl, either loose or contained in a pouch. Light the candle and recite the following incantation:

"In all aspects of my life, I seek an abundance of wealth. I seek good fortune, and I seek good health. I seek a bounty from the harvest that I can share with others. I am grateful for the love I have for my sisters and brothers. I know that when favor smiles upon me, I should spread it around. I shall share with those in need what is yielded from the ground. And should the time come when I am the one in need, I hope that, like me, your wisdom they heed?"

If you want to personalize your spell, you can add specific examples of anything you are thankful for receiving recently. Doing this brings a stronger amount of positive energy since having a more focused incantation allows for increased potency with magic. But remember not to go overboard when performing an abundance spell. You don't want to come off as being greedy or too fixated on material gains. Using the spell for food, health, or other similar facets of your life, as opposed to financial wealth, is the best way to avoid this pitfall.

Luck Charms

Luck charms come in two different varieties: charms to increase your good luck and charms to rid yourself of bad luck. Due to the very idea of "luck" being fairly abstract, it's very important to make your intent crystal clear when casting these charms. It's unlikely that you would succeed in luck charms that work across every aspect of your life, as that is too wide a field for the magic to target. The best idea is to pick a specific area where you need more luck or want to reduce your bad luck and cast the charm in connection to it.

Increase Good Luck

As with other spells and charms, finding the right herbs to supplement your magic can greatly affect how well your incantation performs. Some common choices include allspice, cinnamon, mint, basil, ginger, and poppy seeds. In addition to one or more of these herbs, the charm to increase your good luck requires the following:

- Your altar
- 3 candles
- A token to house the energy for the charm (any small item you can keep on your person)

Initiate the charm by placing the token on top of your altar. Set up 1 candle behind the item and the other 2 on either side of you. Light the candles and repeat these words:

"I ask for a boost to my luck. Through the power of the gods and goddesses, I seek..."

Complete the statement by describing exactly what part of your life you want to have increased good luck in. This can be something like getting a new job, finishing a project, having comfortable weather for an event, or making tasty food. Whatever your desire, be specific, and concentrate all your energy on seeing the outcome in your mind's eye. Next, hold your hands over the token on the altar and say:

"Into this [name of item], I send positive energy and good luck. So long as I have it by my side, I will reap its benefits."

The token should now be charged with the energy you directed into it. You can keep it in your pocket or purse, and its proximity to you will improve the chances of success at your stated goal. If you want, you can pick up the token and hold it in your hand or rub it to recharge the positive energy it gives off, but this isn't necessary for it to work. The power within the item will remain in effect until you've achieved whatever you set out to do.

Purge Bad Luck

If you have been having a string of bad luck, it might be beneficial to cast a charm that will purge it from you, rather than simply performing a good luck charm. If you decide to do these in conjunction with one another, remove the bad luck before casting the good luck charm. This will prevent any negative energy from interfering with the spell. To purge bad luck, you'll need:

- Your altar
- A candle

- Several crystals or stones

First, set the candle on top of the altar and light it. As with the other spells, you will state your intentions for performing the charm at this time. It can be as simple as:

"I seek to purge myself of negative energy and bad luck. I wish to replace it with positive energy and good luck."

You can offer more detail about the specific bad luck you have encountered. After you finish stating your intent, set the crystals or stones around your body, placing them at an equal distance from one another. You'll now channel the negative energy into them, saying:

"As I expel the breath from my lungs, so too do I purge the negativity from my system. I can feel it being drained away, leaving me cleansed and purified."

Finish casting the charm and snuff out the candle. Move the crystals or stones outdoors to let them be rejuvenated. If you are casting a good luck charm at this time, you can leave the candle on your altar lit, adding in the other two and the rest of the materials for it.

Love Spells

To be clear, love spells aren't meant to make someone fall in love with you. Manipulation of thoughts and emotions is a dangerous form of magic that is best not messed with. When talking about love spells in this context, it refers to spells that encourage you to open your heart to the love others give you. It can be difficult to allow yourself to be vulnerable, especially around the holidays, and many people close themselves off emotionally for this reason. These types of spells will allow you to peel away that shell and accept love being freely offered without resistance or hesitation. What you need to cast a typical love spell is:

- Your altar
- Herbs (basil, lavender, rosemary, lemon zest, cinnamon, bay leaves, or cloves)
- A bowl
- 2 Candles
- A feather

Start by placing your chosen herbs in the bowl atop your altar. Set 1 candle behind it and the other in front of you. Light the candles and let your intentions be known, saying:

"I seek to unlock my heart and open myself up to love."

Pick up the feather and brush it across your chest, approximating the area where your heart is located. Close your eyes and meditate on the people in your life who you care about and those who care about you. Visualize a blockage of energy being pulled free, allowing that energy to flow into you freely, and state:

"I am no longer closed off from feeling the love. My heart is open to accept love into it once more."

You can repeat this spell as often as you need until you have broken through the barrier preventing you from receiving and returning the love shared by others. When this happens, you should feel a weight lifted from you, as if shedding a dense layer of petrification from within. If you find yourself closed off from love again, you can try to increase the spell's power by augmenting it with crystals or stones to help siphon excess negative energy polluting your system.

Memory Spells

With how much information people are exposed to these days, it can begin to feel like it's impossible to retain it all in your head. Memory spells can help you sharpen your mind and deepen your ability to organize this information without losing anything. The materials required for performing memory spells include:

- Your altar

- 3 candles

- Herbs (saffron, ginkgo, lemon balm, gotu kola, bacopa, spearmint, or lion's mane mushrooms)

- A bowl

- A glass of water

Set up your candles in a triangle shape atop your altar, with one point directed toward you. Light them and speak the following words:

"I light these candles to fend off the darkness. I illuminate my mind to clear away the fog."

Next, place the herbs in the bowl on the altar. These are chosen because of their association with strengthening the mind. Hold your hand over them and recite:

"As a whetstone sharpens the edge of a blade, I sharpen my mind. I can reach back through the years and retrieve any memory I desire."

After you finish saying this, move your hands over the glass of water. Feel the energy being redirected from the herbs into the water and state:

"Into this water, I pour the power of a sharp mind. It is charged with the energy drawn from this offering."

Drink the water, allowing the energy to permeate your entire body. You should now find that you can recall memories more easily and completely than before. If need be, repeat the spell until you get the desired result.

Chapter 10: Lughnasadh Prayers and Blessings

Most religions have a litany of prayers and blessings for many different occasions. Wicca, Druidry, Celtic paganism, and other neopagan traditions are much the same. During Lughnasadh, there is a selection of appropriate prayers and blessings you can recite to help you honor the harvest festival.

Wicca

To prepare for the Wiccan prayer on Lughnasadh, light a white candle before you begin. This will emit positive energy and draw the light toward you. Light is a very important aspect of the harvest season in Wicca. The length of daytime has begun to shrink, but the sun is still critical to keeping your crops healthy and alive. Open any curtains or shades over your windows to allow as much natural light into your space as possible. The first prayer is a general thanks given to Lughnasadh. Once you are ready, recite the following:

"I thank you for these blessings

I thank you for this time of peace, rest, and reflection

I appreciate it all, and I embrace it all

I am patient, and I am open to waiting until your gifts are ready to harvest

I embrace the power of the light that ripens the fruits

I embrace the warm air that fills my lungs

I embrace the elements: the sun, the wind, the water, and the earth

May this energy imbue me with the power to be a better version of myself

Blessed be."

Another Wiccan prayer focuses on blessing your food, particularly Lammas bread. You can recite it after baking the bread or just before serving and eating it. This prayer is as follows:

"We give thanks for the grains we have harvested

For the bread, we have made and freely offer

We give thanks to Mother Earth for all she provides

For the food in our bellies and our stores for the winter

We give thanks for the loved ones who share our good fortune

For the time spent together and the bonds reaffirmed

We would be lost without your guiding hand

So, thank you for the gifts granted on this day

Blessed be."

The final Wiccan Lughnasadh prayer pertains to the sun. It venerates the benefits of the natural light that is integral to growing crops and fending off the cold. Perform this blessing outside while the sun is at its apex:

"I honor the sun standing vigil in the sky

Bathing the earth in its rejuvenating light

The plants and the animals need it to grow

Keeping them hale for when they are needed

I honor the sun that brings warmth to all living things

I bask in its embrace and give thanks for its power

Its light staves off the darkness, its heat repels the chill

I honor the sun and offer my gratitude

May it always be there until the end of days

Blessed be."

Druidry

Druids are preoccupied with preserving nature and restoring the resources too often wantonly stripped from the Earth. The prayers given during Lughnasadh follow these themes, including elements taken from both ancient blessings and updated modern ones. The most popular among these is known simply as the Druid's Prayer:

"Grant us, O [Great Spirit/Goddess/God/Holy Ones], thy protection

And in protection – strength

And in strength – understanding

And in understanding – knowledge

And in knowledge – justice

And in justice – the love of it

And in that love – the love of all existences

And in the love of all existences, the love of the [Great Spirit/Goddess/God/Holy Ones] and the Earth, our mother, all goodness."

Another common druidic prayer is an old Irish blessing called the Prayer of Deep Peace. It allows you to concentrate on achieving inner tranquility by balancing your spirit with the serenity of nature. The Prayer of Deep Peace says:

"Deep peace to you

Deep peace of the calming waves to you

Deep peace of the gentle air to you

Deep peace of the still earth to you

Deep peace of the shimmering stars to you."

Celtic Paganism

Celtic pagans have numerous prayers dedicated to Lughnasadh that the Christian church has adopted for recitation during Lammas. The first of these is known as the Blessing of the Seasons:

"The Earth is the Mother's

As is everything upon it

Everything created and creativity itself

Fruit and fruitfulness

The springtime and summer

Seedtime and harvest

For the promise of the harvest

Contained within each seed

We thank you, Mother Earth

For the oak tree within each acorn

For the bread within each grain

For the apple within each pip

The mystery of nature is wrapped as a gift

That we shall sow

We thank you."

The next Celtic prayer is a blessing for the harvest time and gathering an abundance to keep you fed throughout the winter. It is called the Prayer for the Harvest:

"As summer passes, we see the signs in golden leaves

The days grow shorter; the mornings become misty

And we see it in the glow of the tapestry of autumn
We can sense the summer passing in the rains that fall
The winds that chill, and the trees left bare
The bounty of our harvest is placed on show
Brought forth by the will of the Earth, our Mother
From green shoot to hoar frost
From sunrise to sunset
We give you our thanks
For the seeds that have grown
For the crops we have harvested
For our storehouses filled
For mouths fed and bellies filled
And, as your good earth rests
Throughout the cold embrace of winter
We await its rebirth
With spring's first bloom."

Another blessing you can perform gives thanks for creativity and fruitfulness. During Lughnasadh, this can include items baked or crafted from the harvested crops, venerating the artisan aspect of Lugh. This is called the Litany of Lugh at Lammas:

"We give you thanks, mighty Lugh
For creativity in all its forms
For the skill of the weavers
The potters, the artists, the sculptors, the needleworkers
And all who take that which you have given
Transforming it into a thing of beauty
We give you thanks, wise Lugh
For fruitfulness in all its forms
For an unselfish love
For grace, knowledge, wisdom, and sacrifice
For all who take that which you have given
Creating with it a thing of great skill."

The next prayer honors the Grain Mother. It can be recited together with a group, or you can speak it alone on behalf of yourself and others. The Prayer for the Grain Mother is as *follows:*

"We bless you

Goddess of Seed and Harvest

Mother of Earth and Grain

We bless one another

So that the beauty of our world

And the love with which it was shaped

Shall be expressed throughout our lives

And thus become a blessing unto others

For now, and for always

Thanks be to you."

The last Celtic prayer can be recited with others in a "call and response" format. Designate one person to read the passages, and the rest of the group will answer in unison with "we thank you." This prayer is:

"For the passing of the summer

And the harvest we have at home...

We thank you.

For the seed in the earth

And the promise of spring...

We thank you.

For the sun that shines

And the rain that falls...

We thank you.

For the love that we share

And the people we've met...

We thank you.

For all things good

And the glory of the world...

We thank you."

Other Neopaganism

There are plenty of non-denominational prayers available that can work across any neopagan tradition. These venerate various aspects of the harvest and the gods honored during Lughnasadh. The first is a Prayer for the Grain:

"Fields of gold and waves of grain

The summer has come to a close

The harvest is ready, ripe for threshing
As the sun fades into autumn
Flour will be milled; bread will be baked
And we shall eat for another winter."

The next prayer is meant to honor the warrior aspect of Lugh:
"The warrior soul, the fighting spirit
Follows a code of honor and wisdom
Strength is not found in arms
The knife, the gun, or the sword
But in the sharpened mind and purified soul
I call upon the warriors of the past
Those who would stand up and fight
Those who would do whatever is needed
Those who would make sacrifices on another's behalf
Those who would die that others may live
I call upon them this night, on Lughnasadh
To give me strength of heart, soul, and spirit."

Another prayer is dedicated to Lugh as a craftsman. It is as follows:
"O Great Lugh
Master of artisans
Leader of craftsmen
Patron of smiths
I call upon you and honor you this day
You of many skills and talents
I ask that you shine your light upon me
And bless me with your gifts
Give me strength in skill
Make my hands nimble and my mind deft
Shine your light upon my talents
O Mighty Lugh
I thank you for all your blessings."

The final prayer honors the many deities of the harvest in general. It invokes the names of gods and goddesses from across the pagan world. It says:

"The fields are full; the orchards are blooming

And the harvest has arrived

Hail to the gods and goddesses who watch over the land

Hail to Ceres, the goddess of the wheat

Hail to Mercury, the fleet-footed

Hail to Pomona and her bounty of apples

Hail to Attis, who dies and is reborn

Hail to Demeter, who brings on the winter

Hail to Bacchus, who fills our goblets with wine

We honor you all in this time of harvest

And set our tables with your bounty."

Creating Your Own Prayers

If you would like to attempt crafting your own prayers to recite during Lughnasadh, the good news is that it's easy to do. As with all other spells, blessings, and prayers, you need to start with a clear conception of intent. Pick an aspect of the festival, harvest, or gods you wish to honor. Decide what specifically about them you seek to venerate and give thanks.

Once you have chosen what you want the prayer to be about, the next step is to find the right words to use. Again, your intent will guide you here – if you're giving thanks, you will say so. If you are asking for a blessing, you can start with that. You can address a god or goddess individually or as a collective. There's also the option to pray to the earth or nature. Any of these are viable for creating a personalized prayer. Make sure you decide if your prayer is on behalf of a group or only yourself. This will alter the language between using "We/our" and "I/me/my" throughout the prayer.

The last part of the process is expanding on the primary themes you wish to address. If you want your prayer to concern the harvest, add in details about your crops or plants being gathered during this time. If your prayer is honoring a god or goddess, describe the benefits granted by the natural forces associated with them or their sphere of influence. You can always include lines pertaining to your own life, especially when giving thanks. This will allow you to express your gratitude for any gifts or positive energy in your life.

After you've created your first prayer, give it a try, and see how it feels. You can always add to, remove, or edit the lines until satisfied with the results. So long as you remember to make your intentions clear, just about anything you say will be acceptable. The actual words aren't nearly as important as the meaning you imbue them with. Unlike certain Abrahamic religions, paganism doesn't have a codified set of prayers or blessings that are expected to remain the same across the board. The decentralized nature of paganism avoids making demands as to how you choose to worship, which makes anyone who values ideal individualism followers.

Conclusion

Now that you've finished reading this guide, you should have a pretty firm grasp on the festival of Lughnasadh, how it's celebrated, and what you can do to participate in the religious traditions during this Sabbat. One of the main things to take away from this book is that individualism is a major aspect of neopaganism. Every blessing, prayer, ritual, or spell is something you can do alone if you wish. While interactions with your community are encouraged, it is not a necessity. You are free to honor the gods, goddesses, and Lughnasadh however you see fit.

Another important lesson to remember is how much your intentions matter when performing any rites within the pagan religions. This cannot be overstated enough. Almost everything practice involves going in with a clear mind and a strong understanding of what you hope to accomplish. This isn't just a skill you will use in worship. It can be applied to every facet of your life. Being efficient and setting firm goals will benefit everything you do.

Celebrations of Lughnasadh stretch back thousands of years, but as paganism has evolved, so too have the rituals associated with the festival. Despite its mythical origins, it has a very real effect on practitioners of these religions. The harvest is an important time during the year when crops are first reaped for consumption and stored away to keep people sustained through the winter until the spring returns. This cyclical nature of the crops and seasons is reflected in the beliefs of paganism, which holds the cycle of life and Wheel of the Year in high regard.

The history and lore associated with paganism carry a rich tradition that has permeated cultural depictions all over the world. Even popular fiction has derived influence from paganism. The comic book character Thor and all associated Asgardians were based on the character from Norse mythology. While often criticized for its inaccurate portrayal of real-life Wicca, the television series Charmed was still filled with terms and concepts from the religion. Of particular importance is the number three, which is expressed in the show as the "Power of Three."

In the Lord of the Rings legendarium, J.R.R. Tolkien names the magical bread that can sustain a mortal for days with just one bite "Lembas bread." This was derived from Lammas bread, a tradition the author was familiar with due to its adoption by Christianity. His elvish and human cultures took inspiration from Celtic and Gaelic sources, including a group of secretive wild men called the Drúedain, who watch over the forests and are believed to possess nature magic. The similarity to the term "druid" is striking and almost certainly used to evoke such an image in the reader's mind.

On the whole, the pagan and neopagan religions share the common beliefs of the power of nature. Practitioners don't necessarily have to reject the conveniences of the modern world, but finding a balance between them and our planet's natural resources is highly encouraged. As society embraces eco-friendly alternatives to things like fuel, electricity, and other power sources, interest in paganism has started to grow. Many people are worried about pollution and deforestation, which have long been a concern to the pagans and neopagans. If these are causes you believe in, you might already share a lot of common ground with long-time practitioners.

When it comes to paganism, there is very little barring you from simply diving right in. You don't need extensive instruction, and many of the concepts can be learned through experience. Unlike other religions, there isn't a narrow list of specific materials required to participate. Most of the herbs, decorations, and other paraphernalia can be gathered from nature or purchased for a very low cost. You also don't need to attend services in a church or temple, instead of being free to worship at home, with friends and family, or anywhere else you desire.

Part 7: Mabon

The Ultimate Guide to Autumn Equinox and How It's Celebrated in Wicca, Druidry, and Paganism

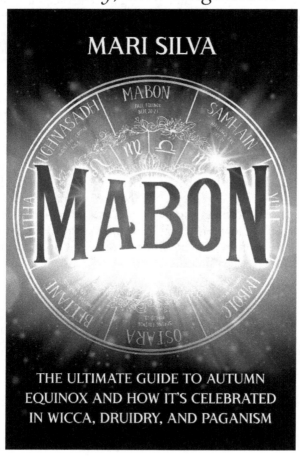

MARI SILVA

MABON

THE ULTIMATE GUIDE TO AUTUMN
EQUINOX AND HOW IT'S CELEBRATED
IN WICCA, DRUIDRY, AND PAGANISM

Introduction

Mabon, also commonly known as the autumnal equinox, is a sacred time of celebration for many Pagans and Wiccans. It is a time to celebrate the harvest season and pay tribute to the deities associated with the harvest. This is not just a time of celebration but also a sacred time of shifting balance when day and night are equal in length. This makes the season-changing festival even more significant to many modern pagans and Wiccans because it is a time to reflect on the blessings received. Thus, many rituals and spells are performed throughout the festival, each deeply connecting to the autumnal equinox.

Whether you have just developed an interest in esoteric religions or are a newly practicing Wiccan or pagan, this book is perfect as an interesting yet uncomplicated guide to help you celebrate Mabon as a Pagan and make the most out of the autumnal equinox through your rituals and spellwork. You will have to understand various aspects to celebrate this festival with full fervor and make use of this sacred time for important spells.

To fully understand Mabon and its rituals, you must learn about the lore and various mythical stories associated with each event. This includes not only the story of the Celtic god Mabon but also short stories and myths about other deities associated with this holiday. Then, this book introduces you to the different fruits, plants, and herbs associated with Mabon. Fruits and plants play a significant role in this festival because they signify the harvest season and its many benefits.

To make the festival even more festive, decorate your home with the special homemade decorations we have added to the book. You will find easy step-by-step instructions for some really great and unusual harvest goodies to get you into celebration mode.

Your Mabon altar is also a very special part of the festival, and an altar has a sacred value. So, to celebrate the autumnal equinox properly, you will have to learn how to set up the Mabon altar. It is also essential for the many rituals and ceremonies that surround Mabon. However, there is no need to look elsewhere; in this book, you will find a detailed list of traditional rituals and ceremonies performed on the autumnal equinox.

Finally, there is a whole chapter dedicated to Mabon food. So, if you are a food lover, this is what you will want to read. It is full of Mabon recipes with signature ingredients of the autumnal equinox. Plus, the chapter will also tell you how to bless your food with the magical properties of Mabon.

The time of the autumnal equinox is full of magic, and the high spiritual energy should be manifested to its full extent. To properly celebrate the festival, it is important that you properly understand every aspect of the equinox.

Chapter 1: Introduction to Mabon

Wiccans and many other pagan groups celebrate eight Sabbats yearly, which are significant festivals. The Sabbats are considered great opportunities to get in touch with the unity of the universe. They serve as a reminder that the Earth and the extraterrestrial, or the physical and the spiritual realms, are intrinsically linked. The sunset of the day of the Sabbat marks the beginning of the festival, and the sunset of the following day marks its end. Magic and rituals are carried out at night.

The Sabbats are divided into two groups, greater Sabbats and lesser Sabbats. The former group originates from western European, or ancient Celtic traditions, while the latter group marks the transitions of the seasons. As you can tell, the Sabbats alternate between earth-centered and solar-based events, creating what we know as the Wiccan Wheel of the Year. Each Sabbat is associated with a certain deity, who is honored by pagans on that day. The festivals are also an opportunity to celebrate the cyclical essence of nature, conduct healing rituals and magic, and use spiritual powers. People who live in pagan communities get together to celebrate the Sabbats and engage in communal rituals.

The four seasonal, or lesser Sabbats, comprise two Equinoxes, Spring and Fall, and two Solstices, Summer and Winter. Besides celebrating the changing weather, harvesting seasons, and singular qualities each festival symbolizes, the Sabbats also acknowledge the change in darkness and light. The Spring and Fall Equinoxes are the two points of balance or stability; this is the time of year when the length of day and night are the same. On the other hand, the Solstices are transitional periods, where light shifts to greater darkness or darkness shifts to great light.

1 November marks the start of the Wheel of the Year. Yule (Winter Solstice) starts on or around the 21st of December and is the first festival of

the year. Imbolc, the second festival, falls during the earlier days of February and marks the signs of fading winter and the onset of spring. Ostara, which is the Spring Equinox, takes place in March, followed by Beltane, which falls in early May.

Litha, who is also known as Midsummer, is the Summer Solstice. This is the longest day of the year and takes place any day between the 19th and 23rd of June. Lughnasadh, the sixth festival, falls on 1 August. This Sabbat is followed by Mabon, our topic of interest throughout this book, which falls any day from 21 - 24 September. Mabon celebrates the Fall Equinox and the abundant harvest. Samhain, the last Sabbat of the year, falls on 31 October 31. Alternatively known as All Hallows' Eve (Halloween), this festival is the most popular pagan holiday. All the dates we just mentioned are in accordance with the Northern Hemisphere.

Now that you understand what the Sabbats are and where Mabon falls on the Wheel of the Year, the rest of this chapter will dive into this celebration's historical and cultural origins. You will learn everything you need to know about Mabon's ancient and current traditions. We will also explore the various perspectives of the holiday. Finally, you will come across the most significant Mabon symbols, colors, incenses, herbs, plants, animals, and stones.

The Origins of Mabon

As we have said, Mabon, one of the eight Wiccan Sabbats, celebrates the Autumnal Equinox. Since this is a seasonal festival and dates differ between the hemispheres, the Northern hemisphere celebrates it around September 23, while in the south, it falls around March 20. In the north, the festival of Ostara is celebrated on this day. Ostara is the Spring Equinox (Mabon's counterpart). Besides marking the Autumn Equinox, Mabon is associated with the mid-harvest or second harvesting season.

Mabon falls on a day when everything is in perfect balance. On the equinox, day and night are exactly the same lengths, creating a sense of balance and equilibrium. This stability is not only limited to the daytime and nighttime. It is merely a symbol of the duality of nature, which can be seen in the masculine and feminine, dark and light, inner and outer, and the physical and spiritual, all falling into balance. Not only is this state of idealism and perfection celebrated, but the transition to the time when the darkness overshadows the light is also acknowledged. Mabon is a reminder that the cyclical nature of the world is slowly approaching a stage of completion. From that moment on, the days will shorten as the nights become longer. The weather will grow cooler as the sun's vigor declines. Green wanes as golds, browns, oranges, and reds take over the scenery.

This Sabbat is named after Mabon, the God of Welsh mythology. Mabon is also called the "Child of Light" and is the son of the Earth Mother Goddess (Modron). The festival was not named until the 1970s as a part of the reconstructed paganism movement. You may be surprised to learn that there is little evidence regarding the celebration of Mabon in Celtic regions, and the celebration of the Fall Equinox is not exclusive to Wiccan or pagan practices. The harvest is an important time for many civilizations, and it was the time of year that brought an abundance of food—the reason there was so much celebration. The Bavarians have long held harvest festivals filled with feasting and joyful celebration. The chances are that you have come across the word Oktoberfest or heard of this festival before.

Other cultures, including those in the USA, celebrate the second harvest, viewing it as a time to give thanks. This makes sense because Mabon is when farmers check on their summer crops and animals to see if they will be able to sustain their families throughout the harsh winter. This is a time when people express their gratitude for what they had in life—food, animals, and future wellbeing. The original US holiday fell on October 3, which is more logical in an agricultural sense because the harvest season is practically over by the time November arrives.

Apple picking is often incorporated into this festival. The picking of the apples provides food for the celebration and is also symbolic of reaping what was sown. Dedications are given to the gods and goddesses as the apples are picked and eaten. Many rituals are performed at this time of the year, most associated with balance and harmony. You can set up an altar at this time of year or decorate it with the suits of the harvest. Considering that it is deeply associated with concepts of gratitude and giving thanks, the celebration is best observed with family and friends.

Since Mabon is at harvest time, it is a good time for evaluating one's own efforts in terms of harvest, crops, and animals. It is the time of year when you "reap what you sow" in all aspects of life. In Mabon, people look back at the goals and hopes they set for the year at Imbolc and Ostara. They take a moment to evaluate their current situation, how their plans have unfolded, and whether their aspirations have manifested. Mabon is the perfect time to complete plans and projects that you've been putting off. It is also a reminder that you must let go of what no longer serves you as you prepare for the coming of winter, which is essentially a period of deep reflection.

Mabon Then

Unlike the names of other Sabbats, which are linguistically tied to other ancient pagan or Christian holidays, Mabon's name cannot be traced back to any single significant event in the past. However, as we have mentioned, celebrating the Fall Equinox and harvesting season has been considered a legitimate holiday by numerous cultures. The English festival, the Harvest Festival, was always held during the early autumn but never tied to a specific date. People played games to celebrate the holiday and conducted rituals to honor the harvest. They made corn dollies, had parades, and held feasts. Even though not everyone who celebrated was necessarily pagan, Harvest Festival is essentially pagan, considering that it celebrated the cyclical nature of the universe and is linked to agricultural cycles.

In early agricultural societies, it was of utmost importance to develop close relationships with one's neighbors. Besides being hospitable, people wanted to ensure that their neighbors would help them out whenever they could not sustain their families at the end of the harvesting season. This is why communal feasts were held, especially in rural areas, where people celebrated their harvest with their neighbors. Feasting and drinking with bread, cattle, wine, and beer were involved.

Mabon Now

Most Wiccans and pagans still view this time as a period to foster communal ties, relationships, and kinship. Many people associate pagan Pride Day with Mabon, where food is one of the most important factors in the festivities. This symbolizes bountiful harvests and encourages people to share the abundance with those who are less fortunate.

If you wish to celebrate Mabon, the best thing that you can do is express your gratitude and thankfulness and reflect on all the good aspects of your life. Honor the balance, as well as the darkness and light within. Even if you are the only one who celebrates Mabon in your community, you can explain the concept of the festival to your friends and family and invite them over for a feast. Modern-day celebrations include seasonal foods and drinks, such as tomatoes, eggplants, grapes, grains, carrots, peppers, potatoes, pumpkins, and onions. If you think about it, it is a lot like thanksgiving.

The Various Perspectives on Mabon

Ancient Britain and Ireland

As we have explained above, Fall Equinox has been celebrated for centuries by numerous civilizations. In ancient Britain, the solstices and equinoxes were highly significant occasions for those who came long before the Celts, Saxons, and the Romans. Stonehenge is a prime example of the structures built to measure time, particularly the equinoxes.

Stonehenge.
https://unsplash.com/photos/aIj87xsnVQA

These celebrations cover all of the Celtic nations. In Ireland, cairns were built to measure the falling of the equinoxes, much like Stonehenge, and they are positioned to capture sunlight in a specific way at a specific time of the year. These cairns were designed in a way that the rising equinox sun slipped right into a long corridor, lighting up a back stone. Astronomical symbols were engraved on the back stone.

Christianity

The Christian church did not take to other deities being revered, and they disagreed with most pagan rituals. This meant that the solstices and equinoxes were disliked, but instead of outlawing them, they changed the festival to align with Christian values. That is why many Christian celebrations fall on the same days as Pagan celebrations, such as Christmas and Michaelmas.

Native American Tribes

Various ancient Native American groups built stone structures that are still intact to this day. A modern-day researcher named one of these structures Calendar One because of the way it can be used to determine the occurrences of the Summer Solstice, as well as the Fall and Spring Equinoxes. This structure, which can be found in Vermont, is built on land that is around 20 acres and looks like a natural amphitheater.

The Southern Californian Native American Tribe Chumash conducted sun ceremonies during Hutash, or September, in celebration of the Fall Equinox. This festival was celebrated after collecting, processing, and storing the year's harvest. According to Chumash's myth, we are all the children of the sun, which shows how significant this celebration was. At that time of the year, the tribe pondered concepts of unity, the harshness of the winter, and the cyclical nature of life that is birth, death, and ultimately, rebirth.

Ancient Celts and Druids

The ancient Druids also had their own take on the festival. During the Fall Equinox, the Celts at the time made figures out of wicker that represented the spirit of vegetation so they could "sacrifice" them. Many suggest that this practice led to the belief that the Druids used to conduct human sacrifices. Although no one actually witnessed a human sacrifice at any Druid ritual, many people shared this belief, particularly because the rumor was given credence by Julius Caesar.

France

The calendar was permanently changed when the French revolution spread across France in the late 1700s. The fall equinox became New Year, and Vendemaire (the grape harvest) became the first month. However, they allotted 3o days to each month and left five of six extra days when the end-of-year celebrations took place.

The Mayans

You are probably familiar with the popular ancient Mayan pyramid in Chichén Itzá. The number three has always been powerful, and triangles were placed together to create pyramids, multiplying the number. You will also find many Mayan pyramids that reflect the light in a certain way during the equinoxes or solstices. This served as a guide during important times of the year.

Mayan pyramid Chichén Itzá.
https://pixabay.com/es/photos/chich%c3%a9n-itz%c3%a1-m%c3%a9xico-pir%c3%a1mide-1025099/

Neo-paganism, as you already know, is a movement aimed at the revival of ancient pagan traditions, spirituality, and religion. Wicca is the most popular of these religions and combines ancient Celtic ideas, beliefs, practices, and modern magic rituals and ceremonies. The difference between Neo-pagan and Abrahamic religions is that the former view time as cyclical. In contrast, the latter perceive time as linear, starting with God's first creation and ending at a decided time.

To an extent, these two beliefs have coexisted peacefully for millennia. That was until December 21 (or 23) 2012 arrived. Based on ancient Mayan calculations, this date would mark the end of their calendar, signaling a shift to a new one. Not many years before that date, on December 30, 2000, our calendar entered a new millennium, signaling a similar transition. Numerous authors confused this date with the monotheistic concept of the end of the world, regardless. They thought that this Mayan calculation was an estimation of the universal destruction that would end all life on Earth. This, however, was a misinterpretation of the Mayan calculation of prophecy, which sent out a wave of terror among many people, particularly Christians. Those who benefitted, however, were authors, filmmakers, and publishers.

The Norse

The Norse celebrated the Autumnal Equinox with a festival named Haust blót. This term could be translated to Autumn Sacrifice. Many Neo-pagans, especially those who worship and honor the deities of the Norse pantheon, still celebrate this festival. Considering the season's color and essence, with darkness and cold taking over, this prompts communities to large light bonfires. Thus, the Fire element is of great significance. During the celebrations of Haust blót, people would perform fire rituals and base their celebrations around the flames. They covered the fields and pastries in red, orange, and dark yellow fields and believed the red shades found in the sky during dusk to be a symbol of blood. This, they thought, was a warning of the hardship that the harsh winters would bring. It was believed that winter was a challenge presented by the gods themselves, which is why acceptance and resilience were necessary.

Japan

The Japanese traditionally celebrate the Spring and Fall Equinoxes over a period of six days. Six is an important number in Japanese culture, signifying their six ideals: effort, wisdom, perfection, perseverance, giving, and meditation. According to traditional Japanese spiritual beliefs, these qualities are essential before one reaches a higher level of consciousness. To them, the Spring and Fall Equinoxes are both ideal for reflecting and pondering on life's true meaning and essence.

Important Correspondences

Symbols

- Pinecones
- Seeds
- Cornucopia or horn of plenty

Color

- Red
- Orange
- Brown
- Yellow
- Copper
- Dark yellow
- Dark green

Food

- Beans
- Corn
- Apples
- Squash
- Cider
- Pumpkin
- Pomegranate
- Root vegetables
- Wine

Herbs

- Rosehips
- Mugwort
- Rosemary
- Yarrow
- Sage

Plants

- Elderberry
- Chamomile
- Star anise
- Ginger
- White oak bark

Stones

- Aventurine
- Sapphire

- Amber
- Cat's eye
- Jasper

Incense

A Mixture Of:

- Lavender flowers
- Myrrh resin
- Rose petals
- Cinnamon
- Apple peel

Flower

- Thistle
- Marigolds
- Sunflowers

Animals

- Stag
- Owl
- Blackbird
- Salmon

Deities

- Mabon
- Persephone
- Inanna
- Pomona
- Morgan
- Demeter
- Green Man

It is said that the goddess reveals herself in her most abundant, motherly form during the Fall Equinox. The god manifests as the governor of harvest and the king of corn. The deity had sacrificed himself to provide humanity with the last harvest of the year before the winter took over. Mabon aims to honor the deities for their sacrifices and generosity. It is also an opportunity to recognize that the deity will be reborn during Yule. Since most people sustained themselves off farming in the past, this festival was a literal celebration of the harvesting of crops. However, in the modern-day world, people started applying this concept to the manifestation of wishes, aspirations, hopes, and dreams, or the "seeds" they had planted earlier in the year. Rituals that honor the deities should be conducted while reflecting upon everything that has unfolded in your favor. Even if the "harvest" was not abundant, you should still thank the deities for putting in the effort.

Chapter 2: Mabon Deities and Lore

In Celtic mythology, Mabon is the god of youth, music, and the sun. In Welsh literature, he is often referred to as "Maponos," which means Divine Youth, Divine Son, and the Great Son. According to the Gauls, he was the son of Dea Matrona, the embodiment of the triple goddess. In Welsh mythology, Dea Matrona was a personification of Modron, and he is called Mabon ap Modron, which means the Divine son of the Divine Mother. He was also the son of the god of the underworld, Urien. A few legends mention that he had Mabon as a brother. Ancient Celts believed Mabon was associated with light, while his brother was associated with darkness. Mabon also had the title of "The Divine Hunter" because he enjoyed the sport and was known to be one of the best hunters.

It is believed many of the Celtic deities were once real people, and Mabon was no different. One night, three days after his birth, Mabon was kidnapped from his mother, Modron. He was held captive in a Gloucester prison called CaerLoyw, which means "the City of Light." However, no one knows why Mabon was taken from his mother and imprisoned. According to the Culhwch and Olwen story, which narrates his kidnapping, imprisonment, and release, there was a hero called Culhwch. Culhwch fell in love with a woman named Olwen. Olwen's father, Ysbaddaden, set him a series of difficult, and some believed, impossible, quests before he could take his daughter's hand. One such task was to hunt a magical boar. However, he would not be able to find the boar without a specific hunting dog named Drudwyn. No one in the heavens or on Earth could control this dog except for the Divine Hunter himself, Mabon. Finding Mabon was an impossible task in itself because ever since he was kidnapped, no one knew where he was or even if he was dead or alive. Some people did not even know who Mabon was. Or if he was a real person.

Only one person could find Mabon, and that was his cousin, Eiddoel. However, Eiddoel was also imprisoned in Gloucester. Folklore has it that many events took place during the search for Mabon. Culhwch and his friends went around asking all the old and wise animals to help them find him. This fact was emphasized to show that Mabon was ancient, and so was his imprisonment. In fact, it was believed Mabon had been imprisoned since the beginning of time. However, none of the animals knew where he was kept. They came across the oldest salmon (Llyn Lliw) in the water, also the oldest of any animal. He told them that he had heard Mabon wailing in his prison in Gloucester. When Culhwch found this information out, he sought his cousin's help, who just happened to be the legendary King Arthur (other legends referred to Arthur as his uncle).

Arthur, together with his knights, rode together to free Mabon. On arrival in Gloucester, the shouts of pain from Mabon could be heard by all. So, they attacked the prison with hopes of freeing Mabon. They were successful in their endeavors, and Mabon was set free, opting to go and hunt as the first thing to do. He hunted Twrch Trwyth, the great boar, on his great horse, aided by his dog. He killed the boar and used combs and blades fashioned from the boar's tusks and bones to cut Ysbaddaden's hair and shave his beard. Ysbaddaden died shortly after, and the two lovers, Culhwch and Olwen, were finally able to get married.

Mabon became the ruler of Wales and even came to Arthur's aid in the battle of Badon. The god of youth was highly revered by the Celts and Romans alike, and to this day, people speak his name. There is a village and a standing stone in Scotland named after him.

No one knows for a fact if the Mabon Sabbat was named after him, although it makes sense if it is. Mabon is a day to recognize the gods' sacrifices (their deaths and rebirth). The festival takes place in September, right before the dark days of fall and winter, and is a time when people hunt to prepare for these few months. Mabon was the Divine Hunter. With his skills, strengths, and the suffering he endured in prison, his memory should be kept alive. He was also the Sun god, associated with the sun's rebirth after the dark winter days. His imprisonment and eventual release resemble the sun being kept away by the cold and dark winter and finally being set free when spring arrives.

Mabon was talked about in various tales and poems. He was once mentioned as Mabon ap Madron, one of Arthur's knights, and also as Mabon ap Mell, which means Mabon, son of Lighting. This mention links him to Apollo, the sun god, and his father, Zeus, the god of lighting. This explains why the Romans referred to Mabon as Apollo Maponos. He was portrayed in the Mabinogion stories as a kind and giving god who was always there to lend a hand to mankind.

In ancient myth, the boar was used as a symbol for the underworld and the winter. When Mabon defeated the boar in the Culhwch and Olwen story, it represents how the sun defeats the winter every year to bring us light again.

The boar was used as a symbol for the underworld and winter.
https://pixabay.com/es/vectors/jabali-salvaje-animal-38001/

Wine also plays a role on this special day. September is the month or the "Wine Moon." This was a traditional time to harvest the grapes that had been planted earlier in the year. Ancient pagans believed that grapes and wine were sacred as they symbolize transformation and rebirth, which are themes for the Mabon festival. For this reason, many wine deities were linked to it. Now we are going to take a look at all the deities who are associated with the Mabon festival.

Persephone

The Greek goddess Persephone's story is one that captures the spirit of the Mabon festival. The story of her kidnapping at the hands of Hades and how the Earth suffered (as a result) resembles the darkness our world experiences during the winter months. Persephone was the daughter of Demeter, the goddess of harvest and agriculture, and Zeus, the sky god and the chief of all Greek deities.

Statue of Persephone.
Carole Raddato from Frankfurt, Germany, CC BY-SA 2.0
<https://creativecommons.org/licenses/by-sa/2.0>, via Wikimedia Commons
https://commons.wikimedia.org/wiki/File:Detail_of_Persephone-
Isis, Statue group of Persephone (as Isis) and Pluto (as Serapis), from the Sanctuary
of the Egyptian Gods at Gortyna, mid-
2nd century AD, Heraklion Archaeological Museum (30305161481).jpg

Persephone was the goddess of fertility. She was known to be a very beautiful girl, and many gods were mesmerized by her beauty and willing to do anything to win her heart. However, Demeter was very protective of her. Some would say she was even obsessed with her daughter, so she did not let any of the gods near her.

Hades, the god of the underworld and brother to Zeus and Demeter, wanted to marry Persephone but Demeter refused. One day, Persephone and her nymphs went to pick flowers. She wandered off alone, and while walking, she saw a strange flower that had a beautiful smell which, according to the legend, was a narcissus flower. As she leaned down to pluck the flower, the ground beneath her feet suddenly opened up, and Persephone fell. She screamed her heart out, but someone caught her in a chariot and rode off. Still screaming for help and scared, Persephone took a look at her captor to find it was Hades, the man she secretly had feelings for.

Needless to say, Demeter was livid and wanted her daughter back. She was heartbroken and miserable and had only one thing in mind, Persephone. She neglected her duties on earth as the goddess of agriculture and harvest, and the earth suffered as a result. People were starving and dying. Zeus saw no other option but to intervene. It is believed that Zeus aided Hades with the kidnapping. He sent for Persephone, who was now married to Hades and became the queen of the underworld and reunited her with her mother. However, Persephone had tasted a pomegranate seed in the underworld. According to the laws of the underworld, anyone who tasted pomegranate could not leave, and so she was stuck in the underworld.

The great god considered a compromise—Persephone would spend a part of her life in the underworld and the rest of the time with her family. All parties agreed to Zeus's decisions. When Persephone was on earth, her mother would rejoice, and the earth would blossom as well. This happened during spring and summer. However, when she went to the underworld, Demeter was consumed with grief, and the earth became barren during the months of fall and winter.

Persephone, like the sun, disappeared during the winter and returned again in the spring. She was both dark and light, and these two parts of her were always fighting with each other, just as Mabon, the light, fought his brother, the darkness.

Demeter

We cannot talk about the autumn equinox without mentioning Demeter, who is responsible for the cycle of the four seasons. The Autumn equinox marks the time when Persephone travels to the underworld and reunites with Hades. It is also the time Demeter spent grieving and abandoned the earth to suffer.

Bust of Demeter.
Museo nazionale romano di palazzo Altemps, CC BY 2.5
<*https://creativecommons.org/licenses/by/2.5*>, *via Wikimedia Commons*
https://commons.wikimedia.org/wiki/File:Demeter_Altemps_Inv8596_n2.jpg

The Greeks believed that the gods were responsible for everything. For this reason, they believed Demeter, Persephone, and Hades' story explained the cycle of the four seasons. Demeter was the one responsible for Earth's withering during the months of autumn and winter and its rebirth and transformation during the months of spring and summer.

Hermes

Hermes was the Greek god of the roads, herds, folks, and the souls of the dead. He was also the messenger of the gods. Hermes had a unique gift that made him stand out from any other Olympian god. He was the only one able to cross the border between the living and the dead. Delivering the souls of the dead to Hades allowed Hermes to travel to the underworld. He was even referred to as the "leader of the souls." Hermes played a role in many legends as the messenger of the gods. In fact, he was the one Zeus sent to bring Persephone back from the underworld.

Hermes is associated with Mabon since he was the one who brought Persephone to Demeter, so, in a way, he brought the sun and life back to earth, allowing Demeter to bless the world again. Being able to travel to the underworld meant that Hermes had a light and dark side. You might say Hermes had had a dark side ever since he was an infant. When he was a toddler, he played a trick on his brother Apollo and stole his cattle. He was known as a trickster and enjoyed pranking people. However, he was beloved by the gods, and even his brother Apollo, whom he often tricked.

He wasn't evil per se, but we cannot say that he was good either. He would do anything to amuse himself, no matter the consequences. He could be good just as easily as he could be evil, which is why he was the patron of both thieves and merchants.

Thoth

Thoth was one of the most prominent gods in ancient Egypt. He was the god of writing, the moon, languages, wisdom, medicine, and secrets. Thoth was often compared to Hermes as both gods were associated with communication and wisdom and acted as messengers to the gods. Like his Greek counterpart Hermes, Thoth was also connected to the underworld and able to travel between the realms. In the afterlife, the souls of the dead cannot pass on without a ritual that is referred to as "the weighing of the hearts." Thoth was the one responsible for this ritual by weighing the deceased's heart against a feather of mat. If the scales balanced, this meant they had been a good person who did no harm, so their souls were permitted to move on to the afterlife. However, if the scales were not balanced, then they were sinners whose souls would be devoured by a beast.

Thoth was born from the lips of Ra, the sun god. As the son of the sun god and someone who was able to travel to the underworld and back, Thoth can easily be compared to Mabon, the sun god, and the son of the god of the underworld. Thoth, just like all the gods mentioned, is also celebrated during the Mabon festival.

Dionysus

Dionysus was the Greek god of wine and fertility and patron of the arts. We have mentioned the importance of wine for ancient pagans and how they considered it sacred. Dionysus was the creator of wine which connected him to the Mabon festival as both represent rebirth and transformation. Dionysus' story includes themes of death and rebirth as well. He was the son of Zeus and a mortal woman called Semele. Dionysus was the only god who had a mortal parent. Semele knew that the man she was having an affair with was a god, but she had no idea that it was Zeus, the chief god. When Hera, the goddess of marriage and family and Zeus's wife, found out that her husband was cheating on her, she was consumed with jealousy. Hera disguised herself and went to Semele and persuaded her to talk to the god Zeus and convince him of who he truly was.

Zeus paid a visit to Semele, and she informed him that she had but one desire in her heart, and after some talking, he promised to grant her desire. He was persuaded to show his true form and did so out of love for Semele. Zeus was heartbroken by the request because he knew what would happen if he did, but he also could not go back on his word after taking an oath. When Zeus revealed his true form, Semele as a mortal, was not able to handle his glory, so she was burned to ashes. However, she was pregnant at the time. Zeus saved the fetus and stitched it to his thigh until he was born. The fetus was Dionysus, who became immortal because he was birthed from Zeus, not his mortal mother.

Hera could not cope with the knowledge that the boy her husband had fathered with another woman was still alive and decided to have him killed. She sent the Titans after him, who ripped him apart. However, Rhea, Zeus, and Hera's mother, who was also the mother of the gods, brought Dionysus back to life. Hera could not hurt Dionysus again because Zeus had him protected.

Just as he was brought back to life, Dionysus was one of the few gods who were able to bring the dead back from the underworld. He wanted to meet his mother, who was always on his mind, even though they had never met. So, one day, he traveled to the underworld and brought Semele back. Themes of rebirth are repeated a few times in Dionysus' story, which makes him one of the gods that should be worshiped during the time of the autumn equinox. He was also connected to Demeter as both were considered prominent deities and were very kind towards mankind. Just like the earth, Dionysus was unhappy and would wither during the fall and winter. However, he was full of joy during harvest seasons.

Bacchus

Bacchus was the Roman counterpart of Dionysus as he was also the god of wine. It was believed that Bacchus was the one who was responsible for religious devotion, creativity, and ecstasy. He would also grant drunkenness to anyone who asked for it. Bacchus' birth and rebirth story share many similarities with that of Dionysus. His father, Jupiter, king of the gods in Roman culture, fell in love with the goddess of agriculture, Prosperina, Persephone in Greek culture. Jupiter took the form of a snake, sneaked into the underworld, and made love with Prosperina. As a result, Bacchus was conceived. However, he was first called Liber. Liber/Bacchus was one of the Roman gods who fought during the battle of Titanomachy. During one of these battles, Liber was killed, and like his Greek counterpart, he was torn apart.

Jupiter, who was consumed with grief, took his son's remains and placed his heart in a potion. He then gave the potion with the pieces of the heart inside to the king of Thebes' wife, who was called Semele and who was also a mortal. Semele drank the potion and became pregnant. However, just like in Dionysus' story, Semele was murdered because of Juno, Jupiter's wife and chief goddess. Jupiter took the fetus from Semele's womb and sewed him to his thigh until he was born. He was born Bacchus. Just like Dionysus, the story is about birth, death, and transformation, which are the themes of the autumn equinox.

Cernunnos

Cernunnos was one of the most prominent Celtic deities. He was the god of wild places, nature, fertility, and beasts. Cernunnos was also referred to as "the Horned One." Not much is known about him because many of his myths have been lost. For this reason, he is often considered more of a mysterious god. He often acted as a mediator between nature and man. The Horned One was also considered the lord of life and death and experienced death and rebirth. Cernunnos, just like mankind, would grow old over time. However, instead of dying and perishing, he would start over and begin a new cycle of life, just like earth and the four seasons, with the earth transforming or dying during the winter to come back to life in the spring.

The Morrigan

The Morrigan was the goddess of war, death, and witchcraft. It is believed that she was a triple goddess and went by many names like Morrigu, The Morrigan goddess, and Thye Great Queen. She could predict which soldiers would die in a battle. She would usually appear on battlefields taking the form of a crow to motivate the soldiers and frighten their enemies.

As mentioned, The Morrigan was a triple goddess and existed between life and death. One aspect of the triple goddess was Macha, who was a horse goddess. She came back from the dead to predict the future. The second aspect of the triple goddess is Badb, who was the Crone goddess of the underworld. The third aspect of her is Anu, who was the mother of gods. The Morrigan can also be associated with the Mabon festival with themes of death and rebirth. As one of her aspects came back from the dead, which represented rebirth, and the other was the goddess of the underworld, The Morrigan represented themes of rebirth and death, which are what the autumn equinox is all about.

Mabon's story is both sad and exciting. Being imprisoned all his life, Mabon was saved from danger and spent his days helping mankind. Full of mystery and bravery, Moban was an interesting and popular figure featured in various Welsh, Celt, and Gallic literature legends. Although some people believe that the Celts never celebrated Mabon, and this is more of a modern idea, Mabon represented many things associated with the autumn equinox, like transformation and rebirth. It is believed that Mabon was simply a hero in an Arthurian legend, while there are others who believe Mabon and Maponos are not the same people and that Maponos is a god while Mabon is mortal. However, we can all agree the story of Mabon is fascinating, and its festival is a special day to give thanks to mother earth,

All the deities mentioned here symbolize the earth's transformation and rebirth that occur annually. When celebrating this special day, make sure you call upon any of the gods connected to Mabon.

Chapter 3: Magical Fruits, Herbs, and Flowers

Now that you are familiar with the myths and lore surrounding Mabon, you can understand how some special fruits, flowers, and plants came to play a significant role in the festival. Not only are they used to decorate an altar, but they are also important ingredients in various Mabon rituals and rites. The great Mabon feast also comprises various recipes using these specific fruits to pay tribute to the season's harvest. These fruits, flowers, and herbs have unique symbolism and meanings, making the festival even more special. This chapter will dive into the many types of fruits, herbs, and flowers used in the Mabon festivities.

Magical Fruits

Mabon is a harvest festival, and numerous fruits and other crops that flourish in this season are integral to the festival.

Some fruits are considered to be magical.
https://unsplash.com/photos/K0efSg5xy9w

These magical fruits are deeply connected with the ancient lore associated with Mabon. Over time, the use of these fruits has become common in the tradition, followed faithfully by all who celebrate it. Some of the most famous Mabon fruits include:

1. Apples

Apples are the main fruit symbol for this season. They have been used for centuries in many sacred traditions, symbolizing life, healing, renewal, regeneration, and health. Where did you think the saying, "An apple a day keeps the doctor away." came from? This fruit also has a deep symbolic meaning connected to the lore surrounding Persephone and Demeter. Demeter being the goddess of earth, and a nurturing soul, used to present people with apples, the fruit of life.

From a pagan perspective, apples are widely loved symbols representing health and vitality. When cut widthways, the center seeds show a pentagon, which according to pagan tradition, represents air, water, earth, fire, and spirit at the top. Apples are used in various dishes and food items for Mabon, including apple pies, roasted apples, apple stuffing, and apple cider.

2. Pears

Pears go along perfectly with Mabon festivities and are one of the most prolific fruits found in the autumn harvest. Many pagans consider pears to be the true harbinger of fall. Cultivated pears go far back in history, with countless recipes evident in every culture. Pears have also been considered sacred in many cultures, but most prominently so in ancient pagan civilizations. The slightly curvy shape of pears echoes the feminine shape and is how they became associated with the feminine body, Aphrodite, goddess of love. Mabon feasts have a fine selection of pear dishes, ranging from simple pear slices to delicious baked pears or pear tarts.

3. Persimmons

Persimmons are less familiar woodland fruits and have been used for Mabon feasts and festivities for centuries. These sweet and slightly chewy fruits add a delicious flavor to Mabon recipes. Moreover, they are used to create scents, especially to be used during Mabon festivities. This fruit has numerous health benefits and is largely associated with Demeter's harvest in a pagan culture. Recipes range from sweet persimmon jams and muffins to savory persimmon risotto.

4. Pomegranate

Pomegranates deserve special mention with regards to the autumn equinox festival. You have read the story of Persephone and Demeter's tragic love in the previous chapter, and while there are many variations in this story, pomegranate fruits have a prominent role in them. Hades used pomegranate seeds to trick Persephone into staying in the underworld. This is why pomegranates are often called the fruit of death. It was served to Persephone and made her stay in the underworld. Modern Mabon festivities have many pomegranate dishes as part of the feasts. These fruits are not just good for health reasons; they are also quite tasty and symbolize the lore associated with Mabon. Pomegranate juice is also a famous beverage for Mabon festivities.

5. Grapes

The autumnal equinox has a special place for grapes because there would be no wine without them. Pagan myths and lore are full of stories and tales that involve wine and the gods. It is used to honor themselves and many other beings. These mainly include Dionysus, Bacchus, and other fermentation deities. According to Wiccan culture, grapevines are associated with fertility and magic and can also be used in fertility rituals. Mabon marks the perfect time for the ripening of wines, and so wines have long been used as a sacred symbol during this festival. This time is also when new wines are set up to ferment. So, if you are hosting a Mabon event, be sure to get a large barrel of wine for everyone to drink. Grapes can also be served fresh or added to fruit salads and other recipes.

6. Berries

Mabon berries include wild damsons, rosehips, sloes, elderberries, hawthorn berries, blackberries, and more. They are not only used to symbolize the rich harvest provided by the goddess Demeter but also symbolize the sweetness in life. Various berries are included in the feast in the form of jams, juices, smoothies, margaritas, baked items, and frozen items. They can also be used to decorate the Mabon altar in a cornucopia. The cornucopia itself is a significant symbol for Mabon. Also called the horn of plenty, the cornucopia is filled with Mabon fruits to represent the wealth of the harvest season.

Magical Flowers

The autumn equinox or Mabon is largely associated with the mythical lore of Demeter, Persephone, and Hades. When Persephone was kidnapped and taken to the Underworld, Demeter's sorrow and rage destroyed nature on earth. As soon as Persephone was allowed to return to earth, Demeter was overjoyed and restored all the plants, herbs, and flowers to full bloom. This is how flowers became deeply connected to festivities during the autumnal equinox. Many very pretty flowers are associated with Mabon festivities, and they are used for both decorations and rituals. These are some of the flowers most often chosen for Mabon festivities.

1. Asters

Asters are one of the most prolific seen during Mabon festivities. Asters can be found in many colors, from pale reds to bright purples. The most common aster color associated with the autumnal equinox is blue

These symbolize devotion, loyalty, and abundance. In addition to being used in decorations, these flowers are often used to encourage metaphysical spiritualism in celebratory rituals. This flower is usually associated with the goddess Aphrodite and is thus used in love spells and rituals. These rituals can be done during Mabon to increase the intensity of the manifested power. They can also be used in tarot card readings and other similar rituals.

2. Chrysanthemum

Chrysanthemums are often used for protective purposes, especially *metaphysical protection*, and come in handy when you are dealing with the spirit world. They are a significant part of Mabon, and their petals are used to decorate the equinox altar. They are also used in rituals and herbal recipes. The unique thing about this flower is that it is available in a range of colors, and each is used to symbolize different things. For instance, white chrysanthemums represent healing and purification, whereas red or purple ones are associated with passion and power. Yellow and orange shades depict the sun's fiery energy.

To use these flowers in your Mabon festival, you can make wreaths or hoops to hang on your home's front door or windows for protection. You can also use this flower's yellow, orange, and red shades to create an autumn equinox crown for yourself.

3. Sunflowers

Sunflower seeds are sown naturally in fertile soil in springtime and reach full bloom during early September. As these flowers grow, they turn their face toward the sun, demonstrating the divine power of the sun. And as the center of the flowers begins to swell, its petals begin to droop and wither until the flower turns back towards the ground, from where it started. The birth, growth, death, and rebirth of these flowers represent nature's cycle, which is associated with the goddess of the harvest, Demeter.

4. Thistles

Another flower most commonly associated with Mabon is the thistle, mainly used for protective spells and rituals. It can also be used to improve your financial and spiritual blessings. You can do many rituals and spells during the autumnal equinox using the thistle flower or seeds to improve your chances. Throw these flowers in a fire to have a protective shield around you that protects you from natural elements like lightning. The beautiful flower represents vitality, joy, energy, and protection. If not used for rituals, you can always use thistle flowers to decorate your Mabon altar.

5. Marigold

This gorgeous flower is not only suited for Mabon decorations, but it is also useful in many natural remedies and, naturally, pagan rituals. Marigold flowers are associated with the element of fire, and the sun, both symbols of autumn and Mabon season. Marigolds have magical properties attributed that make them perfect to be used for rituals and spells during Mabon. These include clairvoyance, psychic readings, prophecies, love, dreams, and renewing of personal energy. The best time to do these rituals would be at noon on the autumnal equinox. The flower can also be used as an herb and has many medicinal applications as well. These include treating swelling and inflammation or healing sprains or wounds.

6. Russian Sage

Sage is one of the most common flowers used in pagan and Wiccan rituals and rites. This is mainly because of the plant's healing and purifying properties which make it irreplaceable for many modern pagans. Almost every pagan festival makes use of sage flowers in one way or another. You can simply use sage to physically and spiritually clean your home. This ritual, known as smudging, can be done by burning sage and wafting its smoke throughout your house. Mainly used for protective, prosperity, and clarity spells, sage is considered to bring health and vitality. However, when using it for magical purposes, you should not cut sage with a metal knife. Rather, it should be plucked.

7. Hydrangea

For Mabon celebrations, you can use hydrangea flowers and leaves to create beautiful scenic decorations within and outside your house. These could include wreaths, flower bouquets, leaf paintings, or simply bunch them together for a colorful arrangement. Hydrangea flowers are often used for banishing purposes and are more common at Samhain but are also used throughout the autumnal equinox to banish any evil entities coming your way. They are associated with psychic shielding, moon magic, and purification.

Magical Plants and Herbs

Magical plants and herbs also play a major part in Mabon festivities, preparations, and the sacred day itself. Demeter's association with nature is the main connection between plants, herbs, and Mabon. These are used throughout the festival to perform different rites and rituals. Plants are said to have not just healing and therapeutic properties for physical ailments but also work wonders for your spiritual healing. Some of the most common plants and herbs associated with the autumnal equinox include:

1. Lavender

Lavender has been used for centuries in pagan rituals, especially during the time of the autumnal equinox. Rumor has it that this herb is used to encourage healthy communication and attracts love and serenity. This herb also has well-known medicinal uses, as it helps reduce inflammation and also soothes burns and bites. For Mabon, you can make a lavender essential oil blend to sprinkle around the house or make some delicious herbal tea to soothe your – or your guests' - nerves. To use as decoration, bundle up sprigs of lavender with other herbs and place them near the Mabon altar. You can create an incense blend to reflect and purify your energy for ceremonial purposes.

2. Grapevine

As you know by now, grapes are a symbol of abundance and fertility. A healthy and abundant grape harvest signifies a prosperous year ahead. In modern practices, many Wiccans and pagans use grapevines for various ritualistic purposes. Some ways you can incorporate grape vines into your Mabon rituals and decorations include:

- Wrap the beautiful grape vines around the altar, or create garlands out of these plants
- Make a simple grapevine pentacle to hang on your wall
- Use grape leaves in your rituals and spells to bring abundance and fertility to your crops
- To create a simple good luck charm, wrap a grape leaf around a silver coin and tie this with a green string.; keep this talisman in your pocket to bring you prosperity.

3. Witch Hazel

Witch hazel is one of the most commonly used herbs in witchcraft and ritualistic practices. It has countless herbal and medicinal uses, including treating poisons, rashes, sunburns, inflammation, eczema, acne, burns, bruises, eye strains, achy muscles, bruises, insects' bites, and sprains. Witch hazel is often referred to as the wound healer herb. It can be blended with other herbs or incense for ritualistic purposes to keep away evil spirits and anyone harboring ill intentions.

4. Rose

Rose is the ultimate herb to use in love spells and rituals. Also, one of the autumnal equinox herbs, rose herbs, have various therapeutic properties, most often used for treating skin diseases and enhancing beauty. For ritualistic purposes, rose herbs can be used to lift your mood and help open up your creative space. So, if you are an artist with a block, perform a ritualistic cleansing with rose herbs to open up your creative channel.

5. Cinnamon

This spice can mean spiritual happiness, wealth, and peace. It was an ingredient used a lot in harvest celebrations as apples were bountiful, and cinnamon pairs well with them. The spice is still plentiful today and used as a flavoring in pies, offers, and other autumnal foods and drinks. The spice also provides many health benefits, from aiding digestion to managing cholesterol. So, even if you overindulge with the Mabon feast, cinnamon added to various dishes will be a useful balm against this habit. Cinnamon can be added to incense for ceremonial purposes to purify the house and even outdoors.

6. Oak

One of the better-known symbols of the equinox, Oaks are known for their many herbal and ritualistic uses during the Mabon season. Oak used to be one of three sacred druidic deities and has many magical properties for use in various spells and rituals. Medicinal uses include treating hemorrhoids, or sinus infections, whereas ritualistic purposes include positive manifestations of healing, longevity, power, order, protection, love, financial success, fertility, and fortune. You can perform a protective ritual involving oak acorns and place them near your windows to ward off lightning or other natural disasters.

7. Myrrh

As it is associated with multiple goddesses, myrrh is one of the most sacred herbs of Mabon and is used to heighten your spirituality. Myrrh is sacred to the Egyptian goddess Isis, as well as Demeter. It can thus be used for various ritualistic purposes during the Mabon season, including protection spells, healing rituals, blessings and meditation rites, and consecration of objects like rings, amulets, crystals, and other ritualistic tools. To purify and protect an area, you can burn myrrh plants and use their smoke for the purpose.

8. Passionflower

As its name indicates, Passionflower has herbal and magical uses in protection and love magic. When this herb is used, it brings peace and calmness to your home. For protection rituals, you can dry these flowers and sprinkle them over the doorstep or right in front of your home's front door to keep harm away. Burning these herbs can help promote love and understanding between people. You can also use this herb to create love potions.

9. Calendula

Calendula flowering herbs were named after the ancient Romans and have been used for healing and magical purposes for more than a century. These herbs are used to release feelings of joy and happiness and bring strength to a weak heart. You can use these plants for a ritual bath during the autumnal equinox to attract praise and admiration from others. You can also make spell bags consisting of calendula flowers to attract success and be triumphant in love-related matters. Its herbal uses include the treatment of skin rashes, insect bites, sunburns, and minor infections.

10. Peppermint

Peppermint has many therapeutic and magical properties, which has kept this herb on the front line for ritualistic and healing purposes for many years. Associated with purification, healing, protection, and love, peppermint herbs can be used in many ritualistic practices ranging from aura cleaning to home purification during the sacred time of Mabon.

Chapter 4: Crafts and Decorations

Any festive occasion is incomplete without matching festive decor to get you in the mood for the festival. And this is true for the autumnal equinox celebrations. Mabon is a time of joy and happiness, and to celebrate it fully, there should be ample amounts of decorations and crafts. The best way to pay tribute to this joyous occasion is to create crafts and decorations that have a significant meaning for a holiday. So, whether you are celebrating the autumnal equinox as a Wiccan practitioner or a pagan, there are many DIY crafts that you can make to add a celebratory air to your Mabon festival. In this chapter, we discuss themed Mabon crafts and give you easy step-by-step guides on how to make your own special decorations. You will also learn the background, how items became associated with the autumnal equinox and its traditions.

Autumn Fairy

This autumn fairy dolly is created with natural materials, which are all connected with Mabon's theme. Whether you believe in fairies or not, they are a symbol of the mythological lore associated with Mabon. This cute piece will not just make an interesting curiosity for the little ones but will also add a whimsical charm to your Mabon altar.

Materials Needed:

- Autumn leaves (red, orange, brown, green, and yellow shades)
- Pine cone (small or medium-sized)
- Acorn cap (large sized)
- Rusty-colored orange wool
- White felt (1 ball)

- String (small piece)
- Hot glue gun

Steps:

1. First, prepare the fairy's head with the white felt ball. You can also use a large cotton wool ball in its place.

2. Use the rusty orange wool to make the fairy's hair by parting the wool into two parts. Glue the hair on top of the white felt ball. Hold it until the glue has dried.

3. Now, take the acorn cap and stick it on top of the fairy's hair with the glue gun. Hold it in place until stuck.

4. Use the pinecone to make the fairy's body. Place it upside down and add glue to the base of the pinecone. Stick the fairy's head here and let it dry.

5. Take two bright-colored autumn leaves to make the fairy's wings. Make sure that the leaves you pick are equal in size. Stick these to the back of the pinecone from the stem side.

6. Tie a string to the acorn's stem to hang the dolly wherever you want.

Apple Garland

As discussed in the previous chapters, apples have long been associated with the magical time of Mabon. They are not just used in food but also to make various decor items as well. Garlands are one of the most common decorations during Mabon festivities. They add a touch of nature to your house and are not that hard to make or purchase.

Materials Needed:

- Oranges (3 to 5)
- Apples (2 to 3)
- Bay leaves (15 to 20)
- Cinnamon sticks (1 bag)
- Twines (arm's length)
- Embroidery needles
- Foil
- Cookie sheet
- Oven

Steps:

1. First, cut the oranges and apples into thin slices. Use a sharp knife to do this; otherwise, the slices will be uneven. The apples will resemble hearts when cut perfectly, and the orange slices will be circular.

2. Place these slices between drying sheets and press to squeeze the juice out. This makes the drying process much easier.

3. Preheat the oven to high heat, and slide in the fruit slices arranged neatly on cookie sheets. Turn over the slices every few minutes to avoid burning.

4. Once the fruit slices are done being dried, line up the materials together and start to put a piece of twine through them.

5. Add the orange slices, apple slices, and cinnamon sticks to the garland, one at a time. Once done, hang it on your doors or simply on the wall.

Candy Corn Pine Cones

Pine cones are pretty common around Mabon season, and a combination of pine cones and candy corn is the perfect craft for this festive day. Pine cones are great for decorating purposes, especially during the fall season. Combine this with beautifully applied paint and glitter, and you have got the perfect eye-catching decoration for your autumnal equinox festival.

Materials Needed:

- Pine cones
- Parchment paper
- Oven
- Spray paint
- Glitter
- Mod Podge

Steps:

1. First, arrange the pine cones on a parchment sheet and heat them in the oven at low heat for about 30 minutes. This will help kill any critters or insects that may have survived the harvest.

2. Start by painting the first layer using orange spray paint. Make sure you cover the whole pine cone with the paint.

3. After the first coat has dried, take the white spray paint, and spray the tip of the pine cone white.

4. Once the white coat has dried, hold the top of the pine cone, and spray the bottom with yellow spray paint.

5. Let the pine cones dry overnight, and then use a mod podge and brush to apply the glitter to the cones.

6. Put the pine cones in baskets or decorate the Mabon altar with them however you would like.

Waxed Fall Leaves

Is there anything more beautiful than the different shaded autumn leaves that fall to the ground during the autumnal equinox? If you are an admirer of the vibrant colored leaves of fall, this craft is perfect for creating an inexpensive yet stunning look.

Materials Needed:

- Fall leaves
- Mini crock pocket
- Paraffin wax

Steps:

1. Melt the paraffin wax in the mini crock pot or any other container and pour the melted wax onto a sheet.

2. Start dipping the leaves in the wax. Be careful not to let your fingers touch the hot wax while doing so.

3. Let the leaves stay there until the wax dries completely. This should take a minute or so.

4. You can make more than one coat on the leaves for a more solid foundation. About 2 to 3 coats should be enough for this purpose.

5. Once they are done, you can place them wherever you would like. For instance, place them on the Mabon altar or the dinner table, or string them on a thread to make a garland. You can also paint these waxed leaves to make them more vibrant and aesthetic.

Apple Candles

Again, as apples are closely associated with Mabon and Harvest goddess Demeter, and seeing that they are plentiful at this time of the year, Mabon wouldn't be Mabon without them. To make the most of these fruits, you should use as many as you can, not just in the grand Mabon feast but also in your crafts and decorations. One such craft can be these creative apple candles. The best part is, they are super easy to make! This craft doesn't even need a lot of supplies, time, or effort on your part but ends up being one of the most creative crafts on Mabon.

Materials Needed:

- Apples
- Tea lights/Candles
- Hole saw
- Spoon

Steps:

1. Take an apple and wash, and dry it completely. Red apples will be perfect to match the theme, but green or yellow ones will work just as well.

2. Use a hole saw bit to drill out a circular hole the size of the candle top from the apple. Make sure you make an accurately sized hole to match your candle or tea light, or the craft will end up looking uneven.

3. Use a spoon to pry out the extra material from the hole you made.

4. Finally, place the candle inside the hole until it sits snugly inside. Light the candles and place them wherever you would like.

Acorn Wreath

If you want a simplistic yet beautiful-looking wreath for your front door, an acorn wreath would be the perfect thing. It is not just easy and inexpensive to make; it also matches the theme of the autumn equinox celebration. Acorns are another of the symbolic food items that are associated with Mabon.

Acorn wreath.
https://pixabay.com/es/photos/guirnalda-oto%c3%b1o-corona-oto%c3%b1o-3041838/

Materials Needed:

- Acorns (large or similar-sized)
- Hot glue gun
- Floral wreath

Steps:

1. Gather as many acorns as you can find. If you can't find some close to your home, order some online.

2. Wash and dry the acorns to clean them, and then put them in the oven at low heat for 30 minutes to get rid of any insects infesting them.

3. Use the glue guns to glue the acorns to the straw or wooden wreaths one by one. Make sure there are no gaps, and every space has an acorn in it.

4. Use a ribbon to hang the wreath on your front door. If you want, spray-paint the acorns any color you like. White works best against a darker background.

Leaf Sun-Catcher

Leaves are a major symbol of the fall season and are seen all around the Mabon festivities. There are all kinds of crafts involving leaves that are not just creative but also easy to make, and this one is no exception. This decor will showcase autumn's real beauty using leaves of various colors, shapes, and sizes.

Materials Needed:

- Fall leaves
- Laminator
- Laminating sheets
- Yarn
- Hole punch
- Rubber band
- Scissors
- Masking tape
- Stick

Steps:

1. Go outside and collect some leaves and a three-foot-long stem from a bush. Make sure you cut off all the little twigs from the stick before you bring it home.

2. As for the leaves, make sure they are straight and moist, do not collect dry or curled-up leaves.

3. Let the stick soak in some warm water to make it easier to bend when you make the sun catcher.

4. While the stick is soaking, pick out the most beautiful leaves that you have collected and place them individually in the middle of the laminating paper. Laminate away!

5. Bend the soaked stick slowly into a circle. Make sure that you do it gently so that the stick does not break. Tie the two ends together.

6. Cut the laminated sheet in a circular shape while keeping the leaf in the middle.

7. Punch holes in the edges of the sheet and use masking tape to temporarily hold the laminated leaf between the circular stick.

8. Thread the yarn through the punched holes, and tie it around the stick to hold the laminated piece between the circles.

9. Hang this sun catcher somewhere in direct sunlight so that the colors of the leaf are enhanced.

Cornucopia Basket

As discussed in the previous chapter, cornucopia baskets are hugely symbolic of the autumnal equinox. They are used to store various Mabon fruits, nuts, and charms. Cornucopia baskets symbolize the abundance of harvest and bounty and are thus important features in a Mabon festival. So, this easy-to-make cornucopia basket will be the perfect addition to your Mabon decorations.

Materials Needed:

- Wicker cornucopia (2 ft. long)
- Burlap (2 yards)
- Raffia (200g packages)
- Binder clip
- Spool of jute string
- Hot glue gun
- Scissors

Steps:

1. Wrap the burlap sack around the wicker cornucopia to cover the entire basket, and tuck the extra material inside. Cut away and burlap that hangs over the edges to neaten it.

2. Use adhesive to stick the burlap to the frame. Make sure you secure the whole thing perfectly.

3. Now, it is time to make the ropes to cover the cornucopia. Take your raffia and bind it with the string to create a long length of raffia cord. Take your jute and bind both ends to each other. You will need to create 9-10 of these for the frame—until it is covered.

4. Now wrap these raffia ropes around the cornucopia basket and hot glue the edges to secure them to the frame. Make sure that you add enough glue to the ropes to tightly secure them to the basket.

Mabon Corn Dolly

Considered to be one of the most sacred symbols of Mabon, corn dollies have been historically significant throughout Wiccan and pagan traditions. Early practitioners believed that the spirit of the grain, or harvest, lived in the field with the crops. However, once all the crops were reaped, she no longer had a place to stay. So, the last sheaves were reaped and used to make corn dollies to preserve the spirit of the harvest and keep her safe and warm all winter. When spring came, the corn dolly would be put back into the earth to bring fertility to the land. Many of these traditions have remained almost the same throughout these years. Thus, the corn dolly still has spiritual significance and is a common part of Mabon rituals. Plus, they are pretty easy to make and do not require more than three materials.

Materials Needed:

- Corn husk
- Scissors
- Embroidery thread

Steps:

1. First, you need to soak the husks for a few hours to make them more pliable. Once they have soaked enough, take them out and pat them dry with a towel.

2. Now, select 3 or 4 of the husks that are similar in size. Tie a string around the narrow part of the husks. Secure the knot twice, and then start folding the layers downward.

3. Tie a string around the upper part of the husk where her neck should be. Use another husk for the arms. Roll the husk tightly and push

the arms all the way under her neck.

4. Use another piece of thread to tie her middle to resemble a torso. Now, take two long, thin pieces of husk, tie them around her shoulders, and bring them to the front. This will be her shawl. Use another piece of string to secure her shawl to the front.

5. Quickly put the corn dolly configuration in the oven to dry the husks properly so that they do not shrivel.

6. Take a stick and some twigs to make a miniature broom for the corn dolly.

Mabon Broom

Mabon is a sacred time and is filled with ritualistic cleansing and purification. This is where brooms or besoms come in. You are probably aware that brooms have been associated with witchcraft for centuries, but do you know why that is? It is because brooms or besoms are often used for hand fasting or cleansing ceremonies, especially during sacred times like Mabon. Thus, crafting a styled besom broom will be the perfect addition to your Mabon festival.

Materials Needed:

- A stick
- Pine needles, grass, or straw
- Natural twine
- Hot glue gun

Steps:

1. Gather the pine needles around the base of your stick. Make sure some of the portions of the stick are completely submerged in the pine needles.

2. Now, place this configuration on twine, and tie it around the pine needles and the stick. Make double knots to secure the broom.

3. To further secure the broom, pour some hot glue on the back of the twine knot. Now, carefully wind the twine around the broom in a circular manner. This should completely secure the twine around the broom.

4. To make your besom special, you can decorate it using gemstones, dried flowers, ribbons, or even old jewelry.

5. Anoint your broom with essential oil and ritualistic blessings of Mabon.

Twine-Wrapped Pears

Pears are another symbolic fruit associated with Mabon. They are used extensively in Mabon festivities and are used to celebrate a successful harvest. While this object does not make use of real pears, it is used to represent the pear shapes and perfectly match the theme of the autumnal equinox. Plus, it is a recycling project and makes the perfect way to reuse old light bulbs. Stick them in the cornucopia basket or somewhere on the Mabon altar to add a rustic touch to your decor.

Materials Needed:

- Old light bulbs
- Twine
- Small stick
- Scissors
- Hot glue gun

Steps:

1. First, to make the stem of the pear, use the hot glue gun to fix the small stick to the narrower side of the light bulb.

2. Now, put some hot glue right next to the end of the stem, and glue one end of your twine there.

3. Start wrapping the twine around the body of the light bulb, adding hot glue once in a while to make the wrapping solid. Make sure that you do not leave any space between the twine so that no part of the light bulb is visible.

4. Keep doing this until you reach the bottom of the pear and finally secure the other end of the twine with glue.

5. Voila! You are done. If you want, you can add shades of green and yellow to these twine pears for a more realistic look.

Crafts and decorations are an essential part of any celebratory event. Add to that the sacred symbolism in Wiccan and Pagan celebrations, and these crafts become irreplaceable. While many of the above crafts are mainly used for decorative purposes, some bring ritualistic significance to the table as well. Plus, all of these crafts are pretty easy to make and require little to no supplies.

Chapter 5: Setting Up Your Mabon Altar

Not all pagans consider setting up an altar as a fundamental part of their practice, but those who do, agree that having a sacred space has many advantages. In this chapter, you will learn about the benefits of setting up an altar in your home and how to use this sacred space in your Mabon celebrations. We will suggest several beginner-friendly tips on how to care for your altar before, during, and after the festivities. It is important to note that the advice from this chapter should only serve as *general guidelines*. As with any other magic-enhancer tool, an altar only enhances your powers. It is definitely recommended that you add your personal touch to the space to fully empower your altar, helping you achieve all your magical goals at the second harvest.

The Purposes of an Altar

For most people, an altar is viewed as a collection of objects placed strategically in a purposeful place. For pagans, however, this space signifies much more than that. It provides a connection to nature, spiritual guides, or any other entity you want to communicate with during your practice. The objects you place on your altar and the place itself are also emotionally, mentally, and spiritually linked to you. Moreover, the surface where you lay your magical tools becomes your sacred space, regardless of its size and purpose. Altars come in many shapes and sizes, depending on their intent, type of practice, and place you have available.

The Benefits of a Sacred Space

As in other religions and practices, a spiritual center for one's practice is a critical part of pagan traditions. Having a sacred place dedicated to your practice comes with many benefits for you, your magic, and those around you. Here are some of the gifts you can gain by setting up an altar in your home.

Inviting Positive Energy

We have already established that an altar is a space where you can harness spiritual energy whenever it is needed in your practice. However, it must be noted that it can also serve as a tool for permanently inviting and retaining this positive energy in your home. Setting up an altar at times like Mabon will ensure that the positive energy keeps flowing through your space, following you wherever you happen to be in your home.

Invoking Spirituality

Paganism is a spirituality-based practice, and each object you place on your altar has a connection to your spirit and the spirit of the entities you want to evoke. They represent emotions, intentions, and symbols of deities and spiritual guides that can help you deepen your own spirituality. Even if you are not familiar with spiritual practices, building an altar will help you get in touch with your inner self. The more times you repeat this, the more spiritual power you garner for your magical practice. From the first stone you put on the altar to the first candle you see flickering in front of you, it will all touch your spirit. It will also help you connect with the spirit of whatever entity with which you are working. Earth-based altar decorations like those used at Mabon often include simple items that enhance spirituality. Growing your spirituality involves using your altar for several days, often placing new items on the sacred surface each day. Whether you opt for exchanging the existing ones or adding new objects depends on the purpose of the ritual. Either way, it will enhance the power of the practice and deepen your spiritual connection to it. If your act involves many people, their contribution to a common altar deepens the spiritual bonds within their community, whether they share the same beliefs.

Expressing Your Creativity

Setting a sacred place for your practice is a form of art. Figuring out which items will give you the best results needs a lot of creative thought, even if you have a guideline like the one provided in this chapter. However, we will teach you how to take a creative approach to every situation in your practice and even in day-to-day life. At the same time, it allows you to create something of your own and express your thoughts and emotions through your creation. Whether you draw, write or craft, you can do something for yourself and the cause your altar is dedicated to at any given moment. As your art is also something to be harvested, placing your creations on the altar during Mabon, along with the offerings and symbols, will enhance the spiritual connection to this Sabbat.

Turning Negatives into Positives

Part of the lure of pagan practices is that they allow you to turn negative experiences into positive ones. By building an altar, you gain a space where you can do something about negative influences, regardless of their source. Whether the negativity comes from living beings or malicious spirits, having a sacred place will empower you to fight them and keep them away from you and your space.

Learning Symbols

There is no better way to learn the correct use of existing pagan symbols than displaying them in a space you visit regularly. And this applies not only to written characters but also to colors, animals, and the favorite items of your spiritual guides. Learning the symbols will teach you their purpose and let you see how they work best. This information will help you create your own symbolism in the future with symbols you will have come to know intimately.

Creating a Meditation Center

Whether you wish to devote your practice to a particular spiritual guide, nature itself, or to developing your spirituality in another direction, an altar can be the perfect place for mindfulness practices. By bringing together the right combination of elements, you can create a space where you can unwind after a busy day at work. As the spirits you choose to evoke your senses, your body and mind relax, and your experience becomes deeper. You can use specific symbols geared toward helping you focus your intent on relaxation or, better yet, choose the ones that feel right for you to use in this situation. There is no better way to ground yourself than by meditating in front of the offerings dedicated to the spirits that allowed you to have a bountiful harvest.

Focusing on Your Magical Intentions

Whether you practice magic daily or only during the major pagan celebrations, having a sacred space can help you focus on your intent every time. The way to choose to set an altar sets the tone for each spell you choose to cast, divination technique, or ritual you perform. If you practice magic with others, an altar can bring each person's intention together and focus it on the intended purpose. And if you are a solitary practitioner, you can tailor the space to your specific taste and preferences, which also helps enhance your magical powers.

Remembering Your Ancestors

Pagans regularly turn to spiritual guidance for answers, particularly when they find themselves in a difficult situation in life. That said, the collective wisdom of ancestors can be a great empowerment tool for your practice on any day of your life. Before Mabon, you can ask your ancestral spirits about their practices and better understand this Sabbat with their help. Or you can simply devote your altar to remembering loved ones who have passed away. Create a space that is a reminder of their presence in your life, and they will accompany you on your life's journey. At Mabon, this can include your ancestors' favorite colors or food, an object which they cherished during their life, or whatever item you associate with a particular person. Pagans who practice in groups often choose to add details symbolizing several ancestors and express their gratitude to each of them individually.

Welcoming Nature into Your Life

Establishing a connection with nature is another way to develop your spirituality and empower your practice. Many pagans choose to grow medicinal herbs and plants for food, even if they only do this in a small corner of their home. By placing your harvest bounty in a special place, you can express gratitude for them, which will bring you closer to nature. An altar can be the perfect spot to display these items. Here, you can also use them to channel nature's power to gain insight, cast a spell, or perform any other magical act. Whichever way you choose to connect with nature, you will most likely leave the offerings on the altar for a number of hours and days. This allows the spirits of nature to notice them and provide many blessings in return.

Sharing the Magic

Whether introducing someone to pagan practices or finding common ground with another experienced practitioner, decorating an altar together can be a great way to share your spiritual beliefs. This is common practice for celebrating major Sabbats in larger pagan communities. Helping you set up an altar for a specific purpose is also the perfect way to share the magic of nature with children.

Where to Set Up Your Sacred Space

Before you start setting up your altar, you must choose a suitable place for it. Ideally, it should be away from any high-traffic areas or possible distractions. Otherwise, you will not be able to relax, let alone focus on your intention during your practice. Many pagans choose to set up their altars in their home office or bedroom, as these are the rooms where they spend most of their time. Having a sacred place in your bedroom would also facilitate morning and evening prayers and quick divinations if your practice includes them. If you do not have much space for a full table to serve as an altar, you can always set up a smaller area on your dresser, vanity table, or even inside your closet. If your practices involve mediation, yoga, or similar activities, it is a good idea to set up an altar in a room that can also accommodate these. A functional basement, garden, backyard, patio, and deck areas are also suitable for setting up an altar. In fact, many pagans prefer having a sacred space outside of their home as this makes them feel closer to nature and appreciate its grounding and empowering effects even more.

How to Set Up Your Mabon Altar

As you have learned early on from this book, Mabon is the celebration of the second part of the harvest. This means that when it comes to food offerings, the best ones to use are those harvested during this period. These may include root crops, squashes, pumpkins, gourds, grapes, potatoes, onions, chili peppers, carrots, red apples, and dried Indian corn. Other nature-themed objects you may include are wreaths made of straw and herbs, acorns, nuts, and leaves in various stages of dryness.

The items listed above are associated with purple, burgundy, crimson, orange, yellow, gold, and other earthy colors. If you can choose the basis of your altar, make sure to use polished wood incorporating these colors. If you have a pre-made surface that looks different from the Mabon color scheme, you can always drape a colored cloth over your altar. Deep brown or red are recommended for larger surfaces as this will be a perfect background for the colors of other items you plan to place on your altar.

If you can only use a small number of tools, such as a few candles, crystals, and symbols, and now harvest produce, use the most colorful pieces of cloth to represent these. For example, you can place a large golden-brown cloth on the altar to symbolize nature and a smaller, purple-colored one on top to represent grapes and red wine. Place a red piece of cloth diagonally across the purple one to illustrate the other fruits of nature.

You will need a centerpiece around which you can place your essential tools and, at the same time, accentuate the down-to-earth feeling you are trying to create with your altar. While a basket made from natural materials would be the best for this purpose, if you only have a plastic bowl at your disposal, use that instead. You can always cover its sides by adorning it with leaves and elements of nature. If you have a small space, you can simply put your offerings inside this bowl or basket. Another idea for a centerpiece would be to use potpourri decorated with tiny scarecrow figures, a common Wiccan practice.

Candles, pillars or taper, and crystals should follow the same color scheme as the other items. They can have a spicy fragrance that reminds you of the season, but if you prefer to use candles without a scent, you can do that too. You can always add more natural scents with ointments if you need specific scents to help you focus. The candles should be placed in a glass jar. This will reflect their light and makes it easier to extinguish them between uses. Light the candles only before casting a spell or performing a ritual, and don't leave them unattended, even if the act needs several hours to complete.

Additional Tips for Setting and Caring for Altars

As you can see, there is a lot to be gained from having a sacred place for your practice and not just for celebrating Mabon. There are also very few rules on how you can or cannot set up an altar for this festivity. As long as you include some of the traditional elements associated with Mabon, you can go on to personalize your space as you like. For newbies, it is generally recommended to have only one main altar in your home as this will allow you to concentrate your power. However, if you are a frequent traveler, you may want to have a mobile altar in addition to the one in your home. Even if you reside in one place, you may not have enough space for an altar in your bedroom. In this case, you can build your main altar elsewhere in the house, and if you would still love to say a dedicated prayer or spell before going to bed, set up a small space for this purpose on your nightstand. Or you may find it helpful to create small shrines in addition to the main altar. The energy will envelop your entire living space, empowering your practice and allowing you to access the power for any purpose from anywhere in your home.

Apart from adorning it with decorations and offerings, there are many other ways to use your altar. In the following chapters, you will find plenty of rituals, spells, and ideas on using your altar in interesting ways during your magical practice, particularly around Mabon. Whichever way you use your altar to celebrate the second harvest, you must not forget to cleanse it regularly. What this cleaning entails depends on how you use the space in the first place. For instance, if you only use it to express your gratitude with a quick prayer, you will only need to cleanse it occasionally. You may need to perform cleanings more frequently if you have a mobile altar. These spaces often come in contact with a larger number of sources of negativity than fixed altars, and you will sense their presence often. In case you plan to make offerings or perform a powerful ritual at your altar during a larger pagan sabbat, you must banish all the negativity from your space first. The purification can be performed in several ways, from smudging to using prayers to calling on spiritual guides.

Chapter 6: Recipes for a Mabon Feast

Mabon is known to be the "Pagan Thanksgiving" by many people. This is why we are here to tell you how to put together the perfect Mabon celebratory feast to enjoy with your friends and family. This chapter serves as a Mabon cookbook that includes delicious seasonal recipes. You will also find a section toward the end of the chapter which will help you understand how you can bless your food with prayers and magic.

Bread is an important part of the feast.
https://unsplash.com/photos/HJ3tXZpY1Qw

Dark Mother: Mabon Honey Wheat Bread

Mabon is an opportunity to celebrate the Dark Mother goddess even in her least comforting forms. This is a time when her presence must be acknowledged, regardless. During Mabon, we celebrate the goddess' wise old woman archetype. There is no better way to do so than by baking a delicious dish that was named in her honor. This appetizing loaf of bread is ideal for celebrating an abundant harvest. You can serve it with Mabon-esque dips like apple butter or herbed oils.

Ingredients:

- Flour: 4 cups
- Flour (whole wheat): 3 cups
- Water: 2 cups
- Honey: 1/3 cup
- Vegetable oil: 1/4 cup
- Butter: 2 tablespoons
- Dry yeast: 1 tablespoon
- Salt: 1 teaspoon

Instructions:

Step One:

1. Take a large bowl and mix the water and yeast. Stir until the yeast is incorporated, and then add the honey.
2. Stir in the vegetable oil, whole wheat flour, and butter. Mix well until you are left with stiff dough,
3. Gradually mix in the all-purpose flour.
4. Lightly flour your countertop before turning your dough out. Knead it for around 15 minutes.
5. The dough should be more malleable and elastic, so you can shape it into a ball.
6. Oil a bowl and place the dough inside. Use a warm, damp cloth to cover it, letting it rise for 45 minutes. It should have doubled in size.

Step Two:

1. Forcefully pat the dough down before you cut it in half, making two loaves of bread.
2. Grease a loaf pan, placing both halves inside. Let them sit and rise.
3. Once they have risen 1 or 2 inches over the loaf pan, move them into the oven.
4. Let them back for an hour at 375 degrees.
5. Remove the bread loaves when they are golden brown and allow them to cool for around 15 minutes.
6. Remove them from the pan and brush them over with melted butter.

Spiced Apple Pie

Apple trees, and apples in general, play a significant role in numerous pagan rites, stories, and lore, especially the ones that relate to Samhain and Mabon! Many people place apples on their altars, presenting them as offerings to the deities. They are also used as a way to thank the gods for an abundant harvest. Besides the significance of apples during the Harvest Festival, there is no better way to welcome fall than by baking a warm and comforting spiced apple pie.

Ingredients:

Ingredients for the Crust

- Flour: 1 1/3 cups
- Cubes of unsalted butter (chilled): 1/4 cups
- Frozen solid vegetable shortening (cubed): 1/4 cups
- Ice water: 3 tablespoons
- Salt: 1/2 teaspoon
- Sugar: 1/2 teaspoon
- Apple cider vinegar: 1/2 teaspoon

Ingredients for the Filling

- Sugar: 2/3 cups
- Flour: 2 tablespoons
- Melted unsalted butter: 2 tablespoons
- Ground cinnamon: 2 teaspoons
- Peeled and cored Granny Smith apples (sliced): 3 1/4 pounds

Topping Ingredients

- 1 cup of all-purpose flour
- ½ cup of sugar
- ¼ cup of packed golden-brown sugar
- 6 tbsp of chilled unsalted butter, cut into cubes (around ½ an inch each).
- 1 ½ tsp of ground cinnamon
- ½ tsp of salt

Instructions:
Crust Instructions
Step One:
1. Add the salt, flour, and sugar into a large bowl and mix well.
2. Add the shortening and butter. Make sure to use your fingertips to rub them in until they are coarse.
3. In a small bowl, mix the apple cider vinegar with 3 tbsp of ice water.
4. Drizzle the liquid over the flour mixture. Use a fork to mix well and break down any clumps. If the dough is dry, add more water.
5. Shape the dough into a ball before flattening it out into a circle.
6. Wrap the dough in plastic and leave it to refrigerate for half an hour.

Step Two:
1. Place your oven's rack in the center and preheat at 400 degrees.
2. Lightly flour your countertop, rolling out the dough on top. You should make a 12-inch round.
3. Move the dough to a 9-inch glass pie dish. Cut any excess dough, so there is a slight overhang. Turn the edge underneath the crimp in a decorative manner.
4. Let it refrigerate as you prepare the filling and topping.

Filling Instructions
Step Three:
1. In a large bowl, mix in all the filling ingredients to coat the apples.

Topping Instructions
Step Four:
1. Blend the all-purpose flour, brown sugar, ground cinnamon, and salt in a processor.
2. Use on and off turns (or the pulse function if your processor has one) to cut in the chilled butter cubes. Your mixture should end up looking like wet sand.

Step Five:
1. Toss the filling, making sure that the juices are well distributed.
2. Transfer the filling to the center of the crust.
3. Pack the topping over and surrounding the coated apples.

Preparing the Pie

Step Six:

1. Place the pie on a baking sheet before placing it in the oven.

2. Let it bake for around 40 minutes until the topping turns golden. If the top is becoming golden too quickly, you can use a foil covering to slow it down.

3. Turn down the heat to 350 degrees, allowing the pie to cook for another 45 minutes.

4. Stick a fork into the middle to check that the apples are soft. You should also see the filling start to bubble through the crust.

5. Leave for an hour to cool.

6. Serve with fresh cream or ice cream.

Recipe Notes: This recipe makes eight servings.

Vegetable Pot Pie

Vegetable pot pies are traditionally served during Mabon. This hearty, vegan-friendly recipe is scrumptious and filling and celebrates the essence of the holiday like no other! This is because it incorporates a wide array of seasonal vegetables, allowing you to share the bountiful harvest with everyone you love. As you cook, think of the variety of vegetables that you get to enjoy in a single dish, thanking nature and the deities for this blessing.

Ingredients:

- 8 medium-sized potatoes
- 1 large, finely chopped onion
- 2 9-inch high-quality (preferably whole grain) pie crust.
- 3 cups of your choice of diced vegetables - choose 3 or 4 of the following: broccoli, cauliflower, leeks, carrots, kale, yellow summer squash, mushrooms, zucchini, corn kernels, peas, etc.
- 1 cup of fine whole grain bread crumbs
- 1 cup of home-made or ready-made vegetable stock
- 1/4 cup of minced fresh parsley
- 1/4 cup of nutritional yeast. This is an optional ingredient, but we highly recommend that you use it
- 2 tbsp white flour (unbleached)
- 2 tbsp extra-virgin olive oil
- 1 ½ tbsp of all-purpose seasoning blend

- 1 tsp of dried thyme
- Salt to taste
- Pepper, freshly ground to taste
- Paprika for topping

Instructions:

Step One:

1. Cook the potatoes (or microwave them) in their skins.
2. When they have cooled down a bit, peel them.
3. Dice four of the potatoes and coarsely mash the rest.
4. Set the potatoes aside and preheat the oven to 350 degrees.

Step Two:

1. In a large skillet, heat the oil, and then place the onions. Set fire to medium heat and allow the onions to sauté until they're golden.
2. Mix in the vegetables of your choice. Make sure to add vegetables that require more cooking time, like leeks, broccoli, and cauliflower. Layer the quicker ones on top, such as zucchini, corn, and peas.
3. Add a little water to the pan before covering it. Allow the vegetables to cook for around 5 minutes, so they are tender but *not overcooked.*

Step Three:

1. Sprinkle the flour into the skillet before pouring the stock as well.
2. Mix in the optional nutritional yeast.
3. Cook for one or two more minutes, stirring until the liquid becomes thicker.
4. Add the diced and mashed potatoes, mixing them in well.
5. Stir in the thyme, parsley, and seasoning blend, then add salt and freshly ground pepper to taste.
6. Once done, place the mixture inside the pie crusts, patting it in well.
7. Sprinkle the bread crumbs over both pies, distributing them evenly. Finish off with a sprinkle of paprika over each.
8. Place in the preheated oven and allow them to bake for 35 to 40 minutes.
9. Remove the pies when the crust is golden, allowing them to sit at room temperature for around 10 minutes.
10. Cut into wedges and serve.

Recipe Notes: This recipe makes two pies and around 12 servings in total.

Mabon Roasted Turkey

As you already know, Mabon and Thanksgiving go almost hand in hand. While Thanksgiving is a national holiday, both celebrations are centered on the idea of giving thanks.

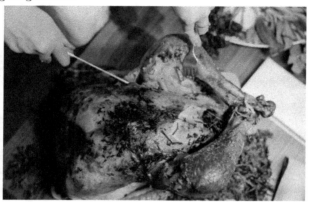

Roast turkey.
https://unsplash.com/photos/cgcteFH-azk

They are also associated with the end of the harvesting season. While there is no symbolic reason as to why turkeys are served on either holiday, it is a tradition that has stood for generations. Perhaps one of the reasons why turkeys are preferred over, say, chicken, on celebrations like Mabon, Thanksgiving, or even Christmas, is that they are large enough to sustain a feast. The following roasted turkey recipe will surely make your Mabon celebration a memorable one.

Ingredients:

- 1 thawed whole turkey (9 pounds)
- 1 medium-sized red onion cut in quarters
- 1 lemon cut in quarters
- ¼ cup of olive oil
- 1 tbsp of dried rosemary
- 1 tsp of dried thyme
- 1 tsp fine sea salt
- 1 tsp of dried tarragon
- ½ tsp of black pepper, freshly ground

Instructions:
Step One:
1. Set the temperature of the roaster oven to 325 degrees to preheat.
2. In a small bowl, start making the herbal rub by mixing in the olive oil, tarragon, rosemary, thyme, pepper, and salt.
3. Remove the neck and the giblets from the turkey. If you are making stock or gravy, you can use the neck and giblets to make them.
4. Use cold water to wash the turkey, then pat it dry.
5. Loosen, but don't remove it from the breast using your fingertips. Spread a tablespoon's worth of herbal rub on the meat below the loosened skin.
6. Spread more of the rub on the meat at the neck and body cavities.
7. Spread the rest of the rub on the skin outside the turkey.

Step Two:
1. Quarter the lemon and onion and stuff them into the body and neck cavities. In most cases, you will be able to fit one lemon quarter in the neck cavity, and the rest will be stuffed in the body.
2. Use toothpicks to secure the neck skin at the back. Fold the turkey's wing tips underneath its back and bind its legs in place.
3. If you wish, you can pause at this point and store it in the refrigerator for a few hours.

Step Three:
1. The turkey should be placed back down on the tray or rack. Lower it into the roaster and place a meat thermometer on its thigh. Make sure to stick it into the thickest part, steering clear of the bones.
2. Leave the turkey to roast in the preheated oven for around 2.5 hours. As a rule of thumb, each pound of turkey should take 15 to 20 minutes to roast.
3. Baste the turkey every half an hour. If you do not start out with enough pan juices, add one or two tablespoons of olive oil.
4. When the turkey turns your desired shade of brown, use aluminum foil to create a loose tent to cover it with. This will help you avoid over-browning. Lift it up when it is time to baste.
5. Allow the turkey to roast until the meat thermometer reads 165 degrees.

Step Four:

1. Turn the roaster off and remove the lid.

2. Allow the turkey to rest for 5 minutes before lifting the turkey using the rack from the oven.

3. Place the rack with the turkey on a platter, leaving it to rest for an additional 10 minutes.

4. Remove the rack and carve the turkey on your platter.

Recipe Notes: This roasted turkey recipe makes around ten servings. It works well with a small to medium-sized turkey (follow the 15 to 20-minute per pound rule). 1 pound of a whole turkey should feed a bit over one person.

Keep in mind that turkey meat is easy to dry out. This is why you should not skip over the olive oil and the frequent basting.

If you wish to stuff the turkey, avoid bread or grain-based savory stuffing, as they can hinder the cooking process. Instead, choose juicy vegetable and fruit stuffing instead. These provide flavor and moisture and may even be discarded later. You can add savory stuffing in the cavity right before you serve the turkey.

Winter Squash with Peas and Mashed Potatoes Stuffing

If you are not a carnivore, or if you have many vegan guests coming over, this is yet another vegetable-based delectable meal to keep everyone satisfied. This recipe uses seasonal ingredients like squash and potatoes, getting right to the essence of the celebration.

Ingredients:

- 6 medium-sized potatoes. They should be peeled and diced.
- 2 medium-sized squash - butternut or carnival. Each should weigh around 1.5 to 2 pounds.
- 1 large carrot cut into thick, 2-inch-long sticks
- 1 large onion chopped
- 1 cup of frozen petite green peas thawed
- ½ cup of rice milk
- 1 tbsp of olive oil. You can use an alternative vegetable oil of your choice
- 2 tsp of salt-free seasoning blend
- Nutmeg - a pinch

- Salt to taste
- Pepper, freshly ground to taste

Instructions:

Step One:

1. Preheat the oven to 400 degrees.
2. Cut the squash in half - vertically. Remove all the fibers and seeds.
3. Line a shallow baking pan with foil.
4. Cover the squash with aluminum foil, placing both cut halves, side up, in the lined baking pan.
5. Allow them to bake for 4o to 50 minutes. They should be firm yet easily pierced with a knife.
6. Remove when done and allow them to cool down.
7. Use a spoon to scoop out the pulp. You should have around a ¼ or ½-inch of firm shell all around.
8. Mash the pulp and set it aside.

Step Two:

1. Place the potatoes in a large saucepan and cover it with enough water.
2. Bring the saucepan to a simmer. Cover it and let it simmer steadily for around 10 to 15 minutes or until the potatoes are tender.

Step Three:

1. Heat the oil in a medium-sized skillet as you wait for the potatoes to cook.
2. Add the carrot and onion to the skillet to sauté them. Remove them when the carrot is crisp yet tender and the onion is golden.

Step Four:

1. When the potatoes are cooked, drain the potatoes and place them in a mixing bowl.
2. Pour in the rice milk and mash the potatoes until they're smooth.
3. Add the onions and carrots and mix well.
4. Stir in the ginger, peas, and nutmeg, followed by the squash pulp from earlier.
5. Mix gently, so everything is well-integrated into the mashed potatoes.

Step Five:

1. Distribute the mixture among the four squash shells.

2. Bake for 15 minutes.

3. Serve each half as a large portion or cut each half horizontally to make eight smaller portions

Recipe Notes: This recipe makes four large portions. If this is not one of your main dishes, you can cut each squash half into half to create eight small portions to make a great side dish.

Homemade Chai Tea

Nothing embodies the spirit of fall like chai tea! The comforting, warming, and relaxing combination of seasonal spices, milk, and black tea makes the ideal Mabon beverage. Serve this aromatic drink to your guests after dinner for a full celebratory experience. Not only is chai tea flavorful, but it can also aid with digestion and help them unwind after a busy day.

Ingredients:

- Black tea: 5-8 bags
- 2 sticks of cinnamon
- One knob of ginger, thinly cut
- 6 pods of cardamom
- 10 cloves
- Cold water: 6 cups
- Whole milk: 2 cups
- Golden brown sugar: 1/2 cup
- Black pepper: 2 teaspoons

Instructions:

Step One:

1. Add the spices and pepper to a large pan.

2. Muddle the spices together, crushing and grinding them with a wooden spoon.

Step Two:

1. Add the water and bring the mixture to a boil.

2. Reduce the heat and simmer for 8-12 minutes.

3. Add in the tea and allow to simmer for 4 minutes.

4. Strain the mixture.

Step Three:

1. Add sugar and milk to taste.

2. Continue to monitor the heat and simmer the mixture, stirring to incorporate the sugar.

3. Serve the tea.

Recipe Note: This recipe serves six people.

How to Imbue Your Food with Magic

People have used prayers, magic, blessings, and grace for centuries to imbue their food with magical powers. Numerous cultures have their own special ways of making food sacred. If you think about it, each religion comes with its own eating rituals, which involve practitioners saying blessings over their food. The primary intention behind this practice is to express thankfulness and gratitude for having something to eat.

Saying grace, however, can be tied to much more than being thankful. Grace is the feeling of joy that you get whenever you replenish your body after being hungry. In a sense, grace resonates with "salvation" more than it does with thankfulness. If you have tried fasting, then the chances are that you can resonate with this feeling.

Not only is food a blessing and essential to life, but it also requires sacrifices to be made. Whether you are eating meat or a vegetable, something has to die so you can have food on your plate. This is why you should thank the Earth and god for it.

There are several things you can do to bless your food. You can say a prayer of grace over your meal or practice invocation and other types of magic.

Theophagy

You can practice theophagy as a method of imbuement by combining visualization with the physical interaction with food (cooking and ingestion). Theophagy is essentially a ritualistic practice where food or drinks are substituted with the body of a god. These substitutes can be grains, vegetables, entheogens, animals, etc. Since no one can get hold of a physical object that relates to a god, you can imbue your food with the name or qualities of your desired god while you are cooking it or before you ingest it.

Grow Your Awareness

Did you know that our digestion is affected by our mood and mental state? If you eat when you are angry, for instance, this can negatively impact your ability to digest food. Performing rituals and saying grace can help us clear our energies and balance our emotions, which would then allow us to benefit from the food that we are eating. Bring your awareness to your emotions while you eat. Try to be sincerely thankful, joyful, and grateful throughout the entire experience.

Say Prayers

Bless your feast with the following prayer before you eat:

"In this sacred time and place,

we celebrate the balance of the equinox

around our community feast table.

We've set a bountiful feast, for which we are thankful.

We enjoy many blessings of our harvests this turning,

and we receive them with humility and gratitude.

May this food and drink nourish our bodies,

and this assembly of friends nourishes our hearts

so that we may be strengthened for our journey into the coming dark.

At this time of our bounty, we remember times of lack.

We remember that life gives itself in sacrifice so that others may live,

Knowing there are those who are suffering,

we hold them in the light of Divine love, and we offer a pledge to give of ourselves as we are able

in service for a greater harvest.

May the blessings of Spirit flow through us.

We are love and light, sacrifice and shadow,

toil and harvest. We are complete.

For all that is lost, there is gain.

When all is lost, we look to hope.

When our hearts ache, we still have happiness.

I can only rise again if I first fall.

But give me not too much of any one thing.

May we remain ever mindful, in deepest gratitude.

Blessed be."

Now that you have read this chapter, you are ready to prepare and plan a Mabon feast. The recipes above will guarantee a memorable second harvest feast. Imbuing your food with one of the spiritual essences we have explained can help you further incorporate the magic of the holiday into the cooking and feasting experience.

Chapter 7: Family and Group Activities

Festivals and holidays are meant to be commemorated with friends and families, and Mabon is no different. As Mabon is a festival that revolves around harvest and history tells us that pagans and Celts used to celebrate this day to thank Mother Nature for a good harvest.

So, when celebrating Mabon, your plans should also swirl around nature, harvest, and promote natural resources.

Moreover, one of the main reasons behind celebrating this day is to pray for the yield to last throughout the winter season. Therefore, as a follower and believer, you have to nurture this idea in younger generations to keep them in touch with the holy tradition of Mabon.

To celebrate the real essence of this festival, you must plan activities accordingly to make the day interesting and enjoyable for your family and maintain its educational aspect.

And to help you with the planning group and family activities during this festive season, we are sharing some tips in this chapter to help to make it a memorable time for you and the people closest to you.

Planning a Mabon Feast

Mabon is a holy festival and carries a lot of significance for all pagan believers. As a matter of fact, Mabon shares a lot of similarities with Thanksgiving.

Interestingly, the concept behind Mabon, as well as Thanksgiving, is to celebrate the harvesting season. Therefore, the meals usually made in a Mabon feast are symbolic, too, much like we have in our Thanksgiving dinners.

Some foods symbolic of the Mabon feast are nuts, pomegranates, bread, mutton, goose, and carrots.

Tips for Organizing a Mabon Dinner/Feast

Mabon is a big and hearty dinner with several guests. It is imperative to plan it well beforehand to avoid any inconvenience on the day. Also, it is a must to assess your budget while planning so that the expenses will not get out of your hand during preparations. Keeping that in mind, here are some tips to help you with the arrangements for the Mabon dinner.

1. Use of Mother Nature

The common theme of all rituals and festivities concerning Mabon is to respect Mother Nature, so arranging a nature-friendly themed dinner is appropriate. Use natural resources to decorate the area and create a Mabon altar. It is also better to keep your meals season-friendly by using fresh vegetables and fruits. Some of the most common things you can get your hands on during the festival days include walnuts, hazelnuts, berries, mushrooms, corn husks, pinecones, and seasonal vegetables.

2. When to Hold the Mabon Feast

In most countries, the festival comes right at the beginning of the school year, and it will be nearly impossible for most families to hold a huge celebration every year, especially if it does not fall on the weekend. But it does not mean you cannot celebrate the festival.

The best way to celebrate Mabon with your family is by holding a family meal at the end of the day. In that case, arrange a delightful yet simple dinner, put bouquets of fresh flowers or candles on the dinner table, and give each family member a chance to let out their thoughts about things they are grateful for and what they want to achieve in the coming season.

3. Plan Every Detail

In normal circumstances, a Mabon feast would be a huge gathering comprising family members, friends, and relatives, and to organize a dinner of that scale, you have to be spot on with every little detail while planning.

4. How to Plan a Menu

First, make a list of the guests and send them invites. Once you know the number of guests, it will help you keep a count of the preparations. The second and one of the most important things is to plan a menu. Always consider the dietary priorities of your guest before finalizing the menu. It is better to arrange both veg and non-veg options for varied preferences. Add a dessert, too, because a sweet delicacy is a wonderful way of wrapping up things. Arrange a handful of drinks, too, because no matter what you put on the menu to eat, drinks can enhance the whole feel of the menu.

5. Organize the Spot

The thing you just cannot do is overlook the place where the actual dinner is going to take place. The dinner arena should be cleaned a day before the festival. Make sure your place is decorated according to the selected theme, and the dishes are done beforehand. It is always a great idea to decorate the entrance with fresh flowers and traditional autumn greenery. Another thing to ensure as a host is to arrange enough garbage bags so that the actual dinner place will stay tidy the whole day of the festival.

6. What to Avoid

Now that we have discussed everything that needs to be done in order to make your Mabon feast a hit, it is time to point out some of the chores that should be avoided to prevent any inconvenience on the prestigious occasion.

- Never make a mistake by inviting guests to dinner before making a manageable plan. For a special dinner, you must make a well-versed plan at least a month before the day of the festival.

- Understandably, you would want to invite everyone you know in your circle to this day, but it is imperative, too, that you think realistically about your budget, time, and the spot of the dinner.

- As we have discussed earlier, it is a must to consider the guests' dietary preferences while finalizing the menu. Try to prepare a multidimensional menu that includes vegetarian and non-veg meals to accommodate guests with different dietary preferences and needs.

- Do not forget to arrange enough cutlery, plates, pots, pans, and forks according to the decided menu to avoid any inconvenience during the dinner.

- The quantity of food is one the most important part to consider while planning. It is the part where people often miscalculate things, and it will eventually become the reason for embarrassment for the host. Also, you do not want to send your guests home starving on the Mabon feast.

- As with the food, always calculate the number of drinks you are going to need for the day. Always arrange some spare bottles just in case. A common mistake you would want to avoid is to arrange only alcoholic drinks. A bottle of wine is good, but it is imperative to arrange a handful of non-alcoholic drinks too for people who do not like or want to drink alcohol.

- Another big mistake people make is becoming a control freak and doing everything on their own, which generally takes a toll on their health physically and mentally. As a result, they do not get to enjoy the actual event at the expense of preparation. So, it is always good to ask for assistance and bring some help in the kitchen to ensure everything goes smoothly.

- I am not sure why, but many people make the mistake of trying new recipes out on that day, and it is always a risk and must be avoided at any cost. Suppose you have found some new exciting Mabon feast recipes and are itching to cook them at the festival. In that case, it is better to try those recipes beforehand to ensure everything turns out well to avoid any inconvenience (or embarrassment) in front of your guests.

- Cooking leaves a handful of dirty pans, pots, and utensils, and it is always a good idea to do to wash them up as you go. It will eventually save you a lot of time and hassle at the end of the day.

- Obviously, the main activity in a Mabon feast must be eating, but you cannot ignore the fact that if you do not have anything else planned besides dinner, your guests will be bored. To avoid that, arrange some fun activities for the children, turn the TV on for sports lovers, or engage your guests in some fun party games, all while they wait for the food to be served.

- Another thing you can do is arrange regular snacks for your guests to keep everyone tidy and fresh until dinner is served.

- Lastly: people often tend to forget the main idea behind the Mabon dinner – to enjoy and celebrate with friends and family. So, it is imperative that the host must take some time out of the preparatory hustles of the kitchen and enjoy the moment.

An alternative to a Potluck Mabon Dinner

For some people, hosting a Potluck Mabon dinner is not really possible for many reasons. But that doesn't mean that if you cannot hold a Mabon dinner, you cannot celebrate the festival at all. There are many other ways to celebrate and enjoy the festivity with your family, and this section is all about that.

1. Bring All the Apples

Apple is the most prominent symbol of the Mabon festival. You don't need to go all out with your feast at this time of year; even just consuming apples (in their various forms) will suffice.

2. Built Your Very Own Mabon Altar

This is the most satisfying thing to do at the Mabon festival. An altar represents a significant portion of the spiritual aspect of a Pagan. Creating an altar in your home on this prestigious occasion is a form of celebration in itself. The Mabon altar is created for numerous reasons, to pray, cast spells or hold ceremonies.

You can build your Mabon altar anywhere you want or have space in your home. Be sure to incorporate the four elements into your altar, symbolizing fire, water, air, and earth in different ways. You can also include something representing your faith, e.g., a goddess candle or a book of shadows.

Another major element that you can add to a Mabon altar is seasonal and ceremonial symbols and colors. Mabon is usually represented with fall colors like brown, gold, and orange. Hence, Mabon is a festival to celebrate the harvest. You can also add symbols to represent the seasonal harvest, including apples, wheat, pomegranate, corn, pumpkin, and other seasonal vegetables.

3. Mabon Balance Meditation

As Mabon is that time of the year when, for a short period, day and night appear to be of the same length of time, or, as it is referred to by the ancient pagans, the periods of light and dark come into balance. Pagans widely believe that the energy of the planet is ideal for meditating and seeking balance in our own lives too.

You will need a black and white candle and a place devoid of stress, confusion, and clutter. Light both candles and close your eyes to begin entry into your meditative state. Breathe in and out while focusing on your breathing, and think about what you need help with in your life. Now right after that, turn your focus on things that are more or less a reason for your happiness or goals that you want to achieve in your life in the near future.

Now the most important part, it is time to acknowledge the blessings of god and understand that with every negative, there is a positive too that comes side by side.

4. Connect with Mother Nature

As we have discussed in the earlier part of the chapter, the real idea behind all of this is to celebrate the harvest and thank god for its countless blessings. Besides all those rituals and indoor festivities, the best way to celebrate it is to connect with nature. You can do that in many ways depending on the time, resources available, and the commitment you would like to give. Whatever you plan, encourage your family to take part in these healthy activities too.

For starters, it is easier to go for a walk at any nearby park or go hiking on trails located in your vicinity with your family. If you can commit, pack up and go camping or sleep with the stars – one of the most amazing things you can do to appreciate and celebrate nature. If you have small children, teach them to appreciate and respect the blessings of the environment.

Various Mabon Activities to Indulge in

Let us discuss some other Mabon activities you can indulge in on the day besides those we have talked about up until now. In this section, we will focus on those activities that can be adapted by the Pagans, especially Wiccans and Druids.

1. Mindful Autumn Cleaning

Mabon is when the balance of light and dark shifts towards the other side of the horizon, and the planet earth experiences a change in temperatures. It is considered an ideal time to clean and organize your home.

Take the negative energies out of your home by decluttering, and put some effort into completing any outstanding repairing work on your home. After you are done with physical cleaning, it is time to move your focus toward the spiritual side of it. This is considered the most important part of this activity, and pagans usually go through a candle ritual that involves several traditional rituals, charging protection, ritual smudging, and healing crystals. Adopt any one of these rituals by following your heart.

2. Extend Your Blessings to Others

Besides following the central concept of the Mabon festival, which is to thank and pray to god for the harvest and blessings, it is also a time when you should reach out to the less blessed people or the ones struggling to make both ends meet. You can do that by sticking to the basic symbol of the festival, harvest, holding a food drive for deserving people, and encouraging others to do the same.

In case you are not in a position to help others financially, it is ok, as most of us have gone through that phase too. In that case, if you can keep your positive energy going, you can physically participate in that holy cause by working for food banks organized by others. The idea is to keep your mind fresh with positive energies.

3. Planting Bulb Flowers

One fun and positive activity that you can indulge in is planting. And this is the ultimate time of the year to plant different tree seeds, especially bulb flowers. They usually hide in the earth throughout the winter, which helps them stabilize and germinate in darkness until the spring arrives, when you will see your planted seeds germinate and appear on the surface.

4. Write a Gratitude Journal

If you have a collection of those beautiful little notebooks you have never bothered to touch after bringing them home years ago, this is the time to use them for good. Gather all your positive thoughts about the things that happen to you and which you feel good about, and write them in that notebook. It will make you feel better about yourself and your surroundings.

Plus, it will work as a signal to the earthly heavens that you need those moments to happen more often in your life in the future.

5. Host a Bonfire

A tradition not really original to the Mabon festival but recognized worldwide and throughout known history is that harvest festivals are meant to end on that very activity, burning a fire. So, it is a no-brainer to arrange something traditional that also has significance in the history books. Invite your friends, loved ones, and other closely related people and set the scene in the environment. Be sure to burn all those things that are not good for you and your loved ones, tell stories, listen to other people, and raise a toast for everyone's safety and health.

Kid-Friendly Mabon Activities

Mabon is the festival meant to unite us with our families, loved ones, and friends, and we are meant to thank Mother Nature for her blessings upon us. And our kids certainly are an integral part of the blessings of God upon us. So, if you are lucky enough to have those little munchkins at your home, involve them in this prestigious occasion and arrange some interesting and enjoyable activities to make them feel better about this holy festival. And if you cannot think of one, here are some fun activities you can arrange for your kids to indulge in.

- To create a Mabon altar, you will need a handful of natural resources such as acorns, nuts, apples, seasonal vegetables, colorful flowers or leaves, ivy, and other natural items you think your kids will love. It would be great for your children if you could take them out and handpick these items so that your children can appreciate the beauty and blessings of nature.

- You can start the festival by making a flavorful apple pie in the morning. Try to engage your children in the baking process too. It will help them grow as human beings and make them appreciative of you and other fellow humans.

- If you are holding a Mabon feast at home, keep the children busy with some fun games and activities. A healthy activity you can organize for them is to engage them in creating paper bouquets, especially autumn flowers.

- Show your kids the old family albums and answer their questions. Also, tell them the stories behind those pictures and tell them about the people and legacy they left behind respectfully.

- You can also honor the wildlife in your vicinity by making bird feeders and inspiring your children to do the same in the coming years.

- Keep a close eye on your family habits and try to find the appropriate solutions to those manners that you feel are inappropriate for the environment and your fellow human beings. For example, use less water, do not waste food, keep a light tone while conversing or recycle more garbage. Your children will learn a lot, making them better people altogether.

- Read stories to them about harvest, Autumn season, and Mabon. It will educate them and give them the whole idea behind the celebration.

- Arrange a question-and-answer session for children so they can ask whatever they have in their minds about the festival, traditions, and religious practices of Pagans.

Chapter 8: Sacred Rituals and Ceremonies

Traditional rituals and ceremonies related to Mabon revolve around celebrating abundance and being thankful. However, many other ways to celebrate the fall equinox include inward reflection, forming spiritual connections, or planning for what you will plant next year. This chapter includes several rituals and ceremonies you can incorporate into your Mabon celebrations. Some of them are more suitable for groups. Others can be performed by solo practitioners and will take only a few minutes of your day.

Mabon Meditation

Mabon is the ideal time of the year to release any negative emotions you carry on your shoulders and harvest some positive ones instead. Meditative practice can help you do this and will not take much time from your schedule either.

Many crops are harvested during Mabon, but at the same time, you cannot help but notice the first signs of nature dying as it prepares for the harsh winter months. The equinox represents a unique balance between the bright side of the year that is now ending and the dark side that is yet to come. Day and night are of equal lengths, another sign of natural balance. It reminds you that you cannot expect the light to come out the following year without experiencing darkness in this one.

Ideally, you should meditate in the evening and preferably outside, as this will give you a stronger connection with the spirits of nature. You can also do it at an altar you have set up inside your home. Here is how to perform a Mabon meditation, regardless of the place you have chosen for it:

- Decorate your altar or an outside flat surface with leaves, acorns, nuts, small amounts of fruit and vegetables, and other autumn symbols mentioned in this book.

- Place a black and a white candle at the center of your working area, and light them both.

- Sit comfortably, take a deep breath, and close your eyes so that you can start to relax.

- Now recall everything you have been struggling with lately and everything that caused you harm or made you anxious.

- Repeat the following:

  "I seek the balance of day and night,

  brought on by this Mabon night

  I seek balance in my life

  as it is found in nature.

  The back candle is illuminated because we all have to suffer at times.

  and the candle will help to remove my suffering.

  The white candle is illuminated for the happiness in my life

  and all that will come my way as I dedicate my life.

  This is Mabon when the light and dark are equal,

  and the balance transcends my soul and brings inner peace,

  and the harmony shall continue within me."

- Continue meditating on everything you wish to change in your life, leaving hurtful memories behind.

- When you feel cleansed from negative energy, start invoking abundance and positivity into your life.

- Open yourself to receiving every spiritual gift possible, and be prepared to express your gratitude for them.

- Let the scent of the burning candles permeate your senses, carrying renewed energy and purpose with it.

- Accept that there are and always will be challenging times in life, and embracing them is the only way to move past them.

- Once you can finally embrace the balance of light and dark, you will be ready to finish your session with a deep exhalation.

- Bring the present back to your mind's focus, stand up, extinguish your candles, and go to sleep.

Dark Mother Ritual

This ritual celebrates all Dark Mothers, and, as such, can be personally tailored depending on which entity you feel spiritually connected to. Inanna, Demeter, Hecate, Tiamet, Nemesis, Kali, and Morrighan are just some of the female deities you can evoke, one or more of them at a time. The Dark Mother is an aspect of goddesses that you may not find too appealing, but its existence is essential for balancing the more comforting aspects. By acknowledging the Dark Mother with this ritual, you are repeating and honoring an ancient tradition of creating an energetic balance for healing from past traumas.

You Will Need:

- Symbols of a pagan goddess known to have a dark side
- Red, yellow, purple, and black flowers
- A basket full of wheat, Indian corn, and other crops representing the second harvest
- A black candle
- A yellow or red candle
- A cup of wine or juice from a red fruit
- A pomegranate
- A bowl, a knife, and a spoon

Instructions:

1. Place all of your items on your altar and perform your usual preparatory practices. Whether you call to cast a circle, call on your spiritual guides, meditate or perform any other mindfulness exercise, it will be up to you.

2. After that, turn back to the altar, light the dark candle, and recite the following:

   "As the land begins to die, and the earth grows cold.

   What once brought life does not anymore.

   As the Dark Mother comes to harvest,

   So does nature continue its descent into night.

   As we mourn the death of nature

   We also mourn the long daylight

   and prepare for winter as it approaches us."

3. The yellow/red candle can be illuminated, incanting:

> *"Anger and pain bring the Dark Mother to the world.*
>
> *The harvest shall wither as the time of change becomes upon us.*
>
> *She travels around us looking for the bounty,*
>
> *forgoing darkness as the crops meet their end.*
>
> *We share in the grief that she takes on for us,*
>
> *And we hope she finds the light that she will bring to us.*
>
> *We cannot have the light without the darkness."*

4. Cut the pomegranate and remove six of the seeds, placing them in your receptacle. Place on the altar and incant:

> *"Six months of light can only follow six months of darkness.*
>
> *We rise back to life only after death has touched us.*
>
> *Great Mabon, let this be your night,*
>
> *And let us celebrate it with you.*
>
> *We embrace the darkness,*
>
> *And celebrate the life of the Crone.*
>
> *Blessings to the dark goddess on this night."*

5. Lift the cup of wine or juice from the altar and place it back and hold your hand out as if you would reach for the goddess.

6. Reflect on the darker aspects of your life, including the pain you are carrying from past traumas, any anger or frustration still worrying you, and unsaid grievances towards others.

7. Now, focus on turning all this negativity into positivity by saying the following:

> *"Bringer of darkness,*
>
> *I am ready to embrace you tonight.*
>
> *What is love without first experiencing loss and grief,*
>
> *What is joy without knowing pain,*
>
> *What is light without the dark,*
>
> *and what is life without first death?*
>
> *O Dark Mother of the night, I thank you."*

8. When you are ready to accept every aspect of your soul, you may end the ritual and extinguish your candles. Leave the wine and other offerings out for the goddess.

Mabon Gratitude Ritual

This short gratitude ritual incorporates elements you and your group can use to express your gratitude for everything you have. You can also perform it by yourself, although it holds even more power if a tight-knit pagan community performs it during Mabon night. It can be incorporated into other traditions or beliefs or, kept as it is, a short pagan rite for giving thanks. It includes symbols of those aspects of your life that you are grateful to have.

You Will Need:

- Gold or green candle to represent abundance. The number of colors you need depends on the number of participants
- Basket of apples or grapes
- 1/8 cup of neutral oil of your choice
- 5 drops of rose oil
- 2 drops of vetiver oil
- 1 drop of agrimony oil
- A pinch of ground cinnamon
- Cornucopias as the symbol of bounty
- An abundance symbol (preferably hand crafted)
- Representations of things you are grateful for (health, career, family, etc.)
- Pieces of cloth or craft material in colors associated with abundance

Instructions:

1. If you do not have it already prepared, make your oil blend by mixing all the oils with the cinnamon.

2. Start decorating your altar with all the items by placing your fruit basket in the middle. Then put the symbols in front and the two candles on either side of the basket. Scatter the other items and colorful pieces of material around the larger centerpiece.

3. Gather around before going to sleep, let everyone take a deep breath, and close their eyes.

4. Take a moment to consider what you have in abundance. Keep in mind that means much more than having plenty of material goods or a high income.

5. Think about friends and family ties, even with those who have already passed away. You can be thankful for all the wisdom the ancestors

provided during their life and even after that.

6. If you have a trusty spiritual guide you use regularly, you may include them in your intention for saying thanks.

7. Everyone should anoint a candle with the oil mixture and light it.

8. One by one, each participant can express their gratitude. Start at one corner of the altar and slowly work towards the other one until everyone has said their thanks.

9. Here are some ideas on what to say:

"I am thankful for my health because it makes me feel well.

I am grateful to my children because their love keeps me happy.

I appreciate my job because I can do what I love while having financial independence.

My garden fills me with joy for the abundance of food and medicine it brings.

I am grateful for my friends and family because they make me feel complete."

10. Let everyone meditate for five minutes after the last person has expressed their gratitude out loud.

11. If you are conducting this ritual as a group, the members can also express their appreciation for each other. If you are a solitary practitioner, you can call or message people you appreciate having in your life. There is always a way to let them know how much their presence means to you; it is just a question of taking the time for it.

Group Apple Picking at Mabon

The best part about large pagan holidays is that they always unite communities. Whether you and your loved ones share the same spiritual beliefs or not, everyone will find their fill of joy and happiness, particularly during this ritual. It involves picking apples as a group and strictly as a group, with a side of gratitude. After pumpkins, apples are probably the most commonly harvested fall fruit. In pagan communities, apples are grown for several purposes, but group pickings are among the most important. Gathering apples with your loved ones is one of the best ways to appreciate the gifts of nature.

You only need apples and perhaps comfortable clothing for this ritual.

Instructions:

1. Gather people from your community, go to the nearest apple orchards and pick as many apples as possible.

2. After harvesting the apples, gather around and sit on the ground in a circle. If the weather is getting colder, you can all converge inside and sit on the floor.

3. Hold an apple in your hands and start expressing your gratitude. Each person should have a few minutes to say what or whom they appreciate most in life.

4. When the last person in the circle has said their thanks, get up and continue with your Mabon celebration.

Group Expeditions

Another way pagans can express their gratitude as a group around the fall equinox is by going on short expeditions in nature. You can go hiking or for a walk, whatever the group decides, and observe nature around you. Make sure to notice all the changes in the landscape and acknowledge the necessity for these changes. You can also repeat this at the spring equinox and compare the transformation you see then with the one you experience before winter.

Your group can also visit a farmer's market or a farm where you can buy fresh organic produce. Everyone can choose a unique ingredient to take home and add it to a celebratory meal you all make together. This can be a fun activity for children as they can learn more about natural food sources while bonding with their family members.

Making Donations

Just as they do at any other festivity, people in pagan communities are famous for sharing what they have with those in need. If you live in such a community and practice together as a group, all of you can gather food and supplies you can donate. However, solitary practitioners are just as welcome to inspire others with their generosity. There is no better way to express gratitude for the abundance of anything you have in your life than by sharing it with the less fortunate.

Morning Gratitude Ritual

While most people express their gratitude on the night of the equinox, there is no reason that you could not do this for several days leading up to this date. The best way to do it is to begin your days with a ritual of appreciation. Start bright and early on the first morning of the Mabon celebrations. Write three to five things you are grateful for on a piece of paper. You can write more if you can think of them immediately, but do not worry if you can only come up with three at first. Create your crafts and recipes, and start decorating your altar to get inspired and find more things to be grateful for. You will soon start adding more and more items to your lists and by the night of the equinox comes, your list will be rather long.

Autumn Cleansing Ritual

While most people get inspired to clean their homes in spring, fall can be just as great a time to catch up on some much-needed chores. And, yes, even chores can be a Mabon ritual. You can perform spiritual and energetic cleansing by smudging your place. Or you can literally dust and air out your home preparing it for the bounty of the harvest and some positive energy you'll need during the cold winter months.

Solitary Grounding Ritual

While you can explore nature around you in a group, conducting a solitary grounding ritual is a good idea to form an even stronger bond with nature. Performing it in solitude will allow you to connect directly to the vital energy. It will also provide a place to feel safe during a transition period such as the fall equinox. By placing your feet on the ground, you can feel how the energy travels from the earth, enters your legs and travels upward through the rest of your body.

Mabon Ritual for Good Harvests and Other Rewards Ahead

Like a Mabon meditation session, this ritual also has the purpose of balancing the dark with light. It is the perfect way to ensure that the second harvest will be just as bountiful as the first one and that you will receive spiritual rewards in other parts of your life.

You Will Need:

- A white or clear crystal to represent light
- A dark gemstone to represent the dark
- A white candle that symbolizes the light side of harvest (the bounty)
- A black candle that symbolizes the dark side of harvest (dying nature)
- White sage, copal, and other herbs for smudging
- Your favorite essential oil or natural perfume

Instructions:

1. Place the light tools on the left side of your altar and the dark tools on the right side. Keeping them apart is crucial before you cleanse them to avoid mixing energies.
2. Keep the essential oil in the middle for now.
3. Create a smudge stick from your herbs, light them, and use them to cleanse the rest of the items. Start the smudging with the lighter

items and slowly move on to the darker ones.

4. Take a deep breath as you inhale the smoke created by the smudging stick and try to sense the energy of each tool you have on your altar.

5. If you have trouble deciding how to start integrating your tools into one balanced whole, call upon your spirit guides to find out how to approach this process.

6. When you feel that one of the candles is ready to be moved, pick it up and place it beside the stones on the opposite side. Shortly afterward, you can move the other candle and light them both.

7. As you see the light candle shining over the dark stones and the dark one over the light crystals, you will feel a balance forming between light and shadow.

8. Enjoy the liberating experience mixing sides brings. Start embracing it and continue mixing and matching by rearranging the stones until you feel that a balance has been fully established.

9. Step back and gaze at the play of light and dark. Consider the lessons you can learn from this experience while you breathe deeply.

10. At this point, you may receive messages from your spiritual guides to make sure to keep an open mind about them.

11. Bring your hands forward in a prayer position in front of your heart and express your gratitude for everything you have achieved and learned.

12. At this moment of balance, welcome whatever the future may still hold and promise to integrate it into your life, whether there are good or bad experiences.

Finding the Right Mabon Traditions for You

As you can see, there are many ways to celebrate Mabon. Practices can be based on things like your spiritual beliefs, the number of people celebrating, or the flora and fauna you have available where you live. Feel free to use the rituals and ceremonies discussed in this chapter, but do not forget to add your own twist to them. By listening to your intuition, you can make your Mabon celebration as simple or complicated as you want them to be.

If you prefer to express your gratitude alone, choose simple rituals focusing on spiritual opening and development. On the other hand, if you are open to social celebrations, you can invite fellow practitioners and even non-pagan friends and family members to join you. Everyone shares the fun during Mabon, from cleaning to gathering supplies to enjoying delicious feasts.

Chapter 9: Spells, Charms, and Baths

Mabon can also be celebrated with different spells, baths, and even by creating your own harvest charms. This chapter brings you plenty of spells to enact centered on the second harvest, with user-friendly instructions on how and when to say them. Most of them use harvest-related ingredients presented in the previous chapters and can be tied to rituals, prayer, or meditative practices suitable for this spell. As expected, Mabon spells are all about celebrating abundance, expressing gratitude, and preparing to transition from summer to winter.

Healing Apple Magic

As apples are one of the most plentiful products around Mabon time, they are often used in spells and rituals as symbols of abundance and something to be thankful for. However, this same quality makes apples perfect for healing magic spells. As you reflect on what you need to be grateful for, you may uncover some unpleasant memories and emotions. You can use this spell to put those to rest and heal. It will remind you that for us to have apples in abundance, nature had to turn dark the year before. So, to experience happiness again, you must go through some dark stages in your life.

You Will Need:

- 1 apple
- A knife

Instructions:

1. Cut the apple horizontally, and place the halves on your altar. The center reveals the ancient pagan protection symbol, the pentagram.

2. As you look at the pentagram, try to visualize your grievances or areas of life that are out of balance. This can be a health issue you are going through or a mental or emotional issue.

3. Having identified the source of negativity, take the seeds out of the apple. You may need to cut the entire center out to remove all the seeds.

4. Once the seeds are removed, take both apple halves into your hands, and look at their center again. Envision a sphere of light in it and feel this light entering your hands.

5. Now take the seeds and bury them underground. If you have a large enough backyard, you can plant the seeds there so they can grow into a tree. If the space is tight, you can place them in a small pot and consider the planting symbolic.

6. Say the following when you are planting the seeds:

"With the healing energy of this apple, I nourish my mind, body, and soul. As the earth nourishes these seeds, taking my worries away, so shall nature nourish me by healing me and making me stronger."

7. As you are about to cover the seeds with soil, focus on feeling your negative emotions and thoughts disappear.

8. After the seeds are planted, wash your hands, and eat the apple while sensing its healing energy coursing through your body and soul.

Releasing Spell

The falling autumn leaves are the perfect ingredient for a releasing spell. Besides all the other significances, Mabon is also the time for letting go. As the leaves fall from the trees to the ground, they symbolize things weighing you down. You can lift this burden from your shoulders by simply using these leaves in a Mabon spell.

You Will Need:

- A bunch of leaves of different colors, shapes, and sizes
- A marker

Instructions:

1. Gather the leaves in a bowl and place them on your altar. You can put them on a table too, but an altar can help you set your intention better.

2. Take a leaf and focus on something you want to release from your life. Write a word or short phrase representing whatever you want to let go of.

3. When you are ready to let go, take the leaf into your hands and recite the following spell:

"With this leaf, I release my attachment to anything that does not align with my values.

I'm letting go of [what you have written on the leaf] and all the hurt it caused."

4. Repeat the process on a different leaf and feeling, setting your intention for letting go of each individual sentiment. Repeat until you run out of things you want to release.

5. Place each marked leaf back into the bowl and take it outside.

6. Release them one by one, letting the wind carry them away, along with your hurt.

7. As the negativity makes its way out from your body, you will feel it leaving more room for positive, healing energy.

Mabon Bath

The abrupt temperature changes brought on by the approaching winter can take a toll on your body and spirit. You will need a hot bath to warm you from the inside out. Taking a bath on the eve of the fall equinox is another great way to celebrate Mabon. A hot bath can be a tool for spiritual opening, healing from past trauma, or protection against the effects of the upcoming cold and dark period.

You Will Need:

- 1/3 cup of sea salt
- 1/3 cup of powdered milk or milk substitute
- 1/3 cup of oatmeal
- 1 teaspoon of dried calendula flowers
- 1 teaspoon of dried chamomile flowers
- 5-10 drops of myrrh essential oil
- 5-10 drops of frankincense essential oil
- Several candles, white and autumn-colored ones
- The incense of your choice (optional)

Instructions:

1. Scoop the oatmeal into a blender or food processor and blend until it reaches the consistency of flour. Pour it out in a separate bowl.

2. Mix the sea salt with the powdered milk or substitute in another bowl, and slowly mix in the dried flowers.

3. Now add the oatmeal and make sure that it coats the rest of the ingredients.

4. Add the essential oil and mix until well combined. You can add less or even a little more if the number of drops in the recipe does not get you the desired fragrance strength.

5. Fill your bathtub with warm water and add the mixture to it.

6. While you are waiting for the mixture to dissolve, decorate the edges of your tub with candles.

7. If you are using incense, light them up. You can skip this step if you find the scent of dissolving flowers relaxing enough.

8. Get into the bath, close your eyes, and meditate on whatever you wish to come to terms with for 30 minutes. You can also ask your spiritual guides for protection by focusing your intention in that direction.

Mabon Balance Spell

While a balancing spell can be performed at any time, its potency around an equinox is magnified. During this time, nature's dark and light sides are in balance, but not for a long time. With the fall equinox, the balance soon shifts towards the dark side, only to shift back toward the light one at the spring equinox. With this spell, you can celebrate this balance, empower it, and make the shift even more beneficial for you.

You Will Need:

- An 11-inch-long white ribbon
- An 11-inch-long black ribbon
- A white pencil or marker
- A black pencil or marker
- A charm or an object that symbolizes balance in your life
- 1 black candle
- 1 white candle
- Incense of your choice
- Acorns, nuts, leaves, and other harvest symbols
- Pieces of cloth or craft material in colors associated with Mabon

Instructions:

1. Before you cast the spell, search out areas in your life that you want to balance. Keep in mind that you should look for polar opposites. For each problematic area, the opposite is the solution.

2. The trick is to take the quality you find problematic and channel it in a different direction to balance out its past effects. Having done that, you will be ready to re-establish the balance.

3. Sit at your altar and place all your tools on it. Light the candles and the incense and arrange the rest of the items around them.

4. Take the black ribbon and the white marker or pencil and write down the quality you feel that you have in excess.

5. Then take the white ribbon and the black marker, and write the quality you lack or of which you need more in your life.

6. Line the ribbons on top of each other and tie them together at one end by leaving an inch off. While you do this, recite the following spell:

   "As winter is to summer, as dark is to light,

   As a god to a goddess, as the day is tonight,

   Let me find the perfect balance within me

   So, I may live in harmony."

7. Tie another knot an inch below the previous one and repeat the spell. Continue this until you have eight knots on the ribbons.

8. Tie the other end of the ribbon around the object that symbolizes balance for you and say:

   "By the ancient powers of three times three,

   this balance is my will, so let it be!"

9. You have successfully created a charm that you can take anywhere around Mabon, so you will always have a reminder of the power of this holiday.

10. Carry the charm close to your body until you gain the balance you were looking for.

Second Harvest Gratitude Spell

As the second harvest is in the middle of the fall season, we have plenty to be grateful for. If you have a garden or a field full of crops, you will be preparing to harvest your bounty or have just done so. And if you do not grow your own produce, getting close to the transition from the third quarter of the year can remind you of everything else you have achieved (harvested spiritually) throughout the year. Putting away your bounty fills you with relief, but it can also be a bittersweet experience as you know that nature is about to die. This spell can help you express your gratitude for your bounty as you are putting it away.

You Will Need:

- A black candle
- Dried sage
- The carrier oil of your choice

Instructions:

1. Place your tools on the altar and mix the sage with the oil.
2. Anoint your candle with the oil herb mixture and light it.
3. As you gaze into the candle flame, visualize yourself putting your tools down as you prepare to rest after a productive harvest season.
4. Take a deep breath and recite the following spell:

   "The harvest is over, so I can allow myself

   to rest and relax.

   I am thankful for all I have gathered

   as I prepare for the next season."

5. Let the satisfaction of a productive year fill you as you send out gratitude to all your guides and nature itself.

A Charm for Finding Peace

Albeit magical, the fall season is a stark reminder that winter is just around the corner, something many of us have trouble coming to terms with. Not to mention how stressful preparing for the Mabon festivities can be, especially when planning a large family gathering or community event. This charm can help you find peace, so you can enjoy the festivities and await the winter without stressing out or worrying about anything going wrong.

You Will Need:

- 1 small rose quartz
- 1 small hepatite stone
- 1 teaspoon of dried calendula
- 1 teaspoon of crushed sunflower seeds
- 1 teaspoon of sage
- 1 teaspoon of lavender
- A small white bag made of cloth

Instructions:

1. Put all of the above ingredients into the bag and close it.
2. Charge the charm you have just created with the following spell:

"Surging waves of peace

Wash over me, envelop me fully

So, I can relax and feel the calm fill me

So, I can relax and enjoy this time fully."

3. Take the charm with you everywhere you go. When you feel stressed out, just take the charm into your hands and let its magic permeate your soul.

4. Repeat the spell once again in your head if you are in the company of others or out loud if you are alone.

Transition Spell

Unlike the previous ones, this spell is geared toward the transition from summer to autumn. It helps you accept that while the warm days are over, not everything is dark yet. It also allows you to pause mid-harvest, take a step back from your busy schedule and find the balance that will prepare you for the winter.

You Will Need:

- An open space full of greenery
- A packet of dried herbs

Instructions:

1. Go to a park or find any patch of nature around you. Take your packet of herbs with you.

2. If the weather is still warm enough, sit on the ground or bench. If it is too cold, just stand in one place for a few minutes.

3. Take the packet of herbs into your hands and take it into your environment. Observe every detail in nature, and appreciate the beauty that surrounds you. If there are other people around you, look at them as well.

4. The more you focus your attention on the little details, the more you feel the time slowing down. Now say the following:

"As I take in the abundant gifts of nature's divinity,

I sense the protection that covers us.

Mabon comes with a precious balance,

The second time of the year.

Abundance still flows,

and through our labor, our bounty grows.

While winter's cold is coming soon.

Mabon still brings hope and joy.

Challenging times are drawing near,

I am blessed with an abundance this year.

Mabon brings color to land and tree

As it dresses nature, preparing it for slumber.

As my spirit embraces the dwindling light,

So, I will be ready for the long and cold night."

5. Let go of your worries and judgments and embrace the balance that Mabon brings.

Autumn Blessing Spell

This simple blessing spell can give you peace of mind before you lay your head to rest as you prepare for the coming winter. It can be conducted for a few days leading to the equinox, and by the time Mabon night comes, you will receive the blessing you need for your spiritual balance.

You Will Need:

- 1 white candle
- 1 black candle

Instructions:

1. Place the candle at the side of your altar and decorate the space around them with leaves, grapes, and other fall fruits.

2. When you are ready, light the candles and say the following:

   "I light these candles to honor the harvest season

   and to acknowledge the abundance in my life.

   I strive to remember each blessing I have received

   and for which I haven't said thanks throughout the year.

   I now want to share these gifts with those around me

   and with those who are not as blessed as I am now.

   I am grateful for having my spiritual guides, and I thank them for all the gifts they have yet to give me this season."

3. Let the candles burn for a couple of minutes as your body and mind relax, then extinguish them and go to sleep.

Corn Dolly Spell

At the heart of the Mabon harvest lies gratitude and generosity. As they are made from parts of the crops harvested the previous fall, corn dollies are great tools for giving thanks for the bounty in your life. This spell will enable you to express your gratitude and share your harvested goods with others. You can perform it alone, but it will be even more potent if enacted by a group.

You Will Need:

- A corn dolly for every participant
- A bonfire or candle

Instructions:

1. If you want to enact the spell alone, sit at your altar and light a candle. If done as a group, you should start by building a bonfire and sitting around it.

2. Each participant should pass a corn dolly through the smoke of your fire source while reciting the following:

   "I ask this dolly to protect my home and those inside it.

   I ask it to keep any disaster, illness, or human malice away from us."

3. Upon finishing the chant, throw the corn dolly into the fire or remove it from your altar if you are casting the spell inside your home.

Spiritual Preparation Bath

Take this bath a week before Mabon and repeat it on the night of the equinox to cleanse your spirit and prepare it for the upcoming changes.

You Will Need:

- Red and purple candles
- A handful of sea salt
- 5-10 drops of jasmine oil
- 5-10 drops of apple blossom oil
- 1 teaspoon of dried calendula petals
- Seeds from one pomegranate

Instructions:

1. Place the candles around your bathtub and light them.

2. Draw warm water into the tub and pour in the rest of the ingredients.

3. Get in the tub and rest for at least 30 minutes.

4. While you soak, set your intention on accepting balance and asking for protection from your spiritual guide.

Chapter 10: Mabon Prayers and Blessings

This final chapter explains different types of prayers and blessings that can be read during meditation or to celebrate Mabon. It starts by highlighting the significance of this practice and also states the prayers for various pagans, particularly Wiccans and Druids. Finally, the chapter provides details that can help readers create or personalize their prayers and blessings according to their spiritual beliefs.

Significance of Mabon Prayers

Mabon is a time when pagans get the opportunity to reflect and celebrate the results of their hard work and patience. Pagan rituals are inspired by farming activities and are held when crops have been harvested. The celebrations are intended to give thanks to the gods and goddesses for bestowing blessings on families and communities through a solid supply of food during the colder winter months. This is also a time for sharing; those who were blessed with abundant food supplies share with the less fortunate.

Falling on the day that light and dark periods are equal, this is also the right time for individuals to focus on the god and goddess that are represented by the sun and moon, which are fundamental to the pagan belief system

You can choose any way that suits your belief system to celebrate Mabon. However, the focus should be on the balance between dark and light or the second harvest. The following are some of the few rituals you may want to try for your celebration of abundant gifts from the earth.

Modern Celebrations

Modern Druids still celebrate Mabon, but they name the celebration: Alban. It is also a celebration at a time when light and dark are equal. The

Asatru groups use it to honor the fall of the equinox, while Neopaganism and Wiccans use the time for community and kinship activities. Depending on your spiritual beliefs, the following are some of the prayers you should know.

Abundance Prayer

Mabon is meant to acknowledge the bounty of harvests and share with the less privileged members of your society. When you celebrate Mabon, you should give thanks for everything you have. This is a time to focus on balance and harmony within your person and around you. It is a good time to be around family and friends and show gratitude.

It is good to be thankful for what you have, including food, health, or even material blessings. Take time to realize that not all people are fortunate. A prayer for what you are grateful for is appropriate here. The following is a simple prayer for Thanksgiving and showing gratitude for the things you have.

Prayer of Gratitude

"I am blessed with all in my life,

and cannot help but give thanks.

I have an abundance,

and am grateful for what I have been given.

Some are not as fortunate as I,

and I know this to be true.

So, I pray for them as I accept my blessings,

to those who watch over and protect me:

please shower others with what I have been given,

and bring blessed balance to all."

When you honor the god or goddess, remember to recite this prayer. You can also provide an offering of your choice.

Mabon Balance Prayer

The light and the dark are in perfect balance. This can affect people in many ways, where some use the time to honor the darker elements of the goddess. Because of the balance, people can be drawn in both directions, and this can make a soul restless.

This can be felt through indecision or a feeling of intuition that everything is not as it should be. You can meditate through this or offer prayers.

Mabon Prayer of Balance

"The light and dark are balanced,

and we give thanks to Mabon for this,

and to all the gods and goddesses for their blessings.

We cannot have the bad without the good.

And hope is only apparent when we feel despair.

And love is what conquers the pain.

And we cannot rise once more without falling first.

That is the harmony we seek,

and we pray for it to grow within us."

Mabon Prayer to the Vine

The Mabon season is also characterized by rich vegetation, more pronounced in vineyards. During this time, grapes are in full season, and they should be used to celebrate the deities linked to the vine's growth and winemaking. The god of the vine must be honored in harvest celebrations.

Use the following prayer when you conduct your Mabon celebrations. Feel free to include anything that makes it more personal to you. Remember to ask the gods for more blessings in your prayer. You can also use it to ask anything you want the gods to provide during the next season.

Prayer of the Vine

"Hark! Hark! Hark!

We have harvested the grapes!

Their blood has become our wine!

The barrels are filled to the brim!

Hail Dionysus! Hail Bacchus!

Come celebrate with us,

And give us your blessings!

Hark! Hark! Hark!"

Prayer to the Dark Mother

If you have a strong connection to the dark elements of the year, you can consider hosting a ritual to honor the Dark Mother. Use this time to honor the Dark Mother because even though she is the one who brings the darkness, we cannot have the light without her.

While many people associate darkness with evil or bad things, several positive aspects can be obtained from embracing the dark component of life. However, this should only be for a short time. Let us call upon those who bring the dark and give them a blessing at this time.

Prayer for the Dark Mother

"Day gives way to the night,

just as life gives way to death,

and we dance with the Dark Mother.

Hecate, Kali, Tiamet,

Nemesis, Demeter, Morrighan,

those who bring destruction so everything can be rebuilt,

I still give thanks even as the darkness comes,

and the world descends into that darkness."

Thanksgiving Prayer for Mabon

This is a time to recognize the blessings in your life and give thanks for what you have. What do you have that brings you joy? How has the world blessed you? How have you benefitted from the gods and goddesses? Think about all you have, big and small.

Mabon Prayer of Thanksgiving

"We have reaped when we have sown,

the ground becomes barren.

The animals have come home for the season.

But we are not short on blessings,

for our plates are full,

and we give thanks to the gods and goddesses."

Count Your Blessings

Mabon is a time for giving thanks for everything we have. In some instances, people may take their fortunes for granted, which is not a good thing to do. Take time to reflect on your fortunes and blessings. Create a gratitude list including all the things you are happy to have in your life. No matter how small or big the things you have, they should get equal recognition in your prayers. Keep your list in a place where you can access it easily to perform your simple rituals.

Home Protection Prayer

The goddess Morrighan will help to bring protection to your home and the land surrounding it. This can be in advance of any threats you might face or because you have felt unsafe in the place you live.

"Oh, Morrighan! Oh, Morrighan!

Protect this land from those who would trespass upon it!

Oh, Morrighan! Oh, Morrighan!

Protect my lands and all who live within!

Oh, Morrighan! Oh, Morrighan!

Keep an eye over my family and me!

Oh, Morrighan! Oh, Morrighan!

You know a good fight, so fight for me,

The welder of the shield and protector of all,

Please listen to my call.

Turn back all those who seek to trespass on my land,

Show them that you show no mercy to those with evil in their hearts.

Keep my land in your heart,

And repulse wrongdoers.

And show your wrath.

Oh, Morrighan! Oh, Morrighan!

We are thankful for your blessings!

Oh, Morrighan! Oh, Morrighan!"

Raise Some Energy

Apart from conducting a prayer for Mabon balance, there are also other rituals you can celebrate to raise energy. Working in groups with family and friends to celebrate Mabon will raise group energy, and one of the most effective ways to achieve this is to use drums, bells, rattles, and other instruments. Others without instruments can clap their hands.

Begin the ritual with a regular but slow rhythm and increase the tempo gradually. End the drumming and clapping at some pre-arranged signal, and you will begin to feel the energy flow in waves. Chanting accompanied by dance is another method that can be used to raise group energy.

Mabon Balance Meditation

Another way of raising your energy is to engage in Mabon Balance Meditation. When you have been feeling spiritually or emotionally low, you can use meditation to re-balance your energy. Start by finding a comfortable place to do your meditation. You want to choose a place where you will not be disturbed and where you will also have room to do the meditation.

You will need a black candle and a white candle for the meditation. Start by placing the candles in a secure place and lighting them in any order. Start to breathe—breathe in and out slowly, focusing on your breath. Shut your eyes, and start to see in your mind all the obstacles blocking the harmony and balance in your life. See what positive change would look like. Focus on the solutions to your problems.

See the negative in your life slipping away, being replaced by positive energy. You might see this as streams flowing to and from you. Take stock of your goals, your friendships, and the romance in your life, and be thankful for the good while drawing positive energy toward you. Know that there is hope, no matter how you might feel right now. When you finish meditating, you should remember all the lessons you have learned and apply them in the future.

Celebrate Home and Hearth

The colder months naturally draw us inside for longer periods. This is the perfect time to declutter your home, your life, and your energy. You can perform a smudging along with cleaning your home. Sweetgrass is traditional for smudging.

When you are building an altar or decorating your home during Mabon, remember to use what might have been harvested in ancient times. Use imagery of the harvest, both the crops and the tools. You can also use this opportunity to give away the things you no longer need. Make repairs to your home in preparation for the hearth celebrations.

Hold a Ritual of Gratitude

To begin this ritual, decorate your altar with appropriate seasonal symbols representing abundance. Some of the items you can consider for your altar include the following:

- A gold or green candle signifies abundance.
- Baskets of fruits such as grapes and apples since they are associated with harvest.
- Create Gratitude Oil to use for the ritual. You need five drops of rose oil, 1/8 cup base oil of your preferred choice, two drops of vetiver oil, a pinch of ground cinnamon, and one drop of agrimony oil.
- Colors associated with abundance, especially green and gold.
- Cornucopias symbolize the season's bounty.
- Craft an abundance mandala. You can paint one or create a piece of art with three dimensions.
- Photos of important people.

- Symbols of the items for which you are thankful.

Take time to reflect on the things you have in abundance. These are not only limited to financial or material possessions. A satisfactory career, loving family, and abundant friends are some of the things you can be thankful for. To begin the rite, use gratitude oil to anoint the candle and light it on your altar. Pray to the gods and goddesses that are more powerful at this time of the year, and offer thanks and gratitude for what is bountiful in your life.

The next step is moving around your altar, reciting the things for which you are happy and thankful. You must also state why you are thankful for something and ask God to continue blessing you. If you do not want to do this alone and prefer to have people around, you can all offer gratitude.

The act of gratitude can be as simple as saying out loud what you are thankful for or taking a minute to meditate on your gratitude. Think about the things, people, and energies you are thankful for. It is essential to understand that gratitude is a gift, so you should continue giving to needy people. Giving something to another person helps you realize that you are fortunate to have the things that someone does not have.

When you make your gratitude ritual, you may need to let the individuals who make you happy know about the occasion. This will also help them to appreciate you. If you wish to send your gratitude directly to someone, you should let them know your intentions. This will also help them appreciate you, which can increase your blessings. Being appreciated by many people means that you are likely to enjoy more gifts from the provider. Make sure you end your ritual by tidying up everything you have covered and ask the god or goddess to continue blessing you.

Decorate Your Mabon Altar

Setting up and decorating your Mabon Altar is a critical component recognized by many pagans. An altar is used for different purposes, such as worship or prayer, a sacred place where you can perform ceremonies, meditation, or cast spells. The altar must be decorated with items that symbolize abundance and should also have fire, water, earth, and air elements. You can also include other items like a goddess candle or anything representing the gods you worship. When you decorate your altar, you must be guided by your spirituality.

Many pagans use their altar to keep spells or ritual-casting tools they use regularly. Other people decorate their altars for specific seasons and ceremonies. For Mabon, the act of choosing colors like reds, yellows, browns, and oranges shows gratitude and thankfulness. You can also include other things that symbolize the harvest season, such as wheat, apples, corn, and seasonal vegetables.

Mabon celebrations are associated with thanking the god and goddess for the things you have in life. They are usually held during the time of the second harvest and are conducted to honor the providers for blessing you with the things you need in life. Most celebrations are accompanied by prayers and different rituals depending on your spiritual beliefs. Most pagans use various items that symbolize abundance in their celebrations. When you perform any ritual, remember to include everything you want and thank the gods and goddesses for what you already have.

Conclusion

Whether you look at it from a religious perspective or an astrological point of view, the time of the autumn equinox is when a lot of changes are taking place. For Wiccans, this time of the year has considerable importance and is celebrated as one of the most joyous occasions of the year. It is one of the eight Wiccan Sabbats celebrated throughout the year. Many people consider this time to be celebrated to show gratitude for a successful harvest. This is usually done by various rituals, ceremonies, and grand feasts.

You can try any of the delicious recipes provided in the chapters, but make sure to add at least one of the dishes to your menu, which features signature ingredients such as apples, pomegranates, turkey, or potatoes. Make the most of this event by planning some ritualistic and general family activities to give thanks to the deities for the harvest of the autumn equinox. Whether you try a bonfire, a picnic, or simple foraging, make sure that you go in groups to spend most of the time with your friends, family, and loved ones. While you are performing these activities, do not forget to count your blessings and celebrate the harvest's abundance by saying a few Mabon prayers and blessings.

Fill your Mabon festival with abundance spells and charms to manifest the power of the equinox into your spells. Other purification and cleansing spells will work best during this time. Make sure that you follow the step-by-step instructions provided in the book to cast the various spells and charms. Deviating from the steps could make the spells less effective and ruin your spellwork.

Mabon is a time of celebration, and as such, many crafts, decorations, activities, and rituals are performed to commemorate this joyous time. You can tell stories associated with Mabon or make delicious feasts filled with the book's savory and sweet Mabon dishes. Add the different blessing rituals to this mixture, and you have got the perfect Mabon festival.

Part 8: Samhain

The Ultimate Guide to Halloween and How It's Celebrated in Wicca, Druidry, and Celtic Paganism

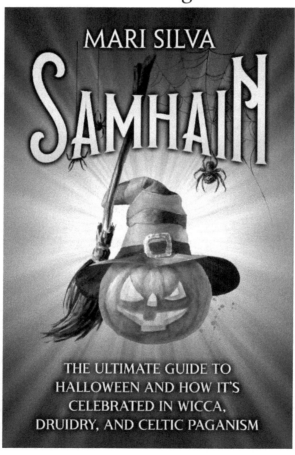

Introduction

As a modern witch or Wiccan practitioner, you are likely to have heard about Samhain, or as it is more commonly known, Halloween. However, there is a big difference between the two. What is it, you may ask? You will find out in the upcoming chapters. The gist of it is that Halloween originated from Samhain. While they are very much alike, Samhain is celebrated with much more serious intensity by members of the pagan persuasion. Considered one of the biggest celebrations in pagan and Wiccan culture, Samhain brings a lot of festivities and enthusiasm to the table. While many people consider it a dark occasion, this time is a celebration to honor those who have moved on from our world.

Ancient Celts lived in fear during this time, as they believed it to have been a dark time when the connection between the land of the dead and the land of the living was at its strongest. While many of these beliefs still exist in modern cultures, fear has been replaced by curiosity and the need to honor the dead. Many people still believe that Samhain is a dark and dangerous time, where evil spirits are out in the open, looking to attack. While a smidgen of this belief may be true, people consider Samhain a celebratory event. Because of this, numerous traditions and rituals are practiced with great passion to this day.

Samhain has a rich history and folklore, making it one of the most enjoyable holidays in Wiccan and pagan cultures. Plus, its connection with Halloween makes it even more fascinating for people. The mythology surrounding Samhain and its associated gods is captivating and discussed in later chapters. The myths and legends are each more enthralling than the next. Thus, this book is perfect for people interested in pagan folklore and mythology.

Filled with detailed instructions on various crafts and decorations you can make to celebrate the season with full enthusiasm, you will not have to look elsewhere for ideas. Plus, you'll find a detailed chapter about how you can set up the sacred altar of Samhain to follow the rituals associated with the ceremony properly. Then, you'll discover how several plants and herbs associated with Samhain are used for ritualistic purposes. These plants help with the remembrance and clairvoyance process.

A grand feast follows the rituals for Samhain, which may interest you because of the unique dishes specially prepared for these festivities. You'll have to read on to find a whole chapter dedicated to Samhain meals. It's easy to read and provides step-by-step instructions on preparing certain meals.

Finally, you'll find chapters covering various activities and rituals especially reserved for the Samhain season. These include hands-on exercises with easy-to-follow instructions and details for every ritual. There are even some child-friendly rituals and activities if you want your kids to participate in this festival. So, whether you're a practicing Wiccan or a newly converted witch learning the basics of centuries-old Celtic culture, this book is suitable for all audiences.

Chapter 1: From Samhain to Halloween

While Halloween is the most popular October celebration in modern times, we can trace its roots back to the Gaelic festival of Samhain. Today, many people treat the two as interchangeable or think Samhain was essentially the "same" as Halloween.

However, this could not be further from the truth. In this book, you will learn about celebrating Samhain in its various iterations in paganism, including Wicca, Druidry, and Celtic paganism. However, before you can start celebrating, you should first understand Samhain's history and traditions.

Understanding Samhain

Samhain is a traditional Gaelic festival signifying the conclusion of the harvest season and the beginning of winter, with Celtic calendars dividing the year into two halves: Light and dark. Just as the day begins at sunrise, the New Year was thought to begin with the arrival of darkness. Samhain functioned as a new year's celebration for the Celts.

The main events of the festival were celebrated on November 1. However, initial celebrations would commence on All Hallows' Eve, October 31. Thus, this clarifies why Halloween occurs at the end of October, not on All Hallows' Day, November 1.

Samhain descends from Gaelic and Celtic tradition and was first cited in ninth-century Irish literature. However, there is a strong possibility that its history stretches back even further, as some Neolithic passage tombs dating to 4000–2500 BC align with sunrise on Samhain, indicating it was a day of high importance.

The choice of November 1 for Samhain celebrations is unlikely to be coincidental and held symbolic importance to the early Celts. As mentioned, the celebration of Samhain included the ushering in of the New Year and was seen as a time of both death and rebirth. These events happened to coincide with the end of the harvest season and the beginning of the dark and cold winter.

There is limited information on how Samhain was traditionally celebrated. Most of our sources come from legendary Celtic sagas, which explain the celebration in a more mythical manner, or Roman authors.

While the Romans kept a record of many Celtic customs, these were likely modified in their writings to act as propaganda against the Celts. Given that the Romans were constantly fighting wars against the Celts, there is some doubt among experts about how accurately they recorded cultural information and how much—if any—exaggeration existed to make the Celts look "barbaric."

This does not mean we know nothing about ancient Samhain celebrations.

There is evidence that Samhain was celebrated with grand feasts and special bonfires. People believed that the bonfires had protective and cleansing powers, and there were likely to have been rituals that involved them. It was also an event that saw the slaying of livestock and cattle taken from summer pastures.

Samhain was also considered a liminal festival—a day when the boundaries between the human world and the Otherworld were fragile. On this occasion, ancient burial mounds were unsealed due to the belief that they were portals to the Otherworld. It was also believed that Samhain was a day when the Aos Sí and other pagan gods were able to travel to the human world.

The ancient Celts would leave food and drink offerings for them to appease these gods, spirits, and fairies. Some sacrifices were symbolically burned on bonfires to act as a protective measure against mischievous and harmful spirits. The offerings were also believed to have been a way to ensure people and animals survived the harsh winter ahead.

Besides gods and the Aos Sí, spirits could also leave the Otherworld and travel to the human world on Samhain. This meant that the souls of dead relatives could visit and be welcomed by family members and loved ones. An additional plate was set at each family's table to ensure they were received with hospitality.

Harmless tricks and pranks were also common, though these were generally attributed to mischievous spirits and fairies making their way from the Otherworld. This tradition of playing pranks on Samhain can be seen in the modern tradition of children calling it "trick-or-treat" when knocking on doors. Like the spirits of Samhain, they ask for a treat that serves as protection against being pranked.

Additionally, Samhain was considered a time of looking at the future. Druids believed that the presence of spirits from the Otherworld in the human world made it easier for them to make predictions about the future, and fortune-telling rituals were a common part of Samhain celebrations.

From Samhain to Halloween

Some of the primary Samhain traditions can be seen in today's Halloween celebrations.
https://unsplash.com/photos/MYRG0ptGh50

One of the primary Samhain traditions that can be seen in today's Halloween celebrations is the practice of dressing up. During Samhain, the Celts would dress as mythical monsters and animals in the hope of confusing spirits who may wish to take them back to the Otherworld with them. The belief was that if a spirit could not identify its target, the person in question would remain unharmed until the veil between worlds was once again opaque.

This belief, of course, can be seen in the modern tradition of dressing children up as animals or mythical and fictional creatures on Halloween. However, the transition from Samhain to Halloween took centuries to accomplish.

Samhain was originally an oral tradition, with celebrations and rituals passed down from parent to child without being written down. However, this changed with the introduction of Christianity to the British Isles.

In the Middle Ages, Christian monks documented Samhain beliefs and practices, and these documents form some of the primary sources we have today that document how it was celebrated. At the same time, the Catholic Church realized that the transition from paganism to Christianity would be smoother if pagan traditions were incorporated into Christianity.

The church began a tradition of reframing these Celtic celebrations in a Christian framework, allowing them to make the most of popular pagan festivals while spreading this new religion. The best-known example of this reframing is Christmas, where the church reframed the Yule/Yuletide celebration to suit the Christian narrative.

In 609, Pope Boniface II announced a new celebration, All Saints' Day. In Middle English, this celebration was also known as All-Hallows or All-Hallowmas. In the eighth century, the date was fixed as November 1, and November 2 was declared All Souls' Day. These days were both to honor Christian martyrs.

These new festivals were celebrated in a similar way to Samhain. Bonfires were lit, and food and drink were offered, though Christians offered meals to the poor and destitute rather than to the spirits, Aos Sí, and pagan gods. Like with Samhain, celebrations would often begin before the official date of All Hallows' Day. Since celebrations would start on the evening and night of October 31, this became known as All Hallows'' Eve—like the evening and night before Christmas is known as Christmas Eve.

All Hallows' Eve would, over time, evolve into Halloween, with children and adults dressing up as animals and monsters to protect them from demons that may cross the thin veil between the two worlds. Over time, this evolved into the modern secular tradition of Halloween, which remains popular even among people who do not believe in pagan or Christian origins. Instead, it has become an enjoyable evening for children to dress up and go trick-or-treating for candy.

An important part of the evolution of Samhain and All Hallows' Eve into modern Halloween was the arrival of Irish immigrants to America. When Americans learned of such traditions, they modified them, such as the example of trick-or-treating, which was initially an adults-only occasion to wear a costume and visit neighboring houses to ask for food or money.

Americans also revived some of the more traditionally pagan aspects of the celebration that had been lost following its Christianization. For example, on Halloween, young women would use yarn, mirrors, and apple parings to discover the name or appearance of their future husbands.

In the 1800s, newspapers and community leaders started working toward Halloween to become a more community- and family-based holiday. Parents were encouraged to leave anything scary or pagan out of their celebrations, which eventually led to the day not having any religious or superstitious overtones and becoming more about community.

After Halloween parties in the 1920s and 1930s led to a spate of vandalism, community leaders further moved to transform the celebration into a day for children and young adults. By the 1950s, Halloween, as we know it today, had taken shape, and a new American tradition was formed.

Other Halloween traditions also have roots in Ireland and Scotland, though not in Samhain. For example, carving pumpkins can be traced to the Scottish myth of *Stingy Jack*. The story is about a man who tricked the Devil. He was not let into either Heaven or Hell following his death through this trick. Rather, he was cursed to wander the earth with nothing but a piece of coal handed to him by the Devil.

To carry this piece of coal, Jack made a lantern out of a turnip and has roamed the earth carrying it ever since. The first Jack O'Lanterns were carved from turnips and potatoes, both easy-to-find crops in Ireland and Scotland. The ghoulish faces carved into them were done so to repel Stingy Jack and other evil spirits from the home when the veil between worlds was thin. When Irish immigrants brought the tradition to America, Jack O'Lanterns transitioned from turnips and potatoes to pumpkins, which were easier to find in this new country.

While Samhain is undoubtedly the root of modern Halloween, Halloween has evolved to be something completely different from the pagan celebration. Today's secular celebration for children bears little resemblance to the harvest festival that the ancient Celts would have celebrated. Many modern Halloween traditions have other roots, such as Scottish folklore and Christian traditions.

Samhain Then and Now

Samhain Then

As mentioned above, Samhain was a time for celebrating the harvest and the world's transition into winter. It was marked with bonfires, feasts, and rituals and was when divination was considered particularly effective.

The veil between the Otherworld and the human world was thought to be at its thinnest, so offerings were laid out to appease pagan gods and spirits that would have been able to reach the human world. People dressed as mythical monsters and animals to protect themselves from being abducted back to the Otherworld at the end of Samhain.

At the same time, there is a good chance we have lost a lot of information about the original Samhain celebrations due to a lack of primary sources. Thus, while pagans still celebrate Samhain, modern celebratory traditions have evolved to combine ancient practices and modern rituals.

Samhain Now

Modern pagans celebrate Samhain similarly to how it was celebrated in the past. There are differences, and different types of pagans also have unique celebrations.

Wiccans

Wiccans generally celebrate Samhain as part of their covens. This includes a feast for coven members and a ritual. This ritual is often public, allowing non-practicing people to experience Samhain and participate in a Wiccan ritual.

Wiccan Samhain rituals often involve honoring the dead, especially those who have died and crossed the veil since the previous year's Samhain celebration. Those who have died are named, and the four elements are called upon to help build a circle and begin the ritual. The specifics of the ritual differ from coven to coven.

Some covens observe a "dumb supper" as part of the feast. Originating in the Middle Ages, this is a tradition where the feast meal is held in silence, with a different place set at the table to honor the dead. Unlike the ritual, this is generally held privately with the coven and family members.

Wiccans who are not part of a coven also follow similar traditions, observing a personal ritual and meal, though non-practicing friends and family are often invited to the latter. Like coven rituals, the altar is central to the celebration and holds ritualistic objects, such as candles, cake, and ale.

Some Wiccan covens will also host a bonfire, generally open to the public. Non-coven Wiccans will often celebrate a bonfire with friends and family. They may also take the time to conduct divination rituals and construct a symbolic Samhain centerpiece representing the celebration, the year, and the winter ahead.

Other Wiccan Samhain traditions include telling stories of ancestors among loved ones and visiting those who had passed at the local cemetery. As it is the New Year's celebration, it is also the time to renovate at home.

Druids

As with Wiccans, Druids usually incorporate the supper into their Samhain celebrations and participate in divination rituals. Druids, in particular, saw Samhain as the ideal time to perform fortune-telling magic, and this practice continues to modern times.

Some traditional Druidic methods of divination on Samhain include:

- Pricking an egg and letting the contents drip into a glass of water, and using the shapes to tell the future.

- Using apple peelings to help young women determine the initial of the man she will marry.

- Using hazelnuts for matrimonial divination. Hazelnuts marked with the names of eligible men and women are placed in a fire in two groups (one for men, one for women). As the nuts pop, the names of those destined to be together are revealed.

Druidic celebrations of Samhain are generally relatively similar to those of Wiccans, though Druids (as mentioned above) focus more on the divinatory aspect of this day. Local Druids and Wiccans will sometimes combine celebrations and mark the day together in communities home to both a Wiccan coven and Druidic organization. One of the byproducts of this is that the celebration is generally larger and more boisterous, making it more enjoyable for everyone involved.

Other Pagan Traditions

Pagan celebrations of Samhain are relatively similar to Wiccan and Druidic traditions, given that they all draw from the same roots. However, pagan practitioners often celebrate the day individually or with close family and friends.

Some common traditions include:

- Decorating the altar.
- Participating in a private ritual.
- Making Samhain bread.
- Taking part in a Samhain nature walk to feel closer to nature. This can be done in a natural area around the practitioner's home and does not need to be an organized walk.
- Using a seven-day white candle to perform a ritual to guide the spirits to rest.
- Performing bonfire magic.
- Holding a séance.
- Performing divination magic, including through the use of runes, scrying, tarot, and other methods of divination.
- Taking the time to correct misconceptions other people may have about Samhain and working to build community connections with other pagans and non-practitioners alike.

Samhain Correspondences

Here are some Samhain correspondences that can play an important part in your day's celebration. This section will introduce these elements, and the rest of the book will go through them in detail.

The Samhain Symbol

This symbol is a looped square called a Bowen knot that joins with two inter-lapping oblong shapes, making a cross. The Bowen knot is believed to help ward off harmful spirits and bad luck, making it the perfect option for a celebration that involves appeasing the spirits and protecting oneself against the harmful attention they may bring.

Tools

- **Black and white candles.** The number you will need will depend on the rituals you are participating in—some may require small candles, while others, like the guiding ritual mentioned above, may call for larger seven-day candles.

- **Incense.** Generally handmade and incorporating the scents and elements of the season. Some ingredients to add to your incense include cinnamon, cloves, rosemary, and sage.

- **Herbs, spices, and plants.** There are many associated with Samhain, including autumn flowers like marigold and chrysanthemums, apples, mugwort, pomegranates, pumpkins and other gourds, rosemary, and rowan. Others include acorns, allspice, catnip, mountain ash, oak leaves, pine cones, sage, and straw. These can be incorporated into your celebration in many ways, including making them a part of your feast, incense, and altar, or they can be used around your home as decorations.

- **A censer for burning incense.**

- **Ritual bell.** If needed for your ritual.

- **Crystals.** Some crystals used in Samhain rituals include amethyst, labradorite, obsidian, selenite, and smoky quartz.

Animals

Animals associated with Samhain include bats, black cats, owls, ravens, and spiders. You can incorporate animal carvings of these animals in your Samhain rituals, donate to shelters and conservation organizations focused on them, or honor them in another way that works for your celebration of Samhain.

Samhain and Halloween, though often associated with each other, are, in fact, two distinctly different celebrations. Samhain has its own rich history and lore, and you will explore this lore in this book.

In the next chapter, you'll learn about the pagan deities and lore associated with Samhain and better understand its connection with death and renewal. You'll then have the chance to more deeply understand the crafts associated with the celebration and how you can decorate your home in preparation for your Samhain ritual and feast.

This book will also explain how you can set up your Samhain altar if you plan on incorporating one in your observation of this festival. If you are unsure whether it is the right option, we will cover some of the pros of having a sacred space in your home. We'll explore how to create both a seasonal and an ancestor altar and explain why the two are different.

Other parts of this book include discovering the sacred herbs and plants associated with the celebration, which you can, in turn, incorporate into your observance and feast. Additionally, we'll offer some traditional recipes you can make as part of your Samhain feast and explain why these dishes are connected to the festival.

We'll also suggest some family and group activities you can take part in as part of your celebrations, allowing you to allow non-practicing loved ones to get a better understanding of this important day. We'll additionally cover the rituals and ceremonies that you can use in your Samhain celebrations, including kid-friendly variations when practicing with your children.

Finally, you'll learn about spells, charms, and baths that are highly potent when worked on and around Samhain, including love magic, abundance charms, divination magic, and protection spells. We'll also cover some prayers and blessings you can read during your Samhain observance and meditation. This will include prayers and blessings for Wiccans, Druids, and pagans, so you'll know how to incorporate the traditions of your loved ones and friends into your own celebration of the day.

By the time you have read this book, all your questions about Samhain will have been answered. All you need to do is turn this page and keep reading!

Chapter 2: Samhain Deities and Lore

This chapter will discuss the gods and goddesses related to Samhain. Since Samhain is connected to death, the deities connected to this holiday will also be associated with death and the underworld. So, let us dive into this chapter, and you can learn everything about the deities of Samhain.

The Crone

Firstly, we will discuss the Crone, who is one-third of the triple Goddess and made up of the Mother, Maiden, and Crone. The Crone represents death and wisdom and is the guardian of the underworld. The Crone is most powerful during Samhain. She goes by many names since every culture has its own Crone. The ancient Greeks called her "Hecate," the Welsh's Crone was "Cerridwen," and the Scottish and Irish Celtic Crone was "Cailleach."

Hecate

Hecate is the Greek Crone. She is the goddess of ghosts, crossroads, magic, the moon, necromancy, the night, and witchcraft. She was the daughter of the Titan Perses and the nymph Asteria, both minor deities. Hecate was associated with the dead, ghosts, and the spiritual world, explaining her connection to Samhain. In various depictions, Hecate was portrayed holding a key that was believed to be the key to the underworld or two torches to guide the spirits of the dead. She was very powerful. In fact, Zeus gave her power over the sea, earth, and heaven. Hecate was also known for her healing powers and vast knowledge.

There is not much known about Hecate. This may be because this goddess loved to remain mysterious, while some believe historians were afraid to utter her name. The best time to call on Hecate is on October 31, the night of Samhain. This is because it is the day when the veil between the physical world and the spiritual world is at its thinnest.

Hecate can take the form of the Triple Goddess and can easily travel from the underworld to the physical world.

Persephone

The gods and goddesses of the underworld can speak to us on Samhain, but the loudest voice of them all is that of the goddess Persephone. She was the queen of the underworld since she was married to Hades. She was the daughter of Demeter, goddess of fertility and agriculture, and Zeus, the god of the sky and the chief deity. As well as being the queen of the underworld, Persephone was also the goddess of fertility, just like her mother. She was a very attractive girl with many gods who fell in love with her, but her mother was obsessed with her daughter and would not allow any of these gods to come near her. Hades wanted to marry her, but Demeter refused, so he kidnapped Persephone and married her, and this was how she became the queen of the underworld.

Naturally, Demeter was not pleased that her daughter had been taken from her. Zeus interfered, and they reached a compromise. Persephone would spend one-third of the year in the underworld with Hades and two-thirds with her mother, Demeter. Persephone spent all autumn and winter in the underworld, and it is believed that she ascended her throne in the underworld during Samhain. As the queen of the underworld, Persephone also became the goddess of death. She was initially called "Core," which means "the maiden," when she was only the goddess of spring and before marrying Hades and becoming the queen of the underworld.

However, in various ancient texts, instead of her real name, Core, the goddess is referred to as Persephone, a name which means "the bringer of death"—ever since she became the ruler of the underworld after marrying Hades. Although the name may imply something negative, Persephone was portrayed positively in many myths. The goddess helped mortals and provided them with wisdom, making her the goddess of rebirth. Death and rebirth are regarded as strong themes for Samhain, as many people associate the gods of the living and the dead with this day. Persephone had another connection with Samhain as she controlled the gates between the worlds of the living and the dead. These gates are responsible for thinning the veil between both worlds, especially during Samhain.

Cerridwen

If you wonder why the image of the cauldron is usually associated with Samhain festivities, it is because of the Goddess Cerridwen. Cerridwen was a very powerful Celtic goddess who lived in the underworld. She was the goddess of mystery, transformation, magic, inspiration, enchantment, regeneration, knowledge, and death. Cerridwen had a magical, powerful cauldron containing a potion, and whoever drank it would get immense knowledge. Cerridwen was the Welsh's Crone and represented the darker side of the Triple Goddess.

She had two children, a beautiful girl called Crearwy and a hideous boy named Afagddu. Cerridwen wanted to give her son an advantage, so she created a potion to grant him knowledge and wisdom. The potion required brewing for a whole year and a day. The goddess made her servant Gwion responsible for the brew until it reached full potency. However, three drops splashed out and scalded his thumb while stirring the potion. Without thinking, he put his thumb in his mouth and, in turn, consumed the potion droplets. Gwion was then gifted with all the knowledge and wisdom Cerridwen wanted to give her son.

Gwion escaped out of fear, with Cerridwen chasing after him. Each of them would transform into a different creature during the chase until she managed to catch him and consume him. She then became pregnant and knew the child was her servant who had been reborn. This chase has become a symbol of transformation, rebirth, and death, which are themes associated with Samhain.

Cerridwen is one of the goddesses strongly associated with Samhain. As a representative of the Triple Goddess's dark side and as a goddess of the underworld, Cerridwen visits her worshippers during the time of Samhain as the world transforms from light into darkness (the end of summer and the beginning of fall).

Cerridwen uses her cauldron to help transform us as well by helping us place our bad habits and negative thoughts into the pot. Since Cerridwen is associated with Samhain and the cauldron is a symbol associated with her, it has also become a symbol for the festival. The cauldron represents transformation, magic, mystery, and inspiration, which are all themes associated with Samhain, a time of mystery and magic.

Fun Fact: It is believed that Cerridwen's cauldron is the Holy Grail mentioned in the Arthurian legends.

The Morrigan

The Morrigan is the goddess of war and could predict who would die during a battle. She could transform into a crow and fly over the battle. She served as an inspiration to the soldiers so that they kept fighting and instilled fear into the hearts of their opponents. The Morrigan's association with Samhain resulted from her role in the battle of the Plain of Pillar (Cathe Maige Tuired), which took place during Samhain. The battle was between the Tuatha Dé Danann (a supernatural race of deities in ancient Ireland) and the Fomorians (a hostile supernatural race in Irish mythology). She met with the chief god of the Tuatha Dé Danann, Dagda, around the time of Samhain and gave him the advice to help him in the battle. The battle began on Samhain when the Morrigan appeared to the Tuatha Dé Danann soldiers to motivate them to keep fighting so they could defeat their opponents.

The Morrigan's assistance worked as the Tuatha Dé Danann defeated the Fomorians. She also played a crucial role in the battle of Cattle Raid of Cooley (Táin Bó Cuiligne), which also took place during Samhain. Similar to her role in the battle of the Plain of Pillar, the Morrigan also inspired the soldiers of this battle to fight to win the war. As a goddess prophesied death and played two major roles in battles on Samhain, we can easily see how she is now associated with this day. In fact, some pagans choose to celebrate the Morrigan during the festival due to her connection to Samhain and because she does not have another day associated with her.

Hel

Hel is the Norse goddess of death and the queen of the afterlife. Her father is Loki, the god of mischief, and her mother is the giantess Angrboda. Although she is often called a goddess, Hel is considered a half goddess since her mother was not a deity. She was abducted along with her brothers and was sent to the underworld. She was responsible for the souls of the dishonored dead. Hel can also release the spirits of the dead back to the physical world. When her father Loki killed her uncle Baldr, the god of courage and wisdom, Odin was distraught, so his other son Hermóðr, the messenger of the gods, decided to ride to the kingdom of the dead to bring his brother back. Hel agreed to send Baldr back, provided that all living and dead creatures would weep for him. As the goddess of death and ruler of the underworld who can release the souls of the dead, Hel can be connected to Samhain.

Cailleach

Cailleach, as mentioned earlier, is the Scottish and Irish crone. She is the goddess of winter, sorcery, and diseases. She can also control the weather. Her season begins on Samhain, October 31, and ends on May 1 or Beltane. She represents the death that takes place during the winter and the rebirth that occurs during the spring.

Anubis

Now we shall discuss male deities, starting with the Egyptian god Annubis. You are probably wondering how an Egyptian god is connected to Samhain. Since he is the god of death in ancient Egyptian culture, his association with this festival makes sense. He was also the god of the afterlife, mummification, the underworld, and tombs. Anubis is his Greek name, while his Egyptian name is Anpu which means "to decay."

You will not find a holiday similar to Samhain in ancient or modern Egypt. However, the ancient Egyptian religion was filled with themes about death, the spirits of the dead, the afterlife, and many other similar themes. Even the pyramids were built around the idea of death and the afterlife.

Anubis is also considered a guardian and protector. He resided between the underworld and the earth to help guide the spirits of the dead to the afterlife. Annubis is also associated with the Sirius star, which connects him to the mysteries of the astral realm. Since Samhain is a time associated with the spirits of the dead and mystery and secrets, naturally, Annubis, the god of death and the master of secrets (Hery Sesheta) and keeper of the mysteries of the universe, is connected to this day.

Osiris

Osiris is another Egyptian deity and a god of the underworld. He was one of the most important gods in Egyptian mythology. He was married to his sister, Isis, the goddess of death, rebirth, and magic. According to certain legends and myths, Osiris and Annubis were related. Some legends say that Osiris was Annubis's nephew, while others say they were father and son. Although they were both connected to death, both gods played different roles. As mentioned, Annubus helped guide the spirits of the dead to the underworld, while Osiris ruled over the underworld and judged the souls.

Before ruling over the underworld, Osiris ruled over Egypt. He had a brother called Seth, who was consumed with anger and jealousy toward Osiris. Seth killed Osiris, cut his body into pieces, and scattered them all over Egypt. Seth then ruled Egypt with his wife, Nephthys (his sister). Isis, Osiris's wife, and Seth and Nephthys's sister were heartbroken over her husband's death and wept for him every day. Nephthys took pity on her sister, and both decided to find Osiris's parts to bring him back to life. Annubis also played a role by inventing embalming—a process to protect the body from decay—until Thoth, the Egyptian god of the moon, taught Isis the magical rituals necessary to resurrect her husband. When Osiris came back to life, Isis conceived a child with him named Horus, who became the god of the sky. Osiris did not stay long in the world of the living and went to rule the underworld.

So how is all of this connected to Samhain? Isis collected Osiris's parts during Samhain from October 28 to November 2, and he was resurrected on November 3. Samhain is also considered the pagan new year, a time of rebirth and resurrection. This meant that Osiris, Isis, Anubis, Toth, and Nephthys were all associated with Samhain.

Cernunnos

Now we will go back to the Celtic gods with Cernunnos, the horned god of the forest. He was associated with vegetation, fertility, and male animals. According to Neo-Wiccan traditions, Cernunnos died during the fall, which affected vegetation during this time of year. However, he was resurrected in the spring and impregnated by the fertile goddess of the land.

Unfortunately, there is not much known about Cernunnos. However, his associations with the themes of death and resurrection and many of his images that depict his association with the underworld create an association between Cernunnos and Samhain. Some Wiccans seek the help of Cernunnos when they want to open the portal between our world and the world of the dead.

Dionysus

Dionysus is the Greek god of wine, mirth, and fertility. So how is the god of wine connected to Samhain? Well, Dionysus is associated with death as a result of his legend. He was the son of Zeus and a mortal woman named Semele, who Zeus was madly in love with. Semele knew her lover was a god, but she had no idea he was the chief deity, Zeus. Hera learned about her husband's infidelity and went to Semele to convince her to ask Zeus to show her his true form. When Zeus visited his lover, she made this request and made him swear he would oblige. Zeus could not break his oath and couldn't refuse his lover's request. Once he appeared in his real form, Semele burnt to ashes since no mortal could handle the sight of such a glorious god. Semele was pregnant at the time, so Zeus rescued his unborn child by stitching the fetus into his thigh until he was born.

When Dionysus was born, Hera was still consumed with jealousy over her husband's betrayal and sent Titans to kill the little boy. They succeeded and ripped his body apart. However, Rhea, Zeus's mother and the goddess of fertility and motherhood, resurrected her grandson. Dionysus was one of the few gods who could travel to the underworld and bring a dead person back. Although he never met his mother, she was always on his mind. One day, he decided to travel to the underworld and bring her back to the world of the living, and he succeeded. Since he is associated with death, resurrection, and the underworld, Dionysus is another god connected to Samhain's festivities.

Arawn

Arawn is a god closely associated with the Druids. He is the Celtic god of death and revenge and ruled over the underworld. He is depicted as a tall man wearing a gray cloak with an intimidating appearance. However, Arawn's kingdom was known to be a very peaceful place. He was also an honorable and fair ruler but showed a ruthless side to wrongdoers. The god of death is also associated with the decay that usually occurs during the winter and the fall. It is a time of death and transformation, themes that both Arawn and Samhain shared.

Arawn guarded the spirits of the dead and watched over the underworld to ensure no spirit escaped to the realm of the living. However, every year he makes an exception that takes place on the night of Samhain when the veil between the world of the living and the dead is at its thinnest, and the portal of the underworld is opened, allowing the spirits of the dead to enter the realm of the living.

Hades

We cannot talk about gods of death and the underworld without mentioning Hades, the Greek god of the dead and ruler of the underworld, and Zeus's brother. As mentioned earlier, Hades lived in the underworld and only left it to kidnap Persephone. His name means "the unseen one," which was appropriate for a god who ruled over a world that was "unseen" to the living. As the god of death and the ruler of the underworld, Hades was feared by many. However, he was not an evil god as he is often represented. In fact, Hades was extremely selfless, a quality that not many ancient Greeks were aware of. He only cared about his realm and defending the rights of the spirits of the dead. However, Hades would get very angry whenever anyone tried to steal souls from his realm and bring them back to the world of the living. His punishment could be ruthless. Since Hades mainly resided in the underworld, he is not featured in many legends, but his connection to the dead and the underworld accounts for his association with Samhain.

Pluto

Pluto is the god of death and the ruler of the underworld in Roman mythology. He shares many similarities with his Greek counterpart, Hades. He resided in the underworld and showed no interest in the world of the living. Nor did he interfere with the matters of the gods. Just like Hades, Pluto also abducted the goddess of fertility, but in Roman mythology, she was called Prosperina. Similar to how Hades was associated with Samhain, Pluto is also connected to this day as the Roman god of death and ruler of the underworld.

Mictlāntēcuhtli

Mictlāntēcuhtli is the Aztec god of death and ruler of the Aztec underworld, similar to his Greek and Roman counterparts, Hades and Pluto. Unlike Greek and Roman gods, Mictlāntēcuhtli was not the son of another deity. He was created by Huitzilopochtli (the god of war), Tezcatlipoca (creator deity), Quetzalcoatl (the god of wind), and Xipe Totact (the god of agriculture and the seasons) when they were building the universe. However, unlike his counterparts, Mictlāntēcuhtli did not need to kidnap his wife, Mictēcacihuatl. She was created simultaneously with her husband, and they both ruled the underworld together.

As the ruler of the underworld and the god of death, Mictlāntēcuhtli is also associated with the night of Samhain. Mictlāntēcuhtli focused on his domain and only wanted to establish order in the land of the dead. According to the Aztecs, all the spirits of the dead had to face Mictlāntēcuhtli. There was no heaven or hell—or any equivalent of a good or bad place after death—and all spirits shared the same fate. However, according to other myths, the Aztecs believed in various forms of paradise. Those who didn't get to paradise would travel to the underworld and suffer at the hands of Mictlāntēcuhtli, who enjoyed torturing them. For this reason, he is often portrayed as an evil god. However, he still had good character since he would sometimes grant life.

Hermes

According to Greek mythology, Hermes is the messenger of the gods and the god of flocks, roads, thieves, and commerce. He is associated with the underworld since he helped the spirits of the dead and provided them with guidance. Hermes was connected to the goddess Hecate since they could easily travel between worlds. As a result of this connection, just like Hecate, Hermes is also honored during the festivities of Samhain. Of all the Olympian gods, Hermes was the only one to travel between the living and the dead realms and delivered the spirits of the dead to Hades in the underworld.

Samhain is when the spirits of the dead can travel from the underworld to visit our physical world. Naturally, all the gods associated with this day are gods of death, the underworld, and resurrection.

Chapter 3: Samhain Crafts and Decorations

How you decorate your home for Samhain can reveal your spiritual beliefs and passion for this special time of year. Ominous rites and traditions mark Samhain, and the occasion would certainly be incomplete without eerie décor. Using Samhain crafts to decorate your home will help create the ideal ambiance for the sacred occasion. Here are some simple Samhain crafts and decorations ideas to inspire you on how to decorate your house for Samhain.

Samhain vs. Halloween Decorations

Halloween and Samhain share a common history and are celebrated on the same date. However, there is a contrasting difference between the two. While Halloween is simply a spooky holiday, Samhain is a unique spiritual experience. Samhain is a day for honoring the dead and is a serious occasion in Celtic paganism. When darkness falls on Samhain, the veil between the living and the dead is at its thinnest. Spirits are considered to visit the land of the living, and thus, the decor adorning your house should be inviting to certain spirits while warding off evil ones.

Color Scheme and Symbols

Samhain is the last harvest season out of the three celebrated in Celtic tradition, and thus, a harvest theme should be followed when decorating for this occasion. The color palette you should adopt includes warm fall shades like orange, maroon, red, and mustard. Other tones include dark pink and dark purple.

Proper decor should also include symbols, sigils, runes, and crystals that depict the Samhain tradition and values. These can include:

Symbols

The symbol for Samhain is the Bowen knot, represented by a looped square and two oblong shapes that form a cross. The Bowen knot is a symbol of protection to ward off evil spirits. Considering the spooky time of Samhain, this symbol is often displayed on front doors and windows to repel any evil spirits or negative energies.

Runes

There are several runes you can carve or inscribe into various decoration items. Each of these has a specific meaning. Important runes for Samhain include:

- *Eihwaz* — Invites the spirits from their realm.
- *Perthro* — Symbolizes sanctuary for the spirits.
- *Kano* — To brighten the way for the spirits.
- *Elhaz* — Protects against evil spirits.

Crystals

Amethyst.

Samhain crystals can be used to honor the beginning of darkness and death. They can be used as decorations or in Samhain rituals. Important crystals for Samhain include:

- *Obsidian* — A pitch-black crystal with protective energy to help ward off evil spirits and repel negative energies.
- *Labradorite* — A shiny blue-gray crystal that can be used to help communicate with the spirits as they cross over into the realm of the living.

- *Amethyst* — A unique violet-colored crystal that is said to form a protective bubble around its owner to ward off evil spirits.

- *Smoky Quartz* — This crystal can help draw spirits close to you and facilitate conversation between you.

- *Selenite* — A white crystal with high-frequency energy is ideal for achieving mental clarity.

Ancestor Altar Cloth

Many people tend to practice ancestor-focused rituals during Samhain, and there is nothing better than using an ancestor altar cloth for this. The altar cloth can also be used to decorate your house and give off a spiritual Samhain vibe. This is easy to make and requires little effort.

Materials Needed:

- An unpatterned white piece of fabric
- Fabric markers or embroidery cotton
- A fabric pencil
- Your ancestral genealogy

Instructions:

1. Using a thread and needle, embroider the names into the cloth or write down the genealogy chart with a fabric marker.

2. Start by writing your name in the middle using a lightweight fabric pencil. Add your date and place of birth as well. Make sure you distribute the space to fit the names in evenly.

3. Branch out and add the names of your parents, your spouse's parents, and their grandparents and move as far up the ancestral line as you can.

4. You can use Post-it notes to place the names on the cloth first to ensure you do not make any mistakes. Once you have done this, either embroider the names or write them down using fabric markers.

5. In the end, you can add pictures of yourself, your parents, grandparents, and ancestors if you have any you wish to add.

Grave Rubbing

Pagan culture considers death not an ending but the beginning of a new journey. This is why grave rubbings are pretty common during Samhain. While most people use their relative's or ancestors' headstones, there are no limits, and you can use any headstone you find striking. However, be very careful when doing grave rubbing, as it can be destructive for headstones if done incorrectly.

Materials Needed:

- Lightweight paper
- A large dark-colored crayon
- Rubbing wax
- Masking tape
- A paintbrush
- A cardboard tube (optional)

Instructions:

1. Use the paintbrush to wipe dust and debris off the grave's headstone.
2. Place the paper over the area you want to trace, and use masking tape to secure it over the headstone.
3. Try to cover the rest of the headstone to avoid getting crayon marks on the stone.
4. Use the crayon to start filling the outer edges of the carved area. Then, move to the center and shade outward toward the edges until the complete headstone is covered.
5. Step back and observe your rubbing. If there is any color variation, add more definition to that region.
6. Carefully remove the masking tape and place it in the cardboard tube, so you do not damage it.
7. Frame the rubbing when you get home and hang it near the Samhain altar.

Bowls and Baskets Galore

What better way to follow the Samhain theme than by displaying a variety of traditional food? Traditional Samhain food dishes are discussed in a later chapter, but some food items can also be used as decor items.

Materials Needed:

- Bowls and baskets from a thrift store
- Harvest season foods, e.g., corn, apples, small pumpkins, etc.
- Autumn leaves

Instructions:

1. Take a basket and fill it with seasonal fruit and vegetables, including pumpkins, apples, red grapes, cabbage, etc.

2. Place these baskets on tables and counters all around your house.

3. Place the autumn leaves beside and under these baskets to create a seasonal atmosphere.

Pumpkin Carvings

Ancient Celts used to carve scary faces into turnips and other vegetables to ward off evil spirits during Samhain. While times have changed, and so have many traditions during Samhain, carving up a pumpkin is still one of the most practiced traditions for Pagans and Wiccans. Carved pumpkins adorned with Samhain symbols and runes make the perfect decoration for this time of the year.

Materials Needed:

- 1 pumpkin
- A small food knife
- A scooping spoon
- A sharpie
- A small container

Instructions:

1. Thoroughly wash your pumpkin and wipe it down to dry it and remove any dust particles.

2. While you can try to draw Samhain symbols and inscriptions by hand, a much easier way is to download Samhain stencils and secure them over the pumpkin with masking tape to draw flawless symbols or even scary faces.

3. Once you have traced the design on the pumpkin, it is time to start carving. Keep a big container close to you to dump the pumpkin fillings in.

4. Use the food knife to cut a circular lid around the pumpkin's stem and pull it out. Start removing the pumpkin seeds, and put them aside.

5. Use the scooping spoon to remove all the pumpkin fillings and throw them away. Make sure you remove as much material as you can.

6. Once you've finished removing your pumpkin's innards, rinse it thoroughly to get rid of all the stickiness.

7. Using the same food knife, start carving the design you traced earlier from the stencils. Do not worry about being neat right now; simply make the carvings.

8. Now, use a craft knife to neaten the edges. Once you have finished carving, place a candle inside the pumpkin and set the lid back on top.

Crystal Balls and Candles

Crystal balls are the perfect Samhain decor items, with their witchy feel and ornate designs. Plus, there are a ton of crystal balls available at affordable prices, with so many features. Some crystal balls have built-in light and blurred glass designs to create an eerie vibe. Candles are also a cliché Samhain decoration, without which the festivities would be incomplete. Black candles are particularly suitable during Samhain festivals and can be placed all around the house for a dark, spooky vibe.

Skeleton Decor

Samhain is a festival for the dead, where we celebrate our ancestors and honor their spirits. What better decorations could you use than skeletons and bones around your house? There are many options for creating skeleton and bone decor pieces for Samhain. Skulls are common items for Samhain, bringing a spooky vibe to the room. So, here are some ideas for skeleton decor for Samhain.

1. Take a regular old skull decoration and spray-paint it black. Connect some butterfly decor pieces to the skull.
2. Take small-sized skull decor pieces, place them on a stand, and put a transparent dome on top.
3. Take a few skull decor pieces and tie them together with a rope. Alternate their colors and hang them outside your front door.
4. Spray paint a regular skull piece golden and decorate it with some vibrant flowers to catch attention.
5. Take the upper part of a skull and adorn it with sequins and rhinestones for a sparkly look. Place a large pearl piece in the eye socket for an even more creative look.
6. Place a few skulls and bones on your dinner table and combine them with long white candles for an eerie, Victorian look.

Corn Dolls

Corn dolls have been a part of the pagan culture for centuries, where they were used in various rituals. According to old witch traditions, corn dollies bring their owners health, wealth, and luck. Today, they are still a part of Samhain traditions and make the perfect spooky decorations for this festival. They can also later be used in different rituals during Samhain.

Materials Needed:

- A bowl of water
- Corn husks
- Glue
- Old fabric
- Paints or markers
- Scissors
- String

Instructions:

1. Place the corn husks in the bowl and soak them until they are soft.
2. Using a piece of string, take a few husks and bind them together.
3. Keep the bunch in one hand for the head and fold the husks downward.
4. To make a face, level out the husks and use another piece of string to tie them around the neck.
5. For the arms, roll up one piece of husk and tighten it with a string from both ends.
6. Bring both arms together in the front and bind them with more string.
7. Use another piece of string to tie in the middle and form the waist.
8. To make the legs, divide the husks into two sections, and bind them at the knees and ankles.
9. To add accessories and clothes, use fabric to design the clothes or hats for the doll. Use the markers to draw on a face for the dolly.

Garlands

While you can easily find Garlands matching the Samhain vibe you are trying to create. There is nothing better than DIY-ing crafts for holidays like these. Plus, garlands can be hung in any room or even outdoors and are quite easy to make. This easy-to-make garland will have three different shapes: Spider, pumpkin, and ghost, each portraying a Samhain symbol.

Materials Needed:

- Twine
- Scissors
- Orange, black, and white yarn

- 1 dining chair
- Green and black pipe cleaners

Instructions:

1. To make the spider, wrap the black yarn around the upper part of the dining chair. The more yarn you wrap, the thicker your shape will be.

2. Wind the black yarn about 75 times around the chair and then slide it off. Tie three loops around the yarn in a perpendicular direction to the yarns.

3. Now, equally cut three portions of the yarn bundle between the middle two loops. Trim the yarn from both sides, so it looks like a spider.

4. Take two black pipe cleaners for the spider's legs and cut them in half. Attach these pipe cleaners to the spider's body with some glue. Use the loop thread to hang the spiders.

5. Wrap the orange yarn around the chair for the pumpkin and slide it off.

6. Cut the yarn into three pieces as you did with the spider. Trim the pumpkin, and add a stem using the pipe cleaners.

7. Simply bend the cleaners around the tied loop and connect them with yarn to hang the pumpkin.

8. Finally, to make the ghost, wrap the white yarn around the chair, slide it off, and cut it from one end, so you get a long bunch of yarn.

9. Tie one piece of the yarn in the center to get two separate portions of the yarn. Fold the two portions together and tie another yarn toward the upper end to create the head of the ghost.

10. Hang these shapes using the twine and set it over the fireplace or anywhere else you would like—be careful that it does not create a fire hazard.

Luminaries

Luminaries can be used to decorate walkways and staircases with brilliantly illuminating pieces that will create a mystical look in your house. You can make luminaries of all shapes and sizes and place them around your house, on staircases, and even outdoors. Plus, this craft is one of the easiest to make and does not require many supplies.

Materials Needed:

- White paper sheets
- Crayons, markers, and colored pencils
- Tape
- Tea lights (battery operated)
- Glass jars
- A sharpie

Instructions:

1. Get printable stencils to draw different scary faces, Samhain symbols, runes, and sigils.
2. Tape the stencils to the white sheets and trace the patterns with a sharpie, markers, crayons, or colored pencils.
3. Once you have done that, remove the stencils carefully without spreading the color.
4. Fold the sheet in a circular shape, with the patterns on the outer side of the sheet, and use tape to enclose the sheet.
5. Place the tea lights inside a glass jaw and turn them on.
6. Place the luminary on top of the jar to enclose the whole thing; the sheet starts glowing.

While Samhain used to be a spooky and eerie season for the ancient Celts and pagans, it is now celebrated with full fervor to honor the dead. Although Samhain is considered different from Halloween, the decor for both holidays comprises spooky items and ornamentations. However, Samhain consists of much more eerie adornments that portray the beliefs behind Samhain. As a modern witch, these decor ideas will assist you when looking for ways to decorate your home for Samhain.

Chapter 4: Setting Up Your Samhain Altar

As previously discussed, one of the ways for Wiccans and pagans to celebrate Samhain is by decorating their altar and using it in a Samhain ritual. If you have never had an altar at your house, you may wonder how to make and use one. Other common questions about altars include whether there are different types and the benefits of having one in your home.

If you've asked yourself any of these questions, this is the chapter for you. By the time you've moved on, you will know all there is to know about setting up your Samhain altar.

Benefits of Setting Up an Altar

An altar is a sacred place in your home that you can use when performing rituals. Altars have been associated with and used for divine practices for millennia. Each tradition has variations on an altar and how it is used, from Catholicism to Buddhism to pagan religions.

The altar essentially serves as an outward representation of your inner spirituality. It is a place that helps honor your ideas and beliefs and serves as a calming space in your home that you can go to when you want to connect with yourself or your gods.

While an altar is often considered a formal space for worship and ritual, many practitioners find it a place where they can pause, reflect, and center themselves. It acts as a space that provides a sense of comfort and calm and a place where you can stay connected to your spiritual side.

An altar at home is a good place to start nourishing the part of yourself that needs more self-care due to a gap in your spirituality. It can also serve as a reminder to be less harsh and more mindful of yourself and your needs and to take time to meet your self-care needs.

An altar also serves as a focal point for your spirituality. It allows you a space where you can focus while praying, meditating, or simply practicing breath work and gratitude. It allows you to connect with the deities you worship more deeply. You may even find that an altar makes it easier to develop pre-existing rituals into personalized ones tailored for you and your needs.

Types of Altars

There are numerous types of altars you can build. Most are personalized to you and your practice. However, there are two major categories that most altars fall under: Ancestor altars and seasonal altars.

Ancestor Altars

An ancestor altar is pretty much what it sounds like—a way for you to honor the people who came before you and helped shape who you are today, and this is a popular option on Samhain. After all, Samhain is a time to honor the dead, and an ancestor altar is one of the ways to do so.

An ancestor altar can be as big as you want. You can use a full table for it or just the corner of a shelf. The size does not matter, only your intent. Though called an "ancestor" altar, it is a way to honor all those who have gone before you, whether they are pets or cherished friends.

Seasonal Altars

Like ancestor altars, a seasonal altar is almost exactly what it says in the name—an altar you set up and change as the seasons change. It is a way for you to honor the cycle of the seasons and help you feel more in touch with nature. It can also be a focal point when working seasonal magic or celebrating the Sabbats.

These altars are generally made by incorporating parts or symbols of the season into your altar. For example, you would honor new life and rebirth for a spring altar and incorporate elements such as fresh flowers and images of maiden goddesses on the altar. Similarly, the space will change and evolve as the seasons do, ensuring you keep connected to nature.

Creating an Altar

When creating an altar, first make space for it in your home. As mentioned, this space does not have to be big, especially if you do not have much space to spare—but you should first create a dedicated place where you can build your altar without it being intruded upon by other parts of your life.

Ideally, the space should be a flat or raised surface. When creating an altar, first create protective boundaries around it. If possible, ensure the altar is in a quiet, out-of-the-way space in your home that does not see much traffic. After all, you don't want it to get knocked over or damaged by mistake.

Additionally, be very aware of your emotions. Does the space you are choosing feel "right?" Is it quiet and peaceful? Do you think you will be able to practice and perform rituals in this space? Does the energy feel bright and happy? Though you may not be able to categorize it empirically, you'll likely be able to tell if a space is right for your altar or not.

Keep in mind that you can have more than one altar in your home. You can even create an altar in your garden if that feels like it is the best location on your property. There are no hard-and-fast rules on where the altars should be located, aside from ensuring that it's the right spot for you and your needs.

Once you have chosen a space, clear it of any debris and clutter, and make sure it will remain that way.

Ancestor Altars

The first step toward creating an ancestor altar is physically cleaning the chosen altar of dirt and debris. You would not invite a loved one to sit in a dirty chair, and you should not invite them to use a dirty space as an altar.

Consider consecrating the area or smudging it with sage or sweetgrass to help make it feel welcoming. You can also sprinkle some consecrated water or consecrate it with the four elements. You will need a white candle, water, salt, and incense to do so. Each item links to a cardinal direction and an element:

Candle = fire/South

Water = water/West

Salt = earth/North

Incense = fire/East.

Light the candle and incense, and pass each item over the altar, facing the related cardinal direction. Speak or chant, asking the element and direction to consecrate your altar. Once you have done this for all four, finish by asking the sky and the spirits to do so.

Add an altar cloth to help welcome the ancestors. Depending on your practice and spiritual traditions, this cloth may need to be very specific or could be anything at all. For example, some practitioners believe that a red cloth should be used, while others require the cloth to have a fringe. Use a neat cloth that corresponds to your beliefs.

Welcome the ancestors to your altar by choosing photographs of them that have some meaning to you. If you do not have photos, use an item that may have belonged to them or an item representing who they were. You can also use symbols representing those that came before—for example, if you have a family crest, you can add that to your altar to symbolically represent all your family members who have passed.

Once you've added items representing the people you want to honor, add other items you can use in your practice when honoring your ancestors. These will differ based on what you use, but some options include votive candles, a symbol of your spirituality (like a pentagram or an ankh), and a cauldron or cup to symbolize the Earth Mother.

You can also leave food offerings on the altar so that the spirits can share your meal with you. Some people leave portions of their meal, while others leave representations of a meal—either as ingredients, like wheat or herbs, or through representational items like bread made of plastic or metal. What you choose will depend on your personal beliefs.

Taking care of your ancestor altar is relatively stress-free. Make sure it is well maintained and clean at all times. If you leave food offerings, make sure to respectfully dispose of them before they go bad. You can do this by ritually burning or burying them, feeding them to the local wild animals, or eating them yourself.

Your choice will largely depend on your personal beliefs and which option works best for you. For example, someone in a city may find burying food offerings or feeding them to wild animals impractical, and others may believe consuming an offering to the spirits is disrespectful. Choose the method that works best for you and your practice.

If you feel like the energy around your ancestor altar is dulling or stagnant, feel free to move it to a new location. And if you have more space than expected, consider expanding the altar if possible.

While your ancestor altar will come in useful on Samhain, when the veil between the worlds is at its thinnest, you can also use it to honor your loved ones on their birthdays and on other days that were significant to them, such as a special anniversary the two of you shared.

Seasonal Altar

Getting started with your seasonal altar is similar to how you start building your ancestor altar. Clear the area you will be using and consecrate it. Once you have done so, you can start filling the area.

For Samhain, you will be building a fallen altar. While Samhain signifies the start of winter, winter has not yet started when celebrating this day.

Some items you can add to your altar include representations of the waning moon—the moon phase associated with this season and seasonally associated with fall. You can also add herbs, spices, and plants associated with the season, such as marigold flowers, acorns, sage, sweetgrass, and cedar.

You should also add crystals associated with fall, such as hematite and indigo gabbro. Other common additions include leaves that have naturally fallen from trees as the season changes, black candles, and tarot cards linked to the fall, such as the Death card and the Queen of Wands. Some practitioners may also add a Rudraksha seed mala, but this differs based on your beliefs.

Fall is a time to release and let go, so you can also add items representing things, ideas, and people you want to let go of this fall. Finally, you can add images of crone goddesses you believe in, such as Hecate, Baba Yaga, or Elli.

Taking care of your fall altar is similar to how you would take care of your ancestor altar—ensure the area is clean and well maintained, and respectfully dispose of food and other items that may start to decompose if left out. Once fall is over, remove the items that make up your fall altar, clear the space, and re-consecrate before building your winter altar.

Samhain Altar

While you can use your seasonal fall altar for Samhain rituals, building a separate altar dedicated to Samhain for the big day is also possible. Samhain is a celebration of the fall, the harvest season, and the circle of life and death; your altar will represent this.

First, clean and consecrate the area that will be used. Then, start to build the altar. Cover the altar with a cloth (or cloths) representing the season's colors, such as black, deep reds, rich purples, or harvest colors like orange and gold.

The candles you add to your altar should also represent these darker shades. Alternatively, add candles of contrasting colors like white or silver, especially if you use them in rituals.

Samhain is a time to celebrate and honor the dead and the dying of the crops and life so that the cycle of life can start anew. Add symbols of death to your altars, such as skulls, scythes, ghosts, skeletons, or grave rubbings. If you are not setting up a separate ancestor shrine, you can add items representing loved ones, such as the ashes of those who have passed.

Other additions to your Samhain altar should be other symbols of the celebration, such as mulled wine, fallen leaves and acorns, a straw man, dark bread and/or ears of corn and wheat, and similar items. If you do not have a separate ancestor altar, add offerings to the spirits. Add images or statues of deities representing death, such as Hades, depending on your religious beliefs.

Given that Samhain is a harvest festival, you should also add some of the year's last harvest products. If you have a home garden, include some herbs and fruit you have grown yourself. If you live in an agricultural area, opt for local products from a nearby farmer's market. If not, add some apples, pumpkin, squash, and other fruits and vegetables that symbolize the harvest. You can also add some harvest and farming tools, like sickles.

Finally, add any divination tools you may use on Samhain. Samhain is the time when divination magic is widespread and easier to perform, thanks to the thin veil between worlds. Thus, additional tools such as tarot cards, a pendulum, a scrying mirror, and any other tools you will use for this task can be added. These tools should ideally be re-consecrated before you add them to your altar and use them in divination magic.

Once you have your altar (or altars) ready for Samhain, the next step is to use it. As mentioned above, your altar can serve as a focal point for your practice. It is also a good way to honor the spirits and those who have gone before you. However, if you are drawn to ritual and magic, you can use the altar for these purposes.

Keep reading if you are wondering how to use your altar during rituals and while performing spells and magic. The following chapters will cover all you need to know about these topics and offer some interesting ways in which you can use your altar while celebrating Samhain. We will also explore Samhain's sacred herbs and plants, which can be used to decorate your altar.

By the time you have finished with the book, you will be comfortable making use of your altar for rituals and better understand how to perform Samhain rituals, both independently and with a group or coven. We shall also cover how you can personalize these rituals and prayers and how you can celebrate Samhain with non-practicing friends and family.

Chapter 5: Sacred Herbs and Plants

Plants have always played a central role in pagan practices. In ancient times, people depended on their crops to survive the winter—and did everything they could to keep these plants alive. Pagans also relied on herbs for healing—the other reason for their strong connection to the world of plants. Fortunately, contemporary pagan traditions still include the regular use of plants and herbs, which are still considered sacred within this community. Their magical properties are mostly associated with Celtic pagan holidays like Samhain. As this sabbat represents one of the best times to connect practitioners with nature and its forces, the plants linked to this holiday enjoy wide popularity. Their lore is found in all the different pagan traditions practiced nowadays.

Thanks to these ancient traditions, pagan communities worldwide can stick together. It also allowed the ranks of poets and druids to pass down their wisdom to the new generations when all other means were prohibited. Plants have played a fundamental part in this process. They were a neutral topic that carried no danger to those who opposed paganism.

Without the plant's ability to sustain life on Earth, we would not be able to thrive. However, plants and nature have to give up their life after each Samhain for this to happen. Come spring, it will be reborn anew, bringing new life. Working with the plants and herbs discussed in this chapter can also help you understand the significance of doing everything to ensure the spirits of nature will wake up refreshed in the spring.

In this chapter, you will be introduced to the main plant groups used in pagan practice. You will encounter healing herbs, plants, and herbs you can use in the kitchen, herbs to cleanse your energy, and protective plants. Keep in mind that different plants have different magical properties. Some plants in this chapter can be used for multiple purposes, while others are best used for a single purpose. Some are great for healing but may be less than useful for nutritional purposes. At the same time, others are perfect for cleansing your body, mind, and space but should never be consumed as food.

For all these reasons, it is crucial to familiarize yourself with the proper use of each. This will allow you to pick the right plants for each occasion. For example, if you want to protect yourself or your home from malicious spirits on the night of Samhain, you should use herbs associated with good spirits. These plants will invite kindred spirits into your life to have the spiritual protection and guidance you need during the sabbat of Samhain. On the other hand, if your goal is to make offerings for your spiritual allies, you'll use sacred herbs suitable for your celebratory meals. After all, offerings are typically just food you set aside from your meals to honor kindred spirits.

Rosemary

As the plant associated with remembrance, rosemary is the perfect tool for Samhain spells and rituals. According to written Roman sources, rosemary was also used at Celtic pagan ceremonies as protection from malicious spirits. In Celtic pagan communities, rosemary was also used in the homes of those who died from an infectious disease. This was part of the smudging ritual meant to purify the energy of the place and prevent the disease from spreading. Later on, priests in Christian churches adopted the use of rosemary and implemented it during religious ceremonies.

Before performing a Samhain ritual, you can use dried rosemary to cleanse your mind, body, and soul from negativity. Alternatively, you can create a charm from the fresh branches and hang it on your door. It will invite the spirits of your ancestors to your home, prompting them to join you in your Samhain celebrations and protect you from unwanted spiritual influences.

Mugwort

According to Celtic lore, mugwort is closely associated with divination. If malicious spirits torment someone in their dreams, this plant can help them block that influence. You will need to heat a large stone in an oven or fireplace, sprinkle it with dried mugwort, and pour water on top of it to create steam. Inhale this before sleeping so that the steam gets into your lungs and later evaporates, removing all the negative influences.

Another way to use mugwort is to incorporate it into the smudge sticks you'll use in your divination ritual, or you can simply place a dried batch under your pillow to receive the answer you are looking for when sleeping.

Lavender

Lavender has an incredibly relaxing aroma, so it has been used for thousands of years. Its calming effects are good for treating insomnia, anxiety, or focusing your mind when meditating. In addition, lavender oil has anti-inflammatory and antiseptic properties—perfect for treating minor wounds. For this reason, pagans often resort to using lavender in their healing practices.

While lavender can be grown indoors, its healing properties are much stronger if it has grown outside, closer to other natural elements, such as the Sun and the Moon. If you want to use lavender in preparation for the Samhain festivities or even during them, harvest the flowers at night, just before the flower buds have opened. You can also buy fresh or dried lavender. When buying it fresh, hang it upside down in a warm and dry area. After two to three weeks, shake off the buds and store them or use them immediately. Put the dried flower buds into a reusable tea bag and place it on your altar to help you focus on the spells and rituals you perform at Samhain. You can also put a packet of flowers under your pillow to help spells to take effect during the night while you are sleeping.

Peppermint

Peppermint is another popular garden herb that has been a staple in every pagan healer practice since ancient times. It is typically consumed as a tea or used throughout the year to treat a broad range of conditions, such as congestion, headache, toothache, or muscle pain. On Samhain, you can use the refreshing aroma of peppermint to gain strength for all your activities. It can also help clear your mind before summoning an ancestor so you can interpret their messages better.

You can easily grow peppermint at home, even indoors, so you have an endless supply of this beneficial plant, or you can buy fresh or dried and make your own tea, an ointment, or a healing salve. In most cases, you will need to boil it in hot water; the longer you do it, the more potent its effects will be.

Chamomile

Like peppermint, chamomile is an incredibly powerful herb with medicinal properties. This herb is only used as a soothing tea, tisane, or salve. Dried or freshly picked flowers are placed in hot boiling water, and a concoction is brewed to the required strength. The longer you brew it, the stronger it will be.

Place the dried chamomile flowers in a reusable tea bag or cheesecloth and submerge them into your bathwater on the night of Samhain. This will relieve any symptoms of stress and revitalize your skin, cleansing your body and mind from any negative energy. You can also mix chamomile with other relaxing herbs or buy it as Bio-Oil and use it for your bath. A lesser-known fact is that it can also be a source of empowerment during Samhain celebrations.

Whether you practice healing regularly or just want to give back to your community at this time of the year, chamomile is a safe way to do this. Create your own chamomile healing salve and treat skin conditions such as eczema, minor cuts, and burns.

Chrysanthemum

This flower is linked to protection, making it another appropriate plant to use at Samhain. Remember, when you invite the benevolent spirits to join you during this sabbat, they may be accompanied by some malicious ones. Chrysanthemums can help you keep the latter at bay because they bloom around this time, which means they will be full of pure, natural energy.

To ensure no harm will come to you or your loved ones, use these flowers as a centerpiece during the festivities or create a wreath you can hang on your front door. Chrysanthemums are also associated with the sun and fire, which you can use for your benefit during Samhain. Dry the flowers and use them as incense for rituals and spells requiring the power of the sun or the fire element.

Rowan Trees

Rowan is another plant used to keep unwanted spirits at bay on the night of Samhain. Branches and berries are placed outside pagan homes, and this has been performed for many years, but gifting these was also a common custom in Celtic pagan communities. You can implement either of these practices or place the branches and berries over the windows and doors—even inside your home—to protect yourself and your loved ones from evil influences.

It is also believed that planting a rowan tree near your loved one's grave allows them to move on more peacefully. This way, their spirit may guide you and the next generations in the future. If you cut the berries in half, you will notice how the inside resembles a pentagram (a traditional Celtic pagan symbol of protection). Place these around the home for added security and abundance in your life.

Apple

Samhain marks the end of the apple harvest season, and the number of apples gathered each fall was once used to represent how successful the year was. According to the Celtic pagan lore, the more apples harvested, the more likely deities and ancestral spirits would side with mortals. This also meant they were inclined to help with other matters, but only if they were properly thanked for contributing to the bountiful harvest. If you also want to express gratitude to your spiritual guide during Samhain, you can do this in several ways. You can prepare dishes with apples and offer them to your ancestors, or simply leave a basket of fresh apples on your altar as an offering.

If you can find apple branches with mature fruit and flowers, including unopened buds, use them to journey to the spiritual world. Apple flowers and the fruit itself can be used for divination. This can be particularly helpful if what you are interested in is related to your emotions. As the apples are associated with the heart, their peel may reveal something meaningful about your relationships. Likewise, the number of seeds you find in an apple may indicate a new emotional connection in your near future.

Pomegranate

Pomegranate.
https://pixabay.com/es/photos/granada-frutas-comida-rebanado-3383814/

Thanks to their many seeds, pomegranates are often associated with fertility. Used at Samhain rituals and ceremonies, pomegranates can ensure that your next year will be even more fruitful than the current one was. Feel free to incorporate the seeds into your meals and drinks, even the ones you prepared as an offering to ask your deities and ancestral spirits to provide you with abundance.

Pomegranates are also linked to the spiritual world—due to their seeds. Their large number represents the power of nature—something you can always rely on as a pagan when trying to communicate with the spiritual world. Scoop out the seeds into a bowl and place them on your altar. Put them next to represent the spirit you are trying to communicate with, and recite the appropriate spell over them.

Lemon

Lemon has been used as a natural remedy for many conditions and should never be limited to only being used in the kitchen. Its high vitamin content boosts the immune system, making this fruit essential to fight off infections. Lemon is also packed with antioxidants, whether used in raw form or as an oil. However, lemons can be used for much more than soothing a sore throat during the winter or as a refreshing drink in the scorching summer heat.

Lemon trees are not the easiest to grow, so you will most likely get the fruit from a shop or market. If you buy the fruit, get organic lemons to enjoy all their benefits. You can use lemons or lemon juice to prepare light desserts or dressings for the wild meat dishes traditionally prepared for the Samhain festivities. Lemon oil can be used for cleansing baths, meditation, or anointing your candles.

Squashes and Pumpkins

Squashes and pumpkins are also well-known indicators of abundance during the harvest season. Harvested late in the season, they have become a staple decoration for pagans and non-pagans all around the globe. However, these fall fruits can have more purpose than simply being a funky decoration during the Samhain festivities. They can be stored in many forms, providing plenty of nourishment for many more months.

At Samhain, you can incorporate them into your meals or use them for divination purposes. Carving a symbol of protection into the skin of a squash or pumpkin and leaving the carved fruit outside your door or window is another ancient pagan custom you can implement to keep unwanted spirits at bay.

Aloe Vera

Due to its remarkable healing properties, aloe vera has been used for centuries. People from all around the world are raving about the sticky gel you can find inside this plant. It relieves pain, speeds up healing of the skin, and has a moisturizing effect. This beneficial plant can also be incorporated into pagan practices, including the celebration of Samhain.

One of the best things about aloe vera is that it grows indoors. It is one of those plants that thrive on neglect, so you will not have to worry about watering it. Place the plant in moderate sunlight for a stylish decoration, a relaxing sight, and an immediate supply of aloe vera gel whenever you need it. To harvest it, cut off one of the mature leaves and let the yellow liquid drain from it—rinse it with water to speed up the process. Use a clean, sharp knife to remove the edges of the leaf and the top and bottom pieces of its skin. You'll find a translucent gel you can immediately apply to the skin underneath it. If you do not want to use it right away, scoop out the gel, freeze it, cut it into small cubes, and store it in the freezer for up to a month.

Apply the gel onto your skin as a moisturizer after taking a traditional Samhain bath, or use the plant as a tool to relax your mind when preparing for a spell or ritual. The gel can also treat minor burns during the Samhain bonfire ritual.

Tips for Implementing Sacred Herbs and Plants into Your Practice

Depending on the paganism you practice, you may find some ancient customs—such as gifting each other with plant products, including fruit, leaves, and nectar—very much alive within your community. If you do not live in a pagan community or are just delving into this topic, you may find incorporating plants and herbs into your practice challenging. After all, we are no longer dependent on the harvest season because we can find all the produce we need throughout the year in supermarkets, so we often take nature for granted. In this case, you should try to connect with nature through meditation and deep breathing techniques performed amid a patch of nature. Regardless of where you live, you can always find a little green corner to admire nature's work more closely. It will help you appreciate everything the sacred herbs and plants can give you around Samhain.

Moreover, as you observe nature around you, you will be reminded that you are just as much a part of nature as all the greenery you see and the animals feeding on it are. If it is not a protected area, you may even take a few herbal souvenirs when you go home to familiarize yourself with their texture, scent, and colors, or you can simply visit a market and buy some herbs you can experiment with in your budding practice. While you can do this at any time of the year, you must remember that Samhain marks the height of the harvest season. This means that the fresh plants are the most potent at this time of the year—making this sabbat perfect for learning all about them.

One of the best ways to start including sacred herbs and plants in your practice is to prepare a celebratory meal. As you can see from the individual description of the plants, Samhain meals typically use many fruits, vegetables, and foraged goods. However, herbs used as spices also play a significant part in these meals. It's a good idea to establish a home garden. No matter how small the space you have for it is, the plants you can grow in your garden will make you appreciate the true meaning of this harvest festival. You can also use herbs to anoint candles before casting your spells and initiating your rituals. Alternatively, you can opt for pampering yourself in a bath using dried, relaxing, or invigorating herbs and oils made from them.

It's important to note that if you are allergic to any of the plants mentioned in this chapter, you should not use them in your practices. If you are not sure whether you have a sensitivity or not, it's always a good idea to do a patch test before using them. Do this for any new plant or herb you will try, whether fresh, dry, or in oil form. People with certain conditions are advised not to use specific herbs or essential oils, which may aggravate their condition. Some herbs can adversely affect healthy pregnant women and their unborn children, who should not use them. If pregnant or breastfeeding, consult a health care professional regarding what plants are safe for consumption.

Chapter 6: Celebrating with Food

We all love festivals and celebrations. We get to have a great time, and they also remind us where we come from and who we are. Festivals are a great way to bring people together and remind us that, despite our differences or backgrounds, we are united by the things we celebrate despite our differences. Festivals also allow us to share a part of who we are with friends and family members who have different beliefs or who practice other traditions. They are great opportunities to teach children about the essence of tradition and make them feel involved. Most importantly, celebrations play a great role in helping us keep our cultures and traditions alive.

Most celebrations in the world come with a menu of their own. Food is an integral part of all cultures across the globe. Food is more than just the mouth-watering, delectable part of the experience. It is of utmost significance when it comes to ensuring that a tradition lives on for generations to come. Nothing strengthens the bonds within a community more than coming together to share a meal that holds significance to each person.

Hosting a dinner or cooking a meal to enjoy on the day of the celebration is a great way to express your love and gratitude to those who are invited. It also makes you feel like you have accomplished something great during the festival. No matter whom you are inviting, the food you cook always sends a message, whether it is "I care for you," "I want to share a part of who I am with you," or "I'm grateful that I get to celebrate with you."

Food is an integral part of the experience if you're celebrating alone. You do not need to host a huge dinner, or even eat with your family, to cook holiday or festival-related meals. It's an opportunity to press pause on the strenuous nature of daily life and take a moment to "savor" the moments that truly matter and get into the true spirit of the celebration with a special menu. Any festival is incomplete without its unique set of food items. In this chapter, you will come across a wide range of recipes you can cook on Samhain to relish on your own or share with your friends, family, or neighbors. These are guaranteed to help you feel the true essence of the celebration and get the full, authentic Samhain experience, especially once you learn why each recipe is relevant to the festival. Here, you will also come across the different Samhain dining methods, highlighting the different ways you can enjoy a meal traditionally on the day of the celebration.

Samhain Food Recipes

As you know, Samhain is typically a community-centered festival. This is because it usually involves group ceremonies and bonfires, making feasts a natural piece of the celebratory pie. However, there are numerous ways to celebrate Samhain by yourself, and cooking up a festival-relevant meal is definitely one of them.

Samhain is celebrated with a wide range of food items. Besides highlighting the end of the season of light or harvest, the festival honors the passage of loved ones. This is why meals are often cooked, and plates are served to honor those no longer celebrating with us. Since the festival also marks the end of the harvest season, it also makes sense that a feast should be prepared.

Samhain is an ancient practice that has been celebrated for centuries; thus, many traditional recipes have been swept away with time. However, there is still a wide range of recipes and ingredients that you can use to keep the festival's spirit alive. Recipes mainly focus on fall produce and seasonal foods, which will become scarcer throughout the year. Most dishes contain flavorful ingredients like pumpkins, cruciferous vegetables, potatoes, and apples.

Ancient Celts based their harvesting habits and traditions on the farming calendar. They brought all their cattle in during the colder months of the year. It is also said that they slaughtered the livestock during the harsh winter instead of feeding them. This is why meat was also a ubiquitous dish among herding communities at that time of year. Potatoes and oats were dug up and stacked for the fest.

For some people, the festival's menu had to do with story-telling traditions and unique beliefs. For instance, many people worried that the púca (a fairy and shapeshifter) would spit on their produce if it were not collected before Samhain. To this day, some Irish people are still in the habit of leaving out a meal for the fairies to enjoy on Samhain. They often leave a plate of champ and a spoon at the foot of a hawthorn tree. Another tradition is to bake thick oatcakes with holes in the middle so that string can be threaded through them. Children who would go "trick-or-treating" to collect nuts and apples from their neighbors would also leave with an oatcake necklace.

Samhain is a time that is very closely tied to deep reflection. It's an opportunity to look back on all you have achieved throughout the past year and develop goals and plans for the coming period. This is a time when terms like "safe," "wellness," "comfort," and "coziness" are highly relevant. The typical Samhain menu reflects these themes of protection and comfort, considering the warming nature of the flavors and ingredients used. Many recipes are roasted, simmered, casseroled, or roasted. Others are seasoned with cinnamon, rosemary, sage, nutmeg, or even garnished with nuts. The food at this time of year is exciting, filling, delicious, and soul-stirring. The following are some traditional Samhain recipes you can prepare for your celebrations.

Soul Cakes

Soul cakes are commonly served on Samhain. Their association with the festival is uncertain; however, they were originally baked for charity. On the night of the sabbat, the poorer citizens of a town would visit the homes of the wealthy, asking for money or food. They offered to pray for the homeowner's loved ones who had passed away in return for an act of kindness. Soul cakes were usually given to the beggars as blessings. There are numerous soul cake recipes, so one version of a soul cake may differ greatly from another. Here is one quick yet delicious way to make this popular delicacy:

Ingredients:

- 1 softened stick of butter
- 1 ½ cups of flour
- 4 tbsp. of sugar

Instructions:

1. In a bowl, place the softened butter and the sugar and stir well until you are left with a creamy mixture.
2. Add the flour to the bowl using a flour sifter. Mix once more and ensure that the dough is lump-free.
3. Divide the dough in half and shape each half into a circle. Use a rolling pin to spread it out. Each circle should be half an inch thick.
4. Place the dough on an ungreased baking sheet and use a fork to draw lines in the dough. Each half should have eight wedges.
5. Set the oven to 350 degrees Fahrenheit and bake the cakes for twenty-five minutes or until they are light brown.

Colcannon

Colcannon is another favorite dish among those who celebrate Samhain. This dish has been ingrained as part of the tradition probably because its ingredients are in season (potatoes and greens like kale and cabbage). This side dish will make a great addition to your dinner table.

Ingredients:

- 5 medium-sized Yokun Gold potatoes
- 2 diced leeks (use only the white and light green parts)
- 6 tbsp. unsalted butter
- 2 thinly-sliced garlic cloves
- Kosher salt (to taste)
- 2 cups of packed, shredded savoy cabbage
- 1¼ cups of milk
- ½ a cup of heavy cream
- Freshly ground black pepper
- 1 thinly-sliced scallion

Instructions:

1. Place the potatoes in a small pot, cover them with water, and season with a dash of salt. Turn up the heat to medium-high and bring to a boil. Turn down the heat and let the potatoes simmer. Once done, drain the potatoes, let them cool slightly, and then peel. Use a knife to check if it slices right through (you should be able to do that within thirty to forty minutes).

2. As the potatoes cook, put a large saucepan over medium-high heat and melt four tablespoons of butter. Drop in the leeks and let them cook for eight to ten minutes, stirring in between.

3. Once they soften up, add the garlic and stir until fragrant. The edges of the leeks should start browning within three minutes. Afterward, add a cup of cabbage and stir until it has wilted. Add the cream and milk and bring the ingredients to a simmer.

4. Add the potatoes and the other cup of cabbage. Use a masher to mash the potatoes coarsely. Season with salt and pepper.

5. Move the colcannon to a serving bowl and top it off with the rest of the butter and the scallions.

Barmbrack

This traditional dish happens to be a traditional Irish bread recipe. This type of bread is associated with Samhain because it includes trinkets that serve as a form of fortune-telling. For instance, if someone gets a ring, it means they will get married within the coming year. A coin symbolizes wealth, the cloth is associated with hardship, and dry peas resemble a dry wedding spell (no weddings). You can always use trinkets of your own choice!

Ingredients:

- 2 beaten eggs
- 1 large lemon zest
- 1 large orange zest
- 2 cups of hot, strong black breakfast tea
- 3 cups of all-purpose flour
- 1 cup of dark brown sugar
- 2 tsp of baking powder
- 1 tsp of mixed spice (you can also use pumpkin pie spice)
- 1 3/4 cups of raisins
- 1 3/4 cups of sultanas
- Dried fruit

Instructions:

1. Preheat the oven to 325 degrees Fahrenheit.
2. Line and butter a deep nine-inch cake pan and set it aside.
3. Add the sultanas, orange zest, lemon zest, raisins, and sugar to a medium-sized bowl. Pour the tea and mix well. Place cling film over the bowl and leave it at room temperature to set overnight.
4. Place the spices, baking powder, and flour in a large bowl and mix well.
5. Add your dried fruits and eggs. Whisk together until there are no dry streaks.
6. Wrap your trinkets in parchment paper and add them to the mixture.
7. Pour the batter into a lined and buttered pan.
8. Leave the bread to bake for 80 to 90 minutes or until golden. It should spring back up when lightly pressed.
9. Let it cool for twenty minutes and take it out of the pan.

10. Slice it to your desired thickness and serve with butter.

Samhain Dining Methods

There are numerous ways to celebrate Samhain through food. Since this is a communal festival, we recommend that you host a large feast and invite your community over. If you do not know anyone who celebrates Samhain, you can use this as an opportunity to share your beliefs and traditions with your loved ones. You can introduce the concept of Samhain to your close friends or family members and ask them to celebrate this festival with you. You can choose a few of the recipes mentioned above and have them experience the spirit of Samhain with you.

If your neighborhood celebrates the festival, you can all participate in a bonfire ritual and eat afterward. You can also have a large outdoor gathering at night where each person cooks up a traditional dish. However, the most popular way to dine on Samhain is to have a silent (dumb) supper.

Having your dinner in silence is a great way to honor the dead, particularly family members or friends who passed away the previous year. Silent suppers are also commonly held for any ancestral spirits that anyone attending wishes to pay their respects to. The origins of dumb suppers are not very clear. However, according to some sources, this tradition is derived from the Ozarks. Others claim that it originated in the Appalachian Mountains. Regardless of how this tradition came about, it was a very popular practice among neopagans at the time of Samhain.

Hosting a Dumb Supper

The idea of a dumb supper may seem incredibly odd to those still learning about the Sabbats. However, the more you reflect on the practice, the better you will understand the idea behind it. Silent suppers are a great way to acknowledge and reflect on your thoughts, considering this is a time of deep reflection. Think about your deceased loved ones, pay them your respects, and express your gratitude toward those in your life today. The Wheel of the Year and its sabbats represent the cyclical nature of life. Death, an inevitable part of life, is one of the hardest things to grasp and accept. We feel lost, mournful, and depressed after the people we love exit our lives. Samhain presents an opportunity to alleviate some of these emotions and lessen the sense of grief by feeling the presence of those who passed and celebrating with people who care about us.

Dumb suppers may seem inherently depressing. However, there are numerous ways in which you can make them more enjoyable and much more exciting. For instance, you are free to design your invitations in whatever way you like. You can also do the same with the table favors. Find a way to maintain the solemn nature of the event, yet convey the spirit of the festivities. Play around with tiny wooden coffins and even Halloween decorations. You can also use obituary-themed menus and invitations!

Invitations and the Guests of Honor

You need to put in some thought to decide whom you want to invite to your dumb supper. You should also consider inviting children. However, in that case, you will have to make some changes to the overall course of the celebration. You will find more on that in the following chapter. While this can be a great way to introduce your children and other kids in the family to the concept of death, it can be a very difficult topic for them to grasp. You should also discuss whether other parents are open to bringing their children over, especially since children will not remain silent for the entire thirty- to forty-minute duration of the dinner.

You should also determine whom you want your guest of honor to be. This is usually a person who has passed away in the last year. You should set a place for them at the head of the table, marking it with a photograph or any other unique way to represent them. For instance, you can honor them by placing the things they enjoyed in life, such as their favorite book, an instrument they played, or a symbol of their favorite hobby, on the chair. If you do not wish to honor one specific person, the head of the table can be symbolically set to represent numerous guests of honor. Since finding things that represent all the people you wish to pay your respects to will not be possible, you can represent them through a universal symbol, like a candle. You can represent each guest using a candle in their favorite color.

The Atmosphere

The heart of any festival or celebration lies in the general atmosphere. This is why you can try to make the environment mysterious. To set the mood, you can use black tablecloths, candles, and tableware. You can also light up the space using candles and lanterns and even use ingredients like activated charcoal to create a black cocktail. You will find many variations of the recipe online. Using fire for lighting is a great idea since it not only helps you create an eerie ambiance, but many people believe that artificial light sources hinder spirit communication. You should keep all technological devices turned off throughout the dinner.

The Food

Any recipes mentioned above would be appropriate to serve during a dumb dinner. If one of the guests of honor used to cook traditional Samhain recipes, you can include them in the menu. If they don't celebrate Samhain, you can tweak their recipes and add certain spices or legumes to give them a more seasonal feel. If you wish, you can also figure out a way to change the color of some of the dishes to black without affecting their taste—if you decide to go with an all-black theme. If you are hosting a large dinner, it can be very hard to cook everything yourself. In that case, you can turn it into a potluck. You can create a list to avoid repetition.

Silence Level

Silence is crucial because it helps heighten the senses and guide us toward the spiritual world. Make sure to mention explicitly that the dinner will be held in complete silence upon invitation. That way, everyone will know in advance.

When setting up the table, ensure you prepare everything, so verbal communication is minimized. You can serve the plates and ensure that they are well-portioned to avoid having bowls passed around, which can be distracting and noisy. This will require you to take note of everyone's allergies, dietary needs, and preferences. If you want, you can set up an open buffet on a separate table so people can choose what they wish to eat. Once everyone has their plates ready, you can all sit down and start the dumb supper. Make sure you explain that no one can get up for refills once you start.

Social events where everyone is quiet are typically very awkward. However, it is very different when you attend a ritual where no words are needed. You can just sit down, enjoy everyone's presence, savor the food, and reflect without worrying about the next thing to say. It is certainly an experience of a lifetime.

Communicating with Departed Loved Ones

Use this opportunity to communicate with your departed loved ones. It does not matter if you don't believe in an afterlife. You can view this as a chance to let go of the things you never had the chance to tell them. Some people like to write messages on pieces of paper to burn them in a cauldron. However, it's not recommended to do so indoors. You can burn them on an outdoor bonfire after dinner if you would like.

Having a bonfire is a great excuse to get the party going. Everyone can go back to socializing afterward. You can have drinks, read tarot cards, share memories, and make the experience all the more enjoyable. Make sure you fold some Samhain-relevant herbs like sage or cinnamon into the paper and use the herb and essential oil to anoint it before throwing it into the fire.

Food is an integral part of all celebrations and festivals worldwide. It is a great way to revive ancient traditions and keep them going for centuries. It also serves to share your beliefs or culture with your friends and family. You can say a lot just by serving others a meal. Now that you have read this chapter, you are ready to host a memorable Samhain feast.

Chapter 7: Family and Group Activities

Host dinner with your family for Samhain to honor the dead.
https://www.pexels.com/photo/selective-focus-photography-of-man-preparing-food-beside-smiling-women-and-kids-3171151/

Festivals are an important part of Wiccan and Druid community life. People born into Wicca and Druidry worldwide grow up celebrating festivals, regarding them as an integral aspect of life. There are eight pagan festivals, each symbolizing seasonal changes that Wiccans celebrate worldwide.

Despite their religious and cultural significance, festivals are celebrated for various reasons. Neopagans view them as an opportunity to unite the community and reinforce the sense of belonging and togetherness. This time unites all pagans as they celebrate a certain purpose or time of the year.

Besides the excitement and fun, festivals make great learning opportunities for kids. Even though they may not always understand, children enjoy festivals the most. They are introduced to games, decorations, preparations, gifts, and sweets. Celebrating with other friends and family makes your kids excited to see everyone come together.

Samhain allows the family to bond over meaningful experiences. They can all participate in something they truly believe in. This is a great chance to get your kids involved in important events. You can encourage them to help you with the decorations and food preparations. This strengthens familial bonds and reminds us of the things that matter.

Depending on how you choose to celebrate, festivals are associated with exchanging gifts and sharing. This creates a joyous atmosphere and encourages children to donate their old toys or help the less fortunate. You can celebrate Samhain in endless ways! Besides the main traditions tied to this festival, you can use this time to teach your kids about important values like generosity, gratefulness, kindness, and humbleness. You can also remind your kids of their roots and family history by honoring your ancestors on that day. At the end of the day, Samhain is the perfect time to let go of old, unhelpful habits to make way for new and healthier ones.

There is no better way to teach your children about your beliefs than celebrating with them during festivals. During this time, they are likely to learn certain concepts and ideas that they otherwise would not be able to wrap their heads around. Traditional activities and celebrations prompt kids to explore because of their natural curiosity. They will probably inquire about certain rituals or ask why things are done a certain way. This is why stories are shared and oral traditions come to life during the sabbats. You can get your kids excited by helping them understand the significance of these festivals through the generations.

Even if you do not have children, celebrating Samhain can be a great way to reconnect with your community and celebrate your similarities. It's not every day that we find people who share our beliefs and traditions. This is why hosting or going to Samhain gatherings and participating in similar social activities can be quite fulfilling. This chapter will find plenty of family-friendly and social activities to try during Samhain. You will also learn how to throw a Samhain or "New Year" party!

Celebrating with Family

The following are a few families and kid-friendly ways to celebrate Samhain and embrace its spirit:

Set Intentions

As mentioned, Samhain is all about letting go of the old and paving the way for new and more fruitful opportunities. Gather your family around and ask them to write down any intrusive thoughts, feelings, and unhealthy habits they are struggling with. Encourage your children to write down anything that comes to mind, no matter how small it is. Perhaps they wish to stop telling lies or being messy. Once all of you complete your list, throw it into the Samhain fire. Do not forget to state your intentions—letting go of bad habits, emotions, and feelings to create space for better ones. Now that you have done that start writing another list comprising your dreams and ideas for the following year. If you want, you can share the things you wrote down with the rest of the family. If anyone wants to keep them to themselves, keep the lists safe until spring, giving them extra attention during winter.

Get Crafty

You can do several crafts with your family to celebrate Samhain. For instance, you can use seasonal symbols like corns and pumpkins to decorate the festival's altar. You can keep the celebrations going for the entire season, considering that your children will be coming home earlier than they usually do—shorter days and longer nights, remember? Doing simple crafts with just a few supplies is the perfect way to keep them busy and engaged while celebrating. Harvest crafts are very popular during this Sabbat. Go out with your family and gather some leaves. You can get as creative as you want! Paint them in bright colors and use them to make leaf prints or glue them together to create a picture. You can carve pumpkins or even make necklaces out of acorns.

Get Outside

The lights may be going out early, but this does not mean you should not embrace the change of seasons. Grab your jacket and head out for a moonlight walk with your family or have a small bonfire. Build a fire and toast marshmallows while sharing stories about the festival and your ancestors. Ensure you check whether there are any hibernating animals while raking through the things you are going to burn and be careful while handling the fire.

Go for a hike and discuss with your kids why some animals hibernate in winter or why the leaves fall and change color. You can also go for a run to welcome the new season with high activity levels. We usually get lazier during winter, so that is one way to set things off on the right track. Encourage your family to maintain healthy habits throughout the following year. When you're out, make sure you observe and give your thanks to the world around you. Express your gratitude toward the changing seasons and the coming of fall. You can do that in whichever way you desire. You can pray silently, give back to the community, help the less fortunate, meditate in nature, or even yodel in your backyard!

Honor Your Ancestors

Honoring your ancestors and recalling the memories are among the most important aspects of Samhain. The stories you tell and how you plan to approach this idea depend on your kids' ages. If you believe they are too young to understand complex matters like life and death, you can always postpone this tradition to the following year. However, many people view this festival as an opportunity to introduce their children to their origins and ancestors.

If you have not done so already, you can study genealogy and trace back your roots with your children. Have them call their grandparents and ask them if they—or their parents or any other distant relatives—come from other countries. Have them ask them about their childhood and how different things were back in the day. Create a family tree on an ancestor altar cloth using the information you gather.

Light a candle and gather your family around to express your love, prayers, and gratitude to your loved ones. You can also set up an ancestor altar and include photos and heirlooms of those who have passed. Use natural objects, drawings, cutouts, etc., to decorate the altar.

Hold a Ritual

Rituals are usually very challenging to attend to when you have unoccupied kids around, so the best thing to do is get them involved in helping you set everything up. You can also tweak existing rituals or develop new ones to ensure that the process is fun but maintains its spiritual aspect. Before starting, ask your children how they would like to get involved. Some kids would like to participate silently, while others prefer to participate in chants and bang on a drum.

Set up a basic altar—you can use your Halloween decorations. Use candles unless you cannot trust your kids around them. Alternatively, you can use LED tea lights. If you are not setting up an ancestral altar, you can add the pictures and heirlooms of your deceased family members. If you like, you can serve food as an offering. Ask your kids to help you bake the bread beforehand. Prepare a cup of something to drink that you can share with all your family and gather around to think about those who have passed away, current family members, and loved ones.

Start the ritual by setting your intention—celebrating the lives of loved ones who have crossed over—and say the names of the people you wish to honor. Start by naming those who have died recently, working your way backward. You do not need to name every deceased person in your family tree; however, you can go into detail by mentioning how certain family members impacted your life, sharing funny or remarkable incidents, or explaining what they were like. Once done, pass the plate around, so each family member has a piece of food to use as an offering. Each person should approach the altar on their own—eldest to youngest, leaving the offering on a plate. Send out a prayer that carries your intention. You can help younger kids with the offerings and the prayer. Hold the cup and set your intention. Then take a sip and pass it to the next person. Put the cup on the altar, join hands, close your eyes, thank your ancestors, and take a moment to reflect. End the rite in whatever way you prefer.

Have Fun!

Samhain and Halloween are deeply connected for most of us, which is totally fine! This time of the year, in particular, is a crossover between the mundane and the spiritual, and this is probably why your children will likely want to bridge this gap in one way or another. Just as you wish to celebrate Samhain, they are probably more interested in the Halloween festivities. Luckily for you, you can trick-or-treat and dress up in any costumes you like while still making plenty of time for the spiritual aspect of Samhain.

You can suggest mixing it up at Halloween in your neighborhood. Instead of having children knock on individual doors down the street, you can throw one large party. Offer food and candy to anyone who walks by! One person can grill on their porch, their neighbor can offer the beverages, another can layout the desserts, and so on. Have one large bonfire and share stories or read spooky Samhain-related poems! Interacting with the community, having a barbeque, and sharing candy with adults can be twice as much fun.

Extend the Celebrations

Celebrations are always more tasteful when your loved ones are around. Invite your neighbors, friends, and family for a feast of various harvest foods. You can even ask your guests to bring a dish so you can share. Spending time with your community and interacting with others is always a great way to celebrate Samhain. If you wish, you can even celebrate in the traditional Celtic way. Celebrate for three days, just like they did back then. Hold rituals and dances, and have feasts during that time. These are all ways to connect with the energy of Samhain.

Group Activities

The following are some ways in which you can celebrate Samhain with a group of people:

Have a Silent Supper

Dumb (or silent) suppers were a popular tradition, especially during the Middle Ages. Eating a meal in complete silence is considered a way in which you can honor your ancestors. Beside your dining table, you can set up another table with pictures, memorials, and heirlooms of loved ones who have crossed over. You can decorate the table with flowers, candles, and tablecloths. Make sure you pick out symbolic colors or choose ones that tie back to a certain memory. Add extra plates for the souls that you wish to honor. Light the candles and have your dinner in complete silence to welcome the spirits. This is because they are very sensitive to the energies in the room. Take this time to think back to your memories, reflect on your emotion, and express your thankfulness and gratitude (silently).

Light Things Up

During Samhain, the Celts held a large communal fire in the village. They gathered around it and went home with a burning branch so they could see each light in their hearth. Villages typically lit several communal fires around them because they believed it would help guide the spirits to their homes. You can have your own bonfire if you want, but this may be a bit of a stretch. You need to have enough space and, of course, the knowledge on how to build, tend, and handle a fire. This is something you can do with a large group of people to reignite the spirit of Samhain. Alternatively, you can pay special attention to your home lighting. Use candles, purchase new lamps, and decorate your home with colored lights, which is something that can also be turned into a group activity!

Create Centerpieces

Gather your friends around and create Samhain-themed centerpieces to place on tables, mantels, altars, or windowsills as decorations. Use black, red, white, and orange candles, tourmaline, amber, obsidian, or similar crystals, fallen leaves, pine cones, and corn dolls. Ask your friends to think of all their achievements. Tell them to think about the centerpieces you are about to make to remind them to honor all they have achieved. You can even use Halloween decorations.

Hold a Moon Circle

Gather your fellow neopagans and stand under Samhain's bright moonlight. Grab a huge spiral and pour salt and nuts inside. Place a candle in the center of the spiral. Stand at the spiral's edge in a circle, all joining hands. Walk toward the center of the spiral. At this point, everyone should push something bad from the past year out of their mind. If this would make it easier, you can write down the things you wish to leave behind. Scatter the pieces of paper as you move around. Light the candle and have each person grab a nut before moving out of the center of the spiral. The nut is representative of seeds, allowing for new beginnings and energies and making way for growth. Think about your intentions for the coming year as you do so.

How to Host a Samhain Party

If you wish to host a Samhain party to celebrate the New Year, this book is here to help! Before you start planning, you need to decide whether you will invite kids to the party. If most of your community has children, you will probably find that you have to. Thu, you will need to choose kid-friendly activities and decor. At the very least, you will have to consult with the parents about whether they would like their children to participate in the ritual. In that case, you may want to tweak the process to make it more kid-friendly. You should also select at least one of the family-friendly activities mentioned in this chapter to keep them occupied.

Then, you should determine your main event for the party. Dumb suppers are a great way to honor the deceased and your ancestors. However, they may not work if you have children around. You can hold a séance instead. Choosing one main event will allow you to stick to a specific theme. However, you can always hold both.

Plan out additional smaller activities for your party. This will make your party memorable and ideal for parents who have kids around. Pumpkin carving or acorn necklace contests can be great bonding experiences. Ensure everyone feels included.

Acknowledge your ancestors by including a few photographs and heirlooms on the altar. You should do that, especially if someone has recently lost a loved one. If you are holding a ritual, your guests probably will not be anticipating a wide range of food options. You can offer fall-related appetizers and simple dishes. If you are hosting a dumb supper, you'll have to go all out. Ask your guests to bring a dish along.

If you're not inviting children, consider lighting up the place using just fire. You can use a blend of bonfires, candles, and tiki torches to create the ambiance. Use natural decorations instead of sticking to the basic Halloween ornaments. Ornament the scene with pumpkins, acorns, pine cones, etc.

Finally, make Samhain ritual favors. There are endless options that you can choose from.

Samhain is among the most significant festivals in neopagan society. If you're part of the Wiccan or Druid community, you may have someone to celebrate Samhain and the other sabbats or festivals. The more the people around, the greater the joy that everyone experiences. Celebrating Samhain with friends, family, or other community members teaches the kids the need for society and the wonders of working with one another for a certain cause. Allowing them to partake in the preparations for Samhain can help them realize that they are important community members and encourages them to find their place in it. They are also taught the basics of shared responsibilities, delegation, and teamwork. They understand that when everyone puts in the work, great things happen. Even if you do not have kids, you can still experience the great joys of the festival. At the very least, you can host your own New Year party and view this as an opportunity to let go of negative habits, thoughts, and emotions to plant the seeds for new and positive ones.

Chapter 8: Samhain Rituals and Ceremonies

Some of the previous chapters discussed how to celebrate Samhain on a physical level. We have covered building a Samhain altar and how you can celebrate with your family and friends, including non-practicing loved ones. We've even covered some foods you can include in a Samhain meal or feast.

However, celebrating Samhain often involves more than just the physical; it also involves your spiritual side. This chapter will cover everything you need to know about rituals and ceremonies you can include in your celebration and why they can play an important part in your observance of the day.

Samhain is a day of honoring the ancestors, the forgotten dead, and the people who have gone before you. It is also a time to celebrate the deities, especially those associated with the harvest and the god and goddess. In the Wheel of the Year, Samhain marks when the Horned God dies before being resurrected on Yule/the Winter Solstice; therefore, it is also when practitioners celebrate and honor the cycle of life and death.

This chapter will also cover rituals and ceremonies for solitary practitioners and those who practice in groups or covens. For those hoping to introduce their children to the spiritual side of Samhain, it will also cover some kid-friendly rituals you can try.

Note that Samhain rituals often involve acknowledging some elements of the season aloud. You can create your own script for these acknowledgments, find pre-made ones that fit your beliefs, or simply speak from your heart—ultimately, your intent matters more than getting the words perfectly right.

Set Up and Decorate Your Altar

We have already covered constructing a Samhain altar in an earlier chapter, and you can use that chapter as a guide on how to go about setting up your altar. Many people find the process of building their altar to be a spiritually significant one in itself, and it is also something you can do with children or loved ones.

If you are building your altar with a child, use this as an opportunity to explore why you're choosing certain elements to add to the sacred space. You can construct either a Samhain altar, an ancestor altar, or both.

When building your ancestor altar, you can take the opportunity to share stories about your loved ones and ancestors with those around you. You can also take the chance of asking the people you are sharing this ritual with—such as your child or family members—if they have any additions they would like to add to the altar, such as a beloved pet or someone else who has made a difference in their lives.

Solitary practitioners can take the opportunity to speak the story of each person added to the altar out loud—these stories can help charge the altar with energy.

Celebrate the Circle of Life and Death

Samhain, and all the other major sabbats, help mark key moments in the cycle of life, death, and rebirth. Samhain is the day of the Horned God's symbolic death before he is reborn on December 21 (Yule). This makes this day the perfect time to think upon—and celebrate—this key cycle that helps nurture the world.

Ideally, a ritual to celebrate the cycle of life and death should be performed outside, though you can do so inside if there is no other option.

You Will Need:

- A few sprigs of rosemary
- A white and black candle
- Black, red, and white ribbons (there should be a set of three equal length ribbons for each person participating in the ritual)
- An altar

You can perform this ritual as a solitary practitioner or with a group of other practitioners.

Instructions:

1. Decorate your altar with symbols of life and death
2. Start the ritual by casting a circle if it is part of your regular practice.

3. Start by welcoming Samhain and the approaching winter. Acknowledge the day as one of death and dying, during which you honor the ancestors, the Dark Mother, and the Ancient Ones.

4. Place the rosemary on your altar. If performing this ritual as part of a coven or group, pass the rosemary around first and ensure everyone handles it. Rosemary is a symbol of remembrance, and when placing the sprigs on the altar, vocally acknowledge the night as one on which you remember the people who have gone before you.

5. Turn to the north and welcome the spirits of the earth, who symbolize death.

6. Turn to the east and welcome the spirits of the air, who will be by a living being's side as they depart the world of the living.

7. Turn to the south and welcome the spirits of the air, who will transform the dead into death.

8. Turn to the west and welcome the water spirits, who will carry all living beings through the river of life.

9. Light the black candle and acknowledge the turning of the Wheel of the Year into darkness.

10. Light the white candle and acknowledge that light awaits at the end of darkness.

11. Each person should take their set of ribbons. White stands for life, black for death, and red for rebirth; you should acknowledge this symbolism and the memory of those you have lost. After doing so, start braiding the ribbons together. Focus on the memories of lost loved ones while doing so.

12. While you braid, vocally acknowledge the cycle of life, death, and rebirth.

13. The knotted ribbons should be placed on each person's personal altar or another place of significance for each individual.

Ancestor Meditation Ritual

Samhain is a time to honor the dead and commune with those who have gone before. The thin veil between the worlds makes it the best time of year to communicate with the dead.

One technique people often find effective when communing with the dead is meditation. Remember that everyone's experience during meditation differs, and you may find it easier to communicate with loved ones who have passed through the veil through another method.

While some people can commune with specific loved ones, others find meditation provides a way to communicate with archetypes representing the dead. For example, if someone you loved was a war veteran, you may encounter another veteran from the same war rather than the specific person you are thinking of. However, communing and meeting these individuals is still a gift and one that you should honor. They often choose to appear to people to provide them with specific messages, so pay attention to what they tell you and how they act.

Do not perform this meditation ritual with expectations—this is a time to think of everyone who has gone before you, both the good and bad. Some of your ancestors would have been great people, but others may not have been that great—and that is okay. Each of them played some part in shaping the person you are today, and this is a chance to think of them all.

If you find meditation works for you, the first step in an ancestor meditation ritual is to set the mood. Take some time going through old photo albums and keepsakes, allowing you to absorb the energies of those you have lost.

This ritual can be performed anywhere, though night is preferable. Firstly, build your ancestor altar—if performing the ritual outdoors, erect a temporary one on a flat rock or tree stump. Then decorate it. Also feel free to light a candle or some incense.

Then, sit—or stand, though sitting is more comfortable—and close your eyes, breathing deeply. Take a moment to reflect, keeping in mind that you embody the ancestors and loved ones who have come before you. Think about the strengths and weaknesses of your family members and how they have all come together in you.

Recite your genealogy as far back as possible, naming each person you're thinking of and giving a succinct description of their life and importance to you. You should also acknowledge the ancestors you do not know but who are still part of you.

As mentioned, you may encounter an ancestor or archetype during this meditation. If you do, ensure to thank them for visiting. While their words and actions may not make sense immediately, they are important, and you may find you understand better later, so make a note of what they say and do.

Plan a Cemetery Celebration

As mentioned, Samhain is a time of honoring the dead, and one way to do so is by visiting their grave at the cemetery. If you can, visit your loved ones and tend to their graves, keeping memories of the time you spent with them in mind. You can also place an offering on their graves, such as a fresh bouquet of flowers, dried herbs—especially those associated with Samhain, such as rosemary and sage—or freshwater. You can also leave an offering that was personally meaningful to the person whose grave you are visiting, such as a favorite book.

You can also visit graves that seem to have been abandoned or do not have visitors. Check with the person running the cemetery if you can leave offerings at these graves. Even if you cannot always do so, tending the graves and clearing them of fallen leaves and other debris is a good way to honor the forgotten dead.

In the late 1800s and early 1900s, it was popular to have picnics in cemeteries to share a meal with the dead. This tradition is banned in many graveyards and cemeteries to protect them against littering. However, you can double-check the rules at the cemetery where your loved one is buried. If it is allowed, you can also consider sharing a small meal near their grave to include their spirit in your meal.

When planning a cemetery or graveyard celebration, check the rules. Some graveyards explicitly prohibit picnicking or eating on the premises, while others limit the types of offerings you can lay on a person's grave. These rules are often meant to protect the graves in the cemetery, so be respectful and tailor your celebration around them.

Perform Bonfire Magic

Samhain is often celebrated with bonfires, making it a good time to practice bonfire magic. This ritual can be performed by independent practitioners and covens and is a perfect addition to any Samhain celebration involving a bonfire.

Once you have a bonfire going, write down a habit you want to free yourself from. Think about your desire to release this habit and imagine yourself adopting healthier habits in the coming New Year.

While doing so, toss the paper with the habit you have written down into the bonfire.

This ritual can also be performed around a fireplace if you cannot host a bonfire outside.

Perform a Ritual to Mark the End of the Harvest

Samhain also marks the end of the harvest season and serves as a welcome to winter, when very little grows. This makes it a key part of the Wheel of the Year, and it is a time to celebrate the abundance the year has given you.

You Will Need:

- An altar decorated with signs of late fall (such as items that symbolize the dead and the spirit world, harvest foods, nuts and berries, dried leaves and acorns, a filled cornucopia, mulled cider/wine/mead, or any other items you find important)
- A loaf of dark bread and apple cider or wine
- The straw you can use to make a straw man or woman

This ritual is ideally performed with family, loved ones, or a coven, though you can modify it for a solo practitioner. You can perform it on a single day or daily for three days, culminating in Samhain.

Instructions:

1. To begin the ritual, prepare a meal for your loved ones. The meal should emphasize the fruit of the recent harvest season, including fruit, vegetables, and wild game meat if possible (and if you consume meat).

2. Decorate the dinner table with candles and a centerpiece that celebrates fall if possible.

3. Before eating, acknowledge the end of the harvest, the coming winter, and the harvest bounty in front of you. Thank the earth for its fruits.

4. Take the cup of cider/wine and guide everyone outside. You can choose any space outside you can all gather in—a vegetable or garden patch would be best, but any area in your front yard will do.

5. Each person involved in the ritual should sprinkle some of the wine/cider on the earth. While doing so, acknowledge the summer that is gone, the winter that is coming, and the end of the harvest.

6. Each person should use straw to make a straw man or woman. Bring it with you as you reenter your home.

7. Place your own straw man/woman at the table with a seat and plate of his/her own. Serve him food first.

8. Break a few crumbs from the dark bread and toss it outside for the birds.

9. Share a meal with your loved ones, keeping the straw man/King of Winter in his place of honor. He should stay there throughout the season. Once the season is over, you should place him in the garden to watch over the new seedlings before burning him in a Beltane ritual.

10. After finishing your meal, put any leftovers in the garden for the animals to eat.

11. Finish the night by celebrating around a bonfire, playing games, or telling scary stories.

This ritual is the perfect time to involve your children in your practice. They can help you gather the fruit and vegetables for the meal, make the King of Winter from straw, and feed the birds and other animals with bread crumbs and leftovers. Explain the importance of the harvest and sharing your bounty with other creatures while you do so, and explain why honoring the King of Winter is as important as celebrating the fall and the harvest season.

Ritual to Honor Lost Loved Ones

You can perform this relatively simple ritual with children, other loved ones, and coven members. It is a good option for practitioners performing a ritual for the first time and those who want something that children can be involved in from start to finish.

For this ritual, you should set up your Samhain altar with the help of your children. If they are too young to use candles safely, you can add LED candles and tea lights instead.

Ask your children—and other friends, family, and coven members—if there are people they would like to include on the altar. This can include pets and other animals they may have had a bond with. You should also add some photos and mementos of loved ones who have gone before you.

You Will Need:

- An empty plate (to pass around)

- Food to use as an offering (something plain, like bread, so that children are not tempted to eat it during the ritual instead)

- A cup with a drink in it that everyone can share (this can be milk, cider, or any other drink that both adults and children can have. If you are not comfortable sharing a cup, you can also use individual cups or glasses)

Start the ritual by casting a circle if doing so is a part of your normal practice.

Instructions:

1. Ask everyone to gather around the altar and take a few moments to think about the family members and loved ones each of you has lost. For children too young to know a deceased loved one, ask them to think about living the family members and others who are important to them. Reassure them that thinking about a lost pet is

okay, too.

2. Start the ritual by acknowledging the importance of Samhain and your celebration of the people you have lost. Vocally acknowledge each person you will honor, starting with those who have recently died. You do not need to recite entire genealogies, but you should acknowledge those most important to you. If you want, you can add information about who each person/pet was. Others can join in with their acknowledgments.

3. Once you have all acknowledged people you have lost, pass the plate around with the food offerings on it. Each person should take a little.

4. Once each member has an offering, you should approach the altar one at a time, working your way from the oldest to the youngest. Leave your offering on the altar in a dedicated bowl/plate.

5. Ask everyone to pray to the gods or deities they follow or your ancestors, acknowledging their importance and asking them to share in the offerings. For smaller children, this can be as simple as just saying "Thank you"—you can say this on behalf of the littlest ones if need be.

6. Pass the cup around—or ask everyone to get their cups. Take a sip in honor of your ancestors, acknowledging this fact as you do so. If you are passing around a single cup, invite the person you are passing it to share in the drink.

7. Place the cup on the altar when everyone has had a sip. If you use individual cups, place a single cup on the altar. Join hands, close your eyes, and acknowledge and thank your ancestors. Take a moment to reflect quietly on your loved ones before ending the ritual in your preferred manner—sharing a meal with your loved ones if possible.

Other ways to celebrate Samhain, focusing on the spiritual side of things, include spells, charms, baths, prayers, and blessings. The next two chapters will cover all these topics, ensuring you're ready for everything Samhain brings.

Chapter 9: Spells, Charms, and Baths

Spell preparation.
https://pixabay.com/images/id-5659775/

Samhain is the spiritual gate between the lighter and darker parts of the year. It is also a divider between our past and present. With the veil between the worlds made thinner—and us being able to communicate with the inhabitants of the spiritual world at this time of the year—anything becomes possible. However, to learn from the past and for us to invite our ancestors, deities, and other spiritual allies, we sometimes need a little help from nature's magic. This chapter's spells, charms, and baths are designed to bring forth this magic and enhance your powers. With their help, you will receive messages from the spiritual world and interpret them correctly.

You'll also charge your heart with power and gain the ability to bring love into your life. After all, love is the core of every human relationship. All of us are motivated by love in one way or another. However, all love spells and charms should only be cast between consensual parties. You should never cast any spell on others without them approving it first, and, above all, all spells and charms are meant to be positive activities you can participate in during Samhain. They should never be used as part of dark magic rituals. You can use smudging, incense, or anything else you feel necessary to banish negativity from your space and attract all the positive energy you need for your Samhain celebration. To avoid mixing negative energy into them, even accidentally, make sure you cleanse your space before performing any spells.

Ancestor Inviting Spell

Ancestral spirits can be your greatest source of wisdom.

You will need:

- Several black and white candles
- A container
- A representation of your ancestors on your altar or sacred place
- Your spell

To enact this spell:

- At night, when the moon is high, turn off all your lights and place one candle in the center of your altar, with the others around it.
- Light the main candle while reciting the following spell:

   "With this light, I invite you (the name of your ancestors)

   and ask you to join me to celebrate this magical night.

   I welcome my departed loved ones into this home and honor their presence amongst us."

- If you are working in a group, each person involved in the ritual should light one of the remaining candles while sharing something about one of the ancestors you have invited.
- If you are working alone, you can remember each ancestor with a sentence or two, depending on how much time you have.
- When the candles have burned down, thank your ancestors for joining you on this night.

A Simple Samhain Wish Spell

With this straightforward spell, you can make all your wishes come true at Samhain. It is performed during the night and only requires one ingredient.

You will need:

- A glass of juice (preferably organic)

To enact this spell:

1. Pour a glass of organic juice and take it outside. If you cannot leave your home, stand at your window so that you can look at the moon.

2. Set your gaze on the moon and tell her what you wish for. Make sure that you paint as detailed a picture as possible.

3. Raise your glass to the moon and recite the following:

   "Goddess of the Moon, look and see

   This drink that I offer thee

   It is yours for all you do

   O benevolent one of bright hue."

4. Pour the juice on the ground and thank the moon for her assistance. Your wish will be granted soon.

A Spell for Releasing the Past

This spell is perfect for releasing all the pent-up emotions you harbor due to past traumatic experiences. With them, you will also banish the harmful energy from your body, liberating your inner power.

You will need:

- A pen
- Paper
- 1 candle or bonfire.

To enact this spell:

1. Make a list of negative emotions you wish to banish from within yourself. They can be related to people, events, or anything else that brings up harmful feelings.

2. Go outside and either light a bonfire or candle. You can also light a candle in your home—just make sure you have the moon in your sights.

3. Look up at the moon and then look down at your paper and read the list aloud.

4. Put your list into the fire to burn it while reciting the following:

   "With this fire, I banish anything harmful.

   Now my mind and spirit will be clean,

   And I will renew my strength from within."

Dream Ancestor Connection

This is another simple spell to invite your ancestors to join you in your Samhain celebration—this time in your dreams.

You will need:

- Paper
- A pen
- A representation of your ancestor
- A comfortable bed

To enact this spell:

- Before you go to bed on Samhain, say the name of the ancestor you want to connect with in your dreams.
- Hold their picture or personal item that symbolizes your connection to them while saying the following:

  "My beloved (ancestor's name or relation to you)

  I invite you into my dreams tonight

  to ask you for your advice.

  I require your strength and wisdom

  for only this can provide me guidance."

- Leave a piece of paper and a pen by your bed—in case you wake up during the night and want to write down the message your ancestor sent you.
- Lie down, close your eyes, and wait for your dream—and your ancestor—to come.

A Spell for Abundance

This spell will help you invite luck into your life at Samhain. This luck will accompany you through the rest of the year, filling your life with an abundance of everything you need. You will gain everything you desire, even if it takes time.

You will need:

- A candle
- A pendant
- String

To enact this spell:

- Loop the string around the pendant and secure it by tying it before lighting the candle.

- Hold the pendant above the flame and start moving it back and forth while chanting the following:

  "As this candle flickers, this pendant will pass good energy and fortune to me.

  I will gain wealth, power, knowledge, and influence.

  This pendant I will pass into power,

  to attract wealth, power, and influence, come to me!"

- Repeat the spell three times, and then tie the string around your neck to keep this new source of energy close to your body.

- Wear the pendant until you feel life is filled with all the abundance you need, occasionally recasting the spell whenever you feel low on luck.

A Spell to Deepen Love Between Two People

While you cannot create love out of anything, you can use this spell to deepen the connection between you and your loved one if the sentiment is already there.

You will need:

- 2 red apples
- 1 pink or red candle
- Pink or red string
- A Pen
- Paper

To enact this spell:

1. Place your candle on your altar or table and light it.

2. Take the pen and paper and write down your name and your loved one's name.

3. Fold the piece of paper into a square, hiding the names.

4. Cut the apples in half, and place one half from each apple in front of you.

5. Put the folded piece of paper between the two apple halves while holding these closely together.

6. Take your string and tie it around both apple halves to keep them firmly embraced.

7. Take your apple outside and bury it in your garden while reciting these words:

"Our love is bound by this spell.

As the passion burns through us

and kindness rushes through us,

Our love is forever bound by this spell."

8. Let your candle burn all the way, and do not forget to say thanks to nature once you start to feel the deepening of your relationship.

A Spell to Sever Ties with Your Past

Sometimes, the only way to re-invite positive energy into your life and magical practice is to completely sever ties with someone or something that hurt you in the past.

You will need:

- A piece of black string
- A small black candle
- A fireproof container
- Tape
- Scissors

To enact this spell:

1. Place your candle in the container and light it.

2. Use the tape to secure one end of the black string at one side of the container's rim and the other end on the other side.

3. Close your eyes and envision this string symbolizing your connection to the person, event, or item harmed in the past.

4. When you feel ready, use your scissors to cut the string right down the middle while imagining that you are also severing all emotional ties with the harmful entity.

5. Now, recite the following:

"I hereby release this from my heart,

as it no longer belongs there.

The new connection, I invite in its place.

An emotion that is true and fair."

6. Place the container outside your home or on your windowsill.

7. Allow the candle to burn down and enjoy being free from all the negativity caused by whatever you just severed ties with.

A Protection Charm against Unwanted Spirits

Unfortunately, among those spirits that cross the divide at Samhain, there are also harmful spirits you want to stay far away from. Use this charm to keep unwanted spirits away from you and your loved ones.

You will need:

- Rosemary
- 1 clove of garlic
- Salt
- A black stone
- A red cloth
- Black cord
- A picture of the fifth pentacle of the moon

To enact this spell:

- Mix the rosemary with salt, and imbue the mixture with your intention.
- Pour the mixture upon the red cloth you have placed on your altar or sacred place beforehand.
- Add the garlic clove to the mixture and take the black stone into your hands. Envision its protective energy traveling toward you and uniting with your intention of keeping unwanted spirits at bay.
- As soon as you feel this energy encompassing your body, lower the stone onto the herbs.
- Take the representation of the fifth pentacle of the moon and fold it in half by holding it away from your body. This will send the negativity away from you.
- Place the folded picture on the herbs and stone.
- Join the four corners of the cloth at the center and secure them with the black cord. Make sure you tie a triple knot for added security but leave enough cord—you'll need it to hang up the charm.
- Step outside with the charm in your hand and prepare to place it on your front door by taking a deep breath and envisioning the desired outcome.
- At this point, you should sense a barrier that will allow you to keep

unwanted spirits away from your home but that enables you to grant those who wish to invite permission. When you do, repeat the following spell:

"On Samhain night, as all spirits roam,

I cast this spell with herb and stone,

While spirits will wander from their eternal home,

from their spectral haunt, I shall seal my home.

And by hanging this charm,

I'll receive no harm."

- Hang your newly empowered charm on your door and let it do its job. It will protect you on the night of Samhain and keep away any lingering malicious spirits that may have stayed in this world after the veil has been restored.

- You may dispose of the charm anytime you feel that you do not need any additional protection.

Samhain Cleansing Bath Spell

Take this bath on the night of Samhain to banish negative energy from your life and manifest your wishes through your inner power.

You will need:

- Black, white, blue, and purple candles (to represent death, life, the god, and goddess)

- Epsom salt and sea salt

- Food coloring (of your choice)

- Essential oils with refreshing scents (such as eucalyptus and citronella)

- Incense (of your choice)

- Moisturizing oil

- Black, white, blue, and purple crystals

To enact this spell:

- Fill your tub with water and add the oils, the food coloring, and the salts.

- Stir the water clockwise to ensure all the ingredients bend together.

- Light the candles and put them at the four corners of your bathtub. While doing this, say the following:

"With this bath, I cleanse my body, soul, and mind,

I am leaving everything that hinders me behind."

- Now place your crystal around the candles and light your incense.

- Enter the bath and let it relax you. Then affirm your intention by inviting the god and the goddess of the moon to help you cleanse yourself.

- Call upon the four elements of nature to lend their power to you. Then remember your living loved ones through the white candle and the dead ones through the black one.

- Close your eyes and envision negative energy leaving your body, mind, and soul. See it enter the water and evaporate from your life through its steam.

- Lie still until you feel cleansed from negativity, and then wash your body.

- When finished, rinse yourself while stating:

"I am now clean of any negativity or harmful spells cast upon me."

- Get out of the bath, dry yourself with a towel, and moisten your body with oil.

Samhain Beauty Spell

Baths are not the only tools for cleansing your body and soul from negative energy. This simple Samhain spell will help you find the beauty from within, filling your life with positivity and encouraging you to chase dreams.

You will need:

- A mirror
- Moonlight
- A picture of whatever physical characteristic you want to enhance
- A pink candle
- Incense (of your choice)

To enact this spell:

- On the night of Samhain, when the moon is high, take a mirror and walk outside. If you cannot go out, you can open a window to see the moon reflected in the mirror.

- Place the picture on the mirror while saying:

"Sacred moon of Samhain, let the wind carry your light,

let your glow surround my body, and let your shine guide my eyes."

- Repeat this three times and concentrate on the body part you want to change. Then say:

  "Sacred moon of Samhain, shape and mold my body,

  as a rose is granted a blossoming beauty, let me thrive in your light,

  the light that brings me the power of beauty and grants it three times three."

- Repeat this three times as well, and light the pink candle or incense when you have finished.

Chapter 10: Samhain Prayers and Blessings

Apart from rituals and spells connected to the season, your practice can also benefit from uplifting prayers, particularly when celebrating the pagan sabbat of Samhain. This chapter includes various types of prayers and blessings for this holiday. Some are designed to honor your ancestors and the Celtic deities, while others are more about celebrating life around the traditional harvest season. You can also use them during meditation or whenever you need to draw strength during your days at this time of the year. You will also receive a few practical tips for personalizing your prayers and blessings according to your spiritual beliefs. This will help you find a way to take advantage of this holiday, whether your journey takes you toward Druidry, Wicca, or any other form of paganism.

A Prayer for Bountiful Harvest

Whether you wish for plenty of healthy crops in your garden or enjoy a productive harvest in any other area of your life, reciting this prayer at Samhain will help you achieve it. It honors the dying earth that gave its life during harvest to nourish everyone in need. While it will lay dormant in the winter, the prayer will remind you that nature will continue its cycle in the spring.

To ensure nature brings you a plentiful harvest again at every Samhain, say the following prayer:

"The corn has been gathered,

the grain is being prepared, and

the healing herbs are now drying.

Our grapes have been pressed,

our potatoes unearthed, and

our beans are already canned.

After this harvest season,

may our food be ready for winter.

May our souls be ready to give and receive

So, we can eat and live gratefully

for whatever we may have in the following months."

Pagan Ancestor Prayer for Samhain

As you know, during Samhain, the veil between our world and the world of spirits is thinner than ever, which is the best time to communicate with your ancestors. This prayer will help you honor your bloodline so that they can aid you on your life's journey in the coming year. With this prayer, you can express gratitude for the wisdom of those who lived before you—as they made you who you are.

Try to relax your mind as you would do during meditation or yoga, and repeat the following:

"At the night of Samhain, when the divide between the world is thinnest

I call out to those who lived and experienced before me.

Tonight, I honor my ancestors, calling to anyone who carried my blood.

I welcome my ancestors to join me at Samhain

and watch over me tonight and always,

protecting me from bad spirits and guiding me through life.

Tonight, I thank you for the blood that runs in my veins,

for it carries your spirit, which fills my heart,

and tonight, I thank you and will always remember you..."

At this point, you may want to mention the name of a few of your ancestors. Then continue:

"So, with the gift of remembrance

My dead will never be forgotten,

as they live within me,

and within those yet to come."

Wiccan Samhain Blessing

The following blessing is widely popular among Wiccans who wish to be protected from ancestral spirits and, at the same time, express their gratitude while being blessed.

Repeat the following blessing to protect yourself and your loved ones at Samhain:

"On Samhain's Eve,

May our ancestors protect you,

from darkness and malicious spirits among us,

Before the new year begins,

While the old one is saying goodbye,

We honor our dead and old.

To express our gratitude for the bountiful harvest,

we offer it to our ancestors so that they can watch over us,

They'll keep us away from harm,

As we enter the new cycle of life."

Ancient Celtic Samhain Blessing

This is another traditional Samhain blessing that is a homage to the ancestors—only this one originates from the ancient Celtic pagan era. During this period, people expressed their respect for the end of nature's life cycle, which symbolizes letting go of the past and focusing on the future.

Recite the following blessing to honor your Celtic ancestors:

"The veil grows thin at this time, and the dead come closer to us,

We honor them, and we remember those whose footsteps we tread.

As life around us retreats into the bulbs and the roots,

where it waits for the time to pass to bring the flowers and fruits.

As leaves fall and cover the ground,

Mother Nature awaits in stillness profound.

As time stands still for all creatures,

We prepare many feasts.

We seek the wisdom of those gone by,

And ask for help with how to deal with the past.

May we face our shadows and accept our faults,

and may we look now to the future to seek new goals."

Wiccan Food Blessing

This traditional blessing is used to bless the food. For pagans, it doubles as an expression of gratitude for the great harvest and whatever gifts this season may bring.

Here is how to bless your meals when celebrating Samhain:

"May we be blessed with a fruitful harvest,

As the earth quickly turns into darkness,

Blessed be the meal we prepare for family and friends,

For all the abundance of fruits, roots, and bread,

Blessed be nature, who nurtures us with care,

We give our thanks to Samhain and all the crops we gathered.

We wish everyone a blessed Samhain!"

Samhain Prayers for Druids

The following prayers are often recited by Druids, who have a unique way of honoring Samhain and the wonderful benefits this sabbat provides for pagan practices.

Typically, Druids open all Samhain celebrations with the following prayer:

"O great spirits, of the land which upholds us,

the sky that embraces us, and the sea that grounds us.

As we stay in the center as living fire,

let our work be done as we wish to do it."

Grounding for Inspiration

Druids place much emphasis on grounding themselves when seeking inspiration. This prayer will help you with that. Envision your past as a maze of underground roots, representing the foundation of your being. Feel how the roots are grounding you—and how they are always there for you, nourishing you throughout your life's journey.

Light a fire, and when you are ready, you can call upon inspiration from your roots with the following Druidic prayer:

"Our poets, our ancient wordsmiths,

Collect the ancient staves of Knowledge,

And let the eloquence light the fire in our minds."

You may offer tree branches, fruit, dry crops, or anything else you may want to use to the fire while reciting this prayer.

Honoring the Tuatha

As the most influential Celtic spirits, the Tuatha will always be there to help pagans out, which is why Druids often turned to them for guidance. Honoring them with blessings and prayers at Samhain will ensure they hear your call. This can be done either over a fire, water, or a sacred tree.

To do it over the fire, recite the following while anointing your flames with oil or butter:

"O sacred fire of Samhain that transforms me,

let its flame warm my spirit and enlighten my life.

Relight the sacred flames that burn within me,

bring the Tuatha to me."

If you want to do it over water, you will need to say the following while dropping a coin into a sacred well:

"O sacred waters that flow beneath the earth,

help me understand the fluid depths within myself.

To uncover the sacred well that flows within me,

bring the Tuatha to me."

Doing it over a sacred tree will require you to take a branch of the tree and recite the following over it:

"O sacred tree that stands between the realms of land, sky, and sea,

let me feel the power of your depths,

Let me be empowered by your strength.

Revive the sacred tree that thrives within me; bring the Tuatha to me."

Calling on Brigid

Brigid is the pagan goddess who can open many gates and accompany you on your journey, aiding you whenever you need it. You may call upon her at Samhain with this praise:

"O Brigid, sacred goddess of the gates of wisdom,

may I walk on your path as I explore mine."

Repeat this several times while tending to a fire or gazing into a well. As the goddess of domesticity, these are the places where you can easily connect with Brigid. You may also make her an offering to make the prayer even more effective.

Inviting Other Beings

Apart from Brigid, Druids may call other beings living in the spiritual world to their side at Samhain. Badb, Anand, Macha, Airmed, Miach, and Lugh are just some of the ancient Celtic pagan ancestors that can come to someone's aid. Druids can also invite their immediate blood ancestors if they need more of their teachings.

If you decide to go down the latter path, you may do so with the following Druid prayer:

> *"I call out to my closest ancestors*
>
> *Those whose blood I carry.*
>
> *I call out to the ancestors we all learned from.*
>
> *I call out to the ancestors who rest in this land.*
>
> *I call out to the ancestors of my blood, heart, and bone and offer you welcome.*
>
> *I call you as my kin, meet me at the boundary of the worlds, and accept my offering!"*

Make an offering to the ancestors. Then continue with the following:

> *"I call out to the spirits of all the worlds.*
>
> *I call out to my allies from the sacred land of spirits.*
>
> *I call out to the spirits of my land and home,*
>
> *of the mighty sea and vast sky, and offer you welcome.*
>
> *I call you as my kin, meet me at the boundary of the worlds, and accept my offering!"*

After the ritual, make an offering to the spirits, too.

Prayer of Sacrifice

At Samhain, a prayer of sacrifice will also bring you closer to the spirits living in the otherworld. You should include an intention that expresses your willingness to share hospitality to form an alliance with these spirits.

For example, your prayer can read something like this:

> *"I* invite you to the sacred place I have established for us.
>
> I have brought the worlds together and have summoned your spirits,
>
> As well as the spirits of my ancestors and their gods.
>
> Please come to a place you won't find anywhere else, at any time.
>
> Join now the gathering of gods, the dead, and of sidhe.
>
> I offer you this gift so that I might receive your guidance, should you wish to grant it.
>
> Let my voice arise from this sacred fire,
>
> let my voice carry on into the depths I aspire,
>
> may the spirits accept my offerings,
>
> Their ways are the only ones I keep.
>
> Accept my *Sacrifice!"*

At this point, you show the ancestors the sacred place you have set up for them and the offerings you've made. You ask them to sit with you at this place so that you can entertain them throughout the night by telling stories and singing folk songs. Before parting from the spirits, recite the farewell poem, or speak to them about the quiet joys of kinship.

Divination Prayer

This prayer should be recited for divination, typically combined with other tools you would use for foretelling.

For example, Druids often cast ogham for divination by saying:

"*The* few of us fill a future as fated foreseen,

as we ignore the fights of our foes' fury.

May we foretell the fool's failure, warn of fame,

and predict *who may be granted flawless flourish for playing a fair game.*"

In the end, you should speak an interpretation of what you have seen when casting the ogham.

Closing Prayer

Just as Druids use an opening prayer to commence their rituals, they would also conclude their affairs with a meaningful closing prayer. After making new contacts with the Celtic deities and finding new ways to honor ancestral spirits or make good on your old connections, you should recite the following:

"Wave your hand over the flame.

Let the fire be but flame.

Wave your hand over the water.

Let the well be but water.

Wave your hand over the tree.

Let all *be as it was before; let the ways be closed!*"

Personalizing Samhain Blessings and Prayers

Samhain is a time for remembrance, honoring the dead, and letting go of past grievances. All these activities require a deep connection with your spiritual self—something each of us has unique ways of achieving. For this reason, while the prayers and blessings in this chapter could be a great stepping stone for your journey as they are, it is always a good idea to add your individual touch to them. Remember, pagan practices are about what feels right to you. Samhain is also the time of the year when many empowering spells are cast and divinations made. This is another powerful reason to personalize the prayers and blessings you recite during this sabbat.

One way to personalize Samhain prayers is by inviting your loved ones to participate in them. Even if they are not pagan practitioners, being invited to a Samhain-themed supper can get them in the mood for saying a prayer or blessing. This is particularly true if you display a picture or mementos of the dearly departed you were all fond of.

Lighting candles is another way to make a Samhain blessing your own. Candle flame can be the perfect alternative to the traditional Samhain bonfires if you cannot attend one. Light candles in the color of Samhain— black, white, blue, and purple—or whatever color you prefer before reciting your blessing. This will get you in the mood for making a spiritual connection. You can also use crystals in the same colors to further enhance the effect.

You may also pour a small amount of beer, wine, or any special drink you have on hand for Samhain into a glass or goblet. Offering this to the dead upon your altar or table when saying a prayer or blessing is another spin on the traditional Pagan custom.

If you live in a larger community, you can share your way of celebrating Samhain with others. Pagan prayers are typically accompanied by offerings, oaths, healing, divination, or other rites of magic. Thus, what better way to empower these than sharing the flame that connects you to the spirit of Samhain? Larger pagan communities often light a central fire—and the individual members take coal from it to relight their hearth after extinguishing it during this sabbat. If you are a solitary practitioner, you can always envision a perpetual flame and focus on this when relighting your fire and saying a blessing or prayer.

Giving to the less fortunate has always been part of the ancient Samhain tradition. It does not matter how much you have to offer. Whether you celebrate with a large community or not, you can always find someone whom you can share food and other small offerings. If you have the means, you can also help someone with greater needs than yourself. Even if you do not have the means, treating an elderly neighbor to a meal will lift their spirits and yours, too. The possibilities for giving and helping people on Samhain are endless—and doing this at Samhain while reciting a traditional blessing will return to you with unmatched benefits.

Conclusion

As one of the most well-known pagan sabbats, Samhain has always been celebrated with great spiritual conventions and lavish festivities. Its historical connections to the ancient Celtic pagan culture are undeniable, but so are its ties to the modern traditions of Halloween. Throughout the many years it has been celebrated, Samhain has evolved to fit the needs of those who follow the ancient customs and modern Wiccans or Druids alike. With so many symbols, herbs, candles, stones, and other tools available for you to honor Samhain, you can celebrate this magical time of the year in a manner that seems right to you.

You have learned about the deities and spirits associated with this holiday. You have also discovered what this time of the year ultimately represents: The gateway between life and death. At Samhain, the veil between our world and the spiritual world is at its thinnest. You can invite any helpful soul through it to your side—from the crones and goddesses living in the spiritual world and helping those who cross find peace with your long-lost ancestors to malicious spirits; the remnants of those who could not find peace may also cross the divide. Thus, you must be careful with your spiritual practices at this time of the year. Fortunately, with proper preparation, you can gain power and wisdom from the spirits with a positive influence and protect yourself and your loved ones from harm.

While setting up an altar is not required for practicing magic at Samhain, creating this sacred place can help you focus your mind on your intention and the tools you use for each spell or ritual. Whether you are familiar with spiritual practices or are just delving into them, there are plenty of Samhain-themed crafts and decorations to make to get into the spirit of the sabbat. Creating them may also relax you, serving as mental preparation for cleansing yourself and your space so only positive energy can remain.

Make sure you prepare lots of herbs and plants with healing and cleansing properties as you will need them during your Samhain activities. You may also find it helpful to have crystals at hand. You can draw energy from crystals if you need added support when casting a protection spell or performing a divination ritual. Choose stones in the same colors as the candles you'll be using—the traditional colors of Samhain. Do not forget to gather some essential oils for your cleansing bath, which you'll take on the full moon of Samhain.

The spells, rituals, blessings, and prayers you have found in this book can be incorporated into your Samhain activities, regardless of your pagan practices. You can even personalize them further to ensure they bring you the most benefits. Some you might take on your pagan journey even after this sabbat has passed. You can also introduce them to your family, encouraging them to participate in the preparations and the festivities. Whether they belong to the pagan community or have a different spiritual background, they will be happy to recite prayers or blessings with you—especially those created to honor your common ancestors or bring love and abundance to all. And, if nothing else, your friends and family are sure to enjoy preparing some delicious traditional Samhain meals and implementing them into their customs.

Here's another book by Mari Silva that you might like

Your Free Gift
(only available for a limited time)

Thanks for getting this book! If you want to learn more about various spirituality topics, then join Mari Silva's community and get a free guided meditation MP3 for awakening your third eye. This guided meditation mp3 is designed to open and strengthen ones third eye so you can experience a higher state of consciousness. Simply visit the link below the image to get started.

https://spiritualityspot.com/meditation

References

13 ways to celebrate yuletide. (n.d.). Circle Sanctuary. https://www.circlesanctuary.org/index.php/celebrating-the-seasons/13-ways-to-celebrate-yuletide

Brethauer, A. (2019, December 2). Awesome Yule tree decorations for your Winter Solstice holiday. The Peculiar Brunette. https://www.thepeculiarbrunette.com/8-diy-yule-winter-solstice-holiday-tree-ornaments/

Corkhill, L. (2018, November 20). Ten ways to celebrate Yule. The Green Parent. https://thegreenparent.co.uk/articles/read/ten-ways-to-celebrate-yule

Decorate your own Yule Altar. (n.d.). Castlefest. https://winter.castlefest.nl/en/blog/vana-grimoire-yule-altaar

Dictionary.com. (2021, December 16). What's the difference between "Yule" and "Christmas"? Thesaurus.Com. https://www.thesaurus.com/e/ways-to-say/yuletide/

Difference between Christmas and yule (with table). (n.d.). Askanydifference.Com. https://askanydifference.com/difference-between-christmas-and-yule-with-table/

Dunn, M. (2020, December 16). The story of Yule, the raucous Viking celebration of winter that inspired Christmas. All That's Interesting. https://allthatsinteresting.com/yule-viking-christmas

Eisinger, N. (2021, December 15). Rituals of Winter Solstice and how to decorate your altar or make a Yule Log. Glad.Is. https://glad.is/blogs/articles/decorate-your-altar-for-winter-solstice

Facebook. (n.d.). Facebook.Com. https://www.facebook.com/PaganCider/posts/mead-the-oldest-drink-of-them-all-the-pagan-mead-is-about-to-be-released-into-a-/1020643751398720/

Farrell, N. (2019, December 13). How to celebrate the winter solstice, the shortest day of the year. Sunset Magazine; Sunset.

https://www.sunset.com/lifestyle/wellness/winter-solstice-rituals-nature

Geller. (2016, November 18). The Wild Hunt. Mythology.Net. https://mythology.net/norse/norse-concepts/the-wild-hunt/

Gooden, T. (2020, December 21). The curious past and lasting importance of Yule. Nerdist. https://nerdist.com/article/yule-curious-past-and-present-day-importance/

Greenberg, M. (2020, November 30). The legend of the Wild Hunt: The complete guide (2022). MythologySource; Mike Greenberg, Ph.D. https://mythologysource.com/the-wild-hunt/

Imagining History. (2020, December 1). Ancient origins of the Christmas Tree - A guide for kids. Imagininghistory. https://www.imagininghistory.co.uk/post/ancient-origins-of-the-christmas-tree

Insight Network, Inc. (n.d.). Insight timer - #1 free meditation app for sleep, relax & more. Insighttimer.Com. https://insighttimer.com/herbalmoongoddess/guided-meditations/winter-solstice-meditation-for-yule

Journeys, S. E. (2011, December 22). Yule traditions and symbols. Sacred Earth Journeys. https://www.sacredearthjourneys.ca/blog/traditions-and-symbols-of-yule/

Kelsey. (2021, November 9). How to celebrate the Pagan Christmas holiday Yule. Blondes & Bagels. https://blondesandbagels.com/how-to-celebrate-the-pagan-christmas-holiday-yule/

Mankey, J. (2017, December 11). Krampus: The Horned God of yuletide. Raise the Horns. https://www.patheos.com/blogs/panmankey/2017/12/krampus-horned-god-yuletide/

Patterson, R. (2020, December 11). Working magic: Yule/winter solstice spells. Beneath the Moon. https://www.patheos.com/blogs/beneaththemoon/2020/12/working-magic-yule-winter-solstice-spells/

Perez, Y. (n.d.). How to celebrate yule. CityWide Stories. https://citywidestories.com/2017/12/08/how-to-celebrate-yule/

SanSone, A. (2019, January 18). Here are the best evergreens for adding year-round beauty to your backyard. Country Living. https://www.countryliving.com/gardening/garden-ideas/g25367864/best-evergreen-shrubs/

Santa and Odin - Christmas and yule. (2017, December 15). Sons of Vikings. https://sonsofvikings.com/blogs/history/viking-origins-of-christmas-yule-traditions

Saturnalia. (2017, December 5). HISTORY. https://www.history.com/topics/ancient-rome/saturnalia

Sharma, S. (2022, February 16). The best crystals for self-love, to attract new love and heal heartbreak. Elle India. https://elle.in/crystals-for-love/

Stokes, V. (2021, June 17). Love, health, success, or wealth? How to use crystals to manifest your desires. Healthline. https://www.healthline.com/health/crystals-for-manifestation

Teens, C. P. L. (n.d.). Discover Winter Solstice and Yule. Cantonpl.Org. https://www.cantonpl.org/blogs/post/discover-winter-solstice-yule/

Thompson, A. (2019, December 20). The many stories behind the origins of yule. Mental Floss. https://www.mentalfloss.com/article/610507/history-of-yule

Ward, K. (2021, October 22). How to celebrate Yule. Cosmopolitan. https://www.cosmopolitan.com/lifestyle/a38039639/how-to-celebrate-yule/

Weaver, S. (2009, December 18). The Yule Goat. Storey Publishing. https://www.storey.com/article/yule-goat/

What is Yule? (n.d.). Almanac.Com. https://www.almanac.com/content/what-yule-log-christmas-traditions

Wigington, P. (2007a, May 13). History of Yule. Learn Religions. https://www.learnreligions.com/history-of-yule-2562997

Wigington, P. (2007b, November 7). Deities of the winter solstice. Learn Religions. https://www.learnreligions.com/deities-of-the-winter-solstice-2562976

Wigington, P. (2007c, November 13). Hold a solitary goddess ritual for Yule, the winter solstice. Learn Religions. https://www.learnreligions.com/yule-goddess-ritual-for-solitaries-2562986

Wigington, P. (2008a, November 19). How to decorate your Yule altar for the Winter Solstice. Learn Religions. https://www.learnreligions.com/setting-up-a-yule-altar-2562996

Wigington, P. (2008b, November 21). Hold a blessing ceremony for your Yule tree. Learn Religions. https://www.learnreligions.com/blessing-your-yule-tree-2562975

Wigington, P. (2009a, April 14). The triple goddess: Maiden, Mother, and Crone. Learn Religions. https://www.learnreligions.com/maiden-mother-and-crone-2562881

Wigington, P. (2009b, November 15). Ten magical gifts to share for Yule. Learn Religions. https://www.learnreligions.com/magical-gifts-to-share-for-yule-2562952

Wigington, P. (2009c, November 25). Pagan rituals to celebrate Yule, the winter solstice. Learn Religions. https://www.learnreligions.com/about-yule-rituals-2562970

Wigington, P. (2013a, February 23). How do pagans honor their ancestors? Learn Religions. https://www.learnreligions.com/ancestor-worship-in-pagan-cultures-2562898

Wigington, P. (2013b, November 14). Eight things to hang on a Pagan holiday tree. Learn Religions. https://www.learnreligions.com/things-to-hang-on-holiday-tree-2563022

Wigington, P. (2016, August 13). 12 simple prayers for the winter solstice. Learn Religions. https://www.learnreligions.com/about-yule-prayers-4072720

Wright, M. (2008, October 30). How to decorate a Wiccan yule altar. Synonym.Com; Synonym. https://classroom.synonym.com/how-to-decorate-a-wiccan-yule-altar-12078392.html

Yule. (n.d.). Controverscial.Com. https://www.controverscial.com/Yule.htm

Yule. (2018, March 19). Our Lady of the Woods. https://www.ladywoods.org/yule/

Yule history and origins. (n.d.). Renstore.Com. https://stores.renstore.com/history-and-traditions/yule-history-and-origins

Yule origins, lore, legends, and customs. (n.d.). Unityunitarian.Org http://www.unityunitarian.org/uploads/6/1/0/3/6103699/high_feasts_holy_days_lesson_9b.pdf

Yule symbols. (2022, January 19). Ancient Symbols. https://www.ancient-symbols.com/symbols-by-subjects/yule-symbols

Yuletide Lore. (n.d.). Angelfire.Com. https://www.angelfire.com/wa3/angelline/yule_lore.htm

Wigington, P. (n.d.). Pagan Rituals to Celebrate Yule, the Winter Solstice. Learn Religions https://www.learnreligions.com/about-yule-rituals-2562970

Yule. (2021, October 4). The Goddess and the Greenman. https://www.goddessandgreenman.co.uk/yule

9 Thyme Magical Properties and Spiritual Uses. (2021, October 27). Angelical Balance. https://www.angelicalbalance.com/spiritual-protection/thyme-magical-properties/

Angelica Spiritual Meaning And Magical Uses. (n.d.). Sentientmetaphysics.Com. https://sentientmetaphysics.com/angelica-meanings/

Barbara. (2016, January 15). How to make a Brigid Doll (Straw Doll). Colorful Crafts. https://colorful-crafts.com/how-to-make-a-brigid-doll-straw-doll/

Bauer, E. (n.d.). Flourless Lemon Almond Cake. Simply Recipes
https://www.simplyrecipes.com/recipes/flourless_lemon_almond_cake/

Bible Gateway passage: John 8:12 - English Standard Version. (n.d.). Bible
Gateway.
https://www.biblegateway.com/passage/?search=John%208%3A12&version=
ESV

Bible Gateway passage: Leviticus 12 - New International Version. (n.d.).
Bible
Gateway.https://www.biblegateway.com/passage/?search=Leviticus%2012&ve
rsion=NIV

Bible Gateway passage: Luke 2 - New International Version. (n.d.). Bible
Gateway.
https://www.biblegateway.com/passage/?search=Luke%202&version=NIV

Blanchard, T. (2021, May 22). 10 Spiritual Benefits of Bay Leaves (For
Attracting Abundance & Positivity). OutofStress.Com.
https://www.outofstress.com/spiritual-benefits-of-bay-leaves/

BRIGID. (2019, May 30). Goddess Gift.
https://www.goddessgift.com/goddess-info/meet-the-goddesses/brigid/

Brigid: Lady of the Sacred Flame. (n.d.). The Goddess Circle.,
https://thegoddesscircle.net/visionary-writing/brigid-lady-sacred-flame

Brigid: Triple Goddess of the Flame (Health, Hearth, & Forge). (n.d.).
Mimosa Books & Gifts. https://www.mimosaspirit.com/blogs/news/brigit-
triple-goddess-of-the-flame-health-hearth-the-forge

Brigid's Cross: How to Make One for Imbolc * Wicca-Spirituality.com.
(n.d.). Wicca-Spirituality.Com. https://www.wicca-spirituality.com/brigids-
cross.html

BRIGID-unabridged. (2019, June 3). Goddess Gift.
https://www.goddessgift.com/goddess-info/meet-the-goddesses/brigid/brigid-
unabridged/

Build a Campfire. (n.d.). Smokey Bear.
https://smokeybear.com/en/prevention-how-tos/campfire-safety/how-to-
build-your-campfire

Candlemas, a festival of lights. (n.d.). Alimentarium.Org.
https://www.alimentarium.org/en/fact-sheet/candlemas-festival-lights

Candlemas Day, Liturgical History : University of Dayton, Ohio. (2022,
March 17). Udayton.Edu. https://udayton.edu/imri/mary/c/candlemas-day-
liturgical-history.php

Celebrating Candlemas in Old Ireland - World Cultures European. (n.d.).
Irishcultureandcustoms.Com.
https://www.irishcultureandcustoms.com/ACalend/Candlemas.html

Chicken & Goat Cheese Pasta. (2017, May 2). Awesome on 20. https://awesomeon20.com/chicken-goat-cheese-pasta/

Collet, N. (2020, January 28). La Chandeleur. French Cultural Center. https://frenchculturalcenter.org/2020/01/28/blog-la-chandeleur-2020/

Corak, R. (2020, February 8). Phoenix Rising: Fire, Water, and Words: Divination with the Goddess Brigid. Agora. https://www.patheos.com/blogs/agora/2020/02/phoenix-rising-fire-water-and-words-divination-with-the-goddess-brigid/

Eason, C. (2016). 1001 spells: The complete book of spells for every purpose. Sterling.

Elm mythology and folklore. (2019, June 12). Trees for Life. https://treesforlife.org.uk/into-the-forest/trees-plants-animals/trees/elm/elm-mythology-and-folklore/

Every Rowan tree has a story. (n.d.). The Present Tree https://thepresenttree.com/blogs/tree-meanings/rowan-tree-meaning

Feb. 2 Christo-pagan Holiday Candlemas, Imbolc, Oimelc, Groundhog Day. (2017, February 27). Seminary. https://northernway.org/school/way/calendar/candlemas.html

Fleckenstein, A. (2014, November 5). 16 Healing Herbs For The Most Amazing Bath Of Your Life. Prevention. https://www.prevention.com/health/health-conditions/a20472817/healing-herbs-to-use-in-a-bath/

Garis, M. G. (2021, March 15). How To Make a Home Altar That Honors Whatever Energetically Empowers You. Well+Good. https://www.wellandgood.com/how-to-make-altar-home-design/

Green, M. (2018, April 3). Sigils: Barcodes for your Brain. Atheopaganism. https://atheopaganism.wordpress.com/2018/04/02/sigils-barcodes-for-your-brain/

Guardian staff reporter. (2000, October 28). The witching hour. The Guardian. http://www.theguardian.com/theguardian/2000/oct/28/weekend7.weekend3

Hammer, J. (2006). Imbolc poems. Journal of Feminist Studies in Religion, 22(1), 75–82. https://doi.org/10.1353/jfs.2006.0009

Hart, A. (n.d.). 3 Ways To Welcome The Warmth Of Spring This Imbolc. The Traveling Witch. https://thetravelingwitch.com/blog/2018-1-15-3-ways-to-welcome-the-warmth-of-spring-this-imbolc

History.com Editors. (2018, April 5). Imbolc. HISTORY. https://www.history.com/topics/holidays/imbolc

Imbolc. (n.d.). Taracelebrations.Org. https://www.taracelebrations.org/celebrations/imbolc

Imbolc / Candlemas. (2021, October 4). The Goddess and the Greenman. https://www.goddessandgreenman.co.uk/imbolc-candlemas

Imbolc - Symbols and Symbolism. (2021, August 25). Symbol Sage. https://symbolsage.com/imbolc-symbols-rituals/

Imbolc Divination Ritual. (2017, February 1). Tess Whitehurst. https://tesswhitehurst.com/imbolc-divination-ritual/

Imbolc: Traditions, Rituals, and Herbs for the pagan Holiday. (n.d.). HERBSTALK. http://www.herbstalk.org/1/post/2021/01/imbolc-traditions-rituals-and-herbs-for-the-pagan-holiday.html

Info. (2020, February 11). Brigid: Survival Of A Goddess. Order of Bards, Ovates & Druids. https://druidry.org/resources/brigid-survival-of-a-goddess

Irish American Mom. (2021, January 31). Explore the Origins of the Ancient Celtic Festival of Imbolc. Irish American Mom. https://www.irishamericanmom.com/explore-the-origins-of-the-celtic-festival-of-imbolc/

Bhagat, D. (n.d.). The origins and practices of holidays: Ostara, Holi, and Purim. Retrieved from Bpl.org website: https://www.bpl.org/blogs/post/the-origins-and-practices-of-holidays-ostara-holi-and-purim

Cameron J. Woods, Collegian Staff. (n.d.). The history of Ostara. Retrieved from Massachusetts Daily Collegian website: https://dailycollegian.com/2004/03/the-history-of-ostara

Dana. (n.d.). alban eilir – The Druid's Garden. Retrieved from The Druid's Garden website: https://druidgarden.wordpress.com/tag/alban-eilir

Journey, N. S. (2016, March 17). A brief history of Ostara. Retrieved from Nature's Sacred Journey website: https://www.patheos.com/blogs/naturessacredjourney/2016/03/a-brief-history-of-ostara

Kyteler, E. (2020, October 20). Symbols of Ostara: Pagan Easter symbols and spiritual meaning. Retrieved from Eclectic Witchcraft website: https://eclecticwitchcraft.com/symbols-of-ostara-pagan-easter-symbols-and-spiritual-meaning

Mark, J. J. (2019). Wheel of the Year. World History Encyclopedia. Retrieved from https://www.worldhistory.org/Wheel_of_the_Year

McAlister, L. (2019, March 22). Alban Eiler – light of the earth. Retrieved from The Celtic Ranch website: https://celticranch.com/blogs/the-celtic-ranch/alban-eiler-light-of-the-earth

The Editors of Encyclopedia Britannica. (2017). Astarte. In Encyclopedia Britannica.

Wigington, P. (n.d.). History of Ostara, the spring equinox. Retrieved from Learn Religions website: https://www.learnreligions.com/history-of-ostara-the-spring-equinox-2562485

Bott, A. (2011, April 23). The modern myth of the Easter bunny. The Guardian.

https://www.theguardian.com/commentisfree/belief/2011/apr/23/easter-pagan-roots

Jensen, S. C. (n.d.). Eostre and the Easter Bunny; a children's story. Soniacjensen.Com. Retrieved from https://dreamlandmagic.soniacjensen.com/stories/eostre.html

Dana. (n.d.). magical eggs – The Druid's Garden. The Druid's Garden. Retrieved from

https://druidgarden.wordpress.com/tag/magical-eggs

Hecate: 13 Ways to Work With the Goddess of Witchcraft, Chalis, Rodriguez, N., Cristi, Julie, Anonymous, Magical Home Protection Powders & Threshold Folk Magic, & 14 CHEAP Witchcraft Supplies at the GROCERY STORE. (2019, July 15). Egg magick: 11 ways to use eggs in your witchcraft. Otherworldly Oracle. https://otherworldlyoracle.com/egg-magick

How to: Make blown egg ornaments. (2011, April 15). Our Best Bites.

https://ourbestbites.com/how-to-make-blown-egg-ornaments

Khaliela. (2020, March 3). Ostara: Eggs and bunnies. Khaliela Wright.

https://khalielawright.com/ostara-eggs-and-bunnies

Klopfer, B. (2015, April 3). How to color Easter eggs with veggies & herbs instead of store-bought dyes. WonderHowTo. https://food-hacks.wonderhowto.com/how-to/color-easter-eggs-with-veggies-herbs-instead-store-bought-dyes-0160965

Thomas, S. S. (2018, September 25). Color magic: A witch's guide to color meanings and energies. Allure. https://www.allure.com/story/color-magic-witchcraft-meanings-guide

Wigington, P. (n.d.-a). Easter eggs: Pagan or not? Learn Religions. Retrieved from https://www.learnreligions.com/easter-eggs-pagan-or-not-2562481

Wigington, P. (n.d.-b). Egg Magic, Folklore, and Superstitions. Learn Religions. Retrieved from https://www.learnreligions.com/egg-magic-and-folklore-2562457

(N.d.). Loc.Gov. Retrieved from https://blogs.loc.gov/folklife/2017/04/decorating-eggs

Stewart, T. (2017, March 14). How to make flower crowns for Ostara. The Witch of Lupine Hollow. https://witchoflupinehollow.com/2017/03/14/how-to-make-flower-crowns-for-ostara

Wigington, P. (n.d.). Crafts for the Ostara Sabbat. Learn Religions. Retrieved from https://www.learnreligions.com/crafts-for-the-ostara-sabbat-4125905

Workman, L. (2014, March 5). Making a cascarone for Spring Equinox. HubPages. https://hubpages.com/holidays/making-a-cascarone

Zenith, A. (2021, March 5). 35 wonderful Ostara crafts, DIY projects, and décor ideas for the Spring Equinox. Witchcrafted Life. https://witchcraftedlife.com/35-wonderful-ostara-crafts-diy-projects-and-decor-ideas-for-the-spring-equinox

Aal, T. (2020, February 5). Creating your own Ostara spring ritual altar. Sage Goddess. https://www.sagegoddess.com/holidays/creating-your-own-ostara-spring-ritual-altar

Wigington, P. (n.d.). How to set up your Ostara altar. Learn Religions. Retrieved from https://www.learnreligions.com/setting-up-your-ostara-altar-2562484

Conneeley, S. (n.d.). Ostara recipes. Blessedbeebooks.Com. Retrieved from https://www.blessedbeebooks.com/ostara-recipes

Gardiner, B. (2021, March 13). An Ostara celebration - A day of perfect balance. The Outdoor Apothecary. https://www.outdoorapothecary.com/ostara-celebration

Grantham, L. M. (2016, March 17). Ostara & Easter recipe: Deviled eggs. Linkedin.Com; LinkedIn. https://www.linkedin.com/pulse/ostara-easter-recipe-deviled-eggs-lisa-marie-rosati

Moone, A. (2018, March 20). Lemon + Lavender Ostara Cake recipe. Plentiful Earth. https://plentifulearth.com/lemon-lavender-ostara-cake-recipe-2

Ostara (mar 20-23). (n.d.). Recipes for a Pagan Soul. Retrieved from http://recipesforapagansoul.weebly.com/ostara-mar-20-23.html

Pollux, A. (2020, February 14). 11 tantalizing Ostara recipes for an effortless picnic. Welcome To Wicca Now. https://wiccanow.com/11-ostara-recipes

Recipes to celebrate Ostara. (2021, March 10). Awesome on 20. https://awesomeon20.com/recipes-to-celebrate-ostara

Wigington, P. (n.d.). Ostara Recipes. Learn Religions. Retrieved from https://www.learnreligions.com/ostara-recipes-2562441

Rego, E. (2016, February 18). Conscious approach, setting intention, and how it recalibrates your relationship with food. Food Practice.

https://foodpractice.com/conscious-approach-setting-intention-and-how-it-recalibrates-your-relationship-with-food/

Bhagat, D. (n.d.). The origins and practices of holidays: Ostara, Holi, and Purim. Retrieved from Bpl.org website: https://www.bpl.org/blogs/post/the-origins-and-practices-of-holidays-ostara-holi-and-purim

Aradia, S. (2015, March 17). Seekers and guides: Garden magick for Ostara. Retrieved from Between the Shadows website: https://www.patheos.com/blogs/betweentheshadows/2015/03/seekers-and-guides-garden-magick-for-ostara

Burchell, C. (2020, March 12). Sow your magic into your seeds this Spring Equinox —. Retrieved from the TINY RITUAL website: https://www.tinyritual.com/guide/ostara-seed-ritual

Wigington, P. (n.d.). Crafts for the Ostara Sabbat. Retrieved from Learn Religions website: https://www.learnreligions.com/crafts-for-the-ostara-sabbat-4125905

Lisa. (2019, April 4). How to plant a magical garden. Retrieved from The Blade and the Cauldron website: http://thebladeandcaludron.com/how-to-plant-a-magical-garden

Caro, T. (2021, April 12). An Enchanting Prayer for Ostara [5 min chant]. Magickal Spot. https://magickalspot.com/prayer-for-ostara

Ostara Chant. (n.d.). Sacredwicca.Com. Retrieved from https://sacredwicca.com/ostara-chant

Ostara: For Eostre. (n.d.). Northernpaganism.Org. Retrieved from https://www.northernpaganism.org/shrines/ostara/writing/for-eostre.html

Ostara: You Are Ostara. (n.d.). Northernpaganism.Org. Retrieved from https://www.northernpaganism.org/shrines/ostara/writing/you-are-ostara.html

Wigington, P. (n.d.). Ostara Rites and Rituals. Learn Religions. Retrieved from https://www.learnreligions.com/ostara-rites-and-rituals-2562469

Wyrd Designs. (2017, March 19). A prayer for Ostara [redux]. Wyrd Designs. https://wyrddesigns.wordpress.com/2017/03/20/a-prayer-for-ostara-redux

igington, P. (n.d.-a). How to set up your Ostara altar. Learn Religions. Retrieved from https://www.learnreligions.com/setting-up-your-ostara-altar-2562484

What do pagans do? (n.d.). Retrieved from Pluralism.org website: https://pluralism.org/what-do-pagans-do

Wigington, P. (n.d.-b). Hold an Ostara Ritual for Solitaries. Retrieved from Learn Religions website: https://www.learnreligions.com/hold-an-ostara-ritual-for-solitaries-2562480

Grossman, P. (2019, June 6). Here's what being a witch really means. The New York Times. Retrieved from https://www.nytimes.com/2019/06/06/style/self-care/witch-healing-hands.html

Ulbrich, B., & Ulbrich, R. (2009). Ostara: Zeremonien und Brauchtum zu Fasnacht, Ostern und Hohe Maien (1st ed.). Engerda, Germany: Arun.

Fairchild, M. (n.d.). 7 spiritual spring cleansing steps. Retrieved from Learn Religions website: https://www.learnreligions.com/spiritual-spring-cleaning-701537

Ward, K. (2021, September 21). Yeah, there's not just *one* type of witch—there are tons of them. Retrieved from Cosmopolitan website: https://www.cosmopolitan.com/lifestyle/a37681530/types-of-witches

Wigington, P. (n.d.-a). Hold a Spring Rebirth Ritual for Ostara. Retrieved from Learn Religions website: https://www.learnreligions.com/hold-a-spring-rebirth-ritual-for-ostara-2562479

Wolfe, S. E. (2020, February 28). 7 ways to celebrate Ostara, the Spring Equinox. Retrieved from The Witch's Guide website: https://thewitchsguide.com/blogs/the-witchs-guide/7-ways-to-celebrate-ostara

Crowomyn, A. (2021, March 18). A theatrical Ostara ritual. Retrieved from Pagan Song: Music for Your Magic website: https://pagansong.com/a-theatrical-ostara-ritual

Pedroja, C. (2017, March 20). 5 ways to celebrate Ostara (the spring equinox) like a modern witch. Retrieved from Female Trouble website: https://medium.com/female-trouble/5-ways-to-celebrate-ostara-the-spring-equinox-like-a-modern-witch-99d51f23d421

Wigington, P. (n.d.-b). History of the pagan Beltane celebration. Learn Religions. Retrieved from https://www.learnreligions.com/the-history-of-beltane-and-may-day-2561657

Wigington, P. (n.d.-a). Beltane Rites and Rituals. Learn Religions. Retrieved from https://www.learnreligions.com/beltane-rites-and-rituals-2561678

The Wheel of the Year: the calendar of pagan festivals explained. (n.d.). Sky HISTORY TV Channel. Retrieved from https://www.history.co.uk/articles/the-wheel-of-the-year-the-calendar-of-pagan-festivals-explained

MythCrafts Team. (2017, May 1). Beltane: Hail the aos Sí! Myth Crafts. https://mythcrafts.com/2017/05/01/beltane-hail-the-aos-si

Let the Beltane fires burn. (n.d.). Blogspot.Com. Retrieved from https://murderiseverywhere.blogspot.com/2016/05/let-beltane-fires-burn.html

Corkhill, L. (2019, April 23). 5 ways to celebrate Beltane. The Green Parent. https://thegreenparent.co.uk/articles/read/5-ways-to-celebrate-beltane

Bhagat, D. (n.d.). The origins and practices of holidays: Beltane and the last day of ridván. Bpl.Org. Retrieved from https://www.bpl.org/blogs/post/the-origins-and-practices-of-holidays-beltane-and-the-last-day-of-ridvan

Beltane fire – the gathering, Southside, 1st of November. (n.d.). Com.Au. Retrieved from https://events.humanitix.com.au/beltane-fire-the-gathering

A detailed history of Beltane. (2013, March 5). Beltane Fire Society. https://beltane.org/a-detailed-history-of-beltane

Beltane. (2021, October 4). The Goddess and the Greenman. https://www.goddessandgreenman.co.uk/beltane

eltane Fire Society. (2020, January 8). Calling our next Green Man for Beltane 2020. Beltane Fire Society. https://beltane.org/2020/01/08/calling-our-next-green-man-for-beltane-2020

eltane myths & legends. (n.d.). Mythinglinks.Org. Retrieved from https://www.mythinglinks.org/Beltane.html

Beltane series: The May Queen. (n.d.). Sabrina's Grimoire. Retrieved from https://sabrinasgrimoire.tumblr.com/post/616154729597255680/beltane-series-the-may-queen

Ede-Weaving, M. (2021, March 30). Sacred sex – the Goddess and God of Beltane. Order of Bards, Ovates & Druids. https://druidry.org/resources/sacred-sex-and-the-goddess-and-god-of-beltane

The folklore of May Day. (n.d.). Myth & Moor. Retrieved from https://www.terriwindling.com/blog/2015/05/beltane.html

Wigington, P. (n.d.). 12 fertility deities of Beltane. Learn Religions. Retrieved from https://www.learnreligions.com/fertility-deities-of-beltane-2561641

Beltane Fire Festival origins and traditions. (2019, April 28). Cooper Cottages. https://coopercottages.com/beltane-fire-festival-origins-and-traditions

Rae, G. (2016, April 14). A simple Beltane ritual. Sage Goddess. https://www.sagegoddess.com/rituals/simple-beltane-ritual

The Newsroom. (2016, April 20). The magic and lore of Edinburgh's Beltane Fire Festival. The Scotsman.

https://www.scotsman.com/whats-on/arts-and-entertainment/magic-and-lore-edinburghs-beltane-fire-festival-1478298

Wigington, P. (n.d.). Hold a Beltane Bonfire Ritual. Learn Religions. Retrieved from

https://www.learnreligions.com/beltane-bonfire-rite-group-ceremony-2561649

Beltane: The Celtic fire festival. (n.d.). OghamArt. Retrieved from

https://oghamart.com/blogs/news/beltane-the-celtic-fire-festival

Bettis, B. (n.d.). Shall we go A-maying? Traditions of mayday. Blogspot.Com. Retrieved from

Wigington, P. (n.d.-b). Beltane Rites and Rituals. Learn Religions. Retrieved from

https://www.learnreligions.com/beltane-rites-and-rituals-2561678

Wigington, P. (n.d.-c). Cernunnos, the wild Celtic god of the Forest. Learn Religions. Retrieved from https://www.learnreligions.com/cernunnos-wild-god-of-the-forest-2561959

Wigington, P. (n.d.-d). Crafts for the Beltane Sabbat. Learn Religions. Retrieved from https://www.learnreligions.com/crafts-for-the-beltane-sabbat-4126784

Wigington, P. (n.d.-e). Magical Pagan and Wiccan symbols. Learn Religions. Retrieved from https://www.learnreligions.com/pagan-and-wiccan-symbols-4123036

Wigington, P. (n.d.-f). Setting up your Beltane altar. Learn Religions. Retrieved from https://www.learnreligions.com/setting-up-your-beltane-altar-2561656

Witch of Howling Creek. (2013, April 10). Ten Beltane decoration ideas. The Witch of Howling Creek. https://witchofhowlingcreek.wordpress.com/2013/04/10/ten-beltane-decoration-ideas

How to celebrate Beltane with kids. (2021, April 27). KidsKonnect. https://kidskonnect.com/articles/how-to-celebrate-beltane

Wigington, P. (n.d.). Celebrating Beltane with kids. Learn Religions. Retrieved from https://www.learnreligions.com/celebrating-beltane-with-kids-2561677

Beltane Fire Society. (2020, January 8). Calling our next Green Man for Beltane 2020. Beltane Fire Society. https://beltane.org/2020/01/08/calling-our-next-green-man-for-beltane-2020

feralwoodfarm. (2021, April 9). Simple recipes for a quick and easy Beltane Feast. Feralwood Farm. http://feralwoodfarm.com/easy-beltane-feast

Info. (2019, December 15). Lughnasadh. Order of Bards, Ovates & Druids. https://druidry.org/druid-way/teaching-and-practice/druid-festivals/lughnasadh

Malec, C. (2013). Beltane. Createspace Independent Publishing Platform.

National Day Calendar. (2014, June 11). YULE – day of Winter Solstice. National Day Calendar. https://nationaldaycalendar.com/yule-day-of-winter-solstice

Rajchel, D. (2021). Mabon: Rituals, recipes & lore for the autumn equinox. Dreamscape Media.

The Editors of Encyclopedia Britannica. (2013). Imbolc. In Encyclopedia Britannica.

Who were the Druids? (2017, March 21). Historic UK. https://www.historic-uk.com/HistoryUK/HistoryofWales/Druids

Wigington, P. (n.d.). Beltane Prayers. Learn Religions. Retrieved from https://www.learnreligions.com/simple-prayers-for-beltane-2561674

Wigington, P. (n.d.). Beltane Magic. Retrieved from Learn Religions website: https://www.learnreligions.com/guide-to-beltane-magic-2561638

Wright, M. S. (2015, April 14). Magic for Beltane: Simple spells, potions, and other magical inspirations. Retrieved from Exemplare website: https://exemplore.com/magic/Magic-for-Beltane-Simple-Spells-Potions-and-Other-Magical-Inspirations

Beltane, mayday, Rituals, spells. (n.d.). Retrieved from Raven and Crone metaphysical gifts and jewelry website: https://www.ravenandcrone.com/catalog/a41/Beltane,-May-Day,-Rituals,-Spells/article_info.html

Moodymoons, V. A. P. (2019, April 29). Celebrate Beltane: Goddess bath ritual. Retrieved from Moody Moons website: https://www.moodymoons.com/2019/04/29/celebrate-beltane-goddess-bath-ritual

Luna, B. (2018, May 1). Beltane rituals for every element –. Retrieved from The Hoodwitch website: https://www.thehoodwitch.com/blog/2018/5/1/beltane-rituals-for-every-element

About Beltane fire festival. (2013, February 11). Retrieved from Beltane Fire Society website: https://beltane.org/about-beltane

Beltane. (2021, October 4). Retrieved from The Goddess and the Greenman website:

https://www.goddessandgreenman.co.uk/beltane

Mark, J. J. (2019). Wheel of the Year. World History Encyclopedia. Retrieved from

https://www.worldhistory.org/Wheel_of_the_Year

Wigington, P. (n.d.-a). Hold a Beltane Bonfire Ritual. Retrieved from Learn Religions website:

https://www.learnreligions.com/beltane-bonfire-rite-group-ceremony-2561649

Hutton, Ronald (1993). The Pagan Religions of the Ancient British Isles. Blackwell Publishers. ISBN 0-631-18946-7.

Hutton, Ronald (2001) [1996]. The Stations of the Sun. Oxford University Press. ISBN 0-19-285448-8.

Lemprière, Raoul (1976). Customs, Ceremonies and Traditions of the Channel Islands. Hale. ISBN 0-7091-5842-4.

Carmichael, Álexander (1992). Carmina Gadelica. Lindisfarne Press. ISBN 0-940262-50-9

Chadwick, Nora (1970) The Celts. London, Penguin ISBN 0-14-021211-6

Danaher, Kevin (1972) The Year in Ireland. Dublin, Mercier ISBN 1-85635-093-2

Evans-Wentz, W. Y. (1966, 1990) The Fairy-Faith in Celtic Countries. New York, Citadel ISBN 0-8065-1160-5

MacKillop, James (1998). Dictionary of Celtic Mythology. Oxford University Press ISBN 0-19-280120-1

McNeill, F. Marian (1959) The Silver Bough, Vol. 1–4. William MacLellan, Glasgow

Simpson, Eve Blantyre (1908), Folk-Lore in Lowland Scotland, London: J.M. Dent.

Buckland, Raymond (2002). The Witch Book: The Encyclopedia of Witchcraft, Wicca, and Neo-paganism. Visible Ink Press. ISBN 1-57859-114-7.

Gibbons, Jenny (August 1998). "Recent Developments in the Study of The Great European Witch Hunt." The Pomegranate. No. 5. ISSN 1528-0268. Archived from the original on 2003-05-05.

Lewis, James R. (1999). Witchcraft Today: An Encyclopedia of Wiccan and Neopagan Traditions. ABC-CLIO. ISBN 1-57607-134-0.

Rabinovitch, Shelly; Lewis, James R., eds. (2002). The Encyclopedia of Modern Witchcraft and Neo-Paganism. Kensington. ISBN 0-8065-2406-5.

Lewis, James R., ed. (1996). Magical Religion and Modern Witchcraft. State University of New York Press. ISBN 0-585-03650-0.

Luhrmann, T. M. (1994). Persuasions of the Witch's Craft: Ritual Magic in Contemporary England. Picador. ISBN 978-0-330-32946-0

A lughnasadh ritual. (n.d.). Rylandpeters. https://rylandpeters.com/blogs/health-mind-body-and-spirit/lughnasadh-ritual-lammas-day-spell

Accommodations. (n.d.). Doebay.Com.

Amanda. (2016, July 30). Celebrating Lammas with kids. A Spiral Dance. https://www.aspiraldance.com/celebrating-lammas-kids/

Bhagat, D. (n.d.). The origins and practices of Lammas/Lughnasad. Bpl.Org. https://www.bpl.org/blogs/post/the-origins-and-practices-of-lammas-lughnasad/

Blumberg, A. (2016, July 29). 8 facts to know about lughnasadh, pagan harvest festival. HuffPost. https://www.huffpost.com/entry/8-facts-to-know-about-lughnasadh-pagan-harvest-festival_n_579a832ee4b08a8e8b5d6134

Buice, T. (2017, June 26). Blackberry Tarts ~ garden to table. Saving Room for Dessert; Tricia Buice. https://www.savingdessert.com/blackberry-tarts-garden-to-table/

Caro, T. (2021, April 25). An Enchanting Prayer for Lughnasadh [5 min chant]. Magickal Spot. https://magickalspot.com/prayer-for-lughnasadh/

Clerk of Oxford. (n.d.). A Clerk of Oxford. Blogspot.Com. https://aclerkofoxford.blogspot.com/2017/08/a-little-history-of-lammas.html

Cornelius Tacitus, P. (2010). Agricola (J. Delz, Ed.). Walter de Gruyter.

Ellis, P. B. (2005). A dictionary of Irish mythology (5th ed.). Constable.

Farrar, S. (1988). Eight Sabbats for Witches. Phoenix Publishing.

Fitzgerald, S. (2020). The last battle of moytura: The wars of Celtic gods and druids. Independently Published.

Gill & Son. (2009). Fate of the children of tuireann. BiblioLife.

Gwynn, E. J. (Ed.). (1991). The metrical dindshenchas: Pt. 1. Dublin Institute for Advanced Studies.

Lammas. (2021, October 4). The Goddess and the Greenman. https://www.goddessandgreenman.co.uk/lammas/

LAMMAS BREAD and PROTECTION SPELL. (n.d.). Just A Pinch Recipes. https://www.justapinch.com/recipes/bread/other-bread/lammas-bread-and-protection-spell.html

Lembas. (n.d.). The One Wiki to Rule Them All. https://lotr.fandom.com/wiki/Lembas

Linder, L. J. (n.d.). Lammas: The ancient heritage of grains. Witchesandpagans.Com. https://witchesandpagans.com/pagan-culture-blogs/ahimsa-grove/lammas-the-ancient-heritage-of-grains.html

Macalister, R. A. S. (Ed.). (1938). Lebor Gabala erenn: Pt. 1: Book of the taking of Ireland. Irish Texts Society.

O'Rahilly, C. (Ed.). (1976). Táin bó Cúailnge, Recension 1. Dublin Institute for Advanced Studies.

Recipes to celebrate Lammas. (2021, July 18). Awesome on 20. https://awesomeon20.com/recipes-to-celebrate-lammas/

Sally. (2021, June 24). Homemade cherry pie. Sally's Baking Addiction; https://sallysbakingaddiction.com/cherry-pie/

Shakespeare, W. (2018). Romeo and Juliet: The most excellent and lamentable tragedy. Hamburger Lesehefte.

Sinclair, A. (2021, December 10). Celtic Tree Astrology: Zodiac signs & birthday horoscopes. Oak Hill Gardens. https://www.oakhillgardens.com/blog/celtic-tree-astrology-zodiac-signs-birthday-horoscopes

Starhawk. (1989). Spiral dance: A rebirth of the ancient religion of the great goddess (2nd ed.). HarperSanFrancisco.

Taylor, A. (2019, September 25). Easy bath magic to release, heal, and recharge. Starlight Witch. https://www.patheos.com/blogs/starlight/2019/09/easy-bath-magic-to-release-heal-and-recharge/

The. (n.d.). Freyfest (freysblot). Valknut - Viking & Norse Fashion. https://www.valknuthorde.com/blogs/news/freyfest-freysblot

The Current Chief, The Former Chief, & Patroness, O. (2019a, November 27). Druid prayer & devotion. Order of Bards, Ovates & Druids; OBOD. https://druidry.org/druid-way/teaching-and-practice/druid-prayer-devotion

The Current Chief, The Former Chief, & Patroness, O. (2019b, December 15). Lughnasadh. Order of Bards, Ovates & Druids; OBOD. https://druidry.org/druid-way/teaching-and-practice/druid-festivals/lughnasadh

Using crystals in synergistic ritual with essential oils. (n.d.). Baseformula.Com. https://www.baseformula.com/blog/crystals-and-essential-oils

Wigington, P. (2007, July 10). Hold this simple harvest ritual to celebrate Lammas. Learn Religions. https://www.learnreligions.com/hold-a-lammas-harvest-ritual-2562166

Wigington, P. (2008a, July 17). Setting up your Lammas (Lughnasadh) altar. Learn Religions. https://www.learnreligions.com/setting-up-your-lammas-lughnasadh-altar-2562171

Wigington, P. (2008b, August 14). Mabon: The autumn equinox. Learn Religions. https://www.learnreligions.com/all-about-mabon-the-autumn-equinox-2562286

Wigington, P. (2016, June 26). 4 Simple Prayers for the Lammas Sabbat. Learn Religions. https://www.learnreligions.com/lammas-prayers-and-blessings-4057769

Wigington, P. (2017a, May 30). Lammas Craft Projects. Learn Religions. https://www.learnreligions.com/lammas-craft-projects-4136753

Wigington, P. (2017b, May 30). Recipes for the Lammas Sabbat. Learn Religions. https://www.learnreligions.com/recipes-for-the-lammas-sabbat-4140665

Wilde, D. (2015). Witchcraft, magick and spells: A beginner's guide. Createspace Independent Publishing Platform.

Witch of Howling Creek. (2012, August 1). Lammas cornbread recipe + giveaway winner. The Witch of Howling Creek. https://witchofhowlingcreek.wordpress.com/2012/08/01/lammas-cornbread-recipe-giveaway-winner

arithharger. (2017, September 18). The Autumn Equinox. Whispers of Yggdrasil. https://arithharger.wordpress.com/2017/09/18/the-autumn-equinox-2/comment-page-1/

Bhagat, D. (n.d.). The origins and practices of Mabon. Bpl.Org. https://www.bpl.org/blogs/post/the-origins-and-practices-of-mabon/

Crawford, C. (2020, September 15). What is Mabon, and how can we celebrate the Autumn Equinox? —. The Self-Care Emporium. https://theselfcareemporium.com/blog/what-is-mabon-autumn-equinox

Fall Equinox celebrations of Christianity, Pagans, Neopagans, etc. (n.d.-a). Religioustolerance.Org. https://www.religioustolerance.org/fall_equinox2.htm

Fall Equinox celebrations of Christianity, Pagans, Neopagans, etc. (n.d.-b). Religioustolerance.Org. https://www.religioustolerance.org/fall_equinox3.htm

Fall equinox rituals, herbs & recipes to celebrate mabon. (n.d.). Five Flavors Herbs. https://fiveflavorsherbs.com/blog/fall-equinox-rituals-herbs-recipes-to-celebrate-mabon/

Mabon house. (n.d.). Mabon House. https://www.mabonhouse.co/mabon

Mankey, J. (2014, September 16). The triumph of Mabon. Raise the Horns. https://www.patheos.com/blogs/panmankey/2014/09/the-triumph-of-mabon/

Mulhern, K. (n.d.). What are the sabbats. Patheos.Com. https://www.patheos.com/answers/what-are-the-sabbats

Rajchel, D. (2021). Mabon: Rituals, recipes & lore for the autumn equinox. Dreamscape Media.

Wigington, P. (2007, July 30). Mabon history: The second harvest. Learn Religions. https://www.learnreligions.com/mabon-history-the-second-harvest-2562060

Apel, T. (2020, August 16). Bacchus. Mythopedia. https://mythopedia.com/topics/bacchus

Apel, T., & Kapach, A. (2020, August 16). Hermes. Mythopedia. https://mythopedia.com/topics/hermes

Bhagat, D. (n.d.). The origins and practices of Mabon. Bpl.Org https://www.bpl.org/blogs/post/the-origins-and-practices-of-mabon/

Celtic religion - The Celtic gods. (n.d.). In Encyclopedia Britannica.

Dionysus. (2014, September 19). Greek Gods & Goddesses. https://greekgodsandgoddesses.net/gods/dionysus/

Dionysus. (2018, March 13). Greekmythology.Com; GreekMythology.com. https://www.greekmythology.com/Other_Gods/Dionysus/dionysus.html

Don't call me Mabon.... (2017, September 15). Hearth Witchery. https://annafranklinhearthwitch.wordpress.com/2017/09/15/dont-call-me-mabon/

Editors, C. R. (2018). Thoth: The history and legacy of the ancient Egyptian god who maintains the universe. Createspace Independent Publishing Platform.

Harter, N. (2005, September 1). Mabon: Journeying with Persephone. Llewellyn Worldwide. https://www.llewellyn.com/journal/article/893

heartofthewitchspath. (2016, August 11). ABCs of Celtic mythology – Mabon and Modron. Heart of the Witch's Path. https://heartofthewitchspath.wordpress.com/2016/08/11/abcs-of-celtic-mythology-mabon-and-modron/

Hermes. (2018, March 13). Greekmythology.Com; GreekMythology.com. https://www.greekmythology.com/Olympians/Hermes/hermes.html

Hermes and the Cattle of Apollo. (n.d.). Greek-Gods.Info. https://www.greek-gods.info/greek-gods/hermes/myths/hermes-apollo/

Locatelli-Kournwsky, L. (2018). Persephone. Archaia Studios Press.

Mabon: A pagan celebration. (2020, September 27). The Meredith Herald. https://www.meredithherald.com/post/mabon-a-pagan-celebration

Mabon ap Modron. (n.d.). Maryjones.Us. http://www.maryjones.us/jce/mabon.html

Maponos – mabon – Celtic god youth and hunting in Gaul and northern Britain. (n.d.). Celts & Myths

Me, A. (n.d.). Who is Mabon? Go Deeper http://www.godeeper.info/blog/who-is-mabon

Meehan, E. (2020, August 16). Thoth. Mythopedia. https://mythopedia.com/topics/thoth

No title. (n.d.). Study.Com. https://study.com/learn/lesson/egyptian-god-thoth-emerald-tablets-facts-quotes.html

O'Hara, K. (2022, May 21). The Morrigan: The story of the fiercest goddess in Irish myth. The Irish Road Trip. https://www.theirishroadtrip.com/the-morrigan/

The Morrigan: Crow goddess of death. (2015, June 20). Eternal Haunted Summer. https://eternalhauntedsummer.com/issues/summer-solstice-2015/the-morrigan-crow-goddess-of-death/

Worksheet Freelancer. (2019, July 23). Mabon facts, worksheets, history, symbols & traditions for kids. KidsKonnect. https://kidskonnect.com/holidays-seasons/mabon/

Wright, G. (2020, August 16). Cernunnos. Mythopedia. https://mythopedia.com/topics/cernunnos

(N.d.-a). Greekreporter.Com. https://greekreporter.com/2021/09/23/autumn-equinox-marks-solemn-change-of-seasons/

(N.d.-b). Theoi.Com. https://www.theoi.com/articles/what-is-the-demeter-and-persephone-story-summarized/

Caro, T. (2020, September 21). Magickal meaning & Symbolism of the pear tree. Magickal Spot. https://magickalspot.com/pear-tree-symbolism-meaning/

Greenhaven: A Pagan tradition. (n.d.). Greenhaven: A Pagan Tradition. http://greenhaventradition.weebly.com/mabon.html

Herbs sacred to mabon. (n.d.). Tripod.Com. https://cronescottage2002.tripod.com/thecottageaugustmabon2002/id10.html

The FruitGuys. (2021, September 2). Here's your fall fruit guide for 2019. The FruitGuys. https://fruitguys.com/2021/09/2021-fall-fruit-guide/

Wang, H. (2022, June 2). What fruit do you eat on the autumnal equinox? 8 recommended fruits for autumnal equinox. Sihai. https://en.4hw.com.cn/644/150862.html

Altar and Oddity. (2020, December 21). *Sacred spaces: How to make an altar in your home.* https://altarandoddity.com/blogs/news/sacred-spaces-how-to-make-an-altar

Apel, T. (2022, April 28). *Pluto.* Mythopedia. https://mythopedia.com/topics/pluto

Barry, B. (2019, October 31). *Samhain and the thin veil*. Donegal Square. https://donegalsquare.com/samhain-and-the-thin-veil/

Browne, N. (2021, December 22). *Arawn: The Celtic god of death and the underworld, explained*. Ireland Before You Die. https://www.irelandbeforeyoudie.com/arawn-the-celtic-god-of-death-and-the-underworld-explained/

Cartwright, M. (2013, September 22). *Mictlantecuhtli*. World History Encyclopedia. https://www.worldhistory.org/Mictlantecuhtli/

Clever Prototypes, L. L. C. (n.d.). *Rhea: Greek mythology*. Accessed July 1, 2022. https://www.storyboardthat.com/mythology/rhea

Cline, A. (2019, February 17). *Mictlantecuhtli: God of death in Aztec religion*. Learn Religions https://www.learnreligions.com/mictlantecuhtli-god-aztec-of-death-248588

Daimler, M. (2016, October 18). *Irish-American witchcraft: The Morrigan and Samhain*. Patheos. https://www.patheos.com/blogs/agora/2016/10/irish-american-witchcraft-the-morrigan-and-samhain/

The Editors of Encyclopedia Britannica. (2022, March 28). *Zeus*. Encyclopedia Britannica. https://www.britannica.com/topic/Zeus

The Editors of GreekMythology.com. (2018, March 13). *Dionysus*. Greekmythology.com. https://www.greekmythology.com/Other_Gods/Dionysus/dionysus.html

The Editors of GreekMythology.com. (2021, April 9). *Hecate*. GreekMythology.com https://www.greekmythology.com/Other_Gods/Hecate/hecate.html#:~:text=Hecate%20was%20a%20goddess%20in,protective%20goddess%20who%20brought%20prosperity.

The Editors of GreekMythology.com. (2021, October 6). *Hermes*. Greekmythology.com. GreekMythology.com. https://www.greekmythology.com/Olympians/Hermes/hermes.html

Enodian, R. (2018, October 22). *Celebrating Hermes, messenger god & guide of souls, on Samhain*. Patheos. https://www.patheos.com/blogs/teaaddictedwitch/2018/10/celebrating-hermes-samhain/

Enodian, R. (2018, October 13). *Descent and ascent: Persephone claiming her throne at Samhain*. Patheos. https://www.patheos.com/blogs/teaaddictedwitch/2018/10/ascent-descent-persephone-samhain/

Ethical Gains. (2020, October 20). *What is Samhain? The history of the pagan celebration.* Sea Witch Botanicals. https://seawitchbotanicals.com/blogs/swb/what-is-samhain-the-history-of-the-pagan-celebration

Fox, C. (2018). *Hades.* Bantam.

Frasca, C. (2021, October 7). *Cerridwen's cauldron and the origins of Samhain by Caireann Frasca.* Motherhouse of the Goddess. http://themotherhouseofthegoddess.com/2021/10/07/cerridwens-cauldron-and-the-origins-of-samhain-by-caireann-frasca/

Gaia Staff. (2021, October 29). *Samhain rituals – How to celebrate Samhain.* Gaia. https://www.gaia.com/article/modern-paganism-13-rituals-celebrate-samhain

The Goddess and the Greenman. (2021, October 4). *Samhain/Halloween October 31st.* https://www.goddessandgreenman.co.uk/samhainhalloween/

Goddess Garden. (2018, December 17). *The Celtic goddess Cerridwen.* The Goddess Garden. https://thegoddessgarden.com/the-celtic-goddess-cerridwen/

Greek Gods and Goddesses. (2014, September 19). *Hades (Haides).* https://greekgodsandgoddesses.net/gods/hades/

Greeley, S. (2021, October 6). *From Samhain to Halloween: The history of Halloween traditions.* Little Rae's Bakery. https://littleraesbakery.com/2021/10/06/from-samhain-to-halloween-the-history-of-halloween-traditions/

Helena. (2021, January 24). *How to build an altar at home for spiritual self-care.* Disorient. https://disorient.co/build-an-altar/

History.com Editors. (2009, November 18). *Halloween 2021. HISTORY.* https://www.history.com/topics/halloween/history-of-halloween

History.com Editors. (2018, April 6). *Samhain. HISTORY.* https://www.history.com/topics/holidays/samhain

Hurstwic, LLC. (n.d.). *The death of Baldr.* Accessed July 1, 2022. http://www.hurstwic.org/history/articles/mythology/myths/text/baldr.htm

Johannesen, H. (2013, September 21). *Hekate: Goddess of Samhain.* Eternal Haunted Summer. https://eternalhauntedsummer.com/issues/autumn-equinox-2013/hekate-goddess-of-samhain/

Johnson, E. (2018, July 24). *A salute to the seasons: Creating seasonal altars.* WomanShopsWorld. https://shopwomanshopsworld.com/blogs/womanshopsworld-blog/a-salute-to-the-seasons-creating-seasonal-altars

Julian, J. A. (2014, September 30). *Samhain symbols – Animals*. The Pagan Circle. https://thepagancircle.wordpress.com/2014/09/30/samhain-symbols-animals/

Keith, J. (2019, October 13). *Halloween plant lore*. Fafard. https://fafard.com/halloween-plant-lore/

ladyoftheabyss. (2018, October 27). *Samhain goddesses – Hel – Norse*. Witches Of The Craft®. https://witchesofthecraft.com/2018/10/27/samhain-goddesses-hel-norse/

Lang, C. (2018, October 30). *What is Samhain? What to know about the ancient pagan festival that came before Halloween*. Time USA, LLC. https://time.com/5434659/halloween-pagan-origins-in-samhain/

Larson, C. (2019, October 13). *Of light & shadow: Connecting with Anubis at Samhain*. Patheos. https://www.patheos.com/blogs/agora/2019/10/of-light-shadow-connecting-with-anubis-at-samhain/

Larson, C. (2018, October 23). *'Samhain' in ancient Egypt?* Of Light & Shadow. https://anubislightandshadow.wordpress.com/2018/10/23/samhain-in-ancient-egypt/

Locatelli-Kournwsky, L. (2018). *Persephone*. Archaia Studios Press.

Mackay, D. (2021, June 27). *Everything you need to know about Hecate (maiden, mother, crone)*. TheCollector. https://www.thecollector.com/hecate-goddess-magic-witchcraft/

Mankey, J. (2018, October 18). *Samhain deities*. Patheos. https://www.patheos.com/blogs/panmankey/2018/10/samhain-deities/

Marie, M. (2020, October 13). *What is the story of the ancient Pharaonic deity Anubis?* Egypttoday. https://www.egypttoday.com/Article/4/93038/What-is-the-story-of-the-ancient-Pharaonic-deity-Anubis

Mark, J. J. (2021, September 6). *Hel*. World History Encyclopedia. https://www.worldhistory.org/Hel/

McGinley, K. (2019, September 16). *Sacred space: How to make an altar in your home*. Chopra. https://chopra.com/articles/sacred-space-how-to-make-an-altar-in-your-home

McLeod, H. (2021, October 27). *Samhain and the history of Halloween*. The Smoky Mountain News. https://smokymountainnews.com/lifestyle/rumble/item/32445-samhain-and-the-history-of-halloween

Meehan, E. (2021, November 20). *Huitzilopochtli*. Mythopedia. https://mythopedia.com/topics/huitzilopochtli

Meehan, E. (2021, November 20). *Mictlantecuhtli*. Mythopedia. https://mythopedia.com/topics/mictlantecuhtli

Meehan, E. (2021, November 20). *Quetzalcoatl*. Mythopedia. https://mythopedia.com/topics/quetzalcoatl

Meehan, E. (2021, November 20). *Tezcatlipoca*. Mythopedia. https://mythopedia.com/topics/tezcatlipoca

Meehan, E. (2021, November 20). *Xipe Totec*. Mythopedia. https://mythopedia.com/topics/xipe-totec

Mojsov, B. (Ed.). (2005). *Osiris*. Blackwell Publishing Ltd.

Moonshadow. (2021, October 29). *Hecate and Samhain*. Spells8 Forum. https://forum.spells8.com/t/hecate-and-samhain/15764

Myth Nerd. (2021, March 20). *Anubis and Osiris: What is the difference?* https://mythnerd.com/anubis-and-osiris-what-is-the-difference/

Neshevich, V. (2020, October 28). *Five important crystals for Samhain*. Green Moon Apothecary Ltd. https://greenmoon.ca/blogs/blog/five-important-crystals-for-samhain

Newgrange.com. (n.d.). *Samhain (Samain) - The Celtic roots of Halloween*. Accessed July 1, 2022. https://www.newgrange.com/samhain.htm

O'Connor, D. (2022, June 27). *An Cailleach - The Irish goddess of the winter and following her trail in Ireland*. IrishCentral. https://www.irishcentral.com/travel/best-of-ireland/cailleach-irish-goddess-winter-trail-ireland

The Order of Bards, Ovates & Druids. (n.d.). *Samhain festival*. Accessed July 1, 2022. https://druidry.org/druid-way/teaching-and-practice/druid-festivals/samhain-festival

O'Hara, K. (2022, May 26). *The Morrigan goddess: The phantom queen and Celtic goddess (An easy-to-follow tale)*. The Irish Road Trip. https://www.theirishroadtrip.com/the-morrigan/

Pon, D. (n.d.). *The origins of Halloween*. Albany.edu. Accessed July 1, 2022. https://www.albany.edu/~dp1252/isp523/halloween.html

Ravenwood, C. (2021). *Celebrating Samhain: A coloring and activity book*. Independently Published.

RaynaNoire.com. (2019, October 29). *Goddesses of Samhain*. http://raynanoire.weebly.com/blog/goddesses-of-samhain

Rhys, D. (n.d.). *Arawn - The Welsh god of the afterlife*. Symbol Sage. Accessed July 1, 2022. https://symbolsage.com/arawn-the-welsh-god/

Rogador, C. (2021, January 29). *Samhain symbol - history and meaning*. Symbols Archive. https://symbolsarchive.com/samhain-symbol-history-meaning/

Russell, T. (2019, January 25). *Why you need a sacred space in your home (& how to create one)*. Davy & Tracy Russell. Sherman, E. (2020, October 23). *How to celebrate pagan Samhain instead of Halloween this year*. Matador Network. https://matadornetwork.com/read/celebrate-wiccan-samhain-instead-halloween-year/

Spookyscotland.net. (2019, October 30). *Halloween origins: Samhain and the Cailleach*.

Stumpp, B. V. (2013, January 15). *The importance of home altars*. Britta's Dance. https://brittasdance.wordpress.com/2013/01/15/the-importance-of-home-altars/

Theoi Project. (n.d.). *Persephone*. Accessed July 1, 2022. https://www.theoi.com/Khthonios/Persephone.html#:~:text=PERSEPHONE%20was%20the%20goddess%20queen,passage%20to%20a%20blessed%20afterlife.

The Thirsty Soul. (2018, October 18). *Samhain: An Cailleach, our ancestors & Celtic New Year*. https://thethirstysoul.com/samhain-an-cailleach-our-ancestors-celtic-new-year/

Ward, K. (2021, August 23). *How to celebrate Samhain, aka the witches' New Year*. Cosmopolitan. https://www.cosmopolitan.com/lifestyle/a34360772/samhain-traditions/

Wigington, P. (2019, January 12). *Cerridwen: Keeper of the cauldron*. Learn Religions. https://www.learnreligions.com/cerridwen-keeper-of-the-cauldron-2561960

Wigington, P. (2019, January 6). *Consecrate your magical tools*. Learn Religions. https://www.learnreligions.com/consecrate-your-magical-tools-2562860

Wigington, P. (2019, August 14). *Sacred plants of the Samhain sabbat*. Learn Religions. https://www.learnreligions.com/sacred-plants-of-the-samhain-sabbat-3879864

Wigington, P. (2019, March 11). *Samhain spirit incense*. Learn Religions. https://www.learnreligions.com/samhain-spirit-incense-4588980

Wigington, P. (2020, April 29). *Setting up your Samhain altar*. Learn Religions. https://www.learnreligions.com/setting-up-a-samhain-altar-2562711

Wigington, P. (2019, June 25). *Set up an ancestor shrine – Ancestor altar*. Learn Religions. https://www.learnreligions.com/ancestor-shrine-ancestor-altar-2562668

Wright, G. (2021, August 27). *Arawn*. Mythopedia. https://mythopedia.com/topics/arawn

Printed in the USA
CPSIA information can be obtained
at www.ICGtesting.com
LVHW051400261023
762086LV00005B/17